A HISTORY OF
AUSTRALIA,
NEW ZEALAND
AND THE PACIFIC

THE BLACKWELL HISTORY OF THE WORLD

General Editor: **R. I. Moore**

Published

A History of Latin America
Peter Bakewell

The Origins of Human Society
Peter Bogucki

A History of Russia, Central Asia and Mongolia: Volume I
David Christian

A History of Australia, New Zealand and the Pacific
Donald Denoon and Philippa Mein-Smith, with Marivic Wyndham

A History of India
Burton Stein

A History of Japan
Conrad Totman

In Preparation

A History of the Mediterranean World
David Abulafia

The Birth of the Modern World
C. A. Bayly

A History of Western Europe
Robin Briggs

A History of Russia, Central Asia and Mongolia: Volume II
David Christian

A History of Africa
Paul Lovejoy

Elements of World History
R. I. Moore

A History of the Islamic World
David Morgan

A History of the Ancient Mediterranean
Ian Morris

A History of South-East Asia
Anthony Reid

A History of China
Morris Rossabi

A History of the Ancient Americas
Fred Spier

The Early Modern World
Sanjay Subrahmanyam

The Beginnings of Civilization
Robert Wenke

A HISTORY OF
AUSTRALIA,
NEW ZEALAND
AND THE PACIFIC

**DONALD DENOON AND
PHILIPPA MEIN-SMITH, WITH
MARIVIC WYNDHAM**

Copyright © Donald Denoon, Philippa Mein-Smith and Marivic Wyndham 2000

The right of Donald Denoon, Philippa Mein-Smith and Marivic Wyndham to be identified as authors of this work has been asserted in accordance with the Copyright, Designs and Patents Act 1988.

First published 2000

2 4 6 8 10 9 7 5 3 1

Blackwell Publishers Ltd
108 Cowley Road
Oxford OX4 1JF
UK

Blackwell Publishers Inc.
350 Main Street
Malden, Massachusetts 02148
USA

British Library Cataloguing in Publication Data

A CIP catalogue record for this book is available from the British Library.

Library of Congress Cataloging-in-Publication Data is available for this book.

ISBN   0 631 17962 3 (hbk)
        0 631 21873 4 (pbk)

Typeset in 10 on 12 pt Plantin
by Newgen Imaging Systems Pvt. Ltd
Printed in Great Britain by
TJ International, Padstow, Cornwall

This book is printed on acid-free paper

Contents

PLATES

MAPS

FIGURES

SERIES EDITOR'S PREFACE

There is nothing new in the attempt to understand history as a whole. To know how humanity began and how it has come to its present condition is one of the oldest and most universal of human needs, expressed in the religious and philosophical systems of every civilization. But only in the last few decades has it begun to appear both necessary and possible to meet that need by means of a rational and systematic appraisal of current knowledge. History claimed its independence as a field of scholarship with its own subject matter and its own rules and methods, not simply a branch of literature, rhetoric, law, philosophy or religion, in the second half of the nineteenth century. World History has begun to do so only in the second half of the twentieth. Its emergence has been delayed on the one hand by simple ignorance – for the history of enormous stretches of space and time has been known not at all, or so patchily and superficially as not to be worth revisiting – and on the other by the lack of a widely acceptable basis upon which to organize and discuss what is nevertheless the enormous and enormously diverse knowledge that we have.

Both obstacles are now being rapidly overcome. There is almost no part of the world or period of its history that is not the subject of vigorous and sophisticated investigation by archaeologists and historians. It is truer than it has ever been that knowledge is growing and perspectives changing and multiplying more quickly than it is possible to assimilate and record them in synthetic form. Nevertheless the attempt to grasp the human past as a whole can and must be made. Facing a common future of headlong and potentially catastrophic transformation, the world needs its common history. Since we no longer believe that a complete or definitive account is ultimately attainable by the mere accumulation of knowledge we are free to offer the best we can manage at the moment. Since we no longer suppose that it is our business as historians to detect or proclaim "The End of History" in the fruition of any grand design, human or divine, there is no single path to trace, or golden key to turn. There is also a growing wealth of ways in which world history can be written. The oldest and simplest view, that world history is best understood as the history of contacts between peoples previously isolated from one another, from which (some think) all change arises, is now seen to be capable of application since the earliest times. An influential alternative focuses upon the tendency of economic exchanges to create self-sufficient but ever expanding "worlds" which sustain successive systems of power and culture. Others seek to understand the differences between societies and cultures, and therefore the particular character of each, by comparing the ways in which they have developed their values, social relationships and structures of power. The rapidly developing field of ecological history returns to a very ancient tradition of seeing interaction with the physical environment, and with other animals, at the centre of the human predicament, while insisting that its understanding demands an approach which is culturally, chronologically and geographically comprehensive.

The Blackwell History of the World does not seek to embody any of these approaches, but to support them all, as it will use them all, by providing a modern, comprehensive and accessible account of the entire human past. Its plan is that of a barrel, in which the indispensable narratives of very long term regional development are bound together by global surveys of the interaction between regions at particular times, and of the great transformations which they have experienced in common, or visited upon one another. Each volume, of course, reflects the idiosyncrasies of its sources and its subjects, as well as the judgement and experience of its author, but in combination they offer a framework in which the history of every part of the world can be viewed, and a basis upon which most aspects of human activity can be compared. A frame imparts perspective. Comparison implies respect for difference. That is the beginning of what the past has to offer the future.

R. I. Moore

SERIES EDITOR'S ACKNOWLEDGEMENTS

The Editor is grateful to all of the contributors to the Blackwell History of the World for advice and assistance on the design and contents of the series as a whole as well as on individual volumes. Both Editor and Contributors wish to place on record their immense debt, individually and collectively, to John Davey, formerly of Blackwell Publishers. The series would not have been initiated without his vision and enthusiasm, and could not have been realised without his energy, skill and diplomacy.

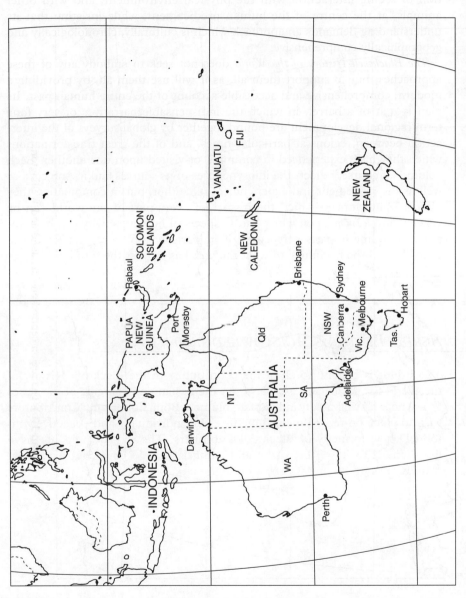

Map 1 Some perspectives, courtesy of the Cartography Unit, Research School of Pacific and Asian Studies, Australian National University.
(a) The region centred on Sydney and Brisbane.

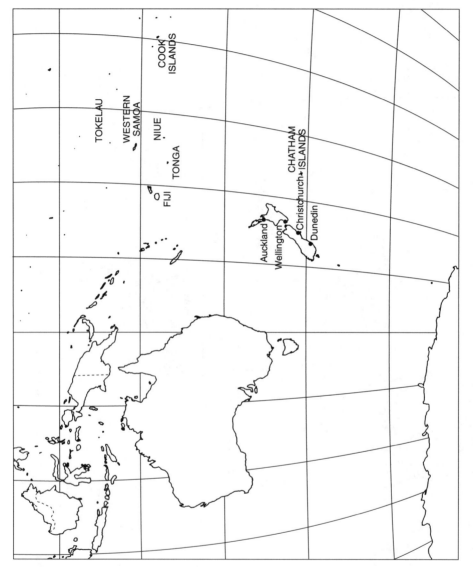

Map 1(b) The region centred on Auckland and Wellington.

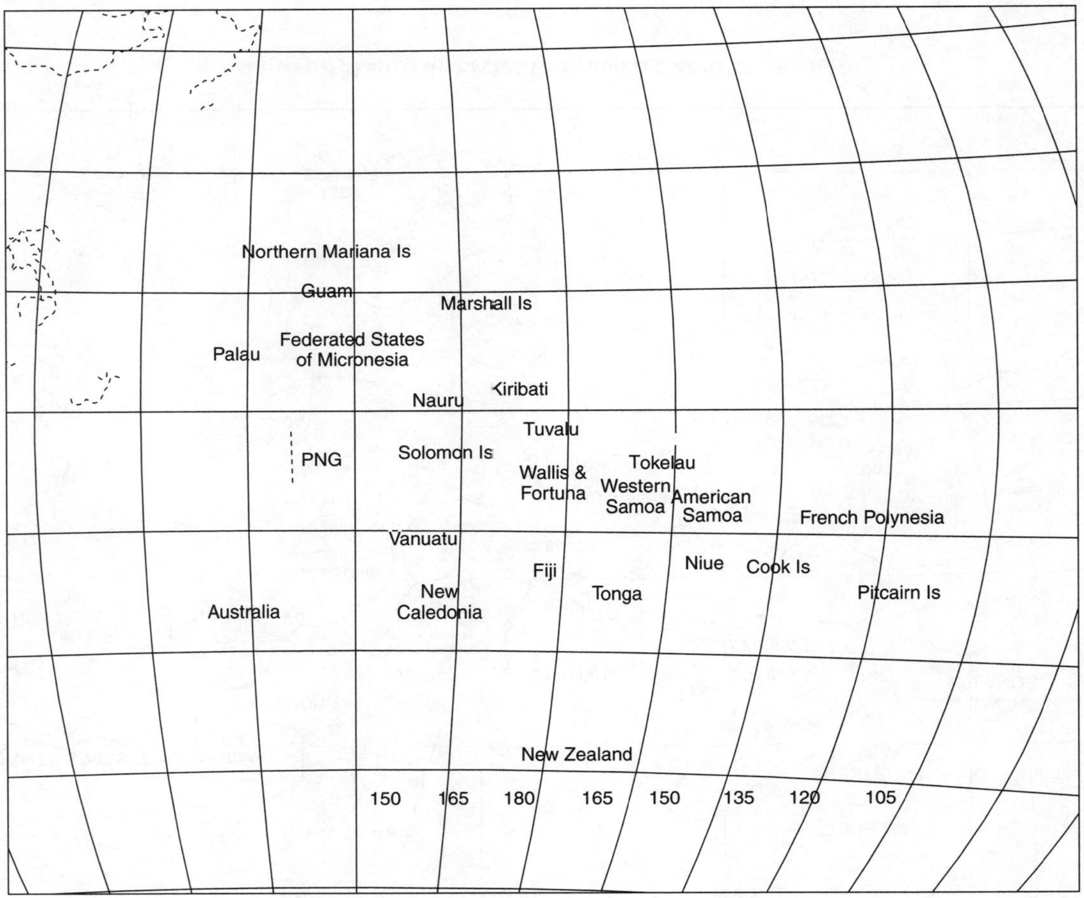

Map 1(c) The region centred on Suva and Noumea.

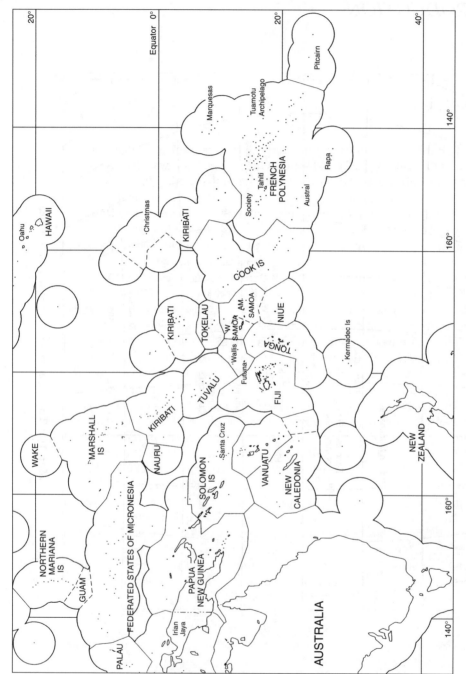

Map 1(d) Exclusive Economic Zones.

INTRODUCTION

Blackwell Publishers proposed this study and its parameters in order to round out its History of the World series. Our first reaction was that the proposal was not only Eurocentric (assembling several societies linked only by their remoteness from Oxford) but perverse. The dominant academic trend is not to build totalizing narratives but to deconstruct them. On reflection, though, we recognized that if national (and especially nationalist) histories are the dominant paradigm and impede fresh understandings, the proposal might have unexpected virtues. Joining national narratives together, or juxtaposing them, may disorient them just as much as the more usual approach of pulling them to pieces.

Australia, New Zealand and the Pacific do not form a self-contained universe, even when we limit ourselves to the South Pacific (a limitation explained below). The region has no name; few scholars have treated it as such; and its boundaries coincide with no major organization.[1] Broad and deep links draw these polities and peoples together, but these ties are not exclusive. Ours is not a self-evident region like Europe or Africa. Several scholars have treated Australia and New Zealand as a single site of social experiment. 'Socialism without doctrines' was the flattering title given by Albert Métin at the turn of this century.[2] The most comprehensive treatment of this line of thought was *State Experiments in Australia and New Zealand* published in 1902 by the New Zealander William Pember Reeves. Since then, most scholars have worked within (and therefore created) national narratives. The originality of our enterprise is to interweave histories which have evolved separately. Like earlier scholars in Australia and New Zealand, the newly independent countries of the Pacific publish nation-building narratives which also tend towards insularity. This tradition obscures the fact that in this unique space political and social identities have formed, interacted and reformed more often, and more recently, than anywhere else. Such volatility results not only from external pressures, but also (and increasingly) from vigorous internal dynamics.

We began this project expecting to compose conventional, positivist history, albeit on an oddly shaped canvas. The comparative method can elucidate puzzles which elude scholars working within national parameters. In a comparative perspective, nations and societies become constituents which respond differently to similar forces, or similarly to different stimuli. It is beyond dispute that national histories have blind spots, and some topics come into focus only in a wider perspective. The most obvious concern

Australia and New Zealand. The federation of the Australian colonies (and New Zealand's decision to stand apart) initiated national historiographies on both sides of the Tasman. Since then, their attempts to 'civilize capitalism', to harness trade unions to Labour parties, to reorder gender relations, to marginalize indigenous societies, and to extricate themselves from colonial networks, have been treated mainly in isolation. Although each nation's sense of itself hinges on the Anzac tradition – fighting alongside each other in the Great War – each national story seeks to ignore the other.

Within our region are not two settler societies but three, although New Caledonia's settlers (*caldoches*) are seldom analysed in French, and hardly ever in English.[3] *Caldoches* have been much more aware of their English-speaking neighbours than vice versa; and within French traditions of administration there has been an unusual variety of practice and ideology from Tahiti and New Caledonia to the unique Anglo-French Condominium of the New Hebrides. These variations make the comparative approach even more attractive. Once we broaden our focus, many topics assume (or perhaps reveal) regional as well as local significance. It follows that they may be better described and understood in a regional context. The more obvious topics are:

- depopulation in the eighteenth and nineteenth centuries;
- the region turned upside down and given new shape as Australia, New Zealand and New Caledonia became significant regional powers;
- the dispossession of indigenes, mainly by force (in Australia and New Caledonia) or despite a treaty (in New Zealand);
- French strategists in New Caledonia seeking to emulate Australia as a convict society and a settler economy;
- the aspirations of British and French settlers alike, to exercise 'sub-imperial' power over neighbouring islands;
- the dramatic consequences of creating states in the islands, and the struggles of successor governments to establish their legitimacy;
- the infinitely varied interactions of gender and race inequities;
- the uneven impact of two world wars, the Cold War, and nuclear testing;
- the lateness – and incompleteness – of Pacific decolonization, which generated unusual difficulties, opportunities and relationships;
- the survival and recovery of indigenous populations and cultures, unsettling the material and ideological bases of settler societies;
- regional environmental issues posed by mining, fishing and forestry;
- diverse reactions to the cultural aspects of globalization;
- reactions to integration into Southeast and East Asian economic networks.

That approach alone, however, would ignore the most arresting feature of these societies. Their identities have been created and transformed locally, although often shaped by ideas generated elsewhere. In the eighteenth century there were myriad communities, mainly small and in some ways vulnerable. It was British colonists who lumped together all inhabitants of 'Australia' and homogenized them as Aborigines, reserving 'Australians' for themselves. The inhabitants of New Zealand, who needed no single term for their islands or themselves, were first deemed New Zealanders and then Maori, by people who gradually became Pakeha.[4] Missionaries and traders nudged Polynesian chieftaincies into centralized 'national' polities. Each tiny society of Melanesia (another neologism) commonly referred to themselves as 'the people' or 'real people': these terms were often seized upon as names for the 'tribe' which Europeans supposed to be inherent in non-European societies. When a land mass or archipelago was annexed (or 'protected') by an imperial power, its inhabitants gained a new collective identity – Papuans or Solomon Islanders. French authorities in the Society Islands used Tahitian interchangeably with Maohi ('the people'), but in New Caledonia they imposed the pejorative term Canaque, derived and debased from Hawaiian (again for people). Briefly some Australian-born British called themselves Australian Natives, until the term settled into its more common and derogatory associations.

From these rough beginnings, identity-politics have been volatile. Interventions from beyond the region – exploration, settlement, conquest – shook this kaleidoscope into fresh patterns. Within the region also, communities adopted and adapted terms for themselves, and imposed them on others. Some communities and their sense of themselves also evolved almost naturally. Settler societies formed as fragments of European diasporas. As exiles and pioneers and their locally born children began to identify with their physical environment, as they became citizens rather than exiles, and as their societies became stable, they toyed with more positive views of themselves. Some thought of their newly accepted home – or aspired to make it – Arcadia with a sturdy yeomanry, a working-man's paradise, or some other improvement upon the British 'home'.

To over-simplify the story, some identities have been imposed from outside the region, others formed as one community interacted with its neighbours, and a few developed largely through their internal dynamics. Many identities make sense mainly in relation to other people within the region. Melanesians in New Caledonia took the odious term Canaque, transformed it into Kanak, and now wear it with pride. It distinguishes them from *caldoches* – another recent invention – although Kanak can embrace those *caldoches* who identify with indigenous neighbours. For Kanak and *caldoches* alike, the French language helps distinguish them from New Zealanders and Australians. Over the same period New Zealand's political landscape has been shaken by Maori cultural and political assertion, which compelled authorities to reconsider the foundations of the country's identity, the historic relations between Maori and colonists, and between both and the land. The increasing official use of Maori terms (Aotearoa for New Zealand, for example) measures this revaluation. Acknowledgement of historic injustices, and attempts to address these, amount to a reassessment of the country's past and present identity which transcends political correctness. Maori and Pakeha (glossed as 'white') are identities which each has given to the other, and which make little sense in isolation.

The Pacific Islands are not immune from identity politics and their sometimes violent consequences. Nine years of civil war between the Bougainville Revolutionary Army and the Papua New Guinea Defence Force compels a reassessment of Papua New Guinea's identity and the quality of its ethnic relationships. In Fiji, two military coups provoked a searching review of relations between the two major communities, ethnic Fijians and descendants of Indian indentured labourers. In devising a constitution to reconcile racial difference and a 'traditional' chiefly hierarchy with democracy, a heated issue is the appropriate term for citizens of Indian descent. 'Indian' makes little sense a century after migration; 'Fijian' is usually reserved for indigenous people; leaving 'Indo-Fijian' as the unlovely compromise. If the nation-state itself is problematic in the South West Pacific, the Polynesian states confront a different identity issue. Samoan and Tongan families routinely place family members in New Zealand, Australia and the United States, and have even been conceptualized as transnational corporations. The state's legitimacy is celebrated, but its relevance is moot.

Australians also debate the identity of their country and themselves. The millennium is one trigger to introspection, but the centenary of federation (2001) also provoked popular reflection as well as official re-thinking about the constitution. In 1998 a constitutional convention proposed a referendum to consider movement towards a republic. More radically, High Court decisions established that 'native title' – indigenous ownership of land – did survive colonization in principle, and in some places in reality. Taken together with reports on the forcible adoption of Aboriginal children, these judgements demanded that government and people reconsider relations between black and white, and between both and the land. Was British occupation an invasion or peaceful settlement? Is a link to the British Crown appropriate for a multi-ethnic society? Australia is no longer predominantly Anglo-Celtic, and that carries implications for literature and art, the culture of worship and the cult of sport, the politics of reconciliation, multiculturalism, visions of Australian identity and place in the sun. The debate is also about seeing (and not seeing) Australia's relationships to 'the world'.

Having accepted that South Pacific societies are integral to a region of interacting identities, we accepted the equator as one boundary, excluding Hawaii and most of Micronesia. The identity politics of Hawaii resonate deeply with those of Aotearoa New Zealand, but can only be understood (as they are practised) in the context of the policy of the United States towards Native American communities, and American academic politics.[5] Micronesia raises similar difficulties, compounded by the islands' exposure to Japanese settlement and government between the wars, and enervating United States economic and social policies thereafter.[6] To do justice to these issues would fatally disperse our energies.

The boundary between our region and 'Asia' is even more arbitrary. Australians, New Zealanders and Pacific Islanders are increasingly integrated economically into an open-ended region. A new focus is APEC (Asia Pacific Economic Cooperation – four adjectives in search of a noun, according to an Australian Foreign Minister) which aspires to shape 'Asia-Pacific', a region which flows from the Association of Southeast Asian Nations (ASEAN) through China to Japan and the Americas. These linkages are often alarming and never predictable. The 'Asian crisis' beginning in 1998 emerged as a currency crisis in Thailand, spreading through Southeast Asia, provoking turmoil and a change of regime in Indonesia and revealing malaise from Tokyo to Kuala Lumpur. What had been evident only to stockbrokers and bankers became universally visible: New Zealand and Australian stock markets were influenced more by Wall Street's Dow Jones than by any other index; and the value of their dollars rested on the worth of the yen. Being 'part of Asia' might be a cultural and political option, but it was an economic reality. 'Asia', 'the Pacific' and 'Asia-Pacific' are different places in economic or cultural or political debates, and we are very aware of the artificiality of boundaries between our region and its neighbours.

New approaches to old subjects help us to make sense of our topic. With the concept of agency, scholars broke down seemingly secure categories of oppressed and oppressors, perpetrators and victims. New perspectives reveal how convicts, women, the colonized, the dispossessed, indentured labourers and other marginalized people negotiated their lives as best they could. Maori cultural and political revival from the 1970s, for example, throws new light on earlier Maori survival and accommodation. The search for indigenous agency was the prime purpose of the Pacific Islands historiography of the 1960s.[7] Among his other recent interventions in Australian scholarship, Henry Reynolds's contribution towards racial reconciliation, *This Whispering in Our Hearts*,[8] addresses precisely this issue.

Our concerns therefore include 'cultural' as much as other branches of history. The term 'culture', alas, often suffers from vague and cuddly associations, but culture also includes the ways in which people relate their direct experience to that of the wider society. Even seemingly neutral narratives sensitize or desensitize us, confront or divert us, legitimize authority or undermine it. The social reformers, visionaries and intellectuals who wept by the bed of the 'dying races' did not cause population loss, but their grieving narratives validated other people's neglect, dulled consciences and marginalized colonized peoples. Edward Said points to culture's further significance as an elevating element – each society's reservoir of the best that has been known and thought, as Matthew Arnold put it – the England of Shakespeare, the Spain of Cervantes, the France of Hugo.[9] Culture is then associated with the ideals of a nation, and even permits discrimination between 'us' and 'them'. Culture in this sense is a source of combative identity, encouraging rigorous codes of behaviour opposed to the liberal philosophies of multiculturalism and hybridity.

To do justice to the dynamic relationships between collective identities, we try to balance comparative histories in which nations or societies are the constituencies, and interactive histories in which each community has influenced the identities of its neighbours. That in turn requires that we balance economic, social and political historical narratives to provide background, and cultural studies in the politics of identity and the social construction of the past. We make no attempt to synthesize established historical studies into a transnational narrative, though we incite others to do so. This is not a short history of the nations, societies, cultures or economies of our region, which are more than adequately narrated in a host of scholarly publications. Our claim to the reader's attention is the novelty of our regional focus, and our concern with the formation and interaction of identities within it.

NOTES

1   The South Pacific Commission did coincide with our region, but it began only in 1948, as a technical body advising colonial administrations. It remains a technical body, and now covers the North Pacific.
2   Albert Métin, *Socialism Without Doctrines*, first published in French in 1901, translated by R. Ward and published in English in Sydney, 1977.
3   A most welcome exception is Isabelle Merle, *Expériences coloniales: la Nouvelle-Calédonie, 1853–1920*, Paris, 1995.
4   I. C. Campbell, 'Culture Contact and Polynesian Identity in the European Age', *Journal of World History*, 8 (1997), 1, 29–55.
5   Poka Laenui, 'Repression and Renaissance in Hawaii', in D. Denoon, S. Firth, J. Linnekin, M. Meleisea and K. Nero (eds), *Cambridge History of the Pacific Islanders*, Melbourne, 1997.
6   David Hanlon, *Remaking Micronesia: Discourses over Development in a Pacific Territory, 1944–1982*, Honolulu, 1998.
7   K. R. Howe, 'The Fate of the 'Savage' in Pacific Historiography', *New Zealand Journal of History* (1977), 137–54.
8   Henry Reynolds, *This Whispering in Our Hearts*, Sydney, 1998.
9   Edward Said, *Culture and Imperialism*, London, 1994.

PART I

Foundations of Contemporary Identities

[1] REPRESENTATIONS OF REGIONAL, NATIONAL AND 'ETHNIC' IDENTITIES

A reader may wonder about the identity of writers who claim to deal with identities. If we try to satisfy that curiosity, however, we find our individual identities almost too elusive to summarize without distortion. Governments take pains to verify passport details, so we might begin with these: yet one of us has changed her name, two of us have changed citizenship, all three have changed marital and academic status, and our past addresses are too many to count. Such multiplicity is not unusual. These accretions – alongside our predictable transitions from childhood to maturity – make us rather typical of Australians and New Zealanders, and especially of academics. For other people in other societies, past and present, the terms of identity may differ, but not the fact of multiplicity. Epeli Hau'ofa was born in Papua of Tongan parents, lives in Fiji, studied in Australia and works in a regional university. None of that public information hints at his movement between disciplines, nor does it explain the qualities of his life and work. Physical mobility alone does not explain elusive identities. In a rare autobiographical account of a rural Papua New Guinean woman, Kwahihi told Michael Young a sequence of episodes in which her father and her successive husbands were the main sources of her evolving identity.[1] A rare individual may experience a diametrical change of identity; much more common is the accumulation of additional facets in response to changing relationships and circumstances.

Group identities are more stable, otherwise a study of this kind would be unthinkable. Even so, their growth and interaction are seldom simple, or unconscious, or consensual. Richard White isolates this quality in his seminal *Inventing Australia*. While 'Australia' is tangible and now self-evident as a geographical expression, it became a concrete political expression only through the continent-wide federation of the colonies in 1901. Further, Australia exists 'pre-eminently as an idea' whose convoluted history is White's subject matter.[2] In the same vein, New Zealand was a country of the imagination long before (and perhaps more intensely than) it became a political entity with the sinews of a state. Equally, 'New Guinea' was the subject of fabrication as well as imagination and speculation by Europeans. Australians and others 'knew' what to expect long before they had any empirical evidence; and some of the speculations by Melanesian villagers about their neighbours were even more febrile.[3]

NAMING RIGHTS

Social identities commonly mingle with physical features, and sometimes treat geographical features as emblematic, so the naming of natural features provokes dispute. When no more than one community has a stake in the names and narratives attaching to a mountain or a lake, imaginative (or tidy-minded) people devise names for them, and these are accepted, or rejected, or modified by their peers, and become conventions, endorsed or contested (or both) until new conventions are proposed or new communities turn up. Whose nominations command such attention? And who are the peers whose imprimatur carries such weight? Naming a place asserts power as well as pro-prietorship and propinquity. Ngai Tahu are a New Zealand Maori *iwi* (or tribe) and their names apply to features within their *iwi* territory, but not to the whole of New Zealand. On a very much larger scale, continents, archipel-agos and oceans are usually larger than any community controlled, or needed to name. Bestowing names on these features is often a perquisite of regional or even global power. Spaniards were late-comers to the greatest ocean on earth. Before they had any sense of its dimensions, they named it the Pacific. The fact of a later Spanish empire on these shores secured the naming rights. Later empires encroached on that domain but honoured its name – otherwise we might call our region Nanyo or Nanyang, Japanese and Cantonese terms for southern lands and seas. A host of features acquired their current names during Europe's self-conscious 'Age of Discovery' – the late eighteenth and early nineteenth centuries – when a strange combination of heroic exploration, imperial hubris and mariners' whimsy allowed an elite of European naviga-tors and naturalists and their patrons to extract cartographic homage.

Scholarly authority can also buttress a claim, lending self-assurance to the claimants. Europeans knew about the Arctic, and their cosmology led them to expect (and name) an Antarctic, long before they found it. Through simi-lar feats of cerebration a conceptual 'Australia' (or Terra Australis Incognita) was prefigured in Europe long before it materialized (in Solomon Islands as Australia del Espiritu Santo)[4] and was then mentally transported to the con-tinent which it now describes. A persuasive advocate for 'Australia' was Matthew Flinders, Royal Navy officer, cartographer and circumnavigator of the continent. He argued that New Holland and New South Wales were no longer appropriate terms, since he had established that they referred to the same land mass. His exegesis covered many of the issues which arise in such namings:

> It is necessary, however, to geographical propriety that the whole body of land should be designated under one general name; on this account, and under the circumstances of the discovery of the different parts, it seems best to refer back to the original Terra Australis, or Australia, which being descriptive of its situa-tion, having antiquity to recommend it, and no reference to either of the two claiming nations [Britain and France], is perhaps the least objectionable that could have been chosen; for it is little to be apprehended that any considerable body of land, in a more southerly situation, will be hereafter discovered.[5]

Plate 1.1 Shane Cotton, *Ko te rakau a Taiamai* (The Tree of Taiamai) 1997, oil on canvas. Collection of the Dunedin Public Art Gallery. Reproduced by kind permission of the artist.

Convenience, geographical coherence, antiquity and acceptability to the great powers: these criteria implied no need to consult the people living on the land whose name was under review. A further political step was also needed. That was provided when Lachlan Macquarie, Governor of New South Wales in the 1810s, was converted to 'Australia', if only to erase the dismal associations of 'Botany Bay'. This may be the earliest Australian instance of the linkage described by Benedict Anderson and applied to Australia by Richard White: the idea of Australia was among other things a powerful marketing exercise.[6]

There are revealing compromises between broad and narrow naming rights. French navigators chose to call a large island after the navigator Louis-Antoine de Bougainville. A century later, German officials accepted Bougainville, and decreed that its dividing range should commemorate their emperor's heir – Kron Prinz – but smaller features like the Kawerong river, rising in the Kron Prinz range, retained the names by which they were known to the Nasioi. The association of European names with large features, and indigenous names with local features, hints mischievously that all Europeans share the broad vision of eighteenth-century navigators, while indigenes care only for parochial physical features. It would be more pertinent and accurate to notice that the struggles of indigenous peoples to modify their ascribed identities and the names of the places important to them, has usually been piecemeal. Many local victories and amendments have been won, but the architecture of knowledge retains its Eurocentric quality.

How the people who named the Kawerong river came to be called (and to call themselves) Nasioi is another question. Many societies in our region simply called themselves 'the people'. Knowing or fearing no others 'against whom identity [needed] to be maintained', they could comfortably equate their society with their species.[7] It is unlikely that 'proto-Nasioi' used any collective name until they lost their freedom to a Hamburg-based chartered company, for whose convenience they were squeezed into a grid of tribal categories.[8] Colonial officials everywhere seem to have disliked the diversity and subtlety of social relations among colonized people. To promote ethnic order they encouraged the delineation of tribes, whether or not these existed or were salient in people's lives. Naming a human community is never politically or morally neutral. If people determine to do it for themselves (as 'normal' Maori did in the nineteenth century) it is to distinguish themselves from others (in this case 'abnormal' Pakeha). If it is done by outsiders, or at their behest, naming reflects – and generates – the outsiders' power. In Pakeha myth and history the Dutchman Abel Tasman was the discoverer, remembered in the name of New Zealand. The historian James Belich observes that this was convenient because it extended New Zealand's European history back from the nineteenth century to the seventeenth. As it did not extend British history, however, it was 'not remembered very hard'.[9] Having named Van Diemen's Land (now Tasmania) after the governor of Batavia, Tasman sailed across the sea named for him until he met New Zealand, and specifically Golden Bay – named since then for its beaches – which Tasman labelled Murderers Bay because the local Ngati Tumatakokiri repelled his men.[10]

The exploring and naming specialists (particularly Captain James Cook in 1774) chose to call a large island in the Southwest Pacific New Caledonia. Thirty languages were spoken on the main island and the offshore (Society) group; and they had no collective term for all of them. French officials applied two terms: canaque, adapted from the English kanak, borrowed in turn from the Hawaiian term for people; and Caledoniens, endorsing Captain Cook's naming exercise. As Europeans became permanent settlers, they appropriated the name Caledoniens for themselves, leaving canaque for the indigenes. In one language, people called themselves Do Kamo, meaning true humans. That term gained wider currency in the 1930s, with the publication of a book of the same name, by the anthropologist and missionary Maurice Leenhardt.[11] A similar appropriation can be observed in the larger settler societies nearby. Until the early nineteenth century the term 'Australians' applied only to Aboriginal Australians: it then moved to describe the colonists, and Aborigines were eventually excluded. Equally, 'New Zealanders' meant Maori before the term was reassigned to the colonists.

In the idiosyncratic logic of naming, it followed from the fanciful choice of New Caledonia that a nearby archipelago must be the New Hebrides. The inhabitants of those islands did not hear these terms until much later; and by that time Nouvelle Caledonie and Nouvelles Hebrides carried the moral authority of European cartography reinforced by the coercive weight of colonialism. The people could not therefore resist the corollary that they were (among other facets of identity) New Caledonians and New Hebrideans. Compared with other names conferred upon – or thrown at – colonized natives, these were more mystifying than offensive. Nonetheless, the advent of political independence prompted some leaders to devise and assert fresh terms to express their sense of themselves. Land – *vanua* – was central to individual and communal identities, so the independence-minded Vanua'aku Pati proposed that colonial New Hebrides become independent Vanuatu, and its colonial subjects niVanuatu citizens.[12] Here, as so often, public identity flowed from the transfer of power – but in New Caledonia the people did not await a political transition. For decades they had been denigrated as Canaques. Inspired partly by the Paris turbulence of 1968, and by their ancestors' own anti-colonial rebellions, students coined and embraced the angular term kanak – un-French in its very letters – and prefigured the independence of Kanaky.[13]

The International Date Line, the Tropic of Capricorn and lines of latitude and longitude (together with the less familiar Wallace and Andesite lines) inscribe the scientific conceptions and global judgements of European cartographers on regional maps. The International Date Line has since been modified so that iKiribati (citizens of Kiribati, formerly the Gilbert Islands) can all live in the same day, but this is merely a modification of an arbitrary imposition. These are traces of a tradition beginning even before Europe's Age of Discovery which carried European naturalists through the Pacific to extend the catalogue of Western knowledge. Joseph Banks, who financed and organized the expedition which was carried in Captain James Cook's first voyage to the Pacific, later became President of the Royal Society and patron of scientists and explorers. That tradition was carried on through the nineteenth century. Charles Darwin was one of many naturalists who treated the Pacific as a natural laboratory (often juxtaposed with 'the Atlantic'), and helped to define its contents and demarcate its boundaries.[14] In our own day the tide of the Age of Discovery has begun to ebb, and so do some of the terms which flooded the world's beaches, revealing in their place a host of parochial terms, categories and identities. But the tidal metaphor is too simple. The subsiding of eighteenth century terms uncovers not pristine pre-European identity, but messy compromise. Australia's best-known physical feature was for decades known to the outside world as Ayer's Rock. It has now reverted to the indigenous Uluru, but the rock has meanwhile become a national (not merely local) emblem. New Zealand's highest mountain was known as Mount Cook. As part of a drive towards bicultural parity it is now Aoraki/Mount Cook. It will probably become simply Aoraki (cloud-piercer) before long, but it will never again be merely a Ngai Tahu landmark. Its distinctive tip has now toppled into the valley, but its national significance is,

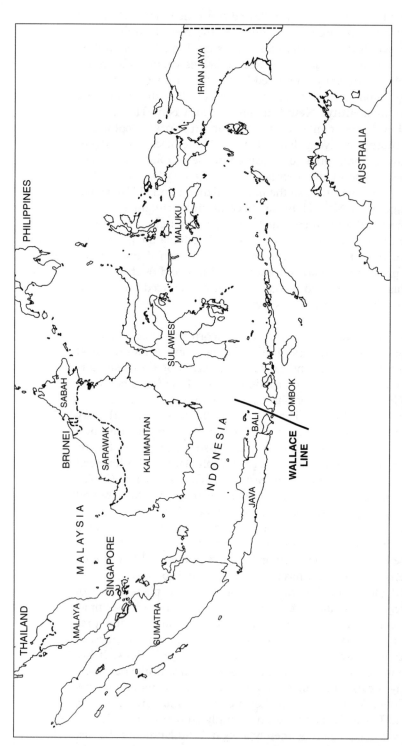

Map 2 Cataloguing and classifying the region, courtesy of the Cartography Unit, Research School of Pacific and Asian Studies, Australian National University. **(a)** Wallace's Line: Placentals to the west, Marsupials to the east, according to Alfred Russel Wallace.

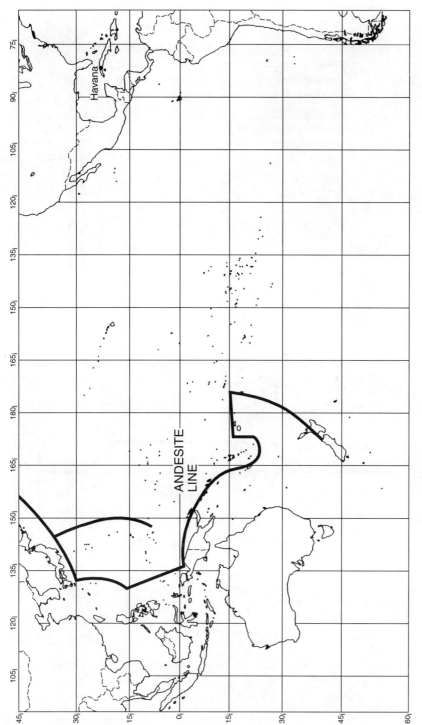

Map 2(b) Andesite Line: natural resources to the west, much less to the east.

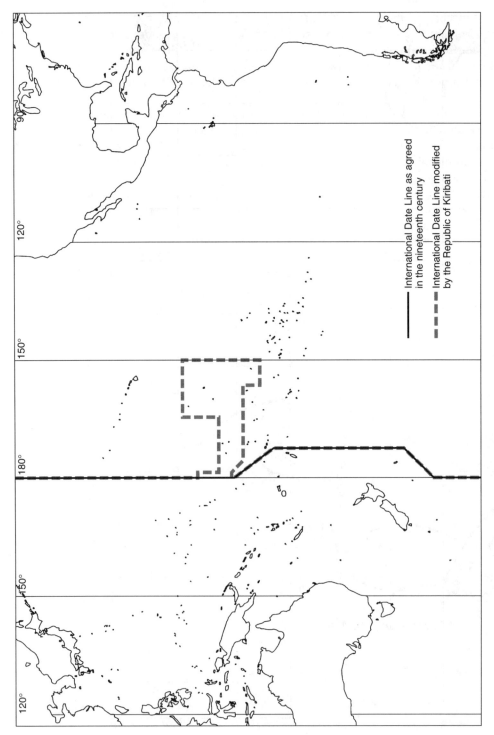

International Date Line as agreed
in the nineteenth century

International Date Line modified
by the Republic of Kiribati

Map 2(c) International Date Line: blurred so that iKiribati can share the same date.

if anything, enhanced by the debate over its name. As for nature, so for culture. The concept and the reality of Vanuatu – a nation-state with a constitution, a government and citizens, an economy and an exclusive economic zone, an incipient national culture and even a national drug – are the apotheosis of a colonial history, not its negation. New Caledonia's immediate future involves a constitutional compromise between colonialism and independence. Past practices are undone, but not the past.

International power relations have had other consequences. Britain and France (and briefly Germany and Japan) created global networks of power and demanded an allegiance which cut across other affiliations. That perspective still informs politics and some of the scholarship in France's overseas territories, although it is challenged by indigenous politics in New Caledonia.[15] Proclaimed in the 1890s, the United States' 'Pacific Century' made a similar assertion, extinguishing the remnants of Spain's Pacific empire and linking Japan and China across the Pacific to a North American centre. Some American strategists continue to imagine the 'Pacific Rim' as a strategic arena, which sometimes includes Australia and New Zealand as its southern quadrant, but invariably portrays the island world as the hole in the doughnut. In that tradition, Hartley Grattan delineated the Southwest Pacific[16] in 1961, long before indigenous peoples were thought to be historically significant; and Oskar Spate's trilogy, *The Pacific Since Magellan*,[17] explicitly excludes indigenous histories in order to focus on the interests and initiatives of the great powers. For all their admirable qualities, these frameworks are too narrow to serve our present purpose.

EUROPEAN FRAMEWORKS

A Whiggish narrative of eighteenth-century arrogance, nineteenth-century colonialism and twentieth-century liberation is merely a first approximation of the ways in which people identify themselves, their neighbours, their allies and enemies. There has never been unanimity about physical, much less human identities; and many are the experts whose proposed terms have been spurned. In their pursuit of political neutrality, archeologists prefer geographical to social markers, but that does not shelter them from controversy. Until about 8,000 years ago, the freezing of oceans and low sea levels meant that Australia (including Tasmania) and insular New Guinea (including many now separate islands) were one land mass. It seemed to many archeologists that Greater Australia suitably described this entity – but Greater New Guinea might be more appropriate since more people lived in the northern sector than in the south. Sidestepping this discussion, archeologists coined Sunda (roughly today's Southeast Asia) and Sahul (roughly Australia and New Guinea) for the land masses exposed by low sea levels.[18] Some such terms were required in order to signal the great differences in flora and fauna between the two regions, divided conceptually by Wallace's Line.[19] These esoteric terms survive largely because lay people seldom see and never understand them. From Sahul to the northeast, archeologists distinguish between Near Oceania (near Australia and settled by humans by about 30,000 years ago) and Remote Oceania (occupied only within the last 3,000 years).[20] That convention may be ignored without penalty, so that Jared Diamond's comparative surveys treat 'Australia and New Guinea' (a similar space to 'Sahul') as one prehistoric continent, analogous with Eurasia, Africa and the Americas – in effect a natural laboratory.[21] The core of our region can also be imagined as stretching east as far as the Andesite Line, another invisible barrier traced by scientists. West of that line, the land derives from ancient continental rocks. East of that line, most islands are coral, and natural resources and rainfall are miserly. The variety of terms and usages is remarkable in a discipline which concerns long-lost environments and unspecific populations, which prides itself on its precise and neutral technical terms, and whose arguments are advanced by specialists. There is no escape from the politics of identity even in the most remote human past.

These semantic convolutions measure scholarly anxiety to escape the linguistic morass which we inherit from the Age of Discovery. The discoverers did not stop at the ordering of physical features, but also classified peoples as Polynesians, Melanesians and Micronesians, and set them apart from both Asia and Aboriginal Australia. Some such division was suggested even before the voyages of discovery.[22] With the moral advantage of exploration, Dumont d'Urville mapped these categories onto the grid of European science, most memorably when he addressed his scientific peers in the Geographical Society of Paris.[23] Alfred Russel Wallace did not content himself with a line between placental and marsupial animals, but traced an evolutionary distinction between Malays and Papuans.[24] In summary, explorers and scientists believed that the region was inhabited by distinct 'races', each with innate qualities. Polynesians (of the many islands) usually lived in hierarchical societies with clearly identified power-holders, so they were ranked above (black) Melanesians whose social arrangements were much less transparent to short-term visitors. Micronesia became a residual category (tiny islands). All were deemed more advanced than Aboriginal Australians, whose hunting, gathering and nomadism condemned them to European condescension. It was implicit (but axiomatic) that the discoverers' societies represented the peak of human attainment, and their societies the acme of human wisdom. Quite apart from awkward boundaries (is Fiji Polynesian or Melanesian; are Torres Strait Islanders Melanesian or Aboriginal Australian; have the people of Irian Jaya ceased to be Melanesians?) this hierarchy is achieved by freezing whole populations into immutable caricatures. To talk of Inner and Remote Oceania avoids some of the expectations which are generated by the terms Melanesia and Polynesia. It would be extremely convenient to dispense with these loaded terms altogether – if they had not been almost universally accepted, not least by Polynesians and Melanesians.

In some sense, European navigators did not merely 'discover' hitherto unknown lands, seas and peoples; they also confirmed or modified what they already thought they knew. Kerry Howe points to the Judeo-Christian tradition of the Garden of Eden, whence mortals were expelled into 'a world of sin, pain, work, and danger'.[25] Europeans were reluctant to abandon hope of rediscovering that earthly Paradise, and that hope revived with voyages to Asia and the Americas. Columbus and others forever found themselves almost within reach:[26] 'I thought I must be near the Earthly Paradise' judged Amerigo Vespucci in 1502, of the Atlantic coast of South America,[27] and 'almost every Spanish and Portuguese commander in Central and South America almost found it, as did the English in their early American colonies'. Howe observes that

> What characterized this 'knowing' was not just what to us is the rather absurd nature of the 'information', but a pre-Enlightenment 'cognitive apparatus' and a classificatory system that was convincingly 'derived from utterly fabulous authorities.'[28]

Despite its artificiality, the trope of paradise has been irresistible to scholars and publishers even today, from Dr Sam Lambert's *A Yankee Doctor in Paradise* through Harry Maude's *Slavers in Paradise* to Oskar Spate's *Paradise Found and Lost*. Gavan Daws's *A Dream of Islands* probes into the lives and ideas of Paul Gauguin, Herman Melville, Robert Louis Stephenson and John Williams, four of the most influential men who were infected by the image in the nineteenth century and whose multi-media work spread the epidemic worldwide.[29] The idea of an earthly paradise carried its converse, an earthly hell. Naturally no place corresponded exactly to these expectations, and in a literal sense the search for paradise was soon blighted; but the rhetoric persisted. Hellish adjectives came readily to the lips of convicts and their gaolers in Botany Bay, Van Diemen's Land and New Caledonia; New Zealand's free settlers took a much more optimistic view of their environs; and colonists' and missionaries' first paradisical impressions of tropical islands often swung violently towards the opposite extreme.

ANTHROPOLOGY

Such broad-brush perceptions were modified in detail, but not erased when anthropology emerged as a formal academic discipline.[30] Most nineteenth-century 'anthropologists' were self-taught and self-appointed, and their scholarship was a branch of European philosophy which reflected upon classical Europe as much as reports from the frontiers of European settlement. Within that tradition, when British officers of the First Fleet and their successors at Sydney Cove began to speculate about Aboriginal capacities, they set their ideas in the frame of contemporary British ideas about the world and its people. Barron Field, Judge of the New South Wales Supreme Court, classed Aborigines as having 'the degenerate Ethiopian character'. His equation of Aboriginal Australians and Africans implied that all these benighted people were not simply stuck in a primitive stage of development, but that they had degenerated – fallen back from it – so that they 'will never be civilized'.[31] The notion of 'degeneration' was not universally accepted, but it articulated Field's sense of the gulf separating his society from that of Aboriginal Australians.

Anthropology assumed its modern form when natural scientists took an interest in human societies, and began the systematic collection and classification of evidence. Most of these adventurous scholars were pondering the implications of Charles Darwin's evolutionary theory for understanding the development of human societies. It seemed self-evident that the societies most remote from Europe would be most fruitfully studied: their behaviour would document early phases of human evolution before contact with 'higher' cultures launched them on the paths of development and self-consciousness (or cultural, if not biological extinction).[32] Much of its data was collected in Australia, New Zealand and the wider Pacific, in the generation from 1890.

In central Australia, the Oxford graduate and Adelaide University naturalist Baldwin Spencer enlisted the support of Frank Gillen, the officer in charge of the Alice Springs overland telegraph office. That partnership combined Spencer's access to social theorists, Gillen's access to Aboriginal practices, and the means of communication with each other and with academic readers.[33] They had an eager audience of European scientists, who knew that Aboriginal Australian societies were concrete, specific and historically contingent – but also saw them as an abstraction which was typical of the earliest phase of all societies in more 'developed' conditions. As in this partnership, settlers, local officials, missionaries and other amateurs were collectors of data, but the research agenda was set, and the information analysed, framed and published, by scholars trained in the natural sciences and working in European academia. In 1897 the Cambridge Expedition to Torres Strait briefly bridged that gap: physicians and photographers brought their experimental equipment to the antipodes in search of an isolated social laboratory in which to explore questions of human perception. Despite the idiosyncrasy of their initial assumptions, some were so fascinated by their human subjects that they reformed their research agendas and began work afresh as pioneers of cultural anthropology. W. H. R. Rivers, a physiologist and psychologist, went on to ethnographic fieldwork in India and the Solomon Islands, and initiated the systematic study of kinship.[34] His colleague C. G. Seligman crossed Torres Strait to organize the first survey of Papuan cultures. Between them they gave empirical substance to the previously vacuous term 'Melanesia'. In that domain they were followed by the intensely focused Trobriand Island studies of Bronislaw Malinowski (another convert from the natural sciences), which set the standards for generations of field-workers.[35]

Anthropology quickly found institutional support in the settler colonies. Rivers' pupil Radcliffe-Brown initiated social and cultural anthropology in Sydney University, eventually reaching an informal division of labour whereby Baldwin Spencer's Adelaide department concentrated more on physical anthropology. New Zealanders had already in the 1890s pioneered Polynesian studies. Reconstructing Maori migration routes and genealogies was more than antiquarianism: it was a vital step in demarcating (with the aim of alienating) Maori land, and it laid the academic foundations for the country's sense of itself.[36] That Polynesian focus was matched in Hawaii, where the Bernice P. Bishop Museum also supported researchers. Before long the vague (almost intuitive) cultural and linguistic category of Polynesia was elaborated and extended. New Zealand scholars were exceptional in organizing their own learned society which published the *Journal of the Polynesian Society*. Nowhere else in the South Pacific did indigenous people play such influential roles in scholarship, mainly as informants but also as researchers; yet they did not subvert the agenda or the methods of the emerging discipline. Like Melanesia, Polynesia was 'essentialized' and people's innate traits classified. While Rivers' early account[37] blended history and ethnography, functional anthropology (inspired by Malinowski, Radcliffe-Brown and their disciples) largely abandoned historical approaches. By elaborating the manner in which every element in indigenous society meshed with every other element, anthropology made it difficult to see how these societies could accommodate social, cultural or economic change, whether by their own agency or through external prompting. Aborigines and islanders might possess complex cultures, but they were portrayed almost as 'people without history'.[38] That approach was tempered but not broken by the Maori anthropologist Te Rangihiroa (Sir Peter Buck), who elaborated the familial relations between all the far-flung Polynesian societies.

New Zealand and Hawaiian scholars were unusual in establishing themselves in the ranks of professionals, rather than colonial data-collectors. Nonetheless the agenda and enthusiasms – and fashions – of the discipline were determined in the academies of Europe and North America. Acknowledging this reality, the new anthropology sought – and sometimes received – support from governments who expected advice on managing change in colonized populations. For Grimshaw and Hart, the transition from 'pure' to 'applied' studies can be seen in the contrast between European scholarship before and after the Great War, and especially in the differences between Rivers and Malinowski.

> Rivers's anthropology took shape in the relatively open atmosphere of the early twentieth century, when established structures were being dislodged and conventional categories questioned, with the modernist explosion a brilliant counterpart to international revolutionary politics, [whereas] Malinowski's anthropology was moulded by a society in retreat. It contained at its core a static version of society.[39]

Although the new (like some of the old) anthropology denied the inherent superiority of one society and its values over another, in some ways it gave support for essentialist categories.[40] While anthropology sought regular patterns in the behaviour of colonized people, history sought unique events in the lives of the colonists. By default, therefore, settlers were seen as historical actors (albeit 'people without culture'), over against the culture-rich but ahistorical indigenes.

Individual anthropologists believed that they moderated the impact of colonial power. Institutionally, the discipline was more complicit in colonialism, but not essential to it. Colonialism was born not of scholarly fashion, but of economic interests, racism, imperial strategies and settler needs, brought into lethal combination. The consequent division of humanity into imperial citizens and colonial subjects bequeathed a series of highly emotive

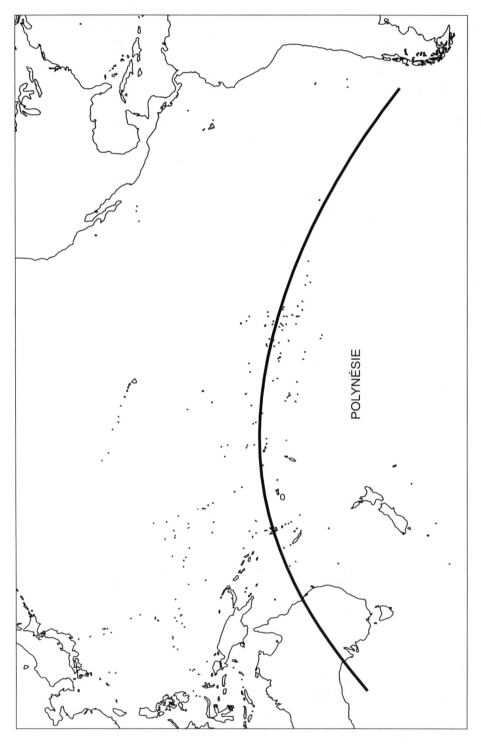

POLYNÉSIE

Map 3 Evolving Polynesia: courtesy of R. Gerard Ward and the Cartography Unit, Research School of Pacific and Asian Studies, Australian National University. **(a)** According to De Brosses, 1756.

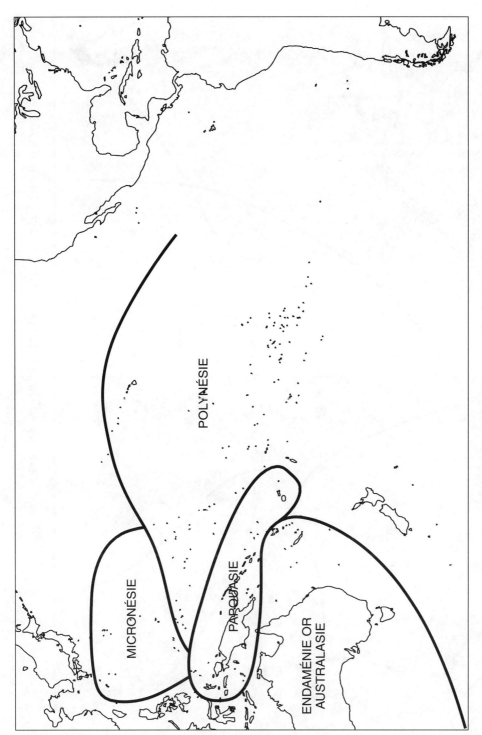

MICRONÉSIE

POLYNÉSIE

PAROPASIE

ENDAMÉNIE OR
AUSTRALASIE

Map 3(b) According to De Rienzi, 1831.

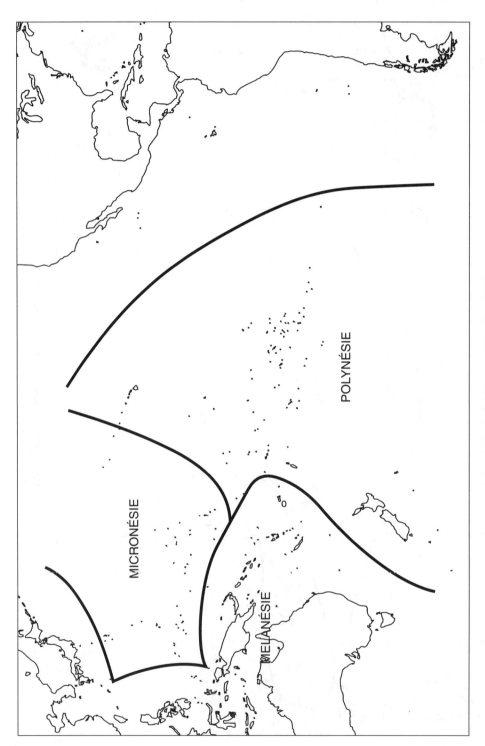

MICRONÉSIE

POLYNÉSIE

MÉLANÉSIE

Map 3(c) According to d'Urville, 1832.

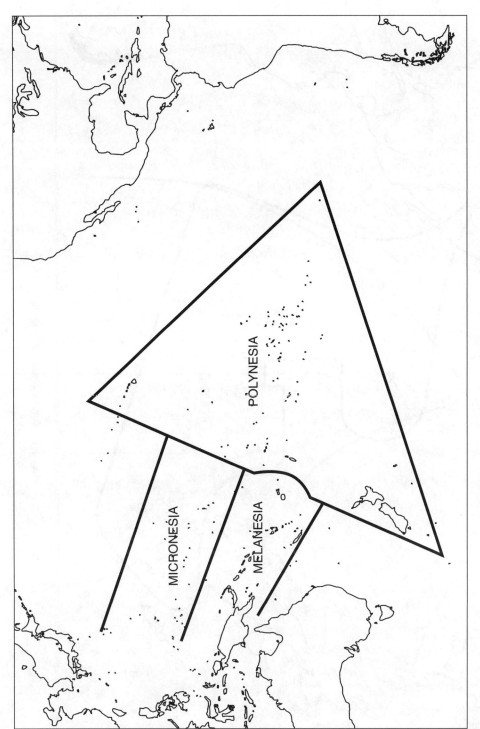

Map 3(d) According to Peter Buck (Te Rangihiroa), 1938.

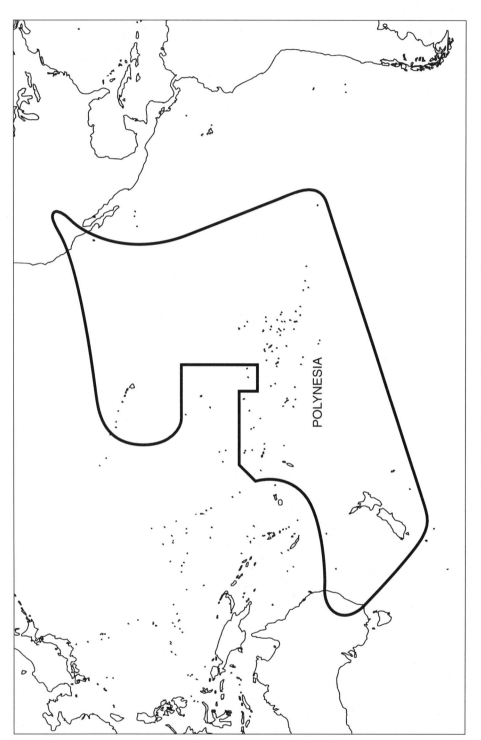

POLYNESIA

Map 3(e) Where are the Polynesians now?

Table 1.1 Regional populations and densities

Polity	Population (1994)	Land area (km²)	Density
Australia	18,000,000	7,682,395	2.34
Cook Islands	19,100	240	79.58
Fiji	777,700	18,272	42.56
French Polynesia	218,000	3,265	66.77
Irian Jaya	1,400,000	420,000	3.33
Nauru	10,600	21	504.76
New Caledonia	182,200	19,103	9.54
New Zealand	3,300,000	270,534	12.19
Niue	2,100	259	8.11
Papua New Guinea	3,951,500	462,243	8.55
Solomon Islands	367,400	28,369	12.95
Tonga	98,300	747	131.59
Vanuatu	164,100	12,190	13.46
Western Samoa	163,500	2,820	57.98

and imperfectly resolved tensions. These are central to our analyses. If the Age of Discovery classed whole communities as savages, colonization made them colonial subjects and natives. Decolonization transformed natives into citizens, but citizens of unequal polities (table 1.1).

DEVELOPMENT ECONOMICS

Inequality was not merely a matter of population or land area. Decolonization brought an invidious distinction between developed and underdeveloped (or the blander term, developing) economies and societies, gutting independence of its liberating potential. Western economic indices struggle to accommodate non-market activity, and therefore (mis)represent islanders as among the world's poorest people. Joel Bonnemaison captures the significance of this arbitrary measure for understanding the perspectives of Tannese in Vanuatu:

> Devoid of cash, the islanders are rich in pigs, kava, and giant tubers, which they trade off with pomp and ostentation from one ceremony to the next. Poor in relation to the outside world, they endeavour to remain rich in their own context, in order to be generous among themselves.[41]

Development agencies acknowledge no such ambivalence. In 1979, for example, an Asian Development Bank delegation reviewed Island agriculture. Epeli Hau'ofa, who took part, was driven to the melancholy conclusion that

> If the Pacific Island societies want to maintain their distinct ways of life and their cultures … then the capitalistic system is certainly not the right one. … [However] the Pacific Islanders seem, by action although not by rhetoric, to have made the choice already and opted for capitalism. By rhetoric, although much less by action, they want to maintain distinct identities.[42]

Table 1.2 Pacific economic statistics[43]

Polity	GDP (Australian $'000s)	Year	Per capita GDP (Australian $'000s)
Cook Islands	89,866	1993	5,195
Fiji	2,077,830	1993	2,716
French Polynesia	4,106,108	1992	19,622
Nauru	206,250	1989	22,418
New Caledonia	3,053,988	1990	17,970
Papua New Guinea	7,269,565	1993	1,882
Solomon Islands	336,572	1993	947
Tonga	176,968	1992	1,815
Vanuatu	267,793	1993	1,678
Western Samoa	212,674	1992	1,305

Table 1.3 Human development indicators[44]

Country	Life expectancy at birth	Adult literacy (percentage of population)	Mean years schooling	GDP (US $ per capita)	Index
Cook Islands	69.8	99	8.4	3,416	985
Niue	66.0	99	8.3	3,051	879
Tonga	69.0	99	7.1	1,396	723
Fiji	63.1	87	6.8	1,991	652
Western Samoa	63.1	98	9.1	722	578
Vanuatu	62.8	64	4.0	1,020	424
Solomon Islands	60.7	23	2.8	529	191
Papua New Guinea	49.6	52	2.1	999	138

The conventions of the regional banker lead inexorably to table 1.2, which suggests, among other things, that the greater the degree of independence, the lower the income.

The picture is equally stark if the statistics are re-processed to measure quality of life according to a 'human development' index (table 1.3).

If economic analysis condemned most islands to 'underdevelopment', political independence allowed intellectuals – including Hau'ofa – to re-imagine their pasts and their futures. Western practice defined political units in terms of land boundaries, and saw islands (and archipelagos) as self-contained land-based polities. Hau'ofa argues that long-distance trade and exchange were fundamental to islanders' way of life:

> The highest chiefs of Fiji, Samoa and Tonga, for example, still maintain kin connections that were forged centuries before Europeans entered the Pacific, in the days when boundaries were not imaginary lines in the ocean, but rather points of entry. ... The sea was open to anyone who could navigate.[45]

Similar long-range linkages have been recreated or invented since independence. A majority of all Cook Islanders and Niueans, and large minorities of other Polynesian communities live in New Zealand. So many Tahitians, Wallisians and Futunans live in New Caledonia that their political preferences can be decisive in contests between indigenes and European settlers. These linkages are not associations of equals, like those of the pre-colonial chiefly families; they do not erase the statistical appearance, nor do they alter the reality, of economic deprivation.

HISTORY

As the most popular of academic forms, history may tell us most about self-perceptions, especially when the subject was taught to generations of school children as civic education. The earliest teachers in state, church and mission schools naturally brought the narratives of the metropolitan countries where they had been schooled. That offered pupils a sense of themselves as far-flung pioneers of the empire or the religion (or both) of the metropole. And although historical studies were written very early in the settler colonies, these essays extended and elaborated 'master-narratives' of empire, civilization, or evangelism. 'Australian history' therefore was not established in university curricula until the 1930s, with W. K. Hancock in Adelaide and Brian Fitzpatrick in Melbourne. Hancock's career alternated between Australian academia and British public service, whereas Fitzpatrick's radical stance was to denounce the pervasive influences of British imperialism in Australian society. For each of them Australian identity was intimately wrapped up in a British context.[46] Only in the 1950s, when Manning Clark began to publish his multi-volume history of Australia, was the British context down-played.[47] At least until the publication of these studies (and perhaps even longer), 'Australians' were represented in print as Britons abroad, peripheral to Europe, yet distinct from indigenous Australians and their Asian and Islander neighbours. In New Zealand, also in the 1930s, J. B. Condliffe's work pioneered the historiography of an emerging nation-state.[48]

The academic representation of New Caledonia remained in French imperial aspic even longer. From Maurice Leenhardt to Jean Guiart, scholarship was led by anthropological studies of Kanak communities,[49] and social histories of any community were sparse until Isabelle Merle's studies in the 1990s.[50] Commonly, New Caledonia was seen as an instance (albeit an unusual one) of French policy and practice in an exotic part of the world.[51] Elsewhere in the Pacific the 'islander-oriented' history of the Pacific – as opposed to narratives of explorers and missionaries – is commonly dated to the 1960s, when the New Zealander James Davidson was appointed to the first chair of Pacific History at the Australian National University. Davidson had researched African History and held a fellowship in Cambridge. Like contemporary African historians he was turning his back on imperial history. Much of his department's work restored agency to islanders, legitimizing the decolonization and independence which transformed the island world during the 1960s and 1970s. It would be simplistic to attach great political weight to academic books directly, but until monographs were published and fed the writers of school texts, any popular sense of identity had no anchor. Until then, books which represented colonial histories as footnotes to narratives of empire or civilization enjoyed great, if contested, authority.

With so many frameworks to work within, few scholars have written about our region in its entirety. At the turn of the twentieth century several treated Australia and New Zealand as related sites for social experiment, following the New Zealand politician and propagandist William Pember Reeves, whose *State Experiments in Australia and New Zealand* set the fashion in 1902. From then on, scholars more commonly worked within (and created) national histories for New Zealand and for Australia, isolating them even from their nearest neighbours. A typical collection of essays avoids naming the region, by adopting the title *Australia, New Zealand, and the Pacific Islands since the First World War*.[52] the authors deal separately with Australia and New Zealand, and devote one chapter to the Pacific Islands and another to Australia–New Zealand relations. In scholarship about the Islands also, it is normal to focus on one island or archipelago or language, although everyone is inevitably (and acutely) aware of the raw power and cultural influences of their larger neighbours.

NOT A SELF-EVIDENT REGION

Alas, no collective term commands general support, to describe Australia, New Zealand and the Pacific Islands. For French scholars, Oceania encompasses the islands but excludes Australia and treats New Zealand as marginal.[53] Some anthropologists treat Oceania in the same manner,[54] but few other English-language scholars use the term at all. The uncertain boundaries of 'Oceania' do, however, draw our attention to the fact that the naming of regions is as political as the naming of communities and countries. There is no self-evident reason why the Pacific Islands are conventionally segregated from Asia – an arbitrary distinction which does violence to the alignments of Micronesians and which implies more internal consistency than anyone has found. Australasia, coined by de Brosses in the eighteenth century, was used sporadically thereafter.[55] It was used interchangeably with Australia in the early nineteenth century, and it was preferred in early drafts of a federal constitution for the self-governing colonies until New Zealand's delegates requested that the term be replaced by Australia. We now treat Australasia as a transitional concept deployed by settlers to distinguish themselves from alarming 'Asia'. Once national identities crystallized in the Australian Commonwealth and in the Dominion of New Zealand, the broad term had no continuing function. For better or worse (and for richer or poorer, in sickness or in health) it is the contemporary state which is the most obvious fount of identity, and the most insistent institution demanding the loyalties of its citizens.

The settler societies brought fully-fledged states with them, in the persons of governors and magistrates and in their conceptual baggage. Governors' authorities and powers were delegated from the crown or the president in whose name they exercised it, and to whom they answered. Those powers were – at least in theory – exercised in accordance with developed legal precedents and traditions. As these societies grew, authority was delegated first to nominated and advisory bodies and later to elected assemblies. Authority descended from the top, even if rhetoric sometimes described it as springing up from the populace. Settlers were from their inception subjects of the state under whose auspices (or in whose prison hulks) they migrated. Within two generations they could elaborate that identity by sharing it with the colony in which they lived. This was not the full extent of their civic baggage: much ink has been spilt on the extent to which they imported, rejected or adapted social-class expectations, and the ethnic traditions which (for example) divided Irish from English and Scots in the colonies. It was clear almost at once that European settlement in Australia would not accommodate indigenous concepts of kinship and affiliation. While indigenous property rights were swept aside, so were identities, consigning every community to the catch-all category 'Aborigines'.

It is unlikely that states existed in the region before the nineteenth century. Polynesian chiefdoms and lineages divided rather than united people who spoke the same language and revered the same traditions. Tongan and Samoan oral traditions were (and are) often organized around dynastic epics and genealogies, but unified rule was rare, and daily life revolved around localized chiefs and familial communities. The speed with which ambitious chiefs co-opted missionaries, traders and castaways for military and ideological aid suggests that the notion of a centralized, monarchical state was neither alien nor unwelcome. Whether or not people became Christian, the political repercussions of missionization were profound. Some chiefs harnessed Christianity to family ambition, creating new structures of belief and authority. As new states emerged, people began to identify themselves as 'Fijians', or 'Tongans', still adherents of local chiefs and lineages, but adding a dimension to their identity. The transition was not easy even in chiefly societies: for fissiparous societies in Melanesia, brought together with neighbouring enemies under the aegis of colonial authority, the transition was more difficult. While Polynesians often live outside the states of which they are citizens, they freely acknowledge its legitimacy; almost all Melanesians live within the state to which they owe allegiance, but their acknowledgement is at best conditional and contingent.

National identity – a very 'modern' notion – is often contrasted with 'traditional' tribal or ethnic identity: the former is clearly an imagined community while the latter may perhaps be a matter of demonstrable kinship. That dichotomy does no justice to the imaginative uses of kinship ideologies and other mechanisms of inclusion and omission. At any rate the first European settlers in Australia could only see themselves as Britons abroad, divided sharply into free, convict and emancipist. Cross-cutting distinctions emerged between 'sovereign' British-born and 'currency' native-born, and as settler populations grew more by immigration than by natural increase, the 'sovereign–currency' divide endured for a couple of generations. Meanwhile colonial identities – 'Victorians' or 'Tasmanians' – were reinforced by the growth of governments in those territories. South Australia and the New

Zealand settlements were free of convicts, giving their settlers an extra sense of distinctness – and superiority. So long as colonies on either side of the Tasman Sea were linked by migration, and by similar social structures, economic enterprises, and political institutions, the term Australasia handily expressed a collective identity. The federal movement, however, expressed and reinforced separate identities. With the creation of the Commonwealth, Australasia was redundant. It was now a matter of urgency to delineate the national cultural traits of these proto-nations.

With the decision not to federate, New Zealand's identity became increasingly insular. William Pember Reeves made that retrospective when he asserted that 'our colony is in no sense an offshoot or outlying province of Australia'. The founders of New Zealand were Britons.[56] Like other societies, white New Zealanders found it convenient and persuasive to define themselves in terms of physical environment, especially to illustrate New Zealand's non-Australian-ness.

> None of the Australian beasts or reptiles, only one bird, none of the eucalypts and acacias...ever found their way across the Tasman Sea. The fertile easy-rolling downs, the park-like woods and dreary endless 'scrubs' of the sandstone continent are replaced in New Zealand by snowy mountains or steep green hills, rich valleys divided by cold mountain torrents, and one of the densest, most luxuriant jungles to be found in the temperate zones. The climates of the Commonwealth and the Colony are as unlike as are the landscapes, and some people think that the two branches of the Anglo-Saxon race which inhabit them are already developing different characteristics.

New Zealand was 'an insular nation. Australia is a continental nation. The history of all races shows that continental races and insular races diverge further and further apart.'[57] New Zealand's distinctiveness rested also on the settlers' relations with Maori, who were, with some reservations, equal citizens; whereas Aboriginal Australians were explicitly denied citizenship and often barred from white society. New Zealanders and Australians represented themselves in the world differently, well before 1900. While both defined Asia as the 'other', they differed over their perceptions of their indigenous peoples against whom, in part, they defined themselves. In doing so, both were identifying a national 'type' as well as an embryonic national culture.[58]

This divergence was even more pronounced as the governments secured their perimeters. As Australians sidled towards a continental federation, New Zealand politicians, presenting themselves as experts in living with Maori, hoped to rule other Polynesian polities. These aspirations touched Fiji as well as Samoa and Tonga, but commanded no support in Westminster, and New Zealand's only acquisition before 1914 was the Cook Islands.[59] Nonetheless New Zealand's self-image remained that of an insular nation whose destiny lay among other islands. Her claim to an island empire rested partly on kinship between Maori and other Polynesians, but also on virtue at home. Some Maori endorsed these claims to expansion (Hone Heke MP supported the 1900 campaign to annex the Cook Islands) and the claims to Fiji were buttressed by 'the good record of the New Zealand Native Affairs Department in administering the Cook group under the stewardship of the Maori Ministers, James Carroll, Maui Pomare and Apirana Ngata'.[60] During debate on annexing the Cooks in 1900, W. C. Walker contrasted New Zealand's ambitions with Australian federation. Even before New Zealand became a colony, Britons imagined that it would enjoy

> a rightful claim to the natural centre of a Pacific world; the colony's moral influence as the Britain of the South would exert such an exceptional gravitational pull on surrounding Pacific islands that its orbit would become irresistible.[61]

The claim to inherent right to dominion was first made by George Grey, on grounds of New Zealand's 'peculiarly enlightened rule'. In 1900 Robert Stout restated the claim:

> The desire of New Zealanders is, whilst seeing the Empire extended, to deal kindly with the Polynesians, to preserve them, to civilize them. This is our mission. If we should fail, we believe foreign nations would not have succeeded.[62]

If the French colonists of New Caledonia aspired to become dominant like the settlers in Australia or New Zealand, they were hamstrung by numbers. As late as 1878 an uprising by Kanak shook the foundations of the colony; there were then fewer than 3,000 free settlers, over 3,000 military and civilian officials, a similar number of deportees after the Paris commune of 1871, and 6,000 convicts. The transportation of convicts continued until the 1890s, inhibiting the growth of colonial society. Altogether there were enough settlers to put down a Melanesian revolt; and enough Melanesians to make the settlers dependent upon metropolitan France for their protection.[63]

The most obvious division in New Caledonian society divides indigenous Kanak from immigrant *caldoches*, with immigrants from other islands commonly aligned with France and the settlers. The opposite situation prevailed in Fiji, where the indigenous population – encouraged by British colonial officials – claimed paramount legitimacy over against the descendants of indentured Indian labourers. In each case political violence made it necessary to seek compromise constitutions. These are rare instances however: few Melanesian states contain such large or coherent constituencies. The artificiality of some post-colonial island states has made it difficult to command the support (or even sometimes the tolerance) of feisty subjects. Governments have usually invoked shared cultural traditions as a basis of nationhood, but these appeals have unpredictable effects. In the 1960s 'the Pacific Way' enjoyed a vogue, with unspecific implications for nationality. In the 1970s the term *kastom* spread through the Southwest Pacific. These constructs, together with 'Melanesian socialism' and the more widely used 'Melanesian Way', may sustain a broad regional identity or lead to a narrow ethnic and linguistic identity: there is no certainty that they will validate national solidarity. More obviously than in Australia or New Zealand, and probably for higher stakes, island governments struggle to reconcile a host of older loyalties and identities with the needs of a nation-state – and the increasingly powerful forces of global cultural tendencies and regional economic integration.

In *The Book of Laughter and Forgetting* Czechs tell Milan Kundera that they will make any sacrifice to attain political power, so as to change the future. Yet in his own experience, the purpose of this struggle is to make it possible to change the past.[64] Our own region differs greatly from Central Europe; at the risk of over-simplifying our agenda, we argue that Australians, New Zealanders and Pacific Islanders make their equivalent sacrifices merely in order to shape each other's identities.

NOTES

1   Michael Young, '"Our Name is Women: We Are Bought with Limesticks and Limepots": An Analysis of the Autobiographical Narrative of a Kalauna Woman,' *Man* (n.s.), 18 (1983), 478–501.
2   Richard White, *Inventing Australia: Images and Identity 1688–1980*, Sydney, 1981; and his 'Inventing Australia revisited', in W. Hudson and G. Bolton (eds), *Creating Australia*, Sydney, 1997.
3   For European speculation, see David Glen, 'The Last Elusive Object', Australian National University, Canberra, MA thesis, in progress. For an extreme instance, John A. Lawson, R. N., *Wanderings in the Interior of New Guinea*, London, 1875. For Melanesian notions, see (for example) Chris Ballard, 'The Centre Cannot Hold: Trade Networks and Sacred Geography in the Papua New Guinea Highlands', *Archaeology in Oceania* 24: 3 (1994), 130–48; and 'The Death of a Great Land: Ritual, History and Subsistence Revolution in the Southern Highlands of Papua New Guinea', Australian National University, Canberra, Ph.D. thesis, 1995.
4   Colin Jack-Hinton, *The Search for the Islands of Solomon*, Oxford, 1969; and Alan Frost, 'Towards Australia: The Coming of the Europeans 1400 to 1788', in D. J. Mulvaney and J. Peter White (eds), *Australians to 1788*, Sydney, 1987, 368–411.
5   Matthew Flinders, *A Voyage to Terra Australis ...*, 2 vols, London, 1814.
6   Benedict Anderson, *Imagined Communities*, London, 1983; White, *Inventing Australia*.
7   I. C. Campbell, 'Culture Contact and Polynesian Identity in the European Age', *Journal of World History*, 8 (1997), 1, 31.
8   Jill Nash and Eugene Ogan, 'The Red and the Black: Bougainville Perceptions of other Papua New Guineans', *Pacific Studies* 13: 2 (1990), 1–18.
9   James Belich, *Making Peoples: A History of the New Zealanders from Polynesian Settlement to the End of the Nineteenth Century*, Auckland, 1996, xx.
10   Anne Salmond, *Two Worlds: First Meetings between Maori and Europeans 1642–1772*, Auckland, 1993, ch. 3.
11   Maurice Leenhardt, *Do Kamo: Person and Myth in the Melanesian World*, Chicago, 1979. See also James Clifford, *Person and Myth: Maurice Leenhardt in the Melanesian World*, Berkeley, CA, 1982. Leenhardt also published *Notes d'ethnologie neo-Caledonienne*, Paris, 1930.
12   Lamont Lindstrom, 'Custom Remade', in D. Denoon, S. Firth, J. Linnekin, K. Nero and M. Meleisea (eds), *Cambridge History of the Pacific Islanders*, Melbourne, 1997, ch. 12.
13   Joel Bonnemaison, *The Tree and the Canoe: History and Ethnogeography of Tanna*, Honolulu, 1994.

14 Roy MacLeod and Philip Rehbock (eds), *Darwin's Laboratory: Evolutionary Theory and Natural History in the Pacific*, Honolulu, 1994.
15 John Connell, *New Caledonia or Kanaky? The Political History of a French Colony*, Canberra, 1987.
16 C. Hartley Grattan, *The United States and the Southwest Pacific*, Cambridge, MA, 1961.
17 O. H. K. Spate, *The Pacific Since Magellan*, 3 vols, Canberra, 1979, 1983, 1988.
18 Jim Allen, Jack Golson and Rhys Jones (eds), *Sunda and Sahul: Prehistoric Studies in Southeast Asia, Melanesia and Australia*, London, 1977.
19 Alfred Russel Wallace, *The Malay Archipelago: The Land of the Orang utan and Bird of Paradise*, London, 1874; and *The Geographical Distribution of Animals*, London, 1876.
20 Matthew Spriggs, 'Recent Prehistory (the Holocene)', in Denoon, et al., *Cambridge History of the Pacific Islanders*, ch. 2.
21 Jared Diamond, *Guns, Germs, and Steel: The Fates of Human Societies*, New York, 1997.
22 Charles de Brosses, *Histoire des navigations ...*, Paris, 1756.
23 J. S. C. Dumont d'Urville, *Voyage de la corvette l'astrolabe ... pendant les annees 1826, 1827, 1828, 1829*, Paris, 1830, II, 614–16.
24 Wallace, *The Malay Archipelago*.
25 Kerry Howe, *Nature, Culture and History: The "Knowing" of Oceania*, Honolulu, in press.
26 Quoted by Howe, *Nature, Culture and History*.
27 Quoted by Howe, *Nature, Culture and History*.
28 Stephen Bann, 'From Captain Cook to Neil Armstrong', in Simon Pugh (ed.), *Reading Landscape: Country–City–Capital*, Manchester, 1990, 214–15; quoted by Howe, 'Nature, Culture and History'.
29 Sam Lambert, *A Yankee Doctor in Paradise*, Boston, 1941; Harry Maude, *Slavers in Paradise: The Peruvian Slave Trade in Polynesia, 1862–1864*, Canberra, 1981; Oskar Spate, *Paradise Found and Lost*, Canberra, 1988; Gavan Daws, *A Dream of Islands: Voyages of Self-discovery in the South Seas*, Brisbane, 1980.
30 Adam Kuper, *Anthropologists and Anthropology: The British School, 1922–1972*, London, 1973.
31 Barron Field (ed.), *Geographical Memoirs on New South Wales*, London, 1825; cited by Russell McGregor, *Imagined Destinies: Aboriginal Australians and the Doomed Race Theory, 1880–1939*, Melbourne, 1997, 7–8.
32 Adam Kuper, *The Chosen Species: Human Nature and Cultural Diversity*, Cambridge, MA, 1994.
33 D. J. Mulvaney and J. H. Calaby, *So Much that is New: Baldwin Spencer, 1860–1929, A Biography*, Melbourne, 1985.
34 Richard Slobodin, *W. H. R. Rivers*, New York, 1978.
35 Kuper, *Anthropologists and Anthropology*.
36 M. P. K. Sorrenson, *Maori Origins and Migrations: The Genesis of Some Pakeha Myths and Legends*, Auckland, 1979.
37 W. H. R. Rivers, *The History of Melanesian Societies*, Cambridge, 1914.
38 Inadvertently sustaining an ideological position which Eric Wolf anatomizes in *Europe and the Peoples without History*, Berkeley, CA, 1982.
39 Anna Grimshaw and Keith Hart, *Anthropology and the Crisis of the Intellectuals*, Cambridge, 1993.
40 Nicholas Thomas, 'The Force of Ethnology: Origins and Significance of the Melanesia/ Polynesia Division', *Current Anthropology*, 30 (1989), 27–41.

41 Bonnemaison, *The Tree and the Canoe*, 108–9.
42 Epeli Hau'ofa, 'A Pacific Islander's View', in R. G. Ward and A. Proctor (eds), *South Pacific Agriculture: Choices and Constraints*, Canberra, 1980, 484–7.
43 Source: South Pacific Economic and Social Database, NCDS, Australian National University, Canberra.
44 Source: UNDP, *Pacific Human Development Report*, Suva, 1994.
45 Epeli Hau'ofa, 'Our Sea of Islands', in Eric Waddell, Vijay Naidu and Epeli Hau'ofa (eds), *A New Oceania: Rediscovering Our Sea of Islands*, Suva, 1993.
46 Brian Fitzpatrick, *The British Empire in Australia: An Economic History, 1834–1939*, Melbourne, 1941; W. K. Hancock, *Australia*, London, 1945.
47 C. M. Clark, *A History of Australia*, 6 vols, Melbourne, 1962–87; and Stephen Holt, *Manning Clark and Australian History, 1915–63*, St Lucia, 1982.
48 J. B. Condliffe, *New Zealand in the Making*, London, 1930.
49 Maurice Leenhardt, *Do Kamo*; Jean Guiart, *La Terre est la sang des morts*, Paris, 1984.
50 Isabelle Merle, 'The Foundation of Voh', *Journal of Pacific History*, 26 (1991), 234–44; and *Expériences coloniales: la Nouvelle-Calédonie 1853–1920*, Paris, 1995.
51 For example, Virginia Thompson and Richard Adloff, *The French Pacific Islands*, Berkeley, CA, 1971; Robert Aldrich, *The French Presence in the South Pacific, 1842–1939*, London, 1990; Robert Aldrich and John Connell (eds), *France's Overseas Frontiers*, Cambridge, 1992.
52 William S. Livingston and W. Roger Louis (eds), *Australia, New Zealand, and the Pacific Islands since the First World War*, Canberra, 1979.
53 For example, the *Bulletin de la societe des oceanistes*.
54 For example, *Oceania*.
55 For example, Alfred Russel Wallace, *Australasia*, London, 1883.
56 W. Pember Reeves, 'Attitude of New Zealand', *Empire Review*, February 1901.
57 William Curzon-Siggers, vicar, Dunedin, NZ Federation Commission evidence, 14 February 1901, 109.
58 See, for example, R. Jebb, *Studies in Colonial Nationalism*, London, 1905.
59 Angus Ross, *New Zealand's Aspirations in the Pacific*, Oxford, 1964.
60 Ross, 'Maori and Polynesian: Race and Politics', in J. D. Freeman and W. R. Geddes (eds), *Anthropology in the South Seas*, New Plymouth, 1958.
61 Angus Ross, *New Zealand's Aspirations in the Pacific*, 9.
62 Robert Stout, 'New Zealand and an Island Federation', *Review of Reviews*, 20 October 1900.
63 Isabelle Merle, *Expériences coloniales*, Paris, 1995; John Lawrey, *The Cross of Lorraine in the South Pacific: Australia and the Free French Movement 1940–1942*, Canberra, 1982.
64 Milan Kundera, *The Book of Laughter and Forgetting*, trans. M. H. Him, Harmondsworth, 1983.

[2] *Patterns of Pre-European Settlement and Interaction*

The navigators and natural scientists of the Age of Discovery, and the scholars who pored over their journals, were captivated by the variety of social and cultural forms manifested in the people they encountered. That fascination expressed itself in ingenious attempts to establish relationships between social forms, in the remote past as well as the immediate present. The first essays in reconstructing the prehistories of the region therefore embodied the intellectual concerns of Western Europe as much as the evidence from the frontiers. Much attention was lavished on Aboriginal and islander origins. That speculation often had a racist agenda which, for example, imagined Aboriginal Australians as the unchanged survivors of a primitive form of humanity (if indeed they had not been degenerating): contemporary Aboriginal societies, especially if they could be observed before they were transformed by Western influences, were therefore expected to throw light on the original state of all human societies.[1] In this stage-theory approach to social evolution Melanesians, with small and opaque political structures, were judged to be primitive or relatively backward. Polynesians, however, usually fairer-skinned than Melanesians or Aboriginal Australians, and commonly living in hierarchical order, seemed to have more in common with (relatively advanced) East Asian societies, and might even be co-opted as long-lost Europeans. To accommodate such a racial hierarchy, from the 1880s colonial scholars devised artful routes whereby ancestral Maori could have reached New Zealand from the Caucasus, as real Caucasians if not Celts or Semites. The trick was to devise a route which avoided Australia, where Polynesians would have been contaminated by Aboriginal people.[2] Later studies shed many of the assumptions (including the essentialism and cultural diffusionism) which prompted such questions. That research confirms clear linguistic indications of historic relations among all Polynesians, and much slighter suggestions for shared pasts among speakers of Austronesian languages (including some in Melanesia as well as Polynesia), but draws very different conclusions from such relationships. Local adaptations are now considered to be at least as important as remote, shared origins in shaping ways in which people live in their environments, and with each other. This research offers no comfort to the simplicities of cultural diffusion – nor to those who would romanticize pre-European conditions.

'INDIGENOUS' COMMUNITIES

Since *homo sapiens sapiens* originated in Africa, and human occupation of our region is probably not much older than 40,000 years, 'indigenous' is an elastic and relative term, and every 'indigenous' community descends ultimately from immigrants from (or through) Southeast Asia. A central element of many community identities therefore is the order – and the social condition – in which ancestral groups arrived. For some societies the odyssey of arrival is so remote that it is overlaid by narratives of autochthony, in which human beings emerge (from other life forms, or from the landscape) not far from where their descendants now live. When Rod Lacey asked an Enga man in the western highlands of New Guinea to tell him the origins of the community, he was told

> the possum Komaipa begot Kombeke. Kombeke began the Mulapini people in Yoko. These two, Komaipa and Kombeke, are right at the base of the centre post in our men's house. Like the centre post these two founders of Mulapini ... hold together our whole group.[3]

Nobody was intended to take this as a literal account; what was important was the claim to have occupied and owned that land through all human experience. Equally important to the informant was the image of the men's house centre post, hinting at the importance of genealogical narratives for the coherence of the lineage. As Lacey and others have found, it is naive and impertinent to reduce the richly allusive poetry of these narratives to historically specific events.

For other societies, old and new, voyages of discovery and narratives of settlement have become epics, and some do serve as historical charters legitimizing contemporary claims. We might therefore imagine that all those whose ancestors arrived first would enjoy the highest status. We might also expect that those whose ancestors arrived as refugees or under duress would keep quiet about it. In fact many other circumstances have to be taken into account – not least, 'race'. It is not only the historical record that determines hierarchies of esteem, but the narratives which their descendants weave around the records and legends.

The pioneers who first settled in Australia and New Guinea were part of a great exodus from southern China, mainly through island Southeast Asia. Many small parties of men and women crossed the narrow seas by canoe or raft and colonized the great land masses by 40,000 years ago. The more remote islands were inaccessible until people devised navigation techniques to get there, and uninhabitable until they developed and refined their agriculture to feed themselves. Pioneering into remote islands therefore continued until a few hundred years ago. The more recent European Age of Discovery took a quite different tack, identifying small and remote islands before they made landfall and began charting Australia and New Zealand. Unlike their predecessors, they also distinguished between the voyages of discovery and the consequent fleets of settlers to predetermined destinations.

Plate 2.1 Taro digging, Papua New Guinea. Kerry & Co., Sydney. Macmillan Brown Collection, Macmillan Brown Library, University of Canterbury.

Initial human settlement leaves more evidence than the ensuing 40,000 years, for which we can discern only a handful of episodes. It is sometimes suggested that Aboriginal Australians experienced little social change once they had adapted to new environments, or that Islanders always formed the myriad small communities seen in our own era. The histories of which we do have knowledge deny that vegetative portrait. Notable narratives include the evolution of agriculture in the New Guinea Highlands by about 9,000 years ago; the separation of New Guinea from Australia soon afterwards; the evolution of diverse social forms and survival strategies among Aboriginal Australians; the rise and fragmentation of a Lapita culture-complex in the Western Pacific; the evolution and expansion of Polynesian societies and the effects upon the rest of Melanesia.

The earliest arrivals were hunter-gatherers. Like their American and Eurasian cousins they wiped out the mega-fauna. In our region that act left no animals which could be domesticated (like the sheep and goats, buffalo and cattle which sustained pastoral civilizations in the Old World). In Australia, warrigal (dingo) which came later was the only creature incorporated into human society and survival strategy. Aboriginal communities spread throughout the continent from the wet tropics through the arid centre to chilly upland Tasmania, devising a plethora of ways of living. All had in common the simplicity of multi-purpose tools, the mobility and very small scale of each group, and the impossibility of accumulating possessions.

Islanders brought in pigs and chickens as well as dogs.[4] Even before these creatures arrived, however, the pioneers fared reasonably well in an environment of great forests and rivers, and dense and diverse vegetation. Bone, shell and stone allowed them to make tools with which to fell trees and shape timber for canoes, houses and shields. Fish and shellfish were easily harvested, although hunting was complicated by the elimination of large fauna. Even before they developed their systematic agriculture, pioneers lived well enough in small, mobile communities of a few dozen souls.

Some coastal New Guineans were engaging in agriculture more than 9,000 years ago, with taro, yam, sago, banana and coconut. Only taro flourished at high altitudes, where it became the staple food. Highlanders, having cleared forest, began draining and irrigation; regular food production allowed them then to domesticate pigs (and in some areas, cassowaries).[5] Taro-based irrigation eventually spread from New Guinea into the Solomons, Vanuatu and New Caledonia and Fiji, but evidently not Australia. The great highland irrigation systems ceased three or four hundred years ago with the arrival of sweet potato, which yields better than taro at altitude. Smaller communities could then flourish, liberated from the need for large-scale water management and sustaining themselves by swidden farming, growing taro or yam.

AUSTRONESIANS, LAPITA, POLYNESIANS: CHRONOLOGIES AND CHARTERS

A great family of related languages – Austronesian – stretches from Hawaii and Rapanui (Easter Island) to Madagascar, with the largest numbers in Island Southeast Asia. This diaspora can be the result only of an immense human adventure. In the Western Pacific, volcanic action has created a host of islands, and atolls in the shallow waters above underwater mountains (seamounts). These offered stepping stones for migration, but outside this area the plates of the seabed drift apart without disturbing the 'empty ocean' in the Northern and Eastern Pacific, so that islands are fewer and further apart. The Austronesian diaspora occurred too long ago to survive in oral tradition or to remain a conscious element of identity, but within this large saga, the Lapita cultural complex requires a more modest feat of imagination.[6] Archeologists named these artefacts and traditions for the New Caledonian village where they first noticed the distinctive pottery. Systematic research revealed related settlements, with stone adzes, distinctive ornaments, domestic animals, and villages of rectangular houses. Their agricultural way of life is implied by their pottery, animals, tools and villages. Their boat technology must have been advanced, and their crops (breadfruit, taro, bananas and yams) and animals enabled them to colonize places which lacked other resources, taking human settlements further east than ever before. They irrigated fields of taro on the larger islands, and dug taro pits down to the water table on atolls. These methods supported sustainable farming. Most of the distinctive features of Lapita settlements derived from Southeast Asia, although the centre of the settlements was the Bismarck Archipelago. From there, settlements spread and prospered from Manus in the west to Tonga and Samoa in the east, from about 3,500 to 2,500 years ago. The first Lapita groups were perhaps fewer than a hundred people. Some settled in places where their neighbours spoke non-Austronesian languages. There, the Lapita community grew partly by natural increase and partly by attracting neighbours through their advanced technologies. Farther east, they were the first to occupy some islands. In either situation they brought the latest social and production systems of Southeast Asia.

We know about the Lapita complex entirely through archeology. The creation and more recent dispersal of Polynesian societies, however, is fundamental to current social and political identities. All Polynesian communities descend from Lapita, and they had occupied parts of New Guinea and its archipelagos, and Fiji, Samoa and Tonga, by two or three thousand years ago. Tahiti and the Marquesas were settled from central Polynesia (Samoa or nearby), one or two thousand years ago, and only then was New Zealand settled, from Eastern Polynesia, between AD 1000 and 1200. The progress of voyaging and navigation was clearly critical in making these feats possible, and agriculture was then vital for survival in new environments.

The Eastern Polynesian ancestors of the New Zealand Maori probably sailed from the Marquesas or Society Islands, and possibly from Pitcairn and the southern Cooks.[7] In Aotearoa New Zealand they found the largest, widest and coldest land in Polynesia, much more diverse than the small islands of the tropics, and having a temperate climate which ranged from cool to freezing, and was notable for erratic seasonal extremes. Much of this land was covered with tall timber such as *totara* and *kauri*. Pigs and chickens did not survive the voyage, but Aotearoa teemed with fish and shellfish, marine mammals such as seals, and birds for hunting, among them naive, flightless birds, of which the moa yielded the easiest meat supply. Fishing predominated over hunting. While marine stocks were readily replenished, some animals and birds were not. Atholl Anderson deduces that colonization led to the moa's extinction through overkilling, combined with the ruin of their habitat and the depredations of the rats and dogs which arrived with the Polynesians.[8]

Rats, dogs and fire from swidden agriculture transformed the northern North Island landscape, leading to widespread soil erosion and forest clearance. South Island bush became grassland, while in the north, fern and scrub replaced the forest cover, offering more scope for harvesting bracken fern root and for *kumara* (sweet potato) gardens.[9] The colonists learnt by trial and error what effort would yield the best return, and developed conservation practices in areas where climate and environment constrained horticulture.

Kumara grew no further south than the Banks Peninsula, while taro and yam in the north were at the margin of their tolerance. Aotearoa proved a grave instead of a garden for Polynesian coconut, breadfruit and bananas.[10]

Cycles of abundance and dearth demanded the invention of adaptations. *Kumara* became the staple, as in Hawaii, but relied on unique storage techniques. The people who became Maori built insulated underground storage pits to provide *kumara* for winter food and for seed tubers to plant in spring. They heated the ground for *kumara* in stone gardens, planting it under stones covered with soot to absorb the heat. Dried sea lettuce and wild plants and fruits such as *karaka* berries were dried and stored, and fish and birds were caught young when they were plump, and stored in their own fat to carry the people through seasonal cycles.[11]

Where the climate did not allow wide cultivations, these farmers transformed what were famine foods elsewhere in Polynesia into staples, notably fern root. Bitter, even toxic plants became 'festive fare' in 'a remarkable example of "added value"', using methods of prolonged cooking and soaking that were already familiar across the Pacific.[12] Perhaps it was fern root rather than moa that sustained the pioneers while they struggled to adapt their tropical agriculture to the cool climate.[13] Migrating to the largest, coldest islands in the Pacific, Maori embodied the youngest islands of Eastern Polynesian culture, though their *marae* suggested some Western Polynesian influences.[14] From whatever sources, by about AD 1500 the leading features of Maori culture and society had been established: clearly defined concepts of tribal (*iwi*) identity, settlements centred on the fortified *pa*, sporadic warfare between them, and elaborate wood carving. In the hundred years after the first recorded European visits, Maori society managed to remain 'apart, inward-looking, closed, vigorous' – and competing among themselves, each community held together by land and kinship and by clusters of values which elevated obligations to kin above all else.[15]

While Maori developed into fiercely competitive groups with a warrior culture, a splinter group – Moriori – found their way from the South Island to the Chatham Islands between AD 1000 and 1300 and were isolated as the surrounding seas cooled, from about 1400. This youngest group of Eastern Polynesians gathered food in autumn and summer to preserve in the cold months.[16] The harsh environment limited their food resources and shaped a simplified material culture whose efficiency (like that of Aboriginal Australians) both Europeans and Maori misunderstood. While a warrior class developed among Maori, Moriori adapted to be non-violent, sedentary hunter-gatherers, living among their key resource, the fur seal, until European and Polynesian sealers from 1791 and a Maori invasion in 1835 wrought havoc on them.[17]

FRAGMENTATION

Despite the categorical clarity of Western terms for language and ethnic identities, the isolation of the region from its neighbours and the separation of its own components are recent in archeological terms. Until 8,000 years ago

New Guinea and Australia were still joined by land at Cape York, and even after Torres Strait was flooded, a string of islands allowed a flow of people and technology. Influences and items did travel both ways in the nineteenth and twentieth centuries, and presumably earlier. At the moment of separation, people on either side of the incipient strait practised hunting, fishing and foraging. Soon a contrast appeared, however, between agricultural groups in New Guinea and some islands of Torres Strait, and continuing hunter-gatherers in Australia and in other Torres Strait islands. New Guineans made regular voyages across great bodies of water, but their migrating enthusiasm seems to have been for further island settlement rather than contacts with Australia. If the ideas of agriculture and sedentary settlements were known to Aboriginal Australians at least in Cape York, the practices did not catch on.

The separation of the region from Island Southeast Asia is no older than three thousand years: that was when Lapita migrants brought Southeast Asian technologies and social forms east into the Pacific. Thereafter Indian Ocean networks, centralized states, Hindu and then Chinese and Islamic influences reshaped Southeast Asia, tapering off through eastern Indonesia and almost disappearing at the west coast of New Guinea. But to imagine (as Wallace himself did) a cultural Wallace's line between New Guinea and Halmahera is to deny real linkages. The conceptual separation of Pacific from Southeast Asian cultures and polities owes more to European classification than to historic connections and discontinuities. As on other cultural boundaries, there was no inhibition against the exchange of commodities, ideas and even people.

These communities were small, and many were highly mobile. As there was seldom any compelling reason for large-scale settlements, the atomized language and political patterns of most of Melanesia were established very early. Commonly,

> the *political* units (i.e. effective fighting units, under unified leadership) ... were small and relatively unstable – probably averaging no more than about 200–300 people, and subject to frequent fragmentation and realignment.[18]

Natural hazards – cyclones, drought, frost – put a premium on food security, especially as root crops were difficult to store. These circumstances created the dilemma that small societies were self-reliant for most of their daily needs, and able to defend their land from predators, but relied on unreliable neighbours not only in emergencies, but routinely for marriage partners. The elaboration of several hundred languages (most in Melanesia, but also in Australia) suggests that many people liked their societies to be small in scale and socially aloof. In the Islands, farming groups built hamlets of up to thirty people who often shifted residence. In the New Guinea Highlands, the collaborating groups were larger, to maintain the drainage systems; but the arrival of sweet potato removed that incentive for concentration, and the fragmentary pattern of the region reasserted itself. To survive climatic and human hazards, such mini-societies needed appropriate technology, exchange partners (preferably in different environments) and schemes of social relations to provide security.

Tools were not visually impressive, and were multi-purpose rather than highly specific. Nowhere in this region were there metal implements of any kind. On the atolls, tools were made from calcified shell; cowries were used to scour breadfruit; and limestone was often used as mortar. Many Polynesians created stone foundations to support elaborate wooden spiritual centres (*marae* in Maori). The great double-hulled canoes evolved into many designs, different again from the cargo vessels carrying bulky goods around New Guinea. Where spades and gardening paddles were used, they were wooden, as were the towering *haus tambaran* of the New Guinea coast. Carvers enjoyed high status in these contexts, while carpenters were the most respected artisans in the Fijian towns of the Viti Levu deltas. Almost all buildings, and shell and bone decorations, were made by stone tools, which underpinned most production systems.[19] Stone masonry was commonly a male preserve, whereas women mass-produced pots for exchange, in sites on the Papuan coast.[20] Shell valuables were also mass-produced in many islands, and served as something like currency.[21] Among the best known were the looped fathoms of *tambu* shell which represented wealth for the Tolai in New Britain. Whales' teeth performed much the same function in other islands. In Fiji, for example, the islet of Bau projected its power far beyond its horizons through its chiefs' access to *tabua* (whales' teeth). Among Samoans, a similar function was served by *ie toga* fine mats, each with its own narratives. Although people possessed wealth, *tambu* became 'capital' only in the late nineteenth century, when social relations were commercialized. As demand changed, so did production and exchange networks. We have seen how sweet potato transformed production in the New Guinea Highlands. The later expansion of highland quarrying responded to a flood of goods from the coast, though neither the masons nor traders recognized the linkage. Polynesian and Melanesian exchanges comfortably accommodated European commodities alongside more 'traditional' items.

Relations with the land were crucial for production and for identity.[22] In this pattern of small-scale communities, each family needed access to a variety of soils and environments; conversely the same piece of land was often accessed by different groups. One might own the trees on a plot while another owned the crops beneath them. In Lakeba, Fiji, groups held wedge-shaped portions of land from the coast to the high interior. On larger islands, communities enjoyed ecological variety by other means, including exchange networks. Land, kinship and social identity were facets of the same reality. Particular kin to a landholder had grounds for seeking a gift of land. People marrying into a community might be given land (and a social affiliation) which grew into ownership and community membership. Refugees might gain protection, shelter and land, and eventually be absorbed. Communities could divide, and in that case they must either divide their land or occupy new territory.

WHAT HELD SOCIETIES TOGETHER?

In one of the most often-cited passages describing pre-conquest Aboriginal society, Captain Cook reckoned that they were far happier than Europeans like himself:

> being wholly unacquainted not only with the superfluous but the necessary
> Conveniences so much sought after in Europe, they are happy in not knowing
> the use of them. They live in a Tranquillity which is not disturb'd by the
> Inequality of Condition: The Earth and sea of their own accord furnishes them
> with all things necessary for life.

That description, summarizing limited and casual observations, resounds
with the continuing (albeit fading) expectations of Europe's age of expansion.
Such is the residual power of that vision, however, that it has taken generations
of scholarship to dispel it. The three thousand people living near the site of
Sydney, for example, went to some trouble to furnish the things necessary for
their lives, using stone and bone and wood, in the absence of metal. On the
coast they caught fish and gathered shellfish; inland they hunted and trapped
fauna, and extracted toxins from plant foods. Each band comprised a handful of families, whose tranquillity was disturbed from time to time by ceremonial occasions which brought bands together, casual encounters, the
engraving of figures on sandstone, the exchanging of gifts – and the resolution
of disputes.[23] The variety of Aboriginal environments and survival strategies
are impossible to summarize, but it is clear that each involved intimate
knowledge of a dangerous environment prone to fire, flood or drought, and
that specialist skills had to be learned. Similar judgements could be made of
island communities. Stone, shell or wooden tools made forest clearance or
house-building or canoe-building laborious, but co-operation made it feasible.
A group was safer than an individual, as well as more congenial. Specialist
services – canoe-building, spiritual intervention, carving – also had to be rec-
iprocated. Most important was the need for protection, so that every individual's interests were best served by participation.

Underpinning all social relations were those of gender. The Nyungar were
a significant population in the extreme southwest of Australia, no more (and
perhaps no less) 'typical' than any other Aboriginal community. Men usually
did not marry until they were thirty or older, and they might marry more
than one wife; whereas women married when they reached puberty, their
marriages were arranged for them (often at birth) and each had only one
husband. Each family was self-sufficient, and the key structural division of
labour was that between women and men:

> Women gathered plants and small animals. They prepared these foods for the
> family, looked after the children, made the clothing and built the huts. Men
> defended the family. They fished, hunted large animals and manufactured
> implements.[24]

Relations were complementary, though not equal. On the question of gender equity, Europeans reckoned that Polynesian women enjoyed more respect
and comfort than women in Melanesia or Australia. While many European
visitors and commentators felt that Melanesian and Aboriginal women needed
to be 'rescued' from harsh and servile conditions, some felt that the eminence

and autonomy of some Polynesian women was a fault that required remedy.[25] These observations certainly shaped the ways in which missionaries and others intervened in the social lives of the people, but they cannot be treated as informed judgements of relationships which were conducted in languages and idioms unfamiliar to the observers. Whether relations seemed equitable or repressive, however, all involved complementarity, otherwise they could not have encompassed survival and social reproduction. In most of Melanesia, male dominance was expressed in ideas of female pollution: most highland societies even flaunted their ideas of male superiority, especially in male cults which centred upon men's houses and secret rituals. Men commonly spent most of their time together in the men's house, while women (and children, and sometimes animals) were dispersed among scattered family houses. That arrangement made manifest the centrality of men in forming the community. A central function of the cults was to transform boys into warriors, which required that boys move from their mother's house to the men's house, while their sisters remained with their mothers. Most Polynesian societies attributed sacred spiritual power to women, yet Polynesian women were the equals of men in status and rank, and some wielded power through kinship relations or as chiefs. In Highland New Guinea women did most of the productive work, whereas women in the matrilineal societies of Island Melanesia owned and passed on the land, and both sexes worked in the gardens. Matrilineal descent did not ensure that men respected women, nor that women were equal decision-makers. However, although distinctions between men's work and women's work were clear in principle, there was no reason for them to be absolute in practice, and Linnekin points out that in most societies men and women helped each other when needed. In planning the New Guinea Highland exchange ceremonies, a man's wife influenced distribution to exchange partners who were not related to her: 'women are essential in shaping and defining the partnerships that nominally belong to men'.[26] Gender ideology also helped to shape many transactions which Europeans consider ungendered. In the New Guinea Highlands the sweet potato is a 'female' crop, unlike 'male' taro, ginger and sugarcane, tended by men. Pigs are also 'female' in contrast to 'male' dogs and cassowaries. Since pigs eat sweet potatoes, men's ceremonies intrinsically depend on women's work. Marylin Strathern has explored how these ascriptions conform to a gender logic.[27] Many societies considered gender relations so basic that they were quite unable to conceive of gender-free relationships.

DEALING WITH OUTSIDERS

Dealing with strangers was no casual matter. When white settlers established themselves on the lands of the Nyungar in Western Australia, they ought to have approached and deferred to Nakina, to secure his permission to settle. In fact an impasse resulted since the settlers (correctly) saw no chiefs and (wrongly) assumed that there was no authority to consult – whereas Nakina would not lower himself to approach the intruders.[28] Aboriginal bands did not always interact with each other peacefully, but they certainly knew how to do so, just as they knew the consequences of ignoring rights and proprieties. In the Islands, only particular people enjoyed the right to interact with outsiders. On Tanna island in what is now Vanuatu, individual men inherited this right and proper interaction was restricted to hereditary spokesmen and messengers. Throughout the Pacific, contractual arrangements prevailed between groups known to each other, and prescribed how to interact and how to signal their intentions.

Many Polynesian societies believed that common people belonged to the land, but their chiefs were demi-gods from the sea. Unlucky arrivals, argues Kerry Howe, must conform to the protocol for castaways:

> The newcomers then surrendered what possessions they held, such as their canoe…as a sign of humble acceptance of and token compensation for the food and shelter they would be offered. If later they wished to leave, they might be supplied with a canoe and provisions, and given a send off.[29]

Migration of whole communities was rare, except when politics or climate made them refugees. Melanesian agriculture promoted gradual movements as communities expanded, and abrupt movement when they split, but the commonest migrations were individual as women (or in some societies, men) took up residence with a spouse from another community. Usually it was goods rather than people which moved. So often were they exchanged by Aboriginal groups that a casual observer could think it irrational. A white policeman in the Lake Eyre basin in the 1870s was puzzled that

> Their whole life is spent in bartering: they rarely retain any article for long. The articles received by them in exchange one day are bartered away the next, whether at a profit or loss. Should any one of them, more shrewd than another, profit on one occasion by this traffic, he is sure immediately after to sacrifice his advantage, and the majority of their quarrels are caused by bartering or refusing to barter.

This impression rested partly on European notions of commerce, and their expectation that ritual and mundane world would not intersect, much less merge into each other.[30]

In the Islands similar patterns prevailed. Shell from the New Guinea coast was bartered into the highlands through many hands, so that the eventual recipients were not aware of the ultimate source. On the coast and between the islands trade was organized formally and often involved large-scale expeditions. The *kula* ring in the Massim fascinated the pioneer anthropologist Malinowski, whose account of it became the staple for generations of anthropology students.[31] Such exchanges required social as much as economic analysis, of a high order. Some exchanges were, of course, more narrowly 'functional'. Greenstone from the South Island of New Zealand was widely traded and exchanged for weapons as well as ornamentation. In the Torres Strait in the late nineteenth century some islanders acquired stone and bone tools, bows and arrows from the Papuan coast.[32] In many situations people exchanged or bartered with their neighbours, and did not need specialist traders or ritualized behaviour. But every exchange had a critically important social context. Huli people conceived that their closest neighbours shared a remote common ancestor, whereas more distant people, albeit human, were not related. For others the world was made up of several human societies similar to themselves, but with different languages and customs. In high island Polynesia each island was shared (or contested) by different chiefdoms, and their common culture and language created only precarious unity among them. For Melanesians, outsiders were either (and only) allies or enemies, depending on circumstances, but never neutral. External relations were mediated by gifts of women and valuables, and the creation of kinship through such strategic marriages offered hope of peace. Trade and exchange could connect people with their ancestors as well as their neighbours. So 'the Huli universe is constructed upon a notion of exchange between living humans and ancestral and non-ancestral spirits.'[33] Knowledge and skill were exchanged just as eagerly as material items. Seeps of mineral oil were 'critical nodes within Huli sacred geography' essential for the survival of the Huli universe.

Each society aspired not merely to survive but to produce a surplus for exchanges. These relations were competitive. Michael Young describes them as 'fighting with food',[34] and they often involved lavish display. In the New Guinea Highlands, Big Men harassed their clients to produce the vegetables to fatten the pigs whose ceremonial distribution was the climax of the cycle. On the Papuan coast in the late nineteenth century Motu villages were sailing twenty multi-hulled vessels each year to the Gulf of Papua, carrying about 26,000 pots and returning with perhaps 500 tons of sago. By then the whole island of New Guinea was surrounded by exchange networks, drawing in the produce of the interior. Long-distance trade and exchange relations were, argues Hau'ofa, fundamental,[35] just as they were for Aboriginal societies. Missionaries, like the Eyre Basin policeman, were disapproving when they saw that chiefs seemed to be always travelling, presenting food and exacting tribute. This was no diversion. Every society had to work hard and consistently at their ritual and mundane exchanges, their gendered tasks, and the distribution of gendered goods. Only in these ways could they produce their daily necessities and sustain and reproduce their family and individual lives. In so doing they also ensured the vitality of the societies which were the sum total of their families, and gave not only shelter and protection, but context and meaning to those who contributed to it.

NOTES

1 Adam Kuper, *The Chosen Primate: Human Nature and Cultural Diversity*, Cambridge, MA, 1994.
2 M. P. K. Sorrenson, *Maori Origins and Migrations: The Genesis of Some Pakeha Myths and Legends*, Auckland, 1979.

3   For example, R. J. Lacey, 'Oral Traditions as History: An Exploration of Oral Sources among the Enga of the New Guinea Highlands', University of Wisconsin, Madison, Ph.D. thesis, 1975.

4   Jared Diamond, *Guns, Germs and Steel: The Fates of Human Societies*, New York, 1997.

5   Jack Golson, in Donald Denoon and Catherine Snowden (eds), *A History of Agriculture in Papua New Guinea*, Boroko, n.d. [1981].

6   Matthew Spriggs, 'Recent Prehistory (The Holocene)', in D. Denoon, S. Firth, J. Linnekin, K. Nero and M. Meleisea (eds), *Cambridge History of the Pacific Islanders*, Melbourne, 1997.

7   J. M. Davidson, *The Prehistory of New Zealand*, 2nd edn, Auckland, 1992, 23–4.

8   Athol Anderson, *Prodigious Birds: Moas and Moa-Hunting in Prehistoric New Zealand*, Cambridge, 1989, 7–8, 187. In Easter Island, only the chicken survived.

9   J. M. Davidson, 'The Polynesian Foundation', in G. W. Rice (ed.), *Oxford History of New Zealand*, Auckland, 1992, 7; *Prehistory of New Zealand*, 38–41.

10 Helen Leach, 'In the Beginning', in J. Phillips (ed.), *Te Whenua, Te Iwi: The Land and the People*, Wellington, 1987, 21–2; Davidson, *Prehistory of New Zealand*, 115–16.

11 Davidson, *Prehistory of New Zealand*, ch. 6; Leach, 'In the Beginning', 22.

12 Leach, 'In the Beginning', 23.

13 Davidson, *Prehistory of New Zealand*, 146. According to Diamond, Maori population growth resulted from gardening; according to Flannery, from eating out the moa. But there were more moa in sparsely populated South Island than in the North Island, which supports Diamond. Flannery also suggests a crisis of resource depletion by the time of European arrival – hence Maori warfare and cannibalism. That is, the extinction of the moa led to destructive forest fires to encourage fern root to proliferate and nutrients to seep into estuaries to nourish marine life, and on to warfare and cannibalism as resources declined. But if this were the case, why were Maori physically large?

14 Davidson, 'The Polynesian Foundation', 15–16.

15 A. R. Parsonson, 'The Pursuit of Mana', in W. H. Oliver with B. R. Williams (eds), *Oxford History of New Zealand*, Wellington, 1981, 162.

16 Davidson, 'The Polynesian Foundation', speculates that they might also have travelled from elsewhere in East Polynesia, but Sutton and King infer that the final migration came from southern New Zealand. D. G. Sutton, 'The Whence of the Moriori', *New Zealand Journal of History*, 19: 1 (1985), 6; Michael King, *Moriori: A People Rediscovered*, Auckland, 1989, 20–2. King suggests the thirteenth or fourteenth century.

17 King, *Moriori*, 35, 38; Sutton, 'The Whence of the Moriori', 8–10. See also Diamond, *Guns, Germs and Steel*, 55–60.

18 Douglas Oliver, 'Some Social-relational Aspects of CRA Copper-mining on Bougainville', 1968, cited in D. Denoon, *Getting Under the Skin*, Melbourne, 2000.

19 John Burton, 'Axe Makers of the Wahgi', Australian National University, Canberra, Ph.D. thesis, 1984.

20 Geoffrey Irwin, *The Emergence of Mailu, Terra Australis*, Canberra, 1985, 10.

21 Matthew Cooper, 'Economic Context of Shell Money Production in Malaita', *Oceania*, 41: 4 (1971), 266–76.

22 R. Gerard Ward and Elizabeth Kingdon (eds), *Land, Custom and Practice in the South Pacific*, Canberra, 1995.

23 J. L. Kohen and Ronald Lampert, 'Hunters and Fishers in the Sydney Region', in D. J. Mulvaney and J. Peter White (eds), *Australians to 1788*, Sydney, 1988.

24 W. C. Ferguson, 'Mokare's Domain', in Mulvaney and White, *Australians to 1788*.

25 Jocelyn Linnekin, 'Gender Division of Labour', in Denoon et al., *Cambridge History of Pacific Islanders*, ch. 3; Margaret Jolly, ' "Ill-natured Comparisons"?: Racism and Relativism in European Representations of ni-Vanuatu from Cook's Second Voyage', *History and Anthropology*, 5: 3 (1992).

26 D. K. Feil, 'Women and Men in the Enga tee', *American Ethnologist*, 5 (1978), 268, 272.

27 Marylin Strathern, *The Gender of the Gift: Problems with Women and Problems with Society in Melanesia*, Berkeley, CA, 1988.

28 Ferguson, 'Mokare's Domain'.

29 Kerry Howe, *Where the Waves Fall: A New South Sea Islands History from First Settlement to Colonial Rule*, Sydney, 1984, 85.

30 Isabel McBryde, 'Goods from Another Country: Exchange Networks and the People of the Lake Eyre Basin', in Mulvaney and White, *Australians to 1788*, 252–73.

31 Bronislaw Malinowski, *Argonauts of the Western Pacific: An Account of Native Enterprise and Adventure in the Archipelagos of Melanesian New Guinea*, London, 1922.

32 Appendix to *British New Guinea Annual Report* for 1905.

33 Chris Ballard, 'The Centre Cannot Hold: Trade Networks and Sacred Geography in the Papua New Guinea Highlands', *Archeology in Oceania*, 29: 3 (1994), 130–48.

34 Michael Young, *Fighting With Food: Leadership, Values and Social Control in a Massim Society*, Cambridge, 1971.

35 Epeli Hau'ofa, 'Our Sea of Islands', in Eric Waddell, Vijay Naidu and Epeli Hau'ofa (eds), *A New Oceania: Rediscovering Our Sea of Islands*, Suva, 1993, 2–16.

[3] INTERSECTING WORLDS

A satellite above the equator, at about 149 degrees West, sees a watery world.[1] Sydney and California are barely visible on either horizon. Without such assistance European sailors had great difficulty navigating an unimaginably vast ocean, devoid of landmarks other than a few islands and innumerable reefs, none of them securely charted. The Dutch East India Company's newest flagship, *Batavia*, with a seasoned captain in charge, ran aground the Abrolhos islands off the West Australian coast in 1629, confident that land was still 600 miles distant.[2] Longitude could be determined, but latitude was near impossible. In the 1770s, the most urgent task of Captain James Cook was to test navigation instruments to address that problem. Apart from the narrow latitudes used by Spanish fleets shuttling between Manila and Acapulco, there were no reliable sea routes; so vague was their cartography that Europeans traversed the Pacific for two centuries without charting the southern continent or even the Hawaiian islands.

Nearly three centuries separated the conquest of central America from the incorporation of Oceania into European maps and power systems. That delay was profoundly significant, materially and ideologically. From 1567 until 1608, Spaniards sought Terra Australis and islands for Christian colonies; from South America Alvaro de Mendaña led two expeditions and a third was captained by Pedro de Quiros and Luis Vaes de Torres. They failed to identify Australia but they did find several islands in an archipelago which they named Solomon Islands. In the same optimistic spirit they named one of these islands La Australia del Espiritu Santo, and in that island chain they also aspired to build a new Jerusalem. Often they were greeted with curious civility, but they always arrived famished and making insatiable demands for food; and their faith proved less infectious than their diseases. Relations with the islanders were subverted also by radically different cultural assumptions. On Guadalcanal, typically, a soldier seeking pigs killed an islander; his kin retaliated by killing and eating nine Spaniards; and the Spaniards killed and mutilated corpses. Every settlement failed, with great loss of life.[3]

Spanish interest then shifted north to the Mariana Islands where it was easier to act out notions of appropriate relations with indigenous people. Islanders were subjected to conversion and strict religious control. By 1695 their resistance had been crushed and survivors were resettled from dispersed settlements into concentrated villages. Through the limitations of Spanish navigation, and the apparent dearth of easily exploited resources, most Polynesians and Melanesians escaped a particularly rapacious era. A further consequence was an imaginative realignment of people. The papal arbitration which drew the line of Tordesillas to demarcate Spanish and Portuguese spheres of operation helped to determine shipping routes and international relationships. Portuguese fleets preferred the eastern route, via the Cape of Good Hope, to reach their possessions in India and the Moluccas; Spanish fleets preferred to risk Cape Horn or the Straits of Magellan or to cross the ocean from Mexico, en route to the Philippines. This arrangement both inhibited excursions across the Tordesillas line and promoted a conceptual division between the two hemispheres. In the process, Spanish fleets helped to confine China and Japan to coastal ventures, so that the Pacific became (in Oskar Spate's phrase) a Spanish Lake.[4] Although Japan and China confined European merchants to a few prescribed ports, on the open ocean the dominant naval power was exercised by a succession of non-Asian powers from the seventeenth century to our own day. Interactions between East Asia and the islands were interrupted for two centuries, and 'the Pacific' was gradually reified not merely as a geographical expression. The holders of power increasingly construed it as a series of related societies: these became vividly represented in European imaginings, and deemed to be socially as well as biologically distinct from their closest continents.

'SCIENTIFIC DISCOVERIES' AND CONCEPTUAL MAPS

Europeans of many nationalities shared the Spanish experience of 'discovering' other people and publicizing their impressions. Spanish authorities were deeply suspicious (with good reason) of English and Dutch and French expeditions intruding on their domain; but in terms of conceptualizing 'Asia' and 'the Pacific' their reports complemented each other, reinforcing categorical distinctions. During the seventeenth century the Dutch explored the Pacific, seeking Terra Australis; but Jan Carstensz was deeply dismayed when he found its arid west coast in 1623. The wreck of the *Batavia* six years later, and the failure of its crew, its castaways or the rescue party to identify useful resources or to make contact with the inhabitants, confirmed this discouraging impression. Unlike the Spaniards, Dutch explorers and merchants wanted neither to convert nor to colonize, but these distinctions made little difference in their encounters in the Pacific. Isaac Le Maire's and Willem Schouten's men were attacked by Tongans when Le Maire inadvertently offended a welcoming party.[5] These and many other meetings created precedents and analogues for strange societies and environments, and by the eighteenth century specialist institutions had been created in order to plan and commission expeditions. Joseph Banks, and other naturalists who sailed with Cook and his successors, were despatched by the Royal Society. They hankered for the respect of other scientists, and they expected islanders (as well as flora and fauna) to be exotic.

These expeditioners were not only agents of European power and science; they were also acting out dramas scripted by and for Europeans, in the sense that they brought articulated expectations of a tropical island paradise – 'sweet airs, glorious abundance of flora and fauna, running fresh water, riches, and their human inhabitants living in a natural innocence and ready for cooption in imperial designs'.[6] That expectation encouraged Mendaña to ignore the actual experience of his first expedition and attempt to create a utopian colony in Santa Cruz. Even the catastrophic failure of that venture did not cause explorers immediately to abandon their expectations, which continued to flourish in utopian literature.[7] Quiros also contrived to disregard the violence of his encounters with islanders, and the doleful experiences of his own crew, and asserted that

> the lands I saw ... are better than Spain ... [and] should be an earthly paradise. ...
>   It is a decent people, clean, cheerful, and reasonable, and as grateful as we have found them. On all these grounds there is reason to hope that, with the aid of divine providence, and by gentle means, it will be very easy to pacify, to indoctrinate, and to content them.[8]

In other words, Europeans encompassed this region imaginatively, even before it was mapped. The ancient notion of Terra Australis (balancing the land masses of the northern hemisphere) was one such projection. Charles de Brosses took the taxonomy a stride further in 1756, when he divided the – still unmapped – southern lands into Magellanic, Australasia and Polynesia.[9] Discovering, naming and classifying was what Europeans did globally, conferring identities which made more sense in London or Paris than within the region.

The expectation of paradise meant that disappointments, when acknowledged, naturally generated images of hell, allowing little possibility of a middle way. After an era of savage images, therefore, islanders were again transformed by Louis-Antoine de Bougainville's accounts of Tahiti. Tahitians first met Europeans in 1767 when a hundred canoes greeted the English Captain Samuel Wallis. The first encounters were marred by what the English believed was Tahitian theft, which provoked gunfire.[10] The Tahitians were secure on land, the English at sea; but it was difficult to move beyond this standoff. The English seemed to possess everything they needed – except women. After some days, groups of naked young women were displayed in an apparent ploy to distract the crew from an attack. After other scuffles, a tentative peace was established, and the Tahitians began to offer women. Howe explains:

> Tahitian chiefs, intimidated by British firepower, had discovered an effective way of placating the strangers ... some women of low birth were ordered to prostitute themselves as a political strategy. Not only did this ensure the goodwill of the English, it also brought considerable economic advantage to the chiefs.[11]

When Bougainville called nine months later, therefore, his ship was surrounded by canoe-loads of young women, most of them naked, and the French understood that they were being offered for sex. The alacrity with which Polynesian women offered themselves to seamen made a major contribution to the legend of the South Seas. Some observers saw their actions as evidence of the exploitation of women, others commented on the apparent independence of Polynesian women in trading their services; none could ignore this phenomenon.[12]

Sex was not the only element of Europeans' readings of Bougainville's island paradise, but neither was it trivial, and it was a tumescent Tahiti that became grist for philosophical speculation on the original condition of humankind and critiques of contemporary European societies. The explorers had more practical concerns, but preconceptions also shaped their perceptions. Bernard Smith shows how Europeans built their knowledge of new societies through well-established tropes such as the 'noble savage', which later gave way to bleaker images. At first Tahiti was 'like Paradise before the Fall of Man', but this 'soft primitivism' was opposed by a 'hard primitivism' as evangelical missionaries saw only 'depraved and benighted savages'.[13]

In either depiction, the objects of discovery were less than fully adult. With more and more 'discoveries', childlike natives became a cliché in European popular cultures. Nearly two centuries later therefore, at the tail end of this process, Australian gold prospectors in the New Guinea Highlands brought movie cameras, confident that they would be able to record the puzzlement of highlanders for the entertainment of Australians.[14] Although the Australians had very different information, arms and technology to those of sixteenth-century evangelists or eighteenth-century scientists, 'explorers' in every era expected to baffle 'natives', and to be surprised and entertained. Edward Said goes on to argue that these stereotypes are not merely historical, but persist in Western scholarship. Like the giving of names, representing the culture (or the past) of another society is an exercise in political power.[15]

For each side, the other posed not only practical problems but cosmological puzzles which had profound implications for the identity of one's own community.[16] Just as European explorers and philosophers did, islanders tried as much as possible to squeeze the strangers into their existing categories of kinship, alliance or enmity. Many Polynesians believed that common people belonged to the land, whereas chiefs were demi-gods from the sea. That hypothesis cast the newest maritime strangers in a powerful and favourable light, but it had to be abandoned when the strangers behaved in ways which struck it down and made it necessary to imagine new explanations. The problem of strangers bursting the bounds of established categories recurred throughout the era of 'first contact'. In 1934, for example, homicidal prospectors passed through Huli country in the New Guinea Highlands. They described themselves as living off the land; in practice that involved shooting domestic pigs and shooting their owners if they protested too vehemently. The expedition killed on average one highlander each day, and always refused to enter into conversation. Since Huli had no categories for predators who refused any kind of human relationship, they never found suitable terms in which to comprehend these encounters.[17]

First impressions were bizarre and ultimately tragic. Even if the newcomers intended no harm, they brought dysentery, tuberculosis and smallpox. That was especially true in the eighteenth century. Despite the steady improvement of public health and the measures to prevent and contain infections, however, outsiders continued to represent a serious health hazard. Dutch authorities explored much of West New Guinea only in the twentieth century, with Dayak carriers and Dutch East Indian troops. There were also British scientific expeditions. During the second of these, some mountain families came to beg the expedition for food. The outsiders could not feed them all, and sent them home; but before they arrived home, thirty or forty died. Whether they died through hunger or epidemic infection, their confidence in the strangers was misplaced.[18] The impact of disease might be a matter of luck, but the social and political impact of these early encounters suggests a pattern. Aboriginal Australians probably fared worse than New Zealand Maori or most other islanders because of the nature of the cultures which came together. The problem was exacerbated by neither Aborigines nor Europeans having anything that the other wanted; nor had they any means to communicate, at least until some Aboriginal Australians learned some English – it took vastly longer for any of the colonists to get their minds around Aboriginal languages. And in any event Europeans encountered Aborigines after having had their minds blown and their expectations raised in Polynesia.

The dynamics of interaction were significantly different in New Zealand, such that contact over the *moyenne durée* intensified rather than devastated Maori cultural economy and in the longer term 'overcooked' things. First encounter was tragic in its path dependence as well as its acts and moments. But encounter also offered opportunities and a new currency of competition, in the form of engagement with outsiders, as well as new means to advertise competitive capacity in the old natural currency – food.[19] It was the encounter with European outsiders – Pakeha – which constructed the Maori. It sent the *Tangata Whenua* – the people of the land – on a journey to become Maori, a word and category which they created to describe themselves, who had hitherto thought in terms of *hapu* (kin group) and *iwi* (tribe). In the new categories they were the 'normal' human beings, in opposition to the Pakeha.[20] Maori society and culture a century later, therefore, was not the same as that which first discovered Europe, for those *hapu* and *iwi* had yet to conceive of themselves as Maori.

Encounter between the 'normal' – Maori – and the other was of its nature abnormal, and mixed rare opportunities with calls for exceptional restraint. Culture contact generated a new culture of contact.[21] It created multiple cultures in the encounter zone, which varied with the baggage of those who met, and the nature of their engagement. The Maori–Pakeha interface entailed glimmerings of understanding amid misconceptions. Interaction proceeded by trial and error, and common human requirements dominated over cultural particularism, driven on the European side by the need for water and food.

Dening uses the metaphor of 'islands and beaches' to explain ways in which humans construct their worlds and their boundaries, and relate to strange people and circumstances. People surround themselves and their cultural islands with metaphorical beaches to define their identities; and the remaking of islands and crossing of beaches can be painful.[22] Indigenous and European discoveries of a larger world happened on actual (and created metaphorical) beaches, and culture was altered in action. Actions expressed norms and beliefs, but also created them, while myths and stories reflected culture, but also shaped it. As Sahlins maintains, 'if friends make gifts, gifts make friends'.[23]

Good historians always balance structure and agency; so did people in a contact situation. They juggled their structures with their will to survive, their curiosity and their opportunism. Cultures in contact misread meanings and found their meanings transformed by the flow of events. In New Zealand's Te Ika a Maui (the fish of Maui – North Island) and Te Wai Pounamu (the river of greenstone – South Island), the 'beach' differed, with the cultural terrain, from the Bay of Islands in the populous and temperate north to the sealing seas of chilly and sparsely populated Foveaux Strait in the south. The nature of the beach varied also with the visitors' behaviour. In a tribal account of a visit by pale-skinned people to the east coast of the North Island, well before Cook (and possibly Spanish), the locals' first response was fear because they saw the strange ship as a war canoe. Fear turned to curiosity and excitement when they watched the strangers fish, which confirmed their humanity, and saw that the pale, fairy people were good fishers.[24] Across the beach, the pale ones were rendered ordinary by the culture of food, and worth knowing, by their fishing.

The identity of the first Europeans to meet Maori is a matter of great moment to New Zealand scholars. Robert Langdon proposed that Spanish (and especially Basque) sailors from the wrecked caravel *San Lesmes* in the early sixteenth century found their way to the north island of New Zealand, among other landfalls.[25] That proposal is extensively argued and not inherently impossible, but it has provoked ferocious reactions among other scholars. The widely accepted narratives of culture contact begin a full century later: Europe remembered the first documented encounter with Maori as 'brief but violent'.[26] Having named Van Diemen's Land, Abel Tasman sailed across the sea to Golden Bay – which he labelled Murderers Bay because the Ngati Tumatakokiri repelled his men. By ramming the cockboat that shuttled between his two ships, killing four sailors, and evading retribution, the Maori undermined the Dutch intention to learn 'whether there is anything profitable to be got or effected', so they were deemed 'savages'.[27] For both Dutch and Maori this episode was bizarre. The Dutch did not understand the *haka*, although they understood it, correctly, as warlike; the Maori were angry that the Dutch fired a cannon and interpreted it, rightly, as a threat; and the Dutch killed a Maori who may have come in peace, after the ramming of the boat. It was the repulsion which was remembered, and rendered the Maori fierce in Europe. This encounter flattered neither Maori nor European. What shocked the strangers was that the first violence was Maori, at the expense of the European explorer. Maori social control prevailed.

CAPTAIN COOK

In New Zealand Pakeha mythology and history Tasman was the discoverer, remembered in the name of New Zealand. Belich observes that this was

Plate 3.1 *The Landing at Mallicolo*, one of the New Hebrides, painted by William Hodges, engraved by J. Bafire and J. K. Sherwin, published February 1777 in *Cook's Voyages: Atlas and Plates*. Courtesy of the Macmillan Brown Library, University of Canterbury.

convenient because it extended New Zealand's European history. But it did not extend British history, so it was 'not remembered very hard'.[28]

Captain James Cook, as an English hero, is remembered as the 'discoverer' who really founded both Australia and New Zealand. It was British settlement rather than his voyage that rendered Cook the founding ancestor. For Australians he is infinitely more suitable than the Spaniards who probably saw Northern Australia on their way through Torres Strait, or Carstenz who certainly saw (and failed to be impressed by) the coast of Western Australia, much less the two Dutch mutineers and murderers who were reprieved from judicial execution and set down as the first Europeans to set foot on the coast of (Western) Australia.[29] Cook assumed an important role in school books since, in Ken Inglis's words, 'He was British, unsectarian, rose by merit from modest beginnings, sailed the world, enlarged scientific knowledge, prevented scurvy and discovered Australia. He was only too well fitted to be a secular and compulsory hero of the classroom'.[30] Cook literally put New Zealand on the map by charting its full outline. His accuracy and skill as a navigator helped him to be remembered, but so did his Britishness; for settlement from the United Kingdom allowed Australians and New Zealanders to look back to the voyage of the *Endeavour* as the opening chapter of their founding stories. Through school books, Cook became a 'founding father' for the 'new nations of the Pacific', who took possession in the name of Britain – and bore the British name to New Zealand.[31]

The humanist myth or the Enlightenment view of Cook as the foremost ancestor of the white colonizers does live in New Zealand history, as Smith and Obeyesekere maintain.[32] He is just as vital to most Australians as to

Plate 3.2 *The Landing at Erramanga*, one of the New Hebrides, painted by William Hodges, engraved by J. Bafire and J. K. Sherwin, published February 1777 in *Cook's Voyages: Atlas and Plates*. Courtesy of the Macmillan Brown Library, University of Canterbury.

New Zealanders because he also charted Australian coasts, and in 1970 his celebrated 'Bicentenary' included Aboriginal collaboration; but he has recently assumed a rather less eminent position in white Australian historical narratives, as mythological emphases have altered their balance. At the other extreme Cook's Britishness has made him an awkward and problematic figure in the narratives of European settlement in French New Caledonia.

The New Zealand historian has become the mythmaker. Every major New Zealand history, from Sinclair's Penguin *History of New Zealand* and Beaglehole's *The Discovery of New Zealand*, to Salmond's *Two Worlds* and Belich's *Making Peoples*, cites Horeta Te Taniwha who as a small boy was given a nail by Cook.[33] In the story as cited by Salmond, taken from White:

> When our old men saw the ship they said it was an atua, a god, and the people on board were tupua, strange beings or 'goblins'. ... As our old men looked at the manner in which they came on shore, the rowers pulling with their backs to the bows of the boat, the old people said, 'Yes, it is so: these people are goblins; their eyes are at the back of their heads; they pull on shore with their backs to the land to which they are going.' ...
>
> There was one supreme man in that ship. We knew that he was the lord of the whole by his perfect gentlemanly and noble demeanour. He seldom spoke, but some of the goblins spoke much. But this man did not utter many words: all that he did was to handle our mats and hold our mere, spears, and waha-ika, and touch the hair of our heads. He was a very good man, and came to us – the children – and patted our cheeks, and gently touched our heads.[34]

Here is the archetype of 'the redoubtable white harbinger of civilization', which Obeyesekere thought was given 'peculiar application' in New Zealand.[35] This became a tradition, an example of collaboration by Maori and Pakeha in constructing myth. But he noted that in 'an unequal power structure the white version triumphs and is eventually accepted by the subaltern culture.' Obeyesekere hears no Maori voice here, only a European one. This is certainly a white story in that Cook is the paternalistic father figure to Maori children. He is the benevolent white father and they are the dear children, according to a humanist framework which set the pattern whereby many Pakeha New Zealanders and Maori came to believe that New Zealand set an excellent example in race relations. The noble Cook touched the children's heads – yet heads were *tapu* ('taboo' to European ears) to Tangata Whenua. Were this a Maori story, Cook would more likely be depicted as foreshadowing disaster for not respecting this powerful *tapu*.

This is not simply a European myth accepted by Maori: it is a hybrid. A filtered Maori voice endures in this story, providing evidence that Maori, like Hawaiians, revered the captain as a chief according to their own hierarchies, and that their elders sought to bring the strange beings into their own frameworks in order to control them. This story itself confirms that Maori, like Hawaiians, did not apotheosize Cook even on his first voyages. The ship was a god, not Cook. (In another story, from further east, the *Endeavour* was a great bird.)[36] The 'supreme man', the 'lord', was like a chief. Indeed, in a Maori account of the meeting of worlds, Cook was 'that Pakeha chief'.[37] To the Tangata Whenua trying to establish who or what these strange beings were it must have been a relief that their *kaumatua* (elders) deduced that the strange beings were goblins, who could be less, not more, than human and therefore easy to dupe.

The latest historian to use the Horeta Te Taniwha myth, James Belich, cites it as evidence that meetings between Maori and Pakeha were like attending a circus. Both employed militaristic encounter rituals and symbolic performances, salutes of cannon and *haka*, and laughed at the bizarre. In Horeta's story, 'as we could not understand them we laughed, and they laughed also ... we gave our mats for their mats, to which some of our warriors said "ka pai" [good], which words were repeated by the goblins, at which we laughed and were joined in the laugh by the goblins'.[38] In Salmond's version, ostensibly citing the same source, 'Perhaps they were asking questions, and, as we did not know their language, we laughed, and these goblins also laughed, so we were pleased.'[39] Where speech failed, laughter communicated the experience of the extraordinary, and fostered interaction. But it need not follow that 'on the whole the direct effect of the explorers on Maori was not vast.'[40] The culture of contact remembered in such stories was a rehearsal for the drama to follow.

Criticism of Cook originates in Enlightenment thought as well, among Europeans who advocated people's rights to decide their own destiny, and whom it suited to discredit the Great Navigator to advance their own interests.[41] In depicting a very different Cook, Obeyesekere cites Cook's journal for what he believes is Cook's first contact with Maori at Queen Charlotte

Sound, in 1769. It was sudden, and fatal:

> I am aware that most humane men who have not experienced things of this
> nature will cencure my conduct in fireing upon the people in this boat nor do
> I my self think that the reason I had for seizing upon her will att all justify me,
> and had I thought [that] they would have made the least resistance I would not
> have come near them, but as they did I was not to stand still and suffer either
> my self or those that were with me to be knocked on the head.[42]

He presents this extract as evidence of Cook's attitude to natives: 'any
resistance cannot be tolerated.'[43] This encounter was not at Queen Charlotte
Sound, which came later in Cook's itinerary. The quotation is from Cook's
visit to Poverty Bay – named by him in disillusionment – in October 1769.
Nor was this a first contact. By the time Cook tried to justify this capture and
killing, he and his crew had killed nine Maori, including a chief, Te Maro, in
Poverty Bay the day before.[44] According to Cook's defence, it was sufficient
that cultural contact was extraordinary; and he did not expect Maori resistance. But why did he expect no resistance when he had already encountered
it? We need to locate his act and defence in their true time and place, to
establish whether Obeyesekere's depiction of Cook the Violent was misplaced as well as out of context.

The day before, four youths in Cook's crew had failed to understand a
Maori challenge on the beach. The European response was 'swift and lethal':
they shot Te Maro and crossed the river to inspect the body.[45] The next day,
9 October, groups of 50–100 warriors challenged a large armed party from
Cook's expedition. Both sides used 'noise' to strike fear into the other;
to stop the Maori *haka*, the Europeans fired their cannon. At this point
occurred one of several crucial interventions by Tupaia, the Tahitian who
accompanied Cook. Tupaia enabled Maori and outsiders to communicate,
because he called out in Tahitian and Maori understood. He explained that
the Europeans wanted food and water – the ordinary essentials of humanity –
and offered iron in exchange. The warriors responded with bitter complaints
about the killing. Through speech, if not language, Cook knew that they
were angry, and that iron would not appease them. Maori then resorted
to ritual to restore cosmological order: one swam out to a spiritually powerful rock where a formal greeting took place with Cook. This rite brought
the outsiders within the scope of Tangata Whenua law and convention.
Having incorporated the Europeans within their global structures and
resumed control, they sought enterprisingly to exchange weapons. The
Europeans refused. One seized a sword, and violence followed.

After these bloody encounters, Cook decided to kidnap some Maori, presumably to inspect and classify the elusive 'Native'. He cut off two canoes, and
fired a musket over their heads. The young fishermen responded by hurling
missiles, stones, paddles and fish. Cook's crew shot four, and captured three
who were terrified that they might be eaten. He gave them wine, bread and
water. Tangata Whenua were deeply distressed by the killings and kidnapping.
Only after Tupaia talked to them across the water did an old man carrying a
green branch – according to a custom known throughout Polynesia – swim

across, embrace the fishermen (thus normalizing them), extend the green branch to Tupaia in a gesture of reconciliation which both recognized, and perform a *tapu*-raising ceremony over the body of one of the dead.[46] This evidence suggests that Cook did react violently to the bizarreness of contact and was disconcerted by Maori resistance. He did not expect the Native to behave that way, given the superiority of British firepower.

As Dening observes, it is significant that Cook is an English hero, and not French. Identity is shaped by interactions over the *longue durée*, and the French and English wove alternative narratives of 'discovery'. The French viewed Cook as violent; French visitors pointed to his use of physical force, attachment to property and discipline, and the wounded and dead left behind. According to Dening, they were right: Cook 'never discovered how he could moderate the behaviour of others whose systems of social control he could not understand nor use, except by violence.' Cook died in Hawaii because he had not learned.[47]

Piecing together narratives of the Great Navigator that are black and white, racially as well as metaphorically, throws more light on identity-politics as shaped through stories about cultures of contact. Australian Aboriginal histories of Cook record the violence of shooting and dispossession, and how the strangers brought nothing of use. In Captain Cook stories by Percy Mumbulla as told to and 'translated' by Roland Robinson on the South Coast of New South Wales in the 1950s,

> The big ship came and anchored out at Snapper Island. He put down a boat an' rowed up the river into Bateman's Bay. He landed on the shore of the river. ... When he landed he gave the Kurris clothes an' those terrible big sea biscuits. Terrible hard biscuits they was. When they were pullin' away to go back to the ship, ... they were throwin' the clothes an' biscuits back at Captain Cook as his men were pullin' away in the boat.[48]

Cook arrived from the sea, the source of disorder for Aboriginal Australians. As Chris Healy notes, in Aboriginal stories the beach is a place of exchange, which Cook initiated. But fruitful exchange proved impossible because Aboriginal Australians and Europeans on the beach had no shared philosophical and social categories.[49] The clothes and ship's biscuits were of no use or value to the indigenous people.

Theft, however, was theft, to European and islander.[50] It was normal for eighteenth-century Europeans to punish theft severely. In Polynesian society it was shameful to take other people's *taonga* (treasures), especially if they were kin, though strangers were more susceptible to raiding. It was not simply that the outsiders could not understand the Maori in their own terms or that the visitors, whose 'lives were in their baggage', became 'jealous custodians of property'.[51] Each tested the other's limits, and their perceptions, in the contact drama of trial and error. Encounter always required extraordinary conduct, and breaches of the strangers' mores – and one's own. In European perceptions, the bizarreness of culture contact excused their own lapses from restraint, but they reserved this excuse for themselves. Quite conceivably the islanders were equally unfair in excusing their own and denouncing others' lapses.

Salmond has an argument about Polynesian agency that reconciles these different views. She demonstrates that Polynesian understanding of Cook's experience as a repeated beach-crosser makes the most sense of how and why he died. Entangled in a web of tensions which precipitated killings of his men, Cook and his crews changed their concepts of and behaviour towards Polynesians. On his final voyage the Polynesian world of light and the European enlightenment were at war within him; in effect he had become part of Polynesia. By his third voyage, his ships were not pure representations of Europe. Many men had previous experience, 'scientists' were absent, and the presence of Mei (a traveller from Tahiti and England) affected the encounters. Cook's decision not to seek revenge for previous deaths left his men puzzled and contemptuous. According to Salmond, Cook felt the sting of contempt in Maori and in his men. The sequels of excessive thieving, the flogging of Tahitians and increasing violence had no precedent. Some of the Polynesian life force (*hau*) had entered Cook, resulting in a mingling of selves. In Maori thinking, Cook found himself caught between two sets of gods. He died as he lived on his last voyage, caught in contradictions. Polynesian and European thinking is necessary to understand this: that within Cook swirled the world of light and enlightenment.[52]

A melding of approaches is revealing in other ways. In killing Cook's men Maori confirmed that the strange beings were not superhuman but human (or less than normally human) and capable of being overpowered. Familiarity bred contempt as well as understanding and friendship. Partial understanding added to the confusion, as shown by the role of Tahitian intermediaries who, through speech, influenced how both Maori and European accommodated strangers in their mental maps. Obeyesekere argues for greater prominence to be given to speech, to allow for improvisation and agency in cultural collision and contact: in effect, for another 'turn' beyond the linguistic turn, to incorporate life's messiness and unpredictability.[53] Tupaia and Tahitian dictionaries were central to the New Zealand story. Cook's crew could speak to Maori through Tupaia, and reach a partial understanding. Speech soothed, if only imperfectly.

DU FRESNE

The French found the same. Marion du Fresne embarked from Mauritius in 1772 with the idea of returning Ahutoru, a Tahitian who had been to Paris with Bougainville, and to search for the southern continent. By the time du Fresne reached New Zealand, Ahutoru had died of smallpox, but Tahiti had left its mark. His crew tried out a Tahitian vocabulary with Maori, and could make themselves understood. Maori too, through Polynesian vocabulary, conveyed the whereabouts of boundary markers, for example in the market of sex. They made clear the message to leave married women alone, though the men could approach the girls.[54] Speech, however, did not stop du Fresne from crossing the *tapu* boundary.

Du Fresne failed to enter the white New Zealand pantheon because he was French. And he did not undergo apotheosis although (like Cook in Hawaii) the Maori ate him, consuming his life force and his *mana*. Inevitably, this Maori world view – and agency – influenced the Pakeha response to du Fresne's sad story. In tandem with the humanist myth of Cook, du Fresne deserved his sticky end. He was killed in the Bay of Islands after a 'series of blunders', and his deputy, Julien Crozet, confirmed French inhumanity, relative to the English, by massacring 250 Maori in retaliation.[55] The story of the inhumane French also suited Maori, as it justified the ritual cannibalism which tarnished the image of the Noble Savage, and of the 'civilized' Maori. Elsdon Best recorded in 1902 that 'It was a source of pure, unadulterated joy for the old time Maori, to be able to say to an enemy, "I ate your father" or "your ancestor", although the occurrence may have occurred ten generations before.'[56]

In a local account, the chief Te Kauri killed Marion because he went fishing at a *tapu* cove, which his hosts had taken pains to explain was *tapu*. The Ngati Pou told the French not to fish on the beach where some of Te Kauri's people had recently drowned, but du Fresne persisted, despite the warnings of the Ngati Pou who had become his friends and who, complicit in the offence, accompanied him on his fishing.[57] Evidently du Fresne did not understand the contradictions in his Maori friends taking him to fish in a rival's territory, where they told him not to fish. Making more efforts than Cook to befriend the Tangata Whenua did not enlighten him.

Tapu was a 'central cultural metaphor' throughout Polynesia to classify the environment, space, class, actions and events, and cultural time.[58] Scrupulous observance of *tapu* stemmed from dread of spiritual power. If a chief were insulted, or strangers trespassed on food-gathering grounds, the people were compelled to demand *utu*.[59] Du Fresne's insult to Te Kauri stemmed from his breach of one of the most potent death *tapu*, which provoked not just human anger but spiritual wrath from ancestors. In a Maori account, Te Kauri exacted *utu* by killing and eating Marion because 'The foreigners [had] violated the *tapu* of Manawaora [the cove] by netting fish there and eating those fish; it was this that made the desecration of the *tapu* such a grave offence.'[60] The fish 'had been touched by the *tapu* of death, and had perhaps nibbled the bodies of the drowned men. To catch these fish was bad enough, but to eat them was tantamount to cannibalism, an attack on the *tapu* of the corpses and that of their tribe, and on the *mana* of their tribal gods.'[61]

Marion du Fresne's expedition discovered, but did not grasp, that Maori accommodation of outsiders required them to respect Polynesian *tapu* boundaries and thus to step beyond their own cultural metaphors. This expectation led to tragedy. Not just Marion was killed, but many Maori, especially Ngati Pou. Te Kauri's people tormented the French by flaunting and wearing du Fresne's and other dead officers' clothes, with cries of 'Tacouri

[Te Kauri] mate Marion'. The French responded by attacking a Maori *pa*, and killing 250 people. The French were appalled to have their greatest horror realized, that Te Kauri had eaten Marion, to consume his life force, destroy his *mana* and snuff out the evil of the French for ignoring the death *tapu*; and the Maori were appalled that the French had fished and feasted at such a *tapu* cove.[62] Each exacted vengeance according to their own cultural constructs, which included their construct of the Other. After this, the balance of power shifted in the Bay of Islands. European intrusion added to the ferment by producing an alliance of otherwise enemies – Te Kauri of Nga Puhi and the Ngati Pou – to drive out the French. More broadly, people rearranged the way they defined themselves, their neighbours and outsiders. Conversely, Europeans rearranged their self-image in their encounter with the Ignoble Savage.

These obscure incidents, and the character of their participants, have had to perform prodigious feats of representation and bear a staggering weight of investigation. The mutiny on HMS *Bounty* is in the same case, being seen by Hollywood (several times) as a (variable) parable as well as an adventure story. The Bligh narratives have fascinated Australians in general as well as Australian scholars, partly because he became Governor of New South Wales, where he was the victim of another (military rather than naval) mutiny. Greg Dening underlines a critical feature of the early contact period and relations on the beach: the absence of a 'contract to understand one another'.[63] To remedy that defect he has probed the events of the first mutiny and produced a highly suggestive reconstruction of islander perceptions. Tahitian ideas made provision for domesticating sea-borne strangers and their awesome powers. Ritually powerful feather girdles were 'the currency of authority. They conferred title and rank.' When Bligh returned to Tahiti in pursuit of the mutineers, he saw and sketched one of these girdles.

> The Tahitians had sewn into the feather girdle a thatch of auburn hair belonging to Richard Skinner, one of the *Bounty* mutineers. ... [Bligh] was mystified that somebody as insignificant as Skinner should be remembered in so sacred an object ... Skinner was the ship's barber. He had astounded the Tahitians ... by producing a barber's model head and wigs styled in the latest fashion from London. In Tahitian eyes, Skinner was somebody special. As a barber, he had a special power to touch *tapu* places. And his own head was red – *tapu*, as special as a parakeet's feather. One could wave a red feather to catch 'Oro's attention ... one could do it with a lock of a stranger's auburn hair as well. ...
>
> [Bligh also saw] a British red pennant sewn into the body of the girdle, as a lappet or fold of its own. ... It was the pennant that [Wallis] had erected on a pole on June 26, 1767, when he took possession of Tahiti for King George III. The Tahitians had taken down the symbol of English sovereignty and incorporated it into a symbol of sovereignty of their own.[64]

While British and French navigators and scientists were trying to accommodate Tahiti in their cosmologies, Tahitians were doing something similar. They had not overthrown their categories, but incorporated the collective *mana* of Britain, and that of Skinner, within existing conceptions.

ENCOUNTERS IN THE TWENTIETH CENTURY

Analyses of eighteenth-century encounters rely on few documents, some oral traditions recorded several generations after the events, and inferences informed by ethnography. In the highlands of New Guinea, on the other hand, mutual discoveries were occurring as late as the 1930s, so the documentation is fuller, and some participants have been interviewed by professional researchers. An incident in New Guinea in the 1930s need not be relevant to New Zealand in the 1770s, but this material does offer insights. Presenting a collection of modern studies, Schieffelin and Crittenden comment that the arrival of the first outsiders

> is usually recalled as an exciting but deeply unsettling event of apparently cosmological import. Strange Beings broke into their world from outside its known horizons. Sometimes these Beings were thought to be mythical heroes coming back to their lands of their origins; sometimes they were thought to be ancestral beings returning.[65]

In one episode in 1930, Gorohonota villagers mistook prospectors for ancestors and welcomed them back:

> We all gathered around to look, we were pointing at them, and we were saying 'Aah, that one – that must be ...' and we named one of our people who had died before. 'That must be him.' And we'd point to another one and say that that must be this other dead person ... and we were naming them.[66]

Although these worlds intersected only in the 1930s, legally highlanders had been German subjects since the 1880s and Australian protected persons since 1921. They could not conceivably know that, nor did Australian officials expect them to; but patrol officers who came to explain how matters stood had no doubt about the legitimacy of their authority. By far the largest expedition of the Australian period was the Hagen-Sepik Patrol led by Jim Taylor and John Black, travelling 3,000 km over 15 months in 1938–9. The historian Bill Gammage describes it as 'the last of the great European explorations which began with Diaz 450 years before', and Taylor himself saw it in that context.[67] The patrol travelled from Mount Hagen in the highlands to the Dutch border and to the mouth of the Sepik river, before returning to Mount Hagen. The minister who authorized this patrol was interested in oil as well as governance, and asked the administrator for a program 'whereby special attention might be given to concentrating upon the penetration of areas in which oil prospecting companies are likely to be interested'. Taylor and Black also had an interest in gold, and each spent some time panning and prospecting. But Australians were only three of 350 people in the patrol. Most participants were carriers, recruited on the march. Taylor recognized that exploration relied entirely on the carrier,

> with his 40 or 50 lbs packs, his blanket and bush knife or tomahawk, who struggles through the sago swamps, his hard calloused feet pierced with the

needle-sharp thorns, often in water to the waist. ... If his spirit falters it means death and a grave in a foreign land.

Rather more important in establishing relations with new communities were the New Guinea police, who saw – and often seized – opportunities for sex, acquiring pigs, and building the social foundation for local leadership when they retired from the police. The police were *de facto* in charge of day-to-day encounters, and often used that authority to advance their individual and collective interests. Some had joined the expedition for adventure and renown, but

> most would strive as well to expand their influence. Obeying the forms and displays the *mastas* expected, they nonetheless sought in the police what the clan taught them to admire. They wanted power, wealth, fame, battle, good food, sex, to understand the *mastas* and to rival the deeds of ancestors and kin. They would pursue these confident that their ability and magic could outmatch any restraints *mastas* might impose.

It is in the memories of New Guineans that some of the significance of these encounters becomes clearer.

> Europeans assumed that Highlanders who treated travellers as unearthly therefore thought them powerful and inviolate. They thought being supernatural gave them protection. At best this was only briefly so. Highlanders quickly sought to discover what the travellers were – men, ghosts, spirits of deities – in order to control them. On that depended their well-being, even their lives. Endlessly they asked the newcomers, 'Who are you?'

That was a cosmic as well as a mundane question. After much experience and long reflection, Taylor reckoned that

> familiarity bred contempt not because people had decided that the strangers were not spirits but because, unlike whites, they believed that spirits could be tricked or overpowered as well as placated. That a spirit was weak mattered more than that it was a spirit.[68]

Violence was always implicit and often explicit in pioneering patrols. Whatever highlanders thought about the visitors, they were not overawed. On one occasion Taylor noted that a man turned up with a rope 'to tie up his share of the loot', and almost all patrol leaders judged that sooner or later it would be necessary to kill someone, in the course of establishing permanent relationships.

Academic narratives of first contact tend to be bilateral. In the Hagen-Sepik Patrol, however, highlanders met other (hitherto unknown) highlanders, and they formed relations with police who were mainly from coastal New Guinea as well as meeting a couple of Australians and seeing their first manifestation of a state. In the long run it may be more important that (for example) Melanesia was mainly evangelized by Polynesians, than that Europeans directed the operations.

MAORI DISCOVERY OF ABORIGINES

It was certainly important that Maori widened their social and geographical horizons. Maori first discovered Aboriginal Australians in 1793 on a voyage to Port Jackson and Norfolk Island, in the framework of their continuing encounter with Europe – Maori had become entangled in the European desire for flax and for visiting rights for whalers in New Zealand. The first Maori to visit Australia, under duress, were Tuki, a priest, and Huru, a warrior, from the Bay of Islands. These young beach-crossers boarded George Vancouver's supply ship in 1793, against their elders' advice, and found themselves kidnapped by the strangers: transported to Norfolk Island via Sydney to fulfil a request by Philip King, the convict commandant and future Governor of New South Wales, for Maori to teach convicts how to dress flax. King had neglected to factor in a Polynesian gender division of labour: dressing flax was women's work. Serendipitously, Tuki and Huru's stay with King and his family evolved into what Maori perceived as an alliance between King and chiefs in the Bay of Islands. Dozens of Maori took overseas trips to Sydney as heads of state, traders, tourists and students. Their discovery of Aborigines left them singularly unimpressed. Because Maori encountered Aborigines in the aftermath of convict settlement as a product of their own contact with convictism, the Aboriginal Australians they met had already had their world dramatically disturbed by dispossession and disease; Aborigines around Sydney had already been devastated by smallpox.[69]

The most accessible illustration of the Maori view of Aboriginal inferiority comes from Te Pahi, a northern chief who decided to ally himself with King and the English at Sydney, and on a study tour with his sons in 1805 stayed as the Governor's guest at Government House. Governor King recorded Te Pahi's, and Tuki's earlier, contempt of Aborigines in January 1806:

> Of the natives of this country he had the most contemptible opinion, which both he and Tookey [Tuki] did not fail to manifest by discovering the utmost abhorrence at their going naked, and their want of ingenuity or inclination to procure food and make themselves comfortable, on which subject Tip-a-he [Te Pahi] on every occasion reproached them very severely. Their battles he treated as the most trifling mode of warfare, and was astonished that when they had their adversary down they did not kill him, which it seems is a custom among the New Zealanders and is carried to the most unrelenting pitch; indeed, no race of men could be treated with a more marked contempt than the natives of this country were by our visitors, who, it must be confessed, were infinitely their superiors in every respect.[70]

If we remove the filter of King's voice, imposing a European hierarchy of races, there remains a Maori view of Aborigines deemed inferior in warfare, in the provision of food and in their nakedness. Te Pahi expressed astonishment at an Aboriginal code of conflict which saw no need to kill. Maori held non-violence in contempt; in their world *mana* derived from fighting and particularly from success in conquest, attitudes soon to be compounded by an accelerating engagement with Europe and its artefacts of guns and potatoes, which facilitated Maori strategies of warfare. These Maori visitors, in Sydney to learn about potato-growing and European technology, shared the European disdain for people whom they perceived as nomads rather than as warriors and agriculturalists.[71]

Correspondingly, the Taranaki Maori who invaded the Chatham Islands in 1835 scorned the Moriori as 'black fella'. Through the overlay of assumption by Maori of the European language of race could be discerned a Maori ranking of Chatham Islanders as equally inferior to Aboriginal Australians (a ranking which Europeans subsequently co-opted in portraying Moriori as Melanesian). That the Moriori were Polynesian was irrelevant. It was their code of non-violence which earned Maori contempt. Just as Maori scorned Aborigines for their 'most trifling mode of warfare', Maori condemned Chatham Islanders because they were pacifist. Through their non-violence they allowed themselves to be slaughtered and enslaved. Conversely, Chatham Islanders viewed the Maori who ignored their *mana whenua* as 'flesh-eating demons'.[72]

As these episodes suggest, discovery-encounters between indigenous communities often took place under the aegis of European power-holders. That is more than a picturesque circumstance, since the perceptions of the powerful commonly percolated into the minds of those meeting each other for the first time. A clear and disconcerting instance of this occurred in Northern Australia in 1965. The Australian administrators of Papua New Guinea and officers of the mining corporation Conzinc Riotinto Australia were struggling to persuade Bougainville landowners to agree to the development of a great copper mine. A party of Bougainville men was assembled and escorted through Australia, to inspect large-scale mining operations.[73] They were dismayed rather than reassured by gazing at Mount Morgan – but deeply impressed by a hundred women trimming fruit for the cannery, who worked 'just like machines'.[74] The men also tried to impose their own agenda on the programme of visits: some believed that 'large-scale European development is synonymous with exploitation', and wanted to meet the Aboriginal victims of this process. But when they did meet, they concluded that Aborigines

> had neglected or refused the opportunities given them to better themselves. This impression is in no small measure due to the unfailing courtesy and genuine interest in the party by Australians [*sic*] everywhere – by a complete absence of discrimination and the absolute absence of condescension.[75]

It is easy to see (in fact almost impossible to ignore) in this encounter the consummate ability of white Australians to co-opt Melanesians into a dismissive view of Aboriginal Australians. Not only did they create the physical context for the meeting; they shaped its intellectual context as well. And in these encounters we may perhaps detect the distant, distorted but lingering echoes of Western Europeans' persistent, courageous and self-deceiving pursuit of heaven on earth.

NOTES

1 R. G. Ward, 'Earth's Empty Quarter?', *The Geographical Journal*, 155: 2 (1989), 235–46.
2 Henrietta Drake-Brockman, *Voyage to Disaster*, Sydney, 1963.
3 This melancholy narrative is told by Malama Meleisea and Penelope Schoeffel in ch. 3 of D. Denoon, S. Firth, J. Linnekin, K. Nero and M. Meleisea (eds), *Cambridge History of the Pacific Islanders*, Melbourne, 1997.
4 Oskar Spate, *The Pacific since Magellan*, vol. 1: *The Spanish Lake*, Canberra, 1979; vol. 2: *Monopolists and Freebooters*, Canberra, 1983; vol. 3: *Paradise Found and Lost*, Canberra, 1988.
5 Kerry Howe, *Where the Waves Fall: A New South Sea Islands History from First Settlement to Colonial Rule*, Honolulu, 1984, 79–80.
6 Kerry Howe, *Nature, Culture and History*, Honolulu, in press.
7 David Fausett, *Writing the New World: Imaginary Voyages and Utopias of the Great Southern Land*, Syracuse, 1993; cited by Howe, *Nature, Culture and History*.
8 Clements Markham (ed.), *The Voyages of Pedro Fernandez de Quiros 1595 to 1604*, London, 1904, vol. 1, 478, 479.
9 Charles de Brosses, *Histoire des navigations aux Terres Australes*, Paris, 1756.
10 Howe, *Where the Waves Fall*, 85. Nicholas Thomas, 'The Force of Ethnology: Origins and Significance of the Melanesia/Polynesia Division', *Current Anthropology*, 30: (1989), 27–41.
11 Howe, *Where the Waves Fall*, 88.
12 David Chappell, 'Shipboard Relations between Pacific Island Women and Euroamerican Men, 1767–1887', *Journal of Pacific History*, 27: (1992), 131–48.
13 Bernard Smith, *European Vision and the South Pacific 1768–1850*, London, 1960.
14 Bob Connolly and Robin Anderson, *First Contact: New Guinea's Highlanders Encounter the Outside World*, New York, 1988.
15 Edward Said, *Orientalism*, London, 1978.
16 Malama Meleisea and Penelope Schoeffel, 'Discovering Outsiders', ch. 4 in Denoon et al., *Cambridge History of the Pacific Islanders*.
17 Chris Ballard, 'The Death of a Great Land: Ritual, History and Subsistence Revolution in the Southern Highlands of Papua New Guinea', Ph.D. thesis, Australian National University, Canberra, 1995.
18 C. G. Rawlings, *The Land of the New Guinea Pygmies*, and A. F. R. Wollaston, 'An Expedition to Dutch New Guinea', quoted by Anton Ploeg, 'First Contact in the Highlands of Irian Jaya', *Journal of Pacific History*, 30: 2 (1995), 227–39.
19 A. R. Parsonson, 'The Expansion of a Competitive Society', 51–3; James Belich, *Making Peoples: A History of the New Zealanders from Polynesian Settlement to the End of the Nineteenth Century*, Auckland, 1996, 155.
20 Ideas from G. Dening, *Islands and Beaches: Discourse on a Silent Land, Marquesas 1774–1880*, Honolulu, 1980.
21 I. C. Campbell, 'European–Polynesian Encounters: A Critique of the Pearson Thesis', *Journal of Pacific History*, 29: 2, 1994.
22 Dening, *Islands and Beaches*, 3.
23 Marshall Sahlins, *Islands of History*, Chicago, 1985, xi.
24 Anne Salmond, *Two Worlds: First Meetings between Maori and Europeans 1642–1772*, Auckland, 1993, 62.
25 Robert Langdon, *The Lost Caravel*, Sydney, 1975; *The Lost Caravel Re-explored*, Canberra, 1988; and 'Castaways', ch. 2 of Denoon et al., *Cambridge History of the Pacific Islanders*.

26 Harrison M. Wright, *New Zealand, 1769–1840: Early Years of Western Contact*, Cambridge, MA, 1959, 3.
27 Salmond, *Two Worlds*, ch. 3.
28 Belich, *Making Peoples*, xx.
29 Hugh Edwards, *Islands of Angry Ghosts*, Sydney, 1966.
30 K. S. Inglis, *The Australian Colonists: An Exploration of Social History, 1788–1970*, Melbourne, 1974, 243. Also cited by Chis Healy, *From the Ruins of Colonialism: History as Social Memory*. Studies in Australian History, ed. Alan Gilbert, Patricia Grimshaw and Peter Spearritt. Melbourne, 1997, 27.
31 Bernard Smith, *Imagining the Pacific*, Melbourne, 1992, 228, 238.
32 Bernard Smith, *Imagining the Pacific*, ch. 10; Gananath Obeyesekere, *The Apotheosis of Captain Cook: European Mythmaking in the Pacific*, Princeton, NJ, 1992, 133–7. Smith gives an illuminating account of the Enlightenment view of Cook, as a new type of hero for European expansion and imperialism, who stood for the freedom to make one's own way in the world. He provides insights into Cook as a blend of new and old heroes: old, in being descended from heroes of the past (like Christ, of humble origins, but who confounded wise men and brought a new message; and treated all men as brothers); and new, in his command of new technologies and in circulating information through his journals which was necessary for free trade. Smith explains why Cook proved an ideal exemplar for younger sons who had to leave home to better themselves, becoming a model for British schoolboys from the end of the eighteenth century. Cook's virtues were timely, as the 'new hero of free and civilized trading' for the era of *Pax Britannica*. Smith, *Imagining the Pacific*, 226–38.
33 Obeyesekere noted this account was first taken down by an unknown person in 1852.
34 Salmond, *Two Worlds*, 87–8.
35 Obeyesekere, *The Apotheosis of Captain Cook*, 136.
36 Salmond, *Two Worlds*, 123–4. Joel Polack, a European trader, recorded an account by grandchildren of Tangata Whenua who lived in Poverty Bay when Cook arrived in 1769 that the *Endeavour* was a great bird. The people had a legend of a great bird that had carried an ancestor back to New Zealand after he had been to Hawaii. Here again any suggestion of apotheosis, in likening Cook to the ancestor, is as much European as Maori myth.
37 Salmond, *Two Worlds*, 181.
38 Belich, *Making Peoples: A History of the New Zealanders from Polynesian Settlement to the end of the Nineteenth Century*, Auckland, 1996, 123.
39 Anne Salmond, *Two Worlds: First Meetings between Maori and Europeans 1642–1772*, Auckland, 1991, 88.
40 Belich, *Making Peoples*, 123.
41 Smith, *Imagining the Pacific*, 238.
42 Obeyesekere, *The Apotheosis of Captain Cook*, 6.
43 Ibid.
44 Salmond, *Two Worlds*, 125; she cites the same reference from Cook's journal, 132.
45 Salmond, *Two Worlds*, 125.
46 Ibid., 126–9, 134. Interpretations are ours.
47 Dening, *Islands and Beaches*, 18.
48 Cited in Healy, *From the Ruins of Colonialism*, 52–3.
49 Ibid., 58–64.
50 Campbell, 'European–Polynesian Encounters', 231.

51 Here we are taking issue with Dening, *Islands and Beaches*, 20–3.
52 Salmond, 'The Trial of the Cannibal Dog/The Death of Captain Cook', paper, NZHA Conference, December 1997, Massey University. See also A. Salmond, *Between Worlds: Early Exchanges Between Maori and Europeans 1773–1815*, Auckland, 1997.
53 Obeyesekere, *The Apotheosis of Captain Cook*, 19.
54 Salmond, *Two Worlds*, 371–6.
55 For example, J. M. R. Owens, 'New Zealand before Annexation', in G. W. Rice (ed.), *Oxford History of New Zealand*, Oxford, 1992, 30.
56 Sahlins, *Islands of History*, 59.
57 Salmond, *Two Worlds*, 386–94.
58 Dening, *Islands and Beaches*, 87.
59 Parsonson, 'The Expansion of a Competitive Society', 51.
60 Salmond, *Two Worlds*, 387, 395.
61 Ibid., 387.
62 Ibid., 395–402. Salmond revisits du Fresne's death in *Between Worlds*, 20.
63 Dening, *Islands and Beaches*.
64 Greg Dening, *Mr Bligh's Bad Language: Passion, Power and Theatre on the Bounty*, Cambridge, 1992, Act 2, 207–8.
65 E. Schieffelin and R. Crittenden (eds), *Like People You See in a Dream: First Contact in Six Papuan Societies*, Stanford, CA, 1991, 3.
66 Quoted in Connolly and Anderson, *First Contact*, 36–7.
67 Bill Gammage, *The Sky Travellers: Journeys in New Guinea 1938–1939*, Melbourne, 1998, 2; quotations from pp. 43–4, 39, 1–2.
68 Ibid., 13–14.
69 Salmond, *Between Worlds*, 187, and ch. 9; see also Belich, *Making Peoples*, 144–6.
70 King Papers, 2 January 1806, in R. McNab (ed.), *Historical Records of New Zealand*, vol. I, Wellington, 1908, 267. See also Salmond, *Between Worlds*, 351–2.
71 Bay of Islands Maori were familiar with the potato since its introduction to Northland on Tuki and Huru's return in 1793: McNab, *Historical Records of New Zealand*, vol. 1, 263. On *mana* from fighting and conquest, see M. King, *Moriori: A People Rediscovered*, Auckland, 1989, 76.
72 King, *Moriori*, 67–76. Jared Diamond, *Guns, Germs and Steel: The Fates of Human Societies*, New York, 1997, ch. 2, perceives the brutal Maori–Moriori encounter depicted by King as a 'natural experiment of history' of how environments affect human societies. In Diamond's teleological argument, Moriori pacifists were defeated by Maori invaders with 'more advanced technology and weapons' because the former were hunter-gatherers and the latter were farmers. In fact, the latter were 'hunter-gardeners', as Belich terms them, and gatherers. The disparities in these cultural economies in response to environment are not as great as Diamond suggests. Just as important in this disastrous encounter was the Maori discovery of Europe. The Taranaki Maori who invaded the Chatham Islands were themselves dispossessed, ousted by other (Waikato) Maori with European guns bought in Sydney.
73 66/458, Denehy to DDC Sohano, 7 October 1965, copied to Department. Cited in D. Denoon, *Getting Under the Skin*, Melbourne, 2000.
74 68/4999, Territory Intelligence Committee Paper 3/68 of 12 September 1968. Cited in Denoon, *Getting Under the Skin*.
75 Report to the Australian Department of Territories, cited in ch. 5 of Denoon, *Getting Under the Skin*.

[4] DEPOPULATION AND IMMIGRATION

DEPOPULATION

Every indigenous society lost population through direct or indirect interaction with Europeans. Crosby argues that this was inevitable, and varied only in scale: Europeans imported (not always knowingly) flora and fauna which subverted the ecologies that they invaded. The Pacific Islands were most vulnerable because of their remoteness from the 'earth's continental hothouses of biological and cultural evolution', from which they had been isolated for millennia.[1] New tools, a 'portmanteau biota', new economic principles and opportunities also disrupted biotic communities. But for our purposes the most salient disruption was human depopulation: 'new infections ran amok among island populations with no inherited or conferred immunities.'[2]

To estimate the scale of depopulation, we must estimate numbers on the eve of European intervention; but no census was conducted until much later, when colonial census-takers agreed that numbers had fallen and were still declining. For the Solomon Islands these reports estimated 100,000 to 150,000. Until the 1930s, neither Dutch New Guinea officials nor those of Papua or Australian New Guinea were aware of highland populations – and vice versa. The first census was attempted in Papua New Guinea only in the 1960s, suggesting a population of fewer than two million. In Irian Jaya, the Dutch left in the 1960s leaving perhaps 750,000 people. In these islands the problem is essentially empirical. Elsewhere the extent of decline, its causes and remedies, became more contentious. If numbers had fallen from high peaks, then newcomers must shoulder some blame. Modern scholars therefore suspect that Australian officials underestimated Aboriginal numbers so as to minimize the European impact.[3] On the other hand, pessimistic evolutionists could imagine depopulation – even extinction – without supporting data.[4] The extent to which depopulation became a moral and political issue depends on the rhetorical choices in later generations rather than the scale of population loss.

Estimates of island depopulation rely heavily on three studies, beginning with Norma MacArthur's.[5] She noticed that European sailors estimated numbers by counting people on the beach and multiplying by the presumed land area. While this practice probably exaggerated the population, some of her cases suggest the opposite conclusion. Later, David Stannard argued that Hawaii's population was twice as large as hitherto believed – 800,000 or more – collapsing to perhaps a twentieth.[6] He suggests that similar catastrophes may have occurred elsewhere in Polynesia. Then the epidemiologist Stephen Kunitz placed greater emphasis on social circumstances than on germs, and correlated depopulation with dispossession: he judged that Hawaii and New Zealand suffered much more than Samoa or Tonga because the former suffered dispossession while the latter did not. On this view, social disruption destroyed social networks and was just as destructive as the infectious agents.[7] For Stannard depopulation caused dispossession; for Kunitz it was the other way round. Butlin also made depopulation a cause when he emphasized introduced diseases in decimating Aboriginal Australians; whereas Durie sides with Kunitz and correlates depopulation with dispossession in New Zealand.[8] These disputes reflect the contrast between a medical model of population decline, or a political economy (or cultural) approach. Typically, the medically trained scholars, Durie and Kunitz, treat death and sickness mainly as products of people's ways of living. To get at the most likely numbers we must evaluate the medical against (and with) social, economic and cultural forms of explanation.

Scholars also debate rates of decline, and their conclusions depend on whether they prefer higher or lower population estimates. MacArthur suggested a population loss of 60 to 90 per cent for some islands in Vanuatu.[9] For Fiji, she reckoned a population of about 135,000, but only 110,000 were counted in 1879.[10] Roy Scragg observes that the Solomon Islands – like other island groups – were swept by chicken pox, whooping cough, measles, influenza, gonorrhoea, leprosy and tuberculosis in the nineteenth century. The intensity of sandalwood and bêche-de-mer and labour trades were uneven, and some islands were little affected while others teetered near extinction. But the initial collapse was not always the greatest problem: Aneityum's population fell by perhaps a third before the missionaries came, but fell by another 90 per cent thereafter.[11] Even when populations declined less sharply, the impact was traumatic, and early colonial officials were exaggerating but not fantasizing when they feared extinction.

The impact was uneven. Melanesians far outnumber Polynesians today, but these numbers were probably more equal before European contact: many Melanesian populations were shielded from the worst effects, whereas Stannard's Polynesian survey presents a range of 60 to above 90 per cent. Maori numbers fell by more than half until the 1890s.[12] On islets – wide open to natural or human catastrophe – population decline could be terminal. New Guinea and nearby islands may have experienced less loss of life than other places. They were less attractive to whalers and explorers, at least until the adoption of quinine to fend off malaria.[13] Stannard attributes much of Hawaii's depopulation to venereal diseases in a society whose mores favoured them. Conditions were less favourable in most of Melanesia, and in any event the frontier of labour recruiting, moving north through Vanuatu and Solomon Islands, reached New Guinea and the Bismarck archipelago only in the 1870s. The gold frontier was also late. Under colonial rule, from

1884, restraints continued to operate. A German settlement in New Guinea had to be abandoned, leaving the doctor to lament that 'malaria has conquered'.

Kunitz notes that mortality depended partly on the frequency of infection, and foreign ships were most common in Tahiti, Hawaii and New Zealand; but New Zealand Maori were partly shielded by large land area and sparse population.[14] After the first generation of limited contacts, dispossession paved the way for the diseases of poverty. Kunitz distinguishes between the immediate impact of epidemics and longer decline once people were swamped by migrants and their children. The history of indigenous Kanak in New Caledonia perhaps illustrates that tendency. Whatever the pre-contact population – 100,000 as recent studies suggest, or the 50,000 which early French officials assumed – it probably contracted to 42,000 by 1887, and to 27,768 by 1901.[15] That trend coincided with large-scale expropriation of land and the concentration of main island populations.

Epidemics were serious, but island populations could recover. Measles, striking perfect conditions in Fiji in 1875, killed possibly 40,000 in a population of 150,000. The population increased in the next few years, but then declined for twenty years when new forms of production were being imposed. This decline was less dramatic than the epidemic, but equally significant.[16] Influenza in 1918–19 offers the clearest evidence of the importance of human intervention.[17] The pandemic travelled along the world's shipping routes, so it reached Australia and New Zealand before it struck the islands. Australian measures largely prevented its further spread, but New Zealanders were less well prepared, and influenza reached Tonga (where it carried off 6 per cent of the people) and Nauru (16 per cent) and then Fiji (where 5 per cent of the population died). Finally, in Western Samoa it brought social and economic life to a standstill. By the time it burned out, 30 per cent of adult men were dead, 22 per cent of adult women and 10 per cent of the children. (Due to a naval commander's ruthless blockade, influenza was barred from American Samoa.) However, in the next five years the Western Samoan population grew by 2.5 per cent a year, and in the next decade by 3.3 per cent. Like some other favoured communities, they had retained substantial control of their social forms and the rhythms of daily life.

The impact of epidemics depended largely on the conditions in which people lived, the measures they adopted and the timing. In New Zealand, the great changes came with the exponential increase in the numbers and density of the Pakeha population. Maori chiefs realized this when more settlers than expected – 2,000 – landed in Wellington early in 1840, many more than they could control. To retain autonomy, they moved inland. Pool argues that the Maori decline was most rapid from 1840 to 1874, and that recovery was assured by the 1890s.[18] With tuberculosis, mission schools were probably more lethal than plantations, as they assembled pupils as boarders. The perverse result is that its presence is an index of Christianity. In New Caledonia, where it was also introduced by missionaries, Kanaks called it *christiano*.[19] Unlucky Hawaiians met Europeans at the worst possible time, when tuberculosis and venereal diseases were rampant. Lucky New Guinea highlanders met Europeans when tuberculosis was controllable by BCG and venereal diseases by penicillin.

Before the European invasion of Australia, the people who became Aborigines as a result of this encounter accepted high death rates in their strategies to balance demand and supply of resources. What to Europeans seemed an inability to care for helpless kin was probably their way to ensure material comfort for later generations.[20] Post-invasion depopulation was driven by radically different forces. It also varied greatly over time and space. Some groups suffered irreparable losses while others recovered. Some were severed from kinship and land, others retained more control, and cultural, language and land associations. Later frontiers experienced depopulation distinctive in degree and kind; Northern Australian Aborigines, for example, maintained strong bonds with the land.[21] The case of the Torres Strait islanders differs again. Groups in marine and mountain ecologies typically fared better than those in the plains. Those in pastoral areas were often the worst affected because as hunter-gatherers they had to compete with pastoralists for water and grass. People in central and southwestern Victoria suffered sudden and devastating losses during the great pastoral expansion of 1836–40, which by 1850 claimed most of the fertile land in the colony. Kangaroo, duck, emu and bush turkey fled, while sheep munched seasons' worth of yams and other plants. 'The livestock won, hooves down.'[22]

There are no reliable figures on depopulation. From the 1930s, Australian scholars adopted Radcliffe-Brown's estimate of about 300,000 at the beginning of colonization, of whom at most 50,000 were thought to have survived. This guess prevailed until the 1980s, when Butlin startled other scholars with an estimate of one million in 1788, calculated by reverse-survival techniques, prompting anthropologists also to lift numbers to 500,000 and even 750,000.[23] The worst period was between 1830 and 1890 when land hunger and pioneering were at their strongest: Aboriginals 'went down like ninepins, and made no mark on the ground.'[24] Against this wholesale invasion by exotic plants, animals and people, they had little defence. With no experience of the culture and its dangers, they often ascribed new evils not to the newcomers but to the sorcery and witchcraft of other tribes. As they suffered dislocation and dispossession, the fracturing of tribal society, particularly kinship and land ties, and distortion of gender roles compounded their losses. Specific causes of death included respiratory diseases and their impact on fertility and infant mortality. Smallpox was probably the most serious epidemic, striking several places in the late eighteenth and nineteenth centuries even before permanent white settlement. Respiratory diseases, particularly tuberculosis, and venereal diseases like gonorrhoea and worst of all syphilis – 'that scourge of man's sensuality' – took a heavy toll. Other attributed causes ranged from malnutrition from ecological disturbance to the abuse of alcohol and opium, and distress from dispossession. The kidnapping of women robbed Aboriginal Australia of reproductive power, apart from the effects of rape and disease on women's and children's survival. Frontier violence also killed. Given their number and scope, there are (predictably) few records or recollections of massacres, poisonings, rapes and systematic starvation. Academics still debate whether more people died from disease or violence.[25]

The commonest official response was to invoke the medical model, which attributed mortality simply to disease and shifted responsibility to the realm of accident, acts of God, or the non-negotiable cost of linkage to the outside world. Many new diseases did have profound impacts. Crowd infections could be savage in 'virgin field' conditions.[26] When measles struck Fiji in 1875, officials presumed that the high mortality was partly due to the sudden onset,

> but the heavy mortality was also attributable in great measure to the people's dire ignorance of the simplest nursing precautions, to their blind unimpressiveness, their want of ordinary foresight, their apathy and despair.

As in this case, some blamed the victims. This was the most detailed articulation of that approach, by a commission appointed to investigate the decrease of the Fijian population.[27] Some behaviour was inept, but doctors also toyed with psychosomatic explanations. Before the Great War, W. J. Durrad of the Melanesian Mission pondered 'The Depopulation of Melanesia', attributing much blame to commercial and religious agents.[28] To reverse what he saw as steep population decline, he proposed the regulation of labour recruitment, sumptuary laws to restrict the wearing of European clothes, temperance, providing hospitals and medicines, cash payments for large families, and encouragement of islanders to 'develop' their own lands.

This prescription impressed W. H. R. Rivers, whose ethnographic surveys also suggested that action could and should be taken to reverse population decline. Trained in medicine, Rivers was a pioneer in physiology, who joined the Cambridge Torres Strait expedition in 1898, and enjoyed fieldwork so much that he began to develop anthropology as well. His survey in the Solomons is the basis for the new discipline of studies of kinship. When the Great War broke out Rivers enlisted to give psychiatric help to 'shell-shocked' officers. Equipped with the latest psychiatric theories and his therapeutic experience, Rivers assembled seven other essays to delve into Melanesia's depopulation problem and its remedies. This collection presented the best-informed Western opinion of 1922, all of them elaborating Durrad's argument. Felix Speiser also proposed eugenic measures to increase the birth rate, and extended medical services. Otherwise he pinned his faith on simplifying islanders' lives:

> All products of civilization, except those which have become absolutely necessary to the natives, should be strictly barred, and the natives thereby compelled to make for themselves mats and clothing, weapons and furniture. ... They would become attached to their homes and live industrious lives; and faith in themselves and hope in the future of the race would soon revive.[29]

A former Commissioner of the Solomon Islands and a Lieutenant-Governor of Papua agreed with the report on the 'Decrease of the Population of Fiji', that islanders could not save themselves. The government should therefore take responsibility for social reproduction and provide (or train) maternal and child health medical staff.

Rivers himself debunked the convenient notion that Melanesians were 'already a dying people before the European invasion' and instead blamed new diseases, opium, tobacco and alcohol. Endorsing Durrad, he pointed to the unhygienic wearing of European clothing, and echoed Durrad's criticism of European influence on housing. Rivers became notorious for his further contention that 'modifications and interferences with native custom' had been 'quite as important, if not more important, in the production of native decadence'. In the Solomons, administrators banned head-hunting, despite 'the vast place it took in the religious and ceremonial lives of the people, without realizing the gap it would leave in their daily interests.' In the New Hebrides missionaries dismissed complex beliefs about ancestors:

> Through this unintelligent and undiscriminating action ... the people were deprived of nearly all that gave interest to their lives. I have now to suggest that this loss of interest forms one of the reasons, if indeed it be not the most potent of all the reasons, to which the native decadence is due.[30]

In Rivers' view, some communities who remained independent retained their fecundity. Others, who embraced Christianity, were also increasing: 'Christianity and the occupations connected with it have given the people a new interest'. Indeed the 'psychological factor' seemed more important than any material condition. That view was avant-garde in the 1920s, but recalled ancient perceptions of moral health and a healthy mind in a healthy body. Rivers' fieldwork suggested that in one island at least,

> All the factors [labour recruiting, European clothing and housing, etc.] to which other writers in this book ascribe the decrease of the population of Melanesia are practically absent, and yet we have a striking diminution of population, due in the main to decrease of the birth-rate.

Here he invoked the European preoccupation with a declining birth rate, which eugenists then treated as a sure sign of racial degeneracy. He was acutely aware of political and social circumstances. By inference, he had noticed the shortage of babies which Pool stresses in assessing Maori population decline.[31] Fewer live babies could be a result of high infant mortality, or high mortality among women at reproductive ages, or both. Just as the synergies between land alienation, loss of hope and sick babies varied by region in New Zealand, Rivers saw particular problems affecting the Solomons. One was the Queensland labour trade,

> one of the blackest of civilization's crimes. Not least among its evils was the manner of its ending, when large numbers of people who had learnt by many years' experience to adapt themselves to civilized ways were ... thrust back into savagery without help of any kind. [This misery added to] a state of helplessness and hopelessness [which] have only contributed as much as any other factors to the decline of the population.[32]

The *Essays* were designed to influence policy. Sharing the race and gender values of their intended readers, they were sometimes preaching to the converted. Lieutenant-Governor Hubert Murray in Papua welcomed the writers' endorsement of his methods, 'including even the prohibition of European clothing, the "baby bonus", and native plantations.'[33] Paradoxically Papuan (and New Guinean) fathers were paid the baby bonus which the Australian government had introduced at home in 1912 to boost the white birth rate. Also in line with Australian practice, abortion became a criminal offence (see chapter 12). Meanwhile the Great War created a host of medical orderlies who were recruited as medical assistants. Papuan young men were also trained in the 1930s to serve as community health workers. Clothing restrictions were imposed, but it was not necessary to regulate housing. Papua required villagers to produce copra themselves, although New Guinea and Papuan officials both recruited villagers for work in plantations and mines; and both banned the entry of 'coloured' labour and the emigration of Melanesians.[34]

Lacking hard evidence, Murray nevertheless suspected population decline and (like Rivers) blamed 'this disturbance, moral and material' for 'the decrease in vitality that has often been noticed among coloured races after the arrival of the white man'. Some institutions deserved encouragement, but must inevitably disappear. One of these was the *kula* exchange network recently publicized by Malinowski:

> The KULA...is full of anthropological interest, and...it teaches social discipline and skill in seamanship. But it will be superseded by modern methods as surely as the mail coach was superseded by the railway, and no Government, however sympathetic, can possibly keep it alive.[35]

This was a popular mantra. 'As surely as' proved a compelling phrase for believers in inevitable progress. In an often (mis)quoted saying recited by Pakeha and Maori in New Zealand, Pakeha commentators insisted that Maori prophesied that 'Just as the Norwegian rat has displaced the Maori rat, as introduced plants have displaced native plants, so the white man will replace the Maori.'[36] In a version attributed to Von Hochstetter in 1865, Maori agreed that 'As clover killed the fern, and the European dog the Maori dog, as the Maori rat was destroyed by the Pakeha rat, so our people will be gradually supplanted by the Europeans.'[37]

Most authorities prescribed work therapy (also favoured in the treatment of Europeans confined to asylums because of disturbed lives). Work always correlated with 'civilization', husbandry in particular. Murray asserted that to counteract the drabness of metal tools and peace, 'the most obvious and possibly the only solution is...if necessary to compel, the native to work for his own benefit'. Papua's coerced copra production was a case in point, as 'no form of industry is to be compared with agriculture as tending to stabilize the native race, and save it from disintegration'.

To counteract 'moral disturbance', Murray hoped that his government anthropologist would propose methods to assist 'the Papuan' in 'his rapid passage from the stone age to modern civilization', and he welcomed

Rivers' views:

> 'Experience', he says 'has amply shown that Christianity is capable of giving the
> people an interest in life which can take the place of that due to their indige-
> nous religion'.

The emphasis on living conditions was not novel. In 1859 Dr Arthur
Thomson, the Edinburgh-educated Surgeon-Major of the 58th Regiment in
Auckland, had expressed parallel views. On the basis of eleven years' residence, he attributed tuberculosis, 'the curse of the New Zealand race', to
new habits, in particular to Maori living on potatoes instead of their nutri-
tious ancient diet, and eating 'putrid' food such as maize; to insufficient
clothing; and 'living in huts worse than dog-kennels'. He hoped that peace,
trade and civilization would improve diet, ventilation and clothes. But such
progress would not suffice: Maori must also stop 'breeding in and in' by
intermarrying with tuberculosis sufferers who had 'scrofulous blood connections'. His fear revived the old obsession with blood lineage, which moved
from eugenics to genetics; but he was comforted that New Zealand settlers
had acted towards the natives 'in a spirit of Christianity' – quite unlike settlers in Tasmania and Australia.[38]

DYING RACES

A year after the First Fleet landed at Sydney, Watkin Tench published his
'Description of the Natives of New South Wales', inviting readers to 'con-
template the simple, undisguised workings of nature, in her most artless
colouring'. He built on the Enlightenment notion of savagery as a failure to
advance, due not to innate deficiencies but to lack of stimuli, so he distinguished between way of life and innate ability. Accepting the stage theory
(progress from barbarism through savagery to civilization) did not commit
Tench to a romantic view. He wished fervently that

> European philosophers, whose closet speculations exalt a state of nature above
> a state of civilization, could survey the phantom, which their heated imagina-
> tions have raised: possibly they might then learn, that a state of nature is, of all
> others, least adapted to promote the happiness of a being, capable of sublime
> research, and unending ratiocination.[39]

Early governors of New South Wales also reckoned that Aborigines could
become civilized and useful members of society. A quarter of a century after
occupation, Governor Macquarie explained that

> it seems only to require the fostering Hand of Time, gentle Means and
> Conciliatory Manners to bring these poor Unenlightened People into an impor-
> tant Degree of Civilization and to Instill into their Minds, as they Gradually
> open to Reason and Reflection, A sense of the Duties they owe their fellow
> Kindred and Society.[40]

But Barron Field, Judge of the Supreme Court, classed Aborigines as having 'the degenerate Ethiopian character', so that they 'will never be civilized'. To be 'civilized' entailed a work ethic and especially cultivation of the soil. The Reverend Lancelot Threlkeld, accepting (as most did) a single origin for all humankind, also held the popular view that Aborigines' current condition was not 'original' but a consequence of degeneration. Since analyses differed, so did prescriptions, and settler opinion was divided on whether Christian conversion should precede, or only follow, settlement and civilization.[41]

While few queried dispossession as destiny, some had qualms about wiping out Aborigines. In Van Diemen's Land, of an estimated Aboriginal population of 3,000 to 8,000 in 1803, 500 or 1,000 survived in 1824, while settlers exceeded 12,500, half of them convicts. After this bloodshed Governor George Arthur responded with a reward for capturing Aborigines; but that only encouraged killing, and what would now be termed ethnic cleansing. His infamous Black Line of soldiers, convicts and settlers tried (in vain) to drive the remaining Aborigines into captivity. Forcing the survivors into exile on offshore islands worked better in claiming Tasmania for Europe. Arthur was not following official policy because there was none. The question was seldom referred to Downing Street, and officials seldom pursued it after they sailed home. Those few who sympathized with Aborigines mainly mourned their inevitable demise, as did the historian Samuel Bennett in 1867:

> The great old family of man to which they belong has become extinct long since in most other lands. They are almost the last of their race, and they are fast yielding to that inevitable march of humanity which overwhelms and crushes all who do not join its ranks.[42]

As racial attitudes hardened and attempts to convert failed, the doomed race theory came to imbibe the view that the best hope was to protect Aborigines from overt cruelty 'for the short time they had left' and segregate them from the 'civilized community'.[43] As McGregor explains, the notion of doomed races was consistent with contemporary beliefs about civilization and humankind:

> Progress was a law of nature, and those who had failed to elevate themselves would necessarily be swept aside in the universal struggle for survival. If the prospect of the extinction of an entire race [upset Victorians], there was none the less a positive side to the picture. For the extinction of the unfit was merely the obverse of that beneficial law of survival of the fittest that guaranteed the constant elevation and improvement of mankind.[44]

In New Zealand, it was Isaac Featherston, a doctor who became a businessman and politician, whose name was linked with the saying:

> The Maoris are dying out, and nothing can save them. Our plain duty, as good, compassionate colonists, is to 'smooth down their dying pillow'. Then history will have nothing to reproach us with.[45]

He made his oft-repeated comment in 1856 at the inaugural meeting of the Wellington Philosophical Society. This text passed to Walter Buller, an ornithologist, in a paper on 'The Decrease of the Maori Race' in 1884, and thence to Te Rangi Hiroa in his 1924 article, 'The Passing of the Maori', and even to Keith Sinclair in his 1956 account of the New Zealand wars. Its significance lay in its effect on later generations, in their constructions of national identity.

Widely assumed to be dying in art, drama, stories and poetry, Maori survived and recovered. Swamping by Pakeha proved more important than Maori loss of numbers in tilting power relations towards Pakeha. Numbers were roughly equal in 1858, but big changes then came with the exponential increase in Pakeha numbers and density, boosted by migration and high natural increase. Those labelled Maori in the census declined to barely 5 per cent by the turn of the century. Put another way, Maori outnumbered Pakeha by 99 : 1 in 1840; they were themselves outnumbered by 10 : 1 only 38 years later, and by 16.5 : 1 in 1901. And yet by the 1890s Maori were already proving to be stubborn survivors.[46]

Aboriginal Australians also defied 'inexorable' laws. Despite general violence and social dislocation, by the 1860s many had patched together their community life, albeit in the shadow of whites. In farming regions they often resumed control over part of their original land, as their homes or patches for cultivation. In grazing land they secured a role in the pastoral industry, living in camps with access to their lands. The 1890s Depression and the ascendancy of cultural and biological chauvinist theories of racial superiority of the 1900s threatened these accommodations. Renewed predictions of imminent demise owed as much to the devastating effect of state and federal interventions into their individual and community lives, as to the wishful thinking of policy-makers that the 'indigenous problem' might disappear altogether.[47] Predictions of inevitable demise exonerated the state from confronting the causes and effects of dispossession, and made it easier to reduce funds for remedies. Federation shifted responsibility for 'smoothing the dying pillow' from local police, missionaries and pastoralists to state welfare officials. Hand-outs of food and blankets to the aged and the sick gave way to institutional palliation. If nineteenth-century marches of 'progress' shattered Aboriginal links with the land, twentieth-century 'solutions' to the 'indigenous problem' threatened the other pillar of Aboriginal culture: kinship. As Daisy Bates asserted in relating 'the passing of the Aborigines' in 1938: 'I did what I set out to do – to make their passing easier and to keep the dreaded half-caste menace from our great continent.'[48] By then, fortunately, the 'dying race' theory was obsolete in New Zealand and in most of the islands: it was losing credibility in New Caledonia, although it was useful for officials and colonists; and now in Australia it was becoming untenable in the face of population gains.

DISPLACEMENT

Claims of the peaceful settlement of Australia belong in the same tradition that described Terra Australis as quiet, silent or empty. To paraphrase

William Blake, they stained the water clear, transforming British invasion and dispossession into a triumph of colonization. Such readings are understandable and convenient. Most Aborigines lived out of sight of Europeans, and those aspects of their culture that were 'seen' were not easily understood. Such blindness was more cultural then physical. Often the European eye did not see what was inopportune.[49] New data and new interpretations overturned the triumphalist narrative of peaceful settlement, revealing the dark side of exploration, the small settlers' battles to survive, the grand visions of pastoralists, as well as their role in disrupting Aboriginal culture by seizing land and dispersing kinship.

Exploration was the Empire's scout: settlement and pastoral expansion were its bulldozers. Each contributed to depopulation. Each history is laced with the violence (physical and spiritual, individual and collective) of the undeclared war over land and resources. Each provided ways to justify invasion and occupation and their tragic consequences. The British had the advantage of numbers, gunpowder and knowledge of their own designs, but their occupation of Australia posed a particular moral dilemma. New South Wales differed from other colonies, for it was neither unoccupied nor obtained by conquest and driving out the natives, nor by treaty.[50] The peculiar status of Aborigines under the crown, still unresolved, forced their rulers to find moral justification. As one observer asked,

> What right have we to impose laws upon people whom we profess not to have conquered, and who have never annexed themselves or their country to the British Empire by any written or even verbal treaty?[51]

Thus, while Aborigines devised survival strategies – co-operation, acquiescence, resistance, armed struggle – many British strategies concerned moral justification. Explorer texts of blank 'undiscovered' tracts; legal pronouncements of *terra nullius*; scientific theories of racial superiority and the assumption of dying races: all served such strategies.

Moral justification was underpinned by certain 'facts', notably Aborigines' material backwardness and moral depravity. Europeans saw a culturally blank landscape, with no monuments or remains of temples or cities. They recoiled at nakedness, and misread the extravagant dress of Aborigines – paint rather than cloth – as proof of material want rather than appropriate to nomadic life. People's hand-to-mouth existence, to those from settled societies a sign of poverty, was practical. To Europeans, Aboriginal abundance was barely conceivable, yet in terms of 'food, health, shelter and warmth, the average aboriginal was probably as well off as the average European in 1800'.[52]

While the earliest explorations were maritime, to secure ports, water routes and supplies, the needs of the convict settlements for food, fuel and shelter, and later for arable land, shifted the priority to the interior. By 1799, with the east coast mapped from Sydney to modern Brisbane, and Van Diemen's Land secured as a second convict colony, the adventurous were looking to expand their frontiers. The crossing of the Blue Mountains in 1813 by Gregory

Blaxland, William Lawson and William Charles Wentworth, and the end of Britain's wars with Napoleon in 1815, unleashed eagerness for land as well as capital for investment. The European population grew rapidly to nearly 30,000 by 1821. They were soon outnumbered by sheep and cattle. The Wiradjuri people resisted, and were massacred with the help of martial law. By 1830, 3,500,000 acres had been appropriated. Settled areas stretched from the River Manning in the north to Shoalhaven in the south, and inland to Yass and Cowra. By then there were stations as far as 200 miles from Sydney.[53]

Exploration was critical to empire-building. Some acts of exploration served as expressions of British imperial design.[54] Others legitimized and consolidated prior British claims. Governor Phillip's orders were to annex about a third of the landmass – from Cape York to South Cape and inland to 135 degrees East – as well as adjacent islands. The whole continent was proclaimed British with the settlement of Perth in 1829. Such claims constituted a massive expansion of empire with neither population nor forces to back it. It was the role of exploration to breathe life into these imagined spaces.[55] 'The explorer's gaze' helped establish power relations between land and conqueror. The construction of the explorer-as-hero, in extravagant tales of courage, legitimized the act and the implications of occupation. These are powerful texts in the triumphalist narrative.

The literature of exploration produced images and interpretations of Terra Australis which shaped Australian experience and identity. The (incredible) image of the solitary explorer is profoundly compelling, especially in the context of the inhospitable bush. One famous explorer, Edward J. Eyre, reflected in his *Journals of Expeditions of Discovery* that 'our presence and settlement, in any particular locality, do, in point of fact, actually dispossess the aboriginal inhabitants'. The 'law of nations', he mused cynically, 'merely lays down rules for the direction of the privileged robber in the distribution of the booty of any newly discovered country'.[56] The first explorer, the pioneer, constructed his own cult through journals and diaries. But often such original frankness was filtered out. Through stories of exploration and settlement, the explorer foreshadowed the bushman of the Australian Legend and the pioneer legend shared with New Zealand.

Australia was not 'found' or 'born' but pieced together by European imagination and exploration. The First Fleet did not know its size or shape. Even that it was a continent remained unproven until Flinders circumnavigated it in 1801–2. 'At the centre of the colonists' minds were not picturesque places, but what preceded them, horizons, possible tracks, bounding spaces.'[57] Explorers' maps established spatial possibilities – 'conceptual geographies' – for settlers to inhabit:

> The historical significance of the explorers' journals and the settlers' diaries [reside in] their open-endedness, their lack of finish, even their search for words … for it is here, where forms and conventions break down, that we can discern the process of transforming space into place.[58]

Exploration always preceded settlement and the creation of colonies. The pattern was set early: Norfolk Island in 1792 and Port Phillip Bay in 1802,

Plate 4.1 William Mein Smith (1799–1869), *Exploring Party in the Wairarapa*, 1840s–1850s. Note the dry landscape and the woman guide. Alexander Turnbull Library, Wellington. Collection Reference no. B-062-021.

the latter comprising over 450 people including 300 convicts. The explorer's task was to give shape, size and substance to the concept of Terra Australis. Vast tracts remained blank in the European map well into the nineteenth century. Leichhardt's exploration of Northern Australia in 1842–8 and Charles Sturt's of Central Australia in 1844–6, E. J. Eyre's search for an overland route from Adelaide to Perth in 1840–4 are prime examples.

Exploration and settlement were not peaceful: boundaries were marked in blood. Henry Reynolds knew this from living in Tasmania and north Queensland, and has spent an academic life disclosing overwhelming evidence about warfare between the indigenous people and white Australia. Aboriginal identities could only be understood by acknowledging a history of violence. The Victorian pioneer Edward Curr wrote what he perceives as the 'best overview of frontier conflict':

> In the first place the meeting of the Aboriginal tribes of Australia and the White pioneer, results as a rule in war, which lasts from six months to ten years, according to the nature of the country, the amount of settlement which takes place in a neighbourhood, and the proclivities of the individuals concerned. When several squatters settle in proximity, and the country they occupy is easy of access and without fastnesses to which the Blacks can retreat, the period of warfare is usually short and the bloodshed not excessive. On the other hand, in districts which are not easily traversed on horseback, in which the Whites are

few in number and food is procurable by the Blacks in fastnesses, the term is usually prolonged and the slaughter more considerable.[59]

At the same time, identities in European Australia were shaped by this violence, only in ways forgotten rather than remembered as in Aboriginal stories. White Australian identities were shaped by fear and anxiety.[60]

In the history of exploration as elsewhere, Aboriginal Australians played ambivalent roles. Their apparent collaboration – as scouts and trackers for explorers, and later as shepherds and stockmen, and the feared Native Police – might be explained by their innocence of the Europeans' designs, or as survival strategies. By making themselves useful – and in exploration, indispensable – they ensured a measure of care and protection from their masters. There is no doubt of the key role of blacktrackers in advancing exploration and settlement. Nor is there doubt about the tragic irony of this collaboration, as guides led the way for dispossession. This pattern was near-universal: Aboriginal co-operation, as well as resistance, followed by the usurpation of their resources. As settlement encroached on their space, 'Aborigines were trapped inside white space and pushed to its margins.' The ambivalent role is most evident in Queensland, where Aborigines – not convicts – were the staple pastoral workforce. One historian argued: 'but for the anonymous toil of generations of Aborigines, the process of colonization in more remote and economically marginal areas might have been impossible to sustain.'[61] Explorers used Aboriginal paths, known to link water sources, which were sacred sites, and would resort to capture to gain this knowledge. Explorers did not seek empty land but land peopled by Aborigines which told of water, food and fired grassland suited to settlement. Eyre discovered life-saving wells by following paths along the Nullarbor; Sturt followed a track to a well full of rain water; Aboriginal guides negotiated access to neighbouring country, and directed the travellers to water. Burke and Wills paid the ultimate price for rejecting Aboriginal expertise.[62]

The invention of New Zealand likewise presumed boundaries shaped by the European imagination and transferred to maps, plans and survey pegs on the ground. Maori had their own boundary markers, and where marker poles signified possession, the survey peg could mark European encroachment or their own reassertion of ownership. Just as Maori resisted surveys in laying out New Zealand Company townships, in Otago, Canterbury, at the start of the wars of the 1860s and after later confiscations, Maori assisted surveys and worked for, and with, surveyors. Surveyors and explorers depended on Maori guides, especially in canoeing up and crossing rivers. Some guides were women. In 1841, Maori expected payment of two shillings each to ferry surveyors across the Manawatu River once night fell.[63] When S. Charles Hartley canoed up the same river with Maori to 'discover' the site of Palmerston North in 1846, he was on a day trip to a historic *pa* site, Papaioea, built by the Rangitane, in the clearing that provided room for the town. In the south, passes across the Southern Alps were revealed by Maori guides who regularly travelled alpine routes to sources of greenstone in rivers on the West Coast. Surveyors lived in the cultural encounter zone. While they extended territory and boundaries, they crossed cultural boundaries during the survey, and so did Maori in their encounter with the surveyor and his theodolite. Consequently the surveyor William Mein Smith, an officer in the Royal Artillery sent to plan Wellington in 1839, stands as one of the *tekoteko* (stockade figures) at Papawai Pa in the Wairarapa, the one Pakeha among the chiefs whose carved figures guard the *marae*, looking inward as a sign of peace.[64]

Explorers and surveyors wrote over the indigenous landscape and histories in drawing their maps, and relied on Aboriginal and Maori guides and their mental maps in shaping their own. Dependent on their guides, they made paths for others.

COLONIZATION AND SETTLEMENT

The British were not the first foreigners to come to Australia, but they were the ones to stay and impose a system of resource management, making Aboriginal Australians 'interlopers in their native places'.[65] Gardening and pig-raising, imported from New Guinea, for example, had been a prospect for Aborigines, compatible with semi-nomadic life. Management of land and resources was not alien: Aborigines had evolved management systems involving bush clearing by fire. But such interventions were small, controlled and less devastating than the technology of the invader whose interventions – agricultural and ecological – initiated a process of 'future eating'.[66]

Not everyone agrees on the trigger for that process. Blainey has argued that British occupation of Sydney and Hobart and a few points of coast had little effect. In his view, innovations in Europe and the demand they generated for wool, minerals and other materials, pressing British migrants ever deeper into the interior and along the coast, sealed the fate of Aboriginal Australia. But there is no doubt about the role of settlement, and pastoral expansion in particular, in overturning the old order.

When Phillip departed in 1792, and due largely to his vision, the British could anticipate development into free settlement. Early governors enjoyed limited control over the spread of the settlement, and effective steps were not taken until the 1820s, when limits were set for the occupation of land for grazing. Even so, 'squatting' – the illegal occupation of crown land for grazing – was hardly checked for the first half of the nineteenth century. Emboldened by their increased power and status, squatters pressed their preemptive claims on crown land. The Australian Land Sales Act of 1846, and the Order-in-Council of 1847, eventually satisfied them. As momentum built towards self-government, the squatter became a major political force.

A decade after occupation, it was clear that the land was not suited to small settlers. Yet small land grants of 60 to 100 acres to turn convicts into yeomen (not peasants) or 500 to 1,500 acres for 'hopeful landed gentlemen' allowed individuals room for pasture and to take risks.[67] The grants were prescribed not by conditions in Botany Bay, but by the empire in the West Indies and Canada, and by pastoral images from Europe. Sentimental ideas about the redeeming qualities of rural life continued to dictate inappropriate land policies in Australia and New Zealand (see chapter 6).

Immigration – like depopulation – was decisive in shaping an Anglo-Celtic, White Australia. The first free settlers arrived in February 1793, but their numbers were few. Throughout our region it was Western European officials, or settlers of Western European descent, who determined the ethnic composition of migrants. Not all migrants were from Europe. In the latter nineteenth century Melanesian young men were recruited to work in Queensland, New Caledonia and Fiji (see chapter 8). In Fiji they were followed and displaced by Indians under indenture; in New Caledonia they were followed by indentured Vietnamese; and in Queensland they were simply repatriated. These were large numbers, but they had little influence on the terms of their movement. Colonial governments determined who should come, for how long, to do what kinds of work, and whether they might remain. Unlike white free settlers, they would not become full citizens without a sustained struggle.

Distance deterred free settlement. It cost more, and took longer to travel from Britain to Australia and New Zealand than anywhere else in the New World. This produced small-populated settler societies, and required state assistance to enable humble Anglo-Celtic folk to migrate. Distance also gave Australian settlements an edge over New Zealand, of a quarter of a million Europeans by 1840. Most were English, and many Irish, particularly after the 1846 famine. Smaller numbers came from Scotland, and South Australia's Germans were the first bloc from continental Europe. Here at once emerged a major difference in settler Australia and New Zealand's ethnic identities. The Irish comprised a quarter of white Australia in the nineteenth century and brought a heavy dose of anti-authoritarianism, Catholicism, and folklore. New Zealand, where large-scale settlement post-dated the famine, and authorities strongly opposed Irish migration, attracted more Scots. These legacies, roots of identity, continue to shape identities through 'our sense of the body, social class, the nation, and cultural tradition.'[68]

As the remotest of the large land masses, Australia and New Zealand were the last to be peopled from Europe. Migrants sailed in four main waves. First came the convicts from 1788 to 1856, with the odd runaway across the Tasman. Second came free and assisted migrants from 1830 to 1850, including the systematic colonizers who built Adelaide, Wellington, Dunedin and Christchurch. The New Zealand Company dispatched nearly 10,000 settlers to New Zealand in the 1840s, among them more children (3,800) than adult males. Third came gold-seekers from 1850 to 1870, to Victoria and then New Zealand and eventually the islands. The waves created huge imbalances and expectations, the biggest being an excess of men. Fourth came the real tsunami (tidal wave) of large families and planned migration from 1860 to 1890.[69] New Caledonia is a land mass of comparable size to New Zealand but even greater remoteness, partly because of French policies and local circumstances. There the first wave of convicts began half a century later than in Australia; free settlers were also half a century later; gold seekers were only one generation late. All numbers were smaller (both absolutely and relative to the indigenous population) than across the Tasman; and the tsunami – such as it was – came only in the middle of the twentieth century.[70]

The lure of gold carried the European population of Australasia over its first million, and drove settlement out from New South Wales and Van Diemen's Land to Victoria, Queensland, and beyond the coastal townships of New Zealand. In 1861 13,000 immigrants arrived in Otago, most of them miners from Victoria. Gold on the West Coast in the 1860s drew diggers from the workings in Otago, elsewhere in New Zealand, and Australia, leaving an 'Australian' legacy in Westland's identity. Sir Julius Vogel followed gold from Victoria to New Zealand, and in the 1870s launched his national migration scheme to build a nation, but he could not have done so without the Native Land Court which, from the 1860s, individualized title to land (see chapter 6). Vogel's immigrants featured largely in Pakeha swamping of Maori, with the gold rush wave second. The 100,000 who arrived under Vogel's scheme in the 1870s added their imprint to national identity, with a strong stamp of Methodism. Some 195,000 fortune-seekers followed gold's glimmer to New Zealand, two-thirds from Australia and the rest from Britain; but many men left, producing a net gain of 114,000 from gold in the 1860s. More came to settle. New Zealand gained nearly 300,000 residents from migration between 1861 and 1890, but from the mid-1870s Pakeha society grew mainly by having children.

From 1861 to 1900 net migration totalled 331,000 to New South Wales, 8,000 more than to New Zealand; 256,000 to Queensland, mostly in the 1880s (as in New South Wales); and 134,000 to Western Australia with the 1890s gold rush. Western Australia's gains in the 1890s were losses for Victoria and South Australia. Victoria, New South Wales and Queensland accounted for 80 per cent of the mainly Anglo-Celtic population of Australia. The kink in Victoria's population structure created by a bulge of single men had worked itself out, not just by natural increase but because single men moved on. Pakeha New Zealand was also settling. Together, Australia and New Zealand were home to 4.6 million Europeans by 1901 (3.8 million in Australia). The migration narrative in New Caledonia is less striking. The long-term reluctance of French people to emigrate was as strong in respect of New Caledonia as anywhere else. Even convicts, whenever they could, chose to serve their sentences near home. Many of the first free settlers came from Australia, becoming French but retaining some Australian cultural inheritance. These settlers became, over time, a consciously colonial community, distinguishing themselves from the metropolitan French who staffed the administration.[71] By 1911 there were 5,700 convicts or ex-convicts (many of them required to remain after their sentences) and twice as many free Europeans. Immigration from Europe then almost ceased until the 1950s, although it continued from the New Hebrides and Indochina, so that the total of immigrant descent caught up with the indigenes by the mid-twentieth century at 30,000 to 40,000 each.[72]

Immigration created instant towns, entrepôts for globalization and empire. By 1850 urbanization had become a leading trend; 40 per cent of white Australians were already 'urban'; Sydney had 54,000 residents, Hobart and

Melbourne 23,000 each, and Adelaide 14,500. Auckland, a port town of 15,000 in 1857, had much in common with the cities built by free settlement in Eastern Australia. Gold fever pushed Melbourne and Sydney to 125,000 and 96,000 by 1861. While Sydney lost its lead to 'Marvellous Melbourne', this lasted for but two generations, with gold and its echo effect in the 1880s from children of gold rush migrants. Sydney again overtook Melbourne in the depressed 1890s. By 1900 both had burgeoned into metropolises by world standards, of over half a million people including their suburbs. By the international definition of urban place (over 2,500 people), 49 per cent of white Australians were urban in 1891, more than in any other New World country. New Zealand's percentage was 38.[73] Urbanization became a distinctive trait of Australian identity. It was massively coastal: Australians are still fringe dwellers living in coastal cities.[74] New Zealanders also live by the sea, but New Zealand came to be characterized more by the small town, because of the nature of its rural development, which diverged from Australia's from the 1890s. In New Caledonia, Noumea was from the first the entrepôt, decidedly more cosmopolitan than the hinterland and to that extent divorced from its milieu.[75]

This 'urban frontier' existed in more than economic terms.[76] The former convict port towns and the new 'grasslands' towns whose hinterlands were committed to commercial farming and pastoralism – and mining, in Australia – metamorphosed into 'commercial cities'; the non-convict ones such as Melbourne and Adelaide (and New Zealand's main towns) being 'pure' commercial cities.[77] This is crucial to identity: the Australasian 'urban frontier' provided entrepôts to the world, ensuring in the context of late settlement that globalization began early. Indeed the urban frontier began as a global phenomenon. As communication hubs, Australian capital cities and principal towns, and New Zealand's four main centres, were pivotal to the frontier as a zone and thus in fashioning identities.

For much of the nineteenth century the town symbolized development, civilization and taming the wilderness. Women preferred towns. Mental maps of home insinuated the city or the small town to new arrivals; urban was European and cosmopolitan as well as civilized. Moreover the suburban idea carried with British migrants was accessible only to a few at home. Migrant ambitions for a plot of land, space, privacy and independence could be realized in the city more readily than on the land, with the help of higher incomes for artisans, cheap public transport and small houses on their own allotments. It is no accident that Australian and New Zealand capital cities, born urban, quickly grew suburban, or that the English country cottage became the model for the suburban house in Australia and New Zealand. Arcadia would prevail in the city, if not in the bush.

Unique among French colonies, New Caledonia's government from the first assumed power to expropriate native-owned land.[78] Rather than take everything, administrators tried to distinguish between occupied and vacant land – a distinction impossible to apply to a regime of shifting cultivation. The Parisian practice of granting tracts of land even beyond the areas controlled by the infant state, also made that policy unworkable. Instead,

Governor Guillain in the 1860s determined to create reserves. As was happening in Fiji (see chapter 6) Gullain systematized indigenous land ownership and management in a form which he believed to be traditional but which was truly revolutionary. Instead of localized and complex rights and obligations, ownership passed to the *tribu*, and decision-making to chiefs.

> The *tribu*, as a proprietor of land, was in fact a fictional, administrative concept. The traditional proprietory rights of individual families and clans ... and the traditional authority of the customary *maitres de la terre*, although they persisted ... were administratively overridden.[79]

Cantonnement not only stripped most mainland Kanak of their land and attacked the social, cultural and spiritual values attached to particular sites; it lumped together clans and families who were not always compatible. But if these arrangements had no validity in tradition or in equity, they did enable the state to alienate tracts, and to introduce settlers. Part of the justification offered for these actions was the past decline of the Kanak population and the presumption – difficult to challenge – that they would continue a remorseless slide into statistical oblivion.

Human displacement was mirrored in the realms of flora and fauna, as Europeans' unacknowledged allies and deliberate introductions filled niches and revolutionized landscapes. Exotic species could be beneficial: the potato, grain and livestock multiplied food capacity and quality, while new crops, notably vegetables, aided human health. But native species suffered. Several 'hired assassins' attacked native species instead of the pests they were supposed to control, such as cats, stoats, weasels and ferrets brought to kill rats. One invader cleared a path for the next. John McNeill sees rats as 'shock troops of ecological imperialism in the Pacific', for example in their destruction of New Zealand birds.[80]

The rat analogy proved a powerful metaphor. The Norwegian rat which Maori viewed as inedible annihilated the Maori rat in the North Island in the 1830s and 1840s. Ernst Dieffenbach, naturalist to the New Zealand Company, analysed New Zealand's potential for colonization. He saw this potential in the replacement of the indigenous rat by the English rat:

> There exists a frugiferous native rat, called Kiore maori (indigenous rat) by the natives, which they distinguish from the English rat (not the Norway rat), which is introduced, and called Kiore Pake[h]a (strange rat). On the former they fed very largely in former times; but it has now become so scarce, owing to the extermination carried on against it by the European rat, that I could never obtain one. It is a favourite theme with [Maori] to speculate on their own extermination by the Europeans, in the same manner as the English rat has exterminated their indigenous rat.[81]

It was important that the rat be English. Only when New Zealand was a truly British colony, could the victor be acknowledged as Norwegian, or generically European.

After Captain Cook, ecological and economic forces transformed environments. Pacific ecosystems linked to the wider world, and were touched by demands from consumers in Europe, America and China. Landscapes, seascapes and human societies were transformed and often replaced,[82] but the effect on human identities was not simple. Much depended on how these were described and explained. At one rhetorical extreme stands Alan Moorehead's sensational 'fatal impact' account;[83] but recent analyses emphasize either a medical (and bacterial) model or one which focuses on human action. However dramatic, and however quantifiable, human pasts generate identities only through the mediation of contemporary concerns.

NOTES

1   A. W. Crosby, *Ecological Imperialism: The Biological Expansion of Europe, 900–1900*, Cambridge, 1986; quotation from J. R. McNeill, 'Of Rats and Men: A Synoptic Environmental History of the Island Pacific', *Journal of World History*, 5: 2 (1994): 299–300.

2   McNeill, 'Of Rats and Men', 312, 315.

3   J. Peter White and D. J. Mulvaney, 'How Many People?', in D. J. Mulvaney and J. Peter White (eds), *Australians to 1788*, Sydney, 1987, 115ff.

4   Kerry Howe, *Nature, Culture and History*, Honolulu, in press.

5   Norma MacArthur, *Island Populations in the Pacific*, Canberra, 1967.

6   David E. Stannard, *Before the Horror: The Population of Hawaii on the Eve of Western Contact*, Honolulu, 1989.

7   Stephen J. Kunitz, *Disease and Social Diversity: The European Impact on the Health of Non-Europeans*, Cambridge, 1994, 188 and ch. 1.

8   N. G. Butlin, *Economics and the Dreamtime: A Hypothetical History*, Cambridge, 1993; M. Durie, *Whaiora: Maori Health Development*, Auckland, 1994, ch. 3.

9   Evidence is set out in D. Denoon, 'Pacific Island Depopulation: Natural or Unnatural Causes?', in Linda Bryder and Derek Dow (eds), *New Countries and Old Medicines*, Auckland, 1995.

10 Ibid., and MacArthur, *Island Populations*.

11 M. J. T. Spriggs, 'Vegetable Kingdoms, Taro Irrigation and Pacific Prehistory', Australian National University Ph.D. thesis, Canberra, 1981.

12 Ian Pool, *Te Iwi Maori: A New Zealand Population Past, Present and Projected*, Auckland, 1991.

13 S. Lātūkefu, 'Oral History and Pacific Island Missionaries', in D. Denoon and R. Lacey, *Oral Tradition in Melanesia*, Port Moresby, 1981.

14 Kunitz, *Disease and Social Diversity*.

15 Alan Ward, *Land and Politics in New Caledonia*, Canberra, 1982.

16 MacArthur, *Island Populations*, 27.

17 Sandra Tomkins, 'The Influenza Epidemic of 1918–1919 in Western Samoa', *Journal of Pacific History*, 27: 2 (1992), 181–97.

18 Pool, *Te Iwi Maori*, 58, 60.

19 Bronwen Douglas, 'Discourses of Death in a Melanesian World', in Donna Merwick (ed.), *Dangerous Liaisons: Essays in Honour of Greg Dening*, Melbourne, 1994, 353–78.

20 Geoffrey Blainey, *The Triumph of the Nomads: A History of Ancient Australia*, Melbourne, 1975, 225–8.

21 Ann McGrath, 'A National Story', in Ann McGrath (ed.), *Contested Ground: Australian Aborigines under the British Crown*, Sydney, 1995, 42–3.

22 Ibid., 129; Butlin, *Economics and the Dreamtime*, 228.

23 W. D. Borrie, *The European Peopling of Australasia: A Demographic History, 1788–1988*, Canberra, 1994. See N. G. Butlin, *Our Original Aggression: Aboriginal Populations of Southeastern Australia, 1788–1850*, Sydney, 1983; J. Peter White and D. J. Mulvaney, 'How Many People?'.

24 W. E. H. Stanner, late 1930s, in 'The Aborigines', in J. C. G. Kevin, *Some Australians Take Stock*, London, 1939, 108.

25 Peter Read, *A Hundred Years War: The Wiradjuri People and the State*, Sydney, 1988; R. Broome, *Aboriginal Australians: Black Responses to White Dominance, 1788–1994*, 2nd edn, Sydney, 1994; David Day, *Claiming a Continent: A History of Australia*, Sydney, 1996; Butlin, *Economics and the Dreamtime*, 216.

26 Ian Maddocks, 'History of Disease in Papua New Guinea', in Clive Bell (ed.), *The Diseases and Health Services of Papua New Guinea*, Port Moresby, 1973.

27 B. G. Corney, J. Stewart and B. H. Thomson, *Report of the Commission appointed to inquire into the Decrease of the Native Population*; analysed by Vicki Lukere, 'Mothers of the Taukei: Fijian Women and the Decrease of the Race', Ph.D. thesis, Australian National University, Canberra, 1997.

28 W. H. R. Rivers (ed.), *Essays on the Depopulation of Melanesia*, Cambridge, 1922.

29 Ibid.

30 Ibid., 94.

31 Pool, *Te Iwi Maori*, 100–3.

32 Rivers, *Essays on the Depopulation of Melanesia*, 105.

33 Hubert Murray, 'The Population Problem in Papua' (1923), copy of text in Australian Archives, Department of Territories, A 452, 59/6066 part 1.

34 Donald Denoon with Kathleen Dugan and Leslie Marshall, *Public Health in Papua New Guinea, 1884–1984: Medical Possibility and Social Constraint*, Cambridge, 1989.

35 Murray, 'The Population Problem in Papua'.

36 Durie, *Whaiora*, 32, citing Walter Buller, 1884.

37 Pool, *Te Iwi Maori*, 60. Pool cites Te Rangi Hiroa, 1924, who cited Archdeacon Walsh, 'The Passing of the Maori', 1907, who cited Von Hochstetter.

38 A. S. Thomson, *The Story of New Zealand: Past and Present – Savage and Civilized*, London, 1859, vol. 1, 212–16, vol. 2, 284–5, 288–9.

39 Tench, cited in Russell McGregor, *Imagined Destinies: Aboriginal Australians and the Doomed Race Theory, 1880–1939*, Melbourne, 1997, 1–3.

40 Quoted in McGregor, *Imagined Destinies*, 51.

41 Ibid.

42 Samuel Bennett, *The History of Australian Discovery and Colonization*, Sydney, 1867. The massacre of Tasmania's Aborigines is reviewed in Day, *Claiming a Continent*, 99–105.

43 McGregor, *Imagined Destinies*, 18.

44 Ibid., 58.

45 Derek Dow, ' "Smoothing Their Dying Pillow" Lingering Longer', *New Zealand Doctor*, 21 January 1998, 45. Featherston graduated MD in 1836 and in 1853 was elected first superintendent of Wellington province.

46 Pool, *Te Iwi Maori*, 61, suggests the Maori population reached its nadir in 1891 rather than 1896, (table 5.2, p. 76).

47 McGrath, *Contested Ground*, 59.

48 Daisy Bates, *The Passing of the Aborigines: A Lifetime Spent Among the Natives of Australia*, 1st edn, London, 1938, 243.

49 Paul Carter, *The Road to Botany Bay: An Essay in Spatial History*, London, 1987.
50 Henry Reynolds, *Aborigines and Settlers: The Australian Experience, 1788–1939*, Melbourne, 1975, 9.
51 Ibid., 103, quoting E. W. Landor, *The Bushman, Or Life in a New Country*, London, 1847, 187–9.
52 Blainey, *Triumph of the Nomads*, 225–8.
53 J. J. Auchmuty, *The First Australian Governors*, Melbourne, 1971; Frank Crowley, *A New History of Australia*, Melbourne, 1974, ch. 2; Alan Atkinson, *The Europeans in Australia: A History*, 2 vols, Melbourne, 1997, 345–6.
54 Carter, *The Road to Botany Bay*, xviii.
55 Auchmuty, *The First Australian Governors*, 48.
56 Reproduced in H. Reynolds, *Dispossession: Black Australians and White Invaders*, Sydney, 1989, 27, 30–1.
57 Carter, *The Road to Botany Bay*, xxi.
58 Ibid., 69–71.
59 E. Curr, *The Australian Race*, Melbourne, 1886, vol. 1, 100–6, reprinted in Reynolds, *Dispossession*, 26; also quoted in H. Reynolds, *Why Weren't We Told? A Personal Search for the Truth about Our History*, Ringwood, Victoria, 1999, 110.
60 Reynolds, 'Confronting the Myth of Peaceful Settlement', in *Why Weren't We Told?*, 135–51.
61 Carter, *The Road to Botany Bay*, 342.
62 Reynolds, *With the White People*, ch. 1.
63 G. M. Byrnes, 'Inventing New Zealand: Surveying, Science, and the Construction of Cultural Space, 1840s–1890s', Ph.D. thesis, University of Auckland, 1995.
64 G. C. Petersen, *The Pioneering Days of Palmerston of North*, Levin, 1952; J. Drummond, 'The Guardians of Papawai', *NZ Historic Places*, no. 63, May 1997, 22–3.
65 Reynolds, *Aborigines and Settlers*, 86.
66 T. F. Flannery, *The Future Eaters: An Ecological History of the Australasian Lands and People*, Melbourne, 1994, 725.
67 Atkinson, *Europeans in Australia*, 218–19.
68 Miriam Dixson, *The Real Matilda*, 3rd edn, Melbourne, 1994, 14.
69 Borrie, *The European Peopling of Australasia*.
70 J.-L. Rallu, 'Population of the French Overseas Territories in the Pacific, Past, Present and Projected', *Journal of Pacific History*, 26: 2 (1991), 169–86.
71 Frederic Bobin, 'Caldoches, Metropolitans and the Mother Country', *Journal of Pacific History*, 26 (1991), 303–12.
72 Rallu, 'Population of the French Pacific'.
73 L. Frost, *Australian Cities in Comparative View*, Melbourne, 1990, 17.
74 Philip Drew, *The Coast Dwellers: Australians Living on the Edge*, Ringwood, Victoria, 1994, 44.
75 Rallu, 'Population of the French Pacific'.
76 R. C. Wade first used the term 'urban frontier' in relation to North America. It has been used by M. Fairburn, 'The New Urban Frontier', and Hamer, *New Towns in the New World*, and most lately in Australia by Lionel Frost, in *New Urban Frontier*, Sydney, 1991.
77 J. W. McCarty, 'Australian Capital Cities in the Nineteenth Century', in J. W. McCarty and C. B. Schedvin (eds), *Australian Capital Cities*, Sydney, 1978.
78 Isabelle Merle, *Expériences coloniales: la Nouvelle-Calédonie 1853–1920*, Paris, 1995; Ward, *Land and Politics in New Caledonia*.

79 Ward, *Land and Politics in New Caledonia*, 3.
80 McNeill, 'Of Rats and Men', 316–18, citing Druett, Thomson, Wodzicki, Clark, Crosby.
81 Dieffenbach, *Travels*, vol. 2, 185, cited by Byrnes, 'Inventing New Zealand', 221–2.
82 McNeill, 'Of Rats and Men', 325.
83 Alan Moorehead, *The Fatal Impact: An Account of the Invasion of the South Pacific 1767–1840*, London, 1966.

PART II

New Societies and Economies

[5] NEW SOCIAL FORMS

Britain was a global power after 1815. 'In region after region the British government set out to maintain British interests – however defined – as cheaply and as uncomplicatedly as possible.'[1] Largely through the written word, it pursued its concerns in ways which shaped Pacific identities. In Australia, convictism produced a distinctive political culture in defining the relationship between government and people.[2] New Zealand, even more remote from the British Isles, began – according to European pen and paper – as an extension of New South Wales, like Queensland and Victoria. But New Zealand's colonial identity specifically excluded convicts and would not be besmirched by the 'convict taint'. While a trading partner of New South Wales, New Zealand stood apart emotionally. From the moment it existed in British ink as a colony, it assumed high moral ground relative to New South Wales, a position premissed on a document which itself represented British economy and expediency: the Treaty of Waitangi, carried around the coast for Maori signatures in 1840, after the initial signing in the Bay of Islands on 6 February. Contemporary concerns generated different spirals of identity-weaving in Australia, where intellectuals tried to create an image that associated things convict with things British, and where local 'currency' lads and lasses, born to convict parents, embodied 'Australian' virtues. Environment proved important, as always, in allowing the Pacific-born to grow big and strong in these imaginings. This view held less weight outside Australia. The Australian colonies had to overcome bad press about the convict taint, which its neighbours exploited in their own marketing. These tiny, remote societies aspired to a difficult goal: trade with Europe, which its settlers saw as the 'real world'.[3]

CONVICTS AND SETTLERS

Governor Phillip's instructions for a convict colony at Botany Bay presumed it would be both a gaol and free. Distrust of French designs justified British expenditure, but was extremely expensive.[4] Alan Atkinson identifies two principles in the early convict settlement: brotherhood by which 'cocks managed hens' in contemporary terms; and 'benevolent dictatorship, or dictatorial benevolence', a product of the Enlightenment. These principles produced distinctive relations between men, women and the state. While this brotherhood was closed to women, women and children were vitally important for identity-building, especially when they were so few. The British government took responsibility for women through transportation, and their presence proved central to authority. Women and marriage were vital for an orderly community.[5]

The presence of children was one reason for not seeing the colony as a gaol, because of the universal wish that they do well.[6] Offspring born free in New South Wales acquired the identity of 'currency', while 'sterling' who came free enjoyed credentials parallel to British money, of being socially acceptable outside the colony. As a means of exchange, 'currency' embraced the 'ragtail collection' of dumps and dollars and promissory notes used until the Bank of New South Wales was established in 1817.[7] Convict settlements ran on pen and paper, not money: for promissory notes, the primary currency, as for tickets of leave and all forms of social contract. Convictism transcended its origins as its creators intended, with all the dynamic of a capitalist economy and a sense of destiny to subdue its physical environment and its inhabitants. Ex-convicts, as small capitalists, proved central to this process.

John Hirst judges that 'this was not a society which had to become free; its freedoms were well established from the earliest times'.[8] Britain still thought of Botany Bay as a gaol, but by the early 1800s, according to insiders, it already belonged to ex-convicts and their children. Manning Clark's picture of Australian convicts is negative, unlike Russel Ward's redeeming one which wrote 'the founding fathers' into the Australian Legend. Convictism was always important outside Australia. Its rediscovery as a redeeming, distinctive imprint on Australian identity is relatively recent, highlighting the significance of the Irish component, and the shortage of white women, but not Aboriginal Australian women. The last point is taken up by feminist critiques, which clarify that convictism helped define relations of indigenous women to the state and to men.[9] Miriam Dixson, who was avant-garde in thinking about women and identity in the 1970s, agrees with Manning Clark's gothic view, and blames the 'curious pious cruelty' of the British elite. Her psychoanalytic feminism leads her to judge as psychologically inadequate the positive view of convictism, that living standards were better than in Britain. The statistics which gave rise to the positive view suggest that convicts were well-fed and well-rested. The standard ration was higher in levels of energy and nutrition than currently recommended levels, delivering an average of 4,000 calories a day. The average convict in government service worked 56 hours a week, much less than other coerced labour and less than most British free workers. Living space was also better.[10]

This raises questions of rights of the subject, the responsibility of power, and attachment to a land of exile in Australian identity-making. Transportation in the traditional interpretation was invented to rid England of its criminals.[11] Brought to Australia by force, convicts 'did not eagerly become Australians'.[12] Nor would they accept moral responsibility for the fate of Aborigines. The number of Aborigines surprised Governor Phillip, who did not expect a peopled land. Historians have rediscovered the remarkable beach-crosser Bennelong and his efforts to come to terms with convict Sydney – though Phillip, like Cook, had first to kidnap him before he could try to speak with him – and how Aborigines incorporated newcomers into kinship networks, for example Phillip as 'father'. Phillip hoped for an indigenous sense of place among Europeans: 'Parramatta' (now in Western Sydney) is a European version of an Aboriginal place-name. But the convicts and their guards did not engage with the environment and Sydney took its name by default from Sydney Cove.[13] Despite its grand harbour the cove was *terra rasa* to the European eye, its inhospitable climate and soil offering neither sufficient shelter nor food, nor animals for agriculture. Even fish were scarce, a problem compounded by the absence of fishing skills in the first convicts. Phillip admitted that 'No country offers less assistance to the first settlers', nor was any 'more disadvantageously placed with respect to support from the mother country'.[14]

Transportation was reformative in purpose: convicts were kept healthy and the men given hard labour to inculcate 'habits of industry'. This meant regular work, which required commercial progress – and family values.[15] Humble men would become prosperous and honest proprietors and cultivators of land, as farming was necessary for a civilized community. The idea-merchants hoped the exiled would ultimately support themselves on their own land. The model materialized in James Ruse, a 'husbandman' from Cornwall, who was given land and convict labour to clear it in 1790, and then married. But he ended up a wage labourer. Global understandings about the state, family and gender informed the whole enterprise: well-behaved convicts received 30 acres, 20 acres more if they married, and 10 acres per child. Grants were made on the same terms as to the military along the St Lawrence river in Canada. The British aspired to settlement generally, and to this end 'deserving' convicts were allowed to have their wife and family sent out free, from 1816.

The good health of convicts and fair living standards are relevant to individual, and particularly group, identities by keeping people alive and well, and inculcating loyalty in subjects – not to the bogey of convictism, but to some idealized 'state'. The exercise of power by the colonial state through the nurture of bodies shaped the rules people grew accustomed to, and thus identities. Ordinary folk entrusted decisions to the state (for example, Revd Samuel Marsden as colonial chaplain). Practicality played a part here; Phillip worried more about keeping convicts alive than reforming them.

In the more wholesome 1990s narrative, historians consider that Australia gave women status, and that the convict system in some ways advantaged women over men.[16] From Macquarie's time, women were expected to marry. Single women received more support than in the Poor Law system in the United Kingdom. Women and children in need drew government rations, and the state supplied a midwife at the hospital. This is a long way from Dixson's famous judgement: 'Australian women, women in the land of mateship, "the Ocker", keg-culture, come pretty close to top rating as the "Doormats of the Western World".'[17]

Marian Quartly makes the point that 'the woman convict as prostitute ... seems to have seduced later historians with her sexual availability'. Anne Summers, by her use of stereotypes of Damned Whores and God's Police, 'confirmed their reality'.[18] In the view of the Australian-born, convict mothers produced honest currency lads and lasses, the stereotype of whom asserted their cultural rights to the land through their pioneering skills, while in the British view the 'imagined prostitute' influenced the decision to end transportation 'and she has seduced historians ever since'.[19] Sleeping together was usual among the British working classes where young couples without property did not bother to marry and polite society accepted mistresses as well as wives. European ideas about proper relations between men and women were transported to New South Wales, and the gender division of labour was part of this (see chapter 8).

In this chapter we are interested in how power shaped identities. The state itself was not monolithic. State intervention became more problematical after 1820, once Commissioner Bigge determined to make transportation 'more terrifying and less expensive'. His solution was to contract-out convicts to private employers. State punishment grew more severe with changes in British penal policy, extending to secondary punishment at outposts such as Moreton Bay. From 1819 women 'at public labour' in New South Wales were confined in the Female Factory, which became more prison-like. The convicts also changed as policy shifted, and it is significant that 60 per cent of all convicts were transported after 1830, once the system grew harsher. Not only were there counter-symbols of the woman convict as prostitute and the honest emancipist-turned yeoman; but convict women as mothers, and orphans, became particular sources of anxiety.[20]

The contradictory identities which Joy Damousi explores in her analysis of women convicts and their children belong to this later period.[21] This underscores the point that convict identities were dynamic and elusive, and offer ample scope for conflicting interpretations. Writing at the height of second wave feminism, it is easy to see how Dixson deduced that Australian women encountered more testy gender relations, because Australian women's 'founding mothers' were convicts. She therefore queried Shaw's conclusion about convictism that 'socially it did no great harm'. But Shaw was looking at society, not identity.[22] Sources for gothic views of how the 'convict stain' left an imprint on Australian identity come from the anti-transportation movement. The Molesworth Committee which sought to end transportation in 1838 made the oft-cited statement that convict women were 'drunken and abandoned prostitutes', and historians still interpret this material in different ways.[23]

According to Hirst, the convict system's enemies shaped how we think about it. 'The British bequeathed to Australia not only disreputable origins, but scathing accounts of just how demoralized and debased the first European settlement was', and their sarcasm stuck. Shame is a key word. The ex-convict Magwitch in Dickens's *Great Expectations* shamed Pip by bequeathing him his fortune, and many potential migrants avoided Australia because of its 'convict taint'.[24] Dignity and vanity worked to shape various

Australian identities according to 'good' and 'bad' accounts of convictism, depending on whether those doing the defining lived in convict settlements or not; while those to whom it became important to be non-Australian, notably New Zealanders, made it a matter of dignity to avoid pollution from the convict stain. Timing is significant. New Zealand was created after the hardening of British penal policy in the 1830s, which strengthened New Zealanders' belief that they could be nothing but morally superior to Australians.

Emancipists saw themselves as patriots, and Australia as home. The power of shame as well as pride infused people's views of themselves. Both free and freed expressed faith in the future and in the next generation of native-born, who turned out miraculously wholesome. The native-born, in turn, naturally believed that they were the true Australians, while their advocates such as W. C. Wentworth sought the contemporary virtues of respectability and a work ethic, and found them in the next generation.[25] Free migrants either chose not to emphasize their Britishness because convicts too were British, or determined to flaunt their Britishness. Colonists who had travelled to the other side of the world wanted to be noticed, but favourably, and encountered difficulties with the emphasis on deterrence in the 1820s and 1830s, which meant that it suited Britain even more to promote tarnished images of convict Australia. The Australian colonies lived with constant anxiety about how others saw them.[26]

Those who wore an Australian identity responded drily to the bad press, their sardonic humour itself becoming labelled as 'typically Australian'. The Molesworth Committee drew on dark evidence from colonists visiting Britain about the depravity of horse racing, fancy dress balls and sexual perversion and hijinks in New South Wales, which prompted conservatives living in the colony to utter anti-British statements, while the respectable were dismayed to receive pity from family at home about their having migrated to such a cesspool. So they defended it. 'Convict contamination was a myth, but since outsiders believed it the colonists had to take it seriously.' The local anti-transportationists stood up to Britain to show how worthy and British they were, and proclaimed New South Wales 'born again by large-scale free emigration and the anti-transportation movement'. But shame stuck about the convict 'birth stain'.[27]

New South Wales and the outposts of secondary punishment called to mind tropes of hell rather than visions of paradise in the popular (outsider) image of Australia, and received wide circulation in the British tabloid press. The spectrum of convict experience, from the harshness of Norfolk Island to light work in the service of a kindly employer, could be used to different ends. Horror was necessary to frighten children and encourage virtue, as Dickens used it. Fear of the unknown, exile, brutality, cruelty, were all well publicized in England. Respectable middle-class people feared not transportation but contamination from the convict stain, like Pip exposed to Magwitch. Both insider and outsider views shared a poor opinion of the convicts – the former in order to encourage free migration. Only late in the nineteenth century did Australians move to condemn the brutality of the system rather than the depravity of convicts. The convicts themselves always believed that they were victims, the real villains being those who exiled them.[28]

French social planners and philosophers of the nineteenth century (including de Tocqueville) debated large questions – crime and punishment, sin and redemption, personal and social responsibility – and small ones such as cost-effective ways of isolating and punishing wrong-doers. The Botany Bay settlement, along with penal experiments in the United States, was one of very few sources of empirical evidence.[29] The intervention of the revolution and the Napoleonic wars limited access to antipodean information, but that did not dampen the rhetoric or constrain the speculation. Perversely, just as a new French government – that of Napoleon III – determined to emulate the Australian example, the British were deciding to abandon it. When the Navy annexed New Caledonia in 1853, an image of Botany Bay was very much in the mind of authorities, and the first convicts arrived there in 1864. The venture was not successful, perhaps due to divided responsibility between the naval governors and the penal establishment, the fast turn-over of governors, France's limited knowledge of actual Australian conditions, and the emphasis on punishment to the exclusion of planning a free society. Some commentators judged the venture to be beyond any chance of redemption; others pinned their faith in specific reforms. One of the latter was Henri Riviere, who insisted that a prosperous settler society could be built if (for example) time-expired convicts were 'unequivocally restored to full civil rights' and allowed full scope for their ambitions. What actually happened was that most people whose sentences expired were required to remain in New Caledonia, but their rights were severely limited there. Accordingly, many became what Australians would call 'bushrangers'. Riviere also believed that immigration should be limited to those who had substantial means.[30] Despite these sensible notions, Riviere drew the criticism of a later commentator, that his writings were 'one more example in the large collection of distorted French perceptions of Australia'. Only the very last naval governor – Pallu de la Barriere, the Governor Macquarie of New Caledonia – made any serious attempt to use the convict settlement as a springboard towards a society of free immigrants. Arriving in 1882, Barriere quit in 1884 before he could make any great impact.[31]

PROTESTANTS AND POLYNESIANS

Two major sources informed the novel social and political and economic forms which irrupted into the Pacific from the late eighteenth century. Settler societies were an obvious well-spring, bringing developed institutions, traditions and practices which embodied Western European history, and the capacity to impose these values and relations on their environment. The less obvious source was Islanders' impressions of their visitors. These enigmas were often explained by 'bicultural' mediators, stray beachcombers or the first generation of Protestant missionaries.

Hard on the heels of Cook, Protestant missionaries began work in the Pacific. The non-denominational London Missionary Society (LMS) was followed by British Methodists and the American Board of Mission from New England. British missionaries focused on Tahiti, Tonga and Samoa, with logistical support from New South Wales. Polynesian chiefdoms were already alert to some possibilities arising from European visits (see chapter 3). The centralization of Tahiti was already under way when the *Duff* brought the first party of LMS 'godly mechanics' in 1797. Centralization suited both monarchs and foreigners, although neither fully understood the other. Europeans generally viewed Polynesian chiefdoms as potential monarchies which should be stabilized. On the other side, island leaders keenly followed Napoleon Bonaparte's battles with King George, reading them in terms of their own ambitions.

Early missions included printers, and literacy made an immediate appeal. Tongans made such demands that the Methodists brought in a press and a printer, who published 3,000 copies of a school primer within ten days. New Zealand Maori expected the written word to reveal the dynamics of European society and economy, the source of their technology and *mana*, but were initially disappointed.[32] Before 1840 literacy did not unlock Pakeha literature and technology, nor did it provide the basis for new approaches to government. The cultural misunderstandings over the Treaty of Waitangi illustrated the limits of literacy. Nonetheless Maori showed new enthusiasm for reading and writing in the 1840s because of the opportunities for competition.[33] Missionaries introduced new ways of pursuing rivalries on the assumption that they could transform Maori objectives, whereas they merely provided new techniques for competing within an old framework of values. Through their enthusiasm for printed language, literate Maori preserved their language and converted Christianity to fit their own evangelism. Similarly the LMS created Malua College in Samoa, while Tupou College in Tonga educated 'choice young men who would ultimately fill important positions both in the Church and the State'.[34] They produced a generation who were adept at dealing with foreigners.

Matavai Bay in Tahiti was an early favourite for provisioning. Pomare encouraged trade and befriended visitors, who accepted his claim to hegemony, gave him firearms, and helped in his battles. Before his death in 1803 he was acknowledged by visitors as Pomare I, and during the next dozen years successive visitors endorsed the ambitions of Pomare II, as the guarantor of the pork trade and rest and recreation. From the 1790s the LMS also pinned their faith to the Pomares, helping to create a unified archipelago, in which power was wielded by the Pomare dynasty with support from LMS personnel. Mass conversions followed. Missionaries were not only advisers, but architects and managers of a new structure. Henry Nott, Pomare's teacher, was the principal author of the 1824 constitution which established a parliament. As parliament's first president, Nott presided over the drafting of codes of laws.

Ten LMS missionary artisans landed in Tonga in 1797, but withdrew in 1800. Later sorties fell foul of disinterested chiefs and priests, traders and beachcombers until two Tahitians were sent in 1826, and built a church and a congregation which British missionaries took over. The decisive initiative, however, was taken by Tāufa'āhau:

> Increasing contact with Europeans and the superiority of their weapons also helped to undermine his belief in the traditional gods. ... After several trips to Tongatapu in 1827 and 1828, where he met the missionaries and some of his [Christian] relatives ... he began to imitate some of the ways of the Christians. He also tried to make his people learn them.[35]

Tāufa'āhau fought and negotiated to combine the essential dynastic titles. As George Tupou (a name reflecting his respect for the British monarchy) he ruled a united Tonga in which Methodism was almost the state religion. The Vava'u Code of 1839 endorsed Christianity and propounded the new social and political order. A revision in 1862 addressed economic issues as well; and in 1875 King George proposed a new constitution, drafted by the missionary Shirley Baker.

> The form of our Government in the days past was that my rule was absolute, and that my wish was law and that I could choose who should belong to the Parliament and that I could please myself to create chiefs and alter titles. But ... a new era has come to Tonga – an era of light – and it is my wish to grant a Constitution and to carry on my duties in accordance with it and those that come after me shall do the same and the Constitution shall be a firm rock in Tonga for ever.[36]

With few modifications, this constitution still serves the kingdom.

When John Williams arrived in Samoa in 1830, his access to chief Malietoa Vai'inupo was facilitated by Fauea, a Samoan who had lived in Tonga. In his 1830 journal Williams paraphrased Fauea:

> He told them also of the number of Islands which has become [Christian] ... and he said they are all much better. ... Wars have ceased among them. Ships visited them without fear and anchored in their harbours and brought them an abundance of Property. ... On hearing Fauea's speech they all exclaimed it would be good to lotu [become Christians] too.[37]

In New Zealand there was no paramount chief, rather a few *ariki* and numerous *rangatira*. A variety of European institutions attracted Maori leaders, while younger chiefs engaged more with new social forms.[38] The Bay of Islands chief, Ruatara, invited Samuel Marsden (the 'flogging parson') and his missionaries from Sydney in 1814, and used his monopoly of the first Anglican mission to create a leading role in developing Maori agriculture. The missionaries were 'his' Pakeha; he distributed their goods and knowledge selectively, and shortened Marsden's sermons as he translated them. Maori heard Ruatara's words, not Marsden's; as a mediator he used his status in one world to raise his status in the other.[39] For the formidable northern chief Hongi Hika, Christianity similarly connoted a business interest. Until Hongi's death the Anglicans found their mission confined to Northland by Maori sponsorship. The 'musket wars' that Hongi waged in the 1820s, with guns bought in Sydney, were made possible by an agricultural revolution that compounded his and his Ngapuhi tribe's wealth and *mana*. His raids emanated from Ngapuhi's new capacity for mass-producing potatoes, while the Ngapuhi raids on other *iwi* rounded up *taurekareka* (slaves, captive in war) who were set to work raising pigs and cultivating yet more potatoes.

With Hongi's death in 1828 Christianity spread from Northland to the rest of New Zealand, conveyed by released slaves who developed Maori versions of the gospel. *Taurekareka* had attended mission schools as well as planting potatoes, and came home not in shame from captivity but with *mana* as theologians. While the missionaries, widely used as mediators, claimed they had ended the wars, in fact the coming of peace spread Christianity. European missionaries followed in the path of Maori preachers.[40] The French who colonized Akaroa in the South Island in 1840 were astonished to find a cool reception for Roman Catholicism from Maori already converted by Maori Wesleyans. Catholic and Protestant missionaries could not agree to divide territory, but Protestants usually agreed among themselves on a geographical division. Wherever missions did compete, Islanders could play one off against the others, so that sectarianism became another dimension of factionalism – and pre-European relationships also inflected sectarianism, complicating identities.

Missionization often helped traders. Once Christianity was adopted, lineages and congregations competed to give contributions (*vakamisioneri*) to the church, and the practice was carried into Melanesia by Polynesian evangelists. Islanders were urged by Protestant missionaries to produce for the mission and for God. In Fiji, missions collected and sold copra. Equally in New Zealand, Maori saw the value in the European agriculture that the missionaries brought with them, which was as a conduit for trade. They sought to maintain and enhance Te Mana Maori by acquiring the material culture that they saw as attractive and necessary to participate in the new society. Maori had the early advantage as the major producers of food, as well as monopolizing trade and transport.[41] With the impetus of missionary instruction and example, Maori agriculture developed to the extent that Maori supplied the dependent Europeans with pigs, potatoes, maize and wheat, using a cross-cultural mix of cultivation methods, and exported to New South Wales. It was not missionaries who bestowed the urge to farm, but the presence of a market.[42] In 1835–7 the chief Paratene became New Zealand's first commercial dairy farmer. Tutored by the missionary Davis, he ran cattle at Kaikohe and churned butter which he sold at the Bay of Islands. While the mission farm at Waimate failed because the missionaries persisted with European methods on land covered in fern, scrub and tree stumps, Maori cleared and cultivated land by adopting European tools. Use of the *ko* (digging stick) was rare by 1850 and ploughs were in demand.[43]

Food served as the natural 'currency' of this competitive society and expertise in procuring food proved more effective than anything else in securing a chief's *mana*. Pakeha commerce, crops and artefacts affected the momentum rather than the basis of gift exchange, at first intensifying the Maori cultural economy. With more crops, new foods, improved techniques and more peaceful relations, prestige-enhancing feasts became more spectacular. In the 1820s and 1830s, feasts extended to walls of food five feet high and of great length, with dried fish, berries and watermelons piled on top of kumara or on wooden stages packed with baskets.[44]

Maori agency made Auckland the commercial centre of New Zealand from 1840. The Ngati Whatua chief Te Kawau sold Auckland to Governor Hobson, to ensure that the Pakeha seat of government shifted from Kororareka in the Bay of Islands, with the governor, so that the Ngati Whatua could reoccupy their lands at Orakei on Auckland Harbour under the shelter of Pax Britannica. Auckland became a centre of commerce as Maori headed for the town's markets in canoes and schooners with produce which they exchanged for manufactured goods.[45]

Missionaries encouraged such frenetic commercial activity. Maori motives and methods continued to dominate in the new economic order, although European influences and local circumstances varied. Flour mills and ships became symbols of *mana*, offering new ways to conduct inter-*hapu* rivalry. In the Waikato, the Anglican missionary, John Morgan, encouraged Maori to build flour mills, while Hauraki Maori developed an appetite for schooners that far exceeded their needs for trade. In the Waikato, where Maori produced for the Auckland as well as the local market, Maori invested heavily in ploughs and horses as well as mills. Flour mill fever spread, heavily draining *hapu* resources. High-profile investments in flour mills and schooners sucked Maori into debt and into selling land.[46] Prosperity from the new economic order was short-lived with the collapse in Australian markets for food in the 1850s, increasing disillusion with European ways, and a crisis in Maori–Pakeha relations. The appearance of weeds – intruders from Europe – fortuitously symbolized disturbed political and social unity.

THE CATHOLIC REVIVAL

Catholic missionaries (except in Spanish Micronesia) arrived later than Protestants, and relied largely on the French navy for support. Commonly some Islanders had already committed themselves to Protestant faiths, leaving the Catholics to work among opposition factions or less attractive islands. In Tahiti, an Anglo-Protestant establishment crystallized around the monarchy, and even after the French navy extended a protectorate over the islands in the 1840s, discouraged Catholic evangelism. Rotuma island received Samoan, Tongan and Fijian mission teachers and pastors from 1839. European Catholics followed in 1846, but withdrew in 1853. An English Wesleyan then consolidated the work of his Polynesian forerunners, so that French Catholics – who returned in 1868 – found themselves at a disadvantage. Conversion was complicated by dynastic politics, and the 1870s were marked by warfare between traditionalists, Protestants and Catholics until 1879, when the leading chief petitioned the governor of Fiji for incorporation. Whether the wars were religious (as missionaries believed) or both dynastic and religious (as Rotuman traditions describe them), secular and sacred issues reinforced each other, confirming the hostility of Catholic and Protestant workers. In the New Hebrides, Marists were despatched from New Caledonia at the behest of commercial interests, to redeem the archipelago from Protestantism and forestall British annexation. A veteran Marist missionary wrote resignedly:

> What pains me is the thought that we're going there accompanied by the military and at the behest of political agitators ... God help us!

His forecast was accurate.

As elsewhere, Maori took the initiative in inviting missionaries. While the God of the Pakeha appealed for his power and wealth, allegiance to Roman Catholicism provided a gesture of resistance to Protestant missionaries. Before the arrival of the French Catholic Bishop Pompallier in 1838, Hokianga chiefs had sent two young Maori to Sydney in 1835 to be instructed in Catholicism, influenced by local Irish. Catholicism provided an alternative politics, a means to assert an independent identity in opposition to British overlordship and to compete with Protestant neighbours. That the Catholicism which arrived with Pompallier was French, conveyed by priests and lay brothers attached to the Society of Mary, enlarged the gesture of defiance in the alternative imperial and spiritual power it represented. Sectarianism became incorporated into Maori politics. Aware of English–French hostility, Maori like the chief Papahia played off the British resident, Busby, against Pompallier, and subsequently the governor against the bishop. Pompallier, an image-maker, dressed for the part. He completely outshone the plain black dresses of the CMS missionaries at the signing of the Treaty of Waitangi and was deliberately liberal in distributing gifts, including the fine French woollen cloaks worn by certain chiefs at the Treaty signing in 1840. The French consciously competed with their Protestant foes, incorporating Maori beliefs in their theology and condemning only those customs contrary to 'natural law'.[47] Maori were responsive to such flexibility. They also liked to try something new as part of their *mana*-seeking.

THE NEW LAWS

Where chiefs exercised control, missionaries could act out their principles and prejudices. Civil and domestic laws reflected Western cultural and class biases, and the rules of commerce gradually became as prominent as Protestant morality. The new codes governed land tenure, taxes, and the rights of foreigners. In the extreme case of Hawaii, land itself was privatized in the 1840s. In New Zealand, some Maori and Pakeha land use was at first compatible, such as early pastoralism under Maori leases in the Wairarapa in the 1840s and the traditional gathering of food resources. But problems erupted when settlers began to fence and to assume freehold. Pakeha grew restless that the Maori remained outside British law, and disputes over fences and stock trespass disclosed that English common law could not be transferred to all settler societies. In England, livestock farmers were obliged to fence in animals to protect farmers' crops. In New Zealand, fences were built around crops to keep animals out. Settlers were irked that Maori were not compelled to fence, while Maori, who customarily shifted cultivations every few years, maintained that settlers should see that their livestock did not destroy Maori cultivations, a position consistent with English common law. As more land was alienated and fenced, they also lost access to food resources.[48]

As the Maori ordering of social relations was disturbed, some looked to the Bible for guidance, and others to British codes of law. For some Maori, the British legal system appealed as a means to shake off their laws of reciprocity and retaliation, of *utu*, *tapu* and *muru* (plunder). In particular, Maori showed interest in British justice as a way to resolve disputes over women and land.[49] As Natanahira Waruarutu of Ngai Tahu put it in 1860: 'now we have a garment which we find to be very warm; I mean the Laws which preserve us from the deep pit. ... Friends I have had two garments – my old one is worn out and my whole desire is for the new.'[50] The living symbol of the new garment was the Treaty of Waitangi.

A formal treaty was unusual in these circumstances, but not unique: a similar pact was negotiated between France and the Tahitian monarchy. What was unique was the great range of meanings which the Waitangi Treaty has sustained. Maori sought to retain control, not lose it, through the European pen and ink used to sign the Treaty at Waitangi, in the Bay of Islands, on 6 February 1840. The treaty did not mark a transition from informal to formal British empire. These terms are too crude to explain the situation in New Zealand, where a range of zones operated, from Pakeha-controlled coastal towns, to Maori-controlled zones with a minority of (or no) Pakeha.[51]

Before treating with the Maori, the British pursued expansion-on-the-cheap by posting a minor Sydney official, James Busby, to the Bay of Islands in 1833 as resident, ostensibly to check European miscreants. Busby arranged for a flag chosen by local *rangatira* to allow Maori traders and their ships free entry into Australian ports in 1834, a flag which the chiefs flew as a symbol of independent Maori identity, and followed with a Declaration of the Independence of New Zealand in 1835, signed by fifty-two northern chiefs under the designation of the United Tribes of New Zealand, which declared Nu Tireni an independent state and entreated the British crown to be its protector. This declaration resembled petitions by other Polynesians, but the northern Maori, who already had their flag, believed that it affirmed their sovereignty; to Busby, it provided a means of making a British protectorate of New Zealand. Here the past shaped future identities. In the 1990s a reinvented United Tribes of Aotearoa based in Northland asserted their independence from the fisheries settlement drafted to settle Treaty of Waitangi claims on the grounds that their *tupuna* (ancestors) had signed the Declaration of Independence.

The same chiefs were the first to sign Te Tiriti o Waitangi. In their view they had not ceded sovereignty. Under the treaty, *rangatiratanga* stayed with them, but Anglican missionaries drafted different texts of the treaty, in Maori and in English. Most signed a Maori version, in which Maori ceded not *rangatiratanga* – sovereignty, or chieftainship – but *kawanatanga* – governorship. 'The Maori version therefore went far to justify the conclusion of the Rarawa chief Nopera Panakareao that "the shadow of the land will go to him [the governor] but the substance will remain with us" .'[52] The missionaries in their ethnocentrism did not believe Maori had a full concept of national sovereignty and so applied the new term of *kawanatanga* in the Maori text. Although the British were prepared to recognize the *mana* of *rangatira*, chiefs, at the local level, in the English versions of the treaty the chiefs ceded *all* their rights and powers of sovereignty which they held over their respective territories. In return, the English text guaranteed them possession of their lands and estates, forests and fisheries, a guarantee far short of the Maori text's unqualified exercise of *te tino rangatiratanga* over their lands and all their *taonga* (treasures).[53] Implicitly, the Europeans acknowledged that *iwi* and *hapu* (tribal and local kin) identities were crucial. At the same time, the missionaries responsible for the linguistic slips nurtured the idea that the treaty was a living covenant between Maori people and the British crown.

The discrepant texts inscribed a cultural abyss which could not be bridged. For the new settler society and some Maori, the treaty assisted identity formation by becoming the nation's founding document. For many *iwi* and *hapu*, however, it guaranteed their *rangatiratanga*, and the subsequent breach of that compact by Pakeha only sharpened Maori resolve to assert an independent identity and regional, kin identities. Thus the treaty inscribed the process whereby Maori began to be defined against Pakeha and Pakeha against Maori, a national Maori identity itself being a creation of post-1840 New Zealand. Cultural misunderstanding, mingled with understanding, was part of the package, as the signing of this treaty of cession/affirmation of sovereignty showed.

Important chiefs refused to sign, among them Te Heuheu of Ngati Tuwharetoa, from the central North Island, with significant consequences for constructing identities within Maoridom. (He was the closest Aotearoa had to a paramount chief.) Taonui, a trans-Tasman traveller, while suspicious, signed to keep the settlers in check but put his Australian experience to account in insisting on Maori autonomy:

> We are glad to see the Governor; let him come to be a Governor to the Pakehas. As for us, we want no Governor; we will be our own Governor. How do the Pakehas behave to the black fellows of Port Jackson? They treat them like dogs! ... The land is our father; the land is our chieftainship; we will not give it up.[54]

It is questionable whether Te Tiriti o Waitangi amounted to a treaty of cession even in English. Such was Governor Hobson's concern to secure imperial control that he proclaimed British sovereignty in May 1840: over the North Island by virtue of cession and the South Island by right of discovery by Captain Cook. The treaty was still circulating and southern

Maori signatures had yet to be collected. In effect this suggested that New Zealand's South Island was *terra nullius*, and the treaty-signing rituals conducted outside the Bay of Islands in 1840 equated to survey pegs in pen and paper for marking out Pax Britannica – a very cost-efficient way to acquire territory.

The British government had already decided to claim New Zealand in 1839. Catching wind of this, Edward Gibbon Wakefield's equally treacherous brother, William Wakefield, sailed for what became the site of Wellington in May 1839 to pre-empt annexation by a land-buying spree as agent for the New Zealand Company. With the sailing of the *Tory*, colonizing companies and speculators ostensibly forced Britain's hand.[55] According to James Belich, the myths of empire induced Britain to step up intervention in 1840 and to acquire full or partial sovereignty; empire resulted from its myths.[56] More precisely, in our view, pyramid selling was central to the entire imperial enterprise. The New Zealand Company was Britain's hand, and settler capitalism aided empire-on-the-cheap.

The transition to British rule was equally devious in Fiji. By 1861 Bau was the dominant polity, and its Vunivalu (war chief) Cakobau the leading power-holder. To Consul Pritchard however (one of a dynasty of missionary-trader-diplomats) Cakobau was 'little more than the most powerful, the most influential, the most dignified Chieftain of his race'.[57] The foreign community was approaching 3,000 by 1870, including Australians and New Zealanders who responded to Pritchard's invitation to take up land to plant cotton. Cakobau's authority was widely contested. Defeated chieftaincies awaited their chances to strike out again, and some were courted by Enele Ma'afu, leader of a Tongan community based in Lakeba. Planters and traders were reluctant to recognize any indigenous authority.[58] Cakobau had requested a British protectorate, but in vain. In June 1871 he declared himself King of Fiji, co-opting Ma'afu as his viceroy and other chiefs and traders as ministers. The next year he brought in John Bates Thurston as chief secretary. Thurston was cast away in 1865, aged 29, and worked for the Methodists before he bought land. Unlike most settlers, he studied Fijian politics and language. The task of government was to preserve a fragile peace, to remain solvent and to secure recognition from foreign powers. When British officials changed tack and demanded the cession of Fiji, Cakobau acquiesced: defiance would risk war. Thurston then helped to negotiate the Cession of Fiji in 1875, on relatively favourable terms, so that Fijian lands were protected, and the islands were brought under one government. The chiefly families were entrenched, but without a king.

TENSIONS BETWEEN EMPIRES

Involvement in Islanders' politics could bring the imperial powers close to conflict, but none of them wanted to annex Samoa, preferring that Samoans form their own independent government. By the 1870s Samoans had endured three decades of warfare, often triggered by the question of a head of state. A dual kingship was attempted, and lasted a few months. Then Steinberger, an American adventurer, won the trust of the chiefs and in 1875 proposed an alternating kingship with effective power vested in himself as premier; but a year later he was ousted by the foreign community. In 1887 the Germans installed Tupua Tamasese as king and sent Eugen Brandeis to serve as his premier. This regime established a monopoly of force, but provoked a revolt and almost led to war between the Great Powers. Finally, an international commission conceded that the kingship was a foreign concept and abolished it. Western Samoa became a German colony and the eastern isles, including Pago Pago harbour, came under the United States navy.

This manoeuvring was not unique. While the British were preparing to send Hobson to New Zealand, the French whaling captain Jean François Langlois returned to France with a deed, signed by South Island chiefs in 1838, stating that the signatories had sold him Banks Peninsula. This deed prompted the French government and the Nanto-Bordelaise Company to race the British to New Zealand, with the idea of leaving the North Island to the British and annexing the South Island. Because of the strength of informal British empire, the French government decided first to despatch French settlers to buy and occupy land in 'Southern New Zealand', and then declare sovereignty. Langlois's deed fell short because, in French eyes, claiming the land required occupation. Like the British, the French acknowledged Maori sovereignty and land ownership, not in Maori terms but in terms of their own law. But they reversed the order of proceeding and gave priority to land purchase and its associated occupation.

Had the French not sailed into Akaroa Harbour in August 1840 to find that local Maori had already signed the Treaty of Waitangi, there might have been a different result for South Island Maori. French rules for living would have spawned different local identities. Non-sellers would have kept their *rangatiratanga* as the French understood it, as sovereignty under French law, but sellers would have lost their native title. The French model bought out native title, unlike the Treaty of Waitangi which supposedly preserved it. In New France, the Maori (mainly Ngai Tahu) would have been relegated to reserves. In practice, Banks Peninsula Maori refused to leave their land and live alongside the French at Akaroa. An even balance of power prevailed in the 1840s, as each needed the economic support and security provided by the other. The Maori view dominated over the land, and French occupation would have required further payment. European views changed with numbers, so that with organized English settlement in the south from the 1850s the Maori insistence on their land guarantee could be ignored, for the moment. Numbers proved the issue in power relations between imperial authorities, colonists and Maori.[59]

Throughout New Zealand, Maori were at first keen to convert Christianity to their interests, but by 1870 this view changed markedly in the wake of the land wars (see chapter 6). In the King Country, CMS, Wesleyan, Roman Catholic and Lutheran missions were not long established before they were

forced to withdraw by fighting in the Waikato. Even in areas where missionaries continued to be active, much of the old zeal was gone, as Bishop
W. L. Williams reflected:

> A notion was generally prevalent among the disaffected, though seldom openly
> acknowledged, that they had been deceived by the Missionaries, whose real
> object in coming to the country originally ... had been merely to pave the way
> for the white man to come and dispossess them of their lands; colour being
> given to this notion by the fact that the Missionaries had rendered important
> assistance to the Government in producing signatures to the Treaty of
> Waitangi.[60]

Equally suspect was the missionaries' withdrawal from districts embroiled in
the fighting and the alignment of some with colonial and imperial troops.

The British claimed sovereignty in the belief that they could write empire
into existence with signatures. In the imperial view, full British sovereignty
over New Zealand dated from 1840, formalized in a proclamation by the
New South Wales Governor, George Gipps, in January; in proclamations by
Captain Hobson; gazetting in London; and in the Treaty of Waitangi. Yet
Maori remained substantially in control of New Zealand until 1860, and in
parts until the 1880s.[61] Butlin emphasized, similarly, how long it took for the
European population to match Aboriginal Australians in numbers and for
colonial products to attain the level of Aboriginal Australia in 1788, which
he argued did not happen until 1850.[62] Numbers mattered in the land/
sovereignty game.

Marriage also assisted the reworking of relations between kin and land.
Throughout the new law codes of the Pacific, family law strove to institutionalize Western gender norms through marriage, and Europeanized marriage
altered the bonds of land and kinship. In New Zealand, both Pakeha and
Maori *hapu* arranged marriages to build strategic alliances and *mana* in their
own worlds and between them. But Pakeha differed from Maori for whom
the wider kin group held greater importance than a marriage partner,
especially for women.[63] In the new social forms, the family was central to
New Zealand's future as an idea and as an economic unit. Despite the
variety of family types, missionaries and systematic colonizers 'accepted
the Evangelical idealization of the family that became the Victorian orthodoxy'. They believed the conjugal, patriarchal family was central to civilized
society.[64]

The civilization of Maori accordingly required that they adopt the rites of
Christian, and later civil, marriage. Dr A. S. Thomson assumed this when he
devised his 1859 list of requirements for civilizing the Maori. The government
should teach Christianity and English language, individualize property, form
roads and English settlements, impose the Queen's law, prevent disease, and
promote amalgamation of the races (for example, to breed out 'scrofula': see
chapter 4). To this end, he favoured altering English laws about inheritance
to native land, so as to encourage racial amalgamation, since legal unions
between European males and 'native' females were then discouraged.[65]

Marriage proved the means by which Maori women's land entered European law. Maori marriages increasingly came under Pakeha law, as under the 1909 Native Land Act, which recognized Maori marriage for succession if it were European in style.

SPORT AND CIVILIZATION

That great fashioner of identity through interaction, sport, also became yoked to the civilizing mission and advocated as a means to amalgamate, or assimilate, Maori and Aboriginal Australians. The first Australian and New Zealand sporting teams to visit the Mother Country were both indigenous: the Aboriginal cricket team in 1868 and the New Zealand Native rugby team in 1888–9. English newspapers not only noted their 'dusky' complexions but, according to the *Times*, saw the visiting specimens as a tribute to 'our colonizing faculty. The colonizing race that can imbue the aboriginal inhabitants of the colonized countries with a love for its national games, would seem to have solved the problem of social amalgamation'. The sporting tours took Home the message that indigenous peoples could be 'civilized'.[66]

Sport could serve as a mediating influence amidst the hardening prejudices of 'scientific' racism, which heightened Australian sensitivities about the 'convict stain' as part of breeding. This made it all the more important to

Plate 5.1 Aboriginal cricketers (Coranderrk, Victoria). Photographer: Fred Kruger. Macmillan Brown Collection, Macmillan Brown Library, University of Canterbury.

Plate 5.2 Samson (in cricket gear), Australian Aborigines, Victoria, Goulburn tribe. Photographer: Fred Kruger. Macmillan Brown Collection, Macmillan Brown Library, University of Canterbury.

beat the English at cricket. As colonial identities developed, sport also served as a venue for racial consciousness by putting fit bodies on display. The first English cricket team came to Australia in December 1861 to be greeted in deferential tones in Sydney.

> In inviting you to visit us we had no idea of testing our skill against yours – that would be simply absurd; but we were desirous of having you here to witness British skill in the noble game of cricket. It is a comfort to know that we are beaten by our own countrymen. They cannot find foreigners to beat our cricketers, our masters come from the old country.[67]

From the start, Australian cricket assumed local colour. The Australian style, one contemporary argued, was 'decidedly colonial, agricultural and

Plate 5.3 Samson and family, Australian Aborigines, Victoria, Goulburn tribe. Photographer: Fred Kruger. Macmillan Brown Collection, Macmillan Brown Library, University of Canterbury.

uncouth'. Cricket fields during the first English tour were typically grazing grounds for sheep and goats. Some played the game barefoot. In look and form, the rough-and-ready colonials were no match for their honoured guests, but they inflicted several losses on the English side. The third English tour in 1864 brought more glory to the colonials. In Melbourne in 1877, the Australians won the first test match ever played between the two sides. Colonial newspapers reported the event more in the language of race than sport.

> For the first time a team representing the cricketing prowess of England has been beaten on equal terms out of that country. The event marks the great improvement which has taken place in Australian cricket and shows, also, that in bone and muscle, activity, athletic vigour ... the Englishmen born in Australia do not fall short of the Englishmen born in Surrey or Yorkshire.[68]

Cricket prowess bespoke a common superior race. It also bestowed the mark of manhood on colonial males, evidence of whose strength was presented to the Philadelphia American Centennial Exhibition in 1876 based on the chest, height and bicep measurements of Melbourne cricketers. Cricket successes set the land of transportation in a different context. For colonials it offered a foretaste of the masculine myth-making in the Great War when the ultimate victory was approval from the Mother Country.

We can put this experience in perspective by observing the very different adaptations of cricket elsewhere. In Samoa, where it was introduced by missionaries, it assumed a form recalling its rural English origins. Whole villages took part, committing themselves to days on end of wholehearted rivalry. So serious was the passion that German officials tried their best to suppress the game, as an intolerable impediment to the production of cash crops.[69] Samoan missionaries brought the game to Papua, and in the Trobriand Islands it was again transformed by a host of ritual additions.[70] The point was not to imitate the Europeans, much less compete with them, but to express their own values and local rivalries. (That happened later in Papua, under missionary auspices.)[71] By comparison with the islanders' innovations, the Australians – and New Zealanders, whose wet climate slowed cricket's adoption – played a severely repressed and deferential game.

NOTES

1 Martin Lynn, 'British Policy, Trade, and Informal Empire in the Mid-Nineteenth Century', in Andrew Porter (ed.), *Oxford History of the British Empire*, vol. 3, Oxford, 1999.

2 Alan Atkinson, *The Europeans in Australia: A History*, Melbourne, 1997, ix–x.

3 Ibid., 219, and Richard White, *Inventing Australia: Images and Identity 1688–1980*, Sydney, 1981.

4 A. G. L. Shaw, *Convicts and the Colonies*, London, 1966, 62.

5 Atkinson, *The Europeans in Australia*, 6, 134–5, 144, 269.

6 J. B. Hirst, *Convict Society and its Enemies: A History of Early New South Wales*, Sydney, 1983, 194.

7 Marian Aveling (Quartly), 'Bending the Bars: Convict Women and the State', in K. Saunders and R. Evans (eds), *Gender Relations in Australia: Domination and Negotiation*, Sydney, 1992, 69.

8 Hirst, *Convict Society and its Enemies*, preface.

9 Russel Ward, *The Australian Legend*, Melbourne, 1966, ch. 2; for a feminist critique see Ann McGrath, 'Birthplaces', in Patricia Grimshaw, Marilyn Lake, Ann McGrath and Marian Quartly, *Creating a Nation*, Melbourne, 1994, 7–26.

10 Miriam Dixson, *The Real Matilda: Woman and Identity in Australia 1788 to the Present*, 3rd edn, Melbourne, 1994, 118–19. The positive view developed by cliometric historians is outlined in Stephen Nicholas (ed.), *Convict Workers: Reinterpreting Australia's Past*, Melbourne, 1988.

11 The traditional view, Shaw's, after challenge by Blainey, Frost and cliometric historians, has been updated by Atkinson, *The Europeans in Australia*.

12 Ibid., 195.

13 McGrath, in *Creating a Nation*, ch. 1; Atkinson, *The Europeans in Australia*, ch. 8.
14 Shaw, *Convicts and the Colonies*, 60.
15 Ibid., 19, 62–3.
16 Aveling, 'Bending the Bars'; Atkinson, *The Europeans in Australia*.
17 Dixson, *The Real Matilda*, 11.
18 Aveling, 'Bending the Bars', 147; Ann Summers, *Damned Whores and God's Police*, Melbourne, 1994.
19 Aveling, 'Bending the Bars', 73–4, 78.
20 Ibid., ch. 7; Shaw, *Convicts and the Colonies*, 148; Joy Damousi, *Depraved and Disorderly: Female Convicts, Sexuality and Gender in Colonial Australia*, Melbourne, 1997.
21 Damousi, *Depraved and Disorderly*.
22 Dixson, *The Real Matilda*, 115–16; Shaw, *Convicts and the Colonies*, 358.
23 See, for example, Dixson, *The Real Matilda*, ch. 4, quotation from 136.
24 Hirst, *Convict Society and its Enemies*, chs 1, 4.
25 White, *Inventing Australia*, 24–8.
26 Hirst, *Convict Society and its Enemies*, 195–6.
27 Ibid., 197–217.
28 White, *Inventing Australia*, ch. 2; Shaw, *Convicts and the Colonies*, 359.
29 Colin Forster, *France and Botany Bay: The Lure of a Penal Colony*, Melbourne, 1996.
30 Henri Riviere, *Souvenirs de la Nouvelle-Caledonie*, Paris, 1881, quoted in John Lawrey, *The Cross of Lorraine in the South Pacific: Australia and the Free French Movement 1940–1942*, Canberra, 1982.
31 Lawrey, *The Cross of Lorraine in the South Pacific*.
32 G. S. Parsonson, 'The Literate Revolution in Polynesia', *Journal of Pacific History*, 2 (1967): 39–57.
33 A. R. Parsonson, 'The Pursuit of Mana.' In W. H. Oliver with B. R. Williams (eds), *Oxford History of New Zealand*, Wellington, 1981a, 142.
34 Quoted in Sione Lātūkefu, *Church and State in Tonga*, Canberra, 1974, 76.
35 Lātūkefu, *Church and State*, 61–2.
36 Ibid., 162–3.
37 Richard Moyle, *Samoan Journals of John Williams, 1830 and 1832*, Canberra, 1984, 124, 142, 68.
38 A. Ward, *A Show of Justice*, Canberra, 1995, 19.
39 J. Belich, *Making Peoples: A History of the New Zealanders from Polynesian Settlement to the End of the Nineteenth Century*, Auckland, 1996, 143–4.
40 Belich, *Making Peoples*.
41 Bill Dacker, *Evidence for the Ngai Tahu Claim before the Waitangi Tribunal*, 24, Otakou Marae, Feb. 1988, 10–13; Alan H. Grey, *Aotearoa and New Zealand: A Historical Geography*, Christchurch, 1994, 138–9.
42 R. P. Hargreaves, 'Changing Maori Agriculture in Pre-Waitangi New Zealand', *Journal of the Polynesian Society*, 72 (1963): 101–17.
43 R. P. Hargreaves, 'The Maori Agriculture of the Auckland Province in the Mid-nineteenth Century', *Journal of the Polynesian Society*, 68 (1959): 61–79; 'Waimate–Pioneer New Zealand Farm', *Agricultural History*, 36 (1962): 38–45; 'Changing Maori Agriculture in Pre-Waitangi New Zealand'.
44 A. R. Parsonson, 'The Expansion of a Competitive Society: A Study in Nineteenth-century Maori History', *New Zealand Journal of History*, 14 (1980): 45–60.

45 R. Walker, *Ka Whawhai Tonu Matou: Struggle Without End*, Auckland, 1990, 99–100.

46 Hargreaves, 'The Maori Agriculture of the Auckland Province', 69–70; Paul Monin, 'The Maori Economy of Hauraki 1840–1880', *New Zealand Journal of History*, 29 (1995): 197–210.

47 P. Turner, 'The Politics of Neutrality: The Catholic Mission and the Maori 1838–1870', MA thesis, University of Auckland, 1986, 25–96.

48 Hargreaves, 'The Maori Agriculture of the Auckland Province', 67; 'Farm Fences in Pioneer New Zealand', *New Zealand Geographer*, 21 (1965): 144–5; Ward, *A Show of Justice*, 50.

49 Ward, *A Show of Justice*, 14.

50 Bill Dacker, *Evidence for the Ngai Tahu Claim before the Waitangi Tribunal*, Waitangi Tribunal vol. 24, Otakou Marae, 1988, 6.

51 The best account of these zones is J. Belich, 'The Governors and the Maori', in K. Sinclair (ed.), *Oxford Illustrated History of New Zealand*, Auckland, 1990, 82–6.

52 Ward, *A Show of Justice*, 44.

53 *Facsimiles of the Declaration of Independence and the Treaty of Waitangi*, Wellington, 1976 (1st edn 1877).

54 C. Orange, 'The Maori and the Crown', in Sinclair, *Oxford Illustrated History of New Zealand*, 46.

55 See, for example, Ward, *A Show of Justice*, 31.

56 Belich, *Making Peoples*, 187.

57 Consul Pritchard to Commissioner Smythe, 14 January 1861, cited in Deryck Scarr, *I, the very Bayonet*, vol. 1 of *The Majesty of Colour: A Life of Sir John Bates Thurston*, Canberra, 1973, 23–4.

58 *Fiji Times*, 20 August 1870, quoted by Deryck Scarr, *Fiji: A Short History*, Sydney, 1984, 52.

59 Peter Tremewan, 'The French Alternative to the Treaty of Waitangi', *New Zealand Journal of History*, 26: 1 (April 1992), 99–104. Also Tremewan, *French Akaroa: An Attempt to Colonize Southern New Zealand*, Christchurch, 1990.

60 Quoted in Andrews, 'Aspects of Development: The Maori Situation, 1870–1890', MA thesis, University of Auckland, 1968, 124–6.

61 Belich, *Making Peoples*, 180–7.

62 Butlin, *Forming a Colonial Economy: Australia 1810–1850*, Cambridge, 1994.

63 F. Porter and C. Macdonald (eds), *'My Hand Will Write What My Heart Dictates'*, Auckland, 1996, 253.

64 E. Olssen, 'Families and the Gendering of European New Zealand in the Colonial Period, 1840–80', in C. Daley and D. Montgomerie (eds), *The Gendered Kiwi*, Auckland, 1999, 37–62.

65 Arthur S. Thomson, *The Story of New Zealand*, vol. 1, London, 1859, 301, 306.

66 Greg Ryan, ' "Handsome Physiognomy and Blameless Physique": Indigenous Colonial Sporting Tours and British Racial Consciousness, 1868 and 1888', *International Journal of the History of Sport*, 14: 2 (August 1997), 67–81. Quotation from the *Times*, 4 October 1888, in ibid., 77.

67 *Sydney Morning Herald*, 28 January 1862; quoted in ' "Pommy Bastards and Damn Yankees": Sport and Australian Nationalism', in W. F. Mandle, *Going it Alone: Australia's National Identity in the Twentieth Century*, London, 1980.

68 *Australasian*, 17 March 1877, in Mandle, *Going it Alone*.

69 Jocelyn Linnekin, 'Ignoble Savages and Other European Visions: The La Perouse Affair in Samoan History', *Journal of Pacific History*, 26: 1 (1991): 3–26.
70 Jerry Leach, director, *Trobriand Cricket: An Ingenious Response to Colonialism*, 16 mm film, PNG Office of Information, 1976.
71 David Wetherell, *Charles Abel and the Kwato Mission of Papua New Guinea, 1891–1975*, Melbourne, 1996.

[6] *STRUGGLES FOR LAND*

Contests for land can seem simple in retrospect, and their outcome predestined. In one view, the colonists' fire-power was manifestly superior to that of Polynesians or Aboriginal Australians. In another, the dynamism of capitalist production must surely sweep all (and everyone) before it. In yet another, colonists saw land as a commodity; indigenous people saw it as intrinsic to their lives and therefore inalienable; and neither could grasp the other's point of view. None of these arguments works in every situation, although each has merit. It was not only misunderstanding which provoked disputes over land, but several circumstances including a particular moral perspective which generations of Europeans brought to land ownership and management.

John Locke was perhaps the most lucid protagonist of this point of view:

> God gave the world to men in Common, but … it cannot be supposed He meant it should always remain common and uncultivated. He gave it to the use of the industrious and rational.

That argument prevailed swiftly in Australia. The Presbyterian minister John Dunmore Lang brought Locke to Moreton Bay when he declared in 1856 that God could not have intended the earth for people

> so incapable of appreciating its resources as the Aborigines of Australia. The white man had indeed, only carried out the intentions of the Creator in coming and settling down in the territory of the natives. God's first command to man was 'Be fruitful and multiply and replenish the earth'. Now that the Aborigines had not done, and therefore it was *no fault* in taking the land.[1]

In New Zealand the struggle was protracted – and so was the colonists' search for justification. The largest alienations after the wars of the 1860s occurred only between 1891 and 1911 when the Liberal government bought three million acres of Maori land while another half million were sold on the open market, and by 1911 93 per cent of land held under customary title had passed through the Native Land Court. By then the government and individuals had polished several variations on the theme of 'use it or lose it'.[2] Those who used the land most productively (Europeans, naturally) had the best moral claim to it. Settlers saw Maori land not as Maori property, but as crown demesne and thus colonial property which must be made subject to

British law. Large-scale Maori landownership was equated with feudalism, and individual title was essential for Maori themselves as well as for colonists. No settler imagined that Maori might be superior – or even competent – farmers. Settlers could transform the bush 'from a wilderness into a garden', but Maori could do the same only if they farmed as individuals and ceased to live as Maori.[3]

A general trend was given precise form by Edward Gibbon Wakefield, an influential and ultimately baffling propagandist.[4] His morals were dubious, his knowledge of the colonies minimal, and his prescriptions appear to derive from Adam Smith.[5] Wakefield was not writing about land for its own sake, but as the central mechanism for the systematic creation of a colonial society which would be almost a slice of (somewhat romanticized) rural England. In his vision of colonization, for example, he had much to say about women, their unpaid domestic work and the need for both female and male colonists and a large proportion of young married couples: 'As respects morals and manners, it is of little importance what colonial fathers are, in comparison with what the mothers are'. The creation of such a society also required the separation of Maori from much of their land:

> The concept that large tracts of land could be used for hunting, farming when needed, non-uniform forestry, fishing, and even as a buffer zone between different tribes, was considered unreasonable. The land should be fenced, ploughed, replanted in a neat, controlled, English manner. This unfenced, ecologically controlled structure looked peopleless and unplanned.[6]

One purpose indeed was to 'civilize' the natives, while creating Arcadia.

The key to Wakefieldian theory was its 'sufficient-price concept'.[7] Bountiful land could spell disaster for new colonies: land should sell for a sufficient price to keep the classes of land, labour and capital in balance. The price should not be so low that tracts of land were bought and not used productively, and labourers became landowners too soon; but not too high, lest that discourage migrants. New South Wales tried to finance emigration from land sales in the 1830s, and the full Wakefield system was trialled in South Australia and six New Zealand settlements from 1836 to 1850.

For every visionary and planner, government had a central organizing role, as it must have the capacity and the vision to implement such schemes. Each settlement began with a form of rule which projected the sovereignty of the imperial power and its traditions. In its simplest form, at annexation or occupation or 'protection', a governor possessed all the powers and legitimacy of the monarch (or president) whom he represented, his autocracy limited only by laws and customs which hedged that power 'at home'. For the machinery of government to operate successfully, of course, it had to command the support of local groups of power-holders. In Fiji, British power was thought to derive not only from Queen Victoria but also from King Cakobau. Implicit in the Fijian chiefly act of cession was an expectation that their rights and traditions – and land – would be respected and protected. The raw power of an imperial expedition was also mediated (or perhaps masked) by treaties with local authorities in Tahiti and New Zealand: there, too, respect for indigenous rights and traditions was implicit in the rituals of transferring sovereignty. In some places (British New Guinea, for example) an imperial power promised protection of indigenous land even where there was no indigenous government.

In the settler colonies the settlers themselves accumulated power which found expression in the evolving constitutions. The governor of New Caledonia was advised by a nominated council in which settlers had minor representation alongside that of the penal establishment and the rest of the bureaucracy. Governors of British colonies had more (and more turbulent) settlers to reckon with, who exerted increasing influence on the bureaucracy until London granted a measure of formal autonomy. In the 1840s, when colonists debated their constitutional forms, the key issue was land management and ownership. Discussions turned on liberal themes: the development of free-market forces, the abolition of privilege, philanthropy (real, if shallow), the belief that men of the past were usually wrong or corrupt whereas present ideals were pure.[8] Responsible self-government (entrusted to a parliamentary majority) was attained in New South Wales and Victoria in 1855, South Australia, New Zealand and Tasmania a year later, Queensland in 1859 and Western Australia in 1890.[9] This fell short of democracy as we now understand it; rather, the constitution drafters perceived democracy as dangerous. No women obtained the franchise, nor non-British males; and South Australia was the only colony to adopt the principle of one man, one vote at the outset. While seats in the lower house (Assembly) were filled by election, there was an upper house (a Legislative Council vaguely resembling the House of Lords) whose members were appointed by the governor or elected by a narrow stratum of property owners. The government was formed in the Assembly, where it must command majority support, but it was also appointed by the governor who could dismiss it and dissolve the parliament, and its powers were constrained by the Legislative Council which would always discourage radical change or threats to property rights. The imperial government retained a monopoly right to legislate on some matters where imperial interests resided, such as foreign policy, and could disallow any colonial law; but colonial legislatures did enjoy wide powers over the sale and regulation of land.

Land was increasingly the subject of competition as it became possible to sell rural produce on a world market. Sea transport was transformed by accurate maps. Equally important, ships became larger, their schedules regular, and costs fell. These innovations allowed the long-distance transport of bulky cargoes. As grasslands were turned to grain, sheep and cattle, populations burgeoned, evicting indigenous people from fertile land, reproducing the commercial and urban infrastructure of Western Europe, but with New World imprints in the landscape such as colonial grid towns.

Productive management of the land, in European eyes, was a prerequisite for ownership. In 1992 the Mabo judgement challenged this view, overthrowing the fiction of *terra nullius* which had proclaimed that pre-1788 Australia was a legal desert and an unpeopled land.[10] *Terra nullius* allowed the crown to become the first owner of the land, as its (European) sovereign. On that view, annexation occurred as occupation rather than conquest or cession, on the premise that '"discovered" territory could be annexed and claimed for settlement if land was unoccupied or underutilized'.[11] The High Court in *Mabo v. Queensland* agreed that the crown had gained radical title, but had not become beneficial owner of the land, which was still the property of indigenous people (see chapter 17). The court held that native title had been extinguished piecemeal as waves of settlement washed over the continent, but that native title survived on Murray Island because the Queensland government had never moved to extinguish it. The court's ruling in *Mabo No. 2* (in which the original challenge continued) applied to the whole continent, suggesting that native title had potentially survived elsewhere in Australia. This decision throws a lurid light on struggles over land in the early nineteenth century.

MAORI AND PAKEHA

It is usual to contrast Australian and New Zealand indigenous experiences and to portray Australia as the exception to the British formula of securing consent from indigenous people by a treaty of cession. In New Zealand, the Treaty of Waitangi has become the nation's founding document in official narratives. Australia had no such treaty. It is commonly argued that this presence or absence of a treaty was, and is, a crucial difference culturally and constitutionally between the nations. Pakeha were also nicer to Maori than white Australians were to Aborigines; for instance, white New Zealanders did not dare shoot down Maori like wild animals; on the contrary, they respected Maori military strength, and deemed Maori superior to Aborigines racially and in their degree of 'civilization'. Accordingly race relations were better in New Zealand than in Australia. Nationalist historians wove this myth into their inventions of a New Zealand identity.[12] (This story has parallels in the enlightenment view of Cook, the storybook ancestor.) For Maori, the treaty became a living document, a sacred text; and for all New Zealanders another way to define themselves against (and with) the British and especially as *not* Australians. But did a treaty make a difference to 'the law of the land', which became the focus of conflict on both sides of the Tasman?[13]

Native title is an imported doctrine based on European feudal concepts of property that were alien to Aboriginal Australians and Maori, in which all land was ultimately held from the crown. It was convenient that the doctrine of crown right of pre-emption – written into the English text of the Treaty of Waitangi – provided a means to incorporate aboriginal title within the feudal construct of British common law.[14] Native title was contingent, not merely for hunter-gatherers, and readily extinguished in settler societies. In effect, annexation in Australia and New Zealand was legally self-supporting. In Australia, the theory of *terra nullius* sufficed. In New Zealand, imperial authorities, embodied in the governor, and later settler governments made vigorous use of the crown right of pre-emption to alienate Maori land by consent, through purchase, between 1840 and 1865 and again in the 1890s.[15]

One Australian settler, John Batman, did attempt the gesture of a treaty to establish his claim over a piece of land beyond the New South Wales government's then boundary. In 1835 he asserted he had secured a treaty with Aborigines to buy 600,000 acres at Port Phillip, the site of Melbourne. The New South Wales and imperial governments rejected his claim and accused him of trespassing on the 'vacant lands of the crown'. Earlier interpretations cited the doctrine of *terra nullius* as the reason, because Aboriginal Australians ostensibly had no rights, while recent interpretations (by, for example, Henry Reynolds) maintain that the crown right of pre-emption was at stake. Only the crown could extinguish native title,[16] so Batman's treaty would have 'subvert[ed] the foundation' of proprietary rights in New South Wales, and hence called into question all existing European title to land in Australia.[17] In short, the crown would brook no challenge. There were strong parallels in Australia and New Zealand between Batman's failure to secure a private treaty and imperial moves to check the excesses of the New Zealand Company's land purchases for the Wellington settlement. Australian entrepreneurs who had their eyes on New Zealand's tussock grasslands for sheep – notably W. C. Wentworth – also failed to make private treaties with South Island Maori because of the principle that individual settlers lacked the 'right of pre-emption of the soil', a power they could only enjoy with the 'consent of their government'.[18]

Closer observation of native title suggests that the experiences of Aboriginal Australians and Maori were not absolutely different, despite the Treaty of Waitangi. Both the experience of treaty breaches, and the treaty as sacred text, have shaped indigenous identities. The differences were most pronounced in the 1840s, a key moment for identity formation. British common law appeared to follow different paths between the Australasian colonies according to different readings of imperial missives and the different charters already established by colonists, which in turn shaped and were shaped by the degrees of conflict and consensus across the colonies. In 1847, the same common law principles of land ownership accordingly gave rise to diametrically opposed judgements in New Zealand and New South Wales.

Reynolds observes that the 1847 New Zealand judicial decision in *R v. Symonds* endorsed the principle of native title, that Maori 'had a right of occupancy on all land held under traditional tenure regardless of whether it was cultivated or not'. This decision confirmed the principle of native title upheld in the United States Supreme Court in 1823 and embodied in the Treaty of Waitangi as well as in British common law. In Australia, 'no colonial court ever defended the Aboriginal right of occupancy': colonial legal opinion endorsed the pastoralists' view that Aborigines were trespassers on their traditional lands if these came under pastoral lease or license.[19] At that moment, in 1847, social forms inscribed in case law appeared very different, and the Treaty of Waitangi did live, for settlers and Maori.

But how opposed were these judgements? A longer view suggests parallels in securing actual sovereignty by creating colonial law over land. *R v. Symonds* did not initiate a significant body of case law; rather its judgements were soon eclipsed, in law and in practice. Moreover, the Symonds case was a dispute of Pakeha versus Pakeha rather than Pakeha against Maori. Both parties recognized native title (suggesting a contrast between settler New Zealand and settler Australia), but that was not the issue at stake. Rather *R v. Symonds* was another round of a 'bitter though erudite debate between the Governor of New South Wales, Sir George Gipps and William Charles Wentworth in 1840', when New Zealand, according to pen and paper, was part of New South Wales, about whether private speculators and settlers could purchase land from Maori. Colonial law differed over recognition of aboriginal occupancy and usage rights, but the jurisdictions were not diametrically opposed on the paramountcy of the crown's rights over 'surplus lands' obtained from indigenous people but retained by the crown rather than disposed of to settlers. The essential, shared issues concerned the crown right of pre-emption and the extent of official control over profits from extinguishing native title and selling or leasing land. In fact *R v. Symonds* assisted imperial officials in asserting crown control over colonization at the expense of Maori and Aboriginal interests. Dispossessing Aborigines and Maori while promoting colonization far outweighed any motive of 'protection'. Worried about the threat to their property rights posed by the European notion that right of property to land derived from working on it, Maori protested in 1847 that their land guarantees in the treaty were under threat.[20]

In New Zealand, as in Australia, colonial institutions and relations encouraged extinguishment of native title. Chief Justice Prendergast made this abundantly clear in 1877 when he ruled in *Wi Parata v. The Bishop of Wellington* that courts had no jurisdiction to entertain claims based on supposed native title. In this case Wi Parata, one of the four Maori members of parliament, sought the return of land to his *iwi*, the Ngati Toa, which the tribe had granted to the Anglican Bishop Selwyn for a school in 1850. Maori wished to reclaim the land because the church had not built the school. The chief justice ruled that Ngati Toa lacked legal grounds for their claim.[21] Thirty years on, the Symonds precedent stood for nothing as Prendergast denied that 'native title had any basis in common law'. He also ruled that the Treaty of Waitangi was not a valid instrument of cession since Maori, as a tribal society, had no legal, sovereign status.[22] In effect he recognized the dominance of Maori *hapu* (kin group) and *iwi* identities, but that was not the contemporary interpretation. He ruled that Maori did not constitute a body politic, and used the derogatory term 'primitive barbarians' – a direct parallel with Eurocentric perceptions of Aborigines. Asserted not to be a body politic, Maori therefore had no customary rights enforceable in the courts; and the court had dismissed the treaty as a nullity.

There had been a paradigm shift towards positivism in legal thought, endorsing Locke, whereby land occupied by people who failed to meet positivist criteria of sovereignty could be declared 'unoccupied'.[23] The New Zealand Treaty did not change the situation. Once a crown grant was issued, it was irrelevant whether or not native owners had consented to sell their land.[24] The outcome of this judgement was profound: New Zealand in effect became *terra nullius* to the legal eye, just as much as Australia. It distorted the legal relevance and status of the Treaty of Waitangi, sidelined by the courts for another century. The judgement wrongly disguised the treaty's meaning as a statement of imperial authorities' intended relations with Maori. This assault on the treaty also magnified its symbolic significance and elevated the idea that the spirit of the treaty, not its words on paper, defined the Maori–Pakeha contract. The *Wi Parata* judgement, not native title, was enacted in laws, notably the Native Land Act of 1909. There is also the disjunction between the myth of harmonious race relations, and the reality of lawyers denying Maori status as a body politic. From the start, imperial officers used the crown right of pre-emption to dispossess Maori as well as Aboriginal Australians.

The governor's *mana* was pivotal to relations with Maori until the 1860s. As governor from 1845 to 1853 (and again in the 1860s), Sir George Grey made vigorous use of the crown right of pre-emption to obtain land for settlement cheaply, much in advance of real need. He sought to allay settler land hunger and to promote assimilation of Maori into European society in keeping with Eurocentric concepts of civilization and property.[25] As Ann Parsonson explains,

> The important thing was that Maori should retain enough land for their own 'subsistence', and that they were offered Crown recognition of their right to occupy their reserves 'for ever'. The real payment they would receive for their 'waste lands' was security of title to the lands they kept, and the rising value of those lands as British settlers became established nearby.[26]

We may contrast Grey's predecessor, Robert FitzRoy, who – responding to Maori and settler demands, and short of funds – waived the crown right of pre-emption from 1844 to 1846, when the imperial government reimposed it. Maori generally welcomed squatters as a source of revenue. But the rapid spread of squatting, combined with large land purchases encouraged by the governor, intensified issues of power and sovereignty. The first squatters took up runs in the Wairarapa in the 1840s, followed by an Australian 'rush' to the South Island in 1851–2. Settlers sought freehold title to free themselves from dependency on Maori patrons, to win status and independence, and for security against rivals for the best land; while Maori were anxious to prevent squatters from acquiring freehold title.[27]

AUSTRALIAN SQUATTERS AND SELECTORS

This was not the only struggle. 'Productive management' also proved a criterion in the contest among Europeans, between squatters and selectors, or large and small proprietors ('selector' is an Australian term for small farmer). Soil and climate conspired against small farming in much of Australia, so the early New South Wales pattern of close settlement was soon reversed.[28] From Phillip onwards, the instinct of governors was to assist large settlers. The future belonged to the pastoralists who became the colony's first rural elite, and the same applied at first in New Zealand.

Wakefieldian theory, which prescribed tight official control over landowner-ship, also conspired against the small settler. The substitution of crown grants by sale was seen as a prerequisite for self-government, in promising fiscal self-reliance through revenue from land sales. The Ripon Regulations of 1831–2 made crown land alienable only by auction, at a minimum of 5 shillings per acre. Governor Arthur found means of thwarting this system in Victoria; it was hardly relevant to Western Australians with little appetite for unalienated land; and in New South Wales sales were limited. The regulations were dis-mantled in 1841 when the Australian Land Sales Act provided for sale by auction at a minimum of £1 per acre throughout Australia, with the right of purchase of 20,000-acre blocks at that fixed price.[29]

In Australia, as in New Zealand, there was a push to landownership in the 1860s, intended to promote small farming by allowing selectors to settle on crown land occupied by squatters, provided they improve it. These selectors were to pay for their small blocks in instalments. The impact of dear land on small farmers could be ruinous. By the 1860s, the average Australian farmer paid at least 80 times as much for new land as Americans, and for less promis-ing land. Thousands of families had to abandon small farms in the second half of the nineteenth century after sinking their savings to keep them afloat. The grim experiences depicted by Henry Lawson and 'Steele Rudd' (A. H. Davis), *On Our Selection*, however, depict but one small-farmer stereotype, located in New South Wales and pastoral Queensland; later small farmers in Victoria and South Australia fared much better (see chapter 10), but in general terms Australia was more suited to grazing and New Zealand to more intensive agriculture on the British model. In Australia and the southern half of New Zealand wool was king and pastoralism, uncivilized in Wakefieldian ideas, promised fortunes for squatters who secured their runs early.

Even for those with capital, the Australian soil and 'the tyranny of distance' frustrated the search for viable crops. Expensive irrigation schemes were nec-essary for small arable farming and worked only in limited areas, so that close settlement arrived late. Some crops, like wheat, proved successful for small farmers, in the wheat belt of Victoria and South Australia, but even productive farms had no future unless their produce could be exported. Only wool over-came these obstacles before refrigeration, because of the wool clip's 'ability to master the problems of distance'. Wool was one of the few crops which inland Australia could produce profitably, and conditions were ideal: good climate and seemingly boundless grass, and few predators. Above all, the high price of wool in England repaid its transport. By weight, wool was more lucrative than any other crop: it fetched ten times the same weight of wheat. Still, Australia was on the other side of the world to the big markets, which granted United States wool a huge advantage. The costs of freight helped to shape Australian wool as an industry which 'funnelled great wealth into few hands'.[30]

Wool did not prevail at once. In 1800 John Macarthur bought an extra 1,400 sheep from a departing colleague to add to his existing flock of 600, and in this stock lay the future of Australian wool industry. These merinos also provided New Zealand's first flocks, shipped from Sydney. Macarthur's genius was as a visionary and a publicist. His case to British manufacturers won him Privy Council support for a grant of 500 (plus a further 500) acres to promote fine-wool sheep. He also bought seven rams and three ewes from the royal stock which he exported illegally. Time was on his side; the Napoleonic Wars increased demand for merino wool, but even such advantages offered no immediate success. Wool required large capital to buy flocks, to survive while wool travelled to market, to pay workers and merchants. A pastoralist had to be 'a small capitalist' to begin with.[31] The promise was realized in the 1820s; yet as late as 1833, whaling remained New South Wales's main export industry. From 1830 to 1850, the expansion of pastoralism was the most important factor in the colonies' development. By 1850, wool had become a staple.

The invasion of inland pastures was swift. Pastoralists asserted their claims on land by squatting, where they erected shepherds' huts and sheep yards on scattered parts of their runs, often at the expense of competitors – other squatters, then selectors – who were hemmed in or cut off from water, and moved on to new land. Pastoral expansion was not orderly, but 'more like a gold rush'. Proclamations of 1826 and 1829 setting limits of settlement were widely ignored. As there was no means of policing, occupation practically meant possession. Squatters' grievances centred on the insecurity of their tenure, and they claimed first option to purchase should the crown put their runs to sale.[32] They were encouraged by crown rulings granting them such rights, and 14-year leases. While sheep numbers grew in Victoria and New South Wales, pastoralists set sights on new frontiers. By 1850, sheep grazed 200 miles inland, from Brisbane to Adelaide and beyond.[33]

Land came to provide governments with more revenue than all other taxes. It also raised the credit profile of the colonies, ensuring large loans by British lenders, reassured by 'kingdoms of unsold land'. However, squatters stumbled when they had either to buy their cheap crown lease, or lose the land. By the 1850s many pastoralists needed to borrow funds for their ordinary operations, just like small farmers. Under the New South Wales Lien on Wool and Livestock Act of 1843, and the New Zealand Wool and Oil Securities Act of 1858, they gained the ability to borrow on the strength of a future wool clip, or mortgage their livestock. A move towards freehold was promoted by laws in the 1860s and 1870s. Perhaps surprisingly, banks were reluctant to lend money to pastoralists either in Australia or in New Zealand, largely because of their conservative lending traditions.[34] Only in the 1860s did banks become large lenders to rural producers. Pastoralists had little business knowledge, and their homes were far from the information and financial services they needed. In this predicament they turned to stock and station agents, firms which gave them access to information, and the benefit of economies of scale in financial, technical and marketing services.

ISLAND PLANTATIONS AND CO-OPERATIVES

Tropical conditions modified European enthusiasm for land, since indigenous production was an obvious alternative for generating cargoes. An immediate problem was Islanders' lack of commitment, so that traders had to take pains to encourage regular production, through exchanging whatever the chiefs wanted at the time: cloth, nails, tobacco, alcohol or even firearms.[35] That system still relied on chiefs to mobilize labour, and not every chief was able to deliver. By the 1850s, therefore, some traders were exploring a more direct route to production. The most ambitious was John Higginson, born in Britain, a migrant to Australia, and a settler in New Caledonia in 1859, where he cornered the colony's Australian supplies. For labour, he turned to the New Hebrides, and was disconcerted to find well-established Protestant missions. To forestall annexation of these islands to Britain, he created the Caledonian Company of the New Hebrides and in 1882 set out to buy the islands piece-meal. By 1886 he had paper claims to half the land area, and began to plant settlers who relied on these paper claims. Many Islanders, having no notion of 'selling' land, were outraged when settlers turned up.[36]

Shipping companies were attracted by the expanding commerce of the region as a whole, and some devised new systems of production for the islands. Godeffroy & Sohn of Hamburg arrived from South America in the 1860s, and placed trading agents on islands throughout the Pacific. They bought land in Samoa and laid out plantations which were tended by indentured workers. Ballande of Bordeaux also created a chain of retail outlets and began to recruit labourers (from French Indochina). The coastal shipping firm Burns Philp & Co. also expanded from Queensland into island trade. As in Australia and New Zealand, a key question was a staple crop. In Samoa, Godeffroys raised cotton to take advantage of the shortage resulting from the American Civil War. So did Australians and New Zealanders who took up land in Fiji under the patronage of chiefs. When the cotton bubble burst, coconuts stood alone. Copra had become an industrial raw material (displacing whale oil); it needed less labour than other crops; and labour rather than land was the great constraint to production.[37]

Copra need not be grown on plantations. In the Tongan national narrative the king travels the world and plans the future of his realm.[38] His perceptions of New South Wales provide the negative example which shapes the new Tongan economy:

> [He] could not understand how there could be homeless and poverty-stricken people in a land as large and obviously rich as Australia ... [and] determined that such an appalling situation should never be allowed to arise in Tonga. The King was also very impressed with the leasehold system which he saw in Sydney, and he made up his mind that the land in Tonga should be distributed among his own people along similar lines.
>
> This appears to have been the origin of King George's idea of legislating for the individual ownership of land – a revolutionary change in the system of land tenure in Tonga. The prohibition of the sale of land which appeared in Clause II of the 1862 Code was only a legislation of customary land tenure, but the notion of individual ownership of land by leasehold was something quite new.[39]

The king allotted estates to chiefly dynasties, and provided that every adult male could claim enough land to sustain a family. That regime suited the small population and the conditions of the nineteenth century, and ran out of land only in the next century.

This 'peasant' production which allowed people to retain their land and some of their independence suited many islanders and would have satisfied many more, but traders and settlers and their governments placed more faith in settler initiatives and plantations. Some nascent governments (like Tonga's) banned or limited land sales, and so did the British regime in Fiji, but more often land was transferred and the development of plantations was limited more by labour and climatic difficulties. Michel Panoff compares these imperial land policies, and concludes that

> where the French government was implicitly colluding with planters...its German counterpart [in New Guinea] in all good conscience was declaring and trying to implement a system geared to reducing the New Guinean to powerlessness and exploiting his work in the extreme.[40]

In most of the Island Pacific it was relatively easy to gain paper title to land. To build on these claims was a different matter: if it happened at all, it required protracted struggle. The exception to the island rule was the *grande terre* of New Caledonia. While most land on the smaller islands of the group remained in the hands of their original owners,[41] Kanak on the main island were dispossessed of most of the land. Working from quite different principles than Australian and New Zealand settlers, French officials would achieve just as comprehensive a feat of land appropriation.[42]

LAND, SOVEREIGNTY AND WAR

Until the 1960s, scholars assumed that the New Zealand wars of the 1860s between settlers and Maori were fought over land, a thesis which Belich dismisses as a 'legend'. Since the 1980s, most – Pakeha – historians have argued that these were wars of sovereignty.[43] This shift occurred in the context of Maori renaissance and land claims to the Waitangi Tribunal, resulting in settlements to redress breaches by the crown (see chapter 17). In that context also, it became clear that the 'New Zealand Wars' or 'Maori Wars' are described more fairly as Britanno-Maori Wars. Recent research suggests that the wars in Taranaki in 1860 and Waikato in 1863 were attempts to destroy Maori autonomy (*mana motuhake*).[44] They represented a conflict of aspirations, between British myths of empire and Maori expectations of retaining *te tino rangatiratanga* (chieftainship) over their territories.[45]

The argument for land begins with the perception that the aim of British land policy was to secure land for settlers, who would accept no pause in frontier expansion. Governor Gore Browne in 1859 observed that only 7 of 26 million acres in the North Island had been bought. With weight of numbers, the settlers' progress was not to be checked by an inferior race: 'the Europeans covet these lands and are determined to enter in and possess them'.[46] On this view, settlement drove the desire for Maori autonomy, in order to keep the land.[47]

In the 1850s, pastoralism signalled the future, as in Australia. Two-thirds of New Zealand had been sold by 1861, mainly in the South Island, where Grey acquired huge tracts, like the Kemp purchase of 20 million acres in 1848, for the Canterbury settlement. South Island purchases using the crown right of pre-emption were completed by 1864. By contrast, less than a quarter of the North Island had been sold by 1861.[48] By then settlers outnumbered Maori, but most of them lived on the fringe of Maoridom, in Wellington, Auckland and the South Island. To advance into the North Island's richest farmland, it was necessary to take up arms.

Tracts of the South Island were a grasslands frontier and the few Maori (relative to the North) were no obstacle to pastoralism. Vast blocks were secured by purchase, if fraudulently. In the North Island there was much less grassland, it was under Maori control, and pastoralism was constrained.[49] The first pastoralists in the Wairarapa from the 1840s, and in Hawkes Bay, relied on leases from Maori owners. Leases were seen as a stumbling block to sales because of the incomes they provided Maori. (All leases in Australia were from the crown, not from Aboriginal people.) Over 32 million acres were sold between 1846 and 1853.[50] On the Maori side there were feuds between land sellers and those who declined to sell, and opposition mounted. On the settler side, demand was rising. The government had a vested interest in revenue from the sale to settlers of land bought cheaply from Maori.

The outbreak of war in Taranaki in 1860–1 was more clearly over land than was the Waikato war of 1863. In Taranaki, the Waitara block was offered for sale by a junior chief, Te Teira, and the government made a down-payment. Wiremu Kingi, a *rangatira*, refused, asserting that Teira had no right of sale. Kingi's people interfered with the survey, and war resulted. The issue arose because New Plymouth settlers had access to very little land, and were suffering a decline in agricultural prices. They aspired to large-scale pastoralism; and they coveted coastal land occupied by Maori.

This was no simple struggle between Pakeha and Maori, and the Waitara block became part of the currency of rivalry within Maoridom. Although the land looked empty, Maori returned as settlers arrived. Governor Gore Browne did not consult widely, and determined on his own to apply a new system of purchase, dealing with Maori at Waitara as individuals. In any event Kingi, as chief, should have been consulted: he dwelt on the disputed land, and so had native title to it. Teira and Kingi had already quarrelled over a woman, and Teira was seeking revenge.[51] Similarly, the Kingitanga or Maori King movement (see chapter 9), against whom Governor Grey and the British army went to war in 1863, arose within tribes which opposed the sale of land. The wars started because the government 'programme' for Maori land became 'stuck', so Grey tried to circumvent the chiefs and their authority; but his strategy backfired.

The contrary argument is that resistance to land sales was the most effective way for Maori to demonstrate their sovereignty.[52] The invasion of the Waikato in 1863–4 in essence was a government response to the Kingitanga,

Plate 6.1 Bust of Queen Victoria, Ohinemutu, Rotorua. Courtesy of the Rotorua Museum of Art and History, Te Whare Taonga O Te Arawa, Rotorua, New Zealand.

whose militants had sent support to Taranaki, providing an excuse to punish the Waikato tribes. This pan-tribal assertion of Maori autonomy could not be tolerated. Belich argues that the Kingitanga revealed that the British empire over Maori was false, so it had to be quashed, and this could only be achieved by conquest.[53] The exertion of *mana* over land was prominent in the Waikato war. The British army deliberately crossed the stream that marked the Kingite boundary in 1863; and both sides understood that the invasion challenged *mana Maori*.[54] From the Waikato viewpoint, this violated their treaty rights.

Where Maori power endured, Maori definitions of land sales and residual rights persisted. When the balance of power shifted, Pakeha definitions prevailed. 'Like empire itself, land sales could be myths on maps' – pen and paper again – until Maori customary use came to an end.[55] Further, there was no overall shortage of land for Pakeha: millions of acres were sold to the crown by 1860, mostly in the South Island. If the wars were over land, why was it necessary to exert formal empire and send 18,000 British troops to fight 5,000 Maori?[56] War had its supporters further afield, including the Australian colonies. On this view the motive for war was not greed for land but determination to force Maori to submit – to destroy their *mana motuhake*.[57]

We need not reject either argument totally. In 1967 Alan Ward challenged the land-hunger thesis, judging that the wars had multiple causes, including fear, racism, and a desire to attack the independent power of Maori because of the settlers' inability to rule in Maori zones; that is, sovereignty. The wars also embodied the idea of civilizing Maori through amalgamation, so that Maori would not be exterminated like Aboriginal Australians.[58] An explanation which considers land and sovereignty as inseparable has much explanatory power. It is anachronistic to separate the land from the people, so that contests for land were inevitably contests for *mana*.[59] Orange sees the issue in the Taranaki war, over the sale of Waitara land, as *rangatiratanga* (guaranteed in the Maori version of the treaty). Correspondingly, from a settler – and imperial – point of view, sovereignty was the issue,[60] but this could not be separated from the land in dispute, as the term *rangatiratanga* itself suggests.

Belich's conception of Maori and Pakeha zones is useful here. Maori stayed largely in control of the North Island until 1863, while the Pakeha zone grew through the alienation of land. Conversely, Maori assertion of authority to veto land sales suggested an exercise of sovereign power.[61] It is significant that the governor initiated war in Taranaki and Waikato, since these were Maori zones which did not need to sell land to engage in economic exchange with Pakeha.[62]

The significance of postwar *land confiscation* cannot be overstated. The expropriation of millions of acres after responsible government reinforces both the land and sovereignty arguments. The wars themselves were inconclusive. Effective power shifted from Maori to Pakeha in the North Island with confiscations and individualized title to land through the Native Land Court. Each helped settler governments to seize control of land.[63] Maori rights as British subjects and individuals were invoked in the causes of civilization and releasing their grip on land desired for settlement. The New Zealand Settlements Act of 1863 conferred the power to take land for public purposes. Land was forfeit and became crown land if its owners were thought to be in rebellion. Nearly 3,250,000 acres were confiscated in the Waikato, the Bay of Plenty and Taranaki, although some was eventually paid for or returned. The Waikato *iwi* lost almost all their lands, while Ngati Maniapoto, their allies, escaped unscathed. In Taranaki, the later confiscation of the entire coastal strip – the best farming land – left a deep sense of injustice.[64] Confiscated land was allotted to military settlers, many recruited from the Australian gold fields and rewarded with land for their war effort. Confiscations fell unevenly, on friendly and opposing tribes. The government mistook and muddled groups and the best land was taken, irrespective of the allegiances of its owners. Much land alienated after the wars actually belonged to *kupapa* (loyal) tribes.

By the time of the Native Land Acts of 1862 and 1865, and the creation of a Native Land Court, Maori had become a minority. While *terra nullius* marginalized Aboriginal Australians, Maori found their title extinguished despite the supposed guarantees of the treaty. After the wars, the purpose of the Native Land Acts was to extinguish native title. From 1865 Maori had to apply to the Native Land Court to justify claims to their own land, and the court converted customary land rights into crown title which Maori could then sell or lease. The new forms of 'individualized' title – assigned to a list of owners, limited to a few named individuals – broke collective control on sales. With no protection of customary title in the Native Land Court, there would be no protection in the courts generally – leading to the Prendergast judgement of 1877.[65] Individualizing title had two purposes: to make land available for settler purchase in the North Island, outside the confiscation areas; and to civilize Maori by detribalizing them. The public works of the 1870s aimed to accelerate these processes. The entrepreneurial state depended on diminishing Maori *mana* (see chapter 9) and that meant Maori *mana* over land. On the other hand, politically *kupapa* shared in the postwar settlement: they were bought off with four seats in parliament in 1867 (for *kupapa* tribes), and representation in the Legislative Council. On the other side, confiscations fuelled the drive for self-determination among *iwi* which lost their land.

LAND AND DESTINIES

Indigenous and settler alike, these were all agrarian societies: almost all would remain so for generations, and none could imagine land losing its importance. A century after these events, it is almost impossible to imagine the economic importance of land to its owners and claimants, much less its cultural mass and its centrality to their identity. If colonists believed that their perspectives were rational – or at least more rational than those of indigenes – they were no less emotional. Land was often the subject of collective as well as individual and family narratives, therefore many narratives are combative and contentious.

The experiences of Maori and Pakeha in New Zealand, and Kanak and settlers in New Caledonia, are impossible to comprehend except in the context of struggles over land, and we address this elsewhere in this book. In Australia, the financial success and expansion of pastoralism were matched by the development of the *terra nullius* doctrine, so that ideology and economy reinforced each other: Australia belonged to those who exploited it most profitably. Commercial farming and pastoralism flourished at the expense of Aborigines and at great cost to the land; but these dimensions of rural history were obscured by the dazzling narrative of wool. The dominant narratives pivoted on long struggles between large-scale squatters and small-scale selectors.

Struggles for land had military, legislative and economic dimensions, but they also involved competing narratives. One was of natural abundance, an Arcadian myth in New Zealand, and in Australia too at first. This story endorsed visions dredged from a mythic Anglo-Celtic past of sturdy yeomen and their families, small farmers practising husbandry (and who were husbands), who would become ideal Australians and New Zealanders. Given opportunities for landed independence by nature's bounty and their own industry, this farming stock would fulfil Everyman's – and his Woman's – dream by transforming Australasia into gardens. There could be no more powerful symbol of colonizing the earth than a garden, grown from imported stock and seed. This could be a small farm (an agricultural garden) or a suburban lot, expressing domesticity in geographic terms; and equal opportunity, or fairness. In such complex explanations, rather than F. J. Turner's thesis of free land on the expanding frontier, Miles Fairburn discerns the individualism in the culture of nineteenth-century Pakeha New Zealand, resonating in a political emphasis on self-reliance.[66]

New Zealand learned to deploy Arcadian imagery in defining itself against 'dry' Australia. As New Zealand's federation commissioners of 1901 smugly justified New Zealand's choice not to become a state of Australia: the worthy commissioners,

> with their knowledge of the soil, climate, and productiveness of New Zealand, of the adaptability of the lands of the colony for close settlement, of her vast natural resources, her immense wealth in forest, in mine, and natural scenery, of the energy of her people, of the abundant rainfall and vast waterpower she possesses, of her insularity and geographical position; remembering, too, that New Zealand ... can herself supply all that can be required to support and maintain ... a population which might at no distant date be worthily styled a nation, have unanimously arrived at the conclusion that ... New Zealand should not sacrifice her independence as a separate colony.[67]

Arcadianism proved its own enemy when natural abundance did not produce a promised land. This powerful myth encouraged people to believe that when they acquired property it was because of their virtue and respectability, not because the state enabled them to do so.[68]

Another narrative is evoked in the phrase 'pioneer legend'.[69] 'Pioneer' appeared early in New Zealand, Victoria and South Australia and (like the related Arcadianism) supported a rather conservative centre of gravity in politics. Pioneer myths celebrated settlers as heroes for their manly virtues of courage, enterprise, hard work and perseverance. Pioneers made a path for others. They tamed the land and wrote their names on it, obliterating indigenous names and legends. Explorers entered the pioneer pantheon as the first and most adventurous pioneers, from Captain Cook to Australia's Burke and Wills and New Zealand's Sir Edmund Hillary. While feminist scholars challenge the masculinism of this colonization by male archetype, pioneer mythology was and is friendlier to women (and babies) than legends of solitary rural males, at least allowing women a place as helpmeet (New Zealand) or helpmate (Australia), and babies a place as the first 'native-born' citizens.

Pioneering, like Arcadia, has trouble with constructions of culture and identity in peopled lands, and resolves this through colonialism: by controlling, ordering and cultivating a strange environment, including the indigenous people, and representing the newcomers as pioneers of civilization.

A more successful rival for the pioneer legend in Australia is the 'bush legend' (or 'Australian legend') which also lurks in Kiwi culture, and which Russel Ward codified.[70] The legend which shaped the search for a national identity in Ward's mind centred on the bush, and was built around itinerant single men rather than settler family men, pastoral workers who moved from colony to colony in shearing gangs and who seemed to outsiders to be a 'nomad tribe'.[71] Bushmen saw themselves as heirs to Aboriginal Australians in their bush skills, but these white Australians (and New Zealanders) could also shoot and ride. The bush ethos grew from the quest to 'master' a strange environment. It is an invented tradition, for which the 'founding fathers' were the convicts. Ward's bushman was egalitarian, a good 'mate', anti-authoritarian, practical, an improviser, and racist. A strong Irish influence pervaded the Australian version. This manly stereotype was brutal to Aborigines but not to Maori. Once Aborigines ceased to be a threat, and joined ancient (and deceased) Maori warriors, folk memory could acknowledge a debt to them.

This bush legend celebrated a model of masculinity embodied in the wandering bushman, who preferred not to have his independence sapped by family ties.[72] It grew from pastoralism, bolstered by a masculine convict heritage. Ned Kelly as cultural hero slotted comfortably into the legend. Ned the bushranger, the ultimate 'wild colonial boy', was on the run with the Kelly gang from 1878–80, precisely when a radical nationalist school of thought and writing was digging in. Young, single, male, nomadic, native-born, the son of convict Irish 'Red' Kelly, anti-establishment and anti-English, hostile to corrupt police and the squattocracy, he feared only the Aboriginal trackers who helped the police to capture him.[73] Ned lives as a quintessential Australian folk hero in ballads, songs, art and heritage tourism. Elevated to icon by his hanging (on Melbourne Cup Day in 1880) he captured the public imagination about what it meant to be Australian. Women loved him: a splendid bushman, 'flash' and gallant, loyal to his wronged mother, he became a media idol with his antics and flair for eluding bumbling authorities and because of the belief that he was not given a 'fair go'. Represented as unique in national narratives, he possessed all the traits of a 'non-unique' popular culture hero, identified internationally as the 'social bandit'.[74]

Pastoral New Caledonia produced real bandits by denying ex-convicts the right to go home or the possibility of employment: they did not lend themselves to myth. New Zealand produced no equivalent larrikin (though Barry Crump tried to assume the bushman persona in the 1960s): it peopled the land with respectable heroes and heroines, befitting its emphasis on settling the land and the extra meaning accorded to 'settler'. Conversely, decolonization in a settler society (see chapter 18) would require the displacement of the stereotypes of the 'lone hand' or 'man alone', and the 'pioneer'.

NOTES

1 David Day, *Claiming a Continent: A History of Australia*, Sydney, 1996, 109–10.
2 T. Brooking, *Lands for the People?*, Dunedin, 1996, ch. 8; and ' "Busting Up" the Greatest Estate of All: Liberal Maori Land Policy, 1891–1911', *New Zealand Journal of History*, 26 (1) (April 1992); P. J. Gibbons, 'Non Fiction', in Terry Sturm (ed.), *Oxford History of New Zealand Literature in English*, Auckland, 1998; A. Parsonson, 'The Challenge to Mana Maori', in G. W. Rice (ed.), *Oxford History of New Zealand*, Auckland, 1992, 167–98; James Belich, *Making Peoples*, Auckland, 1996, 258; Harry C. Evison, *Te Wai Pounamu: The Greenstone Island*, Christchurch, 1993; I. H. Kawharu (ed.), *Waitangi: Maori and Pakeha Perspectives of the Treaty of Waitangi*, Auckland, 1989, 172. The process of Maori land loss is mapped in Alan Ward, *An Unsettled History*, Wellington, 1999, 162–6.
3 For example, William Satchell, *The Toll of the Bush*, London, 1905.
4 Friends of the Turnbull Library (eds), *Edward Gibbon Wakefield and the Colonial Dream: A Reconsideration*, Wellington, 1997.
5 Eric Olssen, 'Wakefield and the Scottish Enlightenment, with particular reference to Adam Smith and his *Wealth of Nations*', in Turnbull Library, *Wakefield and the Colonial Dream*, Wellington, 1997.
6 R. Dalziel, 'Men, Women and Wakefield', and N. Love, 'Edward Gibbon Wakefield: A Maori Perspective', in Turnbull Library, *Wakefield and the Colonial Dream*, 6, 83–4.
7 Michael Roe, *Australia, Britain, and Migration, 1915–1940: A Study of Desperate Hopes*, Melbourne, 1995, 84.
8 Ibid., 88–9.
9 New Zealand gained representative government, and established a provincial system, under the 1852 Constitution Act, when it adopted a property vote for British adult males. See W. D. McIntyre and W. J. Gardner (eds), *Speeches and Documents on New Zealand History*, Oxford, 1971, 73–84. On Australia, see J. Hirst, 'Constitutions', in G. Davison, J. Hirst and S. Macintyre (eds), *Oxford Companion to Australian History*, Melbourne, 1998, 153–4.
10 Tim Rowse, *After Mabo: Interpreting Indigenous Traditions*, Melbourne, 1994.
11 A. Fleras, 'Politicising Indigeneity', in P. Havemann (ed.), *Indigenous People's Rights in Australia, Canada & New Zealand*, Auckland, 1999, 213.
12 K. Sinclair, 'Why are Race Relations in New Zealand Better than in South Africa, South Australia, or South Dakota?', *New Zealand Journal of History*, 5: 2 (Oct. 1971), 121–7.
13 Henry Reynolds, *Frontier: Aborigines, Settlers and Land*, Sydney, 1987, 133; Reynolds, *The Law of the Land*, 2nd edn, Melbourne, 1992.
14 Frederika Hackshaw, 'Nineteenth-century Notions of Aboriginal Title and their Influence on the Interpretation of the Treaty of Waitangi.' In I. H. Kawharu (ed.), *Waitangi: Maori and Pakeha Perspectives of the Treaty of Waitangi*, Auckland, 1989, 99.
15 See, for example, Ann R. Parsonson, 'The Challenge to Mana Maori', in G. W. Rice (ed.), *Oxford History of New Zealand*, Auckland, 1992, 176–7; Ward, *An Unsettled History*, chs 6 and 7, pp. 162, 165.
16 Reynolds, *Frontier*, 137; *Law of the Land*, 126.
17 Day, *Claiming a Continent*, 111.
18 Wording from Governor Gipps' speech to NSW Legislative Council, 1840, cited in Reynolds, *Frontier*, 137. Gipps made clear that the doctrine of native title 'applied equally to Australia and New Zealand'. See also Reynolds, *Law of the*

Land, 132. The New Zealand Company's purchases are reassessed in Ward, *An Unsettled History*, ch. 5.

19 Reynolds, *Frontier*, 135 and 156; *Law of the Land*, 146.

20 D. V. Williams, 'The Queen v. Symonds Reconsidered', *Victoria University of Wellington Law Review*, 19 (1989): 385–402; C. Orange, *The Treaty of Waitangi*, Wellington, 1987, 128.

21 Hackshaw, 'Nineteenth-century Notions', 110.

22 Parsonson, 'The Challenge to Mana Maori', 193.

23 Hackshaw, 'Nineteenth-century Notions', 101.

24 Parsonson, 'The Challenge to Mana Maori', 193–4.

25 Ward, *A Show of Justice*, 88.

26 Parsonson, 'The Challenge to Mana Maori', 176–7, citing *Ngai Tahu Report, 1991*, Waitangi Tribunal Report (Wai 27), 257–61.

27 Ward, *A Show of Justice*, 88–9.

28 Frank Crowley, *A New History of Australia*, Melbourne, 1974, 50–1.

29 Ibid., 88–9.

30 Geoffrey Blainey, *The Tyranny of Distance*, Melbourne, 1968, 127.

31 Ibid.; Crowley, *Australia*, 30.

32 Blainey, *The Tyranny of Distance*, 131 and 92.

33 Michael Roe, *Australia, Britain, and Migration, 1915–1940: A Study of Desperate Hopes. Studies in Australian History*, ed. Alan Gilbert, Patricia Grimshaw and Peter Spearritt, Melbourne, 1995, 100–1.

34 S. Ville, 'Networks and Venture Capital in the Australasian Pastoral Sector before World War Two', *Business History*, 38: 3 (1996), 48–63.

35 Dorothy Shineberg, *They Came for Sandalwood: A Study of the Sandalwood Trade in the Southwest Pacific, 1830–1865*, Melbourne, 1967.

36 Joel Bonnemaison, *The Tree and the Canoe: History and Ethnogeography of Tanna*, Honolulu, 1994, ch. 3.

37 Quoted in Doug Munro and Stewart Firth, 'Company Strategies – Colonial Policies', in Clive Moore, Jacqueline Leckie and Doug Munro (eds), *Labour in the South Pacific*, Townsville, 1990, 6.

38 Sione Lātūkefu, *Church and State in Tonga*, Canberra, 1974, 61–2.

39 Ibid., 162–3.

40 Michel Panoff, 'The French Way in Plantation Systems', *Journal of Pacific History*, 26 (1991), 206–12.

41 Kerry Howe, *The Loyalty Islands: A History of Culture Contact 1840–1900*, Canberra, 1977.

42 R. Gerard Ward and Elizabeth Kingdon (eds), *Land, Custom and Practice in the South Pacific*, Melbourne, 1995.

43 For example, J. Belich, *The New Zealand Wars and the Victorian Interpretation of Racial Conflict*, Auckland, 1986, esp. 298–310; Orange, *The Treaty of Waitangi*; Hazel Riseborough, *Days of Darkness: Taranaki 1878–1884*, Wellington, 1989.

44 Parsonson, 'The Challenge to Mana Maori'; Orange, *The Treaty of Waitangi*. Sovereignty has been a key word in Maori politics and land claims since the 1980s. (In 1979 Matiu Rata, who established the Waitangi Tribunal, left the Labour Party to found a political party, Mana Motuhake, which is now part of the Alliance.)

45 Belich, *New Zealand Wars*, 304; Orange, *Treaty of Waitangi*. Note the context of the reinvention (or discovery) of the treaty as a social compact.

46 K. Sinclair, *The Origins of the Maori Wars*, Auckland, 1976, 44–5, 123.

47 For example, K. Sinclair, *A History of New Zealand*, revd edn, Auckland, 1980, 117.

48 James Belich, *Making Peoples: A History of the New Zealanders from Polynesian Settlement to the End of the Nineteenth Century*, Auckland, 1996, 228.
49 B. J. Dalton, *War and Politics in New Zealand, 1855–1870*, Sydney, 1967, 3.
50 Belich, *Making Peoples*, 225.
51 See, for example, Parsonson, 'The Challenge to Mana Maori', 182–3.
52 Dalton, *War and Politics in New Zealand*, 62.
53 Belich, *Making Peoples*, 234.
54 See, for example, Orange, *The Treaty of Waitangi*, 164–5.
55 Belich, *Making Peoples*, 226.
56 Numbers from ibid., 241.
57 Riseborough, *Days of Darkness*, viii.
58 A. Ward, 'The Origins of the Anglo-Maori Wars: A Reconsideration', *New Zealand Journal of History*, 1: 2 (1967), 148–70.
59 M. P. K. Sorrenson, 'Maori and Pakeha', in W. H. Oliver and B. R. Williams (eds), *Oxford History of New Zealand*, Wellington, 1981, 148.
60 Claudia Orange, *The Treaty of Waitangi*, Wellington, 1987, 144, 155.
61 Belich, *The New Zealand Wars*, 298–310.
62 Waikato engaged from a distance in trade with Auckland, by canoe, while both Waikato and Taranaki people established flour mills. See Belich, *Making Peoples*, 216–17.
63 Parsonson, 'The Challenge to Mana Maori', 186, 190.
64 Orange, *The Treaty of Waitangi*, 170, 172; Riseborough, *Days of Darkness*, 17–18.
65 Parsonson, 'The Challenge to Mana Maori', 187, 190–3. For Native Land Acts detail see Ward, *An Unsettled History*, ch. 8.
66 M. Fairburn, *The Ideal Society and its Enemies*, Auckland, 1989; cf. J. Mansfield Thomson (ed.), *Farewell Colonialism*, Palmerston North, 1998.
67 *Federation Commission Report*, xxiv.
68 Fairburn, *Ideal Society*, 236, 265, 270.
69 See, for example, J. B. Hirst, 'The Pioneer Legend', *Historical Studies*, 18: 71 (1978), 316–37; J. Phillips, *A Man's Country? The Image of the Pakeha Male – A History*, Auckland, 1987.
70 R. Ward, *The Australian Legend*, Melbourne, 1st edn 1958; 2nd edn 1966; 3rd edn 1978. For a summary see R. Ward, 'The Australian Legend Re-visited', *Historical Studies*, 18 (71), 171–90. Ward's influence can be seen in Phillips, *A Man's Country?* Feminist critiques and complications of Ward are discussed in chapter 10 of this volume.
71 Ward took this term from Anthony Trollope, travelling in the outback in the 1870s, who used it to describe pastoral workers. Ward, *Australian Legend*, 2nd edn, 9.
72 Marilyn Lake, 'The Politics of Respectability: Identifying the Masculinist Context', *Historical Studies*, 22: 86 (April 1986), 116–31. See ch. 10, this volume.
73 Ward, *Australian Legend*, ch. 6; also White, *Inventing Australia*.
74 E. J. Hobsbawm, *Bandits*, London, 1969.

[7] MINING

The main traits of the legendary bushman were already fixed in the Australian imaginary by 1851, ready to be exported to neighbours in the Pacific. If anything, according to Russel Ward, the discovery of gold delayed the emergence of a bush ethos as national legend. Other scholars, however, surmise that gold transmitted the values of the outback to new immigrants, maintaining that the dominant memory of the gold rushes in Australia and New Zealand extends pioneer and bush mythology, the lone hand and male mateship.[1] To avoid looking like a 'new chum', gold seekers adopted bush characteristics, such as the hat worn by shearers, stockworkers and diggers. Either way, gold is linked to the bush legend through pastoralism, which paved the way for mining.

Often shepherds and station hands found minerals and became diggers themselves. Although the sheep lands proved richer in gold than copper, it was harder to find gold than the bright blue and green copper lodes. A sheep station at Wallaroo, South Australia, yielded the first copper discovery, and the Adelaide merchants who financed its mining formed the 'great pastoral house' of Elder, Smith and Co.[2] Despite such linkages, Turner's frontier thesis, which would embrace both bushman and digger as frontier types, does little to illumine mining in our region.[3] And all that glisters is not gold in understanding mining's regional heritage. Indeed digger myth, sometimes mingled with bush narratives, has obscured and distorted mining history. One reason is the uniformity of tough masculine labour, celebrated in the nineteenth century: the miner's costume resembled that of the typical bushman, as far as boots and hat. We begin with gold, in order to deconstruct the traditions, long claimed to be national, which have so long and so powerfully contributed to narratives populated by masculine archetypes which obscure the fashioning of distinctive regional and local identities.

The discovery of gold at Sutter's Mill in California in 1848 launched half a century of rushes on the frontiers of European settlement, from California and the Yukon to Ballarat, Kalgoorlie, New Zealand, New Guinea and the Witwatersrand. Most discoveries were made in regions where states were recent, weak or absent; and they were made by individual prospectors or small syndicates, mainly European but including some Chinese. These instant communities created their own rules and conventions until the state could impose its laws, and some traditions lasted much longer. Prominent among prospectors and miners were hard-rock men from the declining Cornish tin mines, bringing with them their traditions of team-work and ore-management. Most rushes were brief, and few gave rise to durable industries and communities, so the discoveries sustained a mobile community of men whose lives were transient, unreasonably optimistic and usually disappointed.

News of gold in California prompted the first rush of fortune seekers – the forty-niners. The Australasian colonies were among the first and most affected, as California was several weeks closer to Sydney and Auckland than to New York or Europe, so long as Cape Horn was the shortest route from the Atlantic to the Pacific. The American experience gave Australians and New Zealanders a taste of their future: Sydney became a major supply base for California, for everything from 'pickles to prefabricated houses', as well as many of California's alleged criminals and the worthies who accused and arrested them.[4] It is no accident that E. H. Hargraves, who sparked the gold rushes in Australia, had seen the early phase in California, and combed similar terrain in New South Wales. He was rewarded with occasional specks, but the Cornish Tom brothers who met up with him discovered 'payable gold' near Bathurst, at Ophir, named for the biblical city.[5] The frenzy shifted rapidly to Victoria, with a sequence of alluvial finds at Bendigo and Castlemaine and deposits in buried streams at Ballarat and Creswick in 1853–4, dug by deep mining. The rushes then headed to northern Victoria and New Zealand, with diggers following gold across the Pacific and the Tasman.

As whole new populations dispossessed and displaced others, Californian and Australian goldfields flourished amazingly. Between 1851 and 1860, the United States produced over 40 per cent of the world's gold output, most of it from California; the white population mushroomed and Native Americans dwindled to one in six. Over the same period Australia produced 39 per cent of the world's gold, most of it from Victoria, whose settler population also burgeoned.[6] Its goldfields hosted 150,000 people at their peak in 1858, including 40,000 Chinese. Victoria's indigenous population also melted away, but not without resistance. In 1856 the French consul's wife in Melbourne, Celeste de Chabrillan, wrote: 'The woods are on fire every night. The blacks set them alight in retaliation for being driven away.'[7]

Gabriel Read, a Tasmanian, struck gold in New Zealand's South Island in 1861, at a spot memorialized as 'Gabriel's Gully'. Otago, and then the West Coast, became an extension of the Australian mining frontier, and ships from Victoria were crowded with forty-niners. In 1862, an American and an Irishman found gold in the Cromwell Gorge. More gold glittered in the Arrow River, and the Shotover near Queenstown, now famous for its white water.[8] Two Maori made the lucky strike in the Shotover River, helped by serendipity in rescuing a stranded dog.[9] Mineral wealth – *pounamu*, greenstone – led Maori to the West Coast, while gold led the Pakeha; two Maori unearthing a greenstone boulder in a creek in 1864 found the gold that triggered the West Coast gold rush.[10]

In the newer frontier historiography, a frontier is not a line but a zone, the site of cross-cultural encounter and interaction. Gold did open frontiers in Queensland and the Northern Territory, and to some extent Western Australia, but mining frontiers were cosmopolitan, and the frontier part of metropolitan culture; hence the place of the metropolis in mining frontier societies, represented by 'Marvellous Melbourne' and, on a smaller scale, gold rush Dunedin. The rushes turned Melbourne into 'a second San Francisco' which eclipsed Sydney as the centre of commerce and culture until the end of the century.[11] In brick and stone, elaborate gold rush architecture reflected identities often as superficial and gaudy as the rushes they symbolized.

Australia's major non-coastal centres stemmed directly or indirectly from gold. Ballarat is the largest of five cities and towns (the others being Bendigo, Castlemaine, Stawell and Ararat) which still dominate central Victoria. Rather than becoming ghost towns, these consolidated from canvas shanties to wood, brick and stone. Agriculture and an industrial base conferred a sense of permanency. According to Weston Bate, Victoria's 36 gold towns, with a population of 146,000 in 1871, were 'almost as powerful socially and culturally as Melbourne' with 191,000. While this understates Melbourne's emergence as a world city, Bate notes the different regional identities: an urban myth of 'Marvellous Melbourne' proved powerful in Victoria, while the bush myth later claimed for the nation centred on Sydney.[12] Some gold towns survive only as museum pieces. The towns built on or beside holes in the ground endure, such as Ballarat, Ross and Waihi, while others from the alluvial phase are ghost towns, unless converted to fishing, agriculture or tourism, or reconstructed, like the West Coast invention of 'Shantytown', and the recreated Sovereign Hill at Ballarat.

The image of a 'Ballarat beyond the desert sands' found its way into Ibsen's play *Love's Comedy*. Some men of letters made more than a mental migration. William Howitt, 60-year-old author of *Visits to Remarkable Places*, the poet Richard Henry Horne, and the sculptor Thomas Woolner were part of the gold rush that California began and Ballarat consolidated. Overnight, gold turned Australia into a frontier of opportunity, an alternative to the United States for British migrants, and their preferred destination throughout the 1850s. Half a million came to Australia, or one in every 50 in the British Isles.[13] The Australian settler population almost trebled in the 1850s, from 405,400 to 1,145,600.[14] Victoria absorbed most. Gold also generated huge imbalances as men outnumbered women by three to one, and five to one among the itinerants who followed the lure of gold from Australia to New Zealand, fuelling anxiety about the prospects of new societies, and about the nature of manhood. Australasian colonies responded with campaigns to import women (see chapter 8). The 'excitement' of gold reinforced already competing identities.[15] Would the vision of Arcadia and a settled society prevail over a gaudy exemplar of the free market?

ELDORADO V. ARCADIA

Gold inspired rival dreams of Eldorado and Arcadia. The already settled fretted that gold threatened the maintenance of order, and an ideal society.

Wedded to a yeoman ideal, radicals and conservatives alike feared an 'atomized society', a fear that Fairburn suggests was realized in New Zealand.[16] They worried about the danger of 'excitement', and responded with the first asylums – in Victoria in the 1850s and New Zealand in the 1860s. Both myths were shared with that most triumphant settler society, the United States; but they met different fates in Australia and New Zealand, with variant effects on the formation of identities.

In Otago these rival identities adopted names: the 'Old Identity', of a Wakefieldian New Edinburgh, sombre and sober, competed with the 'New Iniquity' – thousands of adventurous, gambling, whoring, boisterous young men – worse still, who included Catholic Irish and bespoke immorality, in the Kirk's terms. Conversely, the gold miners' songs mocked the 'Old Identity' for their Scots heritage, for wearing kilts in cold Otago, and for being 'dull and slow'.[17] Gold disrupted Arcadian imagery, though in New Zealand its discovery also fed ideas of natural abundance.

The sudden intensity of gold fever confronted all authorities with a crisis of exceptional proportions. What subversive forces would gold unleash, and how to curb them? Governor Gipps's plea to W. B. Clarke who proudly showed him his pieces of gold-bearing quartz suggests great anxiety: 'Put it away, Mr Clarke, or we shall all have our throats cut'.[18] The lure and fear of gold transcended all boundaries. The establishment expressed concern for social order as the labouring classes flocked to the goldfields. Authorities feared lawlessness and violence. By the mid-1850s 'a swarm of traders, entertainers and other camp-followers followed close on the heels of the diggers to every new rush'.[19] Employers lobbied governments to help them to retain labour. The goldfields were in some ways a law unto themselves. Life was disrupted and families split as men took to the fields with their mates, upsetting the pace and colour of life in Sydney, Melbourne, Dunedin and Auckland. California and the Australian colonies therefore created the precedents for dealing with the spectre of anarchy. Concern for order prompted governments to act; in New Zealand they did so before the big rushes. Legislation of 1858 to cover goldfields administration put in place expedients developed in California, Canada and Australia. One, the £1 miner's right from Victoria, became central to Australasian narratives of egalitarianism and democracy.

DIGGER DEMOCRACY

It is often proposed that gold was a 'great leveller'.[20] The hopes of gold were egalitarian, in dreams of riches, and so were practices on the goldfields. The miners who reached New Zealand had 'forged their own democratic traditions in battling autocracy in Victoria'. Uniform was all-important in dressing tradition. If they wore other than the miner's uniform (nugget boots, wide-awake hat and moleskin pants) they risked mockery, especially if they wore a top hat. Charles Thatcher, who followed the rush from Victoria to

"THE COMING MAN."

Plate 7.1 The Coming Man anticipated in *Melbourne Punch*, 13 May 1858, heroic in every respect except the inexplicable head-gear. Courtesy of the National Library of Australia.

Otago in 1862, sang:

On the diggings we're all on a level you know;
The poor man out here ain't oppressed by the rich
But, dressed in blue shirts, you can't tell which is which.[21]

While the gold rushes undoubtedly gave an impetus to early democracy, gold rush narratives and the archetype of the digger himself supply material for both conservative and radical democratic traditions. The individual digger, free, solitary and independent, loathed working for wages.[22] Most who ventured to New Zealand were of modest means, coming from farming, mining and seafaring, occupations which offered scope for enterprise, if fortune allowed. Peter Lalor, Eureka's hero, became a mine owner.[23] The little digger was recruited as easily for the pioneer legend as for the bush legend, and for their rival clusters of identities. But in Australia he acquired his own legend: Eureka Stockade, a miners' rebellion at Ballarat in 1854, persists as a symbol of national identity, as well as a source of identity for Ballarat. The struggle is memorialized in a reconstructed stockade and a nightly re-enactment for tourists at Sovereign Hill's pioneer settlement.[24] According to the federal Labor politician Dr H. V. Evatt in 1940, 'Australian Democracy was Born at Eureka'.[25]

For some, the miners' licence was central to the story. Imported from California, the monthly licence tax on diggers was intensely unpopular. Miners resented it as a means to raise revenue (preferred by the elite to an export duty on gold, which merchants and pastoralists sought to avoid) and as it did not discriminate between the lucky and unlucky, and modes of extraction. The loathed licence came to express the gulf between the diggers and authority, an administration, moreover, which proved inept and corrupt. Blainey argues that Ballarat spawned Eureka because of the nature of the enterprise. Ballarat's deep-lead mining, underground in buried streams, made the licence even more irksome. Others emphasize the poor goldfields administration on one hand, and the Irish element on the other. The Eureka lead was an Irish claim. While Ballarat as a whole enjoyed its best year in 1854, the Eureka lead offered poor returns. In Bate's view,

> Ballarat's deep-sinkings themselves were not as significant as the situation brought about by deep-sinking on part of the field which by chance was Irish. As in an avalanche, the various elements creating tension put weight on each other...a moderate group answered the law and order arguments with claims that the law should be changed to fit altered circumstances.[26]

Outcomes suggest the strength of popular protest. The licence was abolished, goldfields wardens were appointed and the miners won representation in parliament through their miner's right. Serle endorsed Eureka as a 'fight for freedom', just as earlier scholars saw it as a fight for justice. From Eureka flowed constitutional reforms, one man one vote and vote by ballot – in other words, early democracy – that otherwise might have foundered in the Upper House.[27] In the radical democratic, and nationalist, narrative, Eureka was the gold nugget of mateship. It stood for government by the people and led to the 'sweeping away of a whole system of tyrannical goldfields administration', while digger enfranchisement prompted a revision of the new constitution of responsible government in Victoria to provide manhood suffrage.[28]

Eureka unfurled a flag for defiance against authority in the labour movement, and of radical nationalist history. In this narrative, Eureka stood for democracy, anti-authoritarianism, independence, anti-imperialism, republicanism, protest against economic hardship and inequality, egalitarianism, and anti-capitalism. The same issues surfaced in the political battles of the 1890s. No wonder, then, that striking shearers in Queensland in 1891 raised the Eureka flag, for whom Henry Lawson wrote:

So we must fly the rebel flag,
As others did before us ...
They needn't say the fault is ours
If blood should stain the wattle.[29]

In such ways Eureka provided a tradition for Left and Labor politics. Miners, the labour movement, and those of Irish identity elevated Eureka to first place in national mythology in the depressed 1930s – the Communist Party named its youth wing the Eureka Youth League – and again in the Second World War, during the Japanese threat. Above all, it provided an emblem, the rebel flag, the Southern Cross, which has become over-loaded with subsequent invented tradition.

The Eureka legend also provided a narrative (but not a flag) for liberal traditions, because the protest's complex motives allowed multiple inheritances.[30] In this version, Eureka served as a catalyst for a new social compact. Here we should distinguish between the effects of gold and the effects of Eureka. Gold hastened the end of transportation and the decision to grant the Australian colonies responsible government. Eureka did not influence the new constitution of 1856, but it infused the spirit of democracy which informed the laws passed in Victoria's first parliament, securing manhood suffrage, vote by secret ballot and the right of adult men to stand for election to the Legislative Assembly. In this Liberal narrative Victoria developed a distinctive 'liberal-radicalism'. Victoria emerged 'strongly liberal' from the gold rush tradition, ensuring a non-Labor centre of gravity in Victorian politics. In this sense as in others, identity-politics in Victoria resembled those in South Australia and New Zealand more than New South Wales. Locally, Eureka was significant for Ballarat, whose loyal citizens identified strongly as Britons and were proud that their colony was named for Queen Victoria.[31]

This analysis suggests a layering of identities, with the invention of a national tradition (itself turned to diverse purposes) superimposed on local identities of differing political hue. Each group invoked Eureka in its own interests; at Ballarat; to promote Victoria and its heroic past over the (dubious) heritage of New South Wales; and to advance Australian national narratives.

TYPES OF MINING ENTERPRISE

Two intersecting shafts in the mining industry made a peculiar contribution to shaping identities in our region: types of mining enterprise, and ethnicity. Types of enterprise can be arranged in terms of technology and business organization, and in terms of the particular mineral.

First, identities shifted with the transformation from alluvial mining and surface digging to the underground phase, which involved deep-shaft mining. The first alluvial rushes raced across the landscape as diggers came, prospected and moved on. The fast decline in Ophir's gold, half looted after only three months, was typical of the early phase. The nature of alluvial gold shaped a culture of mobility. From tiny pieces to small boulders (nuggets), alluvial gold was mingled with sand, clay or gravel, washed by floods into old river beds. It is the easiest form of gold to mine. Diggers who found this crushed rock in watercourses needed only a pan, a cradle (a wooden box, rocked manually) to separate the heavy gold from the lighter matrix, and picks and shovels.[32] These were supplanted by more sophisticated methods such as sluicing, a technique transported from Victoria to New Zealand. More complicated methods required diggers to organize, for instance in co-operative ownership of miles of water races. At the Tuapeka field in Otago alone there were 542 miles of water races by 1865.[33]

In a short time the wholesale raiding of alluvial gold shifted the focus and nature of gold digging from surface to underground work. The transformation from individual to collective, from small to large enterprise, continued through the 1850s and early 1860s when the last of Victoria's major rushes swept into Gippsland. These alterations gathered momentum after the rushes, when the serious business of mining began, and corporations with new technologies took control.

While alluvial and deep-lead diggings coexisted through the rushes and beyond, the trend was for the alluvial phase to be superseded by a longer, underground, company phase, of hydraulicking, economies of scale and hard-rock mining, and on the remote West Coast of New Zealand's South Island, by dredging rivers. By the late nineteenth century mining had become a business requiring government regulation, technical expertise, capital and wage labour. It encompassed base metals such as copper, lead and zinc, using the latest technologies.[34]

Geology affected organization. Almost all pre-1880 Australian goldfields were set in the younger Palaeozoic rocks of the eastern highlands from Tasmania to North Queensland. Rich in alluvial gold and tin, they were easily mined. At Ballarat, where gold was found in underground streams, the problem was too much water, which had to be pumped out, so miners formed co-operative companies. At Bendigo, they sought outside capital to exploit quartz reefs.[35] Ballarat's community retained control of their mines, which offers another reason for the symbolism of Eureka. Most mining fields after 1880 were in remote places with challenging climates, which incurred large capital outlays. Deep-lead technology, its shafts and tunnels, demanded large leases and large companies. It is from these companies that the returns were greatest. Australia's three largest known metal deposits are all Pre-Cambrian – Broken Hill, Kalgoorlie and Mount Isa – and all were found after 1880.[36]

Technology shaped the environment as well as vice versa. New Zealand became known for the bucket dredge – 150 worked the rivers of the West Coast – where gravel scooped up by a chain of buckets was washed over sluice boxes and tables and the tailings dumped behind the dredge, leaving a landscape of piles of shingle. Australia entered the mainstream of world mining, known around the world for digging holes. Wherever deep-shaft mining began, the landscape was marked by Cornish technology: the beam engine,

engine house, boiler house and chimney stack, and machinery to pump water from deep shafts, tracking ore lodes. Cornish technology and practices were followed by American innovations in metallurgy, and engineers; for example, Broken Hill Proprietary Ltd (BHP) imported experts from the Rocky Mountains in 1886.[37] Similarly at Waihi, 100 km southeast of Auckland, where gold was found in hard-rock quartz reefs, the Waihi Company hired American expertise and technology.[38]

Each kind of deposit bred its peculiar culture and community. Alluvial gold contributed the frenzy of the rushes and the romantic notion of gold as the poor man's friend. While alluvial gold fostered a nomadic community with a get-rich-quick mentality, deep-lead diggings, the norm in most of Victoria in the latter 1850s, were a different story. Diggers camped at alluvial fields, but they lived on deep-lead fields, albeit often in makeshift homes. It was deep-shaft mining which built the solid brick facades of Ballarat. This commitment to one place created different dynamics among resident diggers, between digger and authority, and between digger and land.

Deep-lead diggings – such as Ballarat and Bendigo in Victoria, and Waihi in New Zealand – assumed much longer time frames, which allowed partnerships and alliances to crystallize, and grievances to harden. They also encouraged family life. Women and children made a particular contribution to the culture and life of deep-lead mining communities. Women worked as wives, mothers, diggers, tourists, barmaids, publicans, prostitutes, teachers and domestics. According to the 1861 Victorian census, 129 women were occupied on the goldfields as nurses, 488 as teachers (outnumbering men), 922 in trading, 6,454 (again more than men) in hotel, clothing and domestic work, 935 in agriculture, 136 in gold mining (alongside 78,919 men), and 522 in food and drink; while 63,295 people on the fields were listed as wives and children.[39]

OTHER MINERALS

Other minerals also encouraged family-centred communities and identities. Minerals other than gold proved at least as important for local, if not national identities and perceptions, a point obscured by glamorous gold. Tasmania's minerals, for example, comprised zinc, lead and copper. Since these formed the bases of settled, orderly and long-lived communities, their profile has always been relatively low. But mining centres which grew up around other minerals made no less a contribution to national cultures, despite a lack of legendary profile.

Copper mining preceded the Australian gold rushes; indeed, copper was Australia's first metaliferous mining industry and in South Australia copper was king. The discovery of silver-lead in the Adelaide Hills in 1841 by Cornish miners provoked a mining frenzy into South Australia that lasted until the Victorian gold rush of 1851. More exciting was the discovery of copper in the 1840s, first at Kapunda, 50 miles north of Adelaide. Copper came to dominate mining in the colony, which mined a tenth of the world's copper in some years. South Australia's mining traditions were Cornish, transported by migrants whose ancestors had mined tin and copper for generations. Cornish miners knew minerals and how to work them alluvially, and most important, below ground. They established Cornish communities in South Australia – all based on copper – at Kapunda, at Burra, and at Moonta, Wallaroo and Kadina on the Yorke Peninsula, which became the largest towns in South Australia outside Adelaide.[40]

At Broken Hill in far west New South Wales, a distinctive community grew up founded on silver. Broken Hill was closer to Port Pirie and Adelaide in South Australia than to Sydney in its commercial, geographical and kinship links. It exploded into an 'instant city' of 30,000 in the silver boom of the 1880s. By the 1890s one company dominated the town, which took its name from the site where it was founded: Broken Hill Proprietary Ltd (BHP). Broken Hill proved to be one of the largest silver–lead–zinc deposits in the world. In production for over 100 years, the first mineral claim was made in 1883. BHP began in 1885, with a Celtic heritage bequeathed by the two Scots and two Irishmen who founded it, as well as the Cornish who flocked in to be mining captains. By the 1890s Broken Hill was one of the world's main silver producers. The Broken Hill lode, developed from the 1880s, was 'enormous', which posed technical problems. Innovations in timbering evolved to prevent cave-ins; the open cut (a United States solution) eventually extended almost a mile. Local innovations, such as flotation, ensured the company a strong future and transformed metallurgy worldwide. Surface workings occurred from 1891. Thirty million ounces of silver from the first ore shipment of 1885 to 1891 triggered a boom in silver mining shares. By 1888 4,000 men worked Broken Hill and 100,000 tons of ore were brought to the surface. Its silver was railed out through South Australia. Drought and concern about sanitation, water shortage and pollution from smelters made townspeople angry; their protests resulting in a municipal water supply. Such trials confirmed that their regional identity embraced South Australia, not New South Wales.[41] Broken Hill sported an identity of fierce collectivism. It stars in labour history narratives through the struggle between capital and labour which led to a legendary 19-month strike in 1919–20. Such struggles spawned a labour movement mythology and strong identity pivoted on the idea that Broken Hill had the best industrial conditions in Australia. The town perpetuated its own myth that, with its unique identity, it did not share the problems faced by other Australian mining towns.[42]

Regional identities in New South Wales owe more to coal. The first mineral discovered in Australia in 1797, Hunter Valley coal was the first to be mined, from 1804, using convict labour. Since 1914 coal has earned more than any other Australian mineral, and has often been the leading export earner. Coal as a fuel, for heat energy and mechanical energy, transformed prospects for growth that hitherto depended on wood.[43] Wood continued to be important – Australia and New Zealand mined their forests for wood, and New Zealand icons and homes were fashioned from wood; but coal fired the industrial revolution and new forms of transport. Demand soared, to fuel steam locomotives and especially steam ships which were the biggest consumer in the nineteenth century.

> Factories sprang up on the American and Asian shores of the Pacific and Indian Oceans, reliant for fuel on accessible seams of coal along the coast just to the north and south of Sydney. The shipping and rail routes that linked Asia, America and Australia [and New Zealand and the Islands] to each other and to the world economy as a whole also ran on fuel brought by sailing ships from New South Wales.[44]

Hence the Union Steam Ship Company, the most powerful colonial shipping company, based at Dunedin, bought into the coal industry on New Zealand's West Coast in the late nineteenth century and became the employer of miners. For that reason it became the arch-enemy of labour – and symbol of monopoly capitalism.

The centre of gravity for coal in Australasia is the main coal basin of New South Wales, stretching from the Hunter Valley in the north near Newcastle, to the Illawarra in the south around Wollongong, and west to Lithgow.[45] By 1888 New South Wales and Queensland were self-sufficient in coal while Victoria, South Australia and Western Australia imported theirs from New South Wales. Tasmania mined half its coal, and shipped the rest from Newcastle and Port Kembla.[46] New Zealand, which also imported coal from New South Wales, developed fields in the Grey Valley and the Buller regions on the West Coast from the 1880s, and in the Waikato in the twentieth century, to service Auckland and the dairy industry.

Coal's principal significance for identities is that mining culture was shaped by the view from the 'end of a pick'.[47] This pick's-eye view is celebrated in labour history, although the coal-black version has offered thin pickings for national narratives. We may contrast this view, important on the Left and in ideals of masculinity, with that crafted by extracting other minerals, where mining was increasingly mechanized, and the mining engineer replaced the manly digger. The hewer of coal was at the centre of pit radicalism. He was equally central to masculine identities which emphasized physical strength and skill. Hence the coalminer was elevated in the myths – and ideology – of the labour movement in Australia and New Zealand from the 1880s.

The pick's is not the only view of coal's influence on identities and traditions. The coalminer is remembered in labour narratives for his historic mission to lead the assault on capitalism, towards a workingman's paradise in which the laws of supply and demand were constrained by the power of organized labour.[48] He has been cast as the quintessential proletarian, though he can equally be claimed for pioneer mythology. For he was the independent collier – a skilled artisan – who as well as being the champion of the honest toiler, battled the elements in harsh conditions and remote communities. One such place is the Denniston plateau on the West Coast of the South Island, bleak and often shrouded in mist, where the only way out for coal and people was by coal truck, down the steep and treacherous Denniston incline.

Mrs John Lomas, wife of the unionist leader, walked that incline. That she did offers a clue to how coal coloured family identities. Families in coal communities offer a counter to the wandering bushman, especially in the mythic bushman's home of New South Wales. The frontier camp soon became a village. In the Illawarra region, mining villages developed from the 1860s. By 1901 the Bulli Woonona community had 2,720 people and 525 dwellings. These families were close-knit. By the late nineteenth century, 60 per cent of brides were Australian-born, over a third having grown up in Illawarra. More brides than grooms were from mining families, daughters of miners. On the coalfields the gender imbalance was not nearly as severe as in pastoralism.[49]

Rather than being free of family ties, coalmining communities were determined to support the all-important family life. Mining families depended on the miner as breadwinner, on his physical health and strength, as well as the state of the coal trade. Mining was dangerous, and single men replacing the killed miners would marry the widows. Many miners migrated with their families. Women from mining families had worked above ground in English mines and were involved in radical politics. Families were central in mining towns and values on the coalfields were dominated by the work ethic, respectability, literacy, and education. Husbands and wives alike were loyal to the union.[50]

Dangers and tragedies bonded people. In the Bulli mining disaster of 1887, 81 men and boys were killed. New Zealand had an equivalent disaster at Brunner, in the Grey Valley, in 1896. Of those who died at Brunner, the New Zealand-born were under-represented. All but one were under 21 and had followed their fathers into the pits. Tragedy, too, was a family affair. The 81 who died at Bulli left 37 widows and 120 children.[51] Though migrants were over-represented, family identity remained strong because people migrated in family groups. Brothers, fathers and sons-in-law worked together. They also lived together, for example in Newcastle where mining families bought double blocks of land, and leased to kin such as widowed mothers and children.

This brings us to the question of ethnicity. The coalminer's wife had his bath ready each night by the fire, just as she did on English coalfields. Coalmining families who migrated to Australia and New Zealand were mainly English, from Newcastle-upon-Tyne, Northumberland and Durham, and Yorkshire. English colliers brought what to coal owners were the 'twin evils' of Methodism and unionism, and their English mining practices, such as 'bord-and-pillar' methods of working. Cast by their employers as 'outsiders' lacking the 'pride of colonials', they nonetheless contributed to national narratives, not least in politics.[52]

The Cornish were not associated with coal, but with gold and silver, copper and tin; and they contributed as much to family as to digger narratives. The Cornish miner's wife or daughter baked his lunch of Cornish pastie, in South Australia as she did in Cornwall. The Cornish carried their traditions, names and hopes across the world, and with the Irish and Scots helped make Australia and New Zealand Celtic outposts. A high proportion of Otago gold miners were from Cornwall.[53] So were the bulk of copper miners in South Australia. They contributed not just their technology but their work practices, of payment by tribute (according to the value of the ore) and tutwork contracts (by the volume of ground dug), as well as the pastie, wrestling, a love of rugby, the chapel, and their names and language. It was the Cornish who brought deep-shaft mining to Australasia. In the mining law established in Victoria, too, with its system of goldfields wardens, we can hear an echo of Cornish experience.[54]

National narratives overlook an ethnic patterning by community as well as a patterning by mining enterprise.[55] An exception is the Chinese, whom historians notice living apart in their camps and reworking ground abandoned by Europeans. There were more than 4,000 Chinese gold miners in New Zealand by 1876, most in Otago. As in Victoria – whence they came – those who stayed begat generations of Chinese Australians and New Zealanders. In Queensland, Chinese on the Palmer River field outnumbered European miners by 17,000 to 1,400. When gold was found in the remote Northern Territory in 1871, Chinese provided the labour, outnumbering Europeans in the Territory by seven to one by the end of the decade.[56]

But ethnic patterning was not only Chinese. On every field, communities were marked by ethnic solidarity. We have seen how the Eureka claim was Irish. South Australia's copper towns were Cornish. Newcastle and the West Coast coalfields were northern English. On every goldfield, camps wore their ethnic affiliations: Hispanics, Chinese, Norwegians. On the Otago goldfields, Irish miners congregated at St Bathans, while there was a City of Dublin claim and a Cornishmen's claim on the Tuapeka field. The miners in each camp were related. So, too, at Hamiltons in Otago, where a Cornish community formed in the 1860s and 1870s. This solidarity could serve many purposes. As Philip Payton notes, the Cornish stuck together in Melbourne, and

> even more so on the diggings themselves where, as in California (or New South Wales), ethnic, national and regional groups used separate identity to defend or extend their interests.[57]

Mining also shaped class identities. The biggest trade unions in Australia were shearers, coalminers, and non-coal miners in the Amalgamated Miners' Association of Australasia (AMA), formed in Victoria in 1874, which had its origins in gold mining. It was because of gold, the 'great leveller', that Georgiana McCrae complained in 1852 that 'Women servants are becoming most saucy since their relatives are often in better ease than the house-holder himself'.[58] But class lines soon developed with deep-shaft mining by companies, between miners, mine workers and their unions, and managers. At Broken Hill, a branch of the AMA formed in 1886 and clashed with companies over individual contracts versus closed shop (employing only unionists). In the first strike in the late 1880s, women were typically prominent; they swept out strike-breakers with brooms, and tarred and feathered non-unionists in a gesture of community solidarity.

Coalmining also contributed to the new, mass unionism of the 1880s. The Dunedin businessmen who imported miners from the English coalfields to hew coal on New Zealand's West Coast, through Vogel's assisted immigration scheme, disapproved of the miners' Methodism and unionism. On one hand, the coal companies cast miners as outsiders and radicals who were likely to cause trouble. They did, with their class solidarity slogan, 'united we stand, divided we fall', intended to further the collier's claim to independence through collective action. John Lomas, the Methodist lay preacher who launched mining unionism at Denniston, aspired to one big union, and joined the Australian voice of new unionism, W. G. Spence of the AMA, to promote the objective of one union for all Australasian coal and metal miners.[59] On the other hand, the independent collier, the specialist at his craft – proud not to be the colonial 'jack of all trades' – represented the labour aristocrat. Bearing this identity, the Denniston miners were the first to go to arbitration (see chapter 11).

Mining, then, consolidated regional identities. In the New World as in the old, it produced unique communities. On New Zealand's West Coast, in the peak years of 1865 to 1867, over £5 million worth of gold was sluiced and dredged from its rushing rivers, and the diggers and mining industry left an imprint which, with their tailings, gave this isolated coast a distinct identity.[60] Much of this is Irish – and Australian. Gold provoked an Australian invasion of the West Coast in 1865, from Melbourne. In 1865 to 1867, all new migrants to the West Coast came from Australia.

Through the lens of mining we discern shared populations in Australasia. The Irish trying their luck, seasoned Cornish hard-rock men, English coalminers, or Chinese, shared and created the region's labour markets. Gold and coal crystallize how much these colonies had in common. While the (Catholic) Irish component became a marker of difference (and Australianness), the miners reveal shared experience – and ethnicity – in Australia and New Zealand's Anglo-Celtic populations. These patterns depended on the chronology of mining, which flowed from southeastern Australia to New Zealand; and in Australia, anti-clockwise around the continent from South Australia, Victoria and New South Wales, to Queensland, where gold was discovered in the 1860s, the Northern Territory (1870s) and Western Australia (1890s). Mining helped consolidate identity in Queensland, which by the 1870s boasted a few (but very rich) mining centres. Charters Towers became one of the most productive fields in the country. At Mt Morgan, huge fortunes were made by Walter Hall (benefactor of the Walter and Eliza Hall Institute of medical research in Melbourne), and by William Knox D'Arcy, who made a killing in copper as well as gold.[61]

As in the eastern colonies, gold fever threatened to break out in Western Australia for some years before it boomed: in the 1870s in the Kimberley region where at its peak in 1890 it attracted as many as 40,000 diggers, and more spectacularly in the 1890s in Kalgoorlie, 560 kilometres east of Perth, a field that has yielded more gold than any other in Australia. Between 1890 and 1894 the colony's population almost doubled. While the other colonies suffered degrees of depression, Western Australia boomed.[62] The period 1851–95 saw a comprehensive survey of Australia's gold resources. No new fields have since been discovered. Many new mines have opened, notably in the 1930s and 1970s, but all in areas already known for their gold.[63]

Western Australia relinquished the most riches, proving the biggest source of gold in Australia. Of the 'big sixteen' companies that controlled the Australian mining industry by the end of the century, nine – in Western Australia – had their head offices in London, and the bulk of their profits went into British pockets. Blainey suggests that their impact on Australian heavy industry would have been bigger had they all been directed from Melbourne. These 16 companies, dominated by Western Australia, did finance much of Australia's industrialization in iron and steel, shipbuilding, chemicals, fertilizers, paper, paint, aircraft production, aluminium, and refining and fabricating metals. 'Their technical mastery in the field was the prelude to industrial mastery.'[64] But such gains came at a price of reinforced economic dependency.

MINING IN THE ISLANDS

As Queensland's prospectors and small operators were displaced by companies in the 1870s, many crossed the Coral Sea to create other frontiers in Melanesia. Australians found gold in New Caledonia in 1870, for example, and worked it for some years. Since Melanesian rights to land had been curtailed drastically since the 1850s, there was no impediment either to prospecting or to exploiting ores. But gold ores were limited and the most important find was nickel, in which Higginson predictably gained an interest. His contacts with Australian entrepreneurs and mining magnates were decisive in channelling capital into New Caledonia, but even these sources would not suffice. Nickel prices fluctuated widely, and the industry only stabilized once a global cartel was established in the 1890s. By that time Rothschilds had bought into the industry, and put Le Société Nickel on a sound footing. During the 1890s, nickel production boomed, integrating New Caledonia into world markets. Nickel had more immediate effects locally. Arable farming declined in importance relative to cattle ranching. Ranching, in turn, promoted 'the aggregation of land titles into fewer and fewer large estates, often owned by absentee proprietors or pastoral societies founded by nickel-wealthy [residents of urban Noumea]'.[65]

While New Caledonian mining grew from an Australian frontier activity into a major component of the world nickel market, Papuan mining remained a small-scale enterprise. Papua was more explicitly an extension of the Australian industry and an unhappy hunting ground for Australians. Early mining was alluvial: the exploitation of lodes demanded more capital than storekeepers could lend. Serious investment was inhibited until 1888 when Lt-Governor MacGregor introduced the Queensland mining laws, appointed a mining warden, and provided transport.[66] Prospectors then focused on the islands of Milne Bay, beginning on Tagula (Sudest) in 1888 when 400 miners sailed in, to the astonishment of a thousand islanders. Heavy rain, rough ground, high humidity and a variety of diseases underlined the miners' dependence on islanders for their labour, their food supplies – and their tolerance. As in Australian alluvial finds, the fraternity shrank to forty in two years; but by then islanders were washing their own gold, and earning more money than any other Papuans. Rushes to other islands were equally ephemeral, until the discovery of lodes. Misima and Murua (Woodlark) then attracted Australian capital, and Sydney promoters exploited the provisions for No Liability companies. Thus Kulumadau, on Murua, was promoted by

> stock market manipulation, insider trading, exaggeration (if not falsification) of assays, romantic reserve estimates, bounteous vendor considerations and, ultimately, mismanagement. ... As much as half of the authorized shares were issued free, and fully-paid, to the promoters. The Sydney company paid £20,000 to vendors on floating, almost three times more than it retained for its own use.[67]

Gold was Papua's main export. The colonial state encouraged alluvial mining, curbed violence, and thereby advanced the interests of Australian investors. In Misima the discovery of the mother-lode led to large-scale quartz-mining from 1914 when BHP took over and sustained production until the 1920s. In a radically different labour market than Broken Hill's, BHP employed men at 10 shillings per month. Few Misimans would work on these terms: instead they sold betel nut to BHP, which exchanged them for yams from other islands. The intrusive economy was much too frail to transform the economic networks or social relationships of the island world.

There was a widening gulf between Australian policy and local practice. When a British Protectorate was proclaimed in 1884, Commodore Erskine promised Papuans that 'Your lands will be secured to you'.[68] Endorsing that approach, the Commonwealth parliament decreed that no freehold land would be sold in Papua (quite the reverse of New Caledonian policy). Similarly, once the federal government took charge, the Queensland-derived laws were amended so that anyone wanting to mine in Papua must inform the government, an official must assess likely damage and demand a deposit to cover the cost of compensation. If a mine was likely to damage a village then an official had to obtain the agreement of the villagers before mining could begin.[69] On the mainland especially, prospectors behaved in a very different manner. They had scant protection from government, so they could not assure themselves safe passage through the lands of indignant Papuans. On a violent frontier the policies of consultation and compensation evaporated.[70]

Nitrates began to be exploited at the turn of the century, for Australian, New Zealand and Japanese farms. The Pacific Islands Company got its start when Albert Ellis identified phosphates on Banaba (Ocean Island) and in 1900 procured a 999 year concession from two Banabans. The company was restructured in 1902 as the Pacific Phosphate Company, and in 1907 won similar rights in German Nauru. Later they rounded out a regional monopsony by forming an alliance with French producers in Tahiti. Banabans lost any chance of royalties: in 1927 they were exiled to Rabi Island in Fiji. Matters turned out better for Nauruans. They were marginalized but not deported, and they won their political independence before their resource was entirely exhausted. For most islanders, however, phosphates were a disaster. Rights were cheaply alienated; islanders were not involved in production; and some were eased out of their island altogether. Mining was a great despoiler of environments, especially island environments rich in nitrates, although most island alluvial gold was too limited to provoke large-scale damage.

For prospectors, mining artisans, promoters and developers, the island alluvials were extensions of familiar Australian resources into exotic locations. The evolution of prospects into large enterprises might wrench these resources away from prospectors and small syndicates, into the orbits of metropolitan investors and markets – but that was the fate of alluvial miners everywhere. In that process, white men were squeezed out except as managers and artisans, supervising unskilled islanders, and employers dispensed with most white workers and their laws and expectations. In brief, gold rushes did little to alter the prospectors' views of the mining world, its hopes, its trajectories, its dangers and its disappointments. And they made little impact on islanders' sense of themselves and their environment, whereas islanders unlucky enough to live above nitrates were exposed to the risk of absolute dispossession.

NOTES

1 David Goodman, *Gold Seeking: Victoria and California in the 1850s*, Sydney, 1994; John Molony, *Eureka*, Ringwood, Victoria, 1984; Russel Ward, *The Australian Legend*, Melbourne, 1966, ch. 5.

2 Geoffrey Blainey, *The Rush that Never Ended: A History of Australian Mining*, 2nd edn, Melbourne, 1969, ch. 11.

3 Jeremy Mouat, 'Mining in the Settler Dominions: A Comparative Study of the Industry in Three Communities from the 1880s to the First World War', Ph.D. thesis, University of British Columbia, 1988, 11.

4 Geoffrey Blainey, *The Tyranny of Distance*, Melbourne, 1968, 139–41; Goodman, *Gold Seeking*, introduction.

5 Blainey, *The Rush that Never Ended*, 14–20; Philip Payton, *The Cornish Overseas*, Fowey, 1999, 228–9.

6 Goodman, *Gold Seeking*, introduction.

7 *The French Consul's Wife: Memoirs of Celeste de Chabrillan in Gold-rush Australia*, intro. and trans. by Patricia Clancy and Jeanne Allen, Melbourne, 1998, 125.

8 Erik Olssen, *A History of Otago*, Dunedin, 1984, 56–8.

9 Ibid., 59–60.

10 P. R. May, 'Gold on the Coast (1)', *New Zealand's Heritage*, 3 (31), 842–4.

11 Blainey, *The Rush that Never Ended*, 39.

12 Weston Bate, *Victorian Gold Rushes*, Melbourne, 1988, 57–8.

13 Blainey, *The Rush that Never Ended*, 37–8.

14 W. D. Borrie, *The European Peopling of Australasia: A Demographic History, 1788–1988*, Canberra, 1994, 67.

15 Goodman, *Gold Seeking*, chs 4 and 6.

16 Ibid., 156; Miles Fairburn, *The Ideal Society and Its Enemies*, Auckland, 1989.

17 Olssen, *A History of Otago*, 63.

18 Geraldine Carrodus, *Gold, Gamblers & Sly Grog: Life on the Goldfields, 1851–1900*, Oxford, 1981, 5. In the series *Inquiring into Australian History* edited by Barbara Vance Wilson.

19 Geoffrey Serle, *The Golden Age: A History of the Colony of Victoria 1851–1861*, Melbourne, 1963.
20 Bate, *Victorian Gold Rushes*, 12.
21 Olssen, *A History of Otago*, 56–64 (quotation from p. 64).
22 May, 'Gold on the Coast', 844.
23 J. W. McCarty, 'Gold Rushes', in G. Davison, J. Hirst and S. Macintyre (eds), *Oxford Companion to Australian History*, Melbourne, 1998, 285; Terry Hearn, 'The Wealth of Miners: A Study of the Gold Miners of Central Otago, 1861–1921'. In *Proceedings of the 1998 Conference of the New Zealand Society of Geographers*, University of Otago, Dunedin, April 1998, 230–1.
24 For a useful overview, see D. Goodman, 'Eureka Stockade', in Davison, Hirst and Macintyre, *Oxford Companion to Australian History*, 227–8.
25 R. D. Walshe, 'The Significance of Eureka in Australian History', in F. B. Smith (ed.), *Historical Studies: Eureka Supplement*, Melbourne, 1965, 103.
26 Bate, *Victorian Gold Rushes*, 44.
27 Ibid., 45–6; G. Serle, *The Golden Age: A History of the Colony of Victoria 1851–1861*, Melbourne, 1963, 181.
28 Walshe, 'The Significance of Eureka', 110–11. Walshe cited W. G. Spence, himself an icon for this tradition in the labour movement.
29 Ibid., 124, citing Lawson, *Worker*, Brisbane, 16 May 1891.
30 Serle, *The Golden Age*, 180.
31 Bate, *Victorian Gold Rushes*, 60, 61, 65.
32 Blainey, *The Rush that Never Ended*, 365.
33 Olssen, *A History of Otago*, 64–6.
34 Mouat, 'Mining in the Settler Dominions', 4–6.
35 Bate, *Victorian Gold Rushes*, 11.
36 Blainey, *The Rush that Never Ended*, 248.
37 Ibid., 251–5.
38 Mouat, 'Mining in the Settler Dominions', ch. 7.
39 Bate, *Victorian Gold Rushes*, 37–8.
40 Blainey, *The Rush that Never Ended*, 105–24; Payton, *The Cornish Overseas*, ch. 6.
41 Mouat, 'Mining in the Settler Dominions', ch. 5.
42 Brian Kennedy, *Silver, Sin, and Sixpenny Ale: A Social History of Broken Hill, 1883–1921*, Melbourne, 1978.
43 E. A. Wrigley, *Continuity, Chance and Change: The Character of the Industrial Revolution in England*, Cambridge, 1988.
44 B. Dyster and D. Meredith, *Australia in the International Economy in the Twentieth Century*, Melbourne, 1990, 18.
45 R. Gollan, *The Coalminers of New South Wales: A History of the Union, 1860–1960*, Melbourne, 1963, 3–4. According to Gollan, coal was discovered first in 1796, near Newcastle.
46 G. Davison, 'The Australian Energy System in 1888', *Australia 1888 Bulletin*, 10 (1982), 25.
47 L. E. Richardson, *Coal, Class and Community: The United Mineworkers of New Zealand 1880–1960*, Auckland, 1995, 11.
48 Ibid., 40.
49 W. Mitchell and G. Sherington, 'Families and Children in Nineteenth-century Illawarra', in P. Grimshaw, C. McConville and E. McEwen (eds), *Families in Colonial Australia*, Sydney, 1985, 111–12.
50 Richardson, *Coal, Class and Community*, 3–4.

51 Ibid.; Mitchell and Sherington, 'Families and Children in Nineteenth-century Illawarra', 116.
52 Richardson, *Coal, Class and Community*, 9; Gollan, *The Coalminers of New South Wales*, 19.
53 Hearn, 'The Wealth of Miners'.
54 Payton, *The Cornish Overseas*.
55 This thought owes its genesis to discussion with Terry Hearn.
56 Payton, *The Cornish Overseas*, 299.
57 Payton, *The Cornish Overseas*, ch. 7.
58 Georgiana McCrae's journal, 195, in Carrodus, *Gold, Gamblers and Sly Grog*, 16.
59 Richardson, *Coal, Class and Community*, 3, 9, 34, 105.
60 P. R. May, 'Gold on the Coast' (1) and (2), *New Zealand's Heritage*, vol. 3, parts 31 and 32; and P. R. May, *The West Coast Gold Rushes*, Christchurch, 1962.
61 Blainey, *The Rush that Never Ended*, ch. 20.
62 Carrodus, *Gold, Gamblers and Sly Grog*, 12.
63 Ibid., 13.
64 Blainey, *The Rush that Never Ended*, 256. For details of gold finds, see J. C. R. Camm and J. McQuilton (eds), *Australians: A Historical Atlas*, Sydney, 1987, 118–19.
65 Alan Ward, *Land and Politics in New Caledonia*, Political and Social Change Monograph, Canberra, 1982, 7.
66 Hank Nelson, *Black, White and Gold: Gold Mining in Papua New Guinea, 1878–1930*, Canberra, 1976.
67 W. A. McGee and G. R. Henning, 'Investment in Lode Mining, Papua 1878–1920', *Journal of Pacific History*, 25 (1990): 244–59.
68 B. Jinks, P. Biskup and H. Nelson, *Readings in New Guinea History*, Sydney, 1973, 38.
69 Hank Nelson, 'Frontiers, Territories and States of Mind', Pacific History Workshop, December 1998, ANU, Canberra. The basic land law was passed in 1906 and the Land Ordinance of 1911 'to amend and consolidate the law regulating the dealing with lands' was assented to in 1912. The section quoted is from the Land Ordinance, 1911, s. 5. An ordinance to amend the law relating to mining, and to provide for and regulate mining on native land, was assented to in 1908.
70 Donald Denoon, 'New Economic Orders: Land, Labour and Dependency', in Donald Denoon, Stewart Firth, Jocelyn Linnekin, Malama Meleisea and Karen Nero (eds), *Cambridge History of the Pacific Islanders*, Melbourne, 1997, 218–52.

[8] LABOUR RELATIONS

Labour relations in this region evolved mainly in one of three patterns. In several Australian colonies, and in New Caledonia, transported Europeans laboured as convicts. New Zealand and South Australia received no convicts, and devised forms of free wage labour which eventually prevailed throughout the British settler colonies, except that Aboriginal Australians were subject to paternalist constraints. In many islands, chiefs mobilized people to harvest natural resources, or process copra; then foreigners acquired plantation land and introduced indentured labour. In each case the original form of labour cast long shadows across the nineteenth and twentieth centuries.

For most of our region the earliest forms of labour relations occurred at sea, or on the beach. Until the 1860s most such foreign ventures made little impact on patterns of service to chiefs. By the 1830s, islanders comprised a fifth of all whaling and sealing crews. Swimming divers had begun to collect pearl and turtle-shell, and seal skins and timber were harvested. By 1830 *bêche-de-mer* was Fiji's leading export from luggers employing two or three hundred Europeans, Fijians and other islanders for a season. Sandalwood then drew Sydney traders to Fiji, New Caledonia and the New Hebrides, for timber whose harvesting was (again) organized largely by chiefs. At first, chiefs would accept trivial items; but as they became sated with these goods they demanded pigs, dogs and turtle-shell. Frustrated traders had to devise new rewards. Shineberg summarized the nexus as teaching islanders to smoke tobacco so that Chinese could burn incense – so that Australians could drink tea.[1] This limited commerce could not transform communities or their values.

THE CONVICTS IN AUSTRALIA

Convictism set the outlines for Australian labour relations in class, gender and racial terms. By 1830, Australia's non-Aboriginal population numbered 70,000 of whom nearly 90 per cent had been transported or were convicts' children. Convicts and ex-convicts comprised 71 per cent of the white labour force by 1840. Dickensian images aside, the convicts as a group defy easy description. In the positive view favoured by cliometric historians (see chapter 5), convicts did not stem from, nor did they comprise a criminal class. Nicholas and Shergold charge Australian scholars with perpetuating misleading ideas – the 'fatal shore' and the 'convict stain' – which are unsoundly based on literary rather than quantitative evidence.

> For more than a generation, the received interpretation of our past has emphasized male convicts as hardened and professional criminals, females as prostitutes and convictism as a brutal and inefficient system of forced labour.

Instead, they offer a 'new and dramatic reinterpretation of the convict system'.[2] Drawing on data for 19,711 convicts transported to New South Wales between 1817 and 1840, they insist that the average convict was indistinguishable from 'ordinary British and Irish working-class men and women'. Young and fit, they were productive workers who brought useful skills; much like the working classes they left behind, they were more literate than the English workforce; they included a labour aristocracy; the convict labour market was efficient; and their living standards better than at home. This thesis is that convicts' human capital was vital to Australian economic development.[3]

No well-researched history ever said otherwise. Before Nicholas and Shergold compiled their database, historians already knew that close to 160,000 people were transported to Australia, more than 80 per cent of whom were men (24,960 women and 132,308 men). Most were young, with a mean age of 26, healthy, single, and free of dependents. Most were first offenders who had been workers until their conviction for petty theft. In many cases, their crimes were work-related.[4]

Professionals were few, but craftsmen showed their skill in architecture, building and printing in Sydney and Hobart. Francis Greenway, convicted of forgery, arrived in 1812 and by 1816 had become Civil Architect and Assistant Engineer. A flow of buildings bore his imprint: the lighthouse at South Head, Sydney Harbour; the courts in Queen's Square; churches at Windsor and Liverpool; and his masterpiece St James in the centre of Sydney. George Howe came as a convict and re-established himself as a typical eighteenth-century man of reason. His son Robert Howe published the *Gazette*, the first daily newspaper. His brother George Tery Howe published the first newspaper in Launceston in 1825. The Howes were the real founders of Australian literature, providing the first opportunities for colonial expression. Convicts built every road, church and public building and were beasts of burden in exploration; when they earned tickets of leave they became constables and supervisors of road gangs.

On this view, the convict colonies – Port Phillip Bay (Victoria) from 1802, Tasmania from 1804, and Swan River (Perth) which received convicts from 1850 – could not afford to maltreat their labour. In the convict colonies which were not sites of secondary punishment, at least, concern for discipline was secondary to survival and development. Well fed, clothed and sheltered, convicts enjoyed a relatively high calorie intake to ensure that they performed their work and to encourage a work ethic. Mechanics toiled at their trade, not in agriculture, and could earn good money and an easy life.[5]

To this ruddy picture economic historians have used systematic statistical evidence to add that 60 per cent of convicts were English, 34 per cent Irish and five per cent Scots. Only one per cent came from outside the British Isles. They were not merely ordinary British working-class people: by today's Australian immigration guidelines, they were exceptional. Nicholas and his team maintain that convict men and women were the human capital which underpinned development. They were effective wealth-creators because of their 'unique age distribution', with over 80 per cent aged between 16 and 35, the most productive age. To the evidence of youth they add data on transportees' heights, as a proxy measure of nutritional status, and show the convicts to be as tall – or short – as working-class people at home. They were healthy, and had higher literacy levels than much of the world today.[6]

Nicholas claims that 'traditional' historians 'asked the wrong questions and neglected the data on the convicts' occupations, literacy and height'. They did not ask the wrong questions: they asked different questions. To treat convicts purely as human capital invites the riposte that this mentality parallels that of the authorities who governed them. Our questions, on the formation of identities, underscore that good health is relevant for more than stocks of human capital, by keeping people alive and well – and loyal to some idealized 'state' (see chapter 5). The exercise of power by maintaining people's bodies shaped rules, and thus identities. Also pivotal are issues of morality, and how others saw Australia. From Hirst, who argued that its enemies shaped how we think about convictism, there has been a swing to the Nicholas and Shergold view, which draws on evidence gathered by convictism's friends. Shaw had already found that economically, convicts helped development. They provided a useful labour force, made private income more profitable, and prompted government expenditure, while the sex imbalance soon corrected itself. Nicholas is wrong to assert that convicts were well treated because they were seen as a 'productive asset', rather than for reformist reasons. This elides the point that work *was* reform. There is nothing in Nicholas's argument to refute Shaw's thesis that transportation and assignment proved the most effective reformatory punishment before 1850.[7] The transported turned out well enough; and their heirs continue colourfully to perform the role of 'larrikins'.

In contrast to *Convict Workers* stands the argument that the places of secondary punishment like Moreton Bay and Norfolk Island, established after the Bigge Reports, in the 1820s, were altogether different and brutal. Set up to serve as warnings, they were central to the convict system. For this reason and because of the use of mass quantification alone, without matching it with convict testimony (for example, on what it was like to be flogged, subjected to 100 lashes with a 'cat-o'-nine-tails') *Convict Workers* cannot be said accurately to represent the whole convict experience.[8] This view, too, emphasizes power relations. It usefully introduces the concept of 'penal labour' to capture the condition of penal servitude: the convict was not just 'a worker who happened to be a convict', or a convict converted to a worker (the criminal class thesis), but a convict–worker: a penal labourer, to be both 'punished and worked'.[9]

It is also useful to remember that the insider view of convictism is regional, and outsider views are local. Australian colonial identities depend as much on the presence of a convict heritage as on its absence, especially in South Australia which, like New Zealand, received no convicts. Again, transportation began and ended later in Western Australia than in the east. It is important for Western Australia's identities that it received no women convicts, just as it is for Adelaide's that it was morally untarnished and thus more civilized than, and morally superior to, New South Wales and Queensland.

All convict colonies shared the problems of a harsh landscape, the need to survive, the convict–master relationship, negotiating between 'home' and local needs, and the governor's idiosyncrasies. With no set guidelines, the governor's social instincts were critical. Each wrestled with imponderables: who owned their labour: the convicts or the state?, with payment and reward, punishment and reform. Phillip had the power to grant pardons and used it wisely. King, like Macquarie later, did not want convicts consigned to 'oblivion and disgrace for ever', and enrolled well-behaved emancipists in the New South Wales Corps and in his bodyguard. He also granted them land. The outstanding early governors – Phillip, Hunter and Macquarie – insisted that the future lay with the reform of convicts. By contrast Ralph Darling (from 1825) held a martinet's views.

Assignment, or contracting out convicts, was not, as some claimed, a 'giant lottery'.[10] The early governors were partial to educated convicts, particularly forgers: to be transported for forgery almost amounted to a qualification for a minor public appointment. Other educated convicts were immediately accepted as schoolmasters, and a few were allocated to emancipist merchants. A number became associated with the legal system. Skilled, rural and construction workers were largely matched to the same types of jobs. The system proved less efficient for domestic workers and unskilled urban workers who were assigned to unfamiliar work in agriculture or the public service. Convictism allowed the state flexibility to assign labour to roads or clearing land as need arose. Assigning convicts to private employment was good for individual settlers, and for the state, particularly when masters were required to feed and clothe their convict servants.[11] Government employment was not necessarily demeaning, although it did keep convicts in their own bad company. In Sydney they worked for about nine hours a day or less if employed on task work, and early in the afternoon their time was their own.

Incentives and rewards were integral to the system in New South Wales, if not at Moreton Bay. Skilled workers were naturally more prized and better treated. Care-intensive work was reward-driven, while effort-intensive work (clearing scrub and road building) was more likely punishment-driven. Rewards included extra rations and clothing, indulgences (tea, tobacco and rum), preferred work, apprenticeship training and time to work on one's own account. A major reward was land: by 1795, ex-convicts were granted a maximum of 30 acres to encourage them to reform and to stay, and Corps men gained about 100 acres each, in the hope that they would defend the settlement, but many land grants proved more a curse than a blessing (see chapter 6).

Punishment was inescapable in any penal system. In one view, the 'picture of a brutal and terrorized society' is not at all overdrawn; in another, there is little evidence of a terrorized society. The picture varies not only with the sources used (words or numbers) but also, crucially, with place. Was Brisbane a site of terror and Sydney not? The number and severity of floggings ordered by Revd Samuel Marsden leap from the page because they are uncommon in New South Wales. At Parramatta, he was known as the 'flogging parson'. (In New Zealand narratives, Marsden became a benevolent figure, as missionary rather than convict chaplain, again showing how identities depend on context.) But in the 'typical' year of 1835, 70 per cent of convicts at Moreton Bay were flogged, compared to 26 per cent in New South Wales.[12] Penal health policy presents a more favourable perspective on the convict system. Convicts had free access to hospital care until 1831, and thereafter on payment by employers. Mortality was no greater than in general voluntary hospitals in Britain, and the quality of care was superior to that of English Poor Law infirmaries after 1834. Australia proved a healthy country for migrants.[13]

As the reality of living standards became known, transportation lost its terrors. The 1831 British Select Committee on Secondary Punishments had no doubt that many convicts welcomed transportation. Newgate prison wardens testified to a change in perspective from dreaded to promised land, a place for a convict 'to obtain a degree of wealth and happiness, such as he had no prospect of attaining in this country'. The more educated the convict, the more he looked forward to transportation. By the time of the Molesworth Committee inquiry of 1837–8, it was widely accepted that transportation had lost its deterrent effect. It was seen now more as 'a reward' or 'simply as emigration'. But they could not avoid the convict stain.

WOMEN CONVICTS

The most striking feature of convict society was the scarcity of women. Only 16 per cent of those despatched, they comprise 11 per cent of all convicts in the Nicholas and Oxley database. Governor Hunter in 1796 complained that 'we have scarcely any way of employing them, and they are generally found to be worse characters than the men'.[14] Women bore the added stigma of depravity. Stereotyped as whores rather than ideal migrants, the story of women convicts is crushed beneath the larger story because of their small proportion, and by the weight of moral indignation then and since. Rediscovered by Miriam Dixson as founding mothers whose lives explain the gothic nature of Australian women's history, the trend to 'normalize' convicts in the 1980s led to a re-reading of convict women in a positive sense, in time for the Bicentennial in 1988. Convict women produced the next generation of native-born – currency lads and lasses – cementing the family and family-based morality as the core of new societies.[15] Oxley shows that they brought immediately useful skills as servants, laundresses, kitchen hands, needleworkers and housemaids, but they were undervalued and their skills squandered.[16]

Australia was well served by its convict women. Healthy and resourceful, they proved productive workers, wives and mothers. Most had been 'movers' at home, not wanderers or vagabonds but workers seeking employment, so they were used to dislocation and novelty. Women more than men were the major force in the migration from country to urban centres. Two-thirds could read, about a quarter of these could also write, and many were numerate. Nearly half were skilled, and another 31 per cent semi-skilled. They brought over 9,000 skills and their commonest occupations were housemaid, allwork, kitchenmaid, nursemaid and cook.[17]

Successive governors influenced by the gender division of labour in England were uneasy with the idea of convict women as workers. With the rise of consumerism, women had a particular role in conspicuous consumption, as emblems and wearers rather than creators of wealth. Phillip thought it improper for women to labour in public, so men cleared the bush, cut timber, dug gardens and built against the weather, while women were assigned light work, such as gathering shell to make lime. Some became washerwomen for officers, or hut-keepers and cooks for gangs of convicts. Symbolically, men did 'real' work while women provided unpaid domestic work and sexual services.

Governor King was among the first to appreciate the worth of female labour. They might do 'no public labour', he admitted, but 'their domestic concerns and providing for their families is an advantage to the society they are placed in'. King wanted to supply stores for British ships. In his novel form of 'public labour', the first floor of a new gaol at Parramatta became a 'manufactory' for weaving cloth from flax and wool from 1804. Sixty convicts were employed in the first year, and 96 the next. It was small-scale production but it supplied most of the convicts' needs for clothing, and some of the boat-makers' needs for sailcloth. Even if only a few made textiles, they were vital in establishing linen and woollen manufacture. The Female Factory was no ideal work environment: women were often overworked and unrewarded, but it established the principle of a non-domestic female workforce, and it supplied the basic need for cheap cloth.[18] However, domestic service was by far the most common female employment. It prepared a girl for a life of domestic labour, paid or unpaid, but left her vulnerable to the tyranny of the mistress of the house, and the sexual advances of the master. Women convicts were in demand both for their labour and for their favours, and abuse of the assignment system was common.

Women convicts did have choices, notably marrying or staying 'on the government' even if this merely exchanged the authority of the state for that of a husband. By 1804, two-thirds worked as wives, legal or *de facto*. Marriage gave women security and protection. For some, like those who married into the New South Wales Corps, marriage involved a dramatic rise in social status. For many it became a ticket out, once their husband's time with the Corps expired. A few escaped dependency entirely. The 1806 muster lists fewer than 60 self-employed among more than 800 ex-convict women, and another score with some trade or occupation: 10 per cent in all. A few did well as traders, often in partnership with an officer. Transportation itself – to a more fluid class system – mitigated their victim status. In permanent relationships or not, some could live in conditions better than they had left in Britain.

Feminist scholarship which defines work to include reproduction, mothering and household work has recreated and relocated women convicts, allowing them to enter the larger picture as workers alongside the men – but subject to the state as father. Further re-evaluations become possible once prostitution is un-demonized, and the charges of rampant prostitution are scrutinized. Until Oxley's *Convict Maids* (1996), prostitution was more an 'evident truth' than a researched topic. Contemporary accounts often confused prostitution with promiscuity and cohabitation. Prostitution was not an indictable offence: moral outrage, part of a fixation with chastity, was a middle-class phenomenon. In the politics of survival, prostitution (and the theatre) were occupations where 'a woman without capital could reasonably hope to earn a substantial living by her own efforts'.[19] Prostitution can now be seen as something foisted on women, another category of punishment; or as work, and another option. It was also a structural aspect of common forms of employment: domestic servants were often expected to 'oblige' the master and his sons.

Women were normally assigned to their husbands. Women contracted out in this way could bring up their children themselves. But mothers in the Female Factory could not; their children were removed.[20] This raises the question of maternal and familial identities. Here we have a history of 'lost children' where the mothering offered by the birth mother is not valued by those in a position of cultural hegemony. According to Joy Damousi, their reproduction was valued but convict mothering was not. Convict women by definition were bad mothers: polluted, they would contaminate their children, so 'their identity as mothers was disavowed'. From 1833 babies were removed from their mothers at nine months (on weaning) to make their mothers available for assignment.[21] But according to Shaw, mothers in assignment – contracted out to the private sector, and to husbands – could exercise their identity as mothers. Marriage, then, purified them, rendered them respectable, moral and suitable to rear children. Only those institutionalized were not, and from the 1830s, when the system grew harsher. This suggests a division of maternal identities, centred on marriage and ideas of motherhood which cast a long shadow towards the removal of children from unwed and Aboriginal mothers (see chapter 14).

Few women had their sentences remitted, but tickets of leave were granted to those who arrived with property, which equated with respectability, or were well-behaved and industrious. Most served their term of sentence, becoming 'free by servitude'.[22] In the end, New South Wales provided hope and the chance of an improved way of life for women prepared to work.

FREE SETTLEMENT

Free labour had much in common with convict labour, bringing similar skills and experiences. Convict settlements encouraged free colonization by laying the foundations of economic growth. In Australia, the free outnumbered convicts and ex-convicts in the labour force from the late 1840s, and numbers were significant from the 1820s, when free migration depended on imperial patronage. The first to arrive were the least poor (though some fled the 'great destroyer of respectability – debt'):[23] capitalists who travelled independently: landholders, merchants, professionals and administrators, surgeons and surveyors.

The colonies competed for free labour. It suited New Zealand propaganda to be 'free', lacking the convict taint, as that profile was likely to attract migrants. South Australia and Victoria also emphasized their non-convict heritage for marketing themselves. Respectability and a high moral tone above all required women, the societies' 'moral currency'. In New South Wales women in the free labour force outnumbered convict women from the late 1830s because most women migrated 'free' in both senses (assisted and non-convict), being shipped out to redress the gross gender imbalance. Free settlement needed women as domestic workers, wives and mothers, and their 'civilizing mission', to build new societies.

Free enterprise needed help from companies and governments to secure free labour, and especially women's labour. The preferred source was England, especially for South Australia's and New Zealand's planned settlements. New Zealand set out to avoid Australia as a source of recruitment, but in practice Australia came second to Britain as a source from 1850 to 1914. Before 1850, at least half the white population arrived from Australia. Auckland began and remained the most Australian of New Zealand towns, and developed by spontaneous migration into the most successful settlement. The seat of government and the military from 1840, Auckland grew from trade and commerce with Sydney.

The first free, 'planned' settlement organized by one of the companies which entered the migrant market grew at Swan River from 1829, providing important lessons about relations between land, labour and capital. Land grants to absentees dispersed the settlement, denied labour its use, and threatened all with starvation. The acute, persistent shortage of free labour prompted a resort to convictism from 1849, despite the risks of moral taint. The settlements organized by the South Australian Company, the New Zealand Company and the Otago and Canterbury Associations between 1836 and 1850 were shaped by ideals of 'systematic colonization'. These were devised to avoid the pitfalls of dispersal, and based on American antecedents. Only in South Australia and New Zealand were attempts made to transplant a vertical slice of British society, not just the masses. The slice would embrace English relations between squire, tenant and labourer – a structure imagined rather than understood. Edward Gibbon Wakefield was not the inventor of systematic colonization, but its synthesizer and propagandist. From 1836 to 1842 in South Australia, and in the New Zealand township of Wellington and its satellites, Nelson, New Plymouth and Wanganui, he provided the problems as much as the ideas. Otago and Canterbury followed in 1848 and 1850. Wakefield's 'art of colonization', devised to redeem his reputation for abducting heiresses, was compelling but impractical, and left mainly for surveyors and settlers to work out.

The plan to keep land, labour and capital in balance through a sufficiently high price of land was subverted at once. It was hard to persuade capitalists to migrate. Most of those who purchased land orders preferred to stay home, and only Canterbury attracted the planned proportion of landowners; almost a quarter migrated as 'colonists' – cabin passengers. The great majority, agricultural workers, artisans and domestic servants, travelled in steerage as 'emigrants'. Of the emigrants to South Australia from 1836 to 1840, 56 per cent of men were agricultural labourers, 20 per cent were from building trades, and 64 per cent of women were domestic servants.[24] The systematic colonizers subverted their theory by selling land orders for sections of land which did not exist, or had not been sold by Maori in New Zealand, and by offering 'emigrants' high wages and security. They worsened the imbalance between capital and labour by sending out yet more labourers to claim further land for sales. The companies provided free steerage passages, and (importantly) a guarantee of paid work. From the start, they promised a 'workingman's paradise'.[25] When unemployment struck in the 1840s, free labour became a charge on the companies, and on the British government once company funds drained away. This promise of public work, and its breach in the 1840s, produced a breakdown in labour–capital relations. Nelson resorted to subsistence farming where labourers squatted on small plots. Small men banded together in villages and provided mutual employment and aid. Labour–capital relations were 'more conventional and less disturbed' in Canterbury, where there was no guarantee of public work, only the publicity of prospects, as in Australia.[26] In the event, wool and gold saved the Otago and Canterbury settlements.

The military also supplied free labour as surveyors of towns such as Wellington and Christchurch and Australia's convict colonies, but also ex-India Army officers as 'pilgrims' to South Australia, and pastoralists for the expanding free settlements. Military settlement by 'the fencibles', discharged soldiers of good character, attracted pensioner migrants to Auckland in the 1840s; Waikato military settlers took up confiscated land in the 1860s, together with imperial regulars who were discharged or retired in New Zealand, including some Australians.

ASSISTED LABOUR

Aside from free spirits in search of land and gold, free labour needed incentives to migrate. Britain introduced government-assisted passages in 1831, as subsidized passages, free passages, or loans. By 1839, 27 per cent of English migrants chose Australia (68 per cent preferred the United States).[27] Free labour to the colonies was no 'spillover' from the USA: the colonies attracted rather different migrants, from lower-wage counties of southern England.[28]

In the nineteenth century almost half of British free migrants to Australia were assisted. Gold made Victoria the exception. Excluding Tasmania, for which there is insufficient evidence, immigration to Australia was usually assisted.[29] Assisted passages were limited to specific occupations: unmarried farm servants, married mechanics and farm workers and their families, and single women domestic workers and wives. What distinguished Australia's and New Zealand's assisted migrants was that women came at similar rates to men's, because the colonies needed their labour, and civilization demanded women. Systematic colonizers believed the family central to the settlements' fate, and young married couples the ideal migrants. By the time Wakefield published *A View of the Art of Colonization* in 1849, he emphasized not merely the gender division of labour as the basis of prosperity, but women as moral agents.[30]

The written word spread by promotional literature and letters encouraged women to migrate, and especially widows who joined their kin. People migrated in groups and chains, as colonists nominated friends and relatives and paid part of their fares. This unusually high proportion of free migrants helps explain why Australia and New Zealand recorded high standards of living in the 1860s. The degree of government assistance reinforced a key informal myth of antipodean settlement – the 'workingman's paradise'. Both 'systematic' colonization and government-assisted migration furthered this idea.

The colonies financed their own assisted labour migration following responsible government from 1856, and the 1852 Constitution Act in New Zealand. Australian colonies and New Zealand provinces took responsibility for recruitment, and competed directly. In New Zealand, Vogel's national scheme superseded provincial recruitment in the 1870s, drawing the largest influx of free labour: 100,000 or 120,000.[31] Colonies also tried special schemes: Germans and Scandinavians for South Australia, Queensland and remote settlements in New Zealand; Scottish Highlanders; and Dalmatians to extract kauri gum, all affecting regional and local identities.

Assisted labourers were independent-minded. Most came from rural England, Ireland and Scotland, as pre-industrial labourers, artisans and domestic servants. They were not paupers: almost all women were 'partly-skilled'; and so were most men. They were literate and enterprising. The poor came later: like non-English-speaking white labour, they were a last resort. From the ranks of the skilled emerged proto-trade unionists to agitate for the eight-hour day. Carpenters did well in New Zealand and stonemasons on public works in Australia.

The high proportion of single women made Australian and New Zealand migration distinctive. The colonies recruited women to meet the shortage of domestic labour, as maids and brides, to rectify the gender imbalance, and above all to create civilized societies. Demand for domestic servants did not depend solely on their economic value; in Australia, single women were sought as domestic workers rather than convict maids, stigmatized as immoral; their value continued to be estimated not simply monetarily but in terms of 'moral character', especially after the moral risks and gender imbalance of gold rushes. In Australia from 1832 to 1836, most migration funding was devoted to single women; the same was true in South Australia in the 1840s and Victoria from 1858. In New Zealand in the 1850s and

1860s, 12,000 single women came from Britain, two-thirds to Otago and Canterbury. Canterbury spent almost its entire migration fund on single women. In the 1870s single women made up a fifth of Vogel's national scheme. Private patronage supplemented public schemes. The Female Middle Class Emigration Society, for instance, was organized in 1862 by Maria Rye who selected young, poor gentlewomen for Canterbury and Otago. In New South Wales and England, Caroline Chisholm created a family colonization scheme, reuniting families and supplying industrious workers. The dominant idea was self-help, so that migrants would eventually repay their assistance, strengthening the respectable working class.

Because single women could not contribute to the cost of their passage (half the steerage fare of £10–11 from Britain in the 1850s), women came free. Governments offered more liberal terms for women than for men, so that single women were more visible in the colonies, and the subject of comment. So keen were Otago and Canterbury to obtain women as wives and mothers and domestics that they offered free passages in the 1860s, in response to the gold rushes, and to preserve their foundation myths. Unlike New South Wales, they imposed no indenture for free passage: recipients only had to promise that they intended to work for wages. Irish women were less desired, and their 'moral character' was questioned. South Australia and South Island planned settlements sought English single women, and over half of those to Canterbury were from England. Canterbury preferred Anglo-Irish women: the numbers of poor, Catholic Irish young women rose in the later 1860s with free passages, consistent with the free labour pattern that poor migrants arrived last.

In New Zealand, 63 per cent of single women worked before they migrated in domestic service, eight per cent as dairymaids and farm servants, five per cent as cooks and housekeepers, and four per cent in needlework.[32] Like convicts, most were skilled and semi-skilled. Although women migrants stayed in their own class in labour relations terms, they adopted aspects of their employers' dress style. There was a notable lack of deference, since scarcity of labour influenced social as well as gender relations. Australians told tales of the European lady addressing her housemaid: 'When I wave my hand you have to come', to which the colonial girl replied: 'Yes, Mum, and when I shake my head, then I won't come'.[33]

A FRENCH AUSTRALIA?

Following Australian rather than their own precedents, France in 1855 acquired as vacant, all New Caledonian lands not under cultivation, and assigned them to settlers. Cattle proved more profitable than farming, and mining soon overtook both, but labour shortages constrained them all. Assisted immigration began only in 1887, offering free passage and free land; but French reluctance to emigrate persisted, and only 11,700 were counted in 1906. Convicts were expected to lay the foundation of a capitalist economy. New Caledonia therefore displaced the notorious Guiana as a reception centre, and 11,100 convicts had arrived by 1876, when they outnumbered free settlers by three to two. Most were required to remain in New Caledonia after their sentences, but the 5,000 deportees from the Paris Commune of 1871 were repatriated by 1879. This population was also self-limiting as only two per cent were women, reflecting their preference for metropolitan gaols. Because the punitive purpose prevailed and there was no local policy-making, New Caledonia made none of the adjustments and offered none of the subsidies which attracted free settlers to the English-speaking colonies.

Melanesians were not integrated into this economy but isolated from it, in cramped reserves and off-shore islands. Despite these reserves, and the presence of convicts, demand for labour outstripped supply, as employers were unwilling (and often unable) to pay realistic wages. In these circumstances they preferred to recruit New Hebrideans under indenture. Beginning in the 1850s as a state venture, recruitment continued as a private business until 1929. Over 14,000 arrived, the majority before 1900.[34] Thereafter they were supplemented and then displaced by Vietnamese and Javanese; and as the administration imposed taxes in the Loyalty Islands, these islanders also came to the main island under indenture. Recruits were commonly engaged for three to five years, not only by planters and mine managers, but by the government. Not only could employers pay as little and as late as they chose; New Hebrideans were as 'foreign' as the settlers, so they were more trusted than Kanak or *liberes*, forming a 'natural gendarmerie' in a violent and unsettled countryside.[35] From the 1880s, women comprised 10 or 20 per cent of many ships' manifests of recruits. A few worked as miners and field hands, but most entered domestic service. Male free settlers outnumbered women by a wide margin, and the imbalance was perhaps ten to one among New Hebrideans, and thirty to one among convicts and *liberes*. Many women became concubines, or laundry contractors after their term of indenture. In brief, nineteenth-century New Caledonia never attracted the planning or the investment which underpinned settlement in Australia and New Zealand; so it failed to overcome the ingrained reluctance of French citizens to emigrate.

SEGREGATED LABOUR MARKETS

In convict Australia, no indigenous people were drafted into the labour force. Phillip's opposition to slavery was not the only reason. Many officials and settlers thought Aborigines not above but beneath the simplest task. Rowley argues that settlers saw Aboriginal people as pest rather than potential worker.[36] In an overview of Aboriginal labour, the first step we 'must take is to come to terms with the popular racist assumption that Aborigines and Torres Strait Islanders did not work'. For, as Curthoys and Moore remind us, early European residents lodged Aboriginal Australians in the same racial category as African slaves, only Aborigines were an expedient resource because they were already there. The first step was to chase them away, and second to encourage them on the fringes of white settlement with the enticement of rations because they offered useful labour. Aboriginal workers were not slaves 'in the strict sense, but neither were they free'.[37] According to Markus, dispossession shaped four unofficial rules of labour relations: violence was necessary to establish who was boss; insubordination was intolerable; training for pastoralism was to be by pastoralists; and Aborigines were not free agents. They were 'run down' and 'broken in', as if animals, and then excluded from institutions devised by and for 'free' wage labour.[38] 'White Australia' imposed no constraints on employers' prejudices.

The norm in labour relations in convict society was a male, white worker. The black 'gin', like the convict woman, was almost invariably cast as sexual object, a pathetic creature used, discarded and despised. In the predominantly male workforce of the northern maritime industries, and in pastoral areas, Europeans were known to abduct women and keep them by force. The convict woman and the 'gin' were both sexual objects, but one eventually moved on. Ultimately, the white woman was as much the beneficiary of Aboriginal dispossession as the white man. She often functioned as the oppressor, and with this admission the chain of oppression becomes long and complex. If the woman convicts were 'the victim of the victims', Aboriginal women were doubly abused.

> Aboriginal women's memories of white brutality focus on the domestic violence and confinement perpetrated by the mistress in the home, as well as the exploitation and sexual violence that so often characterized their encounters with white men on the frontier.[39]

Unlike convict women, they had no path, personal or professional, out of their plight.

Aboriginal workers were distinguished by the legislation controlling them, the various acts passed in each colony supposedly for their 'protection'. From the 1880s, and especially after 1897, Aborigines and Torres Strait Islanders laboured under the control of these special Acts of colonial parliaments, and state parliaments from 1901. Indentured labour forms proved unnecessary because of these 'draconian controls'.[40]

Aboriginal labour was mostly employed in the north and west of the continent, in Queensland, the Northern Territory and Western Australia, where few whites were available and most indigenous people lived. Segregated on reserves, it was assumed that Aboriginal people would be tutored in isolation as a reserve labour force and provide itinerant labour for white settlements. In the frontier zone, in pastoralism, mining, the rainforest and maritime industries and agriculture, Aborigines provided reserves of labour. Camps on the fringes of colonial towns, missions and government settlements became bases for the supply of seasonal Aboriginal workers.[41] There were five to ten thousand Aboriginal stockmen by the end of the century, working for rations rather than wages. Cattle stations in particular provided a congenial environment for Aboriginal men, straddling the old and new economies. They adjusted well to raising sheep and cattle: 'I don't know what we pioneers should have done without the blacks', wrote a cattleman in 1884, 'for they can't be beat at looking after horses and cattle.'[42] Aborigines 'born in the cattle'

Plate 8.1 *A Samoan Picnic, or Jack in his Element,* watercolour, sketched on the back of a letter by Captain Edwyn Temple, founder of the Canterbury Society of Arts, New Zealand, reproduced by kind permission of Mrs Elizabeth Temple.

used their situation to stay in their country: 'Aborigines "grew up" the stations. They worked not just for tucker, but literally to "hold onto" their land, and keep it alive.'[43] Yet Aboriginal pastoral workers – underpaid, given no formal training, rarely celebrated and often beaten – had little incentive to increase their efficiency.

Relations were usually more humane in coastal industries, although working conditions for everyone were often harsh and there was a high mortality rate from disease, violence and work-related accidents.[44] Aboriginal men and women were involved in sealing and bay-whaling off the southern coasts in the first half of the nineteenth century and in pearling and *bêche-de-mer* gathering in the north from the second half. Bay whaling fitted easily into old patterns of life, as coastal clans were used to harvesting whales cast up on the beaches. Europeans in turn supplied local Aborigines with quantities of surplus whale flesh. Bass Strait sealers depended on Aboriginal women, while at some bay-whaling stations Aboriginal crews manned boats, receiving the same pay, or share of profits, as whites. Aborigines and Torres Strait Islanders were even more widely employed in the north. In the 1880s a thousand or more worked during the pearling and *bêche-de-mer* seasons. There too, traditional expertise was carried into maritime trades. The northwestern pearling industry relied on local knowledge of the location of beds of shell. The expertise of Tasmanians allowed European sealers to survive on bleak Bass Strait islands.

In the far north, Aboriginal Australians were more integrated into the colonial economy than in the south. In the maritime industries of Torres Strait, labour from the Pacific, including New Guinea and Asia mingled with Torres Strait and Cape York Aboriginal workers. Torres Strait Islanders' experience had more in common with Pacific Islanders than with mainland Aboriginal Australians.[45]

New Zealand Maori working experience was extremely varied, and very different from that of Aboriginal Australians. Maori retained their autonomy in inaccessible areas, and had it eroded elsewhere by the pressures of colonization. Until 1860 they were the main suppliers of food. From the 1860s they moved from work in regional Maori economies and to the Pakeha economy in its various guises, from large-scale farming, trade and collective ownership to casual waged work and poverty with the alienation of their land.[46] In the era of Maori control, and where that control survived, Maori subverted British practices and wove them into their own framework. Hapu undercut expensive Pakeha labour, successfully tendered for contracts, and with *mana* raised from skills in building and agriculture, turned those skills to use in the Maori economy, in food production, trade, and building churches and schools, all new outlets for competition as comprehended by Maori values.[47]

The scarcity of Pakeha labour drew Maori into Pakeha pastoralism as shearers and station hands. Pastoralists depended on Maori labour and their custom of working in kin groups which included women and children. Maori initiated the first shearers' strike, in 1863, and raised the pay rate until local pastoralists combined to recruit a gang of white 'black-leg' shearers. Maori continued to work in kin groups as itinerant rural labourers. Whole families worked on contract in gangs which specialized in felling timber, gum digging, flax cutting and processing, fencing, shearing and roads. Increasingly however, Maori became marginalized by white labour, as in the Wairarapa from the 1860s when pastoralists recruited Maori only for harvesting once they had a pool of small farmers in bush settlements to provide casual labour. In public works, from the late 1870s Maori ceased to receive the preference which until then was deemed politically expedient.[48]

The radical differences between Aboriginal and Maori working experience is largely a matter of Maori power and Aboriginal powerlessness. Among Maori as well, experience varied in proportion to political power and the retention or loss of their land. *Iwi* who retained land received rents and in some regions royalties from timber, kauri gum and gold. On the East Coast Ngati Porou ventured into pastoralism, but such initiatives declined from the 1890s with large-scale land purchase. Elsewhere the lack of fences posed hazards to experiments with stock, although in the King Country the 'sheep craze' initially stalled further sales of land at prices settlers desired. In the Rotorua region with its hot pools and geysers, Maori became guides in the tourism industry.[49] One Resident Magistrate judged: 'Maoris are not suited for constant labour. They are fond of change and novelty, and cannot be induced to remain long at any settled employment.'[50] Yet Maori work patterns in the casual labour force were no different from those of Pakeha.

Loss of land led to poverty in the Pakeha world of labour relations, and loss of food resources meant poverty in the traditional world by 1900. People were forced to leave their settlements to earn a living. When Ngai Tahu in the South Island sought work for wages to survive, they met prejudice against Maori *kai* (food). They helped develop a taste for their *kai* among Pakeha, for example whitebait exchanged in towns for clothes and cash, a cultural exchange that often resulted from poverty, which in turn stemmed from lack of land.[51]

Workers who entered Australia under indenture were almost as powerless as Aboriginal stockmen and domestic servants, although elaborate legislation offered some protection. Melanesians were shipped in to New South Wales under indenture in the 1840s, on the initiative of the pastoralist Benjamin Boyd; but the venture was not pursued. When sugar became an export staple in north Queensland in the 1860s, Melanesia became a 'labour reserve' for Australian planters as well as New Caledonian ranchers. From 1863 until 1904, over 62,000 islanders worked in Queensland, most from Vanuatu and the Solomons, and 95 per cent were men.[52] Melanesians were also recruited for New Caledonia from the 1860s to the 1920s.[53] The first recruits were ill-informed, and often kidnapped. Coercion became rare after 1872 when the British government passed the Pacific Islanders Protection Act and Queensland enacted matching laws. The Royal Navy policed minimum standards, and Queensland and New Caledonian vessels carried government agents. New Caledonian recruiters perpetuated coercive methods; but in much of Melanesia institutional migration made coercion redundant. Tobacco and alcohol were powerful inducements, and returning workers persuasive; but the trickery and violence of the early 'blackbirding' phase made a much greater impact on the public memory of white Australia.[54]

To the emerging white Labor movement, indentured labour endangered free labour, as well as threatening the 'noble European race'.[55] Newly arrived British migrants to northern Australia, more attuned to unionism than earlier streams, fuelled the labourist racism mix in late nineteenth-century Queensland. In the islands themselves, recruiting negotiations were certainly unequal, but recruits and passage masters were sensitive to wages, which did rise over the fifty years of the Queensland phase. Passage masters and recruits took advantage of a seller's market so long as there was competing demand from New Caledonia as well as Queensland and Fiji. The terms of trade moved against them when Indians arrived in Fiji, and after 1900 when Queensland was closed. Thousands of New Hebrideans continued to sign on for New Caledonia, but their conditions eroded as their leverage declined.[56]

Melanesia was not the only source of such labourers. From the 1870s massive diasporas poured out not just from Europe, but from China and India. Eight million Chinese lived abroad by 1922 and four million Indians, of the 16 million who had migrated between 1871 and 1915. Another million Japanese migrated after the 1880s.[57] Japanese and Vietnamese travelled to New Caledonia; and 60,000 Indians sailed to Fiji before 1916. Indians and Chinese were also indentured to work in Australia. Indians were recruited from 1837 to 1844 by New South Wales pastoralists. The first Chinese shipped to New South Wales in 1848 were also indentured, and the gold rushes drew 3,000 men and boys to Australia. British anti-slavery sentiment generated tensions, as did anxiety in the Colonial Office and the government of India, but immigration to Australia was not controlled until the 1850s.

Outside the goldfields, Chinese engaged in market gardening, furniture-making and laundries: cabinet-making and laundries became the focus of labour agitation in Sydney and Melbourne. Anti-Chinese lobbying and other forms of opposition by white workers prevented Chinese from becoming integrated into the labour market. Unions excluded non-whites on the grounds that they undercut wages, and articulated a race mythology which supposed that they would sap the strength of unions. Opposition to Chinese seamen working for the Australasian Steam Navigation Company was explicit in the strike of 1878–9, when strikers argued that the Company had contravened the accepted rule that employers would not bring Chinese into competition with white labour. Employers' interest in cheap Chinese labour waned. Cabinet-making comprised the only manufacturing trade in which there was significant competition with white labour, and furniture was stamped as made by non-European labour. Chinese laundries survived, with the aid of the shortage of domestic servants.

From the 1880s, British colonists built barriers against Chinese. Their migration was restricted through poll tax and other measures; they were segregated in the labour market and excluded from the labour movement: they were also excluded from citizenship. After the gold rushes, therefore, many went home. Even before the adoption of the 'White Australia' policy, the settler societies defined themselves by excluding Aborigines and aliens (that is,

Asians and Pacific Islanders), but not Maori. According to Burgmann, economic conditions provided the catalyst for the Australian labour movement's response to Chinese migration.[58] The labour movement agitated to restrict Chinese because they believed that they undercut white labour with semi-servile competition. In the depressed 1890s economic insecurities worsened and the colonies legislated to restrict other non-Europeans. In New Zealand, the labour movement also feared unfair competition from Asians shut out of, or fleeing, Australia. R. J. Seddon, the populist premier, explained: 'Nothing that threatens Australia and the Europeans there is good for New Zealand', while Australian exclusion policies also fed the irrational fear that 'every steamer that is now coming down from Australia is bringing a large number of Chinese'.[59] New Zealand put up barriers even as it pulled out of depression in the 1890s. For the New Zealand labour movement, populated by Australian unionists, economic arguments cloaked racial prejudice. Pat Hickey, the Australian miner-turned West Coast unionist and politician, asserted that labour had a duty to 'keep New Zealand white. Internationalism did not mean a reckless intermingling of white and coloured races.'[60] While the Immigration Restriction Amendment Act 1920 represented in part a response to lobbying by trade unions and the Returned Servicemen's Association, who couched their arguments in labour terms, New Zealand's laws, like Australia's, reflected ubiquitous xenophobia. Racism proved a powerful political drawcard; it was vote-catching and did not cost anything.

Labour markets were segregated by gender at least as sharply as they were divided into racial segments. In New Zealand as well as Australia, scarcity ensured that European women were in demand. Marriage proved the reality as well as the expectation for most. The principal labour shortage was of *domestic* workers. British ideals of womanhood and a domestic ideology shaped women's paid (as well as unpaid) labour. Since respectability required a male breadwinner, paid work for women was only condoned socially when women were single. How a woman entered the paid workforce was affected by marital status, place in the life cycle, and class. Willy-nilly, the poorest had to be breadwinners. That strong girls were wanted, is suggested by the fact that their work demanded strength and long hours, in Australian heat or New Zealand mud. Wood fires required supervision and houses lacked most amenities. Wages for female domestic workers were high relative to Britain, and secure from fluctuations in the market, but low relative to men.

Domestic service was certainly skilled, but was not seen as such, being fit work for women.[61] Low wages supposedly encouraged women to marry, and certainly they did not stay in a job long. This mobility suggests that domestic workers were undervalued despite their scarcity, because young women became domestic servants not through choice but by force of circumstance. In the late nineteenth century the highest proportions in paid domestic service were found in cities where manufacturing was least developed. In Adelaide in 1871, 62 per cent of the female paid workforce were domestic servants; in Melbourne, 57 per cent. By 1901 these figures had fallen to

46 per cent and 40 per cent.[62] Increasingly, working-class women refused to work as servants. Middle-class women did much of their own housework, and so became 'housewives'.

There were also new openings in clerical and factory work. Factory work was the commonest paid alternative to domestic service, becoming available first in Victoria, then in New South Wales. Over 90 per cent of factory work in clothing and textiles was done by women. While they doubtless enjoyed the company, the free evenings and weekends, and the pay, they had to tolerate stress and noise. Commercial work was more respectable (especially in the wake of the typewriter from 1885) and new jobs for women evolved as shorthand typists, telephonists, and post and telegraph assistants. As in factory work, a dual labour market formed, with men in higher-paid supervisory positions. Once feminization began, it sustained itself and shorthand and typing became 'women's work'. For middle-class spinsters and widows, teaching offered security and respectability. By the late nineteenth century almost half the teachers in Australia and New Zealand were women. Nursing also became feminized, under the influence of the Nightingale model. The colonies followed British tradition, paying women half of the male rate, and slightly more in skilled work.

Old toils still had to be performed. Most colonial women were recorded in paid work in rural areas because this was where the economy needed them. In the commonest pattern they earned as part of the family economy, where all contributed to a family income; farms often employed whole families. Payment as part of a family unit helped to suppress women's wages.[63] The family income strategy was also found among the urban poor. It was not uncommon for urban poor, and widows, to run boarding houses. A family income strategy is evident also in country towns. Women were working partners with men, in running stores and pubs. Publicans' widows resumed their husbands' licences. This was significant when a widow with dependent children represented the second most common family type. Early colonial governments offered most scope for women's paid employment, for example as postmistresses, who often succeeded their husbands. Because of family partnerships and early widowhood, women gained a respected place in commerce.

PLANTATIONS

Europeans' impact in the islands increased as traders sought their own land and wage labour (preferably indentured). The Hamburg-based New Guinea Company was the most ambitious, commissioned in 1884 to rule New Guinea; but malaria and other diseases struck down its officers and indentured labourers, while tropical organisms ravaged crops. In 1899 the Company surrendered its mandate, but by 1914 prosperous plantations had developed in the Bismarck archipelago, based on copra. Samoa remained the focus of German enterprise, where the Deutsche Handels- und Plantagen-Gesellschaft (DHPG) had land, but not labour. Samoans would not work for them, Gilbertese were readily recruited but there were not enough of them, and to recruit Chinese involved frustrating negotiations with Chinese officials. In Samoa, as everywhere else, plantations needed backing from the state. Until 1900 the German consul was the most powerful single figure in Apia: thereafter it was the (German) colonial governor. As in almost every other dependency the governor chose to deal with a large plantation company rather than a host of small planters. In Samoa that was DHPG; in Fiji it was the Australian Colonial Sugar Refining Company (CSR); and in Solomon Islands it was Lever Brothers which amassed no less than 400,000 acres.[64] Those developments brought corporation and state into such cosy association that workers' rights – even those specified in laws – were most unlikely to be enforced. Only in Australian Papua, where a Royal Commission in 1906 also proposed plantations, did that strategy fail: the 'white Australia' policy ruled out Asian labourers, and shipping costs were high; so plantations were replaced by the coerced production of villagers.[65] In Fiji, the archetypal plantation colony, Fijians retained most of the land, chiefly authority was made compatible with British indirect rule, and CSR ordered sugar production on plantations. The government imported Indian indentured workers (*girmitiyas*) for plantations, reserving Fijian labour for the chiefs. The government also delegated to employers the administration of regulations, and plantations became autocracies where lives were governed in detail by CSR.[66]

Throughout our region the segregation of labour markets by gender, and by race, inhibited the recognition of shared interests. Even in the Australian colonies and New Zealand, where trade unions were precocious and powerful, the drive to secure for union members the expected benefits of the workingman's paradise focused on adult white males to the exclusion of women, Asian workers (indentured or 'free') and Melanesians. Labour as much as capital insisted on dividing workers against one another.

NOTES

1 Donald Denoon, 'Land, Labour and Independent Development', in Donald Denoon, Stewart Firth, Jocelyn Linnekin, Malama Meleisea and Karen Nero (eds), *Cambridge History of the Pacific Islanders*, Melbourne, 1997, 152–83. See also Dorothy Shineberg, *They Came for Sandalwood*, Melbourne, 1967.
2 Stephen Nicholas and Peter R. Shergold, 'Unshackling the Past', in Stephen Nicholas (ed.), *Convict Workers: Reinterpreting Australia's Past*, Melbourne, 1988, 3.
3 Ibid., ch. 1.
4 Robson, Shaw, acknowledged by Nicholas, *Convict Workers*, 4. Statistics from Deborah Oxley, *Convict Maids: The Forced Migration of Women to Australia*, Melbourne, 1996, 3.
5 J. B. Hirst, *Convict Society and its Enemies: A History of Early New South Wales*, Sydney, 1983, 83.
6 There is a discrepancy in Nicholas, *Convict Workers*, between p. 8 (over 80 per cent aged 16 to 25 years) and p. 59 (16 to 35 years).
7 A. G. L. Shaw, *Convicts and the Colonies*, London, 1966, 358.

8 Raymond Evans and William Thorpe, 'Power, Punishment and Penal Labour: Convict Workers and Moreton Bay', *Australian Historical Studies*, 25: 98 (April 1992), 90–111.

9 Ibid., 108–9, original emphasis.

10 S. G. Foster, cited in S. Nicholas (ed.), *Convict Workers: Reinterpreting Australia's Past*, Melbourne, 1988, 6.

11 Shaw, *Convicts and the Colonies*, 20–6.

12 Evans and Thorpe, 'Power, Punishment and Penal Labour', 103–4 (figures rounded).

13 Nicholas and Shergold, 'Unshackling the Past', 12.

14 David Meredith, 'Full Circle? Contemporary Views on Transportation', in Nicholas, *Convict Workers*, 19.

15 Monica Perrott, *A Tolerable Good Success: Economic Opportunities for Women in New South Wales, 1788–1830*, Sydney, 1983, 32.

16 Anne Summers, *Damned Whores and God's Police*, 2nd edn, Melbourne, 1994; Joy Damousi, *Depraved and Disorderly: Female Convicts, Sexuality and Gender in Colonial Australia*, Melbourne, 1997. Portia Robinson, *The Women of Botany Bay*, Sydney, 1988, rediscovered a positive role for convict women as mothers (as opposed to Miriam Dixson's negative view, as 'doormats'), while Oxley, *Convict Maids*, restored them as workers.

17 Deborah Oxley, 'Female Convicts', in Nicholas, *Convict Workers*, ch. 6; see also ch. 10; and Oxley, *Convict Maids*, 171.

18 Oxley, *Convict Maids*, 118, 121.

19 K. Alford, *Production or Reproduction? An Economic History of Women in Australia, 1788–1850*, Melbourne, 1984.

20 Perrott, *A Tolerable Good Success*, 31.

21 Shaw, *Convicts and the Colonies*, 243.

22 Damousi, *Depraved and Disorderly*, 114–20.

23 Perrott, *A Tolerable Good Success*, 45.

24 W. D. McIntyre (ed.), *Journal of Henry Sewell, 1853–7*, vol. 1 (Feb. 1853–May 1854), Christchurch, 1980, 13.

25 Douglas Pike, *Paradise of Dissent: South Australia 1829–1857*, London, 1957.

26 W. J. Gardner, 'The Founding of Nelson and Canterbury: A Comparative Study', *Historical News*, 48 (May 1984), 4.

27 Ibid.

28 Oxley, *Convict Maids*.

29 Robin Haines, 'Indigent Misfits or Shrewd Operators? Government-assisted Emigrants from the United Kingdom to Australia, 1831–1860', *Population Studies*, 48 (1994), 223–47.

30 Robin Haines and Ralph Shlomowitz, 'Immigration from the United Kingdom to Colonial Australia: A Statistical Analysis', *Journal of Australian Studies*, 34 (1992), 43–52.

31 Raewyn Dalziel, 'Men, Women and Wakefield', in *Edward Gibbon Wakefield and the Colonial Dream: A Reconsideration*, Wellington, 1997, 77–86.

32 D. H. Akenson, *Half the World from Home: Perspectives on the Irish in New Zealand, 1860–1950*, Wellington, 1990; W. D. Borrie, 'The Peopling of Australasia, 1788–1988', in K. Sinclair (ed.), *Tasman Relations: New Zealand and Australia, 1788–1988*, Auckland, 1988, 202–23. Also W. D. Borrie, *The European Peopling of Australasia: A Demographic History, 1788–1988*, Canberra, 1994.

33 Oxley, *Convict Maids*.

34 See illustration and discussion in Beverley Kingston, *My Wife, My Daughter, and Poor Mary Ann: Women and Work in Australia*, West Melbourne, 1977.

35 Dorothy Shineberg, *The People Trade: Pacific Island Laborers and New Caledonia, 1865–1930*, Honolulu, 1999.

36 Ibid.

37 Ann Curthoys and Clive Moore, 'Working for the White People: An Historiographic Essay on Aboriginal and Torres Strait Islander Labour', in Ann McGrath and Kay Saunders with Jackie Huggins (eds), *Aboriginal Workers*, Sydney, 1995 (*Labour History*, 69, special issue), 2, 4.

38 C. D. Rowley, *The New Guinea Villager: A Retrospect from 1964*, Melbourne, 1965.

39 Andrew Markus, *Australian Race Relations 1788–1993*, Sydney, 1994.

40 Curthoys and Moore, 'Working for the White People', 6–7, 11, 13; Peggy Brock, 'Pastoral Stations and Reserves in South and Central Australia, 1850s–1950s', in McGrath, Saunders and Huggins, *Aboriginal Workers*, 102–14.

41 Ann McGrath, '*Born in the Cattle*': *Aborigines in Cattle Country*, Sydney, 1987, 174.

42 H. Reynolds, *The Other Side of the Frontier: Aboriginal Resistance to the European Invasion of Australia*, Ringwood, Victoria, 1981, 172. See also Patricia Grimshaw, Marilyn Lake, Ann McGrath and Marian Quartly, *Creating a Nation*, Melbourne, 1994, 1.

43 H. Reynolds, *The Other Side of the Frontier: Aboriginal Resistance to the European Invasion of Australia*, Ringwood, Victoria, 1982, 172.

44 Regina Ganter, *The Pearl-shellers of Torres Strait: Resource Use, Development and Decline, 1860s–1960s*, Melbourne, 1994.

45 Curthoys and Moore, 'Working for the White People', 5.

46 M. King, 'Between Two Worlds', in G. W. Rice (ed.), *Oxford History of New Zealand*, 2nd edn, Auckland, 1992, 290.

47 Eruera Stirling, as told to Anne Salmond, *Eruera: The Teachings of a Maori Elder*, Wellington, 1980, 22–4, 69; C. L. Andrews, 'Aspects of Development: The Maori Situation, 1870–1890', MA thesis, University of Auckland, 1968, 64–5.

48 J. Martin, *The Forgotten Worker: The Rural Wage Earner in Nineteenth-century New Zealand*, Wellington, 1990, 38–48, 173–4; C. Orange (ed.), *The Maori Biographies from The Dictionary of New Zealand Biography, Vol. 2: The Turbulent Years, 1870–1900*, Wellington, 1994, xvii.

49 Andrews, 'Aspects of Development'; Orange, *The Maori Biographies*, xviii.

50 Andrews, 'Aspects of Development', 23.

51 B. Dacker, *The People of the Place: Mahika Kai*, Wellington, 1990.

52 Clive Moore, Jacqueline Leckie and Doug Munro (eds), *Labour in the South Pacific*, Townsville, 1990.

53 Shineberg, *The People Trade*.

54 Clive Moore, *Kanaka: A History of Melanesian Mackay*, Port Moresby, 1985.

55 Markus, *Australian Race Relations*.

56 Shineberg, *The People Trade*.

57 Avner Offer, *The First World War: An Agrarian Interpretation*, Oxford, 1989, 168; Manying Ip, 'Chinese New Zealanders', in Stuart W. Greif (ed.), *Immigration and National Identity in New Zealand*, Palmerston North, 1995, 163; Neville Bennett, 'Bitter Fruit: Japanese Migration and Anglo-Saxon Obstacles, 1890–1924', *Transactions of the Asiatic Society of Japan*, 8 (1993), 70.

58 See the articles by Verity Burgmann and others, in Ann Curthoys and Andrew Markus (eds), *Who Are Our Enemies? Racism and the Working Class in Australia*, Sydney, 1978.

59 R. J. Seddon, *New Zealand Parliamentary Debates*, 92, 23 June 1896, 252, 258.

60 Pat Hickey, 1920, cited in P. S. O'Connor, 'Keeping New Zealand White, 1908–1920', *New Zealand Journal of History*, 2 (1968): 58.

61 Oxley, *Convict Maids*; Charlotte Macdonald, *A Woman of Good Character: Single Women as Immigrant Settlers in Nineteenth-century New Zealand*, Wellington, 1990.

62 W. A. Sinclair, 'Women and Economic Change in Melbourne 1871–1921', *Historical Studies*, 20: 79 (Oct. 1982): 278–91.

63 Alford, *Production or Reproduction?*

64 Doug Munro and Stewart Firth, 'Company Strategies – Colonial Policies', in Clive Moore, Jacqueline Leckie and Doug Munro (eds), *Labour in the South Pacific*, Townsville, 1990, 25; Brij Lal, Doug Munro and Ed Beechert (eds), *Plantation Workers: Resistance and Accommodation*, Honolulu, 1994.

65 James Griffin, Hank Nelson and Stewart Firth, *Papua New Guinea: A Political History*, Melbourne, 1979; Brij V. Lal, *Broken Waves: A History of the Fiji Islands in the Twentieth Century*, Honolulu, 1992.

66 Brij V. Lal, *Girmitiyas: The Origins of the Fiji Indians*, Canberra, 1983.

Part III

New States and Social Identities

[9] NEW STATES

AN IMAGINED REGION

In the 1850s Alfred Russel Wallace had identified the line which bears his name, separating 'Asian' from 'Australasian' flora and fauna, and another caesura between Malays and Papuans (see chapter 1). Casual perceptions of this kind helped to isolate New Guinea and all Melanesia from the Malay world, at least in European eyes. Although whalers, timber-getters, missionaries and labour recruiters steadily added detail to European knowledge of the Pacific Islands, New Guinea remained stubbornly opaque to Europeans until late in the nineteenth century. Neither the Port Essington settlement on the north Australian coast in the 1840s, nor the Royal Navy's surveys of the same decade, threw light on it. As late as 1875 the record of an imaginary expedition could be published as a true record;[1] but by then missionaries and prospectors were scouting off-shore islands and the coast, and Australians were feeling proprietorial about the island and its imagined resources.

The missionaries, prospectors and explorers who crossed Torres Strait in the 1870s not only distinguished New Guinea from 'Asia', but were steeped in narratives of recent (but already mythic) European explorations of Africa. Glen judges that they

> restaged the perilous quest into 'darkest' Africa. ... The snaking course of the 'great [Fly] river' inland and the narrative search for unknown sources or fabled kingdoms at its headwaters flowed freely in early explorer accounts. New Guinea's charm met somewhere between the harsh and wild African interior and a softer Pacific vision of tropical paradise.[2]

When the Royal Geographical Society of Australasia formed in Sydney in 1883, its members too were aware of the role of the parent Society in sponsoring African exploration, and treated that as a model to emulate. Members referred to New Guinea's minerals as 'probably of an extreme richness', and argued that the time was ripe for 'an expedition of a scientific nature to visit the dark island'.[3]

Curiosity combined with gold fever and missionary zeal to give Australians a sense of a broader region in which to fulfil their destinies. Evangelization was unpromising in Islamic or Catholic regions, but possible – even perhaps an obligation – in heathen New Guinea. There were already credible rumours of gold, tempting prospectors from Queensland. Queensland's attempted annexation in 1883 manifested the colonists' ambitions; and when Britain did extend a protectorate over 'British New Guinea', New Zealand as well as eastern Australian colonies agreed to subsidize it. Australia with New Guinea and the Melanesian archipelagos perhaps complemented New Zealand and the islands of Polynesia, and certainly formed an open-ended region. Whether or not the islands were parts of Australasia, they had surely been severed from Asia. As Australian federation rendered 'Australasia' obsolete, the continent and the seas and islands were ever more firmly cemented in the colonists' imaginations as a region, and indeed as *their* region.

Some officials and settlers in New Caledonia shared this vision, but few islanders did. Like Australasia, this region's contours were most visible to descendants of Europeans. One effect of imagining these lands to comprise a region was to make it a new source of precedents for communities who usually brought values and procedures from their distant 'home'. No issue was more urgent than land. These were agrarian societies, and most would remain so. We need an imaginative leap to grasp the economic importance of land to its nineteenth-century claimants, let alone its cultural import. If colonists deemed their perspectives more rational than those of indigenes, they were no less emotional about the land which became the subject of collective and family narratives. Many of these narratives were – and some remain – combative. Typical of colonists throughout our region was the behaviour of new settlers in Voh in New Caledonia in the 1890s. By Isabelle Merle's account, for the newcomers the bush

> was like a blank page on which they had to write their own words. ... They organized space according to what they knew, they took possession of the soil by imprinting on it their own land-marks. ... The world of the Kanaks made no sense to the Europeans and they did not even try to make sense of it ... since they considered themselves the pioneers of an empire, the representatives of civilization.[4]

As settler communities became entrenched, destroying ancient social and economic networks and creating new ones, some grasped the machinery of their own government, most amassed political and economic leverage, and all sought to influence affairs in this newly imagined region. The British Navy still patrolled an 'informal empire' south of the equator. Ashore, British influence rested on kingdoms and theocracies whose Protestant orientation dovetailed with British strategy. This regime could accommodate social and political change if it occurred at a gentle pace, but that condition was not always met. Shipping increased as the Australian and New Zealand colonies began to export on a large scale, and British trade with China was consolidated by the development of Singapore and the cession of Hong Kong in 1842. The sea routes which linked China to Sydney and Auckland (as well as all of them to Europe and North America) sustained an ever-growing network of commerce which loosened Spain's control in the Philippines, and destabilized island polities. On one hand 'modernizing chiefs' could be trapped between the new logic of trade and the old obligations of patronage.[5] On the other hand a seeming power vacuum tempted Australians and New Zealanders to see the island region as their natural patrimony: for some a field for evangelism, for others a domain of easy fortunes, and for a few a stage for empire-building. Gavan Daws argues that some quality of the Pacific fostered outsiders' adventurism:

> Whatever they want, whether it is dominion over others or liberation from a civilized self, whether they surrender to the South Seas or impose civilized controls on themselves and their islands, it is here that they come into their kingdom.[6]

Daws was considering four publicists – the novelists Herman Melville and Robert Louis Stevenson, the missionary John Williams and the painter Paul Gauguin – who were instrumental in representing the Pacific as an arena for wish-fulfilment; but wishful thinking did not end with them. John Bates Thurston and Colonel Steinberger (see chapter 5) could be added to that list. So could the Presbyterian minister John Dunmore Lang in Sydney, who formed a prospecting association in 1871 which hoped that in Papua

> a constitution may be formed similar to that which has been so successfully initiated in the Fiji Islands, and by the purchase of large tracts of land from the natives a sure source of immense future profit will accrue to the Association.[7]

That expedition was shipwrecked, so its members lost their chance of peaceful expropriation. In Europe, Charles du Breil, Marquis de Rays, proposed a similar settlement of Europeans to farm, fish and mine at Nouvelle-France, where 'the natives do not share our idea of ownership and do not argue about the land with the new occupants'. Eight hundred landed in New Ireland between 1879 and 1881, but were driven out by illness and hunger. As late as 1897, two San Francisco syndicates sailed south to find and possess an 'Adamless Eden', despite the vehement advice of consuls that such places did not exist or (if they ever had) were already under the control of a major power.[8] The Americans had little capacity for harm: most of the syndicates settled down disconsolately in Fiji, New Caledonia or New Zealand.

A handful of great powers had indeed arrogated to themselves the exclusive right to claim and exercise sovereignty, so British settlers, French *colons* and German traders could not act independently. Instead they pestered their governments for 'forward' policies of annexation. Britain was reluctant to respond as requested, since individual adventurers posed little threat, and even the more substantial new forces could be reconciled with British imperial interests. The increasing French presence was mainly naval and seldom forceful. Marion du Fresne's New Zealand tragedy (see chapter 3) was not untypical in its very limited consequences. La Perouse reached Botany Bay a week after the First Fleet, then disappeared. French settlers landed at Akaroa in the South Island of New Zealand in 1840 (see chapter 5), too late and too cautiously to secure possession of the South before the British entrenched themselves in the North. Shifting their sights eastwards, France annexed the Marquesas in 1841 and 'protected' Tahiti a year later, ostensibly to support Catholic missionaries. Despite this protection, the Pomare monarchy and the Protestant ascendancy continued to dominate for several years.[9] Protestant missionaries and Australian settlers were dismayed (but British officials remained calm) when New Caledonia was annexed ten years later. The colonists were even more indignant – but helpless – when New Caledonia became a penal colony in the 1860s.

German traders caused Britain no anxiety: German authorities (after unification in 1871) were free-traders and seemed content to monitor trade. The biggest enterprise, the Deutsche Handels- und Plantagen-Gesellschaft centred in Samoa, lobbied Berlin to intervene to protect their land, labour and trade. This was perhaps the least of the pressures which persuaded Chancellor Bismarck to reverse course in 1884 and declare protectorates. Even then he chose not to annex Samoa, and elsewhere delegated power to chartered companies including the New Guinea Company (see chapter 8).

Nevertheless the growth of commerce, the centralization of chiefly powers and Christian evangelization raised the stakes in all conflicts and made formal colonialism more likely. In Fiji, Cakobau's government held the island group together long enough to cede Fiji as a whole to the British crown in 1875.[10] Tonga did become a durable kingdom under Tāufa'āhau, King George Tupou I. His longevity cemented his innovative institutions, and a new land-holding system contained dissent.[11] In Samoa, however, neither missionaries nor trader-king-makers could help their allies to sustain a monarchy.[12] Ultimately the great powers struck a deal whereby Tonga became a British protectorate, Western Samoa a German colony, and the eastern isles came under the administration of the US navy (see chapter 5).

Settler agitation did influence the pace, direction and substance of the partition of the Pacific Islands. Bismarck's protectorate over New Guinea in 1884 was prompted by the DHPG's desire to control a source of labour for Samoa, now attracting Queensland recruiters.[13] Queensland had tried the year before, to force Britain's hand by sending a magistrate to annex all New Guinea. In 1883 Downing Street balked; but Australian anxiety about German intervention made a difference. Within weeks of Bismarck's *schutzbrief*, Britain declared a protectorate over Papua, to be subsidized by the eastern Australian colonies and New Zealand. Solomon Islands, of even less strategic value to Britain but valuable to Queensland as a labour reserve, was also 'protected' in 1893, on condition that the Resident Commissioner raise his own revenue.[14]

These protectorates were declared reluctantly. After federation, Britain encouraged Australia to take over the administration of Papua, but only in 1906 did the Commonwealth make Papua an Australian Territory. The terminology is significant: in United States usage a territory was expected to evolve into a state, achieving parity with other states. The ultimate destiny of Papua was therefore left open (see chapter 10). A Royal Commission drafted a policy – development through plantations – which was easier to formulate than to realize. Large-scale investment (like CSR in Fiji, or Lever Brothers in

Solomon Islands) was desired in principle but few Australians had resources or experience, and they would have been foolish to try: the White Australia policy barred the recruitment of Asian labour, and cargo could only be carried by ships manned by (expensive) Australian crews. Australians who did want to be planters found a more congenial environment in other islands. The Papuan government therefore never escaped dependence on subsidies. By 1914 only a third of the territory was under any control.[15] Not surprisingly, negotiations over an Australian role in Solomon Islands never proceeded.[16]

French New Caledonia, failing to recruit French settlers, lured Anglophones. Its most famous entrepreneur, John Higginson, was born in Britain and migrated to Australia before he reached Noumea in 1859 (see chapter 6). Other Australians left their linguistic mark, 'enriching Caledonian French with words such as *le stockman*, *la station* and *le creek*, not to mention that useful exclamation of exasperation, *bagrite!* (bugger it!)'.[17] It was in the New Hebrides that the aspirations of British and French colonists clashed. Until the 1900s missionaries operated in a legal vacuum. Aneityum island, for example, became a Presbyterian theocracy with a church in each village, and a teacher in control wherever there was a church. Courts and an informal constabulary enforced biblical laws.[18] Neighbouring Tanna had opposed missionaries, until one of them summoned a Royal Navy vessel which shelled the island, burned villages and smashed canoes, until some Tannese confessed their crimes and sins, and informed the queen 'that we will kill no more of her people but in future be good, and learn to obey the word of Jehovah'. The other destabilizing influence was recruitment for work on Queensland or Fiji plantations, or New Caledonian ranches or mines. To combat Australian (and Protestant) influence, Higginson launched Catholic missionaries as well as trying to buy the land.[19] One way or another, therefore, Melanesian theocracies imploded like Polynesian kingdoms. In the New Hebrides, Britain first agreed to share policing duties with France under a Joint Naval Commission, then the islanders came under an Anglo-French Condominium in 1906.[20] A later critic declared, with justice, that the condominium was

> the most out-dated and confused form of government that mankind has ever established. ... There were in fact three governments trying to govern the place, the French colonial administration, the British colonial administration, and the Joint administration.[21]

The condominium was often dismissed as 'pandemonium', the antithesis of good government.[22]

Colonial rhetoric, entrepreneurial gambits, sectarian rivalry and metropolitan indifference combined to produce some of the least coherent and worst funded dependencies of the modern era. Settler preferences had some influence, too, on indentured labour schemes. New Caledonia recruited workers from French Vietnam; Fiji and the Solomons recruited in British India; New Guinea from southern China; but the application of White Australia to Papua (and later to New Guinea) barred all Asian workers or entrepreneurs.

If the imperial powers were the arbiters of legitimacy and authority, the Australian and the New Zealand colonists had taken giant strides towards 'sub-imperial' roles as Britain's surrogates, and as actors on their own behalf.

While the colonists were flexing their muscles, however, the wider region was being transformed by the entry of fresh imperial powers, not all of them congenial. The Spanish–American War, triggered by Caribbean events, consolidated United States power in the Pacific, since the conquest of the Philippines in 1898 created quite new power relations. The Spanish empire was extinguished, and the United States became an imperial power in all but name. If this was tolerable, the revival of Japan really alarmed the colonists. In 1867 Matsuhito revived the dormant power of the emperor. His supporters (in the Meiji programme, named for the new emperor) swiftly achieved the industrialization of Japan's economy and awesome military and naval power. The Meiji programme rejected 'Asia', preferred Western to Chinese learning and created deep ambivalence towards Europe.[23] It espoused national unity, modern armaments, and maritime trade. Most alarming was the arrival of Japanese women and men in Australia's north. Muraoka Iheiji stated his ambition and the colonists' nightmare in these raw terms:

> Put a whorehouse anywhere in the wilds of the South Pacific, and pretty soon you've got a general store there to go with it. Then clerks come from Japan. They grow independent, and go into business. A company will open up a branch office. Even the master of the whorehouse will open up a business.[24]

The nightmare took form in the 1890s in Torres Strait.

THE ENTREPRENEURIAL STATES

Although the Pacific Islands and European settlements in Australia and New Zealand were all called colonies, and each British dependency had a governor representing the British crown, the settler societies had a very different political dynamic than the islands. When William MacGregor was 'Lieutenant-Governor' of 'British New Guinea', he embodied the power of the British crown, but his essential task was to bring the concept and the structure of government to Papua. A decade later, as governor of Queensland, he again embodied the role of the crown but he was overseeing a government which was firmly in the hands of the colonists, and was subject to its own dynamic.[25]

Considered in terms of their economies, each Australian colony, and New Caledonia, developed with coastal entrepôts which funnelled and managed rural exports and industrial imports. The New Zealand pattern differed. As a single colony it had one governor and a central administration but several commercial centres, each with a provincial government. The rise of the entrepreneurial state prepared the way for abolishing these provinces and concentrating power and resources in the centre. From 1876 New Zealand's government more closely resembled the Australian colonies. It was unitary and centralized, with two houses, a General Assembly elected on the basis of one man one vote from 1879 (which included four Maori seats as a reward for *kupapa* Maori support during the Britanno-Maori wars), and an appointed upper house of property owners.

Dispensing with the provinces helped to centralize power over land. New Zealand adopted the South Australian Torrens system of land registration in the 1870s, which speeded the taking of Maori land, and rationalized surveying under one department. The wars themselves contributed to abolition. They provided a spur to facilitate Maori land purchase and to halt the 'Maori troubles' which the South Island, especially Canterbury, believed required southern oversight and a united display of settler 'self-reliance'.[26] Pooling land revenue also provided security for government borrowing to finance public works and further immigration.

The 'demands and distribution of progress' helped to bind settler society generally.[27] Governments and business found that collective marketing had more potential than splintered efforts to attract capital and labour. Promoting New Zealand as a product, a destination and a destiny re-reflected into settler visions of progress. Large-scale public-funded progress could be better handled at the top. Debt and depression also fostered collective responses to safeguard images of abundance and tackle problems expeditiously. The wars created the national debt and thus contributed to the toppling of the provinces. To borrow and hope, however, became a New Zealand trademark.

The wars also fed into the shaping of interdependent Maori and Pakeha identities, as Belich observes:

> There is a sense in which Pakeha regionalism foundered on the rock of Maori resistance, and a deeper sense in which the two peoples made each other – as *peoples* rather than tribes and provinces.[28]

Technical advances helped to link people and societies as well as prompt them to think about separateness. The telegraph – a private monopoly built the trans-Tasman cable in 1876 – reduced the range of difference and expanded the scope for shared experience.

Technological and economic contributions to collective identities were substantial – and ambiguous. A rapidly expanding web of communications, such as the telegraph, did not suppress regional identities by imparting news faster and yet in a more complex manner. Rather, transport and communications added layers of collective identity. It was the highest level of government that most appreciated the need for self-advertisement for British capital and labour. That made New Zealand's central government even more identity-conscious than the provinces. According to Livingston, railways contributed little to nation-building in Australia because of the mismatch of colonial gauges;[29] but railway construction in New Zealand led to standardized gauges in the 1870s and added to collective rather than parochial identity. Telegraph was perhaps a higher form of linkage and shrinkage, which Livingston sees as an example of 'technological nationalism', for example in ensuring the simultaneous raising of the 'national flag' (the Union Jack) at all Australian state schools to welcome federation.[30] The phrase 'the wired nation continent' captures this potential for nation-building. Wiring land and sea, however, could assist imperialism just as much as nationalism, as in the case of the Pacific cable of 1902, funded jointly by Britain, Canada and the Australasian colonies.

Australian and New Zealand histories emphasize the unique features of their entrepreneurial states, although these traits were really shared. In an influential thesis, Butlin argued that the Australian colonies devised a 'distinctive mixed economic system' characterized by a close partnership between colonial governments and business, and government borrowing and expenditure in the interests of business, to stimulate economic growth.

> With private individuals leading, Governments were active supporters as large-scale borrowers from Britain, large-scale investors in transport and communication, operators of the largest enterprises (railways) and subsidisers of immigration (particularly in Queensland).[31]

He could have added New Zealand, because this 'distinctive' system was really Australasian. A novel feature was the scale of government intervention, which contemporaries called 'colonial socialism'. Butlin showed this to be a misnomer: the settler colonies eagerly opted for

> a brand of capitalism in which public authorities had important parts to play in the detailed mechanisms of the economy, in the organization of immigration and overseas borrowing and in large-scale capital outlays.

Public rivalled private capital formation especially in communications, in infrastructure such as railways, roads, post and telegraph; public rivalled private borrowing; colonies became leading employers as well as importers of labour; and leading entrepreneurs included public servants and politicians.[32] In New Zealand, Belich calls it 'state-boosted progressive colonization'.[33]

State engagement in enterprise to build capital and people had as its engine the hopes and fears of settlers besotted by a vision of progress.[34] 'Think big' projects needed government investment to achieve in ten years what would otherwise take decades, to multiply the scale and pace of change in order to accelerate state formation as well as economic development. Julius Vogel, New Zealand's treasurer, outlined the strategy in 1870: 'The great wants of the Colony are Public Works in the form of Roads and Railways, and Immigration'.[35] His government sought to 'rekindle the spirit of colonization', to 're-illumine that sacred fire' by borrowing £10 million over ten years for public works and migrant labour. In fact he borrowed £10 million in five years, 1871 to 1876. William Fox, the premier, agreed that this scheme was not original: 'we only desire to do what the business politicians in America, Australia, and other new countries have done'.[36]

This vision was shared by those who dominated the economy and government (often the same people, as Fox's 'business politicians' indicates). Government and business had to co-operate to attract capital and labour, to accelerate progress beyond what private enterprise could achieve alone. This was especially important given the small markets, shortages of labour and capital, the low trust and political instability in the Australasian colonies. Networking between government and business, and government subsidies and incentives, reduced risk as well as magnifying opportunities for entrepreneurs and boosters. The colonies took for granted that governments should intervene to increase the rate of immigration and the stock of physical capital. The entrepreneurial state stepped in to provide women for progressive colonization; for example, wives, domestic servants and postmistresses as well as farm labour. Only governments could access the scale of British capital required to fulfil the dreams of enterprise and state-making.[37] In sum the state aimed to make business – and the business of colonization – profitable by providing extra people and infrastructure. Remoteness, resource deficiencies, the instabilities of climate produced by El Niño, small societies and markets increased risks and encouraged active roles by governments.[38]

Butlin summarizes the workings of the entrepreneurial state:

> In the period 1860 to 1900, public intervention in the areas specified attained such a scale that
>
> - government had subsidized the inflow of some 350,000 migrants, compared to a total net immigration of 750,000 and a total net population increase of 2,600,000;
> - government had been directly responsible for securing the inflow of half the total foreign capital imports;
> - government had accounted for approximately 40 per cent of total domestic capital formation, essentially in the areas of transport and communications;
> - government, by 1900, owned approximately half the total fixed capital (excluding land) of Australia;
> - government, by 1900, conducted the largest enterprises in the economy primarily in transport and communications and in water and sewerage, thereby absorbing approximately 5 per cent of the total workforce in the economy and generating some 6 per cent of gross domestic product.[39]

Colonies with responsible government were freer to act. Looking in from the United States, Davis and Huttenback assessed that of colonies with responsible government, Australia and New Zealand spent the most on 'big government'. Per capita government expenditure between 1860 and 1912 averaged £6.38 in the six Australian colonies and £6.39 in New Zealand: 'If per capita expenditure is any measure of the role of the government in the economy, the Australasian pattern is unmatched anywhere in the world'.[40] Australian colonies were the biggest spenders on public works, averaging £2.99 per person a year, including railways, with New Zealand at £1.97 (but spending more on human capital, including education). New Zealand spent more than the Australians on direct government support for business, averaging £0.95 a person between 1860 and 1912, compared to the Australian £0.51.[41]

New Zealand under Vogel became the archetypal entrepreneurial state. Julius Vogel, a flamboyant, mercurial, big-thinking, big-spending 'business politician', followed gold from Australia to New Zealand and deployed his talents in the media, founding the *Otago Daily Times* before he became the architect of pressure-cooker state formation.[42] His 1870s public works and immigration schemes typified the grandiose visions of the colonies. As a result of the Vogel 'boom' the settler population doubled to 577,000 by 1886, including 157,000 immigrants between 1871 and 1890. Most were assisted. In the North Island, the accelerated purchase of Maori land, closer settlement and massive bush clearance by new migrants prepared the way for dairy farming. An extra 1,200 miles of railway mostly benefited the South Island, the main trunk line connecting Dunedin to Christchurch. Roads, bridges and telecommunications shrank distances; the government subsidized postal services while a cable connected New Zealand to Australia from 1876. The government became a major employer in post offices, railways, railway workshops and primary schools, while political incentives promoted innovations in farming and business to further the 'progress industry'.[43]

The timing differed in some Australian colonies, but not the strategy. In eastern Australia 10,000 miles of railway line crossed the landscape by the end of the century, and main trunk lines joined Sydney, Melbourne and Adelaide by 1890. The entrepreneurial state became a leitmotif of state formation despite changes of government and the transition from factional to party government. It was as characteristic of the New Zealand Liberals in the 1890s with their state advances to settlers as it was of Vogel himself.

KINGITANGA

Perceiving that Pakeha power issued from the queen of England, Maori sought an equal status through a Maori monarchy, and created the pan-tribal Kingitanga (King Movement). The Old Testament, where Israel called for 'a king to judge us', justified the Maori king's election in 1858.[44] The Kingitanga was a Maori institution, with wider Polynesian resonances, founded to preserve independence by securing international recognition. It provided the focus for *iwi* who wanted to hold onto their land. New Zealand politicians could have recognized the Kingitanga, but decided that to acknowledge its sovereignty would deny settler access to prime areas for settlement. Its stronghold, the King Country, became the centre of dairying in the wake of confiscations and the completion of the trunk railway through the North Island, which the Kingitanga stalled until 1908 but could not stop. Settlers bit into the King Country through the individualization of land title in the Native Land Court. In the 1880s King Tawhiao, along with other northern chiefs, went to London to see the queen to seek redress for the wrongs inflicted on them, only to be rebuffed because Britain would not interfere in the internal affairs of a self-governing colony. Unsurprisingly, *rangatira* sought Maori solutions to Treaty of Waitangi grievances and Maori institutions to restore tribal autonomy.[45]

Tribes outside the Kingitanga established another Maori unity movement, the Kotahitanga (otherwise known as the Maori parliament) which met from 1892 to 1902 under *rangatira* leadership. Its seat was Papawai in the Wairarapa, which then housed 2,000 people. Kotahitanga invoked the treaty and the Constitution Act of 1852, showing how parallel institutions might work under the New Zealand Constitution Act, which provided for Maori custom and practice in Maori districts (a section consistently ignored).[46] The centralization of the settler state distanced rather than integrated Maori into national political identity, prompting modernizing Maori to join traditional leaders in seeking engagement with the modern world. There had been an erosion of Maori power but not identity: the poles of kinship stood unfelled.

AUSTRALIAN FEDERATION AND MANIFEST DESTINIES

In 1825 the government of Van Diemen's Land (Tasmania) was separated from that of New South Wales, the first of several excisions enforced by long distances and slow communication. The outcome was seven self-governing Australasian colonies (New South Wales, Tasmania, Victoria, South Australia, Queensland, Western Australia and New Zealand), each headed by a governor representing the crown, but with no formal provision for co-operation among themselves nor for independent regional action. Political fragmentation mirrored economics, as most colonies comprised one entrepôt for imports and exports. Following the Queensland government's failed attempt to annex eastern New Guinea in 1883, the colonies created a Federal Council of Australasia to address the defects. But New South Wales and New Zealand, and South Australia for a time, shunned the council (through suspicion of protectionist Victoria) and it had no authority to act or legislate. Instead the colonies urged Britain to heed their Pacific strategic interests. The New Guinea issue was temporarily patched up by the British New Guinea Protectorate, subsidized by the eastern Australian colonies and New Zealand. The entry into the Pacific of other European powers, and especially Japan, added urgency to the search for security, while economic development gave increasing salience to mundane questions of tariffs, cable and other technical services, and incompatible railway gauges. While imperial federation appealed to a few political thinkers, a regional federation was a much more consequential proposition.

Because New South Wales had disregarded the Federal Council, and yet a federation was inconceivable without the oldest (and most populous) colony, no serious action was taken until 1889 when the New South Wales elder statesman Sir Henry Parkes announced that defence issues, and Australia's racial destiny – the 'crimson thread of kinship' – compelled federation. An Australasian federal conference (1890) and an Australasian convention (1891) made progress, but not enough to impress New Zealand's delegates. Western Australia might also have turned its back on the federal movement. The new goldfields, drawing men from the eastern colonies, had a decisive influence; but there was no rail link until 1917 and no air link for several more years. Separatism persisted, expressed in resolutions of the local

Plate 9.1 Poster issued by the Australian Natives' Association in 1895 depicting G. H. Reid, the New South Wales premier, holding back representatives of the other colonies, all rushing to federate, except Sir John Forrest, who stands aloof in Western Australia with gold nugget in hand. Sir Henry Parkes, no longer at the forefront of the federal movement, looks on. Courtesy of the National Library of Australia.

parliament, beginning in 1906. The shape of federal Australia, despite appearances, was not inevitable.[47] Nor was federation. A convention adopted a draft constitution in 1898, but two colonies did not hold a referendum at all, and New South Wales voted in favour by too narrow a margin to be valid. Only in 1899 did all Australian colonies approve the revised draft, which was then enacted by the British parliament and came into effect on 1 January 1901.

In some of the rhetoric, federation was represented as more dramatic and epoch-making than it seemed to most people then or later. The Fathers of the Constitution (a motherless document, although suffragists supported federation to secure women's franchise for the federal parliament) followed the United States precedent rather than the Canadian, tilting in favour of the centre rather than the constituents; but that was a matter of convenience, not an impulse towards republicanism or even centralism. Sir Edmund Barton, the conciliator and the first prime minister, declared that it achieved 'a nation for a continent and a continent for a nation'. Perhaps: but little changed institutionally or in popular culture. The House of Representatives was elected democratically, but in the Senate each state (as each colony became) enjoyed equal representation and the chance to review the work of the lower house. A High Court interpreted federal law, but each state retained its Supreme Court and its legal traditions. Governors persisted, and a governor-general represented the crown federally – with reserve powers to protect imperial interests. The persistent rivalry between Sydney and Melbourne was resolved by agreeing to create a federal capital somewhere, distant, between these cities (but within New South Wales). Canberra became the capital, and the federal parliament met there as soon as a temporary building was ready, in 1927; but Melbourne housed the federal government until the 1940s, and the permanent federal parliament building was opened (by the queen) only in 1988.

In no sense did federation represent a break from empire. Nor was it a cultural or ideological break. The politicians who negotiated this structure were not radicals. Neither the labour movement in general nor the new Labor Party in particular exercised much influence; and the structure embodied no trace of the *Bulletin*'s republicanism. The enfranchisement of women occurred federally only slightly later than it did in half of the individual states; and Aboriginal Australians were just as marginal federally as locally. Indeed they were even more marginal, since Aboriginal Affairs remained a state responsibility. Westminster was not dissembling when it welcomed the colonists' draft constitution.

Although the door remained open for New Zealand to join as an 'original state', it chose a separate destiny. Since the opening of the Suez Canal it looked in a different direction from Australia to overcome its remoteness, across the Pacific rather than through Suez to Britain. Britain was New Zealand's major export market and from the 1890s refrigeration and the rise of the dairy industry reinforced her identity as different from Australia's, as 'Britain's farm'. Above all, New Zealanders entertained different notions of the 'crimson thread of kinship'. They too belonged to the British race, but entertained different notions of 'the people'; New Zealanders were a 'peculiar' people, 'just a little superior' – without the convict stain – destined to lead the world in social conditions.[48] New Zealand, an island nation, blessed with national abundance, would develop a 'different national type'. Not only did Pakeha believe themselves superior; they saw the Maori as superior natives. A federal parliament of mainly Australians could not be trusted to deal with 'native races', and the 'advance of civilization would be enormously delayed'.[49]

Once the Australian colonies had federated, the Commonwealth's Attorney-General Alfred Deakin explained to a British audience that nearby French and German colonies seemed to an Australian almost an intrusion on property:

> Confidence in his powers of expansion and certitude of future progress are such that he already views the Continent behind him ... as too contracted for his operations, and by no means as confining his sphere of influence.[50]

Not only was there an odious penal colony in New Caledonia; Australians deplored the German annexation of New Guinea – another case of Britain neglecting Australia's security and destiny.[51] The ultimate nightmare was

Britain being involved in European war, her navy committed in the Atlantic, and the Australians exposed to an enemy base near their undefendable coasts.

Whether British and French colonists valued the islands for their real human and natural resources, their strategic significance or their imagined assets, they were too important to relinquish to another empire. So it came as a shock that London and Paris did not attach the same priority to the islands. New Zealand's enthusiasm for island dependencies was buttressed by the Pakeha self-image as deft interpreters of Polynesia, and by a vision of an island empire to balance the continental federation of Australia.[52] Alas, Downing Street would not take these claims seriously. Downing Street was always willing to share costs, but less often to delegate responsibility: Cook Islands were New Zealand's sole acquisition before the Great War.

It was bad enough that European governments preferred to protect the teetering balance of power rather than tamper with each other's real or imagined Pacific interests. When they did intervene, they did not always act in the interest of their colonists. Governor Gordon of Fiji, for example, developed a decidedly protective policy.[53] The governor's legitimacy rested on cession by the chiefs, and he himself was unusually well-connected and clear-sighted:

> We want capital. ... We want a cheap, abundant, and certain supply of labour; we want means of communication; we want justice to be readily and speedily administered; we want facilities for education; and ... we want revenue.[54]

Indentured Indians provided the labour, and the Colonial Sugar Refining Company brought capital and technology for the sugar industry which became Fiji's export staple. If Gordon relied on Australian capital, however, he was determined to avoid the dispossession which had occurred in various ways in Australia and New Zealand. To that end he formalized the Great Council of Chiefs to advise him, and enlisted chiefs in local government. He created a Native Lands Commission to assess settlers' land claims, and to demarcate the land which remained in communal control. This structure reconciled the sugar industry with the chiefs, and both with the empire. And it discouraged poor settlers.

As the sense of region crystallized, so policies and practices came to be seen as having lateral implications, and even seen as precedents. The (mainly negative) influence of New South Wales on Tonga has been mentioned; and in Fiji Gordon's programme was designed to avoid Australian and New Zealand (and Hawaiian) dispossession. For Fijians, the act of Cession and Gordon's dispositions became 'the charter of the land'[55] which would be held to justify perpetual Fijian (and communal) ownership. That understanding legitimized the later lease of land to Indian tenants while denying them the hope of purchase. Gordon's personal views were more flexible: as a director of the Pacific Islands Company he helped to acquire tracts of land in Solomon Islands on 999-year leases. That land was then acquired by Unilever for plantations. With that exception, British, French and German land acquisitions were usually limited by access to anchorages, or impossible to sustain. Settlers who bought land from Higginson believed that they held title to interior as well as coastal land. Only in the 1960s were some ready to occupy this interior land, an ambition which was by then politically impossible (see chapters 4 and 18). In this rare instance two conceptions collided but the indigenous one prevailed. The New Caledonia mainland was doubly exceptional (see chapter 4). Informed by a vague understanding of Australia, this was the only French colony to try wholesale expropriation, and the only Melanesian site of such a drastic strategy. There, too, Kanak understandings about land were not so much obliterated as submerged for the duration of French dominance.

That lateral vision persisted. In the early 1970s Australian planners in Papua New Guinea hoped to bestow the boon of Australian-style development by introducing individual land title to replace 'traditional' landownership which they deemed an obstacle to prosperity. The campaign against 'reform' was led by a passionate Alan Ward, New Zealand historian and consultant on land, and acutely conscious of the link between individual title and Maori dispossession.[56] As he has reaffirmed in New Zealand through his work with the Waitangi Tribunal, many Maori believed, 'with good reason, that the only way they could maintain control of their land was to keep it out of the Native Land Court'.[57] Maori understandings about land, too, were submerged until the re-remembering of the Treaty of Waitangi in the 1970s as a compact to create a national (colonial) identity.

NOTES

1 David Glen, 'The Last Elusive Object', MA thesis, Australian National University, Canberra, 1999, describes the hoax. The work itself is John A. Lawson, R. N., *Wanderings in the Interior of New Guinea*, London, 1875, recording an expedition in 1872 into the interior and to Mt Hercules, at 32,000 feet.
2 Glen, 'The Last Elusive Object', ch. 1.
3 *Proceedings of the RGSA*, Sydney, 1883.
4 Isabelle Merle, 'The Foundation of Voh 1892–1895', *Journal of Pacific History*, 26 (1991); and her *Expériences coloniales: la Nouvelle-Calédonie 1853–1920*, Paris, 1995.
5 Jocelyn Linnekin, 'New Political Orders', in Donald Denoon, Stewart Firth, Jocelyn Linnekin, Malama Meleisea and Karen Nero (eds), *Cambridge History of the Pacific Islanders*, Melbourne, 1997, 185–216.
6 Gavan Daws, *A Dream of Islands: Voyages of Self-discovery in the South Seas*, New York, 1980.
7 J. L. Whittaker, N. G. Gash, J. F. Hookey and R. J. Lacey (eds), *Documents and Readings in New Guinea History: Prehistory to 1889*, Brisbane, 1975, 386–9.
8 Hugh Laracy, ' "Quixotic and Utopian": American Adventurers in the Southwest Pacific'.
9 Colin Newbury, *Tahiti Nui: Change and Survival in French Polynesia 1767–1945*, Honolulu, 1980.
10 Deryck Scarr, *I, The Very Bayonet*, vol. 1 of *The Majesty of Colour: A Life of Sir John Bates Thurston*, Canberra, 1973.
11 Sione Lātūkefu, *Church and State in Tonga*, Canberra, 1974, 61–2, 162–3.

12 Malama Meleisea, *The Making of Modern Samoa: Traditional Authority and Colonial Administration in the Modern History of Western Samoa*, Suva, 1987.
13 Stewart Firth, *New Guinea Under the Germans*, Melbourne, 1983.
14 Judith Bennett, *The Wealth of the Solomons: A History of a Pacific Archipelago, 1800–1978*, Honolulu, 1987.
15 James Griffin, Hank Nelson and Stewart Firth, *Papua New Guinea: A Short Political History*, Melbourne, 1979.
16 Bennett, *The Wealth of the Solomons*.
17 Stephen Henningham, *France and the South Pacific: A Contemporary History*, Sydney, 1992, 20–1.
18 Joel Bonnemaison, *The Tree and the Canoe: History and Ethnogeography of Tanna*, Honolulu, 1994.
19 Ibid.
20 Walter H. Lini, *Beyond Pandemonium*, Suva, 1980, 18.
21 Barak Sope, 'The Colonial History of the New Hebrides', in Lini, *Beyond Pandemonium*, 17–18.
22 Richard Shears, *The Cocoanut War*, Melbourne, 1980, quoted in David Robie, *Blood on their Banner: Nationalist Struggles in the South Pacific*, London, 69.
23 D. Denoon, G. McCormack, T. Morris-Suzuki and M. Hudson, *Multicultural Japan*, Melbourne, 1997.
24 Yamakazi Tomoko, 'Sandakan No. 8 Brothel', in *Bulletin of Concerned Asian Scholars*, October–December 1975.
25 Roger Joyce, *William MacGregor*, Melbourne, 1971.
26 W. P. Morrell, *The Provincial System in New Zealand 1852–76*, 2nd revd edn, Christchurch, 1964, 148, 270–85.
27 James Belich, *Making Peoples: A History of the New Zealanders from Polynesian Settlement to the End of the Nineteenth Century*, Auckland, 1996, 440.
28 Ibid., 441.
29 K. T. Livingston, *The Wired Nation Continent: The Communication Revolution and Federating Australia*, Melbourne, 1996, 10.
30 Ibid., 184–5.
31 N. G. Butlin, 'Australian Wealth and Progress since 1788: A Statistical Picture', in *The Bicentennial Diary*, Brisbane, 1987, 225.
32 N. G. Butlin, *Investment in Australian Economic Development 1861–1900*, Canberra, 1976, 5–6. See also H. M. Boot's overview, 'Government and the Colonial Economies', *Australian Economic History Review*, 38: 1 (March 1998), 74–98.
33 Belich, *Making Peoples*, 375.
34 Donald Denoon, *Settler Capitalism: The Dynamics of Dependent Development in the Southern Hemisphere*, Oxford, 1983, 205.
35 C. G. F. Simkin, *Instability of a Dependent Economy*, London, 1951, 146.
36 R. Dalziel, *Julius Vogel: Business Politician*, Auckland, 1986, 107; Belich, *Making Peoples*, 351.
37 N. G. Butlin, A. Barnard and J. J. Pincus, *Government and Capitalism: Public and Private Choice in Twentieth Century Australia*, Sydney, 1982, 13–16. See also Boot, 'Government and the Colonial Economies'.
38 E. Jones, L. Frost and C. White, *Coming Full Circle: An Economic History of the Pacific Rim*, Melbourne, 1993, 98.
39 Butlin, Barnard and Pincus, *Government and Capitalism*, 16–17.
40 L. E. Davis and R. A. Huttenback, *Mammon and the Pursuit of Empire. Interdisciplinary Perspectives on Modern History*, ed. Robert Fogel and Stephan Thernstrom. Cambridge, 1986, 122.

41 Ibid., 126–37.
42 On Vogel, see Dalziel, *Julius Vogel.*
43 Term used by Belich, *Making Peoples*, 349–60.
44 1 Samuel 8: 5 in Bronwyn Elsmore, *Mana from Heaven: A Century of Maori Prophets in New Zealand*, Tauranga, 1989, 263, cited in Keith Sinclair, *Kinds of Peace: Maori People After the Wars, 1870–85*, Auckland, 1991, 44.
45 Lindsay Cox, *Kotahitanga: The Search for Maori Political Unity*, Auckland, 1993; Alan Ward, *National Overview*, 3 vols. Waitangi Tribunal Rangahaua Whanui Series. Wellington, 1997, 6.
46 Cox, *Kotahitanga*, 67–70; Walker in I. H. Kawharu (ed.), *Waitangi: Maori and Pakeha Perspectives of the Treaty of Waitangi*, Auckland, 1989, 273–4; Michael King, *Maori: A Photographic and Social History*, Auckland, 1996, 160.
47 W. G. McMinn, *A Constitutional History of Australia*, Melbourne, 1979; *Nationalism and Federalism in Australia*, Melbourne, 1994; C. T. Stannage, *A New History of Western Australia*, Nedlands, 1981. On federation as a product of Australian political culture, see H. Irving, *To Constitute a Nation*, Melbourne, 1997. The best summary source is John Hirst, 'Federation', in G. Davison, J. Hirst and S. Macintyre (eds), *Oxford Companion to Australian History*, Melbourne, 1998, 243–4. The most comprehensive account is H. Irving (ed.), *Centenary Companion to Australian Federation*, Melbourne, 1999.
48 Stella M. Allan, 'New Zealand and Federation', *United Australia*, October 1900, 9–11. On the journalist Stella Allan, see p. 318, n. 23.
49 Captain Russell, in G. J. Craven (ed.), *Debates of the Australasian Federation Conference 1890*, Centenary Edition, Sydney, 1990, 128–9. On why New Zealand did not join Australian federation, see P. Mein Smith, 'New Zealand', in H. Irving (ed.), *Centenary Companion to Australian Federation*, Melbourne, 1999, 400–5.
50 Alfred Deakin, *Federated Australia: Selections from Letters to the Morning Post 1900–1910*, Melbourne, 1968, ed. J. A. La Nauze; *Morning Post*, 19 March 1901. See Hank Nelson, 'Frontiers, Territories and States of Mind', Pacific History Workshop, December 1998, Australian National University, Canberra.
51 Deakin in *Morning Post*, 17 April 1902.
52 Angus Ross (ed.), *New Zealand's Record in the Pacific Islands in the Twentieth Century*, Auckland, 1969; Dalziel, *Julius Vogel.*
53 Scarr, *I, The Very Bayonet.*
54 Cited in Brij V. Lal, *Broken Waves: A History of the Fiji Islands in the Twentieth Century*, Honolulu, 1992, 13.
55 Peter France, *The Charter of the Land: Custom and Colonization in Fiji*, Melbourne, 1969.
56 Peter Quinn, in D. Denoon and C. Snowden, *A Time to Plant and a Time to Uproot: A History of Agriculture in Papua New Guinea*, Boroko, n.d. [1981].
57 Alan Ward, *An Unsettled History: Treaty Claims in New Zealand Today*, Wellington, 1999, 143.

[10] NEW SETTLER SOCIETIES

Between the 1880s and the Great War, with immense self-assurance, settler governments set about redefining relations between each other, between themselves and indigenous peoples, between capital and labour, and even between women and men.

Problems of geographical definition were acute for the Australian Commonwealth, expecting to assume control over British New Guinea as well as continental Australia and the Torres Strait islands. Torres Strait and Cape York were old meeting points for Aborigines, Papuans and Makassans. More meetings occurred with whaling, shell-diving and sandalwood-getting, when vessels arrived from Australian ports – and from Japan. These islands came to resemble other Pacific beach communities of Islanders, Europeans, Japanese, Southeast Asians, black and white Americans, and Africans.[1] Some order was created by Australian traders who funded the shell-diving luggers, crewed by Pacific islanders and employing dress-divers, often Japanese. Other sources of colonial order were the missions which ruled Aboriginal reserves. In delineating Australia's physical and social boundaries, Queensland officials and missions defined islanders' status somewhere between white and Aboriginal. Immigration criteria limited Japanese to prescribed jobs, and halted Chinese arrivals. Together with the repatriation of South Sea islanders, these measures created an ethnic hierarchy.

Torres Strait islanders were anomalous in the evolving 'white Australia'; but the addition of parts of New Guinea more seriously spoiled the symmetry of Prime Minister Barton's 'continent for a nation'. Papua therefore raised awkward questions of race relations, national identity and destiny. To meet this case, the Commonwealth adopted a portentous term.[2] United States Territories were expected to mature into fully-fledged States of the Union. In 1901, when Barton formally proposed to make British New Guinea – as Papua – an Australian Territory, he anticipated 'long centuries for which I hope New Guinea is to be a territory, perhaps, a State of this Commonwealth'. He thought that other islands might also be acquired, for a 'federation in these seas'.[3]

The Commonwealth had already moved to halt the entry of South Sea islanders and to deport most of those already at work. The labour trade which brought them had certainly begun in deception but had become 'normalized', especially for men (see chapter 8). When the trade beached in the 1900s, therefore, life changed drastically. In Queensland peoples from a hundred islands began to merge into one community. Those who came home were often reluctant,[4] and they could not easily recruit for other places. When Australia was closed, and Indians displaced them in Fiji, thousands enlisted for New Caledonia, the only continuing labour importer, but their pay eroded.[5] Melanesians could now experiment with commerce and Christianity only in the context of colonialism.

Because of Australian parliamentary instability, several years passed after federation before Papua was brought under Australian rule, offering several chances for politicians to reflect on identity and destiny. Deakin explained to his English readers that 'a "White Australia" may exist, across the straits, but a "Black New Guinea" the territory now is and must always remain'.[6] That became a categorical distinction. Charles McDonald, a Queensland Labor member, hoped that 'the scandals … [in] the treatment of Australian aborigines will not be repeated there. The way in which our own natives have been treated constitutes one of the blackest pages in our history.'[7] 'Pacific islanders' were becoming suitable recipients of paternal and evangelical concern, unlike Australia's more alarming 'Asian' neighbours. Laws governing Papuan land embodied this concern, even if the practice was weaker than the policy.

Until 1910, South Australia straddled the continent from Adelaide to Darwin. In 1910 the Commonwealth debated whether to relieve South Australia of the northern half of this terrain. Comments on the Northern Territory Acceptance Bill differed in tone and content from the Papuan debates. Nobody suggested compensating Aborigines for scandalous mistreatment – they were hardly mentioned. Deakin spoke eloquently in favour of creating another Territory, though it could not pay its way: he insisted that the 'continent is, and must be one and indivisible'. Evidently the only way to secure the north was to fill it with white settlers. For the same purpose the Commonwealth would complete the North–South rail link, whose 'first purpose', said Deakin, was defence.[8]

Nelson suggests two reasons why parliamentarians ignored Aborigines.

> First, the justification for Commonwealth control and the conception of Australia that members put forward had no place for Aborigines. … The defence of the south depended, it was believed, on having white settlers in the north; [their] image … of their new nation was of one people and one continent. Secondly, they believed that the Aborigines were dying out.[9]

Indeed the 1911 census found only 1,223 'full-blooded' Aborigines working for, or living near, whites. The *Official Year Book* believed that the interior was more populated,

> but it is believed they are rapidly dying out. In these regions, remote from contact with other races, the native has maintained his primitive simplicity, and furnishes an interesting subject of study to the anthropologist and ethnologist.[10]

The parliamentarians' vision of Australia accommodated Papuans across Torres Strait, but not Aborigines in 'white Australian' space.

MEN'S COUNTRIES, WOMEN'S RIGHTS

The settler societies predictably included many more men than women. Pastoral frontiers perpetuated that imbalance, and so did gold. Social planners generally, and Wakefieldians in particular, tried (manfully) to remedy this defect. No solution was found in New Caledonia until the twentieth century. Targeted programmes did recruit women for the self-governing colonies; but as most settled in towns, gender imbalance persisted in rural areas.

Some men came to accept this situation as normal, and it was manifest in some of the poetry and prose created in the countryside, and the literature which sought to represent rural life. As it happened, the editor of the Sydney *Bulletin* in the 1880s, J. F. Archibald, an 'unhappily married, childless misogynist', threw himself into a 'self-styled Bohemia' of mateship, drinking, smoking and gambling. In his circle domestic influences were 'emasculating': their pleasures had to be defended from the scorn of their wives.[11] Henry Lawson, too, was unhappily married. As the Bush crystallized in the *Bulletin* it embodied Archibald's (and Lawson's) values and made a particular appeal to men. The heroes of the emerging Australian legend were pastoral workers, stockmen or shearers (seldom farmers), but invariably free of family ties and expressing that loss as freedom. Their world did contain women: sexual relations were common between Bushmen and Aboriginal women, and fiction presented Island women as compliant. In pastoral conditions, the domains of husbands and wives seldom overlapped. The drover's wife was left to care for the children during her husband's long absences. If he took casual work in the town, separation also ensued, with the pub providing his temporary social milieu. In any event many men were bound to be bachelors because of the society's sexual imbalance, and the *Bulletin* made a virtue of necessity, endorsing these men's rejection (or lack) of domestic life.

There were of course other visions of masculinity, shaped by family farming on selections, by urban life, by evangelical Christianity (in bodies such as the Young Men's Christian Association) and by happy domesticity; but these did not generate the same myths. Land reformers visualized a 'yeomanry' of freeholders and their families. In reality lack of capital made them depend on the unpaid work of wives and children. Instead of 'smiling homesteads' many became 'sordid farms', supporting Russel Ward's view that 'cocky' (small farmer) was a term of scorn in nineteenth-century Australia. The 'string-bark cockatoos', selectors on open tableland or mallee scrub country, were the ones despised for their drab lives; not the 'people of the tall timber', forest selectors – and New Zealand's dairy-farming 'cow cockies' – who entered pioneer mythology by winning their valleys of farmland from the bush.[12] One label for the celebration of solitary rural males is 'Lone Hand' narratives, whose New Zealand counterpart was (and is) 'Man Alone'.

The family was the ideal of revolutionaries as well as reformers. William Lane, leading his idealists from the Bush to the Paraguayan chaco, based his vision of a new society on contented families including 'new' men. These were rare in life, and rarer in legend. Marilyn Lake observes that the nationalist writers of the 1890s celebrated a narrowly masculine and pastoral experience in pushing their 'masculinist' politics, and argues that Russel Ward's later *Australian Legend* accepted these part-fictional pastoral workers as archetypes of 'national character'. Like others, he conflated the male with the national tradition, and 'unwittingly made a significant contribution to our understanding of gender relations in Australia'.[13]

It was against these realities and legends that the women's movement grew from the 1880s, grounded in much real violence, alcoholism and uncontrolled fertility. It is suggestive that, as the sex ratio began to equalize in the 1880s, proportionally fewer women married. The social purity lobby hoped to eradicate the masculine ethos along with its sexual double standard. Their high ambition was to make men change – a challenge which the *Bulletin* rebutted with predictable spleen. Explicit masculinism informed cultural production; it was challenged by many women and some men; and its values have been promoted and contested ever since.

Paradoxically, these discouragements helped women to win political equality unusually early in New Zealand and Australia.[14] Consistent with the whole social programme, the vote for women was designed to stabilize society rather than transform it. In building political identity this reform featured as another social experiment – Denoon thought it 'curious that the same generation which consolidated the White Australia policy also consolidated the position of women as politically equal and economically half the value of white men'. The connection between the two is what Carol Bacchi terms 'the mother influence'.[15] Masculinist politicians and feminist campaigners could agree that the white woman must be the 'mother of the race' in building and developing these new states.

The suffragists claimed equal rights on grounds of difference; not just on the liberal grounds of natural justice, but on religious grounds too, as wives and mothers. They sought these rights to improve family and society. Women, they argued, had a natural maternal character, which should be exercised in the state as well as the home. These societies needed the special qualities of 'mother influence'. The suffrage would benefit families and the state, since women were the nation's housekeepers (cartoons showed maternal figures purifying parliament by cleaning behind politicians' ears). That perspective asserted the moral superiority of women whose influence would ensure moral reform and build stable white political identities.

The women's movement aspired to more than political citizenship. In Dorothy Page's view, 'they wanted to change society by their votes, to acknowledge the place of women in it and to protect them where necessary'.[16] The main strands of colonial feminism – moral reform of society and equal rights for women – were woven into the National Council of Women's declared aim in 1896: to unite women's organizations to attain 'justice and freedom for women, and for all that makes for the good of humanity'. The maternal strategy made sense in the context of first-wave feminism. Most suffragists shared middle-class anxieties about the future of the race and civilization, and belonged to wider reform movements to promote social purity and racial strength. These associations enabled women to work alongside men

Plate 10.1 *Leisure Moments*, by Alice Marian Ellen Bale, 1902. Bale was a woman member of the Heidelberg School. Courtesy of the Queensland Art Gallery and A. M. E. Bale Trust.

in reforming states and constructing myths. Men needed them to create and protect the social and moral order.

Women's suffrage was gained in Pitcairn as early as 1838, in Wyoming in 1869, Utah in 1870, Colorado and the Cook Islands just before New Zealand, which was the first self-governing country to enfranchise women in 1893. South Australia followed in 1894, Western Australia in 1899, federal Australia and New South Wales in 1902 (for white women), Tasmania in 1903, Queensland in 1905, and Victoria in 1908. Before 1914 women were also enfranchised in some western American states, Finland and Norway.[17] These were mainly white settler communities which had displaced indigenous peoples and remained frontier societies. Here, men themselves gained the vote early, and pride in their democratic charters drew women into an agenda of nationalist myth-making. The urban frontier in Australasia and the American mid-west expanded in parallel with economic development and political democracy. On these frontiers women won the franchise before other reforms (such as in marriage and divorce). There was an acute need to hold on to respectability and it was widely accepted that 'men in groups – in mining camps, on battle grounds, in Parliament – had a tendency to deteriorate away from women's influence'.[18] Respectable men and women were moved to remedy these ills; women's temperance campaigns were launched first for 'home protection' in laws governing drink.[19]

William Pember Reeves wrote that 'one fine morning of September 1893, the women of New Zealand woke up and found themselves enfranchised'.[20] In one sentence he wiped the suffragists' campaign from the story. He saw the vote as a gift from men, and this view predominated until women's history rediscovered women's quiet, sustained campaigns. Only in the 1990s was Kate Sheppard re-remembered as the leader of New Zealand's suffrage movement, in time for the centennial of the vote for women. Reeves may have rendered women activists invisible because, as agent-general in London, he wished to assuage British (especially investors') fears that they endangered the social order. Or perhaps he found the women in his own household unmanageable.[21]

Men's and women's movements for reform through 'universal' political citizenship succeeded where they were co-ordinated. The major vehicle for women was the Women's Christian Temperance Union, which organized letter writing, mass petitions, leaflets and meetings to raise awareness. In New Zealand, the 1893 suffrage petition rolled onto the floor of parliament boasted 31,871 signatures, about a quarter of all adult women, including some Maori. The WCTU was brought from the United States by Mary Leavitt, followed by Jessie Ackermann who became a catalyst for the South Australian campaign and later in other colonies. The timing of the women's vote, however, did depend on men. New Zealand's politicians had accepted women's vote in principle by 1879, after attaining one man one vote, but the women's vote was not won until 1893, because men's politics enjoyed priority. Earlier moves foundered in disputes over the representation of Maori, and property.

In Australia and New Zealand, women's suffrage squeaked through parliaments in a period of flux. In South Australia this entailed the convergence of Liberal and Labor forces and conservatives' self-interest. Labor did not oppose the measure because it involved no property qualification. The Liberal premier, Charles Kingston, needed the women's vote: urban men like him needed women's aid to challenge the (rowdy) voice of rural workers.[22] This proved a key issue in Western Australia, where men outnumbered women by 212 to 100 in rural areas, but only by 113 to 100 in Perth.[23] The gold rushes of the 1890s tipped the scales. Premier John Forrest opposed votes for women, but made a sudden about-face in 1899. He was worried by the strength of organized labour on the goldfields, who demanded a redistribution of seats as their numbers burgeoned. The women's vote was rushed through parliament before the property qualification was abolished in the hope that women's voice would bolster the conservatives: women were enlisted for settler capitalism, and the property qualification survived until 1907 because of Forrest's fear of Labor.[24]

Western Australia presents the strongest case for women's vote being a gift; but even there the women's campaign was critical. A clue to its importance is that the first election in which women voted (in 1901) ousted Forrest in favour of a women's champion, Walter James. His wife, Eleanora James, was a leader of the WCTU. Their partnership signified a consensus between liberal men and feminists, resembling the alliance in New Zealand between Sir John Hall and Kate Sheppard (and, in Christchurch, between Kate Sheppard and her future husband William Lovell-Smith). Sheppard bundled together in one charismatic person all the identities of a typical suffragist: she was both the 'New Woman' and the 'colonial helpmeet', a nonconformist, and committed to Fabian Socialist politics of 'plain living and high thinking'. Sir John, the voice of property, insisted that the women's vote would 'increase the influence of the settler and family-man, as against the loafing single men', which summed up the argument for stability. If we consider relations between the men's movement (for democracy and fairness) and the women's movement (to remove women's legal 'disabilities'), we see that such gendered alliances worked to promote prosperous, stable societies, believing that men and women together should build free young nations, 'stalwart, sturdy, staunch and strong'.[25]

But the colonial feminist agenda was wider than political citizenship. The 'social purity' movement presented a radical challenge when some sought, for example, to abolish the double standard of morality. They argued that sex should occur only within marriage, and for reproduction: otherwise women were debased to the level of men, instead of raising men to women's moral standard. This agenda required revolutionary change, which masculinist politics found unpalatable.[26] Rival discourses (masculinist, feminist and medical) jostled for a place in the settler states and in shaping gendered identities. Australian feminists argue that a 'battle of the sexes' erupted in the 1890s for no less than control of the national culture, and the same can be said of New Zealand.[27] Consensus was possible over women's demands for autonomy in the political realm, as mothers. Consensus was impossible over economic independence, especially for married women: indeed equal pay for equal work – economic citizenship – is still unmet.

Until federation, Aboriginal women and men had suffrage rights in South Australia, Victoria, New South Wales and Tasmania, as subjects of the queen, but not in Queensland and Western Australia, which had the largest Aboriginal populations. The Commonwealth excluded Aboriginal Australians from political citizenship under the constitution (and women who did not yet have the vote at the state level, initially).[28] Being British subjects did more for Maori. Maori women joined two suffrage movements, first to vote for the House of Representatives and second for the Maori unification movement, Kotahitanga. From 1867 there were four Maori seats in parliament, but women could neither stand nor vote. After 1876 they could vote in local elections, but a freehold property qualification barred most of them. From 1886 the WCTU had a Maori Department: alcohol and family welfare were concerns shared with Pakeha women. In 1893 women were enfranchised on the Maori roll, and joined men in voting for Maori members of parliament, a month after Pakeha women joined Pakeha men at the polls. (Three of the four Maori MPs opposed the vote for Maori women, presumably on traditional grounds.) Maori women and men with freehold property of £25 could vote on the European roll if they wished; that is, they had a choice of ethnic label, provided they showed themselves to be 'civilized' through individualized property title; and from 1897 Maori women could stand and vote for Kotahitanga.[29]

Gender assumptions naturally flavoured colonists' understandings in the islands, infected their narratives, and often shaped policy. Two features of Tahitian and Hawaiian societies which arrested Europeans were the sexual availability of some women, and the public power exercised by some others. Whether these features were 'traditional' or more or less shaped by contact,[30] they were also generalized, so that Europeans expected similar behaviour in Samoa and Tonga (but not New Zealand). These features also presented themselves as conditions demanding reform. Victorian ideas of gender roles were advocated with passion by Protestant missions.[31] We need not imagine mere imposition: the monogamous family, the companionate marriage, the father as head of a nuclear household, could only take root with collaboration – and adaptation. Most evangelists to Melanesia were Polynesian married couples whose training equipped them to exemplify Western domesticity: husbands learned to preach and teach, wives to maintain a Christian household.[32] When communities converted, the authority of the pastor was usually buttressed by local deacons, again exemplifying the maleness of Christian authority.

Europeans often described each Melanesian dependency as 'a man's country'. This was literally true, since men outnumbered women by as much as 10 per cent; but that was not what the phrase meant.[33] Most Melanesians who worked in Queensland, Fiji and New Caledonia were men, and that was true of plantation workers generally.[34] From these engagements they returned with trade goods, some fluency in a pidgin – and new magic.[35] Men were better equipped than their sisters, by language and experience, to deal with outsiders. That advantage was compounded when officials recruited men as police; and ex-policemen were likely to be appointed to the men-only village-level posts – *luluai, tultul,* village constables – which linked colonial power to villages.[36] In theory, girls could attend mission schools with their brothers, but few did. In theory too, mission and government medical services were available to all. In practice almost all doctors and medical assistants (*liklik dokta,* who worked as practitioners) were male, most nurses were female; boys were more likely than girls to be brought to clinics; and racial and sexual taboos restricted contact across ethnic and gender lines.[37]

It was not only collaboration which brought men into cross-cultural relations. The best-known incident in the colonial history of Solomon Islands is the killing of the (Australian-born) District Officer Bell and his Islander police, on the island of Malaita.[38] Whether this was a tax revolt or an insurgency, all participants were men and so were all members of the posse which exacted vengeance. Peter Corris analysed these events as a historian and as a novelist.[39]

Naismith's Dominion differs from his academic work mainly by creating perceptive British and Islander women, reminding us that 'historical records' – oral
and written – are mainly the work of the men who feature in them.

The massacre created and reinforced stereotypes of 'savage' inland tribes
and friendly coastal ones, and branded Malaita as a place of massacre and
menace. In the 1990s the nearby island of Guadalcanal was disturbed by land
disputes. As the most numerous migrants to Guadalcanal, Malaitans were
prominent in these scuffles. Some Guadalcanal villagers suspected that
Malaitans' reputation for violence inhibited police from arresting them
(see chapter 21). In New Guinea too, the 'Rabaul Strike' of 1929 involved
policemen, plantation workers and domestic servants, while male missionaries sought to intercede with the men who wielded authority. One of those
(on leave at the critical moment) was James Taylor, who then led the epic
Hagen-Sepik Patrol which apprised thousands of highlanders of the existence
of government.[40] More than 350 people took part, all but five male. There
were encounters with highland women as some police tried to create strategic
alliances for a comfortable retirement; but Australians found it politic to veil
such liaisons. When Taylor then began to establish control, again he relied on
individual police to maintain order, often through marriage alliances. Colonial
officers and islanders alike came to regard the public domain, and government in particular, as the realm of men.

WHOM TO EXCLUDE

To preserve their identity, the settler polities adopted racial exclusion. Issues
of capital and labour, protection and democracy itself, delivered a consensus
on this point. The rise of the working classes, combined with stereotypes of
Chinese as servile and immoral, and miscegenation horrifying, slammed the
door on Asia. (Islanders were excluded through paternalism rather than
antipathy, but the outcome was the same.) Offer explains that Labor were
the champion of 'White Australia', quoting W. M. Hughes, the future prime
minister, in the New South Wales parliament in 1899:

> [In Queensland] we have a breeding ground for coloured Asiatics, where they
> will soon be eating the heart's blood out of the white population, where they
> will multiply and pass over our border in a mighty Niagara, sowing seeds of
> diseases which will never be eradicated, and which will permanently undermine
> the constitutional vigour of which the Anglo-Saxon race is so proud.

The shortage of labour could not be made up from Asia or the Pacific,
because racism rigged the market. 'The exclusion of Asian labour ... appeared
as a necessary condition of individual prosperity.' These settlements, 'having
wrested their territories from aboriginal occupiers, set about to secure their
possession from what they perceived to be land-hungry Asians.'[41]

Settlers believed that Asians would not fit into their democratic society.
They were a supposed menace to democracy, while racism itself 'arose

directly out of [settler society] virtues of democracy, civic equality and soli-darity'.[42] The first duty of these states was to be 'just to our own people, to our own workers'.[43] In theory Maori belonged to the people and therefore were entitled to the old age pension under New Zealand's Old Age Pensions Act of 1898. Chinese were excluded. In practice Maori received a lesser pro-portion (generally three-quarters) according to their status in the racial hier-archy, despite their supposed equality.[44] Racist assumptions also excluded Indians, who were caught by the term 'Asiatic'; their skin colour trumped their status as British subjects. From the 1890s, however, a new external threat loomed, in Japan.

The way ahead was clear for Australians once Queensland rejected the Anglo-Japanese Commercial Treaty in 1900. The Immigration Restriction Act of 1901, the Commonwealth's first legislative gesture, had its New Zealand counterpart in the Immigration Restriction Act 1899, which prohib-ited immigrants who were not of British or Irish parentage and could not pass a European language test. The use of a language test – the idea came from London – assuaged British strategic interests. That policy culminated in the Immigration Restriction Amendment Act of 1920 which prescribed an undeclared White New Zealand policy. New Zealand's policy had the same purpose as Australia's, but New Zealand's greater need to comply with British imperial strategy involved a more secretive procedure.[45]

Contemporaries recognized that the goal of racial homogeneity was the dri-ving force toward a White Australia. The discourse of Social Darwinism and a flexing eugenics movement provided tools in 1901, when Prime Minister Barton doubted that 'the doctrine of the equality of man' was intended to include 'racial equality'. As federation strengthened collective settler identity on either side of the Tasman, White Australia was both a precondition and an out-come of national self-determination, and the core of emergent national identity. In the first federal parliament, ideas of imagined community overlaid labour movement concerns: as Deakin argued, at stake were 'national manhood, the national character, and the national future'.[46] While nationalism had yet to gain a comparable grip in New Zealand, the shared idea of 'the people' had coa-lesced and permeated public consciousness so that all who were non-white, non-Christian and non-European in culture were labelled 'unassimilable'.[47]

It was this obsession with race which prompted the exclusion of Aboriginal Australians from this community. The constitution avoided the word 'citizen' with its republican overtones, in favour of British 'subject', and determined to preserve states' rights to decide whom to exclude. For several generations they 'systematically excluded Aboriginal people from basic citizenship rights and entitlements', and from the notion of the Australian people.[48]

SETTLER SOCIETIES AND CULTURAL EXPRESSIONS

During the late nineteenth century the colonists groped towards a distinctive sense of themselves as separate (though not apart) from the Mother Culture.

Four generations of native-born British Australians had wrestled with the tyranny of distance from 'home', the exile's nostalgia for the old order and the settler's challenges. 'Home' still embodied the old country but for many it also embraced the new. No serious cleavage of loyalty yet threatened the imperial connection even in Australia, with its nationalist republican tradition. Republicans imagined a 'New Australia' which was radical, democratic and progressive. Republicans dreamed of the 'political architecture' for a new society,[49] but republican radicals remained in the minority. Instead, in 1899 vast crowds turned out in the colonies to farewell troops to support the British empire against the Boers. These 'spontaneous' offers of contingents from the Australian states may have been engineered, and most enthusiasm came from the middle classes.[50] The latter's constructions of colonial identity dominated. The six Australian colonies were approaching nationhood with the boundaries of identity provided by colonial and mother cultures, always permeable, still heavily blurred.

Where tensions existed, they were often framed in terms of class. A different scale of values had taken root in the colonies from 'home', claimed utopians like William Lane, whose vision of an Australian workingman's paradise was the antithesis of the class-bound British system. In some quarters, notions grew of 'the Australian' – the 'coming man' – as a higher physical as well as moral type that maintained, or improved, British racial purity.[51] Colonists' pride was mainly conceit of race, not of nationality (though nationality intruded to the extent of producing *better* British). Most of those areas challenged (often successfully) by the colonials occurred in the context of physical – thus racial – qualities such as sports, as during the 1905 All Black rugby union tour which reassured New Zealanders of their destiny as a nursery for British bodies. To improve the stock was to fulfil the destiny of a British outpost. Though New Zealand laid greater stress on being 'Britain of the South' as a marketing stratagem, Australia's 'radical' nationalism can also be seen in these terms. Rejection of empire in this radical strand stemmed from a critique of British society. Works such as 'A Song of the Republic' (1887), Henry Lawson's first published poem, extolled unionism, socialism and nationalism, and looked to a new order of society 'free from the wrongs of the North and Past / The land that belongs to you'.

Neither in the cocky 1880s nor in the anxious 1890s did this nationalism sustain a coherent campaign of rupture with empire like America's. Rather it appealed to notions of development, democracy and fairness that themselves built upon British radical traditions. Reformers cast Australia and New Zealand, alongside America, as the new moral frontier of Western society, and for Australians and New Zealanders, like Americans, this was a racial frontier. But in the British societies of the Pacific the imperial connection remained, adding pomp and pride to settler dependence.

By the 1890s the proportion of white native-born Australians had reached 75 per cent, and by federation the figure was 82 per cent. The native-born grew in confidence: their impulse 'to take over' manifested itself throughout colonial life, increasingly claiming a place in debates on the future.[52] In Victoria, the Australian Natives' Association led the campaign towards nationhood as a federation. Trade unions were forging alliances with worker organizations and, through these, a nationwide party to represent labour in a federal parliament.

Natural and human disasters – a rabbit plague, floods and drought, financial collapse and struggles between capital and labour – bedevilled the 1890s, shattering the optimism. As the financial crisis worsened, the Australian colonies were wracked with industrial tensions. The Commercial Bank of Australia, the Australian Joint Stock Bank, and the London Chartered Bank of Australia had to suspend payment, igniting panic. In a series of strikes, riot police confronted angry workers with fixed bayonets in Broken Hill. Non-union – 'scab' – workers needed police escorts. The Riot Act was read in Sydney after a clash between unionists and 'scabs' in the wool industry. Queensland shearers refused to modify their demands for higher pay and better conditions, and pastoralists signed up non-union labour. Freedom of contract agreements signed by pastoralists and shearers undermined the moral and effective basis of unionism and drew scathing responses from union leaders. The maritime strike of 1890 spread from Sydney to ports and coalfields in New Zealand. New South Wales miners refused to cut coal for local ships and were locked out. Melbourne gas workers were called out. But by 1893 the flame of protest was sputtering. A Broken Hill strike organized to protest the gaoling of union leaders collapsed. The labour movement's ineffectualness exposed the shaky bases of the 'workingman's paradise' and prompted the first wave of moral exiles. In 1893, William Lane and 200 members of his New Australia Co-Operative Settlement Association and their children sailed to South America to found a socialist (and feminist) colony in Paraguay. By 1899 a disappointed Lane and a rump of followers, having failed to transform work and win economic and gender equality, quit Paraguay for New Zealand, where Lane edited a conservative Auckland newspaper.[53]

On the eve of federation the colonies remained dependent on Britain, for physical as much as economic survival. Real independence would be slower and more difficult than expected. Australians' transition to nationhood, much less costly in human terms than the Americans', would also be elusive. Without a war of independence, Australians had to devise other battlefields on which to define and defend their separateness – not yet independence – from Britain. As Luke Trainor explains,

> the struggles of 1889–90, with the other great strikes and Australian depression of the 1890s, produced a curious result. The shock drove some fractions of colonial capitalism – bankers, merchants, pastoralists among them – into a greater sense of dependence on Britain. Among the working class it produced a nationalist flowering. Finally, the outcome was a compromise.[54]

Energies generated by the reformers' agenda of a workingman's paradise sought new outlets. The cultural field provided journals, fiction, painting, architecture and language for these energies. An Australian folk culture had by the 1890s found a home in the bush, around men's campfires. According to Ward, an oral tradition fostered by nomadic male bush-workers, it had its roots in regions of Britain where ballads and songs were vehicles of news and entertainment. Not merely a culture of the unlettered as in the old country, Australian folk culture comprised a peculiar blend of the educated, self-educated and uneducated. Its major media were 'the song, the narrative ballad for recitation and the yarn'. A largely unselfconscious part of bush-life, it served to pass the time. Altogether other reasons invited the emergence of the bush song, for example drovers' practical need to provide reassuring sounds for their cattle at night.[55] Such a culture belonged in a time and place receding from most colonists' experience; but the wide literacy achieved by the 1890s gave folk culture a new medium: the printed word.

THE BULLETIN

Founded in 1880, the Sydney *Bulletin* 'tapped the folk undercurrent ... running strongly for half a century or more', capturing the tensions within it: harking back to a golden age in European Australia, while locating its springs in the bush. In the *Bulletin* (and to a lesser extent the Brisbane *Boomerang* founded in 1887) talented young writers articulated masculinist 'Australian' values and idealized an 'Australian way of life' and aspirations. The *Bulletin* had wide circulation, especially among men, including in New Zealand.[56] The 'bushman's bible' found its way into clubs and hotels, huts and barbers' shops.[57]

Its motto was 'Australia for the Australians' and its gods were mateship and male egalitarianism which, under J. F. Archibald, became synonymous with being Australian. Archibald was a genius in capturing the anxiety and excitement of a community coming to terms with its colonial past as it anticipated independence. Within a decade it hit a weekly circulation of 80,000, and reflected and shaped the mood of thinking Australia: openly racist and anti-Semitic, and misogynist.[58] Its trademarks were a gay vulgarity and bold defiance of the old order. It flaunted its radicalism and republicanism, and staunchly opposed monarchy and the class system that upheld it. In the 1880s and 1890s it embodied the colonists' impulses towards a distinctive identity and purpose, constructing the first coherent landscape of an Australian culture. Its writers shaped 'a group myth about Australians and their destiny'; in the absence of conventional heroes, visiting the past to claim the bushman as the first 'Australian', the anti-hero in the struggles against empire. The bushman of legend is significant not only for the kind of war – class war – with which he is associated, but also for his anonymity and collective nature. All later national legends – bushranger, digger, Anzac – would rest on the bushman, their heroes also distinctive for their anonymity and collective qualities, and their peculiar tragedy as loser-heroes.

The *Bulletin* voiced a loud position in pre-federation cultural debate, and its writers embraced a spectrum of nationalisms; but its wide circulation did not mean acceptance of its politics. Many who contributed were radical nationalists of a sort, but by no means all. A. B. ('Banjo') Paterson, creator of *The Man From Snowy River* and the colonies' most popular poet, was brought

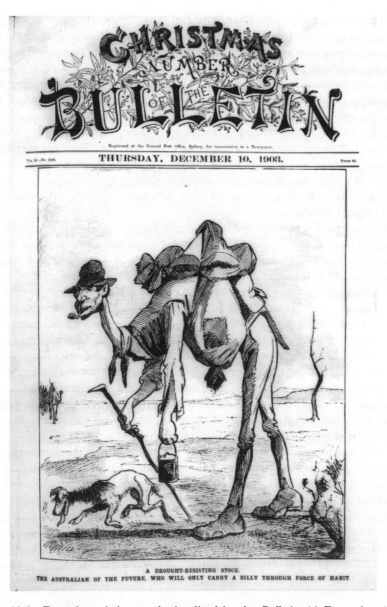

Plate 10.2 Drought-resisting stock visualized by the *Bulletin*, 10 December 1903, after several years of Australia's worst recorded drought, which began in 1895. Aridity and drought distinguished Australia from its neighbours. Courtesy of the National Library of Australia.

up on a station in Orange, New South Wales. A handsome, well-bred solicitor, his works were more concerned with a romantic past than a radical future. His hero was more a pioneer, typically a country gentleman by class, and a bushman by instinct, 'who worked with his men on the run, paid high wages, and sympathized with unionism; who was generous to the passing swagman and just to the drover with his hungry mob'.[59] Henry Lawson stemmed from a different class as his works and their politics reflected. Lawson's were bushmen by class and politics as well as instinct. Theirs is also a different bush, not simply in terms of station versus shed, but in its spiritual character: bleak where Paterson's is bright and optimistic. Son of a Norwegian sailor, from youth he was a nomad, following his family from goldfields to selections, eventually to settle in Sydney. Read as 'the People's Poet', in fact his main medium was the short story, where in *The Drover's Wife* and *The Bush Undertaker* and a dozen others he proved himself a master. In verse and prose he articulated egalitarian democratic protest in portraits of 'shabby slum-dwellers and soured selectors' through whose poignant lives he made crushing critiques of the 'workingman's paradise'.

Lawson found a kindred spirit in Joseph Furphy, alias 'Tom Collins' and author of *Such is Life* (1903). Described by its author as of 'temper, democratic; bias, offensively Australian', the novel was a self-conscious effort to chisel a colonial type against the British grain: brash where the other was polite, outrageous where respectable. Furphy, too, stemmed from humble origins. The son of Protestant Irish bounty emigrants, he was a manual labourer who worked the land, the goldfields, and even a threshing machine in his youth. Furphy described himself as 'half bushman, half bookworm'. He was self-educated, 'soaked in Shakespeare, the Bible, and the *Encyclopaedia Britannica*'.[60] His fame rests mainly with his 'gloriously ambitious novel', a 1,125-page manuscript labelled a masterpiece by generations of critics. Like Lawson, he portrayed a bush soaked in manly sweat and class politics. Ultimately, the literature of these nationalist pioneers constituted more a celebration of bush values than a critique of Australian society.

The genteel nationalism (or pioneer mythology) of Paterson contrasted sharply in tone and approach with Lawson's and Furphy's angry and class-based nationalism. In both, however, the bush stands at the centre of 'Australia' and 'the Australian'. For Paterson it was pastoral country, prosperous, anchored to home and family, church and school; for the others a world adrift, precarious and bleak, a relentless trial of physical and mental endurance. Both have their contexts in the real Australian bush, and in a different mix in New Zealand (which claims the gentleman as a national type, especially where Australians are present).[61]

BUSH MYTHOLOGIES

For over a century the Australian bush resisted alien conceptions of the land and land management. New Zealand's bush proved more compliant, though it took its name from the Australian lexicon. The bush of the Australian imaginary and experience destroyed lives. In this unequal struggle grew awe at its harshness and respect for those who endured. The sagas of generations of failed selectors and insolvent small farmers shaped a mythology which both borrowed from British pastoral tradition a sense of the redeeming qualities of the land – Arcadia – and overturned it, by stressing the land's physical and spiritual bleakness reinforcing, rather than undermining, the bushman's heroism and moral triumph.

Bursts of pastoral expansion also crystallized a quite different model of the Australian (male) rural dweller. 'The farmer', personification of the British occupation of southeastern Australia, belonged in the yeoman tradition, respectable, and proud of his competency (see chapter 6).

> By tradition the backbone of the country, uncorrupted by society, more patriotic and virtuous than the allegedly decadent city dweller, his struggle with the land made the Australian farmer hard and proud, noted for his toughness and independence.[62]

Or so the historians' mythology has it. The pioneer-become-farmer as the 'backbone of the country' took pride of place in New Zealand stereotypes, ahead of and supposedly distinct from the (stereotypically Australian) bushman.

The myth of the bush waxed as the reality waned. The 1870s and 1880s saw rural Australia transformed, with country towns – from 50 to 500 people – forming along new railway lines. It was settled country with towns to service markets for wool and wheat, sugar and shipping industries and a booming timber trade. Men still outnumbered women in pastoral districts, but there was gender balance in farming areas and country towns. The new demographics, of predominantly native-born rather than migrants, with many young people, rejuvenated rural Australia, while the domestic dimension tamed life in the bush. Shearers and other nomadic workers still contributed a disturbing element but there was countervailing sobriety and respectability. The same applied in New Zealand, as the frontier zone shifted to small farming and bush settlements in the lower North Island. A new rural working class of family men, their homes with wives and children in nearby towns, was a key agent in civilizing the bushscape. By 1900, schools, churches and cottage hospitals were as much a feature of the outback as the shearing shed and the pub. Binge drinking and violence persisted but domesticity, civic pride and temperance movements made them less common. The frontiers of civilization now lay in the far north and west of Australia.

Barbara Baynton's short stories, collected as 'Bush Studies', offer compelling insights from this changing culture. Her writing is unsentimental, even brutal; the muscularity in her portrayals of the bush and bushwomen leaves Lawson's bush and bushmen limp. Born in the small town of Scone in New South Wales, Baynton was brought up in the Liverpool Plains where she met and married her first husband, a selector. She left the bush in 1887, when the marriage ended and she moved to the city with her three children. At the turn of the century she moved to London, henceforth alternating between Australia and England. She began writing in the 1890s and her first story was published in the *Bulletin* in 1896. Her fiction draws on her early life and depicts a harsh world devoid of Paterson's romanticism or the spiritual elements that soften Lawson's harsh stories. Her work commands attention both as literature and as social criticism. Her principal characters are women, toughened and victimized by the horror of their daily lives. Among her best stories is *Squeaker's Mate*, where a woman, her back broken by a falling tree, is abandoned by her callous man; and *The Chosen Vessel*, in which a young mother alone in her bush hut is raped and murdered by a strange swagman. Baynton's output was small but her neglect until the second wave of feminist writings was due mainly to the exclusive character of the Australian Legend. For *Squeaker's Mate* presided over the selection and home, and did men's work, such as felling trees. Her broken back from this toil made her reliant on the indifferent Squeaker. Feminist scholarship reveals Baynton's story as subversive of conventional gender relations; restoring the woman, as mate, to dependency exposed Squeaker's unfitness to wear the trousers.[63] The politics of her writing were also radical and nationalist but not in the Lawson/Furphy mould. They resided mainly in subversive portrayals of women as the real bushmen, in their capacity to endure *as women*. Her women bore the horrors of the bush with stoicism and courage like Lawson's men; but they did so without the aid or comfort of their mates.[64]

Modernity, like domesticity and respectability, had also begun transforming the bush. The bicycle brought major changes to life's rhythms as roads improved. Its use grew dramatically in the 1890s. The bicycle brought the first official postal services, and in the outback was used by insurance agents, doctors, shearers, schoolteachers, road and railway workers, and ministers of religion – though it did not at once replace the horse. In the cities the 'New Woman' climbed on her bicycle and became fast.[65] In the same decade, the first milking machines reached New South Wales, and the first public telephone was installed at the Sydney General Post Office. The first moving picture peep-show opened in Sydney and Christchurch. A railway linked Perth and Coolgardie, while Brisbane, still a country town, introduced electric trams. By the end of the decade, Hobart, capital of Tasmania, was lit by electricity.

URBAN AUSTRALIA

By the 1890s Australia, although locked into primary industry and dependence on the rural sector, was among the most urbanized countries in the world. Melbourne and Sydney had become metropolises, yet Australia was not urbanized by modern standards, and suburban bushland surrounded the cities, easily accessible by bicycle, train or horse and trap. This rural context inspired the first major harvest of an Australian creative spirit, from the cities. In one view, the bush beckoned because of disillusion with the city, now reduced to decadent site of mortgages, failed marriages and racial decay.[66] The *Bulletin* is one case, but there are others in painting, architecture and language.

The Heidelberg School (the first Australian school of painting) that flourished in Melbourne in the 1880s offered striking perceptions and images of the landscape. The group comprised native-born and migrants. Its major figures –

A COMPARISON

The Melbourne Girl   ∴   The Sydney Girl

Plate 10.3 The Coming Women. Sydney and Melbourne girls, visualized by *The Lone Hand*, 1912. Courtesy of the National Library of Australia.

Tom Roberts, Frederick McCubbin, Arthur Streeton and Charles Conder – were regarded (like *Bulletin* writers) as 'young radicals in revolt'.[67] Their nationalism was never overt. They may have seen themselves as helping to shape, even crystallize, a distinctively Australian culture, but 'they did not see their work as nation-building'.[68] Their radicalism resided in the form, content and implications of their art.

The Heidelberg painters were challenged by the landscape and the peculiar problems of craft and subject matter for the visual artist. How to free the landscape of the distorting British lens and 'analyse the true values of colour as seen through an envelope of atmosphere'?[69] Their first exhibition of what came to be called Australian impressionism in Melbourne in 1889 displayed for the first time – according to the leading art historian Bernard Smith – 'a naturalistic interpretation of the Australian sunlit landscape'. They analysed eucalypt forest

> in the full blaze of sunlight. They depicted the colour and luminosity of the pale shadows of midsummer ...; the atmospheric effects of dust, heat-haze and afterglow. But they loved most the warm coloured stillness of summer evenings.[70]

They had grasped the significance of the sun and bright light in Australian experience and identity. While the bright sun was shared with the Pacific Islands and New Zealand, these painters recognized that the quality of living in Australia's bright light was distinctive. Indeed, the sun was used as a symbol of Australia.[71] Deemed the truest depiction yet of the distinctive shades and tones of the bush, the exhibition of 150 paintings, mostly set on cigar-box lids, was greeted with scepticism and disdain. A senior critic deemed them mostly 'a pain to the eye'.[72]

The impressionism of the Heidelberg painters was the product of both local and overseas influences. European influence was evident in all their techniques, particularly of the French Barbizon School and English watercolourists, but also from Italy and Spain, and even Japan. They adapted rather than aped such influences. Theirs was 'an original attempt to apply impressionist principles to a different set of visual and social conditions'; their problems of rendering light and colour were 'their own', and their technical solutions 'were also largely their own'.[73] The context of impressionism was the focus in nineteenth-century painting on naturalism as a new approach to portraying landscape, and in Australia, the sunlight and colour of the bush, applying the *plein-air* method. Their principal aim, articulated in the catalogue for their 1889 exhibition of 9 × 5 impressions, was to capture a moment rather than a scene or image: 'to render faithfully, and thus obtain first records of effects widely differing, and often of very fleeting character'.[74]

Educated, male and urban, these painters – like the *Bulletin* writers – 'went bush' to construct their images of Australia. The bush lured them and eluded them. Tired of Melbourne, Streeton went inland – 'away from all polite society' – to 'create some things entirely new', and in the bush he sensed 'great hidden poetry' which he aimed to translate to canvas:

> I fancy large canvases all glowing and moving in the happy light and others bright decorative and chalky and expressive of the hot trying winds and the slow immense summer. It is immense. ... But somehow it's all out of reach. ... I love Australia (and yet have seen so little).[75]

Intellectuals as well as artists, Roberts and McCubbin brought a broad nationalist agenda to their art. Roberts's attempt to capture national life culminated in his celebrated historical portrayals of that life: 'Coming South', the migrant experience and shearing studies. Painters and writers intersected in important places: in the 'urban idealization of the outback', the maleness of the bush, the celebration of the dignity of labour and the cult of the bush-worker (in Roberts's shearing studies for example) and physicality. Roberts's and Paterson's work shared the myth-making about a golden age of pastoralism. Roberts was the most political painter, which is not saying much. While his sympathies lay with the labour movement, his paintings (including his shearing studies, significant given the militant role of the shearers' union) reflect nothing of the political intensity of the period. McCubbin's work has closer links with the bush of Lawson and Furphy. His works are suffused with sentiment and a heavy melancholy, and his ordinary frontier life has a grey lining. They present a raw picture of pioneer life. To Serle, he is 'the painter of life and death and of the hardships of the pioneer'. Like Lawson, his celebrations of pioneers were of a heroism unseen, unrewarded and ultimately futile.[76]

Despite differences in style, setting and politics, important impulses united Streeton's pastoral landscapes and the historical paintings of Roberts and McCubbin. Through their works runs an affirmation of Australia's right to its own identity and spirit of place. As Bernard Smith argued, they brought a 'new sense of optimism, joy, and love of the sun' to the environment, from which the historian Serle deduced that they 'made a major statement on behalf of the school of hope and freedom against the school of exile'.[77] Like Lawson and Furphy, the Heidelberg painters suffered neglect. Local interest was conservative, and greeted nationalism with distaste. Recognition by the local art establishment began only decades later.

Architecture was another field of expression of place, and another index of the coming of age of a new British type. Already by the 1880s, leading figures pondered how to develop a distinctively Australian housing style. Here too there was interplay of local and overseas influences. The 'Marseilles tile', first imported in bulk in 1886, became the vogue, particularly in Sydney and Melbourne, marking the Australian suburbanscape for half a century with the 'uniform tyranny of red brick and orange tile, stretching for countless mile on suburban mile'. Britain's influence was felt with the 'Queen Anne' style which dominated suburbia until the Great War – 'red brick, painted timbers and emphasis on roof-shape; madly broken-up gables and spires'. For all its debts to Britain and Europe, Bernard Smith argued, the end result was 'an Australian style if ever there was one', which merited its own name. To mark its birth in tandem with the Commonwealth, he baptized it Federation.[78] The Federation house claimed a unique place in architecture, even if it offended architects. Australian design was developing in three streams: at one end was the work of a few 'nationally-minded innovating architects', at the other construction by spec-builders, and between them 'minority architect-designed housing'. Australian architecture absorbed as well as contributed innovations. Two which made global impact were the cavity wall and brick veneer.[79]

By 1900 a pattern had crystallized in the quest for a separate small house on its own lot ('section' in New Zealand), with a fifty-feet frontage, a front lawn and a backyard. The opposite applies to public buildings, where virtually nothing Australian can be seen for decades. Philip Drew lamented: 'If buildings were words, then they would say ...: "I don't really want to belong here; I'm not staying; my presence is only temporary. I would really like to be somewhere else, preferably where I came from." '[80] Drew looks to the coast for distinctively Australian architecture; and to the veranda as a signifier of the colonial condition of 'makeshift'.

> The old was left standing. The veranda was added as an improvised light structure. The old provided a strong support at the back while leaving the front open. While the veranda itself was a comparatively new structure, a frail open framework facing the new prospect, it was attached to and supported by the old. This is how Empire worked. The veranda was transitional, a provisional shelter erected during a period of adjustment while colonial society found its bearings in a new country. The temporary character and lightness of the veranda is an apt metaphor for this provisional cultural condition.

The Australian veranda was 'a quintessential colonial gesture made by an insular people intimidated by unlimited space and wide horizons'.[81] It is context which matters, because the veranda – known from India to the West Indies – became as much an identifying characteristic of the New Zealand house as the Australian. New Zealanders, however, built in weatherboard, like Queenslanders and Californians. The styles on the new American urban frontier appealed in Australia and New Zealand for the shared settler society ideals they symbolized, of democracy, privacy, freedom and the nuclear family.[82]

As with shelter, so with speech. The New Zealand and Australian accents, closely related, were developing from the 1850s. 'We are always waging war against the colonial accent', complained Miss Lorimer, headmistress of Nelson Girls' College, in 1912. Teachers and inspectors lamented the 'colonial twang'.[83] Publication in the 1890s of *Austral English* and an Australasian supplement to *Webster's International Dictionary* recognized distinctive forms of speech. A century in a new environment had given rise to a new language to describe fauna and flora as well as activities and functions. Some old terms were adapted from British, American or other English-speaking societies to suit the new context. Words like 'bush', 'paddock', 'gully', 'creek', 'station', 'fossick', assumed new local meaning; and very few – 'barrack' and 'larrikin' – were new or borrowed from Aboriginal languages. Words with meanings extraneous to the scene disappeared – 'meadow', 'woods', 'copse', 'spinney', 'glen', 'inn', 'village'. Australian colloquialisms – 'going crook', 'on the outer', 'get stuck into', 'rough as guts' – and diminutives such as 'bullocky', 'cocky', 'wharfie' – brought local flavour.[84] New Zealand speech adopted some Maori words, but much was Australian, symbolic of shared experience. 'Bush', 'paddock', 'creek', 'station', 'ropeable', 'sheila', 'joker', 'kindy', 'shout', are a few examples.[85]

NOTES

1   Hiromitsu Iwamoto, 'Nanshin: Japanese Settlers in Papua and New Guinea: 1890–1949', *Journal of Pacific History* monograph, Canberra, 1999.

2 Hank Nelson, 'Frontiers, Territories and States of Mind', Pacific History Workshop, December 1998, Australian National University, Canberra.
3 *Australian Parliamentary Debates*, House of Representatives, vol. 6, 1901–2, 7079–91.
4 Clive Moore, *Kanaka: A History of Melanesian Mackay*, Port Moresby, 1985.
5 Dorothy Shineberg, *The People Trade: Pacific Island Laborers and New Caledonia, 1865–1930*, Honolulu, 1999.
6 Alfred Deakin, *Federated Australia: Selections from Letters to the Morning Post, 1900–1910*, ed. J. La Nauze, Melbourne, 1968: letter of 31 Dec. 1901, 85.
7 House of Representatives, 3 Nov. 1904, vol. 23, 6513.
8 Ibid., 4425–37.
9 Nelson, 'Frontiers, Territories and States of Mind'.
10 *Official Year Book of the Commonwealth of Australia 1901–1911*, 1157.
11 Marilyn Lake, 'The Politics of Respectability: Identifying the Masculinist Context', *Historical Studies*, 22: 86 (April 1986), 116–31.
12 Russell Ward, *The Australian Legend*, Melbourne, 1966; distinctions between types of selector are from Peter Hempenstall, *The Meddlesome Priest: A Life of Ernest Burgmann*, Sydney, 1993, 5.
13 Lake, 'The Politics of Respectability', 117.
14 For explanations, see the debate between R. Dalziel, 'The Colonial Helpmeet: Women's Role and the Vote in Nineteenth-century New Zealand', in B. Brookes, C. Macdonald and M. Tennant (eds), *Women in History: Essays on European Women in New Zealand*, vol. 1, Wellington, 1986, 55–68; and P. Grimshaw, *Women's Suffrage in New Zealand*, 2nd edn, Auckland, 1987.
15 Donald Denoon, *Settler Capitalism: The Dynamics of Dependent Development in the Southern Hemisphere*, Oxford, 1983, 186–7, 191; Carol Bacchi, *Same Difference*, Sydney, 1990, 6–28.
16 D. Page, *The National Council of Women: A Centennial History*, Auckland, 1996, 1.
17 C. Daley and M. Nolan (eds), *Suffrage and Beyond: International Feminist Perspectives*, Auckland, 1994, appendix.
18 P. Grimshaw, 'Women's Suffrage in New Zealand Revisited', in Daley and Nolan, *Suffrage and Beyond*, 37.
19 Ibid.
20 W. P. Reeves, *State Experiments in Australia and New Zealand*, 2 vols, London, 1902.
21 Raewyn Dalziel, 'Presenting the Enfranchisement of New Zealand Women Abroad', in Daley and Nolan, *Suffrage and Beyond*, 46–51. Reeves's wife Maud was active in Fabian Socialist politics in London while his daughter Amber had a child out of wedlock to H. G. Wells. R. Fry, *Maud and Amber*, Christchurch, 1992.
22 A. Oldfield, *Woman Suffrage in Australia: A Gift or a Struggle?*, Melbourne, 1992.
23 Ratios of number of males/100 females, 1901, in Wray Vamplew (ed.), *Australians: Historical Statistics*, Sydney, 1987, 40.
24 Oldfield's interpretation supports this reasoning.
25 William Lovell-Smith, poem 1893, in M. Lovell-Smith, *Plain Living High Thinking*. Models of the New Woman and colonial helpmeet from Grimshaw, *Women's Suffrage in New Zealand*, and Dalziel, 'The Colonial Helpmeet'. On Hall, see J. Garner, *By His Own Merits: Sir John Hall – Pioneer, Pastoralist and Premier*, Hororata, 1995.
26 But where couples were in agreement, fertility declined: see ch. 12.
27 S. Magarey, S. Rowley and S. Sheridan (eds), *Debutante Nation: Feminism Contests the 1890s*, Sydney, 1993. This theme is taken up in Patricia Grimshaw, Marilyn

Lake, Ann McGrath and Marian Quartly, *Creating a Nation*, Melbourne, 1994, chs 7 and 8. On New Zealand, see T. Tulloch, 'The State Regulation of Sexuality in New Zealand, 1880–1925', Ph.D. thesis, University of Canterbury, 1997.

28 Most members of the first federal parliament believed that Aborigines could vote only in South Australia, but in 1902 this was also the case for Aboriginal women as well as men in New South Wales. P. Stretton and C. Finnimore, 'Black Fellow Citizens: Aborigines and the Commonwealth Franchise', *Australian Historical Studies*, 25: 101 (Oct. 1993), 521–35. For details of constitutional exclusion, see J. Chesterman and B. Galligan, *Citizens without Rights: Aborigines and Australian Citizenship*, Melbourne, 1997, 67–83.

29 T. Rei, *Maori Women and the Vote*, Wellington, 1993.

30 Bernard Smith, *European Vision and the South Pacific*, Sydney, 1960.

31 Jocelyn Linnekin, 'New Political Orders', in Donald Denoon, Stewart Firth, Jocelyn Linnekin, Malama Meleisea and Karen Nero (eds), *Cambridge History of the Pacific Islanders*, Melbourne, 1997, 185–216.

32 Margaret Jolly and Martha Macintyre (eds), *Family and Gender in the Pacific: Domestic Contradictions and the Colonial Impact*, Cambridge, 1989.

33 Donald Denoon with Kathy Dugan and Leslie Marshall, *Public Health in Papua New Guinea 1884–1984: Medical Possibility and Social Constraint*, Cambridge, 1989. The meaning of the phrase in New Zealand is explored by Jock Phillips, *A Man's Country?*, Auckland, 1987.

34 Ralph Shlomowitz, 'Mortality and the Pacific Island Labour Trade', *Journal of Pacific History*, 22: 1 (1987), 34–55; 'Mortality and Indentured Labour in Papua (1885–1941) and New Guinea (1920–41)', *Journal of Pacific History*, 23: 1 (1988), 70–9.

35 Ann Chowning, 'Recent Acculturation between Tribes in Papua New Guinea', *Journal of Pacific History*, 4 (1969), 27–40.

36 August Kituai, *My Gun My Brother: The World of the Papua New Guinea Colonial Police, 1920–1960*, Honolulu, 1998.

37 Denoon et al., *Public Health in Papua New Guinea*.

38 Roger Keesing and Peter Corris, *Lightning Meets the West Wind: The Malaita Massacre*, Melbourne, 1980.

39 Peter Corris, *Naismith's Dominion*, Sydney, 1990.

40 Bill Gammage, *The Sky Travellers: Journeys in New Guinea 1938–1939*, Melbourne, 1998.

41 A. Offer, *The First World War: An Agrarian Interpretation*, Oxford, 1989, 164–72.

42 Offer, *Agrarian Interpretation*, 198, 170.

43 Collins in debate on Asiatic Restriction Bill (no. 2), *New Zealand Parliamentary Debates*, 94, 13 Aug. 1896, 314.

44 On race and welfare policies, see ch. 14.

45 P. S. O'Connor, 'Keeping New Zealand White, 1908–1920', *New Zealand Journal of History*, 2 (1968), 41–65. See also T. M. Roy, 'Immigration Policy and Legislation', in K. W. Thomson and A. D. Trlin (eds), *Immigrants in New Zealand*, Palmerston North, 1970, 15–24; and B. Moloughney and J. Stenhouse, ' "Drug-besotten, Sin-begotten Fiends of Filth": New Zealanders and the Oriental Other, 1850–1920', *New Zealand Journal of History*, 33: 1 (1999), 43–64.

46 A. T. Yarwood, *Asian Migration to Australia: The Background to Exclusion 1896–1923*, Melbourne, 1967, 24. Deakin's comment is from *Commonwealth Parliamentary Debates*, 4, 2 Sept. 1901, 4864.

47 Manying Ip, *Dragons on the Long White Cloud*, Auckland, 1996, 174–5.

48 Chesterman and Galligan, *Citizens without Rights*, 82–3.

49 Bruce Scates, *A New Australia: Citizenship, Radicalism and the First Republic*, Melbourne, 1997, 7, 208.

50 C. N. Connolly, 'Manufacturing "Spontaneity": The Australian Offers of Troops for the Boer War', *Historical Studies*, 18: 70 (April 1978), 106–17, and 'Class, Birthplace, Loyalty: Australian Attitudes to the Boer War', *Historical Studies*, 18: 71 (Oct. 1978), 210–32.

51 Richard White, *Inventing Australia*. The Australian Experience, ed. Heather Radi, Sydney, 1981, ch. 5.

52 Geoffrey Serle, *From Deserts the Prophets Come: The Creative Spirit in Australia 1788–1972*, Melbourne, 1973, ch. 5, 60–2.

53 Scates, *A New Australia*, 187–93.

54 Luke Trainor, *British Imperialism and Australian Nationalism*, Melbourne, 1994, 138.

55 Serle, *From Deserts the Prophets Come*, 61. Serle's source is Ward, *Australian Legend*.

56 J. O. C. Phillips, 'Musings in Maoriland – or was there a *Bulletin* School in New Zealand?', *Historical Studies*, 20: 81 (Oct. 1983), 520–35.

57 Serle, *From Deserts the Prophets Come*, 61.

58 See, for example, Magarey, Rowley and Sheridan, *Debutante Nation*.

59 Serle, *From Deserts the Prophets Come*, 63, from H. M. Green, *History of Australian Literature, Pure and Applied*, Sydney, 1961. See also J. B. Hirst, 'The Pioneer Legend', *Historical Studies*, 18 (1978), 316–37.

60 Ibid., 67.

61 See chs 15, 20.

62 Buxton 1870–90, in Frank Crowley, *A New History of Australia*, Melbourne, 1974, 180.

63 Sue Rowley, 'Things a Bushwoman Cannot Do', in Magarey, Rowley and Sheridan, *Debutante Nation*, 194–8.

64 Penne Hackforth-Jones, *Between Two Worlds*, Melbourne, 1989, for biographical background.

65 Sue Magarey at the 'Suffrage and Beyond' conference, Victoria University of Wellington, 1993. See Susan Magarey, 'Why Didn't They Want to be Members of Parliament? Suffragists in South Australia', in C. Daley and M. Nolan (eds), *Suffrage and Beyond: International Feminist Perspectives*, Auckland, 1994, 67–88.

66 Graeme Davison, *The Rise and Fall of Marvellous Melbourne*, Melbourne, 1978; David Hamer, *New Towns in the New World: Images and Perceptions of the Nineteenth-century Urban Frontier*, New York, 1990.

67 Serle, *From Deserts the Prophets Come*, 72.

68 Peter Beilharz, *Imagining the Antipodes: Culture, Theory and the Visual in the Work of Bernard Smith*, Melbourne, 1997, 31–2.

69 Bernard Smith (with Terry Smith), *Australian Painting 1788–1990*, 3rd edn, Melbourne, 1991, 68.

70 Ibid., 82.

71 Ibid.

72 James Smith, *Argus*, 17 August 1889, cited in Smith, *Australian Painting*, 77, and Serle, *From Deserts the Prophets Come*, 73.

73 Smith, *Australian Painting*, 79, 82.

74 Ibid., 81; Serle, *From Deserts the Prophets Come*, 73–4.

75 Streeton to Roberts, quoted in Smith, *Australian Painting*, 81, and Serle, *From Deserts the Prophets Come*, 76.

76 Serle, *From Deserts the Prophets Come*, 77. More detail in Smith, *Australian Painting*, 86–92.

77 Smith, *Australian Painting*, 82; Serle, *From Deserts the Prophets Come*, 78.

78 Bernard Smith, 'Architecture in Australia', *Historical Studies*, 14: 53 (Oct. 1969), 90; Serle, *From Deserts the Prophets Come*, 84. See also Robin Boyd, *Australia's Home*, Melbourne, 1952, ch. 6. Smith lamented Boyd's use of the term 'Queen Anne' in this 'seminal book'.

79 Serle, *From Deserts the Prophets Come*, 85.

80 Philip Drew, *The Coast Dwellers: Australians Living on the Edge*, Ringwood, Victoria, 1994, 1.

81 Ibid., 8.

82 William Toomath, *Built in New Zealand: The Houses We Live In*, Auckland, 1996; Lionel Frost, *The New Urban Frontier*, Sydney, 1991.

83 Elizabeth Gordon, 'The Origins of New Zealand Speech: The Limits of Recovering Information from Written Records', *English World-Wide*, 19: 1 (1998), 61–85.

84 Serle, *From Deserts the Prophets Come*, 87–8.

85 See, for example, Joan Hughes (ed.), *The Concise Australian National Dictionary*, Melbourne, 1992.

[11]   CAPITAL AND LABOUR: RESISTING GLOBALIZATION

There is an 'intimate relationship between the market and the imagined community of the nation', as Richard White astutely observes, which 'can be seen in the way the best known expressions of an Australian identity were ... marketing exercises'.[1] New Zealand 'state experiments' also served to market products and attract capital.[2] Britain was the target audience for this marketing. Equally significantly, Australia and New Zealand began to export food as well as fibre to the mother country. The global economy grew rapidly with innovations in transport which saw a collapse in the cost of sea-freight as steamships enabled Australia and New Zealand to sell cargoes in British markets. The British were the only serious global traders before 1945, the pound sterling the dominant global currency, and London the centre of world finance.

Australian and New Zealand visions of progress gave settlers and their governments 'voracious financial appetites',[3] and British capital gushed, providing between a quarter of new capital (in the 1870s and 1890s) and half (in the 1860s and 1880s). Financial crises turned off the tap for eastern Australia from the early 1890s into the 1900s, but mining tempted British capital, especially Western Australian gold. Sterling flowed not only into increasingly unpromising wool, city-building and railways. It enabled settler societies to restructure their economies after the depression, and after Australia's drought of 1895 to 1903. Refrigeration triggered revolutionary developments in economy and culture, reinforcing both dependency and white identity. It drew investment into freezing works to process mutton and beef, dairy factories to process butter and cheese, refrigerated shipping, and banking and finance. Australia and New Zealand used capital to intensify agriculture, but in a different mix. Both expanded from the 'dry' pastoral to the 'wet' dairy frontier.[4] Australia also irrigated wheat. And they competed to supply Britain, now the largest importer of food.

For Australia (as for Canada and Argentina) wheat was the 'great expanding staple of the Edwardian period': New Zealand added meat and dairy products.[5] More than Australia, it took up refrigeration and built dairy factories which were etched on the countryside in landscape painting. Typical was Christopher Perkins's *Taranaki* (1931): the white cone of Mt Taranaki with a dairy factory in the foreground.[6] New Zealand promoted itself as the 'Empire's Dairy Farm', an image ingested by Pakeha. Milk as a cultural icon meshed with 'clean and green' images of an environment in which to rear

Plate 11.1 *Taranaki*, 1931, Christopher Perkins. Courtesy of the Auckland City Art Gallery.

children, where people led an active outdoors life: in short, a country which realized the yeoman model. Australian dairy farmers on the other hand are treated roughly by the bush legend (see chapter 6).

These technical advances promoted exports, inhibiting manufacturing and diversification. They encouraged rural development, restructuring economies within agriculture rather than away from it, and fuelled another round of acquiring Maori and Aboriginal land, now in wet country. S. A. M. Adshead offers insights into refrigeration, the key technical advance. This had great consequences for both food production and consumption. While it transformed production for export, it also ushered in a consumer age.[7] Following Argentine efforts to export frozen meat to France, Australians tried dry air refrigerant, and Queenslanders successfully shipped frozen meat to England in 1880. New Zealand followed with its first shipment in 1882, a joint effort between the New Zealand and Australian Land Company and the Albion Shipping Company. New Caledonian ranchers did not move into dairying, but these engineering advances locked Australia and New Zealand into export-led growth, and the consumption as well as the production of meat and dairy products. Sheep and dairy farmers, and grain growers, realized that they must 'capture minds as well as markets'.[8] Images promoting these products again affected how they saw themselves. Both production and consumption are part of culture and mould identities, and refrigeration affected both.

Food is the first example of culture in nature, and a core medium for expressing identity. Our relations with food are 'one of the most common and pervasive sources of value in human experience', and the effectiveness of a food as an ethnic symbol is a product (among other things) of relations between people and their environment.[9] 'We are what we eat', but Adshead turns this adage into its 'consumerist opposite', that we eat what we are. This is pivotal for grasping identity among settlers in Australia and New Zealand, especially as they fashioned their societies and identities within bilateral, dependent trading relations, in an imperial framework of guaranteed markets, supplying staples for Britain.

New Zealand's rapid diversification into dairy products and the 'Empire's Dairy Farm' therefore offers insights into settler culture and identity, as does the Australian export of wheat. It is no accident that Australia's soldiers in the Great War were known as 'cornstalks' and New Zealanders as 'fernleaves' when the fernleaf brand featured on its butter wrappers. The export of 'good New Zealand milk' as butter, cheese and dried milk had profound implications, as they did on the British breakfast table (and at the mass end of the market). Milk had long had a mythic status as a life-giving fluid, associated with health, youth and purity.[10] Above all, it was children's food. Processing food for Britain, and building British bodies in the United Kingdom and in New Zealand, reinforced colonists' beliefs about themselves as body-builders and brawn for empire, and views of New Zealand as an ideal place to process imperial identity. As late as 1955, New Zealand's first state nutritionist, Dr Muriel Bell, declared that milk was for 'building Britons'.[11] An economy – and culture – based on milk is a long way from one based on minerals (as well as wool), as in Australia.

Refrigeration also had ecological effects with consequences for people's relations to the environment. Global consumerism transformed the environment by intensive agriculture: refrigeration permitted the conquest of Australia and New Zealand by sheep for meat as well as wool, and by the 'Dairy Cow as an Empire Builder'.[12] In this more concentrated ecological imperialism, British flora and fauna provided the basis for 'native' New Zealand and Australian breeds. Innovations included the Corriedale sheep (a Lincoln or Leicester cross with Merino) for wool and meat. Britain's partiality for fat lamb rather than mutton spurred 'pasture improvements' for 'fattening young stock', with implications for 'fattening human stock'.[13] English grasses replaced native pasture and plant in the bush-burn and prompted more innovations in ploughing and sowing. It also destroyed forest cover, imposing a new ecological order. Imperializing the New Zealand landscape was rather simple, as 'English grasses thrive wherever the natural bush and fern are cleared'.[14] But it was harder to turn Australian pasture into English countryside; so South American grasses colonized the landscape.[15]

The *Making New Zealand* pictorial survey to mark New Zealand's centenary in 1940 opened issue no. 11, on pasture lands, with the line: 'In New Zealand more than in any country in the world we find justification for the words of the Bible, "All flesh is as grass, and all the goodliness thereof is as the flower of the field"'.[16] English grasses fed British livestock to serve to British consumers, in an imperial food chain. English grasses were even re-exported to the United Kingdom, as meat and dairy products. The biblical reference alluded to Arcadian myth, which portrayed New Zealand as the land of milk and honey. Significantly, this reference became an anthem, sung on Anzac Day (see chapter 13). Not only did New Zealand process imperial grass into imperial flesh and blood – with more emphasis on 'imperial' than in Australia – but the flesh of its best young men would become the 'flower of the field', symbolized in the poppy.

The economic dependency of settler capitalism thus had immense effect for reordering not only the economy, but also the physical, social and cultural landscapes. Imported grass, sheep and cows and their re-exported products helped to process separate yet parallel white, colonial identities. Restructured export economies revived closer settlement schemes. Refrigeration raised the hopes of those for whom Arcadia meant small farming. Indeed, the way these frozen foods featured in national policies had a bearing on Australian and New Zealand political futures.[17] These governments were accustomed to subsidizing the import of labour, and now offered bonuses to agri-business for innovation in the export of butter and cheese. They also imported dairy experts to advise farmers; John Sawers, from Scotland, became New Zealand's Chief Dairy Expert in 1889 and his brother Cheese Expert to Victoria. They were joined by Danish and Canadian instructors, and an Irish woman to teach farmers' wives butter-making (women's work before it was mechanized).[18] They imposed methods of quality control including cool stores, factory inspection and grading for export. Expansion of food exports, however, had to await the lifting of depression and financial crisis.

BOOM AND BUST

Dependency also reshaped identities through experiments with a new order of capital and labour, as a bulwark against instability. Reordering ('state experiments') then helped define a new phase of identity-making, as devices for balancing capital and labour were elevated to symbols of distinctiveness.

While the eastern Australian colonies and New Zealand shared the financial crisis of the 1890s, they differed in the timing, severity and onset of depression and in their patterns of recovery. New Zealand, depressed in the 1880s, suffered a flight of capital via Anglo-Australian banks and a flight of labour across the Tasman; then from 1895 it found prosperity and a new sense of self in enhanced dependency on Britain through the industries opened up by refrigeration.[19] It therefore escaped the shrinkage of capital which savaged drought-plagued Australia.[20] After the collapse of the Australian 'long boom' from the 1860s to 1890, GDP did not recover until the 1900s. Similarities also interest us. In both New Zealand and Australia the crisis centred on public debt, private mortgages which financed expansion of settlement onto marginal land, and insistence on a voice by organized labour in strategic sectors of the export economy.[21]

There is a moral purpose in studying the 1890s financial crisis: to reveal the effects of greed and avarice (unregulated capitalism). Older sources like Edward Shann sourced the problems to banks canvassing easy money from Britain. Banks then lent in the colonies in the 1880s with foolish optimism, assuming a continuing boom. In a saga of greed and folly, investors lost sight of realities, pastoralists overstocked, and banks lent too easily. Not only speculators but prudent depositors lost their money in a run on banks and bank crashes in 1893. Australia's bankers and financiers

> had failed in their main duty. They had forgotten...that an economy, to be sound, must maintain in equipoise its material equipment and...production... that capital values have no meaning apart from actual net income.[22]

There are parallels in Australia and New Zealand between the 1880s and 1890s and the 1980s and 1990s: financial institutions failed, big businessmen were bankrupted, politicians were involved in speculation, and businesses in governments. However, no bank failed in the 1930s, because of memories of the 1890s.[23] Shann shows how governments borrowed until London pulled the plug. When the crisis struck, politicians sought scapegoats, such as the Victorian Commissioner of Railways who was blamed for excessive railway building. Labour could not prevail over capital during the maritime strike of 1890 while employers were facing massive debts. With the crushing of the strikes, labour leaders moved fast into politics.[24]

Noel Butlin argued that this crisis was internal. His influential analysis is strongly nationalist – an economist's version of Ward's bush legend – attributing agency to Australians in halting domestic expansion.[25] We may accept that some problems of British capital had a particular effect in Australia and New Zealand because of how their societies responded and that this extravagant (or greedy, or desperate) response should be set against the drive to foster enterprise. Butlin's theme of structural imbalance in Australia can extend to New Zealand. He maintained that Australians invested heavily in unpromising avenues: in wool, despite diminishing returns and ruined soils from moving into the arid interior; in activities with a lower comparative advantage (in Australia, dairying and meat); in the public sector ignoring investment criteria (for example in excessive railway building); and in excessive house-building, especially in 'marvellous Melbourne'. According to Butlin, from the 1860s to the 1880s Australia appealed as a destination for migration and investment, hosting a huge capital and population inflow which went steadily wrong. British investors pumped sterling into the pastoral industry even when it had spread onto marginal land and prices fell. Rabbits helped ruin the soil. House-building mushroomed faster than population, the speculative boom fed on itself and, over-stimulated, imploded.

External as well as internal stimuli help explain these colonial economies and the dreams and ambitions which drove them. Bad times struck not merely Australia and New Zealand, but they were most severe in these narrow export-led economies, and in Australia because of drought. The sharp drop in British capital squeezed the financial structure, no matter where that flow was headed, and wounded economies structured for boom conditions. Hence a compromise between internal and external views makes most sense. Luke Trainor, for example, sees the overseas/domestic debate as false. He re-emphasizes the British dimension, noting for instance that the halt in the flow of capital in 1891 meant that Victoria could not recover and depression spread. He also highlights the importance of banks.[26]

On one hand, banking arrangements were deficient, hence the collapse of the finance system in Victoria in 1892–4. Free trade and an expanding global economy called for free banking. Deregulated banking was inherently unstable, and it followed from governments making it easy for business.[27] On the other hand, bank crashes were rare outside Victoria, for example in New South Wales and New Zealand (the New Zealand government rescued the Bank of New Zealand in the 1890s, which helped, as it would again in the 1980s). The finance system that collapsed had served well the thrust of the entrepreneurial state, allowing government and business to borrow and hope. While poorly regulated banking encouraged greed, invited fraud and criminal activity, fraud was not the basic problem. The real problem was the trumpeted solution: that the financial system existed to foster boom conditions, made possible by selling commodities in British markets.

Blending cultural and economic history offers insights. Politically and emotionally, the Australian colonies and New Zealand, saddled with broken dreams and unstable, dependent economies, returned imaginatively to the land. The city, especially Melbourne, came to symbolize sin and suffering. Even Victorians began to suspect that Melbourne had killed the colony, and 'urban disillusionment and rural myth-making were intertwined'. A new start would be made in the bush.[28] But there was regional variety: Western Australia, enjoying a gold rush, did not enjoy providing 'outdoor relief' for the eastern colonies, and its prosperity contributed to its reluctance to join federation.

Australasia as a whole switched from embracing globalization to resisting it. Like all pioneers taking pride in their ingenuity, they set out to reorder relations between capital and labour, buffered from the outside world and the caprice of the free market. Foreign observers like Albert Métin, who praised their 'socialism without doctrines', saw the experiments as Australasian. Although they were a regional phenomenon, politicians and historians claimed them separately as they wove 'state experiments' into the texts and textures of national identities.

ARBITRATION AND PROTECTION

Australia and New Zealand pioneered compulsory industrial conciliation and arbitration, which provided the pivot of industrial relations and (later) welfare states. In the main Australian narrative, arbitration is a 'significant and distinctive institution of Australian society'.[29] It owes its character and rationale to egalitarianism, and to the rise of Labor parties. In the New Zealand narrative a Liberal–Labour alliance produced the distinctive institution.[30] A plank in the programme for the settler as working man – along with Advances to Settlers to settle land prised from Maori and Aboriginal people – this 'experiment' grew from the pioneering experience, as its creator, the New Zealand journalist and politician William Pember Reeves, emphasized.

Arbitration was invented to prevent strikes and lockouts which threatened the export economy. The focus of the strategy was export-led development and growth.[31] Both economies pursued this strategy as they were too small to influence international trade and British trade cycles. Intended to achieve self-reliance, compulsory arbitration between capital and labour came to be seen as the only safe policy to foster colonial enterprise. Australia and New Zealand sought to avoid disputes when times were tough; to 'hold the balance' between the fickle export economy and the desire for security at home, between the world views of employers and workers.[32] They would make something of their reputation as democratic, progressive colonies and ensure a 'fair go' for their joint constituency, the working man, the colonist, 'the people'. The new nations would show the world how to resolve conflict between capital and labour equitably. Arbitration would reconcile the irreconcilable positions of freedom of contract (beloved of employers) and union solidarity (which demanded compulsory unionism). It recognized unions and encouraged them to rebuild. It would serve all 'the people', and restore order and peace as the state nurtured a civilized community. Indeed the arbitrating state represented 'the organized community'.[33]

Arbitration, its supporters hoped, would cushion these states from instability in the world economy. Politicians pressured to find panaceas – Alfred Deakin spoke of 'that spirit of unrest and aspiration…among all civilized people' – decided that the state should act. From the entrepreneurial state developed a political culture of the interventionist state to protect and promote 'the people' and collective identity. That compulsory arbitration is distinctive to Australasia signifies how people comprehended their destinies and sought to control them: they sought solidarity 'to protect themselves from the icy winds of market competition', and ethnic solidarity would shelter them from foreign competitors. Arbitration embodied this feature of settler capitalism. Ethnic solidarity joined forces with equity (*egalitarianism*). 'Socialism without doctrines' meant something to pilgrims and to creators of 'social laboratories';[34] and it equally meant something to the white electorate, beneficiaries of early democracy, in realizing their longed-for white 'workingman's paradise'.

Arbitration became one of the best-known expressions of Australasian identities, claimed simultaneously as distinctively New Zealand and Australian. It was indeed distinctive in that no other settler society adopted it. The shared context of financial crisis and labour militancy, combined with early democracy, ushered in majorities who held a liberal/labourist conception of social justice for 'battlers', and 'the people'. Australian and New Zealand systems influenced one another, making competing claims to the founding document, arguing whether Kingston's South Australian bill of 1890, or Reeves's in New Zealand, the first enacted in 1894, had priority.[35] The centrality of arbitration is also revealed in debates over L/liberals or Labo(u)r men as its inventors. The 'classical' form of Australasian compulsory arbitration characterized by state agencies and registration and recognition of employer associations and trade unions was introduced in New Zealand in 1894, Western Australia in 1900, New South Wales in 1901, the Commonwealth in 1904, and South Australia and Queensland in 1912.

Its creators had to transcend class interests to secure it. Such a 'bargained exchange'[36] required a unifying idea of shared identity, provided by the discourse of a 'new liberalism' which expected the state to assist its citizens.[37] Putting together the Australian and New Zealand narratives strengthens Stuart Macintyre's case that L/liberalism shaped arbitration as an idea and a system.[38] Kingston and Reeves were both Liberals, and Liberals represented the aspirations of the 'new urban frontier': to hold the line on respectability, and hold the balance between labour and capital. A One Nation idea is implied by the liberal discourse of 'the people'. Arbitration would provide one framework for a 'free, prosperous and contented people'.[39] Likewise, in New Zealand, Reeves saw his creation as being for the community as a whole, not labour.[40] The Liberal policy of 'self-reliance' and the culture of respectability and manly independence deemed that 'the capitalist equally with the labourer must be identified, by residence and fulfilling all the duties of a colonist, with the progress and destiny of [Australia and] New Zealand'.[41] This belief enhanced a sense of destiny already consolidated by federation. We cannot separate such constructs from White Australia and New Zealand: both were shaped by the same notions of 'the people', and endorsed by a coalition of wage-earners and 'middling classes' on each side of the Tasman.

In comparing Australia with the United States, Cross argues that long-term settlement patterns more than class conflict and crisis shaped labour movements and models of market democracy. He pinpoints the contributions made by labour scarcity, the absence of a large class of agrarian proprietors (in contrast to the United States), and a 'precocious state sector'. These allowed a cross-class, liberal consensus in Australia which approved the organizing idea of 'comfort, community, and working-class respectability'.[42] We can agree about the role of the entrepreneurial state which allowed social engineering by middle-class professionals. The presence of an older Tory influence helps explain why an arbitration system did not materialize in Canada. But New Zealand's experience subverts the argument about the absence of large numbers of small farmers. The idea of a workingman's paradise extended to the small farmer; its rural equivalent entailed settling the small man and the unemployed on the land. New Zealand Liberals who voted for arbitration also introduced Advances to Settlers, as did small 'l' liberals in Australia.[43] Small farmers, unaffected by arbitration on the family farm, were much affected by it beyond the farm gate in getting produce to market: by rail, sea, and especially on the waterfront, especially when exporting frozen food.

That this experiment was designed for the white worker and his family gives a clue to who was included and excluded, in identity creation. The honest worker in steady employment was a sub-species of 'the settler', and embellished what it meant to be a 'settled family man'. It is significant that the family man was – and still is – seen as a beneficiary of women's suffrage, first in New Zealand and South Australia, which were the first sites also of compulsory arbitration. The new order was possible to concoct because democracy arrived early. People wanted to belong, to nest in security and comfort and create a sense of community, though their desire for equality proved elusive.[44] Arbitration could cut across other loyalties and reinforce ethnic solidarity.

Defeated in strikes by export-focused employers, the labour movement modified its strategy from ethnic – and gender – solidarity in trade unionism to solidarity in labourism, in 'civilizing capitalism' by arbitration, and by regulating and protecting the conditions of white labour. The power of parliamentary labour flowed from labour's early entry into politics.[45] This gender-based labourist ideal embraced what Australian scholars see as a distinctively Australian conception of social justice, although it does extend to New Zealand.[46] Rickard sees arbitration as an 'Australian solution *par excellence* for industrial strife and declining living standards':

> The idea of arbitration began as a means of settling industrial disputes, but in practice it took shape as an institutional guardian of national standards, an enigmatic expression of the Australian psyche.

He notes the artifice in this; popular sentiment followed initiatives by colonial cultural inventors such as the media magnate Reeves and the lawyers Kingston and Higgins.

Rivalry pervaded everything, as Australia and New Zealand competed for the titles of social laboratory and workingman's paradise. They thought it 'normal and proper' that their living standards would exceed those of the old world (as they did in mid-century); falling living standards and unemployment in new societies were 'unnatural', especially in new societies intended to improve upon the old.[47] The restorative package had three parts: compulsory arbitration, followed by New Protection and the male breadwinner (family) wage.

The pain of twenty-year cycles of boom and bust, the hurt and disorder from depression and strikes, jarred with their advertisements and views of themselves and justified a new order of protection, of arbitration, plus tariff protection for industry, plus protection of wages and conditions, plus ethnic solidarity. We cannot separate the new order of capital and labour, intended to resist globalization, from the population imperative to keep Australia and New Zealand safe. Both sought stability with growth to protect living standards for white people.

In Australia state rivalries coexisted with ethnic nationalism. Tariffs and migration became federal powers because they underwrote the priorities of nationhood, of people and money, and keeping citizens secure. Victoria had been protectionist, and New South Wales free trade, which temporarily stymied the creation of an Australian political culture, but in the menacing international climate the new Australia decided on a tariff. A federal tariff should even out disparities between states, create a customs union and thus one domestic market, though Western Australia needed time to adjust. The first federal tariff was low, to benefit farmers and merchants. The tariff itself was made possible by the shift to non-wool exports (non-perishable wool being the stuff of free trade). 'New' Protection provided further aid for nascent secondary industries. This protection was not separate from primary production: process industries serviced the farming sector, for example in farm machinery.[48] Thus protected, the economy could help create the social laboratory. Ironically, the push for social experiment only existed because of technical advances promoting the export sector which was 'periodically hostile' to those experiments.[49]

What was new about New Protection was that *workers'* protection was tied to the protection of industry: security offered to producers by tariffs flowed on to workers. A floor on white male breadwinners' wages was explicitly linked to the buffer protecting employers against competition. New Protection was embodied in the Excise Tariff Act of 1906. Deakin explained that 'The "old" Protection contented itself with making good wages possible. The "new" Protection seeks to make them actual.'[50] It achieved this by levying (beside a tariff on imports such as farm machinery) an excise on local products that was waived if a firm paid 'fair and reasonable' wages.[51]

Although the High Court declared New Protection unconstitutional, H. B. Higgins, president of the Commonwealth Arbitration Court, went on to define the 'fair and reasonable' wage. The result was the celebrated Harvester Judgement of 1907 which enshrined a basic, male breadwinner wage. Higgins had to determine if H. V. McKay, proprietor of the Sunshine Harvester works near Melbourne, paid his employees a 'fair and reasonable' wage which would merit exemption from excise. In refusing, he ruled that such a wage must meet 'the normal needs of the average employee regarded as a human being living in a civilized community'. This being was a white male wage-earner, for whom Higgins deemed seven shillings a day sufficient to support a family of five (a wife and three children) in 'some small degree of comfort'. Skilled working-class and middle-class values of self-control, thrift, order and respectability, that men were entitled to marry, have a family and live in 'frugal comfort', were written into the script.[52] Justice Sim's wage decisions then applied Higgins's ruling in New Zealand.[53] In 1925, the basic wage in New Zealand supposedly provided for a man, his wife and only two children (acknowledging the decline in white fertility, in defiance of pronatalism). From 1936 New Zealand adopted the norm of three children for setting the basic wage, as in Australia, its tendency to skimping already evident.

This judgement became a powerful symbol, though its standard of a family wage based on the cost of living did not become the basis of wage and welfare policy until the 1920s. Macintyre terms Higgins's decision a 'socially useful myth', enshrining the expectation that the state would ensure prosperity for white working-class people.[54] Mythologized as the bedrock of wage determination in both countries, the language and intention of the judgement – and the way people heard it – illuminate the fashioning of destinies and identity. Its complex significance centred on the principle that men must be paid as breadwinners. The male breadwinner therefore became the focus of identity. The objective of the family wage is readily explained. Wage-earners fared better than in most other places in terms of living standards, and these standards came to be seen as a birthright. Yet insecurity always threatened. Families were impoverished suddenly and easily when they had dependent children, and in old age, hence the aim to assist the family breadwinner and support the aged, as well as injured and invalided workers.[55] This family wage incorporated a criterion of human need, based on wage security for the family, as opposed to wages determined by market and profit margins; the market was subordinated to the cost of living in setting wages. That seven shillings a day was the standard before the depression suggests that it was directed at restoring labour's self-respect, as well as protecting living standards.

The family wage became the linchpin not just of industrial relations but of family and social policy. It established the basis of what Castles terms 'wage-earners' welfare states' in which the protection of white workingmen's wages and conditions became the priority. This sent Australia and New Zealand down a path of building workers' welfare states in which the male breadwinner wage was the main means of sustaining the working-class family. It was the nexus between the labour market and the welfare system, with other forms of assistance added on[56] (see chapter 14).

Underlying this formula lurked a concept of social justice where every male citizen had the right to the fruits of *his* labour. The family wage was created for the 'provident' workingman, with a heritage not in socialism but in self-reliance: Antipodean welfare capitalism emphasized individual responsibility, consistent with its Liberal as well as Labo(u)r pedigree. It embraced the concepts of a civilized community, social cohesion, participating and belonging, suggesting settler states' ethnic and gendered identities. Social welfare tailored to wage security for white male workers rendered other social claims secondary. Such arrangements were only conceivable because of policies to ensure ethnic solidarity.

'New' protection consolidated the gender division of labour by defining women as well as children as dependants. The family wage was then used to deny equal pay. In theory a man received a wage to meet the needs of a whole family, so women in the paid workforce were assumed not to be supporting families but single and dependent, and were paid only as individuals.

The enterprise paid lip service to egalitarianism. Welfare capitalism protected wages and conditions by insulating them from the free market so that working- and middling-class families could share more fully in prosperity. It narrowed income differences among wage-earners, but only for white family men. Eugenist beliefs coloured the arbitration and new protection framework: Higgins understood the Arbitration Court to be 'an instrument for raising the downtrodden and for improving the stamina and character of the coming generation'.[57] His ruling helped establish a basic wage from which developed a wage hierarchy based on masculine definitions of skill, with additional payment for skill. According to Olssen, the unskilled accepted the right of the skilled to control the labour process, which he sees as part of a compact about standards of behaviour. In other words, the destinies being moulded expressed the code of respectability, and the emergent societies were for skilled working-class people.[58]

The emphasis on social justice was later compromised in economic downturn by the 'capacity to pay'. A furore blew up in New Zealand when its Arbitration Court reduced award wages in the 1920s because of deflation.[59] Nonetheless the concept of protecting real wages for the white male breadwinner did become the basis of family policy. In 1925, New Zealand's Arbitration Court Judge Frazer summed up the view that had developed from Harvester:

> Instead of a man being paid according to the current market value of his work, he is to be paid not less than a wage that is regarded as sufficient to maintain himself, a wife, and two children. He is regarded as a social unit, rather than as an economic unit. When a trade is prospering the worker can still obtain, and does obtain, the current market value of his work, but he must not, in times of trade depression, be paid less than the wage which is regarded for the time being as sufficient for the maintenance of himself, a wife and two children, plus an additional payment based on his skill and certain other factors.[60]

Specifying two rather than three children could be said to mark earlier economic difficulties in New Zealand as well as acknowledging – when it suited – shrinkage in white families. On Castles' question about whether class politics or party politics was a key factor in creating workers' welfare states, his argument points to class politics. Other studies see the state through other lenses. Garton maintains that Castles made the individual worker the basic social unit and asks what of family policy.[61] Judge Frazer's language does confirm the 'worker' as the basic social unit, but sees him as a social unit precisely because he represented his wife and children. The 'worker' was presumed to be his family's provider.

THE FAMILY AND THE GENDER DIVISION OF LABOUR

The white workingman's paradise, intended to materialize in the 'wage-earners' welfare state', pivoted on the family, which revolved around the man as breadwinner and the woman at home as wife and mother. The family wage merely cemented this ideal as one measure to strengthen the white family: it took for granted that woman's workplace was the home.

The gender division of labour embodied in the family wage itself originated in the home. Women's lower labour force participation (as wives and mothers) resulted in weaker bargaining power and lower wages which in turn reinforced their identities as mothers and providers of domestic labour.[62] Ryan and Conlon, with their 1970s focus on paid work, asked how arbitration shaped women's struggle for equal pay, and criticized the Harvester judgement as 'Higgins' albatross'. They blamed the sexist ideology of the Arbitration Court and the family wage for legalizing women's worth at half the male rate.[63] Settling women's wages at 54–75 per cent of men's systematized their dependence and confirmed the gender order in the home.[64]

Arbitration did institutionalize this obstacle to women's independence, but its real source was the ethnic and gendered division of labour which defined a white male settler – but not his wife or his mother – as a 'worker'. Status attached to a man having a wife at home, not in the paid workforce. The family man had become a model of masculinity and the wife and mother, the Ruler of the Home, the model of femininity. The ethic of a respectable working class encouraged this belief which demanded that a woman be married to a sober husband in secure employment. This ideal presupposed an economic floor.[65] A gendered concept of 'need' ensured that women would be paid less and restricted their paid employment. Arbitration encoded existing rituals. Australia and New Zealand followed Britain in setting women's wage rates at half the male rate, to encourage them to marry. Societies with more men than women placed a special emphasis on this consideration. In New South Wales as early as 1850, the women's wage was established at 54 per cent of the male rate.[66]

After the introduction of arbitration and the family wage, the low percentages of married women in paid work fell further, from 5.7 per cent in New Zealand in 1916 to 3.5 per cent in 1926 and 3.7 per cent in 1936. Working-class people approved of the family wage. A mother at home enhanced family support, assuming a male breadwinner could be had; and inequality within the family was overlooked (see chapter 14). Fairburn notes the irony that the 'family' itself comprised a net of dependent relationships. He argues that this 'did not strike contemporaries as ironic',[67] but it did strike feminists as ironic that the goal of independence was for men, not women.

The feminists who campaigned for political citizenship also sought economic citizenship. They aspired to economic independence for women without a male breadwinner through equal pay, and of women with a male breadwinner through a share of the husband's income. A landmark New Zealand National Council of Women resolution stated in 1896 that

> where a woman elects to superintend her own household and to be the mother of children, there shall be certain part share of her husband's earnings or income for her separate use, payable, if she so desired it, into her separate account.[68]

Such a challenge to manly independence proved too radical for the public. The issues on which feminists argued for a share of their husbands' earnings instead became arguments for a family wage, that a woman (and thus her husband) had foregone income to become a wife and mother, that unpaid work was real work, payment for mother-work was necessary for children's protection, the position of married women ought to be improved, and above all that childrearing had the utmost economic and national importance. White women – and Maori women who lived as Pakeha – deserved equal status as mothers of the race.

The 'dominant construction of women' was as mothers.[69] This was also the majority experience. By 1920 a broad consensus held that the ideal family comprised a family man as provider and defender, and a mother as keeper of the home. The women's movement upheld this model in an effort to improve women's status, privileging the White Mother, but on terms which feminist historians have deemed 'masculinist'.[70] Marilyn Lake in particular argues that a study of gender relations as power relations unearths how men pursued their interests as men as well as class interests and ethnic solidarity. More was at stake than the 'politics of respectability' versus unruly frontier politics: a battle between ideals of masculinity, between the 'Lone Hand' for whom independence meant freedom from family, and William Lane's 'Domestic Man' who was a sober, responsible breadwinner.[71] But there is room for confusion. In this view, the labour movement was a men's affair and independence a white man's privilege; and arbitration and the Harvester judgement were 'masculinist' for retaining independence as a manly characteristic. Yet Domestic Man is depicted as triumphant by the 1920s. To what extent is this refashioning of manly independence (to father the race) also feminist, furthering women's maternal interests? Or was it wholly 'masculinist' to define the White Mother as the dependant of Domestic Man rather than his economic as well as political equal? We prefer the blended interpretation because the family wage suited many parents.

According to Deacon, the 'construction of the dependent woman' was a conscious act in the interests of working-class men, by men of the 'new middle class', public servants and professionals who allied themselves with skilled working-class men in imposing their image of Australia, and the same could be said of New Zealand. T. A. Coghlan, the New South Wales statistician, institutionalized the idea of women as dependants of male breadwinners by reformulating census categories, and had much to say on the subject.[72] Deacon pointed to Coghlan as the most powerful speaker for this male 'new class' which sought to naturalize women's dependence. But there is no need to blame Coghlan, who expressed widely held beliefs when he equated 'progress' with the presence of few female breadwinners:

> [It] must certainly be looked upon as evidence of the superior lot of the Australian women. In most European countries, even the married women are compelled to work for such wages as they can procure, in order to assist in the support of their families; but fortunately the necessity for such labour is not yet general.[73]

By the 1890s the Australasian colonial statisticians agreed that women previously classified by their husbands' occupations (appropriate for family enterprises) should be reclassified as performing 'domestic duties' unless the husband decided otherwise. White women as toilers in the fields sapped hopes for a workingman's paradise where a provident workingman could support a wife and children. In the statisticians' words,

> Although … the female relatives of farmers, if living on the farm, attend as a rule, to the lighter duties of the poultry yard and dairy, it was felt … that the statement that so many females were engaged in agricultural pursuits would create an impression … that women were in the habit of working in the fields as they were in some of the older countries of the world.[74]

Higgins concurred in the Fruit Pickers' judgement of 1912: 'fortunately for society, the greater number of breadwinners are men. The women are not all dragged from the homes to work while the men loaf at home'.[75] 'Progress' and prosperity required women to be seen at home, engaged in unpaid duties as wives and mothers. The strength of this belief rendered much of their work invisible, especially in family enterprises and on the family farm. But it also signalled actual changes in the nature of work and the economy represented in the shift to the family wage, including women's increased domestic responsibilities.[76] Rather than devaluing women, the role of the skilled working-class and middle-class woman was believed to be 'pivotal in demonstrating the wealth and status of the husband, the family and the nation'.[77] This required adopting the identity of White Mother.

Arbitration also entrenched the gender division of labour by formalizing the distinction between men's and women's work. It systematized the advantages of men over women in paid work by endorsing a segmented labour market which accorded 'women's work' lower status and pay. The Mildura Fruit Pickers' judgement of 1912 cemented the barrier, stipulating that women in men's work were paid the male rate only to prevent men being squeezed out.[78] Higgins confirmed the stereotypes of men's work and women's work: men did fruitpicking, and women fruitpacking. 'Women's work' was distinguished from men's, justifying wage differentials.[79] Commonly, women were restricted to work deemed 'fit' for them, often repetitive, light and unskilled. Hence the increasing numbers of single women moving to paid work found a segmented labour market (while married women faced marriage bars, at least in the public service). The labour market was vertically segregated into men's and women's jobs, and a narrow range of feminine jobs. It was also horizontally segregated, with men in positions of authority, and higher pay, even in areas of 'women's work' where the majority employed were women.

Skill was constructed as masculine, so arbitration advantaged skilled male craft workers. Arbitration helped construct gender differences; from 1930 the (male) metal industry became the basis for pay margins for skill, rendering women automatically 'inferior'.[80] In the Sydney Shop Assistants case of 1907, male unionists opposed the feminization of shop work and fought to protect men's jobs, supported by the Court.[81] By comparison, women in the printing industry, a male sphere, received lower margins for skill because they lacked power in their (strong) union and therefore in arbitration. The gender division of labour was not the result of the male breadwinner wage; rather, men constructed and reinforced their own definitions of skill, and succeeded because women lacked bargaining power by leaving to marry and bear children.[82] Political power resided in areas of men's work, in industries of strategic significance for export-led economies, such as mining, wharf-labouring and capital-intensive industries.

The 'living' wage protected men's right to work, and equal pay, where it existed, was intended to retain men's jobs for men. Arbitration did not promote women's unionism as it did men's. If we consider why the Victorian clerical workers' campaign for equal pay failed, it becomes clear that class and multiple identities played a part. Women had to work with men of their own class and occupation to secure better pay and conditions. In the 1920s women teachers and post and telegraph union women in New Zealand fought separate campaigns for equal pay.[83] Most women in paid work remained outside the arbitration system, which covered only a limited range of urban women, working in factories, hotels and restaurants. But there were small successes; tailoresses did win a minimum weekly wage instead of piecework.[84]

Indigenous women were doubly oppressed. Rural Aboriginal women were either paid a 'miniscule' wage or not paid at all, and the demand for Aboriginal women in domestic service increased as white women left it, leading to 'official abduction' for training and assignment. Capitalism, race and gender all underlay the division of labour.[85] This pattern echoed the practices of the Pacific Islands generally (see chapter 8), whereby most plantation and mining work was done by indigenous men under indenture, while a few women were recruited for domestic labour, for even less pay.

In both Australia and New Zealand, development spurred the shift from the family economy to the family wage. The rise of the male breadwinner wage coincided with rising middle-class and working-class respectability, all of which presumed that white women's identity entailed motherhood. Femininity equated with the White Mother, just as masculinity meant the White Father. So much for labour militants and their 'manly independence'. Henry Lawson, 'much read and quoted by the strikers' of the 1890s, invoked Eureka in his memorable verse:

So we must fly a rebel flag
As others did before us,
And we must sing a rebel song
And join in rebel chorus.
We'll make the tyrants feel the sting
O' those that they would throttle;
They needn't say the fault is ours
If blood should stain the wattle.

Geoffrey Bolton thinks this mostly bluff, observing that many strike leaders had no difficulty in later conforming to respectability.[86] Several entered parliament. So did J. A. Millar, the former New Zealand leader of the Maritime Council and of workers in the maritime strike, who became a Liberal member of parliament from 1893 to 1912 and minister of labour; he crossed the floor to help bring in Bill Massey as conservative farmers' premier. Others were co-opted into the public service, joining the new professionals. John Lomas, leader of the miners and treasurer of the Maritime Council, became a mining inspector; Reeves stopped him from returning to England and recruited him for his Labour Department, and he rose in 1909 to be secretary of labour. The state co-opted almost the whole 1890s generation of women union leaders – like Harriet Morison – as factory inspectors or Women's Employment Branch officers in New Zealand's Department of Labour. Women belonged to the 'new class' too. Massey's Cossacks defeated the militant Red Feds on the waterfront before the Great War with the help of former militants, men and women who believed in the new order of things.

These experiments shared their ethnic solidarity and intent to reinforce the privileges of white labour. They institutionalized the gender division of labour, systematized the advantage of men over women in paid work, and encoded the basic wage for women at 54 per cent of men's. The idea of a workers' welfare state sharpened divisions between the included and shut out: ethnic divisions, divisions between men and women, between breadwinners and dependants, and between the respectable and disreputable, between wage and salary earners, and between urban and rural imagined destinies. Farmers helped introduce arbitration and protection for white workers, but their attitudes changed with the rise of labour movements. Class became 'the major determinant of political loyalties in Australia' between 1890 and 1910, producing interdependent traditions of labour and anti-labour.[87] New Zealand differed only in tenor and timing. This political interpretation has much explanatory power, though a re-reading suggests a need to unpack 'class' to delve into the significance of the 'family' wage. Arbitration and the 'new' protection, centred on the white family, refracted who was thought important to forming states as well as nations.

The 'ritual' of egalitarianism, not its reality, shaped the new order. It is always what people believe that matters, and ritual egalitarianism bestowed the bonus that all shades of politics could deploy it.[88] Like the race card, it cost no money, yet the idea offered the resolute a dream. Crusades appeal, and the significance of pride in 'state experiments' cannot be overstated. As well as vanity – and youthfulness – attached to being first, Australia and New Zealand negotiated the shift in terms, from competing for recognition as the workingman's paradise, to the world's 'social laboratory'. A consensus developed, whereby capital and labour shared values of nationhood and masculinity. The breadth of this consensus is revealed in the persistence of arbitration and the 'wage-earners' welfare state' for most of a century, until globalization once again prompted a revolution in social policies.

NOTES

1   White, 'Inventing Australia Revisited', in W. Hudson and G. Bolton (eds), *Creating Australia: Changing Australian History*, Sydney, 1997, 20.
2   David Hamer, *The New Zealand Liberals: The Years of Power, 1891–1912*, Auckland, 1988, 63.
3   Davis, Lance E. and Robert A. Huttenback, *Mammon and the Pursuit of Empire*. Interdisciplinary Perspectives on Modern History, ed. Robert Fogel and Stephan Thernstrom. Cambridge, 1986, 51. (But they merely confirm high levels of British investment, absolutely and per capita, for every *white* settler; see Donald Denoon, *Settler Capitalism: The Dynamics of Dependent Development in the Southern Hemisphere*, Oxford, 1983, 49–51.)
4   W. Frost, 'Farmers, Government and the Environment: The Settlement of Australia's "Wet Frontier", 1870–1920', *Australian Economic History Review*, 37: 1 (1997), 19–38.
5   Avner Offer, *The First World War: An Agrarian Interpretation*, Oxford, 1989, 137.
6   See G. Docking with additions by M. Dunn, *Two Hundred Years of New Zealand Painting*, revd edn, Auckland, 1990.
7   S. A. M. Adshead, *Material Culture in Europe and China, 1400–1800*, London and New York, 1997.
8   Phrase from Offer, *First World War*, 149.

9   Adshead, *Material Culture in Europe and China*, chs 1 and 2; D. W. Curtin and L. M. Heldke (eds), *Cooking, Eating, Thinking: Transformative Philosophies of Food*, Bloomington, 1992.

10   F. McKee, 'The Popularization of Milk as a Beverage during the 1930s', in David F. Smith (ed.), *Nutrition in Britain: Science, Scientists and Politics in the Twentieth Century*, London and New York, Routledge, 1997, 123–41. This association with purity and life was cross-cultural, as images attest of the Indian god Krishna as a baby, fed by the cow-mother. In many Austronesian languages mother's milk, breast and matrilineage are cognate.

11   Draft of letter by Muriel Bell to *Otago Daily Times*, June 1955; copy in file on milk in schools compiled by Flora Davidson, New Zealand Department of Health, Ministry of Health, Wellington.

12   The title of one of six ten-minute movies made for Britain by the New Zealand Dairy Board in 1926.

13   On 'fattening of young stock' see *Making New Zealand*, Wellington, 1940, 1: 12, 30.

14   H. G. Philpott, *A History of the New Zealand Dairy Industry 1840–1935*, Wellington, 1937, 12.

15   Frost, 'Farmers, Government, and the Environment', 35.

16   *Making New Zealand*, 1: 11, 2.

17   An idea borrowed from S. W. Mintz, *Sweetness and Power*, New York, 1985, 31. Offer agrees: family farming led to new forms of social and political life.

18   Philpott, *A History of the New Zealand Dairy Industry*, 72–121. In 1905–6 Nora Breen from Ireland was appointed to visit farms and instruct settlers making butter.

19   C. G. F. Simkin, *The Instability of a Dependent Economy*, London, 1951, 169.

20   See Gary Hawke, 'Australian and New Zealand Economic Development from about 1890 to 1940', in K. Sinclair (ed.), *Tasman Relations*, Auckland, 1987, 110; Herman M. Schwartz, *In the Dominions of Debt: Historical Perspectives on Dependent Development*, Ithaca, NY, 1989, 173.

21   Schwartz, *In the Dominions of Debt*, 174.

22   E. O. G. Shann, *An Economic History of Australia*, Cambridge, 1930, 315. Edward Shann was Professor of History and Economics at the University of Western Australia.

23   Graeme Snooks kindly pointed this out.

24   A. G. L. Shaw, *The Economic Development of Australia*, 5th edn, Croydon, Victoria, 1969. Shaw was influenced by Shann and by Brian Fitzpatrick, *The British Empire in Australia: An Economic History, 1834–1939*, Melbourne, 1941, who saw the colonies as servants of British capital.

25   N. G. Butlin, *Investment in Australian Economic Development 1861–1900*, Canberra, 1976.

26   Luke Trainor, *British Imperialism and Australian Nationalism*, Melbourne, 1994, ch. 10, esp. p. 123.

27   D. T. Merrett, 'Australian Banking Practice and the Crisis of 1893', *Australian Economic History Review*, 29: 1 (March 1989), 60–85.

28   Graeme Davison, *The Rise and Fall of Marvellous Melbourne*, Melbourne, 1978: quotation from p. 257.

29   John Rickard, *Australia: A Cultural History*, 2nd edn. The Present and the Past, ed. Michael Crowder and Juliet Gardiner, London and New York, 1988, ch. 6.

30   E. Olssen and L. Richardson, 'The New Zealand Labour Movement, 1880–1920', in Eric Fry (ed.), *Common Cause: Essays in Australian and New Zealand Labour*

History, Wellington, 1986, 1–14; Erik Olssen, *Building the New World: Work, Politics and Society in Caversham 1880s–1920s*, Auckland, 1995.

31 Denoon, *Settler Capitalism*, 226–8. However, John Rickard, *Class and Politics: New South Wales, Victoria and the Early Commonwealth, 1890–1910*, Canberra, 1976, 161–2, views arbitration as a free market response to industrial unrest.

32 Metaphor from J. E. Martin, *Holding the Balance: A History of New Zealand's Department of Labour 1891–1995*, Christchurch, 1996. The author of the Department of Labour, the Liberal premier, was blessed with the name of John Ballance.

33 R. Stout, quoted in Keith Sinclair, *A History of New Zealand*, revd edn, Auckland, 1980, 176; also K. Sinclair, *William Pember Reeves*, Oxford, 1965, ch. 13. On the collocation 'fair go' see J. Hughes (ed.), *The Concise Australian National Dictionary*, Melbourne, 1992, 195.

34 Donald Denoon, 'Settler Capitalism Unsettled', *New Zealand Journal of History*, 29: 2 (Oct. 1995), 135, 137.

35 S. Macintyre and R. Mitchell (eds), *Foundations of Arbitration*, Melbourne, 1989, ch. 4; cf. J. Holt, *Compulsory Arbitration in New Zealand: The First Forty Years*, Auckland, 1986.

36 Term from Palmer, in Macintyre and Mitchell, *Foundations of Arbitration*, ch. 14.

37 S. Macintyre, *The Labour Experiment*, Melbourne, 1989, 11; Hamer, *New Zealand Liberals*, ch. 2.

38 S. Macintyre, 'Neither Capital nor Labour: The Politics of the Establishment of Arbitration', in Macintyre and Mitchell, *Foundations of Arbitration*, ch. 8.

39 Ibid., 186. cf. Hamer, *New Zealand Liberals*, 9–11 and ch. 2. On the Liberals as the party of ambitious towns as opposed to farmers' towns, and the 'urban frontier', see ibid., ch. 5. Hence also the title of Tom Brooking's *Lands for the People?* Dunedin, 1996.

40 Hamer, *New Zealand Liberals*, 144; also 40.

41 Ballance, quoted in ibid., 53.

42 Cross, 'Labour in Settler-State Democracies: Comparative Perspectives on Australia and the US, 1860–1920', *Labour History*, 70: 1 (May 1996), 1–24. Castles identifies the same ingredients but attributes agency for the workers' welfare state to the labour movement: F. G. Castles, *The Working Class and Welfare: Reflections on the Political Development of the Welfare State in Australia and New Zealand, 1890–1980*, Wellington, 1985.

43 See Brooking, *Lands for the People*. In his *History of New Zealand*, revd edn, 1980, 183, Sinclair saw the Industrial Conciliation and Arbitration Act 1894, together with the New Zealand Settlements Act 1863 which confiscated Maori land, and the Advances to Settlers Act passed in the same year as arbitration, as the 'most decisive' legislative measures 'in moulding New Zealand society'. Similarly, Western Australia established an Agricultural Bank to make advances to settlers in 1894, in effect providing one-way tickets to farms. See N. G. Butlin, A. Barnard and J. J. Pincus, *Government and Capitalism: Public and Private Choice in Twentieth Century Australia*, Sydney, 1982, 57.

44 Olssen, *Building the New World*, 253–4.

45 V. Burgmann, 'Premature Labour: The Maritime Strike and the Parliamentary Strategy', in Jim Hagan and Andrew Wells (eds), *The Maritime Strike: A Centennial Retrospective*, Five Islands Press Associates with University of Wollongong Labour History Research Group and the Australian Society for the Study of Labour History, 1992, 83–96.

46 For example, Macintyre, *Labour Experiment*; Olssen, *Building the New World*.

47 Rickard, *Class and Politics*, 286, 282, 283–4.
48 Butlin, Barnard and Pincus, *Government and Capitalism*, 60–1.
49 Olssen, *Building the New World*, 259–60.
50 Quoted by S. Macintyre, *Labour Experiment*, Melbourne, 1989, 21. Also Russel Ward, *A Nation for a Continent*, Richmond, Victoria, 1977, 47.
51 Macintyre, *Labour Experiment*; Macintyre, *Oxford History of Australia, Vol. 4: 1901–1942: The Succeeding Age*, Melbourne, 1986, 103; Ward, *A Nation for a Continent*; Rickard, *Class and Politics*, 210.
52 Ward, *A Nation for a Continen*, 49; Rickard, *Class and Politics*, 220; also Macintyre, *Labour Experiment*, 24; Castles, *The Working Class and Welfare*, 13.
53 Holt, *Compulsory Arbitration in New Zealand*, ch. 4.
54 Macintyre, *Labour Experiment*, 51; Macintyre and Mitchell, *Foundations of Arbitration*, 15–19.
55 Macintyre, *Labour Experiment*, offers a usefully concise summary.
56 Castles, *The Working Class and Welfare*, especially 102–4; also Macintyre, in Macintyre and Mitchell, *Foundations of Arbitration*, 188.
57 Castles, *The Working Class and Welfare*, 14.
58 Olssen, *Building the New World*, 225, 255. The best source on respectability is McCalman, *Struggletown*, Melbourne, 1984.
59 Holt, *Compulsory Arbitration in New Zealand*, 148–57.
60 Ibid., 157–8.
61 S. Garton and M. E. McCallum, 'Workers' Welfare: Labour and the Welfare State in 20th-century Australia and Canada', *Labour History*, 71 (Nov. 1996), 116–41.
62 R. Frances, 'Shifting Barriers: Twentieth-century Women's Labour Patterns', in K. Saunders and R. Evans (eds), *Gender Relations in Australia: Domination and Negotiation*, Sydney, 1992, ch. 12.
63 E. Ryan and A. Conlon, *Gentle Invaders: Australian Women at Work 1788–1974*, Melbourne, 1975.
64 D. Kirkby, 'Arbitration and the Fight for Economic Justice', in Macintyre and Mitchell, *Foundations of Arbitration*, 334–51.
65 J. McCalman, *Struggletown*; Patricia Grimshaw, Marilyn Lake, Ann McGrath and Marian Quartly, *Creating a Nation*, Melbourne, 1994, ch. 5.
66 K. Alford, *Production or Reproduction?*, Melbourne, 1984, ch. 8.
67 M. Fairburn, *The Ideal Society and Its Enemies*, Auckland, 1989, 57.
68 See, for example, M. Lovell-Smith (ed.), *The Woman Question: Writings by the Women who Won the Vote*, Auckland, 1992. The NCW quotation raises the issue of unequal distribution of resources within the family, an issue ignored by the family wage.
69 Grimshaw et al., *Creating a Nation*, 195.
70 For example, Marilyn Lake, 'The Politics of Respectability: Identifying the Masculinist Context', *Historical Studies*, 22: 86 (1986), 116–31; Judith A. Allen, *Sex and Secrets*, Melbourne, 1990. See ch. 10, this volume.
71 Lake, 'The Politics of Respectability'.
72 Desley Deacon, *Managing Gender*, Melbourne, 1989, and 'Political Arithmetic: The Nineteenth-century Australian Census and the Construction of the Dependent Woman', *Signs*, 11 (Autumn 1985), 27–47.
73 K. Alford, 'Colonial Women's Employment as Seen by Nineteenth-century Statisticians and Twentieth-century Economic Historians', *Labour History*, 51: 2 (1986), 5, quoting Coghlan, *The Wealth and Progress of NSW 1900–01*, Sydney, 1902, 703.

74 Hayter in *Census of Victoria*, 1891, 192, quoted by Deacon, *Managing Gender*, 142–3. Also quoted in M. Lake, 'Helpmeet, Slave, Housewife: Women in Rural Families 1870–1930', in P. Grimshaw, C. McConville and E. McEwen (eds), *Families in Colonial Australia*, Sydney, 1985, 179. Alford's source is the 1890 Conference of Colonial Statisticians: see K. Alford, 'Colonial Women's Employment as Seen by Nineteenth-century Statisticians and Twentieth-century Economic Historians', *Labour History*, 51 (1986), 5.

75 J. A. Scutt, 'Inequality before the Law: Gender, Arbitration and Wages', in Saunders and Evans, *Gender Relations in Australia*, 269; Macintyre, *Oxford History of Australia, vol. 4, 1901–1942*, 111.

76 See, for example, Kerreen Reiger, *Disenchantment of the Home: Modernizing the Australian Family 1880–1940*, Melbourne, 1985.

77 Alford, 'Colonial Women's Employment', 7.

78 Ryan and Conlon, *Gentle Invaders*, 98–100.

79 J. A. Scutt, 'Inequality before the Law'.

80 Kirkby, 'Arbitration and the Fight for Economic Justice', 340–5.

81 G. Reekie, 'The Shop Assistants Case of 1907 and Labour Relations in Sydney's Retail Industry', in Macintyre and Mitchell, *Foundations of Arbitration*, ch. 12.

82 R. Frances, 'Marginal Matters: Gender, Skill, Unions and the Commonwealth Arbitration Court – A Case Study of the Australian Printing Industry, 1925–37', *Labour History*, 61: 2 (1991), 17–29.

83 M. Nolan, 'Sex or Class? The Politics of the Earliest Equal Pay Campaign in Victoria', *Labour History*, 61: 2 (1991), 101–22; and 'Employment Organisations', in Anne Else (ed.), *Women Together: A History of Women's Organisations in New Zealand*, Wellington, 1993, 197–8.

84 S. Robertson, 'Women Workers and the New Zealand Arbitration Court, 1894–1920', *Labour History*, 61: 2 (1991), 30–41.

85 R. Frances, L. Kealey, et al., 'Women and Wage Labour in Australia and Canada, 1880–1980', *Labour History*, 71: 2 (1996), 54–89.

86 Quoted by G. Bolton and H. Gregory, 'Commemorative Address: The 1891 Shearers Strike Leaders: Railroaded?', *Labour History*, 62: 1 (May 1992), 125.

87 Rickard, *Class and Politics*, 307.

88 Idea of egalitarianism as a 'ritual' from ibid., 308–9.

[12] *Be Prepared!*

From the earliest days of British settlement, Australasian colonists were made fearful by their immense distance from Britain. News of Russian or French fleets exacerbated that insecurity, and so did the knowledge that war might have been declared, fought and lost in Europe long before news reached Sydney or Hobart. That background anxiety was intensified in the late nineteenth century, an era of greatly increased rivalry among an expanding number of empires. That development was especially disconcerting to colonists who had grown up to take British naval and mercantile leadership for granted. To heap up their anxiety, the European leviathans now had a deal with a revived Japanese empire, adding a racial dimension to the colonists' fears. Australians and New Zealand Pakeha became obsessed with the need to fill their empty spaces with people like themselves. There were, of course, different emphases. Australians proved to be more preoccupied with home defence than New Zealanders, because of their weaker imperial ties, their immense and visibly 'empty' spaces, and their proximity to 'Asia'. Those circumstances made them especially vulnerable to Japanese sailors and soldiers, as they had felt earlier to Chinese miners and artisans. Far from real kin, on both sides of the Tasman they sought safety in Alfred Deakin's 'unity of race'.[1] The *New Zealand Herald* spelled out the links between White Australia and White New Zealand in 1908:

> Mr Deakin has defined the first duties of the Commonwealth to be: To occupy the land, to utilize it and to keep it British and White, duties which are closely interdependent. For it is manifestly impossible to maintain our exclusionist policy unless we fill with white men and women the place which we deny to Asiatics.[2]

In Pakeha thinking, Maori equated to British standards, as British citizens. They belonged through blood ties to 'the people' and therefore helped to fill the land. White Australians as usual preferred not to think about Aborigines at all, and certainly did not see them as people like themselves. Reflecting on many years of observing Australian race relations, the New Zealand anthropologist Raymond Firth judged that

> Of all the people on this earth it seems to irk white men most of all … to contemplate resources of nature lying undeveloped by their possessors. They are … provoked to a kind of sacred frenzy at the sight, not purely from the desire for

material gain, but quite largely from their conception of utilization as a species of moral duty to the universe which has made such resources available.[3]

Seen in that light, Aborigines were not a help but a handicap in the vital crusade of occupation and development.

DEFENCE

The population and defence policies of the self-governing colonies bounded racially defined polities. Imperial rivalry and international tension therefore helped to consolidate White Australia and New Zealand, and at the same time to draw Australians and New Zealanders, singly and collectively, into Britain's wars. Governments and people had little interest – and less capacity – for analysing the issues in these widely scattered campaigns. Many 'proto-Australians' crossed the Tasman to join the Britanno-Maori Wars; but the first colonial entry into an unambiguously imperial war occurred in 1885 when New South Wales despatched 770 volunteers to the Sudan to help recapture Khartoum from the Mahdi. They arrived just in time for the last rites.[4] The colonies were better prepared in 1899 to join the Boer War. The British decision not to deploy 'coloured' troops against a white enemy made no dent on the zeal of the Australian colonies, who raced each other to raise and despatch troops. In some rural as well as urban areas of Australia the Boer War aroused more interest than the achievement of federation.[5]

Joining Britain's wars involved more than the usual risks. Among Australian officers of the Bushveld Carbineers were 'Breaker' Morant and Lieutenant Handcock. They were charged with the killing of prisoners and civilians, tried by (British) court martial, sentenced and executed by firing squad. (One eventual consequence was the abolition of the death penalty for troops under Australian command.) Since Morant was an occasional contributor of verse to the *Bulletin*, the event was picked up by critics of the British connection. In the 1980s the issue resurfaced when the film *Breaker Morant* revived the popular interpretation of the trial as a characteristic British scapegoating of more-or-less innocent larrikin Australians. That provoked a South African scholar to search the relevant archives, endorse the verdict of the court martial and exonerate Lord Kitchener as Commander-in-Chief. The book made no impact in Australia, against the more comfortable narrative of martyrdom, precursor of the larger Anzac legend. In a continuing celluloid campaign, the New South Wales Film and Television Corporation commissioned research which revealed that Kitchener wanted his commanders to shoot Boers disguised as British soldiers. The makers of the documentary identified with

the campaign to have the remains of the two returned from South Africa for reburial in Australia, and for their names to be restored to the nation's wartime roll of honour.

They expected the documentary to

> help expunge 'Australia's residual cringe about the Boer War, and the Morant/ Handcock stain on the Anzac tradition and the nation's otherwise impeccable war record'.

The news prompted a tart rejoinder from a Bondi reader describing Morant as

> a particularly nasty piece of work (his main sport back in Australia had been assaulting Aborigines and mistreating horses). Morant was guilty as hell and should be left to rot in South Africa.[6]

Ambivalence about the status of Maori created some embarrassment for New Zealand. Some Maori, Te Arawa, Ngati Porou and from the Wairarapa, were keen to fight but they were excluded on English orders. The Boer War was to be a 'White Man's War', but S. Elizabeth Hawdon, proud of her heritage as the first white child born in Canterbury, thought that they took their disappointment with dignity, which showed their character. She wrote:

> The Maoris showed their ungrudging sympathy with their white brothers by making up for each contingent a separate war cry, and the young New Zealanders used these awe-inspiring yells with great effect upon more than one occasion. Is there any record of white and brown of any other land being on such fraternal terms as the New Zealanders?

She cited one such *haka*, the 'Maori war cry' of the third contingent, the New Zealand Rough Riders from Canterbury:

Kia kaha, hi! Kia toa, hi!
(Be strong, yes! Be brave, yes!)
Puritea te mana O te Kuini, hi, hi, ha-a-a!
(Uphold the supremacy of the Queen, yes, yes, yes!)
Ake! Ake! Ake!
(For ever, and ever, and ever.)[7]

The proud mother of a volunteer, Mrs Hawdon wrote *New Zealanders and the Boer War or: Soldiers from the Land of the Moa* for a popular audience (under the pseudonym 'by a New Zealander', because she was a woman), which relayed first-hand accounts of the histories of New Zealand's ten contingents. These contingents included individual Maori, who followed Joseph Chamberlain's advice of not asking London, since 'no one would have known the difference'.[8]

The Boer War was New Zealand's first send-off of soldiers to show its loyalty to the British empire, its rehearsal, its exercise in being prepared, as 'King Dick' Seddon, the premier, explained: 'We should prove to those of our race and those in the dear Motherland that we were prepared, outside all questions of expense, to help them'. The public responded with immense enthusiasm, turning out in crowds of unprecedented size. The first contingents and their horses represented the best of the volunteers; then the provinces sent forces, and finally the government, but the eighth to tenth arrived too late. Some men ended up serving in three contingents, some went to South Africa twice, and off again to the Great War. Rivalry with Australia was a feature: Queensland led the way in offering troops, followed by South Australia, Victoria and New South Wales, which could hardly stand out. New Zealand gloated that, by 'arduous exertions', their first contingent landed before the Australians – except a few New South Wales Lancers who had come from England. The citizens of Dunedin provided horses for special troopers from their different trades and lines of business, and gave the horses names: ' "Pills" represented the chemists; "Butcher Boy", the fleshers' shops; "Sweets" was the horse provided by the confectioners' young ladies'.[9] Troopers expressed their pride in their sense of superiority in the empire in physique and fitness. According to one tall story, the Boer War would have had a different ending but for them, as this rhyme suggests:

DOSE MAORILANDERS

We have heard of mighty nations,
Always ready for a row;
We have heard of dose legations,
Stormed by the rampant Chow;
We have seen our Boers a-runnin'
From der khaki seen afar;
But, I say, we ain'd as cunnin'
As dose Maorilanders are!

We have heard the whiskered Yankee,
With his new invention tales;
We have seen the cornstalk lanky
From the plains of New South Wales;
We have seen the 'Stralian drinkin'
From his flowin' whisky jar –
But they're nodden like, I'm thinkin',
What does Maorilanders are!

We have seen ole Kiplin' writin'
Of his noble Fuzzy Wuz,
An' the way the Burmese does;
When they're fighting o'er the ocean,
Of the Tommy and the Tar;
But dose blacks ain'd got a notion
What dose Maorilanders are!

We have seen the cowboys ridin'
An' a-herdin' on the plains,
An' the city men a-stridin'
For the early mornin' trains;
We have seen the street boy catch on
To the overcrowded car –
But I guess dey ain'd a patch on
What dose Maorilanders are! – E.L.E.[10]

The contrast with New Caledonia is clear. In the face of chronic labour shortage (exacerbated by the low rates of pay which employers offered), New Caledonia had recruited indentured workers from the New Hebrides and Indochina. One outcome was a very narrow stratum of French settlers on the land, in trade or in the professions. Settlers forever grumbled about governors and policies, but they were too few absolutely and relative to New Zealanders or Australians, to aspire to autonomy. There was some sentiment in Australia that Britain should buy New Caledonia and the New Hebrides, and some allusions to an Australian 'Monroe doctrine'; and French authorities were well aware of it:

> The recent development of the Australian Navy coincides with a recrudescence in the attacks in the Sydney and Melbourne press, of which our local administrations in the Pacific... have been the object for nine years [sc. since 1904]. [Presbyterians spearheaded this critique, but the governments of Australia and New Zealand] are given to an often indiscreet attention ... to the actions of our most highly placed administrators and to the recriminations of the least recommendable of our indigenous subjects.[11]

By then the French had dispersed their Pacific fleet, and little could be done to avert an Australian threat. It was clear to the *caldoches* that they needed the patronage of Paris, and it was clear to Paris that Britain was the ultimate guarantor of France's Pacific possessions.

SOCIAL PREPARATIONS

For Australians and New Zealanders, self-government opened up a broad range of policy options. While population policy affected both immigration and natural increase, Immigration Acts defined whom to exclude. The former (whom to include: 'native-born', white Australians and New Zealanders) grew more pronounced from the turn of the century, with profound consequences for the idea of woman as mother. All three imperatives – restricting immigration, fostering natural increase, and bolstering defence – issued from fashioning white racial identities and engineering settler states.

Central to their fears was the rise of Japan, emerging from isolation and using emigration to increase the amount of trade and to encourage shipping. The decisive change for Japan and its relations with Britain and the British colonies came with the Anglo-Japanese Treaty of Commerce and Navigation in 1894, in which the British government gave Japan the status of most-favoured nation and granted her citizens full rights to travel, reside and buy property. Pacific rim settlers immediately resisted.[12] At first Australia and especially New Zealand gave little heed to the alliance because it reduced the threat from Japan and offered a buffer against Russia, the traditional enemy, even though it confirmed their suspicion that British strategic priorities as always were in Europe. Australia harboured more suspicions about the Yellow Peril because of its labour politics; but any equanimity vanished in 1905, and the antipathy persisted until the 1950s.[13] British settlers throughout the Pacific were 'haunted by the apparition of an alien ship, loaded with menace, lying off the coasts of their defenceless cities'.[14] After the decisive naval battle of Tsushima, in which the Japanese destroyed the Russian fleet, the image was no longer of a ship in harbour teeming with Japanese labourers, but a first-class battleship crammed with Japanese sailors.[15] Already in 1896 and 1897 the New South Wales Premier George Reid's voice was swelling the throng urging the settler colonies to extend their restrictions so as to exclude all non-Europeans. He was disturbed not merely by Japan's increasing might, but also by the diplomatic consequences if a Japanese minority were to emerge in Australia.

From the 1890s, therefore, Japanese confronted attitudes which had already developed against Chinese in the British colonies. For New Zealand's Premier Seddon, Japanese and Chinese were one of a kind: 'they are Chinese though they are Japanese'. In his judgement their offences included the spreading of tick to Queensland, so that New Zealand must protect its cattle as well as its women and children.[16] As there were absolutely no Japanese in New Zealand in 1896, the fear was counterfactual: what catastrophes might ensue from a Japanese invasion of Queensland?[17]

Australia and New Zealand were therefore 'antipathetic' to the Anglo-Japanese Treaty. Australians disowned it in 1896, while New Zealand tried to ignore it by passing an Asiatic Restriction Bill which targeted Japanese equally with Chinese, despite qualms about the likelihood of Britain disapproving (or perhaps disallowing) a Bill which violated the treaty. Japan was outraged that New Zealand would pass such a Bill when not one Japanese had set foot there, and lobbied for it to be denied royal assent. Through 1896–7 most of the Australian colonies also rejected the Anglo-Japanese treaty. In an effort to overcome the impasse between Britain's global strategy and its settlers' intransigence, at the Imperial Conference in 1897, Joseph Chamberlain advocated the face-saving Natal language test. (That ingenious device enabled immigration officials to exclude non-Europeans on the pretext that their language skills were deficient. See also chapter 10.) Japanese were indignant that the colonies treated them like Chinese, and Australians and New Zealanders were loath to abandon the label 'coloured races' (or explicitly 'Japanese') in the legislation, but Britain insisted on the 'political expediency of not reenacting legislation so repugnant to a friendly power'.[18] Chamberlain accordingly persuaded the colonial governments to adapt the Natal dictation test. Immigration restriction had mushroomed from domestic politics to an issue of international relations.

The Yellow Peril assumed a military shape in 1905, and commanded a response of Anglo-Celtic unity. The Anglo-Japanese Alliance, rewritten in 1905 and 1911, could not dispel suspicion that Japan was only a temporary British ally. Rather than making the Pacific safe, the Alliance fostered misgivings – and at the same time muted them. It demonstrated that Britain's Pacific interests were not identical with those of her dominions (a status attained in 1907), and yet reminded them that the imperial connection was essential to their security. Unease in New Zealand was tempered more

Plate 12.1 The Great White Fleet. The United States navy, painted white, is welcomed in Sydney Harbour, 1908. Courtesy of the Australian War Memorial.

than in Australia by the need for courtesy and imperial loyalty. Australia, more labourist, was more explicit about its displeasure. It was galling for both dominions that British supremacy in the Pacific depended on Japan. The alert over Japan sounded by Deakin evolved into a general consensus by 1907–9 that Australia had to take independent initiatives to counter a threat for which the Anglo-Japanese Alliance did not compensate. In New Zealand, with its more conservative politics and stronger loyalty to empire, greater tensions between regional and imperial interests showed in political ambivalence; of public statements in favour of the alliance, to please Britain, and private misgivings. The view that Britain could not expect approval when 'exposed to the risk of being turned from white to yellow by her entanglement with an Oriental Power' represented less the mainstream than one end of the spectrum of comment.[19]

The shift in the balance of power towards Japan nevertheless brought a change of attitude to the United States, since 'Uncle Sam' appeared a better champion of Whiteness. The 1908 visit of the Great White Fleet, as Australians called the American Grand Fleet, at the invitation of Deakin in

Australia and Ward in New Zealand, gave palpable evidence of this sentiment. Roosevelt acknowledged that he despatched the fleet, symbolically painted white, to warn Japan that 'these colonies are white men's country'.[20] New Zealand offered a less boisterous welcome, but 'Fleetitis' overtook both countries.[21] In Sydney, the *Bulletin* changed its motto from 'Australia for the Australians' to 'Australia for the White Man', and huge crowds, poetry and hyperbole poured forth about the 'common thread of kinship' of the Anglo-Saxon race.[22] In Wellington the MP for Wairarapa, J. T. Hornsby, was the most outspoken: 'I am thankful that Uncle Sam has come into the Pacific to keep the yellow and brown men busy if there is to be any trouble'.[23]

For Ward, the New Zealand Liberal premier, this show of strength sufficed; but for Deakin a stronger anti-Japanese strategy was imperative to protect Australian interests. While Australia and New Zealand were united in their mistrust of Japan and their determination to defend their whiteness, their differently experienced tensions between nation and empire provoked different naval responses. Australia decided to build its own navy in 1909, while New Zealand offered to buy a battle cruiser for the Royal Navy, for which it had to borrow over £1,000,000.

Australia opted for an independent search for security because it was more preoccupied with home defence. It had immense coasts to protect and a different concept of the Pacific region. It was closer to and more overtly suspicious of Asia, especially Britain's ally. With federation it also commanded more resources, while it was less tied to the empire economically and culturally. Conversely, New Zealand demonstrated more imperial loyalty, out of necessity and from choice. The federation of Australia had made New Zealand smaller, highlighting its vulnerability, and the more the sense of dread and danger, the more New Zealand grew closer to Britain: out of loyalty, because it was too small to build its own navy, and above all because it needed an imperial navy for its protection. Its sense of a separate destiny from Australia, as a distinctive people, also played a part.

These divergent decisions had ripple effects that brought the two closer together as well as distinguishing them. Rivalry prompted Australia to match New Zealand in buying a battleship for the empire; while New Zealand began to co-operate in defence with Australia from 1912. With the outbreak of war in 1914, the British Admiralty assumed control,[24] but in their divergent responses to Japan, overlaid by differing bonds to empire, the settler states had set in train their strategies in relation to Singapore and Pearl Harbor.

While Labor parties encouraged the idea of a White Australia in the 1890s, the call to be White became a plank in every party platform from federation, and on both sides of parliament in New Zealand; the race card consistently appealed as a vote-catcher not requiring funds. In 1901 debate hinged not on the principle of prohibition but on its form. The Commonwealth adopted the Natal test (as had New Zealand and the separate Australian colonies) to satisfy British sensitivities. New Zealand followed a parallel path, though it did not resort to the Australian device of using European languages other than English.[25] This technique was adapted over the years, becoming quite explicit: under the Immigration Restriction Amendment Act 1920, people who were not of British or Irish birth or parentage could only enter New Zealand at the discretion of the minister of customs. 'Aboriginal Natives' of any part of the empire except New Zealand were not 'British' for the purposes of the Act. This dispensed with some iniquitous measures but the poll tax, a legacy of gold rush prejudice, survived. Chinese protests to London fell on deaf ears as China was not a great power which had to be conciliated.[26] Chinese already in New Zealand also lost their right to citizenship from 1908 to 1952.[27]

In a continual process of whitewashing, legislation defined the 'other' by whom they were not: the 'other' was anyone not of British or Irish birth or parentage. Significantly, the 'other' included Australian Aborigines, so White New Zealand followed White Australia in excluding Aborigines, but not Maori, from 'the people'. Rather than being recolonized, New Zealand, like Australia, went through a process of being whitened. 'For better or worse, the character, and self-identity and the historical fate of the Pacific basin was tied up with the settlers' determination to exclude Asians, and reserve their territories for people of British and European descent.'[28]

POPULATE OR PERISH

Shared alarms engendered shared strategies. One was to bar migration from all parts of Asia, and meanwhile to boost the numbers and the quality of white men and women by producing healthy babies. The white child was positioned as someone essential to successful defence and development. In the new century it was axiomatic that 'our population is best replenished and our empty spaces best filled by our own natural increase: the newborn infant, in other words, is our best immigrant'.[29] Health experts and politicians agreed that the falling birth rate was ominous for Australia and New Zealand, and for the empire generally. Settler birth rates were falling just when the need was evident for increase. A slowing population growth normally accompanied a shift from migrant to settled societies dominated by the 'native-born'. The panic about virility and numbers erupted because imperialists and nation-builders seized upon the decline in fertility – a shared experience in the West – and presumed low replacement rates. What did falling fertility portend but race suicide?

There could have been no better fuel for this fear than the 1903–4 Royal Commission on the Decline of the Birth-Rate and on the Mortality of Infants in New South Wales. The commission, half medical consultants, the rest business and professional men, condemned the desire to restrict fertility as 'characteristic of a decadent state of society' and concluded:

> The future of the Commonwealth, and especially the possibility of maintaining a 'white Australia', depend on the question whether we shall be able to people the vast areas of the continent which are capable of supporting a large population. This can only be done by restoring and maintaining a high rate of natural increase, or by immigration on a large scale, or by both. ...
> It is the duty of the present generation of Australians to see to it... that the loss of this fair heritage of the British race... is not made attributable to them

by those who may ... have to sacrifice their blood and treasure in the vain hope of defending it.[30]

Patriotism, pronatalism and ethnic solidarity mingled with forebodings. Moral panic trumped evidence, and the birth rate became a matter for state action.

The commissioners' politics were 'masculinist'. All but one (W. A. Holman)[31] were pronatalist. They blamed the declining birth rate on women's selfishness, particularly the women deemed most fit to reproduce, who were 'bent on gratifying their selfish desires, and on pursuing social advancement'; and they heard no testimony from the women's movement.[32] They half-recognized that parents' expectations had risen with more regular and longer schooling, which particularly benefited working-class girls. But they blocked their ears to the message of Victoria's statistician and birth and death statistics that reduced fertility brought improved life chances. Indeed, they were oblivious to a white health transition, of which falling fertility and infant mortality were major parts.[33]

But the commissioners were less myopic than historians once thought because, poised at the intersection of sweeping changes in health, sexuality and the family, they did register that the 'forward' movement of women played a part in the birth rate decline.[34] In 1901, Dr (later Sir) James Barrett summarized the thinking of his Australasian medical colleagues. Many of them welcomed birth control as a means of protecting women's health and ensuring that 'better children would be reared', but these doctors had not anticipated that birth control 'might become an instrument of national destruction'. Instead, Barrett protested, 'The propagation of the Anglo-Saxon race has been placed largely under voluntary control, owing to the education of its women. The extent to which this control is resorted to may determine the fate of the Empire'.[35] Moralists in medicine, the church, politics and business were right that educated women were the vanguard of voluntary motherhood. Of the first women university graduates from the 1870s in New Zealand and the 1880s in Australia half did not marry, and those who did had only one or two children.[36]

In their critique of the New Woman, the commission drew on the evidence of 96 witnesses, of whom 87 were men. None of the nine women represented any women's organization. They came from health and charity work, comprising one doctor (of the 27, mainly specialists, present); three matrons; two 'nurses'; a factory inspector; an ex-officer of the Salvation Army; and a 'married lady' who represented the general public. The recalcitrant feminists who were charged with 'unwifelike' and 'unnatural' behaviour in rebuffing their husbands and 'defil[ing] the marriage-bed with the devices and equipment of the brothel' expected to be admonished, and refused to appear.[37]

Medical and police witnesses testified to the wide practice of birth control, and their evidence matches a recent Australian study that 'withdrawal, along with sexual abstinence and induced abortion, played a major role in bringing about the historical fertility declines of the West'.[38] They thought withdrawal 'very common' where men earned more than two pounds a week but less common among the labouring classes: 'the man will not submit to it'. They identified withdrawal as the main method, followed by abortion among women of the 'poorer classes' whose husbands seemed less inclined to co-operate than among the 'educated classes'.[39] Such evidence pointed less to women's control over fertility than to men's continued dominance and responsibility, tempered by a trend towards joint decisions above a certain level of income and education. Parents with changing aspirations chose to invest in fewer children. Attitudes changed first, followed by the capacity to produce a higher calibre child.[40] The national identity-makers on the commission blamed women, because of their certainty that mothers were the moral guardians of the family, a belief which women deployed to win space in the public realm and national myth-making.

This was a clash between the demand for more – or better – children for a higher type of man or woman. It exposed competing moral views of the dramatic shifts in gender and generational relations which saw the average white family shrink steadily from six or seven in the 1880s to two or three in the 1920s. Fertility control spelt immorality to the majority of the Birth Rate Commission, as it did to many feminists in the social purity lobby.

Private hopes and behaviour, however, had much in common with the radical feminist position of voluntary motherhood (and fatherhood): that it was immoral for parents to give life to children whom they calculated they could not afford. Ordinary people shared a concept of morality – and therefore identity – that doctors detected among their patients. One doctor reported that 'most respectable women' believed in 'any measure to prevent children being born when the parents are not able to keep them'. Others repeated this view: 'some very nice women ... – very conscientious women – say there is no prospect for children in this country now – no opening; and therefore they think it is not right to bring them into the world'.[41] Mrs Brettena Smyth, Melbourne's birth control campaigner and supplier, insisted on the morality of women's deciding how many children to have. 'Wives have a right to demand of their husbands at least the same consideration which a breeder of cattle extends to his stock', she asserted in her manual *Limitation of Offspring*.[42]

At the public level, angst about remoteness and small numbers bedevilled leaders and bureaucrats and doctors. Australia and New Zealand restricted access to birth control and censored advertisements, but the persistent falls in family size suggested that people harboured heterodox ideals of the imagined community. Identity bred of experience always had family survival as its bottom line, while the Harvester judgement endorsed three children – the new norm – as 'fair and reasonable'. More than family economics was at stake. The numbers game between public and private moralities spilled into a battle over gendered identities enshrining the ideal type of man and (especially) woman to create and nurture these superior societies. For the pronatalist school dominant in public rhetoric, quantity spelt quality: numbers counted in displays of racial vigour, in war and in claiming terrain. For the quality school to which most colonial feminists belonged – dominant in practice, and quick to adopt eugenist discourse – fewer children bespoke worthier parenthood.

Both sides did agree on the sanctity of motherhood as essential for the desired social, ethnic order. They shared the concept of the family as the basis for a better society: it was 'nature's best school for teaching the lessons of life'. Fundamentally they all valued white racial purity, appropriating the language of eugenics which sought the physical, mental and moral betterment of the race. Layers of identity also melded in the focus on the white infant, giving rise to the infant welfare movement. The child would be the saviour of the British race, and Australia and New Zealand its Pacific nursery. Both aspired to be model nations which re/produced the best type of white baby reared on wholesome food, sunshine and fresh air.

Despite their already low rates of white infant mortality, Australia and New Zealand grasped infant survival as an answer to national and imperial anxieties, because angst about defensive unity strengthened by numbers could not be separated from jitters about 'Asia'. The birth rate scare ballooned and so did the cultural significance of 'saving the babies'. In 1901 Dr Richard Arthur, a passionate advocate of White Australia who founded the Eugenics Education Society of New South Wales and later became minister of public health, proposed another method to ensure an increase in population: 'It consists not in increasing the birth rate, but in diminishing the death rate [by saving] a proportion of the children who die in infancy from preventable causes'.[43] To achieve this, the Birth Rate Commission had its brief extended to infant mortality and its contribution to prosperity and racial vigour.[44] New Zealand's portly Premier Richard Seddon who introduced a 'Sale of Preventatives Prohibition Bill' the same year had more success with his Memorandum of Child Life Preservation in 1904 – a direct response to the alarm fuelled by the New South Wales report.

Predictably, if perversely, war heightened the emphasis on the sanctity of life with profound effects for rhetoric and policy. In 1917, after the carnage on the Western Front, New Zealand's icon, Dr Frederic Truby King, mental health expert, declared in a pamphlet *Save the Babies*:

> The Plunket Society in New Zealand was one of the first organizations in our Empire to recognize the germ of degeneration that had begun to sap our own vitality. It saw that if we could not do anything in the meantime to check the falling birth-rate, we could do something locally to lower our infant death-rate, and to improve the mental and physical characteristics of our future generations. ...
>
> It is our bounden duty to save our children and build up for the Empire a stalwart race of men and women and thus avoid the huge number of army rejects and be able to take our place even more fully than we can to-day in any future Imperial crisis.

He built to a crescendo of imperial patriotism:

> Upon Britain depends the civilization of the world. The defeat of Britain means the death of liberty.[45]

> ARE YOU A PATRIOT?
> DO YOU WANT YOUR NATION TO SURVIVE?
> Are you determined that never again shall there be 50 per cent of possible rejects in our Community?[46]

Army medical examinations ranked recruits according to their fitness for overseas service (A1) or otherwise (C2 or 3), and these indexes provided the language for eugenists. In war the discourse about degeneracy revealed more starkly its concern with health, strength and physique as well as numbers.

But pronatalism continued to be favoured by doctors and governments. The war compounded public unease about the birth rate. Dr J. S. Elliott, leading figure in the local branch of the British Medical Association and editor of the *New Zealand Medical Journal*, had served in the South African War and the Great War. He sounded much like Australia's birth rate commissioners when he declared in 1922:

> When many of the best and bravest of our young men have perished in the Great War and when the urgent need of this country and the Empire is population, it is not only surprising that Malthusianism should be advocated by medical men or even by laymen, but it is monstrous. If countries suitable for the white races are not to be fully populated and developed by the white races, it means one of two results, either these countries will be over-run by coloured races, or there will be the most bloody and horrible wars for racial supremacy. The mind shrinks from either alternative ... the general and extended use of contraceptives ... [does] violence to everything that is sacred to the name of nature, morality, science and common-sense.[47]

MEASURES

Although concern for a falling birth rate was provoked by white racial anxiety, some of it spilt over into speculation about – and even measures to address – the possible demise of indigenous people. The government of Fiji was more committed than most, and was appalled that Fijian numbers continued to fall through the 1890s. Numbers of births were pleasingly high, but so was the infant mortality rate. The obvious explanation was that Fijians made bad mothers.[48] Laws and regulations were therefore put in place to criminalize and eliminate abortion, infanticide or neglect. A few years later the government invested in clean water, provincial hospitals, doctors and sanitary inspectors. Later again, the mission bodies began to visit, inspect and advise village mothers; milch cows were introduced; and schools were created in which to train Fijian girls for motherhood. At last, in 1908, the government began to teach Fijian nurses as extension workers. For reasons unrelated to these ventures, the Fijian population stabilized in the 1900s, and increased thereafter. Governmental concern then switched to the immigrant Indian population, returning to Fijian mothers only in the 1920s when the mortality rates of Indians proved to be very much lower than those for Fijians – with disturbing implications for the future.

No other island dependency had Fiji's resources, nor such a developed system of administration. The less developed regimes adopted measures which were either cheaper or simple enough to require no professional intervention: cash payments to men who fathered many children, criminal sanctions against abortion and any other method of birth control, international quarantine and domestic segregation to discourage the transmission of infections from one race to another.[49] Happily almost all indigenous populations began to regain their numbers by the 1920s, no matter which combination of measures had been adopted.

In white societies, the infant mortality rate (measured to exclude those defined as Aboriginal and Maori) became the measure of success in the mission to save babies. At least the baby death rate seemed remediable; as medical knowledge improved, it became possible to prevent the major killer, diarrhoea. It was also important to be seen to do something since the future of the white (British) race had become a major political issue. Interventions to reduce infant deaths moved down a logical chain from the late nineteenth century, from sanitation to clean up the environment on the one hand and infant life protection acts to prevent infanticide on the other, to milk (babies' food), and mothers and their practices. Again, it was simplest to blame bad mothering.

The infant welfare movements in Australia and New Zealand which responded to these white racial anxieties were part of an international movement to 'help the mothers and save the babies' by educating mothers in mothercraft (a word coined about 1910). The movement in every Australian state and in New Zealand varied along a spectrum of shared experience, refracted through different political cultures, health regimes and local conditions.

The New Zealand Society for the Health of Women and Children, established by Dr (later Sir) Frederic Truby King and his wife Isabella in 1907 with the help of wealthy businessmen's wives in Dunedin, was not unique, though it is frequently represented as such in New Zealand narratives. The Adelaide School for Mothers of 1909–10, established on the English model by women's private efforts, similarly aimed to save the babies and improve the physique of the nation by instructing mothers in infant feeding and care. Sydney's movement had its tentative beginnings in 1904–14 with nurse visiting (initiated by the medical officer of health) and a school for mothers established by the National Council of Women, while Melbourne and Brisbane opened infants' milk depots with the object of making bottle feeding safer. But it was the New Zealand society – popularly known as the Plunket Society – which won an international reputation and thus a place in national myth-making, which both capitalized on and promoted New Zealand's image as an ideal place in which to bring up children.[50]

Both countries began to establish maternity hospitals as monuments to motherhood. In Australia metropolitan women's hospitals opened in Melbourne and Sydney in the 1890s and in New Zealand the state St Helens hospitals, of which the first opened in Wellington in 1905, were both maternity hospitals and midwifery training schools.

Australia, however, diverged from New Zealand in opting for a national cash benefit to promote White Australia, consistent with its more Labor politics. The Maternity Allowance (baby bonus) of 1912 paid £5 for a live, white baby. According to the Act, it excluded: 'Women who are Asiatics, or are aboriginal natives of Australia, Papua, or the islands of the Pacific' (in 1926 'Asiatics' changed to 'aliens'). However, we have already noted how paternalist Australian administrators paid Papuan fathers the allowance (see chapter 4). Significantly, white, unwed mothers met the criteria of fit motherhood on race grounds. New Zealand, like the National Council of Women in Australia, could not go this far because of its heavier weighting to deserving and undeserving as moral categories.[51]

But it took the losses of the Great War to provoke public men into putting their weight behind the baby health movement. 'Equally saddening' as the long casualty lists in the newspapers was the 'infants' casualty list', of white Australian and New Zealand babies who did not live to see their first birthday. For the sake of the race, women, as mothers, bore a 'duty' to 'repair that war-wastage'. This was 'war work'.[52]

> Long Live King Baby! The Head of the Home and Hope of the Nation. ...
> The hope of Australia lies in healthy living babies, fewer dead babies, stronger children, and a fitter race. Population means power! The nation that has the babies has the future[53]

proclaimed the advertisement for New South Wales' first baby week in 1920. This message assumed particular meanings in Australia and New Zealand from the Great War, in making a place for women as mothers complementary to the values embodied in their Anzac legends, which became central to tradition and identity-making in these white dominions.

NOTES

1 J. Rickard, *Australia: A Cultural History*, 2nd edn. The Present and the Past, ed. Michael Crowder and Juliet Gardiner, London and New York, 1988, 114–16.
2 Quoted in J. E. Bennett, 'Redeeming the Imagination: A Trans-national History of Australia and Aotearoa/New Zealand, 1890–1944'. Ph.D. thesis, University of Melbourne, 1997, 270.
3 Raymond Firth, 'Anthropology in Australia, 1926–32 – and After', *Oceania*, September 1932, cited by Russell McGregor, *Imagined Destinies: Aboriginal Australians and the Doomed Race Theory, 1880–1939*, Melbourne, 1997.
4 K. S. Inglis, *The Rehearsal: Australians at War in the Sudan, 1885*, Sydney, 1985.
5 Bill Gammage, *Nerrandera Shire*, Nerrandera Shire Council, 1986.
6 *Sydney Morning Herald*, 13 and 14 April 1999.
7 S. E. Hawdon, *New Zealanders and the Boer War or: Soldiers from the Land of the Moa*, Christchurch, c.1902–3, 260, 247. Sarah Elizabeth Hawdon was the daughter of Dr Alfred Barker and married Arthur Hawdon, a pastoralist whose family made money in Australia, in 1872. With thanks to John O'Reilly and Alastair Mein Smith.
8 Ian McGibbon, *The Path to Gallipoli: Defending New Zealand 1840–1915*, Wellington, 1991, 117.
9 Hawdon, *New Zealanders and the Boer War*, 5, 14–15, 20. On the Australian offers, see C. N. Connolly, 'Manufacturing "Spontaneity": The Australian Offers of Troops for the Boer War', *Historical Studies*, 18: 70 (1978), 106–17.
10 Hawdon, *New Zealanders and the Boer War*, 200.
11 Director of the American and Oceanic service to his minister, 1913, cited in Robert Aldrich, *The French Presence in the Pacific, 1842–1940*, London, 1990, 275.

12 Bennett, 'Redeeming the Imagination', 67–83.

13 Neville Meaney, *The Search for Security in the Pacific, 1901–14*, Sydney, 1976, 10, 51–2, 120.

14 Avner Offer, *The First World War: An Agrarian Interpretation*, Oxford, 1989.

15 C-in-C Australia Station to Wellington, 1905, quoted in McGibbon, *Path to Gallipoli*, 162; Joseph Ward (ibid., 164) in 1911 referred to the 'shadow of a great coloured nation which was looming over our country'.

16 Seddon, *New Zealand Parliamentary Debates*, 93, 24 July 1896, 472, 471, also P. S. O'Connor, 'Keeping New Zealand White, 1908–1920', *New Zealand Journal of History*, 2 (1968), 43.

17 As depicted in the *Review of Reviews* in 1896, speeches of Newman and Earnshaw, *New Zealand Parliamentary Debates*, 93, 24 July 1896, 466–7.

18 Bennett, 'Redeeming the Imagination', 74.

19 M. P. Lissington, *New Zealand and Japan 1900–1941*, Wellington, 1971, 9.

20 McGibbon, *Path to Gallipoli*, 165.

21 Deakin to Jebb 1908, cited in Meaney, *The Search for Security in the Pacific*, 167.

22 Russel Ward, *A Nation for a Continent*, Richmond, Victoria, 1977, 63; Meaney, *The Search for Security in the Pacific*, 169.

23 Lissington, *New Zealand and Japan 1900–1941*, 8.

24 Ian McGibbon, 'Australia–New Zealand Defence Relations to 1939', in Keith Sinclair (ed.), *Tasman Relations*, Auckland, 1987, 169–72.

25 O'Connor, 'Keeping New Zealand White', 43; Manying Ip, 'Chinese New Zealanders', in Stuart W. Greif (ed.), *Immigration and National Identity in New Zealand*, Palmerston North, 1995, 172–3.

26 O'Connor, 'Keeping New Zealand White', 59.

27 Ip, 'Chinese New Zealanders', 173.

28 Offer, *The First World War*, 214.

29 *Appendices to the Journals of the House of Representatives*, New Zealand, 1925, H-31, 3; Erik Olssen, 'Truby King and the Plunket Society: An Analysis of a Prescriptive Ideology', *New Zealand Journal of History*, 15: 1 (1981), 12.

30 NSW Royal Commission on the Decline of the Birth-rate [RCDBR], vol. 1, 16, conclusion.

31 W. A. Holman and his wife Ada Holman, an activist for mother and child causes, limited their own family to two children.

32 RCDBR, vol. 1, conclusion. See Judith A. Allen, *Sex and Secrets*, Melbourne, 1990; Patricia Grimshaw, Marilyn Lake, Ann McGrath and Marian Quartly, *Creating a Nation*, Melbourne, 1994.

33 Philippa Mein Smith, *Mothers and King Baby: Infant Survival and Welfare in an Imperial World: Australia 1880–1950*, Basingstoke, 1997, ch. 1.

34 A. Mackinnon, *Love and Freedom: Professional Women and the Reshaping of Personal Life*, Melbourne, 1997, 22, 38. Neville Hicks, *'This Sin and Scandal': Australia's Population Debate 1891–1911*, Canberra, 1978, saw them as men with a grip on the past.

35 J. W. Barrett, 'Presidential Address', *Intercolonial Medical Journal of Australasia*, 6: 1 (20 January 1901), 25, 27. Quoted also in his *Twin Ideals*, vol. 1, London, 1918, 349.

36 On Australia, see Alison Mackinnon, *Love and Freedom*, Melbourne, 1997; on New Zealand, see W. J. Gardner, *Colonial Cap and Gown*, Christchurch, 1979.

37 Phrasing from M. O'Sullivan, 'Presidential Address', *Australasian Medical Gazette*, 26 (20 February 1907), 60. On O'Sullivan's speech see Neville Hicks, *'This Sin and Scandal': Australia's Population Debate 1891–1911*, Canberra, 1978,

48; and L. T. Ruzicka and J. C. Caldwell, *End of Demographic Transition in Australia*, Canberra, 1977, 25.

38 Gigi Santow, 'Coitus Interruptus in the Twentieth Century', *Population and Development Review*, 19: 4 (Dec. 1993), 768, 772, 783.

39 RCDBR, vol. 2, Dr Ralph Worrall, 2 November 1903, q.2933, Dr A. Watson Munro, Hon. Surg. Women's Hospital, 29 October 1903, qq.2662–4, 2668, Dr W. J. S. Mackay, Hon. Surg. Lewisham Hospital, 12 November 1903, qq.3312, 3318, 3330–1.

40 See, for example, Ann Larson, *Growing Up in Melbourne: Family Life in the Late Nineteenth Century*, Canberra, 1994.

41 RCDBR, vol. 2, Dr C. W. Morgan, 24 September 1903, q.1072, Dr Ralph Worrall, 2 November 1903, q.2959.

42 B. Smyth, *Limitation of Offspring*, Melbourne, 1893, 11. See also Susan Sheridan, 'The *Woman's Voice* on Sexuality', in Susan Magarey, Sue Rowley and Susan Sheridan (eds), *Debutante Nation: Feminism Contests the 1890s*, Sydney, 1993, 114–24; Grimshaw, et al., *Creating a Nation*, 184.

43 R. Arthur, 'Increase of Population Through a Diminished Death-Rate', *Australasian Medical Gazette*, 25 January 1901, 43; also quoted in his evidence, RCDBR, vol. 2, 7 December 1903, q.5244.

44 This extension is discussed in Mein Smith, *Mothers and King Baby*, 32–6.

45 Truby King, *Save the Babies*, 1917.

46 Poster, Save the Babies Week, 1917.

47 J. S. Elliott, 'Birth Control', *New Zealand Medical Journal*, 21: 106 (December 1922), 342.

48 Vicki Lukere, 'The Native Mother', in Donald Denoon, Stewart Firth, Jocelyn Linnekin, Malama Meleisa and Karen Nero (eds), *Cambridge History of the Pacific Islanders*, Cambridge, 1997, 280–7.

49 Donald Denoon, with Kathleen Dugan and Leslie Marshall, *Public Health in Papua New Guinea, 1884–1984: Medical Possibility and Social Constraint*, Cambridge 1989.

50 In a common pattern, the society took its name from its patroness, the governor-general's wife, Lady Plunket, who herself gave lectures advertising Plunket methods on 'The Proper Care and Feeding of the Baby'. *Press*, Christchurch, 19 September 1908, 9; 25 September 1908, 7. On the beginnings of the movement in Australia before the Great War, see Mein Smith, *Mothers and King Baby*, ch. 3.

51 Maternity Allowance Act, *Commonwealth Acts*, vol. XI, no. 8, 1912, s.6 (2). The NCW wanted the £5 allowance to have strings attached; it preferred to establish a school for expectant mothers in each state: *Australasian Medical Gazette*, 32 (20 July 1912), 62. Instead New Zealand had a National Provident Fund contributory scheme from 1910 under which new mothers who were insured by their male breadwinners received £6 for childbirth expenses from 1914, while Friendly Societies paid out £4 on the birth of a child from 1916.

52 *Daily Telegraph*, Sydney, 1 October 1918; *Bystander*, NSW, 24 October 1918. Mein Smith, *Mothers and King Baby*, 77–86.

53 *Sunday News*, Sydney, 24 March 1920.

PART IV

Wars and Reconstructions

[13] THE GREAT WAR

ANZAC LEGENDS

Anzac legends are pivotal episodes in Australian and New Zealand national narratives, fundamental to their self-images as unique. These experiences and their narration link and yet separate them from each other, and from Britain, and they serve to distinguish them sharply from their geographical neighbours. A recent speech touches the main themes of the narratives and helps to explain their resonances.

> The story ... lives in our national histories and collective memories. For Anzac is not merely about loss. It is about courage, and endurance, and duty, and love of country, and mateship, and good humour and the survival of a sense of self-worth and decency in the face of dreadful odds.
>
> These were the qualities and values the pioneers had discovered in themselves in what were, for Europeans, the new lands of Australasia. They were tested at Gallipoli and on the ancient battlefields of Europe for the first time in the Great War.
>
> Gallipoli was not the Anzacs' bloodiest campaign of that war. ... But it was the *first*. And it was heroic even in failure. And what makes it unique is that it was where the people of Australia and New Zealand found their nationhood. 'Before the war who ever heard of Anzac?' said their commander-in-chief, the British general, Sir Ian Hamilton. 'Hereafter, who will ever forget it?'
>
> The campaign failed, but the men were not defeated. There is a crucial difference. In a triumph of daring and initiative, more than 35,000 Anzacs were evacuated during eleven December nights, with barely a casualty. ... But their dead – our dead – remained behind on the other side of the world: more than 8,100 Australians and 2,700 New Zealanders. ...
>
> While Gallipoli is Turkish land, it has become a sacred site of our nations.

Thus the Australian Governor-General Sir William Deane, at dawn on Anzac Day 1999, to an audience largely comprising secular pilgrims from Australia and New Zealand, at a site on the Dardanelles now known as Anzac Cove.[1] Articulated, embroidered and moralized in Anzac Day speeches, politicians' allusions, participants' and scholars' books, veterans' meetings and their institutions, 'documentary' and feature films and television programmes, the component stories have become so familiar and smooth that their jagged and extraordinary features can escape notice. For another perspective on these events and their consequences we might compare them with the more limited experience of French colonial dependencies in the Pacific.

Until the *Entente Cordiale* of 1903, French strategists could not rule out Britain as their next enemy, Australians as Britain's belligerent surrogates in the Pacific, and New Caledonia and the New Hebrides as possible targets (see chapter 12).[2] Even when that alarm was (partly) allayed, grave doubts lingered about the defence of these islands. The naval presence could be beefed up to Australian and New Zealand standards only at the unacceptable cost of weakening the home fleet. France therefore went to war hoping that the British navy would protect the Pacific territories. Tahiti hosted one elderly warship, powered by sail and steam. When it was sunk by German ships, Tahiti had no naval defences. The naval commander and the civilian governor then squabbled over their powers: the commander spent two months in gaol in consequence.

More significant was the colonies' role in Europe. A thousand men – Polynesian and European – enlisted in Tahiti and most of them fought in French units in Macedonia. A similar number, mostly Melanesian, joined up in New Caledonia and fought in France: one in ten was killed in action, and two in ten died of illness. These small tragedies were lost in the vast European theatre. No doubt many individuals were transformed, but that did not transform their societies. French views of the colonies were not re-made, nor were soldiers' view of themselves and their relations with France. They saw no action in the Pacific, and in the postwar settlement France gained no Pacific spoils. These events were submerged as undifferentiated elements of the larger tragedy of the European war.

The Anzac experiences, and especially the legends which flow from them, were much more than interruptions to the smooth-running histories of the British colonies. Service in the war was neither a natural culmination of previous trends nor a necessary precursor of national sentiment. It was extraordinary that Australian and New Zealand soldiers fought in the same army corps; it was their first intervention in a European war (and almost the last). Not every adult male was allowed to take part. Maori formed and fought gallantly in a Pioneer Battalion, later renamed the Maori Battalion, which also enlisted Niueans and Cook Islanders. Fijians also fought in British formations, but Aboriginal Australians had a marginal role in reality, and less in legend. A few New Guinean police fought for Germany, but played no other part in the war or its narratives.

The outlines of Australian and New Zealand participation are clear enough. In view of the colonists' strategic and social anxieties (see chapter 12), their governments were keen to display loyalty and commitment to the empire. When war broke out in August 1914, British colonies were automatically engaged, but they also hastened to pledge their loyalty 'to the last man and the last shilling'.[3] Like other papers, the *Sydney Morning Herald* saw this as a moral and potentially nation-building venture and exulted in Australia's 'baptism of fire'. That was not a random expression. Two generations of school children had recited James Brunton Stephens's poem *The Dominion of*

Australia: A Forecast with its evocative line 'She is not yet'. That sentence reflected a general sense that Australia had not only been spared, but had been denied, its baptism in blood.[4] Rudyard Kipling observed to Banjo Paterson that 'You people in Australia haven't grown up yet. You think the Melbourne Cup is the most important thing in the world'.[5] That was not unfair: the horse race on the first Tuesday of each November was the occasion most widely observed across the continent.

The men who rushed to recruit, and the governments which hastened to enlist them, were consciously building a nation as well as defending an empire, and felt no contradiction between the two. There were four million Australians when war broke out, including a million and a half men aged between 15 and 64. A total of 400,000 volunteered and 330,000 shipped abroad. Some 60,000 died and another 150,000 were casualties – nearly two-thirds in all.[6] Of over 120,000 New Zealanders who served (again about 80 per cent overseas), 17,000 died. Nearly all who enlisted early and did survive were wounded.

While the Australian government tried in vain to introduce conscription (in 1916 and 1917), the New Zealand government succeeded. They took this step not because men would not enlist but as a matter of equity, on grounds of equality of sacrifice, the very grounds invoked in Australia to reject conscription: yet the numerical outcome was similar on either side of the Tasman. There were little more than a million New Zealanders in 1914, of whom over 100,000 men served overseas. Their casualty rate was high: 59 per cent killed or wounded. The Australian rate was even higher, at 68 per cent. Since Australians and New Zealanders were often deployed as shock troops, they took heavier casualties than did average British forces. On this scale, the deaths and injuries made a social and political impact which was – and is – almost too great to assimilate.

Some Australians travelled great distances to enlist in the capital cities, but so many mobbed the recruiting offices that medical examiners could raise the physical criteria absurdly high. The First Australian Imperial Force looked different to its successors.[7] At least until May 1915, when newspapers began to list casualties at Gallipoli, public opinion was fiercely behind recruitment: even afterwards, hostility to anything German was so fervent that towns as well as people changed their names, and denunciation of Teutonic wickedness was unrestrained. For individuals, recruitment motives were varied. One recalled that he and his peers joined up

> because public opinion told them to, or if they didn't want to be out of an entertainment all the boys were in; or if they felt they ought to; or if they wanted occupation or excitement or a tour. ... [T]hey may feel that they are seeing life; they may, if they're Imperially minded ...; they may feel they are 'helping civilization'; they may feel among the boys.[8]

They went to war outwardly united and eager. With superiority in war deemed the ultimate test of national fitness, Australia and New Zealand raced to command their maximum effort: the empire was 'everything'.[9] Even after the tragic event, Australia's Prime Minister Billy Hughes ('the Little Digger') hailed the Great War for having 'saved us from physical and moral degeneracy and decay'.[10] War was a stage on which to show how the transplanted British 'type' had progressed, and how the better British stock produced in Australia and New Zealand was evolving into hardy national types. In both national narratives, it was never doubted that the young men who sailed north would excel in the ultimate test of citizenship.

The colonies' first task was to mop up German forces in the Pacific. Their land forces were trivial, but predatory warships caused real damage and psychic trauma for many months, and made it urgent to capture and disable radio communications such as the station at Rabaul. Australia's first engagement therefore was a short, sea-borne campaign in which the Australian Naval and Military Expeditionary Force captured Rabaul swiftly and the rest of New Guinea at leisure, while a New Zealand expedition relieved the Germans of Western Samoa. Those little campaigns eliminated Germany from all lands south of the equator, while the Japanese did the same to the north, in fulfilment of an agreement with Britain: that division of labour dismayed governments in Melbourne and Wellington, especially as it led to Japan's postwar occupation of Micronesia. Within the region however, Australia and New Zealand were consequential powers. Many islands did change rulers (with dire results in the 1940s) but these military bagatelles are now almost forgotten. It was in the Old World that New World heroics must be performed. The soldiers generated the Anzac legends in Europe and the Mediterranean.

The Great War had a surprising shape.[11] This was a world war in the sense that it committed more countries and many more combatants, and inflicted more casualties than any previous war. Following the Bolshevik revolution in 1917 Russia withdrew, but the United States was already engaged. There was fighting from the Pyrenees to the Urals, and few European powers remained neutral, but the little campaigns in Africa and the Pacific had only a limited bearing on the war's outcome, and there was no war at all in the Americas or most of Asia. This was a European war, from the Atlantic to the Mediterranean.

The Central Powers (Germany and Austro-Hungary, joined by Turkey) enjoyed interior lines against Britain and France on the Western Front, Italy to the South and Russia on the Eastern Front. Despite a prewar German challenge in naval armaments, the British navy still enjoyed predominance when war began, and her supremacy in the Atlantic was maintained (partly because the Japanese alliance allowed the concentration of force). Britain and her allies could therefore rely on food convoys from North America, South Africa, Australia and New Zealand. That advantage might have reminded British strategists of the successful approach of their predecessors in the French revolutionary and Napoleonic wars. A naval blockade of the Central Powers was feasible in principle and was visualized but discarded by British planners. It would have exposed British soldiers to less danger, allowing strategists to choose the site of their eventual landing. The dominions would have supplied food rather than men. That was what German planners expected of the British colonies, whose militias had not yet been tested in European warfare.

Instead, of course, there were immense movements and catastrophic defeats for Russia on the Eastern Front; after protracted fighting the Italians prevailed over the Austrians in the South; and the Western Front became the archetypal war of immobility, epic endurance and attrition. Having secured the Pacific, Australians and New Zealanders sailed to the Mediterranean, to detach Turkey from the Central Powers. A landing at Gallipoli would close the Dardanelles to all enemy navies, isolating Turkey and neutralizing her. Over 50,000 Australians fought in a campaign of eight months. Between April and December, one in seven died or were killed in action and buried there. Of the over 8,500 New Zealanders who fought at Gallipoli, nearly a third died and over 4,700 were injured (including men injured more than once). As for disease, hardly anyone escaped. When that operation failed, some Australian and New Zealand light horse went on to fight the Turks in Palestine and Syria, the site of the last cavalry charge of the war, and perhaps the last anywhere. The infantry sailed to France, to spend the rest of the war in the trenches. It was difficult then, and impossible now, to represent this butchery as rational, or even coherent.

Australia's most successful soldier was John Monash, a Melbourne engineer of German–Jewish ancestry, and a part-time peace-time soldier. Promoted major-general in 1916, he commanded and trained the Australian 3rd Division. Lacking the easy sociability of other Australian commanders, he distinguished himself in the meticulous planning of operations so as not to squander lives: in 1918 he showed that an integrated assault by aircraft, tanks, artillery and infantry could indeed break the German line – if planned and executed with sufficient care and precision. For this feat he was knighted, and admired; but he inspired little affection and lived out the rest of his life in relative obscurity.[12] The public much preferred its notion of the Anzacs as lions led by donkeys. Many soldiers were promoted to corporal or sergeant in the field – and broken to private for indiscipline.[13] Uniformed larrikins, not their officers, became Australia's icons.

Australian and New Zealand legends shared similarities in loyalty to country, mates and an egalitarian ethic, combined with anti-British sentiment once the men recognized the nature of the campaign. These legends shared ingredients of initiative, resourcefulness and improvisation. Equipped with antiquated British technology – bayonets – against modern Turkish machine-guns, the Anzacs learnt that they were more likely to survive if they fired and stabbed rather than charged without bullets, in the British custom. Explained Charlie Clark, 67 years later: 'Faced with a joker coming at me with a bayonet I could shoot him straight away'.[14]

In the presence of Australians, however, New Zealand's icons were, theoretically, gentlemen. This is because Australians defined themselves against one reference point, the British, while New Zealanders – the smaller partner in the Anzac corps – defined themselves against both the British and the Australians. Taken together – or when they wished to emphasize their partnership – Australians and New Zealanders were Anzacs, a term which marked them off from the British. At the same time the New Zealand soldier who began the war as Tommy Fernleaf ended it as the Kiwi, a

THE CORRECT WAY

Plate 13.1 Cartoon from soldier's diary, which portrays the stereotypical contrast between the Anzacs' manly chins and the British chinless urban type. The soldiers made an issue of not saluting British officers. Reproduced by kind permission of W. D. McIntyre.

distinctive type, conscious that he was different.[15] 'Kiwi' served to distinguish New Zealanders from their 'Aussie' 'Digger' partners.[16] Soldiers and correspondents believed that the Kiwi was not only better than the English as bearer of all the pioneer's virtues, but also superior to the Australian larrikin digger, heir of the bush legend. Keith Sinclair deduced, wrongly, that there was no New Zealand stereotype akin to the 'drunken Aussie'. The quiet New Zealander had already emerged in Ormond Burton's 'Silent Division', who did not sing. In contrast to the loud digger, New Zealand's icon was a uniformed gentleman.[17]

Only a minority of Australian and New Zealand soldiers fought at Gallipoli; but it was this first (and failed) encounter, more than the interminable (but finally successful) Western Front which gave name, location and substance to the legends. This saga began when troops sailed to Egypt, where the Australian and New Zealand Army Corps was formed and trained for combat under the indifferent gaze of the sphinx. Before dawn on 25 April 1915, as part of a multinational force commanded by the British General Sir Ian Hamilton, they were carried through the Dardanelles and landed at Gallipoli. Before the end of the year they withdrew in an operation as delicate as the assault: remarkably, the retreat incurred no casualties.

The Anzacs of 1915 came to represent the highest form of citizenship, not merely as citizen soldiers but as volunteers. It was as volunteers that they demonstrated that Australia and New Zealand had a distinct role in race betterment through safeguarding British racial supremacy and producing (respectively) better-than-the-British and better-British. It was as volunteers, with the gallantry, chivalry and patriotism that this status signified, that they demonstrated their superiority and died gloriously. It was as volunteers that, sacrificing their lives for the best of causes, they gave birth to the nation at Anzac Cove in both national mythologies.[18]

On the first anniversary of the Gallipoli landing, Anzac Day was marked by a service in Westminster Abbey, attended by the king and queen. If it began as imperial ritual, it soon evolved into local and national forms. As soldiers found their ways home, Anzac Day became the focal celebration of those who survived and the families of those who did not. During the 1920s, on either side of the Tasman, Anzac Day became not only a holiday but a Holy Day. Children learned their patriotism in the parades, standing before local war memorials on 25 April, hearing about the Great Sacrifice. The message was not lost between Anzac Days, as schools, businesses and clubs boasted their honour boards. The dead were buried near where they died: ubiquitous and highly visible memorials became sites of mourning and memory at home, repairing a lack of memorials which had been slightly embarrassing.[19] These were large monuments in capital cities, and modest statues or civic halls in the towns and suburbs, places that were sacred, but not religious. There were eventually four or five thousand in Australia. Few were decorated by crosses; almost all carried the names of the dead, and many included the names of all who served. The purpose of that listing was to honour those who served, and perhaps to dishonour those (Irish, Catholic, pacifist, or all three) who did not.[20] Most striking about the small-town memorials is their simplicity. D. H. Lawrence described the Thirroul war memorial as:

> a statue in pale, fawnish stone, of a Tommy standing at ease, with his gun down at his side, wearing his puttees and his turned-up felt hat. The statue itself was about life size. ... Carved on the bottom step it said 'Unveiled by Granny Rhys'. A real township monument, bearing the names of everybody possible: the fallen, all those who donned khaki, the people who presented it, and Granny Rhys. Wonderfully in keeping with the place and its people, naive but quite attractive, with the stiff, pallid, delicate fawn-coloured soldier standing forever stiff and pathetic.[21]

Inga Clendinnen agrees with Inglis that the memorials are remarkable for their sadness and specificity: 'Nothing grandiose. Nothing larger than life. Just the exact and terrible size of death.' She believes that this 'obstinately horizontal view of society must somehow be connected to our convict past'.[22]

The divisiveness of that time does not loom large in the narrations of our own day. Stories of these deeds fertilized Australians' and New Zealanders' cultural soil like no others. Facts and foes have done nothing to diminish their force. If anything, they have fanned the flames of patriotic pride that make the legends a towering presence in the cultural landscape. In 1927 there were heated exchanges between Australian and British official historians, constituting the 'Gallipoli scandal':[23] since then the Australian version has held public sway. After several wars and a century of nationhood, it remains Australia's premier legend. The same can be said for New Zealand, where Anzac Day competes with Waitangi Day, yet is more hallowed and less contested than this rival date for (publicly) creating a nation.

The Gallipoli legend has no rivals, only contesting definitions and readings. C. E. W. Bean, the official press correspondent with the AIF, landed with the first troops and remained with them until he departed a day before their evacuation. His despatches and diaries played a seminal role in shaping the legend. Two other correspondents – Ellis Ashmead Bartlett and Lester Lawrence, both English – shared the reporting. Bean's preference for the frontline soldier's rather than the warship's experience flavoured his reports with a peculiar urgency and passion. They also endeared him to the men in front and then to generations of readers, even if his credentials as an 'Aussie bloke' were no stronger than those of other intellectuals.

Bean's prolific writings (his diaries and notes amounted to almost 300 volumes) form by far the most comprehensive and sustained account of the campaign. Embedded in them was the makings not only of the official history, but of the suffering and gallantry that laid the basis for the legend. Bean's role was critical in ensuring that one flowed naturally from the other. His sentimental links with and practical knowledge of the Australian bush allowed him to bridge the local and global experience of the bush struggle, and to ennoble both bushman and digger. A seasoned journalist, familiar with the outback and bush-lore, Bean linked the struggle and fortitude of the bushman with that of the digger. The stoic resourceful bushworker was dressd in uniform and sent to war. The lineage of the bush mythology thus stretched to the Gallipoli peninsula.

Bean was well aware of the significance of his writings, in many cases 'the only records available' of 'what happened'. Embarking for London, he felt the burden of his mission. His last diary entry of that fateful year reads:

> These diaries have been a weight on my mind – and so have my photos – I shan't be happy till I get them to a safe place, the diaries duplicated and the photos printed. A single shell or a submarine could destroy nine months' hard work and the best records we have of the Gallipoli campaign.[24]

In his time, Bean was celebrated for his professionalism as a journalist in the classical sense. Others have since praised his vision of the role of the modern war correspondent: 'to report, not criticize' or 'sensationalize'. More recently, yet others have pointed to the mythologizing aspects of Bean's accounts. The campaign, the official historian and the legend of Gallipoli

Plate 13.2 Gallipoli Peninsula, 1 July 1915. C. E. W. Bean's photograph and perspective. Courtesy of the Australian War Memorial.

remain embedded in the collective psyche of Australians as the holy trinity on the high altar of national identity.

Bean was not alone in gilding the lily. Decades of children learned to admire Simpson and his donkey, Simpson being a stretcher-bearer who used a donkey to evacuate wounded men from the front line at Gallipoli, without concern for his safety during the three weeks before he was killed. His heroism was real, but his name was Kirkpatrick; he was an Englishman who intended to work his passage home from Perth by enlisting; he was not unique in using a donkey; and his behaviour was rougher – and his politics more radical – than his first biographer chose to reveal.[25]

The agony of Gallipoli, the tragic waste of Australia's and New Zealand's best 'boys', the Mother Country's betrayal of her Antipodean contingent, the defeat, the shame of the retreat: all form part of the shared story. Revisionist histories emphasize certain aspects of the experience that laid the basis for Australia's national identity. Some even dare undermine the retreat with no casualties, arguing that the bloodlessness reflected the Turks' eagerness to be rid of them; that the Turks were well aware of the planned retreat and chose to let it happen. Recent histories undermining the moral force of the legend – fed by 'a press-inspired sense of national superiority', formed 'of an image of nationhood based around military achievement, real or imaginary' – still cannot avoid its impact. As late as 1995, one author argued in one breath that

'Nationhood based upon the soldier puts the cart before the horse', only to concede with another that

> what was almost unique, and what can be pinpointed, was the sense of nationhood that had supposedly been achieved, which was reflected in a new national image, as though Australians had now won the right to be sole occupants of the vast continent they inhabited. Their national image had changed in four years from that of a rather self-deprecating people into one of a people who had been encouraged to believe they'd almost won the war single-handedly.[26]

The language of the Anzac histories bears the weight of the mythology. It has a defining passion and poetry untypical of the Anzac himself: dour and unruly, vulgar and inarticulate. He is a true mate and that is the core of his philosophy, his claim to fame. In the words of their celebrants, the Anzac would hardly recognize himself and his time and place. Anzacs landed at a 'forbidding coast'. The Gallipoli peninsula – 'this harsh finger of land' – has 'a last-place-in-the-world atmosphere'. Its 'compelling beauty' bewitched new arrivals, only to turn on them. Those who struggled there – 'sweat-soaked and panting, through the spiky bush and up the heart-breaking cliffs and hills' – grew to hate it. The passions stirred by the campaign have not wilted. Seventy years later *'Damn the Dardanelles!' The Agony of Gallipoli* still raged with anger at the British betrayal.[27] The purpose of this book, the author explained, was 'to explain the defeat, to apportion the blame and to let the soldiers speak'. His penultimate chapter is called 'The Guilty Men'. His aim is to transcend the 'general condemnations' of the conduct of the campaign:

> It is time for History to be more specific in apportioning the guilt – for guilt is more appropriate than blame or responsibility – and more precise about the errors and inadequacies of the principal figures involved.[28]

Laffin's accused – a 'Who's Who' of the British military command, including Churchill as First Lord of the Admiralty, and the First Sea Lord, Admiral Lord Fisher – appear in a 'charge sheet' in alphabetical order. Circumstances outside their control may have deprived the Anzacs of victory, so Gallipoli must be a major disaster, blamed on imperial superiors for what one soldier called 'hell heaped up', and another 'sacred ground of lost endeavour'. The mission continues, of rescuing the reputations of 'the soldiers and sailors who went to their deaths in as pitiless a place of war as history can produce'.[29]

The legend moved into film with Peter Weir's *Gallipoli*. That realization erred in significant details: the historical consultant pointed out, for example, that the leading actors were too short to have passed the tests for enlistment in the AIF. Such defects did not weaken the story's immense power: during the weeks of preparation and filming, the 'extras' acquired some of the sardonic, laconic qualities of the soldiers whose lives they represented.[30] For vast audiences, *Gallipoli* 'proves' that British officers let down their Antipodean allies. While British historians would dispute that narrow reading, the Anzac story now has the credibility of a vivid, quasi-documentary account. *Gallipoli* can also be seen as the central narrative of a triptych. In *Breaker Morant*, the

Australians Morant and Handcock are sentenced to death by a British court martial during the Boer War (see chapter 12). In *Blood Oath*, a Second World War Japanese officer is guilty of inhumane treatment of Australian and other prisoners of war in Southeast Asia; but he is saved from the war crimes tribunal by Americans anxious to rebuild government in Tokyo.[31] Each film demonstrates the paranoia which often shadows the development of national sentiment; but Australia is the only society in the region which enjoys the financial and cultural resources to project that perspective globally.

One view is that New Zealand has two legends: the older imperial version which celebrates the superior British type raised in the Antipodes and the glory of the Great Sacrifice; and a reinvented, 'private' narrative, building on the Great Sacrifice, which embalms the horrors of war that the soldiers actually endured.[32] This narrative which invokes the men's hellish experience helped endorse the country's non-nuclear policy from the 1980s. It is part of an assertion of national identity which highlights the 'NZ' in Anzac and New Zealanders' distinctiveness from Australians. Similarly, 'popular memory' interviews of Australian veterans in the 1980s showed how interactions between experiences, memories, identities and the legend had changed over time. 'The role and influence of new particular publics is especially obvious in relation to Anzac memories', because new publics remake the legend.[33]

Since New Zealand had no film equivalent to Weir's to preserve the legend of its heroes, the novelist Maurice Shadbolt set out in the 1980s to create a living memorial to enshrine New Zealand experience and New Zealand places at Gallipoli, such as Quinn's Post and Chunuk Bair, rather than the Australian places featured in Weir's film, Lone Pine and the Nek. The result was a play, *Once on Chunuk Bair*, made into a film (1991). It highlights the New Zealanders' taking of Chunuk Bair on 8 August 1915. For Shadbolt, this is the day when New Zealanders excelled, were betrayed by the British, and lost their innocence. After Chunuk Bair disillusion set in and awareness crystallized that New Zealanders were different.[34] The hero of Chunuk Bair was Colonel W. G. Malone. A true gentleman in uniform, a lawyer, farmer, husband and father, he saved men from disease by sanitation, and by covering trenches against machine-gun fire. A natural leader, organized in defence, in attack he led his men and refused orders when these meant suicide. In the revised legend Malone, with 760 men of the Wellington Battalion and some Maori, took and held Chunuk Bair for 36 hours. They could see the Dardanelles, their ultimate objective, but the British relieved them too late. Only 70 returned. Malone was killed by British naval shellfire. In brief, New Zealanders took the high ground but had their hero Malone felled by the British, who then made him a scapegoat.[35] Shadbolt makes excessive claims for the New Zealanders' significance at Gallipoli and (by omitting the Australians) distorts the national legend just as much as Weir does in omitting the New Zealanders.[36]

New Zealand's public legend also differs in detail from the Australian, and in its cumulative meanings. The New Zealand army's adoption of the Lemon Squeezer as the ceremonial headdress can be read as a non-Australian memorial to Malone, because it began as the uniform of the 11th Taranaki

Rifles, Malone's regiment. More seriously, from 1916 Australia and New Zealand diverged over conscription. New Zealand passed the Military Service Act in 1916 without a referendum, because the government faced no dissent of the kind and degree which confronted the Australian government. Australia's prime minister in 1914 was Andrew Fisher of the Labor Party, who pledged 'the last man and the last shilling' but struggled to hold the party to that commitment. The Scot was replaced in 1915 by the tempestuous Welshman William Morris Hughes. Hughes lacked the parliamentary numbers to legislate conscription. When he tried to achieve by referendum what he could not win in parliament, he split the Labor Party. Federation, then, played a role alongside the early rise of Labor in distinguishing Australia's home front from New Zealand's. Hughes also helped provoke a 'no' vote by his abuse of power in general and of Catholics in particular. The long-established Australian Labor Party was split between those who insisted on the primacy of loyalty to empire and those who believed their first loyalty should be to class. By contrast, the New Zealand Labour Party formed in 1916 in reaction to conscription.

What Ken Inglis calls the left-wing or 'radical legend of conscription' would, logically, emphasize this difference in national traditions and the greater place in the Australian narrative of loyalty to class as well as race and empire. But as Inglis's work shows, patriotism overlaid class and sectarian identities, and opposition to the war and to conscription were not the same thing. He endorses Ernest Scott's account: it would have taken only 36,000 people to vote yes instead of no, for Australia to have conscripts; and conscription might have come if not for the Easter rising in Dublin in 1916:

> The suspicion entertained by [Ginger] Mick in 1914 and discarded later, that he was fighting so toffs could dine on pickled olives, became rather more widespread at home as the war went on. It became so for several reasons: because many Irish Catholics were alienated at Easter 1916; because the controversy over conscription gave an opportunity for all kinds of misgiving, from pacifism to Bolshevism, to cluster around a single unexpected issue; and also, more simply, because the balance of opinion and prejudice among working-class people in Australia was affected greatly by the departure of a very large proportion among them for the war. The working man who joined up was more likely than the working man who stayed behind to let pride of race overcome pride of class.[37]

The same could be said of New Zealanders. The 'shift of identity and allegiance from class to nation' which Inglis identifies in the verse of C. J. Dennis applied also in a shift from province or state to nation. Since loyalty is integral to identity, these shifts point to a developing layer of national identity among the troops – particularly after the August offensive at Gallipoli – not felt at home where people had no idea of the horrors, and did not want to know. But loyalty to nation and pride of race could mean different things. Did pride of race refer to the British race or human race? Or a nationalistic White Australia? Nationalism did not denote independence; so how far did loyalty to nation mean devotion to empire?

The different outcomes over conscription reinforce other signs that Australia and New Zealand occupied different slots on the spectrum of imperial loyalty. While both conscripted schoolboys into military training by 1911, Australia adhered more closely to the principle of conscription for home defence (in other words, for the nation). It drew a sharper line between defence of land and sea because it sought to be more independent than New Zealand did. Australia was also more divided in its secondary British and Irish allegiances and more overtly suspicious of Japan.[38] One widespread notion was that conscripts would defend White Australia against 'Asia', and only volunteers would serve overseas in Britain's wars. That notion set the terms of the conscription battle. As Hirst notes, the 'no' vote to conscription for the empire (as opposed to home defence or pride of race) elevated volunteers to an elite with a special place in and claim on the nation.[39] The best citizen was not just the soldier but the volunteer soldier.

This belief affected the tenor of the Australian and New Zealand legends and reconstruction of their masculine 'types'. Contrary to the radical legend, the absence of conscripts made Australian national identity – understood as masculine – more, not less, militaristic. Again little-but-more-loyal New Zealand could not personify in the Anzac a higher loyalty to empire when not all its heroes volunteered. New Zealanders were all volunteers until after Gallipoli, but once conscription was introduced in November 1916, a dual system operated, and that distinction muddies the public image of the soldiers.

New Zealand's greater emphasis in practice on 'thou shalt fight' invited the creation of a legend of natural nobility and heroism which proved more funereal than in Australia. (It would meld more comfortably 70 years later with the shifting meaning of the Anzac legend in the New Zealand national tradition, as it drew more directly on the remembered experiences of the few.) However, the shared Anzac experience and legends proved more significant than these divergences. That emblem of life and death, the poppy, came from Flanders' fields where the graves lie of thousands of New Zealanders and Australians; yet Gallipoli, the 'baptism of fire' and first test of manhood, is most mythologized, iconized and ritually remembered.

Maori volunteers, in Maui Pomare's words, 'won their spurs on the fields of Gallipoli'.[40] They represented at once Britannia's warriors and Aryan Maori who invoked the tradition of Tumatauenga, god of war. Those bicultural men of the Young Maori Party, Carroll, Ngata, Buck and Pomare, strove to win equality for Maori through acceptance as Pakeha. They believed Maori identity to be defined with, more than against, the British in the spirit of Article 3 of the Treaty of Waitangi. The Maori heroes of the Pioneer Battalion who proved themselves at Gallipoli (notably at Chunuk Bair) fulfilled the wish of Pomare and other Maori parliamentarians that Maori would fight, once they saw that other 'native' – Indian – troops were allowed to do so. For Buck (Te Rangihiroa) pride of race dictated that the Maori citizen soldier be the equal of others, and distinctive, in the empire. Maori volunteers 'gave a new and glorious tradition to the story of the Maori race'. To fight was the highest form of citizenship; it proved Maori 'the equal of the pakeha in the fullest sense', proved 'his hereditary fighting temper as

strong as ever'; and showed 'a larger patriotism' than loyalty to the tribe, tra-
ditionally the strongest source of identity. Doctors Pomare and Buck wanted
to affirm Maori patriotism and identity beyond the level of *iwi* and *hapu* and
thus demonstrate that Maori were the equal of Pakeha. For Maori, too,
Gallipoli was sacred ground because men spilt blood there.[41] In a symbolic
twist to the thread of kinship, it was commonly said that the blood of Maori
and Pakeha mingled in the trenches. The Pioneer Battalion marched into
their national story by shedding blood – while Aboriginal Australians, collectively though not individually, were shut out once again.

MOTHERS, SISTERS AND WIVES

> The mothers, the daughters, the sisters and wives of Australian and New
> Zealand soldiers now walk side by side down the dark path of pain and suffer-
> ing and sacrifice; theirs the common cross, theirs the one bright crown.[42]

Women, too, could participate in the test of national types, as 'mothers of
the race'. To adapt Masefield, mothers were proud to have produced 'the
finest body of young men ever brought together in modern times'.[43] They
heard often that 'YOU are responsible for the future of the race'.[44] Such
pride proved central to the idea of a homogeneously elite people who would
stand in ethnic solidarity: 'the nation'. Correspondingly, the Great War generated eugenic anxieties about the future which would prove central to these
societies' identities. Nagging doubts surfaced about sending the best and
bravest young men, fittest for fatherhood, to make the ultimate sacrifice. For
the majority, the Great Sacrifice by dying bloodily proved young men's manhood as well as loyalty to race and empire. Equally conditioned to believe in
the rightness of war, the anti's in the conscription debate wanted to keep
men home to hold the settler states they had created against Asian invasion,
and some, like Ettie Rout, to father healthy, virile citizens.

All sides invoked equality of sacrifice. Belief in equality of sacrifice led New
Zealand to conscription and Australia to its rejection. In the class version of
the argument, the labour movement demanded equality of sacrifice by capital,
urging the government to conscript wealth instead of working-class flesh and
blood. Ironically, war enhanced the belief that human life was sacred, with
consequences for mothers and babies. There was increasing agreement about
the sanctity of life as the war dragged on and casualty lists grew. Equality of
sacrifice acquired more meaning because of belief in the sanctity of life: why
should only some make the sacrifice for humankind's salvation?

War underscored how it is men's sacrifice which is remembered, though
mothers also sacrificed life – men and women are national subjects in different ways.[45] For women, the Great Sacrifice denoted not just the noble death
of beloved sons, brothers and sweethearts, but a mother's ultimate sacrifice,
not her own life, but her son's. 'What greater joy can a mother experience ...
than the knowledge that her life and example have helped her boy to live a
noble life, and, if needs be, to die a noble death?' asked New Zealand's

Bishop Averill, while verses told how mothers gave their 'bonny Boys…To Die for an Empire's name'.[46] War grief intensified the belief that 'woman's true destiny is sacrifice'[47] and to be truly patriotic she had to give the men she loved, particularly her sons. Their paragon was 'Volumnia, mother of Shakespeare's Coriolanus (who, had she a dozen sons, "had rather had eleven die nobly for their Country, than one voluptuously surfeit out of action")'.[48] This ideal ran from classical myth to Mary, mother of Jesus. Together with equality of sacrifice, the idea of noble maternal sacrifice fed a conviction that all mothers' sons should share the same dangers and all mothers, sisters and wives share the same fear and grief. Hence the majority of Australian and New Zealand women came to support conscription, to make fairer the burden of sacrifice and grief which saw all the sons in one family die or suffer pain or damage, and none in another.[49]

War, then, is gendered, and so is patriotism and the whole 'imagined community'. For women, patriotism amounted to motherhood. As Truby King emphasized: 'Perfect motherhood *is* perfect patriotism'. Citizenship required women to be wives and mothers, in service to the family, and to sacrifice their men for the nation and their race. Citizen mothers could serve in war only as non-combatants. As mothers, however, they were creating Australian and New Zealand identities. They knew that they were 'creating a nation' by building a sense of sameness, oneness and shared values in home and school, and among their men away fighting. Women were not duped into being mothers. They were mothers, and used this identity and its symbolism in contributing to the war effort and to negotiate spaces for women and children in the 'nation', only with greater imperial fervour than in the nineteenth century because of war and ethnic anxieties.

Australia and New Zealand saw themselves as progressive White Dominions where the early vote for women allowed them to aspire to grand ideals. For women this entailed to 'rear and train a noble race'.[50] Having already invoked 'mother influence' to claim a place in the body politic, they did so again in the war, consciously investing in national and racial identity by constructing themselves and being constructed as 'maternal figures'.[51] By giving life but more so by giving life in death, the 'mothers of the race' perversely increased life's value.

The grief of the bereaved worked its way into national narratives, producing secondary narratives of Woman as Mother – white, Pacific Islander and Maori. Just as the volunteer soldier represented the highest form of citizenship for men and supposedly for humanity, the soldier's mother represented the highest form of maternal citizenship. By patriotic and heroic sacrifice, Woman as Mother was further elevated in settler societies, at least rhetorically. The 'ordeals of the silent un-khakied mortals' found speech in women's verse, as did Lorna Anker's 'bereft grandmother' in *Ellen's Vigil*:

Benjamin Isaac Tom
Passchendaele Ypres and Somme
three ovals float
on the cold wall
plastered whiter
than their bones,

young, khaki'd
their bud-tender eyes
premoniton filled.

Ellen,
Her three boys gone,
transplanted seventy years
from Lurgan's linen
no longer counts crops
in season
but digs diligently, delicately,
digs down
further down
her spade searching
her garden for
three lost sons
Thomas Isaac and Ben.[52]

Here we have a parallel tradition to the Anzac legend, which could support it and change its meaning, or develop an alternative identity. Women's grief had much in common with the 'private myth', warning of the horrors of war.

WOMEN'S WAR SERVICE

The Great War nevertheless revealed how keen women were to join the stoush. Proud and patriotic, most wanted to be active participants and clearly saw themselves as at one with the men. New Zealand's Dr Elizabeth Gunn, 'lady doctor', is one example; in 1915–17 she 'donned uniform and went importantly off to war', as a captain in the New Zealand Army Medical Corps, only to be posted to a local measles hospital. Dr Agnes Bennett took herself to Egypt where she worked for the Army Medical Corps without a formal commission. Australia's women doctors were not allowed to join the Australian Army Medical Corps. While this may signify that New Zealand women won a relatively larger space, the difference was marginal and only two women doctors donned uniform.

Nurses came closest to service as honorary men through 'active service' overseas, including close to the front line in France. They served on hospital ships at Anzac Cove, and in Egypt. Some lost their lives: 23 Australians and ten New Zealanders when the *Marquette* was torpedoed in 1915. The nurses' memorial chapel at Christchurch Hospital is the only New Zealand memorial to nurses from the Great War, built in memory of three local nurses who died on the *Marquette*. Australian nurses gained their memorial in 1999, exactly a century after the first of them served in the Boer War. Ken Inglis observes that the women named on Australian war memorials are nurses, whose veiled figures appear, obscurely, inside Melbourne's Shrine of Remembrance and, more visibly, on Sydney's Anzac Memorial. Officials solved the problem of classifying nurses' service by turning them into 'mothers of the race' who tended 'weary and wounded men ... with loving care'.[53]

Women who wanted to serve but were not allowed to enlist joined patriotric groups which raised funds and provided 'comforts' for men. During the Great War membership of the imperialist Australian Women's National League rose to become the largest non-Labor organization in Australia, active in fundraising, soldiers' comforts, encouraging recruitment and conscription. The governor-general's wife in both countries led fundraising initiatives, sewing and knitting, preparing Red Cross food parcels and bandages, and tending returned soldiers.[54] New Zealand women's patriotic organizations numbered 920 by the end of the war, combined as the Women's Patriotic Societies of New Zealand. White Feather Leagues called for conscription and pursued eligibles and refused to dance with 'shirkers', to shame them into volunteering. Lady Stout established the Anti-German League to hound assumed traitors with German-sounding names, while the Women's National Reserve knitted, made up parcels, ran canteens and conducted street collections. Of all this work, knitting had the greatest symbolic significance. *Her Excellency's Knitting Book* stated:

For the Empire and for Freedom
We all must do our bit;
The men go forth to battle,
The women wait – and knit.[55]

New Zealand again showed it was not Australian when the governor-general's wife, Lady Liverpool, and Mrs Miria Pomare, wife of Dr Maui Pomare, joined forces to raise money for Lady Liverpool's and Mrs Pomare's Maori Soldiers' Fund – a consciously joint effort in 1915, to support the soldiers of the Pioneer Battalion. Maori women's committees sent parcels to Maori and Pacific islanders including delicacies such as mutton birds; and Miria Pomare reportedly knitted socks for every soldier in the first contingent, adding a gold sovereign to each pair.[56] Wives of Maori parliamentarians sought like their husbands to secure a position in the dominant culture and to prove their equality through the Maori Soldiers' Fund. Their work could be read as assimilationist, accepting an imperial paradigm, but they did not see it that way; they strove to show how their people were bicultural and equal, like Miria Pomare herself.

Women also played a key part in constructing the requirement of racial purity, as moral mothers of the nation. To be morally pure was to be racially pure, in the eyes of the social purity lobby. Respectability, predicated on a sober breadwinner, was integral to the physical, mental and moral betterment of the race; and moral mothers intent on obliging men to change for the sake of women and children saw the family as the essence of empire and nation. The Women's Christian Temperance Union won a major victory for its view of the collective imaginary with 6 o'clock closing in Australia and New Zealand. New Zealanders voted for pubs to close at 6 p.m. in 1917 – after the largest petition in the dominion's history – while South Australia, New South Wales, Victoria and Tasmania all shut their pubs at 6 p.m. by 1916 after referenda. This expression of gendered identity equated patriotism and national efficiency, and protecting racial strength, with sending men home for dinner. Through 6 o'clock closing Woman as Mother made her vivid mark on the shared national stories.

PACIFISTS

A handful of objectors with mainly Irish, socialist and Christian fundamentalist loyalties – and in New Zealand, particular *iwi* loyalties – refused to fight because they rejected the identity of soldier or the war as immoral, preferring prison. Dissenters helped establish a peace tradition which would become mainstream in New Zealand in the 1980s and help to change the meaning of the Anzac legend. The best-known Pakeha objector, Archibald Baxter, father of the poet James K. Baxter and author of *We Will Not Cease*, found his story of courage and torment merged with Anzac myth because he was sent to the front where his torture under fire merged with the soldiers' experience.[57]

A dedicated minority of women who shared these sympathies argued that women as 'mothers of the world' bore a special responsibility as guardians of moral purity for the entire human race to promote peace and arbitration to end armed conflict. Christian socialists among them protested that the mothers of the nation did not bring lives into the world to be used in the interests of the capitalist class; while an overlapping set of feminists who campaigned for the vote for women co-opted the language of arbitration as a substitute for war as well as industrial strife. They argued that the role of mothers was to educate children in 'reason', not 'brute force'.[58] As mothers, they were responsible for educating about arbitration and peace. Wilhelmina Sherriff Bain caused a stir by airing such views during the Boer War, emphasizing that mothers 'were the arbiters of destiny – the real educators of the next generation'. In fulfilling this 'privilege', 'it would place women beside men in influential positions, so that they might help to mould thought and public action'.[59] By perceiving arbitration as the exercise of domestic skills in the public sphere, they claimed arbitration as a value integral to feminine as well as masculine identity. The demand that women have a 'direct voice in the affairs of the nation' expressed a clear intent to belong in national narratives.[60]

Like most pro-war groups, the anti's also co-opted mother arguments, and with the same ultimate goal, to improve the world. Woman as Mother – specifically White Woman as Mother – blanketed other particular identities. 'Mother of the race' could mean the human, not the British race, and branches of the Women's International League for Peace and Freedom emphasized this global responsibility. Thus the war brought the universal warrior/mother dichotomy into sharp focus. The favourite verse of feminist pacifists came from the English Adela Pankhurst and Cecilia John:

I didn't raise my son to be a soldier
I brought him up to be my pride and joy,
Who dares to put a musket on his shoulder
To kill some other mother's darling boy?[61]

Some Maori were pacifists. War provided evidence of different meanings attached to Maori identity and to ethnic identities more generally because individuals and groups thought of pride of race in different terms. It showed how being Maori denoted, first, pride of *hapu* and *iwi*, and, second, a condition in relation to Pakeha. The divide had been cut in the nineteenth century between *iwi* and *hapu* who claimed local sovereignty under the Treaty of Waitangi and those who imbibed a particularist pan-Maori identity and allegiance to the crown, also derived from the treaty. (Before Maori urbanization, pride of *iwi* was a universal – if institutionalized – condition of being Maori in Maori terms; whereas for Pakeha, to be Maori meant a universal Maori identity, while *iwi* identity amounted to primitive tribalism – as Pomare and Buck thought.) A striking exemplar of dissent and how that affected identity was Princess Te Puea, granddaughter of Tawhiao, the Maori king, who opposed the Maori MPs' support for the war and hence also the position of Mrs Pomare. Te Puea represents, with Miria Pomare, how ethnicity trumped gender. Maori volunteers included in the Anzac legend as members of the Pioneer Battalion came mainly from *kupapa* (friendly) tribes which had supported the government during the Britanno-Maori Wars. The King movement wanted no part in the legend: the Kingitanga asserted that its men should not fight, and none did.

For Te Puea loyalty to the Kingitanga and her Waikato people came first. As a Kingitanga leader she denied that Maori owed loyalty as British subjects. For her, Maori identity denoted a different relation to the nation; a recurring theme in New Zealand. In response to calls for men to fight for king and country, Te Puea replied: 'We've got a king. But we haven't got a country'.[62] Her people had their own king and King movement, while the land wars left Tainui with their grievance, the *raupatu*, the unjust confiscation of most of their land. The traumatic cross-cultural encounter and the weeping sores left by the wars themselves also forged a pacifist tradition through the prophet movements. Waikato had not fought again, according to Tawhiao's prophecy, and Te Puea conveyed her ancestor's message of peace. She urged Maori men to oppose the conscription which the government punitively extended only to Waikato Maori in 1917 in response to the alleged disloyalty of the King movement. In the government's view, including that of its Maori members, Maori owed loyalty to the 'nation' understood in Pakeha terms, as soldiers: for the Kingitanga the Great War was a Pakeha matter.

In the remote Urewera country, the prophet Rua Kenana revealed a parallel gap between some Maori and Pakeha perceptions and the diversity of Maori experience.[63] Rua led his Tuhoe people in opposing the Great War. The Tuhoe remained suspicious of Pakeha because their best land was confiscated in the 1860s as reprisal for the supposed 'Hauhau rebellion' and their support for the prophet Te Kooti. Rua realized his people's poverty when he worked for Pakeha. Conversely the Tuhoe, late to encounter Pakeha, attracted settler resentment for the land they retained as a 'landocracy'. They became targets for the settler ambition to divest them of 'waste' land, for which Rua's opposition to volunteering for the Pioneer Battalion and his involvement in the sly grog trade (whisky helped his visions) provided pretexts to remove him. His arrest in 1916 and unlawful imprisonment for sedition exposed the continual struggle over land and sovereignty and how this translated in the Pakeha lexicon into 'disloyalty': his resistance to recruiting was distorted by rumour and misreading of his visions into sedition and support for the Kaiser.

THE ODD WOMAN OUT: ETTIE ROUT

It remained for Ettie Rout to expose sources of identity in relation to gender as well as the state and ethnicity, by straying beyond the prescribed moral code. She was excluded from the nation by women. She could belong, from a woman's viewpoint, as a New Woman and so long as she assumed the mantle of maternal identity, as when she provided canteens for the troops in Egypt. But she was vilified at home as a wicked woman for breaching the code of moral motherhood. Ettie agreed that woman's racial duty was as Mother, but had her own idea of what this meant. She sinned because she refused to see venereal disease as a metaphor for immorality and treated it as a medical problem. Her campaign for safe sex for soldiers in France made her a 'whore' to women's groups yet, to the soldiers, a guardian angel.[64] If men want beer and women, she argued, then give them beer and clean women. The Australian and New Zealand governments adopted her prophylactic kits without acknowledgement, while censoring her under war regulations. Ettie offended women's constructs of manhood and womanhood, predicated on moral purity, as the WCTU made clear in 1918 when they expressed their

> utter abhorrence of the effrontery of Miss Ettie Rout in implying that our boys must be supplied with remedies to make wrongdoing safe, & sin easy. We contend that we send our sons to fight for purity & righteousness & we utterly discountenance everything that slackens moral fibre & self-control, & place on record our emphatic repudiation of prophylactics & the woman who advocates them.[65]

She had to be suppressed in constructing the legend, to be rediscovered only on the eve of the centenary of women's suffrage.

The Anzac legends sharpened the gender divide, for instance through Anzac Day parades for men, yet women ensured that they were not excluded from the nation, as they understood it: witness Ettie's fate; they showed that they belonged by shutting her out. We may conclude that the New Zealand versions of the legend are more friendly to women. This brings us to Hobsbawm's question, whether the 'nation' is an ethnic group or a sovereign political entity. We need to distinguish between the cultural and political dimensions of identity in relation to the state. Maori did or did not belong depending on their land and kin allegiances; while women were excluded from the Anzac legend as civilians, as non-combatants, but included culturally, as mothers.

The Great War maimed a generation of men, divided families, unleashed torrents of grief, and created legends. Veterans, celebrated in myth, were neglected as returned soldiers. They did not want to talk: their memories were too horrible to share, and the publics chose not to know that men died squealing like pigs, of gore, filth and terror. Seventy years passed before the survivors spoke and their stories regilded the Anzac legends for new groups. Gallipoli became a sacred site from 1915, part of Australia and New Zealand

Plate 13.3 Anzacs and their Protector. Australian, New Zealand and South African soldiers in Paris, August 1918. 'The lady' is Ettie Rout, famous and notorious for making contraceptives available to soldiers. Australians are identifiable by their slouch hats, and New Zealanders by their lemon-squeezers. Courtesy of the Australian War Memorial.

as Anzac Cove. Grief furrowed the landscapes, in public monuments and public policy, as death and grief renewed the importance of birth and life.

NOTES

1 And reproduced in the *Sydney Morning Herald*, 26 April 1999.
2 Robert Aldrich, *The French Presence in the South Pacific, 1842–1940*, London, 1990, ch. 9.
3 Australian Labor government pledge, cited in J. B. Hirst, 'Australian Defence and Conscription: A Re-assessment. Part 1', *Australian Historical Studies*, 25: 101 (1993), 609.
4 K. S. Inglis, *Sacred Places: War Memorials in the Australian Landscape*, Melbourne, 1999, ch. 2.
5 Ibid., 74.
6 Bill Gammage, *The Broken Years: Australian Soldiers in the Great War*, Canberra, 1974.
7 Ibid., 4.
8 Gunner Higgins, quoted in ibid., 21.

9   John Rickard, *Australia: A Cultural History*, 2nd edn. The Present and the Past, ed. Michael Crowder and Juliet Gardiner, London and New York, 1988, 117.

10   Cited by Richard White, *Inventing Australia: Images and Identity 1688–1980*, Sydney, 1981, 127, quoting McQueen.

11   Avner Offer, *The Great War: An Agrarian Interpretation*, Oxford, 1989.

12   Geoffrey Serle, *John Monash: A Biography*, Melbourne, 1982.

13   Gammage, *The Broken Years*.

14   Charlie Clark, interviewed weeks before his death in 1982, remembering Chunuk Bair, in Maurice Shadbolt, *Voices of Gallipoli*, Auckland, 1988, 64.

15   'Tommy Fernleaf' featured (drawn by Amy B. Dawson) in British peaked cap, in *Countess of Liverpool's Gift Book of Art and Literature*, Christchurch, 1915.

16   Inglis, *Sacred Places*, 84. 'Digger' was the men's name for the Anzacs.

17   Keith Sinclair, *A Destiny Apart*, Auckland, 1986. See also Jock Phillips, *A Man's Country? The Image of the Pakeha Male – A History*, Auckland, 1987, 158–92.

18   The term 'public myth' is from Phillips, *A Man's Country?*, 163–9. For a feminist critique, see Patricia Grimshaw, Marilyn Lake, Ann McGrath and Marian Quartly, *Creating a Nation*, Melbourne, 1994, 211.

19   Inglis, *Sacred Places*, chs 2 and 3.

20   Jock Phillips and Ken Inglis, 'War Memorials in Australia and New Zealand: A Comparative Survey', *Australian Historical Studies*, 24: 96 (1991), 179–91. On New Zealand, see M. Sharpe, 'Anzac Day in New Zealand 1916–1939', *New Zealand Journal of History*, 15: 2 (Oct. 1981), 97–114.

21   D. H. Lawrence, *Kangaroo*, cited in Inglis, *Sacred Places*, 5–6.

22   Inga Clendinnen, second 1999 Boyer Lecture on ABC Radio, November 1999.

23   Kevin Fewster (ed.), *Gallipoli Correspondent: The Frontline Diary of C. E. W. Bean*, Sydney, 1983, 9.

24   Ibid., 12–14; quotation from 202.

25   Peter Cochrane, *Simpson and the Donkey: The Making of a Legend*, Melbourne, 1992.

26   John F. Williams, *The Quarantined Culture: Australian Reactions to Modernism 1913–39*, Cambridge, 1995, 80–1.

27   John Laffin, 'Damn the Dardanelles', *Sun*, Melbourne, 1985.

28   Ibid., 197.

29   Ibid., 6.

30   Gammage, *The Broken Years*.

31   Hank Nelson, 'Write History: Reel History', in Brij Lal (ed.), *Pacific Islands History: Journeys and Transformations*, *Journal of Pacific History* monograph, Canberra, 1992, 184–202.

32   Jock Phillips, *A Man's Country?*, ch. 4; Jock Phillips, '75 Years since Gallipoli', in David Green (ed.), *Towards 1990: Seven Leading Historians Examine Significant Aspects of New Zealand History*, Wellington, 1989, ch. 7.

33   Alistair Thomson, *Anzac Memories: Living with the Legend*, Melbourne, 1994, 185.

34   Maurice Shadbolt, *Voices of Gallipoli*, Auckland, 1988, introduction; Maurice Shadbolt, *Once on Chunuk Bair*, Auckland, 1982.

35   Christopher Pugsley, *Gallipoli: The New Zealand Story*, Auckland, 1984, ch. 10.

36   Shadbolt, *Voices of Gallipoli*, 9.

37   Inglis, 'The Anzac Tradition', quotation from *Anzac Remembered: Selected Writings of K. S. Inglis*, ed. John Lack, Melbourne, 1998, 35.

38   Hirst, 'Australian Defence and Conscription'; F. B. Smith, *The Conscription Plebiscites in Australia 1916–17*, Melbourne, 1971, 20.

39   Hirst, 'Australian Defence and Conscription', 627.

40 Pomare cited in Michael King, *Te Puea: A Biography*, Auckland, 1977, 84.

41 King, *Te Puea*, 79–82, 84. Quotations from Buck, cited by King, *Te Puea*, 80.

42 *Canterbury Times*, 26 January 1916, cited in Jane Tolerton, *Ettie: A Life of Ettie Rout*, Auckland, 1992, 104.

43 Cited by White, *Inventing Australia*, 129.

44 For example, by Truby King in *Save the Babies*.

45 Lake asks if 'women' and 'nation' are 'always at odds' or if men and women are national subjects in different ways, in 'Women and Nation in Australia: The Politics of Representation', *Australian Journal of Politics and History*, 43: 1 (1997), 41.

46 'The Cry Of the Mothers to the Brewers', cited in Tolerton, *Ettie*, 167.

47 A phrase used, for example, by New Zealand's Dr Doris Gordon.

48 Cited in Inglis, 'Men, Women, and War Memorials', *Anzac Remembered*, 117.

49 For example, Paul Baker, *King and Country Call: New Zealanders, Conscription and the Great War*, Auckland, 1988, 30.

50 M. Hutching, ' "Mothers of the World": Women, Peace and Arbitration in Early Twentieth-century New Zealand', *New Zealand Journal of History*, 27: 2 (Oct. 1993), 181.

51 Megan Woods, 'Re/producing the Nation: Women Making Identity in New Zealand, 1906–1925', MA thesis, University of Canterbury, 1997. On Australia, see Lake, 'Women and Nation in Australia'.

52 L. S. Anker, *Ellen's Vigil*, Christchurch, 1996, 24.

53 Inglis, 'Men, Women, and War Memorials', in *Anzac Remembered*, 99.

54 P. Maclean, in J. Beaumont (ed.), *Australia's War, 1914–18*, Sydney, 1995, ch. 3.

55 Sandra Coney, *Standing in the Sunshine: A History of New Zealand Women Since They Won the Vote*, Auckland, 1993, 312.

56 Tania Rei, 'Lady Liverpool's and Mrs Pomare's Maori Soldiers' Fund 1915–21', in Anne Else (ed.), *Women Together: A History of Women's Organizations in New Zealand*, Wellington, 1993, 23–4.

57 Writing helped: his book owed much to notes taken by his wife, Millicent Macmillan Brown, daughter of Professor Macmillan Brown of the University of Canterbury, and that institution's first lady graduate, Helen Connon, the first woman to graduate MA (Hons) in the British empire. This became a tradition within a tradition, a radical, left-wing, peace tradition emerging from a notable Christchurch family. Christchurch was home to Pakeha pacifists: the term 'barmy Christchurch', favoured by Aucklanders, mocked this under-belly of alternative identities.

58 J. Damousi, 'Socialist Women and Gendered Space: The Anti-conscription and Anti-war Campaigns of 1914–18', *Labour History*, 60: 1 (May 1991), 1–15; Hutching, 'Mothers of the World', 173–85.

59 Wilhelmina Sherriff Bain, 'Peace and Arbitration', May 1900, in M. Lovell-Smith (ed.), *The Woman Question*, Auckland, 1992, 224–8.

60 Quotation from Hutching, 'Mothers of the World', 183.

61 Anne Summers, *Damned Whores and God's Police*, 2nd edn, Melbourne, 1994, 427.

62 Cited in King, *Te Puea*, 78; also Baker, *King and Country Call*, 213.

63 Judith Binney, G. Chaplin et al., *Mihaia: The Prophet Rua Kenana and His Community at Maungapohatu*, Auckland, 1990.

64 Tolerton, *Ettie*.

65 Cited in T. Tulloch, 'State Regulation of Sexuality in New Zealand 1880–1925', Ph.D. dissertation, University of Canterbury, 1997, 238.

[14] *ANXIOUS PEACE*

The 1920s were years of contradiction, 'roaring twenties', but also the 'troubled twenties'. They and the 1930s were years of social experiment; but the laboratories of the interwar years were much more anxious than they had been at the turn of the century. In economic insecurity and political uncertainty, grand development schemes were proposed and foundered, and the expansion of home amenities and leisure was framed by the Great War and Depression. In Australia and New Zealand new (mainly American) technologies, suburbia and consumerism began shaping landscapes and dreamscapes.

War and depression encouraged the dominions to fashion beliefs about themselves which fitted poorly with world economic trends. Constructions of race and metaphors of claiming the land through settlement, for example, generated empire settlement schemes which were deluded and outmoded. At the same time Australia and New Zealand built on their colonial heritage to claim as modern, their romantic inheritance as places in which to rear healthy children and strong bodies which were exemplars of their 'national fitness'.

> It has rightly been decided that this should be not only a 'white man's country', but as completely British as possible. We ought to make every effort to keep the stock sturdy and strong, as well as racially pure. ... The Great War revealed that from [the pioneers'] loins have sprung some of the finest men the world has ever seen, not only in physical strength, but in character and spirit.

This legacy must be developed, urged health and education professionals.[1] Building the child and the nation, and a white world, acquired special meaning in Australia and New Zealand as ingredients of mutually dependent yet separate national mythologies.

FINANCIAL INSECURITY

Australia and New Zealand shared the problems of dependence on Britain in defence, trade and finance. Power – and marketing national identity – remained in the hands of those who valued the British relationship and accepted London's criteria of sound financial management.[2] Australia and New Zealand became more aware of their independent financial identities.

Both were depressed before the world crisis, because of sagging export prices and declining terms of trade, and were highly vulnerable to external shock. The end of the war and the return to a civil economy in the early 1920s only reminded them of their vulnerability in a British-dominated world market.

The Anzac partners, however, accumulated different sources of debt. New Zealand sought to farm its way out of trouble. The Dairy Export Control Board made six ten-minute movies for Britain in the 1920s, including 'The Dairy Cow as an Empire Builder', to distinguish New Zealand and its dairy products. Pitched at women as consumers, the films expressed a form of domestic imperialism. If Britain would not agree to imperial preference for its kin and allies, then New Zealand farmers would appeal directly to British housewives to prefer the 'pure quality foods produced in their own Empire overseas'.[3] Australia turned instead to manufacturing and industry, borrowing heavily in an ambitious programme for 'Australia Unlimited'. States rather than the federal government borrowed to finance urban and industrial expansion on a scale much larger than in New Zealand.

Australia's population grew by 20 per cent in the 1920s, partly because of migrants under the 1922 British Empire Settlement Act; the British component of 261,000 – 80 per cent assisted – comprised the bulk, intended to propel another round of pioneering and 'open up the country' for development.[4] A few thousand Italians and other Europeans accounted for the rest. As usual, few settled on the land, and those who did were mired in debt. There was a high repatriation rate. At Margaret River in Western Australia, where it was hoped that British migrants would 'force the pace' of development in bushland which had 'defied' settlement, and, through dairy farming, make Western Australia more self-sufficient in food and less dependent on the eastern states, this closer settlement scheme and others like it were doomed.[5]

Unfulfilled expectations fuelled banking difficulties and also flowed from debt. Australia became London's biggest borrower, with an 'extravagant' reputation, and the more the United Kingdom urged restraint, the more the states sought an independent line.[6] The Commonwealth tried in vain to curb state borrowing. Western Australia grew sufficiently disillusioned with the eastern states to vote to secede in a 1933 referendum, although the movement fizzled. New Zealand was frustrated that London did not distinguish it from Australia, so it created its own Reserve Bank in 1933 to assert a separate identity. Political uncertainty heightened anxieties. Disaffected New Zealanders elected conservative minority governments, but conservative politics also dominated federal Australia from the conscription debacle of 1917 into the 1930s. Labor clung on in the states, especially in Queensland (to 1950) and New South Wales.

Urban drift continued, as did the spread of suburbia which, by the early 1920s, was home to most Australians. Suburbia shaped and enclosed lives characterized by a detached house on its own block, a motor car and labour-saving devices – if a family could afford them – all impelled by self-improvement and bought with borrowed money. Consumerism and conformism became signature themes of an 'Australian way of life', shared with New Zealand. The trans-Tasman neighbours already had home ownership rates above 50 per cent by 1911, and these rates rose to 70 per cent in the next 50 years. Advances to soldiers for house-building proved the most successful form of soldier settlement. In Australia home loans were readily available through War Service Home Schemes at five per cent, building societies and government housing, and in New Zealand through State Advances, which offered home loans of up to 95 per cent for a suburban house and section. A Californian bungalow, the basic structure at the bottom end of the market, cost £1,000 or £1 a week at standard low mortgage rates. Many designs came from a pattern book. New Zealand, which adapted its low-cost bungalows from California and Australia, enjoyed a suburban boom in the 1920s, especially in Auckland, with speculation in property values by land speculators, builders, building societies and new home-owners. By the 1920s, some could not then build or sell their over-priced land.[7] Motor cars were also increasingly accessible: a Chevrolet costing £545 in 1920 cost less than half that six years later. Thus the minor boom in car registrations in Australia which had more cars for its population than anywhere except the United States; car numbers soared from 92,000 to 571,000 before the end of the decade. The number of cars on New Zealand roads more than doubled.

A study of advertisements suggests that modernity brought radical changes to the domestic sphere. New marketing strategies targeting 'the housewife' created ever greater needs for 'home comforts', which fostered new industries. By the 1930s new women's magazines – *Australian Women's Weekly*, *New Idea* and *New Zealand Woman's Weekly* – reinforced the stereotype of the modern housewife and advertised 'new ideas' of childrearing, feeding by the clock, and scientific household management. Electricity was a key development, and New Zealand's rural landscape began to carry the imprint of hydro-electric power. Electricity lit up homes and showed the dust. By 1923 a third of Australian homes were electrified. Of this lucky third, 75 per cent had electric irons, 20 per cent radiators, only two per cent vacuum cleaners, and one per cent toasters and kettles. Most Australian and New Zealand homes had no washing machines or refrigerators until the 1950s. Only the comfortably middle class could enjoy the trappings of a consumer society, a new house in the suburbs and resources for scientific mothering, 'domestic economy' and 'domestic hygiene'.[8]

The 1920s saw the beginnings of mass (media) culture. Radio, introduced in 1913, came into its own with twenty stations – government and private – in Australia by mid-decade, and a jump from 130,000 to 270,000 licences between 1926 and 1928. New Zealand created a national broadcasting system in 1925. In their suburban bungalows, people turned to 'the wireless' for music, talks, plays, news, sport and children's programmes. The power of this first medium of mass entertainment did not escape official notice. Radio attracted heavy censorship.

Cinema – silent movies, cartoons, serials, romances and tragedies – blossomed. Admission was cheap. It was mainly American movies that audiences rushed to see, though British documentaries also had an appeal. Hollywood caught the imagination of the glamour-hungry, even if some worried about 'immorality' in American films. The Americanness of the cinema and mass culture generally was vital to their success. Local popular culture suffered a set-back, at least in celluloid, and Australia's fledgling film industry – responsible, Australians believed, for the first ever 'feature film' (now lost) and some good silent films – folded. In New Zealand, Rudall Hayward adapted James Cowan's history of the *New Zealand Wars* to produce *Rewi's Last Stand* in 1927, a benevolently paternal portrait of Pakeha settler pitted against brave Maori. This effort at biculturalism was sadly overlooked because New Zealand history was to be a Pakeha story, and Maori merely the prologue.[9] Fifty years passed before Australian film revived and an industry took root, with state and federal funding. New Zealand's industry revived via a tax loophole in 1981.

The coming of jazz (coinciding with the invention of the phonograph and the cheap record) also involved cultural negotiation. Regarded by the Establishment as tasteless, subversive of morality and above all Black, jazz reached Australia via Chicago rather than New Orleans. The gesture did not assuage opposition from an unlikely alliance of moralists, higher classes and local musicians.

The 'troubled twenties' was an era of unmet aspirations, political and industrial strife, unemployment (never below six per cent) and hardship endured by many ex-diggers. The social polarization sparked by the conscription campaigns continued, fed by working-class bitterness at deteriorating living standards. Postwar militancy was widespread throughout the trade union movement and the Labor Party. Suspicion against so-called old and new enemies of empire – Fenians, Bolsheviks and socialists – was among the legacies of the war and its aftermath. It fed hatred and fear, as loyalists with political muscle and scores to settle moved on their targets. Hughes, his conscription bitterness undimmed by victory, detained Irish dissidents. The rise of Bolshevism and the birth of Soviet Russia in 1917 bred deep suspicion which grew apace with disturbing new developments at home such as the 1917 general strike and the founding of the Communist Party of Australia in 1920 – described by a founder as 'devoutly Stalinist'[10] – and the Labor Party's adoption of the socialization objective a year later. The ferment and fanaticism in the radical Left stirred fears of communist subversion and prompted secret right-wing organizations. John Monash, most famous of Great War 'diggers', formed his own militia, 'The Specials'. By far the most significant militia was the 'New Guard', formed in 1931 by ex-officers of the AIF. With a membership in the tens of thousands – many of them old diggers – this quasi-military, quasi-secret organization was entrusted with nothing less than upholding national traditions and national honour. The Right was usurping the role of Labor as self-appointed guardian of national tradition. Labor's identification with anti-conscription, support for the Irish national rebellion and even Bolshevism and revolution abroad had eroded its moral ascendancy. The party that led the nation into war emerged stained by charges of disloyalty. The rise of 'the Digger' in place of 'the Bush Worker' as the embodiment of national identity crystallized radicalism's fall.

'The Digger', uncontested icon, supreme unifying symbol of the ideals of the people and Commonwealth of Australia, and New Zealand, was caught

Plate 14.1 The Jazz Arrives at Dingo Flat according to *Aussie* magazine, 1920. Courtesy of the National Library of Australia.

between Left and Right in contesting custody of his memory. The Left framed a Digger legend within the broader anti-imperialist tradition of the convict-cum-bushman, and struggles to free Australia from the shackles of empire; and the Right, to reinforce imperial ties. The outcome was never in question. Custody went to the Right which won hands down as the Nationalists forged an alliance with the Returned Soldiers' and Sailors' Imperial League of Australia (RSSILA), and in New Zealand, the Reform Party allied with the Returned Servicemen's Association (RSA). The conservatives guaranteed stability and order, and vigilance against socialism, in return for the RSL's and RSA's authority over Anzac Day and employment preference for ex-servicemen. Implicit in these deals were also unrivalled levels of preference from governments. A decree by the minister for defence in late 1918 to all Commonwealth government departments ordered that the RSL be recognized as the official representative body of returned soldiers, and that its complaints receive immediate attention.[11] Custody of 'the Digger' granted servicemen's associations a powerful moral voice not only with government, but in the whole community. The dearth of Australian icons granted 'the Digger' domination over so-called national values and identity. Custody of Australia's Anzac Legend was and remains among the most potent political weapons for conformity and loyalty on a diverse and divergent population.

Soldier Settlement schemes developed against a broader canvas of economic revitalization in Australia, encapsulated by Prime Minister Stanley Bruce's famous 1923 slogan, 'Men, Money and Markets'. Schemes in both dominions were intended to reward diggers with their own farms, as well as to increase the production of wool, wheat, frozen meat and dried fruits, and so fulfil the agrarian myth after a century of failures. Of returning servicemen, a quarter wanted to become farmers, even if only half had farming experience, and only 13 per cent had the capital. Though there were individual and some regional successes – the Mallee wheat farmers and the doubling of the Victorian fruit crop – these were exceptions. Even with the help of Commonwealth and state authorities to lend money or find land, the 1929 Commission of Enquiry found only 27,000 digger farmers from a total of 37,000 still on the land. For the whole of Australia, the loss on soldier settlements was over £23 million. The blame was laid on small blocks, novice farmers, shortage of capital and poor prices, but the problem went deeper. The schemes were unsustainable, and reflected misconceptions about farming based on denying the peculiarities of antipodean soil. The harrowing tales of hardship were not new in the bush, where a theme of woe links generations of would-be farmers. Costs far outweighed benefits.[12]

A New Zealand parallel is the 'bridge to nowhere'. A concrete bridge sits across a deep gorge, surrounded by bush, in the remote Mangaparua Valley, up the Wanganui River. It is a decaying monument to the 'limits of hope' where fewer than forty returned soldiers took up selections, and none had capital. The road which serviced the bridge has been abandoned to erosion and bush. In 1936 the bridge came too late to stop settlers quitting, defeated by slips and floods triggered by environmental disturbance. As in Australia, returned soldiers felt they had lost their manhood.[13]

THE GREAT DEPRESSION

After the 1929 stock market crash, the free fall in primary product prices hurt Australia and New Zealand, whose per capita incomes fell by 10–20 per cent – much less than in the United States. The trigger was the fall in export prices which lowered national incomes even though farmers produced more. National expenditure was not restored until 1936–7 and unemployment remained high. Real wages only recovered to their earlier level in 1938, while wage and salary earners failed to regain their old share of national income. For many people, the Depression persisted until the Second World War.[14]

Depression hurt Pakeha New Zealanders less than Australians. The reported unemployment rate in Australia was about 30 per cent in 1933, even with unemployed school leavers classed as dependants. There is controversy over the rate in New Zealand. General histories report 12 per cent (40 per cent among Maori), but recent research suggests that nearly 30 per cent of the workforce in the depths of the Depression were 'not formally employed'.[15] Australian and New Zealand experience was not unlike that of other Western societies: disparity in impact between white- and blue-collar workers, networks of voluntary and other community support for local victims, the radicalizing of the intelligentsia, haunting images of the jobless drifting through town and city in search of work, or food, or both. Couples delayed marriage, limited their children (the birth rate reached its nadir in Australia in 1934, New Zealand in 1935), death rates from septic abortion rose, some women starved themselves to feed their families, and teenagers left school early.

Predictably the crisis did not impose equal sacrifice. The experiences of men, women and children could differ markedly. The employed – however poor – were better off than the unemployed; the unskilled were more likely to lose their jobs than the skilled. The groups most affected by declining living standards were those always most susceptible to poverty: elderly men and the unskilled. Labour force participation rates largely measured male employment. Although women teachers were subject to a marriage bar, women's employment rates actually increased. Women suffered pay cuts and discrimination, notably unequal pay, rather than unemployment. This supports an argument that the household absorbed depression shocks. Some employed and those on fixed incomes benefited from falling prices; and the well-to-do hardly suffered. The crisis provided cheap household help. Private schools maintained enrolments and traditional values. Depression reinforced values of mend and make do, and education as a mechanism for social mobility. Extravagant charity balls gave the affluent outlets for their compassion.

Equality of sacrifice was invoked by Left and Right to justify opposing economic policies. The orthodoxy of balancing budgets prevailed – it had to prevail, to assure credit from London – and dented the workingman's paradise on both sides of the Tasman. An Australian Arbitration Court in 1931 ordered a ten per cent wage cut on grounds of equality of sacrifice. A parallel decision in New Zealand reduced public service wages by ten per cent and private sector wages followed. Jack Lang, New South Wales' renegade premier, defaulted on interest payments to Britain twice, in 1931 and 1932, also on the grounds of equality of sacrifice, and was dismissed by the governor. Australia's federal system provided space for such resistance – repugnant to New Zealand and to the Australian federal government – reinforcing despondency about their joint labour experiment.

The crisis also created tensions in the working classes and the labour movement, splitting employed from unemployed, rank-and-file from militants, workers from ideologues. The Unemployed Workers Union, founded in 1930, fought evictions but its known links with the Communist Party undercut its standing and bargaining power. It failed in its main task of pressing government for greater relief. Sustenance – 'susso' – was inadequate, and often depended on harsh tests. In central Melbourne, Dr John Dale opened a market stall advertising 'Dr Dale's New Bread', where he sold the new knowledge of nutrition for seven pence to the city's poor, whose 'daily (daley) bread' was a wholemeal loaf, dried milk, 1¾ ounces of butter, and an orange.[16] The crisis left distrust among and within the classes most affected.

WELFARE

Chapter 11 showed why the white workingman, as family man, became the linchpin of welfare as well as labour experiments, institutionalizing the assumption that women and children should depend on a man for support. Australia and New Zealand formed workers' welfare states, built on the male breadwinners' wage. Cash benefits supplemented this emphasis. The welfare system accordingly extended first to the old, then to invalids, and belatedly to the unemployed, when the Depression revived calls for a 'civilized community'. Women and children received assistance intended to supplement the family wage, but this support was minimal, patchy, and depended on the tenor of local politics.[17]

A number of themes characterized Australian and New Zealand experience in the interwar years. First, the skilled received help with housing (their largest item of expenditure) primarily through home ownership. The motif of land settlement, central to identity, triumphed in suburbia. Second, in terms of cash payments, most public energy, if not resources, bolstered the assumption that the family wage should meet working-class needs (in reality the basic wage fell short). In both countries, the 'desire to uphold the traditional family structure and insist on the male breadwinner's responsibility for his family' overbore the reality of sole women breadwinners.[18] It was in the 'anxious peace' that the family wage, produced by the arbitration system, gained pivotal status, illuminating a league table of white feminine identities ranked in relation to marriage and motherhood.[19] Widows with children received miserly pensions in New Zealand from 1911; war widows at higher rates, according to their husbands' rank (war widows were the first to be provided for in Australia). Third, any measures for mothers and children followed the pattern of Australia's 1912 'baby bonus' in being pronatalist, intended to promote the birth and rearing of the child as a public asset. Fourth, Maori and Aboriginal Australians received separate treatment because of their different places in the imagined community. Fifth, Australia and New Zealand therefore opted for non-contributory social security, which was a regional phenomenon, like arbitration, and an outgrowth of it. Despite persistent tensions between ideals and costs, welfare benefits were determined by citizenship rather than ability to pay, which perpetuated political identities which asserted this welfare model as distinctive.

Eligibility for cash benefits suggests who was accepted and who was excluded from the state and its idea of community. In law entitled to equal rights as citizens and thus to cash benefits, Maori suffered discrimination from bureaucrats who routinely exercised their discretion to pay lower pensions to Maori on the grounds that they held communal land. By the 1920s Maori were paid 25 per cent less than Pakeha, though they had become dispossessed. Two sets of rules applied for those who lived as Maori and Europeans.[20] Aboriginal Australians were denied pensions. In Queensland and Western Australia they were forced onto government settlements and missions, where they received rations, and in Victoria and New South Wales they were forced off reserves and denied rations if they had more than a stated proportion of white 'blood'. Debarred from work and benefits, they lived in shanty towns and camps near the reserves or on the fringes of country towns.[21]

The theme of ethnic solidarity stands out. We might compare the New Zealand family allowance of 1926 and the New South Wales family endowment of 1927. New Zealand's non-Labour government provided two shillings a week for three or more children where the male breadwinner earned less than £4 a week (the notional family wage), subject to moral criteria to ensure that payment went to respectable families. New South Wales' more spendthrift Labor government paid 5 shillings a week for all – white – dependent children, including the illegitimate, as a supplement to the basic wage. In Labor New South Wales, ethnicity vanquished the family wage principle.

Pronatalism justified child endowment, to help with the costs of children. But politicians could not digest the feminist demand of motherhood endowment, or payment for mother-work, continuing the colonial feminists' call for the economic independence of married women. As New Zealand's Mrs Kelso said, on behalf of the Dominion Federation of Women's Institutes in 1937: 'If women in this country had money in their pocket that was actually their own, they would tackle babies much better than they do now'.[22] Instead, childbirth was paid for by taxpayers, wherever (a minority of) Labo(u)r governments allowed, to meet the ideal of equal medical treatment and attendance by a doctor, in hospital. The 'modern woman' and doctors shared, and demanded, the ideal of hospital birth with a doctor, which also satisfied egalitarian tenets. Thus New Zealand's first Labour government introduced its maternity benefit in 1939 under its social security legislation after a wrangle with general practitioners (the state guaranteed the doctor's fee), while Queensland's Labor governments built maternity hospitals funded by a state-owned lottery.

EUGENICS AND KING BABY

The value of the well, white child, economic and emotional, was transforming from the 1890s, evident in the fertility transition, the scare it engendered, and the 1920s campaigns to save baby life and make childbirth safer. Maternity assumed extra significance in national narratives. Women's duties as mothers were a central concern in Australia and New Zealand, and prominent in discourses about national identity. Child health, and then maternal health, came to be seen as central to the nation's wealth. The Great War helped to put mothers and babies on public agendas and accord more respect to patriotic motherhood. New Zealand in particular aspired to be a world model for producing 'His Majesty the Baby'. It enhanced New Zealand's healthy reputation that it had the lowest infant mortality rate in the world; Australia came second. Though this low Pakeha infant mortality rate, and its decline, predated the Plunket Society, New Zealand's women's voluntary infant welfare organization, it was claimed as evidence of the success of Dr Truby King and the Plunket system in the 'systematic pioneering educational health mission'.[23] Truby King himself became a world expert on babies (he was a psychiatrist, not a paediatrician, as his rivals noted) by travelling to London to establish a mothercraft training centre for the 'Babies of the Empire Society' during the war. The Truby King baby became international in the 1920s, promoted as the best King Baby by imperialists – and by Truby King nurses trained in New Zealand and London who took their message home to Australia – helped by the Duchess of York whose daughter, Princess Elizabeth, was advertised as a Truby King baby. Truby King visited Australia often from 1919 to 1931, invited first by Lady Munro Ferguson, wife of the governor-general and sister to Lady Plunket.[24]

Upbringing is central to identity, both in reality and in what people believe, and Australia and New Zealand made beliefs about themselves as places in which to bring up children central to their national narratives. Truby King became a media idol when he made New Zealand a world model with a royal imprimatur. Australians had the effrontery to contest this claim: they must 'work out [their] own salvation' asserted a Sydney specialist, even if the states did send emissaries across the Tasman to discover if there was 'anything more than a mere name in Truby King'. Australia had 'more to teach than to learn' from him. Dr Helen Mayo, leader of Adelaide's voluntary infant welfare movement, expressed a common scepticism:

> The chief drawback to the Plunket system is the fanaticism of the nurses, it becomes practically a religious cult with them. Our system is less rigid, and is probably more adaptable to Australian conditions.[25]

What began as a medical dispute between health professionals grew into a clash of patriotisms. The *Bulletin* ridiculed Truby King for his 'intensely, almost bigotedly, patriotic belief in the merits of his own Dominion', which made him damn 'with bell and candle everything Australian and all who do not blindly follow his methods in every fetishistic detail'. Conservative newspapers, on the other hand, agreed that 'If We Had The Plunket System Here / Our Little Ones Would Live', and denounced unbelievers as 'Herods and Hirelings'.[26] The row spurred Australians to create their own systems and standards and write their own baby-care books. The movement also varied in each Australian state, shaped by local conditions and Labor and non-Labor

Plate 14.2 Nurses and cots (bassinets) on the verandah, Karitane Hospital, Wellington, New Zealand. Plunket Society Collection, Hocken Library, University of Otago.

politics. Where conservative politics predominated, as in South Australia, Victoria and New Zealand, the mixed economy of welfare offered more space for women as public maternal figures.

That this elderly doctor stirred chauvinism over infant welfare services and feeding methods in Australia showed how much the white baby mattered, and that feeding symbolized mind mattering as well, in inflated rhetoric about His Majesty the Baby. At a time when people were seen as 'stock' in the eugenicist discourse, it was imperative that white New Zealand babies and baby-care methods be seen as superior to white Australians and Australian methods. New Zealand and Australia competed for the title of 'social laboratory' in health, just as they competed in sport, to display the biggest, strongest Anzac bodies. As we saw in chapter 8, the exercise of power through body politics shaped rules and loyalty, and thus identities.

The emphasis on King Baby had its dark side. Programmes to 'improve' the race seemed progressive and congenial to a generation of intellectuals given to plans for social engineering. Anxieties that evolution might not lead to progress justified state intervention. Yet Truby King's eugenist attitudes and language were not all-pervasive. Environmentalists in one context could be eugenists in another; 'environmentalist and hereditarian ideas were not polar opposites ... but part of a single and particular discursive formation'.[27] Truby King was one such reformer, promoting strategies for the unfit, the fit and those who could be made fit, from his regimen for the feeding and care of babies to segregation in an asylum, to sterilization because 'it is desirable that obviously unfit and bad strains should be got rid of'. Similarly Dr Elizabeth Gunn, school doctor and founder of health camps in New Zealand, said in the same breath in 1924 that many 'malnutrits' 'improve very much in the health camps', and yet:

> The feeble-minded, and the mentally defective, that we cannot improve in the schools, should be classed and segregated into colonies. I think we might go even further, and if we find children who can give no mental test, and imbecile children, then there should be some medical way of getting rid of them.[28]

Aboriginal mothers were deemed unfit by 'blood', and their children of mixed descent had to be removed for their own redemption, and for the white society, to 'save the babies'. 'The corollary was the construction of the unfit mother: a conception that dispelled moral qualms about depriving Aboriginal, poor white, and unmarried mothers of their babies and transferring them to "fit" mothers by adoption.'[29] Children of mixed descent, 'half-caste' or more, were seen as different from Aboriginal people because of their European blood, and able to be absorbed in white Australia. Their mothers were by definition unfit, so these children had to be taken for their White Father. By 1911 the Northern Territory and every state except Tasmania had 'protectionist legislation' giving the chief protector of Aborigines or a board power to control Aboriginal people, who had commonly been relegated to reserves. In some states and in the Northern Territory the chief protector was the legal guardian of Aboriginal children. The state assumed the role of White Father, and the Aboriginal mother had a status parallel to, but less than, the white unmarried mother.

The first national discussion of Aboriginal affairs, at a Native Welfare conference in 1937, agreed that

> the destiny of the natives of aboriginal origin, but not of the full blood, lies in their ultimate absorption by the people of the Commonwealth ... and that children of 'mixed aboriginal blood' should be educated and trained for employment with a view to assimilation.[30]

By 1937, forcible removal no longer occurred under protection Acts, but under general child welfare legislation designed to protect neglected and destitute children. From the 1920s, babies were also forcibly taken from their mothers under adoption Acts. Fit mothers were white, married and middle class, and implemented the model of childrearing devised for King Baby.

Depression anxieties, especially about nutrition, brought the toddler to the fore because health surveys suggested that the pre-school child was (in bodily terms) the Depression's greatest victim. On a wave of interest in new nutritional knowledge and in child development, the child – hope and problem – assumed a leading place in Australian national narratives. The world interest in the young child and in food in the Depression manifested itself in the first national initiative in child health, the six Lady Gowrie Child

Centres – intended to measure and set standards for the white Australian child, of Australian-born parents – the first of which opened in Melbourne in 1939. These 'shopfronts' for pre-school care adapted the latest American ideas on child health and education in formulating principles of Australianness. New Zealand, however, as the 'Empire's dairy farm', continued to opt for body-building. In 1937 it introduced a school scheme of a free daily half-pint of bottled milk. School milk was not distinctive to New Zealand, but New Zealand school milk mediated emerging identities within the welfare state. Introduced to benefit the dairy farmer and the child, the half-pint bottle came, with Plunket, to signify that New Zealand was a healthy place to rear children.

Acute rivalries developed also on the sports field, underlining the importance of body politics. An Australasian identity – as in Davis Cup tennis – fragmented from the 1920s into Australian and New Zealand identities. The New Zealand horse, Phar Lap, was appropriated as quintessentially Australian. Victory was a spur for national sentiment, notably in imperial games. Rugby union was New Zealand's national game, and cricket Australia's. Against this backdrop, New Zealand responses to the Bodyline Test cricket series between Australia and England in 1932–3 illustrate Australian–New Zealand relations in the Depression.[31] In the New Zealand view, Australians were rude to accuse the English of 'unsportsmanlike' behaviour because of their new – and winning – bowling style. This was 'not cricket', but an excuse to be anti-English.

Consistent with this enthusiastic physicality, the popularity of camping and the great outdoors soared. Cars allowed people to venture on camping holidays and to take snapshots of indigenous scenery. National parks, forest and bird protection societies and tramping clubs attracted enthusiasts. Having banned sea-bathing until the turn of the century, Australia now saw itself as home of surfing. New Zealand pictured itself as a health spa (a Department of Tourist and Health Resorts was created in 1901) centred first on the geothermal regions, with the additional lure of Maori (Te Arawa) culture and geysers at Rotorua. Tourism initiatives were fostered by and foundered in the Depression; the Chateau at Tongariro on the North Island's volcanic plateau stung the Mt Cook Company, which introduced the first alpine flights; while the staircase for tourists to descend the escarpment at Katoomba in the Blue Mountains west of Sydney provided a public works project in the Depression. Settler societies were identifying with and claiming their own landscapes.

The Depression proved a fillip to the health camp movement. Dr Elizabeth Gunn started health camps with surplus equipment from the New Zealand army. The first, on a farm near Wanganui in 1919, housed children in one paddock and stock to feed them in another. Fattening human stock was the aim.

> Mr Lethbridge's land at Turakina is just now fattening more valuable stock than it has ever fattened before … for 95 boys and girls are there under canvas and enjoying wholesome living and fresh air.

After eating and sunbathing, they looked 'rosy and sunburnt'.[32]

Plate 14.3 Cars and camping. Snapshots from the Tremewan family album. Courtesy of Richard Tremewan.

303

FOR ART AND COUNTRY: THE LITERATURE OF NATION-BUILDING

To be a writer in Australia between the wars promised a public place and role, but only at the risk of exposure, accountability and engagement. Lawson and Furphy had set the tone in a colonial context informed by anti-imperialist rhetoric. It fell to the next generation of writers – born with federation, its adolescence shadowed by the Great War, its mettle tested by Depression and the advent of fascism – to shape a landscape on which a national literature would grow and expand. The times challenged Australian writers to do more than spin yarns, and to help realize that society and join in the task of nation-building, and therefore to refashion relations between writer and society, to confront the tensions of the artist/citizen.

The 1920s were a time for charting an explicitly national literature. Framed at one end by Nettie Palmer's survey of *Modern Australian Literature 1900–1923* (1924) and at the other by H. M. Green's *An Outline of Australian Literature* (1930), the decade saw the rise of the first cartographers of such a literature and their attempts to chart its development as a discrete body of writing. Meanwhile, artists were seeking to direct that development with new theories and definitions of Australian art that aimed to liberate the creative spirit from convention and local preoccupations. But a deep-seated cultural cringe persisted, that regarded things Australian as necessarily inferior to things British (and later American). It was nowhere more obvious than in the high-culture set whose literature of nation-building, or 'people's literature' as some chose to call it, bore all the tensions of the cultural politics of the Left: British in cultural affinities, radical nationalist in political rhetoric. Brennan's 1927 piece 'Some Makers of Australia' argued for a universalist approach to the 'poet's "national" task'. Norman Lindsay's *Creative Effort* (1920) posed a bold 'new aesthetic programme' for the country's 'Urban Intelligentsia' which emphasized 'gaiety in art' and defended 'the individuality and freedom of the artist against a wowserish Australian society'.[33]

Then emerged two of the most successful names in Australian creative writing. Ion Idriess and Henry Handel Richardson raised lowbrow and highbrow Australian literature to new levels. *Madman's Island* (1927) launched Idriess as one of the country's most prolific and popular writers. In 1929, Richardson's *Ultima Thule*, last volume of her trilogy *The Fortunes of Richard Mahony*, appeared to rave reviews. One 'particularly responsible London critic' proffered that 'if there has been a masterpiece written in our time, here is that masterpiece'.[34] The novel prompted Richardson's nomination for the Nobel Prize in 1932, the first such honour for an Australian writer. The recognition seemed a portent, as were new developments in the form and content of the novel, and the emergence of women writers in public literary life. Best-selling adventure and travel stories by Idriess and F. J. Thwaites gave local publishing a boost. Increasingly, writers' individual achievements were wed to the fortunes of a national literature.

Some even posited an alliance between art and country. In a 1935 essay on 'The Future of Australian Literature', Vance Palmer, author and leader in cultural circles, saw literature as constitutive and creative, not merely expressing a wider social context. The 'new' literary impulse, he foretold, 'will have a tremendous effect in Australia in the next fifty years. It will quicken its imagination, stimulate its powers of introspection, and make it as interesting to itself as every country should be.'[35] This vision of a holy alliance between art and country caught the imagination of other writers, exploring new relationships between writer and society, culture and identity.

Through the late 1920s and early 1930s, across generations, emerged a new vision of Australia – 'as a civilized nation, instead of a permanent "culture-colony"'[36] – and new tools for expressing it – 'our own – our very own language'.[37] Expatriates of long standing like Miles Franklin made their way back to 'that far, lone, siren land that enthrals us'.[38] Together with kindred spirits they embarked on a mission to write no less than 'a people's literature' that would be neither derivative nor self-consciously Australian, neither hankering after exotic places, nor littered with 'bushrangers, buckjumpers and bandicoots',[39] but springing naturally from the 'spirit of the place'. This was the springtime of a new literature, self-consciously itself and deliberately national. What were its well-springs? The question gave rise to wide debate, and the issue of race surfaced early. 'To be worthy of the name of the race from which it comes', a prominent voice argued, writing 'should express the spirit of the race.'[40] The matter of physical atmosphere – 'the feeling of a place'[41] – also featured, prefiguring what Jindyworobaks later posited as a bold new alliance between art-and-place – or better yet, art and the spirit of place.

The Jindyworobak (adapted from an Aboriginal word meaning to annex, to join) movement was a radical expression of Australian nationalism, a reaction against both an entrenched colonialism and international influences eroding Australia's isolationism through the 1920s. The movement, founded in 1938 by the writer Reg Ingamells, drew stimulus from *The Foundations of Culture* (1936), P. R. 'Inky' Stephensen's aggressively nationalist manifesto for a distinctive Australian culture based on the spirit of place.

Ingamells aspired 'to free Australian art from whatever alien influences trammel it, that is, to bring it into proper contact with its material'. The national culture, he insisted, depended on recognizing 'environmental values' and understanding Australian history and traditions from primeval to modern times. Ingamells's explicit link of Jindyworobak philosophy with Aboriginal culture was ridiculed by many as naive if not outrageous. The intention was not to appropriate Aboriginal culture, but to invoke it as an example of environmental values in action. The movement failed in its principal aim to force Australian literary development into a narrow nationalism. Its assumption that Aborigines were a dying race and misunderstanding of Aboriginal culture and language reflected a widespread ignorance and amnesia, yet it remains significant as a reflection of wider impulses to embrace a sense of national identity with the land, as opposed to the bush.[42]

In these and other ways the literature of nation-building echoed as well as departed from the radical nationalist writing of the 1890s. It borrowed earlier themes of national identity and the cult of the Common Man but avoided unionism or working-class culture. Stemming from a 'highbrow' national consciousness, the new literary nationalism reflected a broader perspective based on familiarity and appreciation of great literatures of other countries. The fact of nationhood also cut sharply across the generations. 'Nationalist' became increasingly an outward rather than inward-looking stance in writing, which now sought to reflect both modern and timeless Australia.

The Depression shook Australian intellectuals like nothing before it, dissolving old certainties and dismissing old truths. A whole generation was scarred by the experience. It beckoned a radical new reading of the role of art, literature and culture. It placed moral accountability on the intellectuals' agenda. 'The human wreckage' that drifted past his town, one of this generation recalled in typically emotive language, 'stamped his consciousness ... the streams of unemployed who trekked across the mountains to the hinterland in search of non-existent work camping in humpy outcrops at the edges of the town'.[43] Far more than either world war, the Depression was the Australian intellectual's call to arms. Like the Great War, it shattered illusions of the country's insulation; more directly than the war, it demanded engagement with global issues. The Depression happened here, the war there. The experience spared no one.

Just when the alliance of art-and-country was poised to yield an early harvest of national literature, the Depression jolted its premises and complicated its mandate. To the task of nation-building it added a new, uncomfortable agenda with its own moral imperatives and visions of social justice. Federation had forged a union which the Depression threatened to dissolve into class struggle. One spoke the language of nationhood, the other of internationalism. Peace and prosperity, economic equality and social justice, once unproblematic, posed difficult questions of priorities and values. What price peace in the struggle for social justice, and vice versa?

The West had barely time to recover from the worst of the Depression when an even more daunting threat arose. The Italians invaded Abyssinia in 1935, Germany reoccupied the Rhineland in 1936, Japan invaded China in 1937, and the *Anschluss* swallowed Austria in 1938, while the democracies watched stupefied. Meanwhile the Spanish Civil War dragged on – for the Left the quintessential symbol of the struggle between the forces of good and evil.

The Australian Left responded with horror and exhilaration, sharing in spirit – and some in the flesh – the burdens of comrades in the International Brigades in Spain. Jean Devanny, novelist and prominent member of the CPA, suffered 'a complete breakdown' at the news of Barcelona's bombing, and determined to pursue 'a policy of detachment. I must or go mad with it all.'[44] The crisis swept aside old antagonisms between Sydney and Melbourne intellectuals, artists and journalists, high- and low-brow writers, to centralize and collectivize resources. With Moscow's blessing, socialism became inclusive, allowing communists and 'fellow travellers', activists and 'armchair' socialists to make common cause against fascism. Restrictions on freedom of expression often welded these allies together, censorship providing a rallying point. From the interplay of professional and political concerns, a rare camaraderie developed among Left intellectuals, its character resembling a crusade to reclaim the soul of Western society. By late 1935 Vance Palmer was proclaiming from England that 'a new order has to come, and very quickly, if civilization is not going to crash in a series of fruitless fascist wars'.[45]

'The Thirties myth' about Western intellectuals fits the Australian context as well as the European. Indeed, this camaraderie of kindred spirits working at opposite ends of the globe towards the same lofty (if vague) goal coated the Australian writing enterprise with almost mystical qualities.

> The Thirties myth goes something like this: ... some of the best writers of the time – were induced by its unfamiliar political pressures to write against their own bents. Uneasily allured by Communism, they professed a fatal interest in unemployment, the Spanish Civil War, the death throes of capitalism, the imminence of revolution and of world conflict. ... To some of them, it appeared that to stand aside and carry on as if nothing in the world concerned them except their own work, narrowly considered, would cause an injury not only to conscience but to such gifts as they felt they had.[46]

Literature had become accountable and sacred, part of a crusade. For writers of the Left, options were narrowing, whatever their position on pure versus applied literature.

In Depression New Zealand the dairy farmer in John Mulgan's classic novel *Man Alone* surmized of protesters over unemployment in Auckland: 'They listen to a lot of reds, a lot of bloody agitators. If they ain't Russians, they're Australians. That's what the trouble is.'[47] The pressures to be 'on the side of history' were vast and growing.

But whose history? For those with pretensions to write a 'people's literature', the global crisis called for large adjustments to conceptions of the national literature crystallized in the more innocent twenties. How Australian could the literature be when those dictating terms were in Moscow? For a people and culture embarking on an independent course, it was inescapably retrograde to subordinate national priorities to another – Soviet – empire. However, such questions were largely academic. The nature of the literary enterprise was changing with a tendency in radical circles to explore and exploit relations between literature and politics, and to link the cutting edge of literary development with the ferment on the Left. Few would have disagreed with one writer's claim that this was no time for 'inventing little fairy tales',[48] but the gap between escapist literature and propaganda could be vast.

So was the gap between moral opposition to capitalism and fascism, and active support of socialism and communism. The spectrum of 'leftish' shades in Australian intellectual circles embraced everything from communism to nineteenth-century liberalism. For some, the cause remained ill-defined; for others, it crystallized in an all-consuming issue like the Spanish Civil War or censorship. Ultimately the question was not the brand of socialism espoused, but engagement with issues. Some writers turned to pamphleteering, broadcasting and other ways of reaching a wide public. Others turned to collective action: major-party politics, campaigns and lobby groups. The Communist

Party exercised a magnetic pull but few intellectuals made the leap from 'fellow traveller' to card-carrier. The party's overbearing image was an obstacle and the fanaticism of some members disturbing. Tales of writers in Europe – so dazzled with Bolshevism that their moral judgement lapsed – fuelled those fears. The dilemma for Australian writers was ultimately ethical. Moscow-ordained social realism offered creative writers one set of guidelines, but raised problems of ethics and aesthetics, of the function of art as ends or means. Art and country, twin pillars of the literature of nation-building, had been superseded by more pressing goals.

Debate over the moral value and implications of literary realism began in Australia in the 1880s.[49] By the 1980s, literature of protest or literature of commitment (as realist writing is sometimes described) had put down roots. Since then, it has been identified with the work of radical nationalists, especially Lawson and Furphy, who wrote 'of the people, for the people, and from the people'.[50] Communist writers appropriated the tradition, linking it with a hatred of economic injustices and a desire for social progress, and reading the work of radical nationalists as 'instinctive, pre-revolutionary attempts at socialist realism'.[51] Furphy's emphasis on aggressive democracy and Lawson's raw evocations of the terror of the bush and the plight of the slum-dweller had shaped a social rather than a political democratic literature lacking political self-consciousness. It was the apparent lack of a set idea or a fixed message, a critic of the 1960s argued, which made Lawson's literature of protest so effective.[52]

Social realism bore instead a distinct and deliberate political complexion. The notion that art must 'have a proletarian ideology and be understandable to the masses' was first promulgated by the Kharkov Conference of November 1931.[53] It culminated in 1934 when at the First All-Soviet Congress of Writers, Stalin's cultural spokesperson elaborated it into the 'method of socialist realism'. Distinct from 'objective reality', this brand of realism was to be permeated with a revolutionary consciousness.[54]

For the Australian writer, in whom neither nationhood nor the rite of passage of Gallipoli had altogether dissipated the sense of estrangement from the 'home culture' (if no longer the Mother Country), Bolshevik-style social realism carried considerable appeal. It may have stemmed from a culturally alien world, but it was an international scheme aimed at consolidating efforts across Western society. In Australia, where the image of the writer as a neglected, misunderstood outcast held sway among the literati, Stalin's description of writers as 'the engineers of human souls' flattered them. So too in New Zealand, where the 'man alone' typos evolved from frontier hero to rebel or social victim after about 1930.[55]

Moscow's attempt to make literature 'the tool of the revolution, rather than an expression of it' raised ethical, methodological and conceptual problems. Attempts to dictate a consciousness and impose uniformity on art negated its spontaneity and dented its integrity. Ironically, a major factor limiting this brand of social realism in Australia was the robust democratic literary tradition already in place. Ideals of social justice and democracy had taken culture-specific forms and meanings. Mateship – 'key-word of the Australian democratic spirit' – was a prime example.[56] Though premissed on egalitarian tenets, the Australian democratic tradition stemmed from and reflected a social rather than a socialist creed. Its springs and manifestations were politically unselfconscious, the outgrowth of personal conviction rather than ideology. In this tradition, a novelist of the 1930s argued, democracy appears as 'in solution, as natural and unconscious as the blood in our veins ... a matter of attitude and subject matter, not of precept and example'.[57]

Australian social realism, as slippery a term as the political radicalism underpinning it, has been described as 'Depression literature', 'proletariat literature', 'reportage' and 'socialist realism'. The writers most closely associated with it were CPA members like Katharine Susannah Prichard and Jean Devanny. Unable to reconcile their socialist with their artistic consciences, most writers diverted their political energies from 'that insistent propaganda, that rabid agitation, that ranting bitterness which made so much fiction of the late thirties awkward and embarrassing'.[58]

THE ISLAND DEPENDENCIES

Peace in the Island dependencies was as anxious as anywhere else, but for other reasons. While Australians were insecure in the face of Melanesian numbers, sexuality and cultural strangeness, New Zealanders were over-confident in dealing with Polynesian cultural nuances in Samoa. Rabaul was the centre of Australian rule in New Guinea. On the evening of 2 January 1929, police and workers withdrew from the town to the Methodist and Catholic missions. The organizers were Sumsuma, a ship's captain and labour-recruiter, and several senior policemen, relatively well paid and respected, and familiar with the structures of colonial authority which denied them their worth. Ordinary workers were usually employed on fixed-term contracts, paid the statutory minimum wage, and likely to be involved in ethnic feuds among themselves. Some of their grievances were industrial, including a demand for a minimum wage of £12 a month (fifty times the prevailing rate), but the protest also expressed a common rage against paternalism and a hope that the missionaries would prove different from other whites. In the event, most of the workers returned to town next morning when the missionaries advised a return to work and asked the government for clemency. The fact that strikers were drawn from all forms of employment underlined the episode's racial dimension and brought down on them the wrath of the government. Charges were laid, prison terms imposed, and men drafted to hard labour. Most were beaten by outraged and anxious officials while awaiting trial or during their sentences.[59]

That portentous event alarmed the settlers and their officials by its evidence of New Guineans' capacity to organize without – and by implication against – white help. A few years later in Papua's administrative centre, Port Moresby, the tiny settler community fell prey to sexual anxiety. Whether or not Papuan men made sexual advances on Australian women – and whether or not they were rebuffed – the settlers plunged into panic. As in Rabaul, white alarm was heightened by suspicion that the most dangerous Melanesian men were those – police – who enjoyed most trust.[60] The panic might have spread to Rabaul, if not for a volcanic eruption which obliterated the town and some villages. Nature seemed to echo the uncertainty of Australian life in the tropical dependencies.

Western Samoans did not doubt that *fa'aSamoa* – Samoan tradition – reflected their superiority, while New Zealanders thought the Samoans 'splendid but backward'. Incompatible values informed a 1919 exchange between an orator chief and a New Zealand official. The chief explained that 'you are ruling Samoa by authority of the Samoans', but the official insisted that 'The allied nations ... gave the control of Samoa to New Zealand under King George of Great Britain and I am governing for New Zealand'.[61]

The influenza epidemic of November 1918 seared memories, especially as Americans managed to keep American Samoa free of infection. An inquiry then exposed official neglect and poor judgement, but the administration could learn little from its mistakes, as Samoa was governed by civil servants on limited-term postings. The local assembly, the Fono of Faipule, had no role in decision-making, and sought legislative powers. By the 1920s many Samoan families and foreigners were linked by marriage, so European residents joined Samoans to protest against New Zealand autocracy.

An ambitious administrator, General George Richardson, arrived in 1923 with a reform agenda. He gave the Fono a key role in governance, at the apex of a structure in which district councils regulated village activities in intrusive detail. The Fono became Richardson's ally in reshaping daily life. For example, to raise productivity Richardson restricted cricket, and tried to prohibit *malaga*, 'travelling parties' who exchanged fine mats ceremonially. When he also proposed to individualize land tenure, the Fono agreed to a scheme whereby *matai* would distribute lands to untitled men. Under the Samoan Offenders Ordinance of 1922, Richardson imposed mortifying penalties:

> Afamasaga is a High Chief who wears trousers, speaks English well and trades as a merchant in Apia. I imposed an additional penalty upon him ... and deprived him of his titles and sent him to his Native Village where he has never lived before but where he can wear a lava lava and get time to reflect on the seriousness of this offence.[62]

Before a Royal Commission in 1927, Samoans complained most about banishment and revoking titles. Interference in *malaga* was the second most frequent grievance.

Opposition took the form of an alternative government. 'O le Mau' was founded in 1926, under the slogan Samoa for Samoans. When Richardson banished two leaders, Samoans began passive resistance. Despite evidence of arbitrary banishment, corruption and other issues, the Royal Commission supported Richardson's position that the Mau had been instigated by a few *afakasi* (mixed-race) and Europeans. O. F. Nelson and two Europeans were deported, and popular support for the Mau grew. When Richardson arrested 400 'Mau leaders', he had to turn away hundreds more who asked to be jailed with them. Tupua Tamasese Lealofi, one of the highest ranking chiefs, was asked if the Mau wanted New Zealand removed from government: 'Yes; it is the wish of the Mau that Samoa should be controlled by the Samoans'.

By 1928, when Richardson was replaced, the Mau was performing many government functions. Nelson presented a petition to the League of Nations, but the Mandates Commission refused to hear it. No fewer than 8,000 of 9,300 adult Samoan men signed this petition. The Mau was also winning support in New Zealand, and in 1929 a new government suspended the Fono. Despite conciliatory gestures, protests continued. On 28 December 1929 – Black Saturday – a procession marched through Apia, and police tried to arrest tax-defaulters. A European policeman fell, and the others opened fire. From a nearby police station machine-guns joined in. Eleven Samoans were killed, almost all high-ranking *matai*. The three highest ranking – Tamasese, Tuimaleali'ifano and Faumuina – were all wounded, and Tupua Tamasese Lealofi later died. Since they wore distinctive dress and were trying to quiet the crowd when they were shot, Samoans were convinced that the police had targeted them.

The Mau was now declared seditious and troops hunted supporters. Men fled to the mountains while soldiers terrorized villagers, and women (as the 'Women's Mau') rallied supporters and staged demonstrations. A stand-off lasted until 1936, when New Zealand's first Labour government came to power and made an immediate policy shift. The Mau was recognized as a legitimate organization, the Samoan Offenders Ordinance was repealed, and a new Fono was elected, composed largely of members of the Mau. The new Fono could select members of the Legislative Council, giving Samoans – and particularly Mau supporters – a direct role in governance.

MAORI AND ABORIGINAL INITIATIVES

There were important debates in urban as well as rural Aboriginal communities between the wars, but disproportionate numbers and the near-invisibility of Aborigines in the eyes of authority, meant that new possibilities added little to the anxieties of the wider community. Maori were never invisible. Dr Peter Buck, who became a celebrated anthropologist based at the Bishop Museum in Hawaii, wrote to his old friend Apirana Ngata in 1934:

New Zealand trots out the Maori people as show case specimens for the outside world to see what they have accomplished for a native people but if it were not for the Maori people themselves and their leaders, New Zealand would have about as much to show in local statesmanship as she has in Samoa.[63]

The 1918 influenza pandemic is one example which would support Buck's scepticism. It struck almost as hard in New Zealand as in Samoa, especially among Maori, who probably suffered a death rate of 42.3 per 1,000, seven times the Pakeha rate.[64] Parallel with Island experience, an estimated four per cent of Maori died in the last two months of 1918. The *tangata whenua* sought their own solutions. From the crisis sprang a new religious, faith-healing movement, Ratana, which appealed to the Maori poor, especially those who had lost land and lived in a poverty which startled Pakeha. Maori numbers were recovering rapidly, but too little land remained for the young people. T. W. Ratana, a Maori farmer who practised Pakeha farming in the lower North Island, had a vision at the height of the epidemic. He and his two sisters were the only survivors of the 'flu from 21 descendants of his grandfather, and there had been no time to make coffins. Ratana's creed comprised the Bible and the Treaty of Waitangi. The Ratana Church, established in 1925, rivalled the Anglicans, the church of the Ngati Porou and Arawa tribes, prominent in the Pioneer Battalion, and also rivalled the King movement. In the Depression Ratana's mission turned to politics to secure for Maori their rightful position under the treaty. The Ratana movement made an alliance with the Labour Party, winning its first seat in parliament in 1932, and by 1943 Ratana members held all four Maori seats.[65] While both Ratana and Labour stood for the workingman, for the carpenter – like Christ – the Ratana movement invented its own symbols and identity, and sought to write the treaty into New Zealand statute. It stood for new ways of looking at the world. In the anxious peace, Maori began to propound a right to have their needs met, and sought equality in meeting those needs through Ratana's pan-Maori identity.

The Depression was a time of defining change for Maori–Pakeha relations, right across politics. Apirana Ngata of Ngati Porou, Anglican and highly educated – the first Maori graduate, and the most educated person in parliament – exerted *mana* in conservative circles. He had helped organize the Pioneer Contingent, and in the Second World War he would organize the Maori Battalion. High Tory, he was the bitter enemy of Ratana as the voice of the people. Ngata cherished a vision of Maori land cultivation, transporting the Pakeha pioneer legend into another context and turning Maori into settlers, farming their own land. He sought farms for returned Maori soldiers, barred from soldier settlement schemes, though he allowed these to be surveyed from Maori land. He wanted State Advances to Settlers to flow to Maori as well as Pakeha. Ngata took the Ngata Porou into dairying and set up two *iwi*-controlled co-operative dairy factories, sending young men not to New Zealand's farms and co-operatives, but to New South Wales to learn the latest methods. As the first Maori minister of Maori affairs from December 1928, he ranked the difficulties of claiming title to land second to land development. From 1929 state advances extended to Maori, and his land schemes helped Maori survive the Depression. But Treasury scrutiny of expenditure and procedures had Ngata ousted in 1934, disgraced, and control of Maori land development schemes passed increasingly into bureaucratic Pakeha hands.[66]

Renewed *mana* for Maori as developers (not just sellers of land) aided the invention of Waitangi Day, in the first official celebrations of the treaty signing at Waitangi itself, in February 1934. In the Depression the governor-general had gifted the Waitangi Treaty House and grounds as a 'national memorial'. Maori boycotted an attempt to remember Waitangi in 1922. *Iwi* recognized that this commemoration also marked the centenary of the Declaration of Independence by northern tribes in 1834, but this event did not enter the government's narrative. On the first significant Waitangi Day – during the 1940 centennial – Ngata led the *haka*, the Maori challenge and welcome, but it was the imperial gift of the treaty site in 1932 which triggered Pakeha writing and thinking about Waitangi as the 'seeds of nationhood'. Until then Waitangi featured in settler narratives as the site where New Zealand became part of the empire. By the 1930s Pakeha were becoming conscious of a national identity and Maori identities were reviving. For some, Waitangi symbolized unity. If Anzac Day was 'new', Waitangi as a national Day was even newer.

'Australia Day' (Anniversary Day in New South Wales until 1932) celebrated the arrival of the First Fleet; but in the 1938 sesquicentennial Aborigines protested with a Day of Mourning. Among white Australians, gestures of social cohesion still had more relevance at the state level. Victoria and South Australia preferred to remember their own 'pioneers' in centennial celebrations in 1934 and 1936. In Australia as in New Zealand, it was too soon to promote national feeling through a day to honour the founding of a nation.

NOTES

1 Report of the Committee of Inquiry into Mental Defectives and Sexual Offenders, 1925, *Appendices to the Journals of the House of Representatives*, 1925, H-31A, 28, quoted in Philippa Mein Smith, *Maternity in Dispute: New Zealand 1920–1939*, Wellington, 1986, 25.
2 P. J. Cain and A. G. Hopkins, *British Imperialism: Crisis and Deconstruction 1914–1990*, 2 vols, London and New York, 1993, ch. 6.
3 *New Zealand Dairy Produce Exporter*, 29 August 1925, 18–19.
4 S. M. Bruce, future prime minister, September 1924, cited by M. Roe, *Australia, Britain, and Migration, 1915–1940: A Study of Desperate Hopes*, Melbourne, 1995, 60.
5 H. P. Schapper, *A Survey of Dairy Farming in the Far South-West of Western Australia*, Perth, 1953.
6 P. J. Cain and A. G. Hopkins, *British Imperialism*, vol. 2, *Crisis and Deconstruction, 1914–1990*, London, 1993, 117.
7 G. Ferguson, *Building the New Zealand Dream*, Palmerston North, 1994, 88–90.
8 K. M. Reiger, *The Disenchantment of the Home*, Melbourne, 1985, ch. 2.
9 J. Dennis and J. Bieringa (eds), *Film in Aotearoa New Zealand*, 2nd edn, Wellington, 1996, 17, 28; C. Hilliard, 'Stories of Becoming: The Centennial Surveys and the Colonization of New Zealand', *New Zealand Journal of History*, 33: 1 (April 1999), 3–19. Hilliard shows how the 1860s wars were excised from surveys commemorating New Zealand's centenary of settlement in 1940.
10 Russel Ward, *A Nation for a Continent: The History of Australia 1901–1975*, Ringwood, Victoria, 1983, 193.
11 Ward, *A Nation for a Continent*, 140.
12 For an Australian case, see M. Lake, *The Limits of Hope: Soldier Settlement in Victoria 1915–1938*, Melbourne, 1987. A contemporary view is given by Edmund de S. Brunner, *Rural Australia and New Zealand: Some Observations of Current*

Trends, Studies of the Pacific no. 2, San Francisco, 1938, a rural sociologist from Columbia University, who found the push for closer settlement puzzling and contradictory.

13 A. P. Bates, *The Bridge to Nowhere: The Ill-fated Mangapurua Settlement*, Wanganui, 1981.

14 G. R. Hawke, *The Making of New Zealand*, chs 7 and 8. On Australia, see G. Spenceley, *A Bad Smash: Australia in the Depression of the 1930s*, Melbourne, 1990.

15 Keith Rankin, 'An Estimation of the New Zealand Labour Force in 1933', economics seminar, Victoria University of Wellington, 1989. Conventional estimates follow J. Macrae and K. Sinclair, 'Unemployment in New Zealand During the Depression of the Late 1920s and Early 1930s', *Australian Economic History Review*, 15: 1 (March 1975), 35–44.

16 Vera Scantlebury Brown, Diary B6, 25 July 1929, 28; 23 Sept. 1929, 4, Melbourne University archives. Also quoted in Philippa Mein Smith, *Mothers and King Baby: Infant Survival and Welfare in an Imperial World: Australia 1880–1950*, Basingstoke, 1997, 221.

17 Useful sources are Stuart Macintyre, *The Labour Experiment*. Themes in Australian Economic and Social History, ed. Boris Schedvin, Melbourne, 1989; Francis G. Castles, *The Working Class and Welfare: Reflections on the Political Development of the Welfare State in Australia and New Zealand, 1890–1980*, Wellington, 1985.

18 M. McClure, *A Civilised Community: A History of Social Security in New Zealand 1898–1998*, Auckland, 88.

19 This league table is discussed in M. Tennant, *Paupers and Providers*, Wellington, 1989.

20 McClure, *A Civilised Community*.

21 Human Rights and Equal Opportunity Commission, *Bringing them Home: Report of the National Inquiry into the Separation of Aboriginal and Torres Strait Islander Children from Their Families*, Sydney, April 1997, 30–1.

22 National Archives, Wellington, Septic Abortion, Committee of Inquiry, Evidence, 1936–7, Mrs Kelso, 6 Oct. 1936, 92, H1, 131/139/15, quoted in Mein Smith, *Maternity in Dispute*, 113. On feminist calls for motherhood endowment in Australia, see M. Lake, 'A Revolution in the Family', in S. Koven and S. Michel (eds), *Mothers of a New World: Maternalist Politics and the Origins of Welfare States*, New York and London, 1993, ch. 11.

23 The infant welfare movement and its response to declines in fertility and infant mortality are analysed in Mein Smith, *Mothers and King Baby*. Quotation from 'Vesta', 'A School for Mothers. The New Zealand Scheme', *Argus*, Melbourne, 19 Sept. 1917, 12, cited in Mein Smith, *Mothers and King Baby*, 70. 'Vesta' was the penname of Stella Allan (née Henderson), a first-wave feminist. Educated at the University of Canterbury, she was New Zealand's first woman law student, and sister of New Zealand's first woman MP.

24 See Mein Smith, *Mothers and King Baby*, ch. 5.

25 Royal Commission on Health, Australia, *Minutes of Evidence*, 1925–6, Dr H. Mayo, Adelaide, 14 May 1925 and Dr W. F. Litchfield, Royal Society for the Welfare of Mothers and Babies, Sydney; General Council, *Minutes*, Report B, 6 Jan. 1920, 12 Feb. 1920, cited in Mein Smith, *Mothers and King Baby*, 107, 115.

26 *Bulletin*, 5 Nov. 1925; *Sun*, n.d. (Nov. 1923); *Sunday Times*, 25 Oct. 1925, 8 Nov. 1925; cited in Mein Smith, *Mothers and King Baby*, 114–15, 127.

27 S. Garton, 'Sound Minds and Healthy Bodies: Reconsidering Eugenics in Australia, 1914–1940', *Australian Historical Studies*, 26: 103 (Oct. 1994), 163–81.

28 National Archives, Wellington, Committee of Inquiry into Mental Defectives and Sexual Offenders, Evidence, Truby King to Chilton, 9 July 1924, 573A; E. Gunn, 30 May 1924, 80–1, H 3/13.

29 J. McCalman, 'Maternity', in G. Davison, J. Hirst and S. Macintyre (eds), *Oxford Companion to Australian History*, Melbourne, 1998, 416.

30 Human Rights and Equal Opportunity Commission, *Bringing them Home*, 28, 32.

31 Greg Ryan, ' "Extravagance of Thought and Feeling": New Zealand Reactions to the 1932/33 Bodyline Controversy', *Sporting Traditions*, 13: 2 (May 1997), 41–58.

32 *Wanganui Chronicle*, 17 Nov. 1922, cited in Mein Smith, *Maternity in Dispute*, 3. M. Tennant, *Children's Health, the Nation's Wealth: A History of Children's Health Camps*, Wellington, 1994.

33 John Docker, 'Norman Lindsay's Creative Effort: Manifesto for an Urban Intelligentsia', *Australian Literary Studies*, 6: 1 (May 1973), 24–5.

34 Quoted in Nettie Palmer, 'The Novel in Australia: A Sudden Flowering', *West Australian*, 14 June 1930. Ethel Florence Lindsay Robertson (née Richardson) wrote under the pen name of Henry Handel Richardson.

35 Quoted in 'Australian Authors' Week', *Sydney Morning Herald*, 4 March 1935.

36 P. R. Stephensen to Nettie Palmer, 20 July 1932, NLA MS 1174/1/4022-24.

37 Mary Gilmore to Frank Dalby Davison, 13 July 1929, NLA MS 1945/1/3-6.

38 'Brent of Bin Bin' (Miles Franklin) to Nettie Palmer, Oct. 1931, NLA MS 1174/1/3769.

39 Isobel T. Hassall, 'Let's Grow Up', *Sydney Bulletin*, 2 Aug.1933, ML MSS 1284.

40 Frank Dalby Davison to Nettie Palmer, 21 Jan. 1933, NLA MS 1174/4185-86.

41 Marjorie Barnard to Nettie Palmer, 15 Feb. 1932, NLA MS 1174/1/3924-5.

42 'Jindyworobak Movement', in W. H. Wilde, J. Hooton and B. Andrews (eds), *Oxford Companion to Australian Literature*, Melbourne, 1985, 371–2.

43 Roger Milliss, *Serpent's Tooth: An Autobiographical Novel*, Victoria, 1984, 9.

44 Jean Devanny to Miles Franklin, 22 Sept. 1939, ML MSS 364/32/97-9.

45 Vance Palmer (from UK) to Frank Dalby Davison, 25 Nov. 1935, NLA MS 1945/1/97.

46 Frank Kermode, *History and Value*, Oxford, 1988, 5–6.

47 John Mulgan, *Man Alone*, Auckland, 1990, 73; quoted by Ryan, 'Extravagance of Thought and Feeling', 48.

48 Vance Palmer to Frank Dalby Davison, 4 July 1937, NLA MS 1945/115:12-13.

49 Doug Jarvis, 'Morality and Literary Realism: A Debate of the 1880s', *Southerly*, 43: 4 (1987), 404–20.

50 Ivor Indyk, 'The Economics of Realism: John Morrison', *Meanjin*, 46: 4, (Dec. 1987), 502. This formula to describe the radical nationalists' work was by A. A. Phillips.

51 Susan McKernan, *A Question of Commitment: Australian Literature in the Twenty Years after the War*, Sydney, 1989.

52 S. Murray-Smith, 'The Novel and Society', in Geoffrey Dutton (ed.), *The Literature of Australia*, Victoria, 1964, 427–40.

53 C. Merewether, 'Social Realism: The Formative Years', *Arena*, 46 (1977), 65–80, 70.

54 Sharyn Pearce, 'The Proletarianization of the Novel: The Cult of the Worker in Australian and American Fiction of the Depression', *Southerly*, 48: 2 (Dec. 1988), 187–200.

55 'Man Alone', and 'Mulgan, John', in R. Robinson and N. Wattie (eds), *Oxford Companion to New Zealand Literature*, Auckland, 1998, 331–2, 385–7.

56 Xavier Pons, '*The Battlers*: Kylie Tennant and the Australian Tradition', *Australian Literary Studies*, 6: 4 (Oct. 1974), 369.

57 Marjorie Barnard Papers, Lecture 4, 'Australian Democracy & Literature', 10, MSS SET 4511 Item 2.

58 Eleanor Dark, *The Little Company*, Sydney-Auckland, 1945, 17.

59 Bill Gammage, 'The Rabaul Strike, 1929', *Journal of Pacific History*, 10 (1975), 3–29.

60 Amirah Inglis, *Not a White Woman Safe: Sexual Anxiety and Politics in Port Moresby, 1920–34*, Canberra, 1974.

61 Malama Meleisea, *The Making of Modern Samoa: Traditional Authority and Colonial Administration in the Modern History of Western Samoa*, Suva, 1987, 124–8.

62 National Archives of New Zealand, Island Territories 88/3 part 1, 1924; Interim Report No. 2 on Native Affairs.

63 M. P. K. Sorrenson (ed.), *Na to Hoa Aroha: From Your Dear Friend: The Correspondence between Sir Apirana Ngata and Sir Peter Buck, 1925–50*, vol. 3, Auckland, 1988; also cited by G. Butterworth, *Sir Apirana Ngata*, Wellington, 1968, 17.

64 G. W. Rice, *Black November: The 1918 Influenza Epidemic in New Zealand*, Wellington, 1988, introduction, ch. 6.

65 J. M. Henderson, *Ratana: The Man, the Church, the Political Movement*, Wellington, 1972.

66 Butterworth, *Sir Apirana Ngata*; M. P. K. Sorrenson, 'Ngata, Apirana Turupa', *Dictionary of New Zealand Biography*, Auckland, vol. 3, 1996, 359–63.

[15] WAR IN EUROPE, AND IN THE PACIFIC

STORM CLOUDS

Australia and New Zealand, dominions since 1907, had their powers enlarged and their autonomy defined by the British government's Balfour Declaration in 1926. They were

> in no way subordinate to one another in respect of their domestic or external affairs, though united by a common allegiance to the Crown, and freely associated as members of the British Commonwealth of Nations.

Despite the declaration and the Statute of Westminster which gave it substance in 1931, most leaders assumed that autonomy meant something like internal self-government and that Britain would continue to represent the collective interests of the empire. That perception helped to draw their governments' attention towards London, almost as much as French colonies focused on Paris.

During the 1930s they were dismayed by the fraying of the world order established at Versailles and notionally supervised by the League of Nations, whose authority also declined as major powers withdrew. The Soviet Union was rhetorically committed to overthrowing capitalism, imperialism and colonialism – the bases of all Pacific government. Although they had no objection to colonialism or to capitalism, Germany, Italy and Japan seemed even more likely than Russia to tip the world into war. While German expansion in Europe and Italy's African adventures were remote, Japan's Micronesian mandate brought her alarmingly close – Rabaul and Apia are closer to Truk (Chuuk) than to any Australian or New Zealand harbour. Japanese authorities in Micronesia were fiercely secretive, fanning the (valid) suspicion that naval and military construction was going on despite the League of Nations mandate rules. The disappearance of Amelia Earhart flying near Japanese territory increased that suspicion, yet neither French nor British Imperial conferences made plans for a Pacific crisis. Nor did Pacific turmoil resonate as much as European calamities, in the hearts of far-flung Europeans. Despite the formal neutrality of British and dominion governments, Australian and New Zealand volunteers – and not only those of Spanish descent – fought in Spain:[1] few were involved in the closer agony of

China. Support for the Spanish republic was organized mainly by communist parties. A handful of Australians and New Zealanders also called themselves liberal internationalists, but they were small minorities, as were Japanese liberals whom they met in the Young Men's Christian Association and in conferences of the Institute of International Affairs.[2]

The Second World War was not one encounter but several. Japan and China had been at war for years before their campaigns were subsumed as one theatre of a world war. In the dominions it was easier to recollect earlier wars than to imagine future ones, so a reprise of the Great War (now re-named the First) seemed likely when Britain declared war on Germany in September 1939. A re-run seemed even more likely when Hitler's armies invaded Russia, creating a new Eastern Front. It was Japan's offensive against the United States in 1941 which transformed a European and Mediterranean conflict into a global war which incorporated – or suspended – other conflicts. The rhetoric of heroism was not confined to the great powers:

> Let us stand here and face them, let us take the wounds in our fronts and not in our backs fleeing, let our women escape with their small sons at the breast, and later bring them back to show them the place where we ... fought and died to the last man, so they will know who their fathers were and who it was that killed them.[3]

That Wagnerian prose was not Churchill's, but the terms in which New Guinea Big Men exhorted their Kawelka followers in parochial wars that we cannot now name. The Kawelka were oblivious to the First World War, and not much troubled by the Second.

WAR IN EUROPE

When Britain declared war on 3 September 1939, dominion responses varied only in timing. South Africa debated for three days and Canada a week, but it was still 3 September when Australia and New Zealand committed themselves. Disarmament had been widespread after Versailles, and the dominions were slow to re-arm. Although they worried about Japan's intentions, they had little strategic intelligence, so they asked the British government to propose the form of their contributions to what they expected to be an imperial effort. Australians and New Zealanders who happened to be in Britain, or enlisted in the Empire/Commonwealth Air Training Scheme, joined British formations (one was the future Australian prime minister John Grey Gorton). Naval co-operation was also close. Britain asked the dominions to reinforce Singapore and India, or send divisions to Europe and the Mediterranean.

Australia raised four infantry divisions (all volunteers, as in 1914), and sent three to the Middle East. Invoking Anzac, they called themselves the Second Australian Imperial Force (2AIF). Ponderous mobilization, cabinet indecision, fluctuating perceptions of Japanese intentions, the unreadiness of the armed forces and a shortage of shipping delayed their departure until early 1940. With the New Zealanders they then helped defeat the Italians in North Africa in 1941; they were deeply involved in the failed campaigns in Greece and Crete later that year; and in 1942 they fought Rommel in North Africa until they achieved victory at Alamein.

On the Western Front, however, Hitler's blitzkrieg swept through the Low Countries, forcing them and France to capitulate by June 1940, and British forces to evacuate. Worse: Western defeats increased Pacific tensions. Japan took advantage to throttle support for China, and revived doubts over the security of the European colonies and dominions. Neither governors nor settlers nor islanders in the French Pacific had prepared for such a crisis. With the fall of France, officials had to choose between General de Gaulle and Free France, or Marshal Pétain and the collaborationist Vichy regime. The resident in the New Hebrides opted for Free France, but other governors prevaricated until September, when settlers in Noumea and Tahiti staged *coups d'état* and installed Free French regimes. Briefly this World War recalled the First in its Pacific theatre: little fighting, most dominion forces sailing to Europe, and Islanders involved modestly (though France did recruit Tahitians and Kanak, Britain did raise Fijian formations, and Tongans paid for an RAF Spitfire).

Some 30,000 Melanesians were living in New Caledonia. They were subjects not citizens, governed by a native legal code and confined to reserves unless permitted to work elsewhere. The 17,000 *caldoches* were represented in the Governor's Council but the council chafed under the tight control of the Ministry of Colonies in Paris and envied the autonomy enjoyed by the dominions. At the Fall of France, a manifesto was circulated by autonomists aggrieved that New Caledonia was 'too much subjected to the [Ministry of Colonies] whose initiatives were frequently untimely and cancelled out the best efforts of governors to organize the colony'.[4] As it was clearly unrealistic to strike out for complete autonomy, on 19 September the colonists instead overthrew the Vichy-inclined governor and declared for de Gaulle. A catalyst to this action was the Australian cruiser *Adelaide* in Nouméa harbour. Her captain saw de Gaulle's representative take command, and organized the withdrawal of the old governor and the Vichy sloop *Dumont d'Urville*. Australians then strengthened the island's defences.[5] Kanak opinion carried little weight: the decisive players were *caldoches*. In a dispute between de Gaulle's Pacific high commissioner and his governor of New Caledonia, the high commissioner had the governor arrested – but the *caldoches* captured the high commissioner and forced de Gaulle to withdraw him.[6]

As in the Great War, German and Italian migrants and their descendants (and Japanese visitors) were in an invidious position. In New Guinea the officials suspected subversion, as German Lutheran missionaries seemed to have links with Nazi and German representatives. There and in Australia 'enemy aliens' were detained in camps with little regard to the compatibility of Germans and Italians, fascists and Jews, communists and conservatives. As prisoners (mainly Italian soldiers) were transferred from North Africa and the Middle East, the prisoner-of-war population eventually grew to 25,000. Most were European and many worked as farm labourers. Later, when Japanese civilians were interned, much stricter constraints were imposed.

WAR IN THE PACIFIC

The Japanese assault on Pearl Harbor on 7 December 1941 was the trigger for simultaneous offensives of stunning success. Japanese forces drove Americans from most of the Philippines by Christmas, when they also captured Rabaul. They soon controlled the north coast of New Guinea and the northern Solomons. More mortifying was the fall of Singapore, assumed to be impregnable, especially as its defenders outnumbered the Japanese assailants. In that lightning campaign the Australian 8th Division was destroyed: 18,490 men were lost, a tenth killed, a tenth wounded, and almost all captured.[7] Smaller groups were captured piecemeal in Southeast Asia and New Guinea, and the fate of these 22,000 Australian prisoners of war in Japanese hands remained a matter of anxiety until the very end of the war. More immediately, Japanese raids on Darwin in early 1942 and the discovery of three midget submarines in Sydney Harbour in May raised the stark spectre of invasion. Three years passed before the threat of Japanese hegemony in the Pacific – the counterpart of a Nazi Europe – was entirely removed.

Australia's prime minister on the eve of the Pacific war was Robert Menzies, leading the United Australia Party; of all leaders perhaps the most committed to Britain. The Opposition Labor Party was led by John Curtin, a conscientious objector in the First World War and a sceptic about reliance on the British navy. Curtin declined to enter a government of national unity, and became prime minister when Menzies lost the support of independent MPs. Although the two men and their parties differed in their strategic emphases, the division was less deep than some later glosses suggest. It was Churchill who suggested that two Australian divisions withdraw from the Middle East. Curtin's cabinet quickly agreed. The issue which provoked angry dissension was Churchill's wish to divert these divisions to Burma, while Curtin insisted on their returning to Australia.[8] Had they sailed to Burma, they might well have shared the tragic fate of the 8th Division. But the episode has more than military significance. In Australian nationalist narratives, British confidence in fortress Singapore and insistence on the primacy of the European theatres amount to *The Great Betrayal* (the title of David Day's 1988 study), a view passionately endorsed by Labor Prime Minister Keating in the 1990s. No such debate ruffled relations between Britain and New Zealand, whose forces remained in the Middle East. From 1942 Australia's war was fought mainly in the Pacific, while New Zealand's was almost entirely in Europe. There was no Anzac re-run.

Curtin at once sought American aid since Britain could clearly play no Pacific role until the war was won in Europe. In March 1942 Douglas MacArthur escaped from the Philippines to take command of General Headquarters, Southwest Pacific, in Melbourne. That boosted Australian morale, but it took time to organize serious resistance to the Japanese. They were poised to take Port Moresby by sea in May when they were turned back by the American fleet in the Battle of the Coral Sea. They then attacked overland, but were bloodied on the Kokoda Track. They were then driven

Plate 15.1 Kokoda Track. Soldiers and carriers enjoy a break in the weather, and a pause in the toil of the Track. Courtesy of the Australian War Memorial.

from the Solomons by a massive American push through Guadalcanal. By early 1943 they were isolated and had begun their long retreat along the New Guinea coast. Towards the end of 1943 the Americans began their westward onslaught from the central Pacific. That made New Guinea marginal strategically; but in late 1943 Allied forces landed in New Britain and fought the Japanese to their stronghold in Rabaul, where 100,000 men surrendered at the end of the war, releasing the people from four years of occupation and hunger. GIs also landed on Bougainville, then moved on: from October 1944 Australians replaced them and were still harassing the Japanese when atomic bombs on Nagasaki and Hiroshima brought the war's last theatre to a close.[9]

The savagery of the island campaigns was extreme. If the war in Europe was fought at least partly over ideology, that was not how soldiers, prisoners or civilians experienced the Pacific war. All of white Australians' history and cultural orientation framed this as the ultimate racial contest foreseen by so many. They took few Japanese prisoners, only partly because tropical forest made that difficult and Japanese soldiers were loath to surrender. Japanese prisoners included civilians interned when war broke out; and over a thousand were held at Cowra in New South Wales. Cowra is so remote from Sydney (or the sea, or anywhere else) that it seemed secure; but in 1944 the internees organized an escape attempt, storming the barbed wire fence. A third escaped and some remained at large for over a week; but 231 died in the break-out, and so did four Australians.[10] That suicidal episode reinforced the Australian belief that Japanese preferred death to captivity, and of course heightened anxiety over Australian POWs. In this do-or-die conflict, unlike the First World War,

Australia seemed to be the front line, a circumstance which united the country. There was an obvious need for economic as well as military planning, and conscientious objection was rare.

The most searing impact of the war on Australians was speculation, followed by fearful knowledge, of the fate of prisoners of war.[11] Although half a million Australians served overseas, there were only 39,000 casualties (against 58,000 in the Great War), and probably more Papua New Guineans died than Australians. A high proportion of Australian casualties were among captives. Both sides saw the conflict as a racial show-down.[12] Japan did not observe the pertinent Geneva conventions, and there was no echo of the respectful treatment meted out to Russian prisoners in 1904. Some Australians (including women nurses) were executed on capture, but many more died of gross overwork, malnutrition and disease. Places and episodes became emblematic of a general horror: Changi prison in Singapore which was the main holding camp; the Thai–Burma railway whose construction provoked the most sustained inhumane treatment; the Sandakan death march which only half a dozen survived. About 8,000 of the 22,000 POWs of the Japanese died (compared with 3 per cent of Australians captured by German or Italian forces). Of Australia's few non-sporting heroes in the twentieth century, Edward Dunlop was perhaps foremost on account of his heroic treatment of POW patients.

Many POWs testified in the War Trials; many more found it impossible to share their experiences with their families. One generation of Australians learned of these privations through novels like Russell Braddon's *Naked Island* (1952) and the British film *A Town Like Alice* (1956). A later generation was reminded by the publication of first-hand accounts and academic studies.[13] These horrors coloured postwar relations with Japan, sustaining a deep suspicion which delayed Australian recognition of the two economies' complementarity. By the 1990s, when the Hawke and Keating governments promoted links with 'Asia', it was necessary to recast the prisoners as pioneers (albeit involuntary) of that geopolitical reconception.[14]

TAKING PART

The closeness of the fighting swept aside some barriers to participation. Australia raised formations for Torres Strait Islanders and for Aboriginal coast-watchers, as well as allowing entry into mainstream regiments. Islanders also experienced a variety of wars. Despite settlers' fears of arming them, a Papuan Infantry Battalion was established, and in 1944 the first New Guinea Infantry Battalion. Together they formed the Pacific Islands Regiment (PIR), feared or respected in jungle warfare. Some 3,500 fought in the regiment, while 3,000 police saw action and 1,000 served as medical orderlies. Fijian soldiers fought in the Solomons alongside the Solomon Islands Defence Force. Most of the 300 volunteers who fought in Africa, Italy and France in the Tahitian company of the French Pacific Battalion were Polynesians and *demis*, and they fought alongside Melanesians from New

Caledonia. The war changed these soldiers' view of themselves: they could now be certain that they deserved respect, and they demanded it. PIR soldiers broke down detention centres to liberate comrades, and generally protested against differential treatment. Although the army did increase pay rates and provide some postwar compensation, men of the PIR waited in vain for appropriate recognition.[15]

Fijians enlisted eagerly. Over 6,000 served in the Fiji Military Forces, including the Labour Corps. One won a Victoria Cross,[16] confirming British regard for these exemplary colonial people. Conversely Fiji Indians' lives as indentured labourers and labour-tenants gave them a bleaker view of empire, and news from India reinforced it. They would fight overseas only if they gained equal pay with Europeans, so the only Indian platoon was disbanded, and further offers to enlist were rebuffed. Nor did they respond to the lure of the Labour Corps. CSR contracts made enlistment impossible for most ten-ant farmers, so only 331 enlisted, but that would be held against them. Fijian eagerness sustained the case for a separate Fijian administration, and in 1944 the government put that regime substantially in the hands of the chiefs. At the head of a Fijian Affairs Board, Ratu Lala Sukuna and other chiefs regulated every Fijian village. Sukuna's vision rejected individualism, so his reign could 'only tend to the strengthening of communal separateness and the intensification of communal problems for the future'.[17]

Many Islanders were conscripted for labour. Around 37,000 Papua New Guineans toiled for the Australian New Guinea Administrative Unit (Angau), which conscripted them for the army and plantations, to build roads, airstrips and camps. Angau had to meet quotas 'even if a temporary sacrifice of native interests is involved'. Many deserted. If not, they carried 40-pound loads of rations and ammunition into the rainforest and ridges of the Kokoda Track.[18] Then they carried the wounded back. The press and newsreels sentimentalized them as 'Fuzzy-Wuzzy Angels':

Using leaves to keep the rain off
And as gentle as a nurse
Slow and careful in bad places
On the awful mountain track,
The look upon their faces
Would make you think that Christ was black.[19]

Other villagers worked almost as hard growing food, clearing tracks, burying the dead, nursing the sick and maintaining village life.

Australians were informed that loyalty inspired these heroics, but villagers also carried wounded Japanese and rescued Zero pilots. When the Australians left his Sepik village in 1942, Michael Somare found the Japanese very friendly.[20] Many villagers welcomed them, but towards the end of the war soldiers had to live off the land, appropriating food and alienating their local allies.[21] Villagers who held positions of trust with them had to change alle-giance deftly, to escape postwar Australian witch-hunts for 'collaborators'.[22]

A Labour government in New Zealand, which included objectors from the First World War, and Labor in Australia, both introduced conscription, but in Australia this was imposed only for 'home defence' in the Pacific war, consistent with attitudes since the turn of the century, though now embracing most of the islands occupied by the Japanese. This time New Zealand did not conscript Maori. Instead Ngata animated the formation of the Maori Battalion whom he divided on tribal lines to ensure a dynamic force, driven by competition among *iwi*. The 28th Maori Battalion became heroes in Italy. Certain that they, too, deserved respect, they fought to have their rights recognized on a tribal basis, as leader Charles Bennett later reflected: 'we knew at that time what the price of citizenship was and we were prepared to pay it'.[23] This time, Maori land was exempted from acquisition for soldier settlement schemes and Maori soldiers were eligible.

Within boundaries set by the dominant culture, the Maori Battalion nudged their people closer to equality through their war-time prowess. In this war Maori 'assumed unprecedented responsibility in the administration of their affairs'. At home the Maori-controlled Maori War Effort Organization, formed in 1942, worked through *iwi* and *hapu* to register Maori, co-ordinate recruitment and all war-time activities. It won responsibility through the need for workers in dairy factories and freezing works. The Maori War Effort Organization involved all tribes, and even won support from the Waikato, Taranaki and Tuhoe people, those most alienated by dispossession, and provided the basis for Maori visions of postwar reconstruction under Maori leadership. Autonomy lasted only for the duration. Not allowed to be Maori on their own terms, *iwi* were denied the 'flax-roots' structure which worked so effectively during the war and which Maoridom hoped to make the basis of a postwar, Maori-led, Maori Affairs Department. Contrary to government promises, control of Maori affairs remained with the central bureaucracy from 1945, though the term 'native' was replaced by Maori.[24]

Aboriginal Australians were at first excluded from the armed forces, but with the threat from the north some were informally recruited into the army. Others performed heavy labour on roads, army camps and airstrips, or were recruited to pick cane or cotton. Northern Aboriginal families were compulsorily removed, 'ostensibly for safety but also because of fears about their collusion with the Japanese'.[25] Nor had the Australian government wanted no black Americans to be sent to Australia. Those serving in the United States army were segregated, but in Melbourne and Brisbane, where American troops were stationed, black Americans were often welcome as objects of curiosity.

WOMEN AND MEN

The arrival of Americans on Australian and New Zealand turf helped to change the images of Australian and New Zealand forces. So did the presence and absence of the British in the European and Pacific theatres of war; and, particularly, the separation of Australians and New Zealanders who fought in different theatres from February 1943. New Zealand's 2nd Division stayed in the Mediterranean, serving in Italy from 1943 to 1945. In Europe,

New Zealanders retained the British as a point of comparison and marker of difference. No longer obliged to identify as not Australian, the soldiers adopted some 'Australian' characteristics. The archetypal New Zealand soldier shifted from the gentleman pioneer to the hard case and hard man, still rugged and muscular, if no longer 'tall'; with a larrikin streak befitting 'General Freyberg's Forty Thousand Thieves'.[26]

Conversely, the British absence from the Pacific and the glamour of the Americans subdued Anzac images at home. The Australians' larrikin bushman stereotype merely lessened their ability to compete with Americans as local heroes and lovers, a galling experience on returning from the war in Europe to defend their loved ones, and way of life, from Japanese invasion.

The home front and war front overlapped for men and women because war came home. Women mobilized for patriotic work, as in 1914, knitting, packing Red Cross parcels for servicemen and POWs, and as drivers. Janet Fraser, the wife of New Zealand's Labour prime minister, Peter Fraser, who served on the Wellington Hospital Board and on an abortion inquiry in New Zealand in the 1930s, joined Dr Agnes Bennett to form the Women's War Service Auxiliary in 1940 as an umbrella for women's organizations to organize registers of 'maids of war work'. This extended to digging up lawns and parks to grow vegetables. In Australia, the Women's Voluntary National Register and Women's Australian National Services were parallel co-ordinating bodies. Women were once again keen to don uniform, and once again authorities opposed their 'playing at soldiers'.

The Pacific war changed this. Women joined official auxiliaries to the armed forces in Australia from 1941, and from 1942 in New Zealand. They also became 'land girls', finally making women's rural work visible. The presence of the Americans also increased the demand for women's work. With the Japanese threat hovering, Australia introduced industrial conscription, obliging all 'unoccupied women' (single and divorced, and women without children, aged 18 to 45 – the (re)productive years) to join the workforce, when they had not performed the war work of having babies. With the exception of the Lady Gowrie Child Centre in Melbourne, which became a war-time centre and extended its hours in 1943, no thought was given to child-care centres in order to recruit mothers, and evidence that both mothers and small children benefited from the Melbourne centre's longer hours was suppressed because it undercut domestic ideals. While middle-class women resisted being 'man' powered, working-class women were conscripted into essential industries; one, whose husband died of war wounds, preferred crying over peeling onions to staying home with her grief.[27] Women fed and clothed people, as always, but they remained auxiliaries, in paid work merely 'for the duration'; those standing in for railway porters became 'station assistants', clerks became 'clerical assistants', and drivers 'tram girls', who daringly wore trousers.

The war brought new controls. Australia and New Zealand rationed petrol (more generously in Australia, with its vaster distances): that lasted until 1950 in New Zealand, with two breaks. Pearl Harbor led to panic buying of sugar and tea, and Australia and New Zealand rationed both in 1942. Butter and meat followed in 1943; butter was for Britain, and meat for the Americans in the Pacific. Austerity clothing prompted new fashions of women's slacks, to ease the wear on stockings, and school socks for girls because stockings were scarce. From shortages and import restrictions New Zealand's rugged Crown Lynn china was born, while the new breed of nutritionists advised how best to use local produce and cook egg-less cakes. 'Priority' customers for eggs (and in Australia, oranges) were expectant and nursing mothers, young children, and invalids. Vegetable growing extended to a New Zealand 'dig for victory' campaign in 1943 to 'make every yard of ground yield'.

A million Americans passed through Australia, mainly Queensland. Brisbane became a garrison town while 20,000 GIs stayed in New Zealand for two years (the United States South Pacific headquarters were in Auckland). Through their influence on Australian and New Zealand food habits they affected culture and identity. Americans were used to vegetables, including frozen vegetables. They were also much larger milk drinkers than New Zealanders or Australians. Prompted by the American presence, New Zealand launched a milk inquiry in 1944 and to its chagrin found that while milk produced for Britain was good – regulated and inspected – milk for local consumption was unreliable, and not required to be pasteurized (Christchurch was proud of this 'freedom' which locals saw as 'British').

Americans influenced much more than milk production; they were objects of desire, exotic intruders with smart uniforms; money (twice the spending power of Australians); and access to luxury goods, notably tobacco, silk stockings and chocolates. Uniformed Americans reflected the romance of Hollywood. They were more courteous than Australian and New Zealand men, proffered gifts, including flowers ('sissy' to jealous locals), and enjoyed women's company. They engaged women in conversation rather than retreating with 'mates' to the other end of the room. They were also here. For young women, the war – through the Americans – offered opportunities for thrills and sexual adventure. For men, they were usurpers, women-takers, a threat to their manhood, and Australian men directed at women their bitter hostility over this loss of sexual power.[28]

Feminine identities, ever fluid, were reinforced by war-time conditions in their shift, at the level of discourse, from an emphasis on ladylike qualities of grace and refinement to sex appeal and allure.[29] Younger women responded to these new representations of identity, which older women active in mother-oriented first-wave feminist organizations found abhorrent and debasing. Young women moving into paid work could pursue sexualized ideals of attractiveness to men by purchasing commodities such as lipstick. If they acquired a Yank boyfriend, however, they risked scorn from local men and their supporters for 'going jeep'. They also risked assault, and bore the costs of new sexual freedoms such as pregnancy. Joy accompanied pain; such risks could seem worthwhile for a young woman or she might block them out when the love of her life was about to leave and might be killed in the Pacific.[30] It was a common saying in Australia and New Zealand – indeed wherever Americans were stationed – that the Yanks were 'over-paid, over-sexed and over here'.

PLANS AND VISIONS OF RECONSTRUCTION

One of many lessons which the war seemed to prove was that government intervention could create full employment and channel energies to national purposes. A long term of Labor government (1941–9) and (from 1944) control over both houses of federal parliament allowed the Curtin and Chifley governments to act on this perception. A new economic and social order was the goal of a Department of Post War Reconstruction created in 1942, staffed by young public servants headed by H. C. Coombs, imbued with Keynesian ideas, and then inspired by the Bretton Woods plans for postwar economic management on a global scale. The Commonwealth sought a permanent increase of powers in economic management, for a permanent reordering of the economy to banish forever the mass unemployment of the Depression. As matters turned out, the Commonwealth faced increasing opposition from the private sector, the High Court and the states, as the threat of invasion receded. Several centralizing options were put – and mainly lost – in national referenda.

If Labor's ambitions were not fully realized, significant elements were continued by Menzies and the Liberal–Country coalition which succeeded them in 1949. The Snowy Mountains hydro-electric scheme, for example, was begun in 1949 under defence emergency powers (circumventing constitutional limits). Had the Menzies government or New South Wales or Victoria opposed the concept, it would have failed. In fact it became the largest engineering feat in Australian history, affecting irrigation and electric power in Victoria and the Capital Territory as well as New South Wales; and it mobilized hosts of European 'new Australians' (and came to be seen as a source of Australian multiculturalism). If its environmental impact was problematic, its boost to national self-esteem was significant.[31]

The department also envisaged a more educated workforce, so ex-service personnel were supported in university courses and trade training. As part of the vision for reconstruction, the new Australian National University opened in 1950, the federal government's first venture into higher education. Its charter was to meet Australia's (and incidentally some of New Zealand's and the Islands') newly identified needs for advanced research and graduate training and as an 'intellectual power house for the rebuilding of society'.[32] Nor would the newly trained and educated workers be left to the mercy of a fickle world market: a public works programme was devised in case employment rates slackened. As it happened there was neither labour nor raw material to alleviate the housing shortage. Also to ensure full employment, manufacturers were encouraged by tariff protection and by formal agreements such as that with General Motors to produce an all-Australian car: the Holden. These programmes were complemented by a drive for European immigration which (again) reached its full potential in 1949, when Labor lost power – but the Menzies government continued the strategy.

Not all Labor's plans worked. The Commonwealth gained wider powers over taxation and in banking, but failed in its attempt to nationalize the banks and to introduce a universal health scheme. Conversely Commonwealth powers to control wages prompted a disastrous show-down with coalminers on the eve of the 1949 election; and continued price controls offered Menzies an easy and popular target. Even at its fullest extent, this programme presumed a vigorous private sector. This was planning, but not socialism.[33]

Socialist alternatives were difficult to develop. Socialists formed the Communist Party of Australia as early as 1920 – or rather, foreshadowing future schisms, they formed two parties, one of which became a loyal client of Stalin and the Communist International.[34] The party was therefore obliged to treat the Second World War as a contest between imperialisms, until Hitler invaded the Soviet Union: that made the party an illegal organization until the expansion of the war. There were over 20,000 party members by 1944. Chifley's assault on the coalminers' strike dented the party's confidence, and its trade union bastions came under attack from Industrial Groups, the anti-communist activists organized by B. A. Santamaria with the encouragement of the Catholic hierarchy. The Menzies government failed to proscribe the Communist Party, but the Petrov Royal Commission from 1954 persistently accused its members of spying for the Soviet Union. That was especially hurtful in view of the party's strenuous attempts to harness Australian nationalism to the radical cause. At any rate the party's strength – largely intellectual in Melbourne, industrial in Sydney – waned through the late 1950s and 1960s. Splits involving accusations of Trotskyism, Stalinism, Moscow-line and Beijing-line further confused the issues and blurred the dream of radical social and political change.[35]

A Communist Party also emerged in New Caledonia. An Association of Friends of the USSR formed in Noumea in 1941, comprising metropolitan and local French radicals. War-time alliances in Europe made the Soviet Union unusually popular among public servants and colonists alike. Despite a large American garrison therefore, and with help from communists and Russophiles in Australia, the association gave the Soviet Union a higher profile than might have been expected. Peace and the rise of General de Gaulle continued that profile, and communists won parliamentary seats and took up some cabinet positions. In Noumea, some activists wondered about the next step. Independently of the party in France, they decided to create a local affiliate. At the moment of the party's birth, however, its crippling internal contradiction emerged. Australian and New Zealand communists could adopt 'progressive' policies denouncing racial discrimination at home or abroad without jeopardizing white proletarian support. In New Caledonia, however, French proletarians were dismayed by the party embracing Vietnamese (whose lives as miners and labourers predisposed them to join), much less Kanak and their anti-colonial ambitions. The communist moment had passed by 1948, but its continuing members had adapted to the local context sufficiently to demand abolition of the *indigenat*, racial equality, and political mobilization for Kanak. In that sense it proved to be a spur to the politics of the 1950s and 1960s.[36]

Across the Coral Sea, war-time enthusiasm for Fuzzy-Wuzzy angels prompted some rhetoric about an Australian New Deal for them: but the minister visited the territory only once, and relied on his department to initiate policies. Policy decisions were tardy, routine issues neglected, and policy and programmes languished.[37] Only once did the New Deal make a difference. The minister cancelled all labour contracts from 15 October 1945 and 35,000 men walked home, halting plantation production. However, soon the planters returned and recruited the labour that might have enriched village life. The New Deal restored white dominance, modified by initiatives in health, education and agricultural advice.

Bureaucratic management was not the only possible route to a new order, although it was the only one tolerated by Australian authorities. The American war-time presence was one of the more arresting features of the war for Islanders, more perhaps where they built air bases than in places where they fought. By mid-1942, 8,700 Americans were stationed in Tonga, over 6,000 in the New Hebrides, 22,000 in New Caledonia, and a whole division in Fiji. A million Americans passed through the island of Manus. Everywhere they created jobs and paid better than colonial rates.

> Having no stake in colonial rule, and consisting of black as well as white troops, Americans came, built airfields, gave away more food than could be eaten, and departed, their place taken by colonial officials who often seized the goods they had just been given. ... New kinds of Australians appeared too, who ignored the Army's rules against fraternization. Informal, egalitarian and disrespectful of authority ... they were not the 'English', who ordered everyone about, but 'Australians', who shared a tin of bully beef or a packet of cigarettes.[38]

In Noumea the Americans assumed control of labour to ensure decent treatment; and many cult movements (see below) built airstrips to give American wealth direct access to their island.[39]

Partly in response to the limitless matériel of war, and the contrast between possible wealth and actual poverty, some Melanesian initiatives were described by officials as 'cargo cults'. That academic term lumped together and condemned a slather of 'political organizations, movements, charismatic sects, and crusades'.[40] Outsiders were incredulous that ritual action might procure Western goods and build a harmonious order within villages, and with Europeans. Peter Worsley proposed that these were proto-nationalist responses to colonialism:

> the activist millenarian movement is typical only of a certain phase in the political and economic development of this region, and ... is destined to disappear or become a minor form of political expression among backward elements.[41]

Other scholars argued that 'the cargo cult was a normal, creative Melanesian form of cultural dynamism'. Peter Lawrence argued that cultists wanted European goods because they represented equality with foreigners.[42] Anthropologists increasingly 'normalize' these ventures: 'What we call "cult" or "movement"' says Roy Wagner, 'is nothing less than the ordinary form of ritual and interpretive innovation in Melanesian societies'. So completely have cults been sanitized and exorcized in academic literature that Colin Filer wonders if we are allowed to mention them at all.[43] However construed, these movements were most prolific in the aftermath of war, when they were most needed to explain villagers' poverty and whites' affluence. Missionaries condemned these movements; anthropologists were baffled by them; colonial governments suppressed them; and independent governments do the same.

Two notable instances disconcerted returning colonial governments. Solomon Islanders in the Labour Corps contrasted American generosity with British meanness, and formed a movement known as Maasina Rule (often rendered as Marching Rule) in south Malaita, where leaders collected tax and revived customary law, cementing the movement with Christian, pagan and other ideas. The movement spread through the eastern and central Solomons, with adherents refusing to pay official taxes. Expecting the return of Americans in 1949, they created beacons for the ships, and built stores for the cargo. The British did not retrieve their position on Malaita until the 1950s, relying largely on mass arrests and a militia recruited in the western islands of the archipelago.[44]

Even better known is the John Frum Movement on Tanna, beginning in about 1940, in which 'kastom received a positive interpretation to counter-balance negative, Christian readings of Melanesian culture. People revived customs of reciprocal exchange, dance, and the kava ritual which they had abandoned on conversion to Christianity'.

> In his first appearances ... John Frum stated the need to revive knowledge which had been devalued during a period of Presbyterian mission control. He also talked of a coming cosmic inversion of relations between land and sea, mountain and valley, and black and white. Cargo elements played a part in his early messages, which predicted the arrival of the American military bringing political freedom and economic largesse. Many Islanders abandoned the Presbyterian, Catholic and Seventh-day Adventist missions. ... Many men resumed drinking kava, thereby honouring their ancestors, and revived ritual exchanges and dance festivities. They also abandoned Christian coastal villages for garden and village sites which their families had deserted a generation before. Some, moreover, rejected money and challenged the presence of European traders.[45]

Repression was counter-productive, and enthusiasm reached fever pitch when Americans arrived, as predicted. Men joined labour corps to work at the United States Base on Efate. And as the movement outlived colonial repression, it transformed into a church (with regular rituals) and a political party. In the 1950s its leaders recruited police and held court, and overcame the structural problem besetting all such movements, how to recreate itself through the generations.

By comparison with Islanders' expectations, most of the colonial reforms of these years were trivial. New Caledonia and French Polynesia became territories of the French Union; special codes of laws for indigenes were withdrawn in favour of French citizenship; and each territory elected one deputy and one senator to the National Assembly in Paris. In New Caledonia therefore Kanaks were no longer confined to reserves: they could live in town without seeking permission and they could be paid the same wages as Europeans.

Transforming legal possibility into reality was a different matter. United Nations trusteeships replaced League of Nations mandates for New Guinea, Nauru and Western Samoa, but with no immediate consequence. Nauru's Council of Chiefs complained that they still had no role in formulating policy.[46] Western Samoan leaders feared that a trusteeship might frustrate their desire for independence; but on reflection the chiefs decided not to ask for amalgamation with American Samoa (which would have brought all Samoa under United States administration) but to seek separate self-government.[47] In these piecemeal ways, high aspirations in the Islands were gradually and incompletely harnessed to colonial programmes. The parallels with Australian and New Zealand reformists' disappointments were not widely remarked.

NEW ZEALAND: EQUALITY OF OPPORTUNITY

Buoyed by confidence in science and a new world order, the optimum had become the norm in child health and development. Concerns abounded during and after the war to avoid dictatorship, promote democracy and prevent aggression in children. Just as the Depression added security, the Second World War contributed training for democratic living as important for child development. The myth of equality of opportunity represented a New Zealand response to ideas in common currency internationally, that a child should be allowed to fulfil his or her potential. The ideals of the 'New Education', to promote the full development of the individual and a rounded education of the whole child, provided a mantra of postwar reconstruction. Clarence Beeby, director of education from 1940 to 1960, penned a much-quoted statement of equality of opportunity for Peter Fraser, then minister of education (from 1940 Fraser was New Zealand's prime minister), in 1939:

> The Government's objective, broadly expressed, is that every person, whatever his level of academic ability, whether he be rich or poor, whether he live in town or country, has a right, as a citizen, to a free education of the kind for which he is best fitted and to the fullest extent of his powers.[48]

Beeby later apologized for the masculine pronouns. His words tallied with the American pragmatist philosopher John Dewey's concept of education as growth. Educators in Australia and New Zealand championed Dewey's hope for the school as an ideal society. In Australia the focus on all-round child development of the pre-school child could be seen in the formation of the model Lady Gowrie Child Centres in Melbourne and other state capitals in 1939–40. In New Zealand innovations occurred first in the school rather than the pre-school, in the infant room, and in new co-educational secondary schools. Equality of opportunity required a broader school curriculum, beginning with the primary school. New Zealand followed the same influences as Australia, adapted from the United States and Britain, but with a focus on the school rather than the kindergarten child. Postwar import restrictions and the emphasis on child development produced Buzzy Bee in 1948, the red wooden pull-along toy for the pre-schooler which became a Kiwi icon. Buzzy Bee and his clickety-clack noise as his wings revolved and wheels turned entered Kiwi culture as the toy of the postwar baby boomers. It was also an exercise in making do: the manufacturers, Ramsey Brothers of Auckland, diversified after the war from toilet-roll holders to wooden toys. By the 1950s they sold 40,000 Buzzy Bees a year.

Such ideals of full development did not apply to indigenous children. In the Maori district high schools established in the 1940s under Beeby, he later acknowledged a failure to allow Maori *kaumatua* (elders) to influence the curriculum. Maori leaders valued academic education, whereas the new Maori district high schools in rural areas emphasized practical skills and a manual education appropriate for training a manual labour force. Aboriginal children remained workers, but were gradually admitted to state primary schools with the shift in policy towards assimilation. The New Education only extended to Aboriginal, Pacific Island and Maori children where (as in New Zealand) they attended mainstream state schools, as two-thirds did by the 1950s.

The pre-eminence of equality of opportunity as an idea coincided with the shift in both countries to a policy of assimilation, in New Zealand of 'integrating' indigenous people, which accompanied a shift from race to welfare thinking. In this changed context, given further impetus by the war, Maori continued to seek to take the initiative. At Wellington Teachers' College, a site of the new ideas under an innovative principal, Frank Lopdell, Kingi Tahiwi was appointed to teach Maori language and culture. His expressed hope was to increase tolerance by educating young Pakeha teachers as well as Maori in Maoritanga. Tahiwi insisted against Maori opposition that his Pakeha and Maori pupils join the Ngata Poneke Maori Club in Wellington, formed to assist Maori on their migration to the cities (see chapter 16), and he made a big impact.[49] More generally, the Maori Battalion's illustrious reputation made it impossible to maintain a system of social security benefits which discriminated against Maori. The Maori Social and Economic Advancement Act 1945 proved a compromise; it ensured that copies of the Treaty of Waitangi were hung on school walls, though pupils had yet to learn about the treaty, and it created the Department of Maori Affairs as a welfare bureau. Some achievement of equality for Maori followed in welfare terms, notably through family benefits. There were noticeable improvements in the wellbeing and dress of Maori children from greater equality in payment of family benefits and Maori women's spending power on behalf of their children. But Maori Affairs remained in Pakeha hands. Without land, tribal councils shifted their demands to welfare concerns, such as better Maori housing.

BRINGING THE AUSTRALIAN INTELLIGENTSIA TO HEEL

The suppression (or co-option) of charismatic Islander leaders and their followers also had parallels in the dominions. Naturally, the mechanisms of containment differed, just as the content and style of their visions diverged.

War imposed new priorities on all citizens, including the intelligentsia. Artists, writers and journalists wore new hats as public servants or information officers, public historians or broadcasters. It was, as one admitted, 'a case of working where one is most urgently needed'.[50] The war effort imposed a duty not a choice, and wide divergences of view surfaced only (and hesitantly or obliquely) in private correspondence because of censorship. Some differences probed the pacifist alternative. A curt exchange between two writers suggests this undercurrent of tensions. The occasion was the release of Aldous Huxley's pacifist manifesto *Ends and Means*. The book – and the discussions it provoked – drove a deep wedge between colleagues and friends. Reacting angrily at the implication that she was 'merely "thinking British"' when she advocated war, Nettie Palmer took pains to clarify the matter: 'It's not *Chamberlain*'s Britain we're supporting: but any country that at last resists Nazism to any degree is our friend, as I see it'.[51] The outburst left Frank Dalby Davison 'a little bit puzzled that you should have thought me capable of such thick-headedness as to accuse you – in the light of all I know of you – of "merely thinking British"'. Unmoved by her argument, he reiterated his pacifist position:

> If our forceful friends the Germans came here, I think it would be best to neither fight nor run away. It might be uncomfortable or even dangerous for a while – and some might even get killed – but I think the world would be in the way of discovering better methods of dealing with difficulties.[52]

Around 150 years into the development of British Australian society, questions of identity and loyalty – to empire and to Australia – still niggled consciences and unsettled relations even in radical nationalist circles.

Pacifism proved less explosive in peace than in war, when it could be discussed outside the emotive dichotomy of 'patriotism' and 'treason'. Feminists led the postwar campaign to ban war. Their most potent symbol of protest was woman-as-mother. War, they argued, imposed peculiar stresses on women's nurturing roles, requiring them to put country first, family second, and embrace a call to battle that might kill or injure husbands and sons. As the mothers of tomorrow's soldiers, therefore, women had a right to demand a greater voice in public debates on issues from foreign affairs to education. Active campaigns were waged by women 'citizen politicians' arguing the need for women's contribution to 'running world affairs'.[53] Convincing the average woman proved no easier than convincing the community of the need for women to use their collective political and moral power, as mothers, to help run world affairs. Once again the gap was vast between educated and non-educated women, as between the intelligentsia and the community as a whole.

In Western radical circles the New Order became a shorthand term for 'the good society'. The vision grew with the war and flourished in the prospect of peace: the New Order would be the reward and tribute for sacrifice and desolation. From the ashes of the Old Order would rise 'a better and saner social organization'.[54] The New Order was the wave of the future for Western society, a catch-all phrase that never gained substance nor clear definition. It was partly this vagueness that allowed it to become all dreams to all people and gave it momentum. It also carried strong moral overtones. In Australia, this vision embraced radical reform in all major aspects of community life. It emphasized education and health, and assumed the development of a new ethical basis to all human organization.

The immediate postwar years shattered radical reformers' hopes of economic parity and social harmony, bringing not the New Order but a new chaos. The romantic anticipation of peace – 'that whatever the world will be when the war ends, the world will be different'[55] – soured into 'a general distilled sense of fear' even before the war ended. Hiroshima and Nagasaki forced a new consciousness in radical circles, filling would-be social reconstructionists with deep 'forebodings'.[56]

Fellow radicals in Europe and the United States shared this dismay. Some urged Australians to regard themselves as blest – not cursed – by distance from the West, telling of anti-semitism rife in 'the home of the free and the land of the brave', and 'red purges' in which writers and intellectuals seemed to be leading targets. Pulitzer Prize winner Karl Shapiro, an American soldier-poet posted to a camp near the Blue Mountains for part of the war, urged disengagement from the West and isolation. His *News to Australia* (eleven verses and 150 lines dedicated to Eleanor and Eric Dark) addressed the spiritual and moral decline of the United States, and pleaded with Australians to

Befriend your insularity, be far,
Hug the antipodes, survive.[57]

The war-time tensions between an American-led Western Alliance and Soviet Russia that erupted in Europe and later in Asia almost as the peace treaty was signed, led eventually to a 'balance of terror', and Australian developments resonated with global tensions. Only a year after the war, 'believers in socialism' were questioning Labor's commitment 'to create a socialist society'. The Left campaigned vigorously to bring the party to heel, accusing it of abandoning its principles and becoming 'the left wing' capitalist party and not socialist at all.[58] For the Left, the ultimate outrage was Chifley's decision in the winter of 1949 to use troops to break the coalminers' strike. Two months before Labor's defeat at the polls, a heavy despondency had settled on radicals: 'Hope Aust. Democracy doesn't fall in bits about us – there seems to be some large cracks appearing'.[59]

The resounding victory of Menzies' conservative forces at the election buried the hopes and drained the moral energies of a unique generation of Australian Left radicals. They were born with federation, raised against the horror of the Great War, called to arms by the world economic crisis of the 1930s, and bonded spiritually to 'socialism' by the Spanish Civil War. A generation elapsed before social reformism was re-ignited by new visionaries who focused on Gough Whitlam. *New Left* voices such as the cultural historian Humphrey McQueen later argued that the social and political conservatism of twentieth-century Australian society – not capitalist conspiracy from within or beyond Australia – defeated both Chifley and Whitlam. The people (this new generation of Left radicals conceded) were not and never had been revolutionary. 'History', a member of the Left consoled himself, 'was on our side', though the community was not.[60] It is no coincidence that in the large corpus – memoirs, cultural and political histories – surrounding the decline of the Left after the war, the word 'dream' recurs, more in sorrow than in hope.[61] A New Order did not redeem the land of the convict, or what Miriam Dixson identifies as the 'class–convict–frontier cluster'.[62]

Parallel developments were at work in cultural circles. Radical nationalism was a spent force except among die-hard Old Left historians carrying the torch of righteous anger for the convict-bushman. It is doubtful that the idealism of a Henry Lawson in his celebration of mateship and unionism, and the populist philosophy underpinning Furphy's *Such is Life*, ever claimed more than sentimental commitment from most readers. At any rate after the war Labor and the Left could no longer claim broad community appeal. Menzies' victories punctured the Left's identification with the masses: the 'Common Man' did not vote for the New Order but for his suburban quarter-acre block. It was time to enjoy the fruits of war and sacrifice.

The veil was lifting elsewhere, too. State patronage of the arts, pursued by 1930s writers as crucial to the development of a distinctive national literature, was flexing its muscle and threatening to compromise the integrity of the arts it was designed to protect. Ironically, the agitators for state support a decade earlier, literary figures of the Left, bore the brunt of repression. Instruments of power, such as the Commonwealth Literary Fund, created to facilitate independence became, in conservative hands, instruments of repression. The new overseers of culture disliked the mingling of literary and political elements that had marked the literature of radical nationalists, and the art and profession of writing suffered setbacks. Independence and autonomy – the pillars of the 'little magazines' industry – were seriously undermined.

State funding was only one of several weapons bringing literature to heel. Censorship had deep roots; indeed, it set Australia apart from other Western societies, so stringent were state and federal laws against certain 'sexual' and 'political' material, and often so savage their application. The case of Robert Close's *Love Me Sailor* (1945) inscribed a new chapter to that history. The treatment of the author and his publisher was the most vicious application of state censorship ever imposed in Australia. Convicted of 'obscene libel', Close was sentenced to three months in jail and fined £100, a warning which other writers ignored at their peril.

The scene was not altogether bleak, particularly for new writers, mostly unfussed if not delighted by the directive to keep literature 'strictly literary', a principle reasonable enough before the Cold War turned the tradition into a dictum, with sinister implications for transgressors. Some of the finest Western literature – classic and modern – fell into this category. The philosophy of 'art for art's sake' had been much debated at the time of federation by those who insisted on the writer's responsibility to society, and those who demanded free license for the writer, arguing that art and country were not natural bedfellows. Among the most passionate advocates of pure literature was Christopher Brennan (1870–1932), a celebrated poet who argued that 'the form makes the idea'.[63] Brennan's brilliant lyrical poetry (notably his volume entitled *Poems*) had long before the Cold War made the case for a 'strictly literary' stream in Australian writing. New voices in poetry such as A. D. Hope and Douglas Stewart shared Brennan's view.

Ultimately it was not 'the political' but 'the radical' that the postwar directives sought to expunge from creative writing. Many new figures like James McAuley were political conservatives, but others like Judith Wright were not – though neither ventured into the forbidden territory of Left politics. Partly by official intimidation, partly by the advent of new writers, radicalism lost its grip, allowing new approaches to writing and to relations between art and society. If the personal had become the political for writers of the crisis-driven 'literature of conscience', the political was increasingly subsumed within the personal in the exciting new 'literature of commitment'.

The strength of the new writing stemmed both from form and content. The revival of interest in poetry and drama (in a push to create a National Theatre) did not eclipse the novel, pre-eminent medium of a whole generation of writers: male and female, urban and rural, popular and 'serious', expatriate and resident. Good, even outstanding novels emerged from established and new writers. It is in this period that Patrick White first stirred interest. Australian literature was expanding and diversifying to embrace biography and journalism. Growth and expansion were evident also in the industry and the market that supported it. Publishers reflected these developments and contributed to them. New Penguin paperback editions reached a wider audience and the trend towards home editions of American or British publications (prompted by war-time conditions) favoured the local market. Literary criticism was maturing and expanding to embrace new forms and perspectives as well as academic and journalistic approaches. Australian literature had ceased to be 'a family affair' run by a dynasty of 'serious' writers. It was a fledgling literary industry.

NOTES

1   Amirah Inglis, *Australians in the Spanish Civil War*, Sydney, 1987. The great majority fought for the Republic against Franco.
2   Tomoko Akami, 'The Liberal Dilemma: Internationalism and Nationalism in Australia and Japan, 1920–1940', Ph.D. thesis, Australian National University, Canberra, 1997.
3   Andrew Strathern (ed.), *Ongka: A Self-account by a New Guinea Big-man*, London, 1979, 58.
4   Bayardelle to de Gaulle, 1940; cited in John Lawrey, *The Cross of Lorraine in the South Pacific: Australia and the Free French Movement 1940–1942*, Canberra, 1982, 8.
5   Ibid.
6   Frederic Bobin, 'Caldoches, Metropolitans and the Mother Country', *Journal of Pacific History*, 26 (1991), 303–12.
7   Gavin Long, *The Six Years War: A Concise History of Australia in the 1939–45 War*, Canberra, 1973.

8   Ibid.; L. Ross, *John Curtin: A Biography*, Melbourne, 1977.

9   Dudley McCarthy, *South-West Pacific Area – First Year. Kokoda to Wau, Australia in the War of 1939–1945*, Australian War Memorial, Series 1, v, 1959; and David Dexter, *The New Guinea Offensives, Australia in the War of 1939–1945*, Australian War Memorial, Series 1, vi, 1961.

10 Hugh Clarke, *Breakout!*, 1965; republished as *Escape to Death*, Sydney, 1994.

11 Hank Nelson, *POW: Australians under Nippon*, Sydney, 1985.

12 Gavan Daws, *Prisoners of the Japanese: POWs of World War II in the Pacific*, New York, 1994; Gavan McCormack and Hank Nelson, *The Burma–Thailand Railway: Memory and History*, Sydney, 1993.

13 For example, the television programmes *Blood Oath* (1990) and *Paradise Road* (1997); David Malouf's novel *The Great World* (1990) and many first-hand accounts in print.

14 McCormack and Nelson, *The Burma–Thailand Railway*.

15 Stewart Firth, 'The War in the Pacific', in Donald Denoon, Stewart Firth, Jocelyn Linnekin, Malama Meleisea and Karen Nero (eds), *Cambridge History of the Pacific Islanders*, Cambridge, 1997, 291–323; Gavin Long, *The Final Campaigns: Australia in the War of 1939–1945*, Australian War Memorial, Canberra, 1963.

16 Brij Lal, *Broken Waves: A History of the Fiji Islands in the Twentieth Century*, Honolulu, 1992, 110; Asesela Ravuvu, *Fijians at War, 1939–1945*, Suva, 1974, 53.

17 Ken Gillion, *The Fiji Indians: Challenge to European Dominance, 1920–1946*, Canberra, 1977; Firth, 'The War in the Pacific'.

18 Neville Robinson, *Villagers at War: Papua New Guinean Experiences of World War II*, Canberra, 1981.

19 Ken Inglis, 'War, Race and Loyalty in New Guinea, 1939–1945', in Inglis (ed.), *The History of Melanesia*, Port Moresby, 1969.

20 Michael Somare, *Sana*, Port Moresby, 1975, 4–5.

21 Richard Curtain, 'Labour Migration from the Sepik', *Oral History* (UPNG), 9, 1978.

22 Robinson, *Villagers at War*; Curtain, 'Labour Migration from the Sepik'.

23 Interview with Mira Szaszy in A. Rogers and M. Simpson (eds), *Te Timatanga Tatau Tatau: Early Stories from Founding Members of the Maori Women's Welfare League*, Wellington, 1993, 316; also quoted in Margaret McClure, *A Civilised Community: A History of Social Security in New Zealand 1898–1998*, Auckland, 1998, 121.

24 Claudia Orange, 'An Exercise in Maori Autonomy: The Rise and Demise of the Maori War Effort Organization', *New Zealand Journal of History*, 21: 2 (April 1987), 156–72.

25 Jan Kociumbas, *Australian Childhood: A History*, Sydney, 1997, 207.

26 See Jock Phillips, *A Man's Country? The Image of the Pakeha Male – A History*, Auckland, 1987, 198–212.

27 Case study 227, Melbourne Lady Gowrie Child Centre.

28 Marilyn Lake, 'Female Desires: The Meaning of World War II', *Australian Historical Studies*, 24: 95 (Oct. 1990), 267–84; Rosemary Campbell, *Heroes and Lovers: A Question of National Identity*, Sydney, 1989. On New Zealand, see Judith Fyfe (ed.), *War Stories Our Mothers Never Told Us*, Auckland, 1995.

29 Lake, 'Female Desires'.

30 See, for example, Sonja Davies, *Bread and Roses*, Auckland, 1984.

31 Siobhan McHugh, *The Snowy: The People behind the Power*, Melbourne, 1989; George Seddon, *Searching for the Snowy: An Environmental History*, Sydney, 1994.

32 S. G. Foster and M. M. Varghese, *The Making of the Australian National University 1946–1996*, Sydney, 1996, 19, quoting Coombs.

33 Tom Sheridan, 'Postwar Reconstruction', in Graeme Davison, John Hirst and Stuart Macintyre (eds), *Oxford Companion to Australian History*, Melbourne, 1998, 521–2; Stuart Macintyre, *Winners and Losers*, Sydney, 1985; Paul Smyth, *Australian Social Policy: The Keynesian Chapter*, Sydney, 1994.

34 Stuart Macintyre, *The Reds*, Sydney, 1998.

35 Tom Sheridan, *Division of Labour: Industrial Relations in the Chifley Years, 1945–49*, Melbourne, 1989; Ian Turner, *Room for Manoeuvre*, Melbourne, 1982; Macintyre, *The Reds*.

36 Ismet Kurtovich, 'A Communist Party in New Caledonia (1941–1948)', *Journal of Pacific History*, forthcoming.

37 D. Denoon, 'Capitalism in Papua New Guinea', *Journal of Pacific History*, 20 (1985), 119–34; Ian Downs, *The Australian Trusteeship Papua New Guinea 1945–75*, Canberra, 1980, 82–3.

38 Firth, 'The War in the Pacific', citing K. E. Read, 'Effects of the Pacific War in the Markham Valley, New Guinea', *Oceania*, 28 (1947), 95–116.

39 For example, Geoffrey White and Lamont Lindstrom (eds), *The Pacific Theater: Island Representations of World War II*, Honolulu, 1989.

40 Lamont Lindstrom, 'Custom Remade', in Donald Denoon, Stewart Firth, Jocelyn Linnekin, Malama Meleisea and Karen Nero (eds), *Cambridge History of the Pacific Islanders*, Melbourne, 1997, 407–15.

41 Peter Worsley, *The Trumpet Shall Sound*, New York, 1968, 255.

42 Peter Lawrence, 'Cargo Cult and Religious Beliefs among the Garia', *International Archives of Ethnography*, 47 (1954): 1–20; and his *Road Belong Cargo: A Study of the Cargo Movement in Southern Madang District*, Manchester, 1964.

43 Colin Filer, 'The Melanesian Way of Menacing the Mining Industry', in Laura Zimmer-Tamakoshi (ed.), *Modern Papua New Guinea*, Kirksville, Mo., 1998, 147–78.

44 Colin H. Allen, 'The Post-war Scene in the Western Solomons and Marching Rule: A Memoir', *Journal of Pacific History*, 24: 1 (1989), 89–99; Hugh Laracy, *The Maasina Rule Movement: Solomon Islands, 1944–1957*, Suva, 1983; Lindstrom, 'Custom Remade'.

45 Lindstrom, 'Custom Remade'.

46 Nancy Viviani, *Nauru: Phosphate and Political Progress*, Canberra, 1970.

47 J. W. Davidson, *Samoa mo Samoa: The Emergence of the Independent State of Western Samoa*, Melbourne, 1976.

48 C. E. Beeby, *The Biography of an Idea: Beeby on Education*, Wellington, 1992, xvi, 124.

49 Barbara Ann Smith (née Staff), WTC student, 1938–9, personal communication.

50 Eleanor Dark to H. S. Latham, The Macmillan Co., New York, 13 Feb. 1943, ML MSS 4545 22 (25).

51 Nettie Palmer to Frank Dalby Davison, 27 Oct. 1940, NLA MS 1945/182–4.

52 Davison to Palmer (1940), NLA MS 1174/1/5917–18.

53 J. Ryall, 'Women's Peacetime World', *Australian Home Budget*, July 1945, 43–7. On women 'doing politics' as 'citizen politicians', see M. Lake, 'Feminist History as National History: Writing the Political History of Women', *Australian Historical Studies*, 27: 106 (April 1996), 154–69.

54 Eleanor Dark, 'Man and Nature', unpublished essay.

55 Originally in editorial, *Meanjin*, no. 1, 1945, in Jenny Lee, Philip Mead and Gerald Murnane (eds), *The Temperament of Generations*, *Meanjin*/Manchester, 1990, 46–7.

56 Frank Dalby Davison to his mother, 'Sunday morning 1945' (during peace cele-
    brations), NLA MS 1945/1/331-332-334. Eleanor Dark, diary entry of 7 Aug.
    1945, MLMSS 4545 18 (25).
57 Karl, *News to Australia*, *The New Republic*, 3 June 1946, 808–9.
58 Originally in J. F. Cairns, 'Wot, No Socialism?', *Meanjin* 2 (1947); in Lee, et al.,
    The Temperament of Generations, 43–4.
59 Eleanor Dark to Brian Fitzpatrick, 27 Oct. 1949, NLA MS 4965/2/163.
60 David Carter, ' "History Was On Our Side": Memoirs from the Australian Left',
    Meanjin (1987): 108–21.
61 David Walker, *Dream and Disillusion: A Search for Australian Cultural Identity*,
    Canberra, 1976; Len Fox (ed.), *Dream at a Graveside: The History of the Fellowship
    of Australian Writers 1928–1988*, Sydney, 1988.
62 M. Dixson, 'The 'Born-modern' Self: Revisiting *The Real Matilda*: An
    Exploration of Women and Identity in Australia', *Australian Historical Studies*, 27:
    106 (April 1996), 14–29.
63 Christopher Brennan, 'Philosophy and Art', extracts from an unpublished resi-
    dential address to the Sydney University Philosophical Society in 1903.
    Reprinted in *Southerly*, 4, 1977, 203–6.

[16] INTERDEPENDENCIES

COLD WAR, THE AMERICAN ALLIANCE AND NUCLEAR POLITICS

The war showed that neither Australia nor New Zealand – much less other regional polities – was secure without a 'great and powerful friend', in the catch cry of the time. Peace revealed only one candidate. Britain quit the Indian sub-continent in months, and became mired in a campaign against communists in Malaya. She did return to the Pacific – to test nuclear weapons in Australia and the Gilbert Islands (Kiribati). Of the other colonial powers, the Dutch tried to regain control of the East Indies from Indonesian nationalists but the United States dashed their hopes of retaining the whole archipelago, and then denied them the chance to retain West Papua or any other outer-island (see chapter 18). France might fend off Vietnamese nationalists and regain Indochina, but that was as much as she could hope for in the short term. Independence was the clear destiny of all colonies in Southeast Asia. If militant nationalisms worried Australians, New Zealanders and Caledonians (as the settlers now called themselves), the Soviet Union – sponsor of international communism – seemed an even greater threat. In the political wilderness, Robert Menzies could invoke old certainties. In 1945 as he rallied anti-Labor forces into the Liberal Party, he damned Labor's anti-colonialism:

> The very arguments used for throwing the Dutch out of the East Indies are the arguments which will be used to throw the British out of Malaya... [and] Burma, India, for throwing the Australians out of New Guinea... the continued existence of the British Empire is vital to the peace and the future of the world.[1]

But in office, neither Labor nor Menzies himself could indulge such nostalgia.

Australians viewed America with ambivalence. Mesmerized by the glitter of American culture, many were also repulsed by its materialism. America did offer positive models: a suburban society in her own right, Australian business and media looked to the United States for ideas and material. Government commissions and individuals journeyed there as pilgrims on fact-finding missions into methods and equipment – medical, scientific and technical – concerning education, race, migration, health, labour relations; but jealousy as well as empathy coloured the relationship.

War fostered both. The New Guinea campaign was a joint Australian–American exercise, whose success smoothed the way to a broader peace-time alliance.[2] Australians' ambivalence was not allayed, but they now knew that without Uncle Sam, the Japanese might have invaded. A blend of postwar bravado, growing identification with the region, and a residual 'depression-bred fear of "Wall Street"'[3] tinged public opinion, but few sought another American retreat into isolationism. The debate on the costs and benefits of the American alliance – including the use of bases in Australia – was fraught. What price security and protection, or at least the illusion of them? A close alliance placed Australia inside the nuclear ring. However, keeping Americans at bay was only half the problem. The other half was keeping them interested.

The Labor Party was more comfortable than Menzies with postwar realities. It fell to Dr H. V. Evatt, as minister for external affairs, to conceive and execute new policies. Poised between old and new dependencies, Evatt and his department headed by John Burton aspired to a role as a middle power in relation to independent Asia. The land of the convict, home of the battler, preached international collective security and championed smaller nations in and through the United Nations. The principle of strength in numbers that underpinned mateship and unionism was globalized. Assuming that the main threat to world peace lay in superpower rivalry, Evatt's watchful eye on American actions was a marked feature of these policies. A committed internationalist, he was an architect and advocate of the United Nations (and chaired the General Assembly in 1948). He also recognized Sukarno's Republic of Indonesia early enough to make a difference.[4] In such moments Australia and even New Zealand seemed willing to deviate from American policy. That flickering independence did not survive the Labor Party's replacement by Menzies' coalition of Liberal and Country parties. Lining up behind America, New Zealand and Australia both deplored the Chinese Communist Party's victory in 1949, and persistently treated the Taiwan regime as China's government. They acquiesced in United States actions which denied West Papua to the Netherlands, and signed off on the Act of Free Choice option in 1962. Their troops travelled to Korea, nominally to support the United Nations but really the United States. After Britain's campaign (the Malayan Emergency), federated Malaysia promised stability in Southeast Asia, but Singapore's secession was troubling – and Indonesia's anti-imperialism alarming. To invoke the 'third world' was disconcerting, but the drive to destabilize Malaysia by *konfrontasi* was potentially calamitous. Nevertheless, following the American lead, New Zealand and Australia turned against President Sukarno only as he fell from power in 1966.

Whatever latitude Australia and New Zealand sought in foreign affairs hinged on the American alliance. This was partly secured by the three-power ANZUS Pact of 1951. It promised, but did not guarantee, American support for her allies: its advocates could only propose that it 'made mutual assistance at least marginally more likely'.[5] More helpful was its animation of the machinery of military, diplomatic and political dialogue: it provided a regular and privileged forum for foreign ministers to enjoy high-level communication with Washington.

Labor and Liberal were not as far apart as their rhetorics suggested. They agreed on the need for a powerful friend; they were equally nervous about a seemingly monolithic communism; and both saw independence as immediately possible in Southeast Asia, but not the Pacific Islands. For the latter, Australia and New Zealand took the lead in creating the South Pacific Commission, a forum for technical co-operation among the colonial powers (briefly including the Netherlands for West Papua). A 1944 agreement (Canberra Pact) between Australia and New Zealand staked their claim to regional influence, calling also for a common policy for the welfare of the people of the region. They sought a regional defence policy, pointedly rejecting the principle that possession of bases constituted a fair claim to sovereignty. (Manus, north of New Guinea, was the reference; and the Americans eventually abandoned their bases there.)

A major regional initiative was the Colombo Plan for Co-operative Economic Development in South and Southeast Asia, adopted in 1950. A diplomatic Indian attributed it to 'the initiative of Ceylon, the enthusiasm of Australia, the friendly encouragement of New Zealand and Canada and the wise guidance of the United Kingdom',[6] but Percy Spender – Australia's minister for external affairs – was sure that the credit was his. His department had been preparing for such a move under Evatt, especially in Professor MacMahon Ball's Goodwill Mission to Southeast Asia, which explored ways of gaining leverage. The Colombo Plan, emerging from a Commonwealth ministers' meeting in Ceylon, was the most important non-military vehicle for Australian and New Zealand influence. Its most visible element was a large and long-term programme of scholarships for students from newly independent countries (Commonwealth members or not) to study in Australia and New Zealand. Exposure to these societies as well as their studies should dispose them to favour their hosts and counteract the migration policies which compelled them to leave when they graduated. Less visible was a flow of funds, experts and machines – planners assumed that 'development' needed merely capital and expertise – for which the Marshall Plan for Europe was an early model.

For the government, the plan's main purpose was to help Asian governments to raise living standards and thereby remove the presumed preconditions for communist influence. A covert but equally vital purpose was to commit America, whose resources were essential to the plan, and whose commitment to regional security was the ultimate prize.[7] This, the most imaginative and expensive foreign affairs initiative taken by the two countries, was not so much an assertion of independence from the United States, but complemented her interests and was baited to reinforce that interest and transform it into regional commitments.

The critical alliance was, of course, ANZUS, whose significance grew as the Cold War intensified. Australia, for example, hosted US communications centres. The most consequential American initiative was in Indochina, picking up pieces left by France after Dien Bien Phu. Support for the Democratic

Republic of (South) Vietnam involved military aid, then military advisers, and finally combat troops. Neither Britain nor France was engaged, so the presence of Australian and New Zealand forces explicitly acknowledged American leadership. By comparison, the United Nations was a paper tiger. The General Assembly, growing in numbers of ex-colonies and anti-colonial zeal, passed Resolution 1514 in 1960, which established the Committee of Twenty-four to monitor decolonization, and declared that a lack of economic and social preparedness would no longer justify deferred independence. That was disconcerting for Australia, whose rule in Papua New Guinea was often defended in those terms, but denunciations of colonialism were vacuous unless endorsed by the Security Council where the United States, Britain, France, Taiwan and the Soviet Union each enjoyed the power of veto. In the 1960s Australian rule in her dependencies rested upon the Western powers' veto of General Assembly resolutions.

These international pressures committed everyone in the region to the Western bloc and mainly to the American camp within it. These alliances were consequential, but they did not play directly into domestic politics; rather, they were refracted by governments, media and popular perceptions. Many Australians and New Zealanders were ambivalent about American power and culture through their 'traditional' attachment to the substance and symbols of Britain's empire (sentiments extravagantly expressed during royal tours). The reorientation of Britain's economic links therefore disturbed many Australians and New Zealanders, even those with no direct economic stake in the issue. Britain itself was divided by the shift of focus from Commonwealth to Europe, and it was not until 1979 that the European Community agreed to her entry, but applications had been lodged in Brussels since the 1960s. The antipodean effects could scarcely be imagined, so the issue reinforced (even for empire loyalists) the realization that the United States was the only possible great and powerful friend.

French ambivalence towards America was even more pronounced. Perversely, though, many Islanders wanted a more intimate relationship with the Americans than their colonial masters allowed. We saw (in chapter 15) that many millenarian prophets identified Americans as the owners or custodians of goods or ideas needed to transform their societies. Fervour for America was not limited to prophets. Western Samoans were attracted by wages in American Samoa, and by careers in the United States army, which they joined in large numbers. The anomalous division of their archipelago allowed Samoans (and Tongans on their kinship-tails) to initiate chain migrations to Hawaii and California. That made them less dependent on New Zealand for jobs, and enabled many families to become purposefully transnational and ride out crises in any part of their diaspora. Throughout Melanesia, however, American enthusiasms were zealously discouraged by officials who suspected criticism of their own efforts, if not disloyalty or even cargo-ism.

Throughout the Cold War, our sparsely populated region was treated (in Firth's phrase) as the great powers' nuclear playground.[8] Britain wanted its own nuclear deterrent and Prime Minister Menzies was delighted to co-operate in 1952, providing the uninhabited Monte Bello Islands off

Plate 16.1 'Event Baker', Operation Crossroads. US underwater nuclear test at Bikini Atoll, July 1946. From Michael Szabo, *Making Waves: The Greenpeace New Zealand Story*, Auckland, 1991.

Western Australia. Other sites were granted with equal alacrity, although Emu Field and Maralinga in the South Australian semi-desert were not vacant. Menzies was evidently so pleased to help that he made a commitment before informing his cabinet; but he did not suffer electorally for subordinating national interests to imperial and nuclear causes.

A generation later, when a Labor government appointed a Royal Commission into the conduct of the nuclear tests, opinion had been transformed. In the 1980s, as the Cold War thawed and nuclear weapons inspired fear and loathing, Britain's strategic needs cut no Australian ice; disregard for the safety of troops on site seemed gross negligence, and casual sweeps to warn Aborigines near-criminal (spotter aircraft merely followed the roads). Some people had been leading 'traditional' lives in the Maralinga Prohibited Zone. This was no mere technical defect, nor was it a narrowly British failure. An official who criticized the search was accused of 'placing the affairs of a handful of natives above those of the British Commonwealth of Nations'.[9] Faced with evidence of earlier negligence, Britain agreed retrospectively to help pay to decontaminate these lands, and Australian opinion had also shifted. After a struggle, therefore, the Maralinga people regained their land in 1984. A decade later they signed a deal for compensation of $13.5 million, the return of the Maralinga village including the airstrip, and a monopoly over nuclear tourism enterprises. But in 1957–8 the programme merely moved to Christmas Island (Kiritimati) in the Gilbert Islands (Kiribati) to test hydrogen bombs. It did not seem significant then, but i-Kiribati were much less likely than Australians to pursue (much less gain) compensation.

Britain then wound up her programme and in 1963 signed the Partial Test Ban Treaty. Her tests were trivial beside the 66 nuclear devices which the United States exploded in Micronesia; but it was French testing which united most of the region in protest. The secrecy which distinguished French from American tests helps explain the distribution of dislike, but Pacific polities could more readily afford to alienate France than the United States or even Britain. France's deterrent was central to her sense of her global role in the 1960s. Humbled at Suez, she had also lost Dien Bien Phu and with it Indochina. The Fourth Republic tottered until May 1958, when General de Gaulle returned to power. Though he ended the war in Algeria, this was not the end of empire. The overseas territories were asked by referendum to endorse the new (Fifth Republic) constitution. Each could choose independence, but most voted heavily to remain in the French community. In French Polynesia though, Tahitian nationalists did campaign for independence, and local officials had to exert overt leverage to produce only a 64 per cent vote for continued association.

The need for manipulation arose from the fact that France could no longer test nuclear weapons in the Sahara, and few places on earth were remote from Paris, isolated from other population centres, and politically dependent. Having secured the territory's vote, De Gaulle reversed the trend towards devolution and unveiled the Centre for Nuclear Experimentation. Building began in 1963, and testing followed in 1966, making the centre the main source of the territory's income, capital and jobs. That brute fact deflected Maohi anger away from the nuclear tests; and Paris was lavish in funding the services and patronage which divided not only the anti-colonial forces, but also the anti-nuclear groups.

> The modern history of French Polynesia then, is a 'nuclear history' in the sense that nothing of importance in its recent politics and economics can be understood without reference to the overwhelming presence of the Atomic Energy Commission (CEA) and the Pacific Experimentation Centre (CEP).[10]

The nuclear significance of French Polynesia also lent New Caledonia some strategic importance. France was not keen to leave New Caledonia, and for the first time the non-indigenous population was increasing through the immigration of displaced and fiercely loyalist settlers from Algeria and Indochina. Those demographics would have made independence difficult; and that argument could now be complemented by the view that a free New Caledonia might undermine France's position in Tahiti. And even New Hebrides could now be seen as a domino which must not fall.

COLONIAL ADMINISTRATIONS RESTORED

Few features distinguish our region more than the fate of colonial regimes after the Pacific war. Nationalist parties were coming into government in former colonies in most of Africa and Asia. In the United Nations and through the Non-aligned Movement, they flexed their diplomatic muscle and denounced imperialism. Yet colonial rule in the Pacific was seldom challenged by coherent nationalist movements, and administrators insisted that Islanders needed and welcomed (temporary but long-term) tutelage. The contrast with other regional bodies (the Organization for African Unity, or NATO) was stark and enabled the colonial powers to behave very differently in the Pacific. France had already quit Algeria and Indochina when she tightened control over Tahiti; and her largest African colonies became independent in 1960 with no Pacific echoes. Britain left the Sudan and Ghana in 1956, when British rule in the Pacific had another generation of vitality. Despite the Americans' general opposition to colonialism, her Trust Territory of the Pacific Islands was run in a decidedly colonial manner, first by the navy, then by the Department of the Interior, using the rhetoric and substance of development as instruments of control.[11] New Zealand decolonized earlier (but less completely) than other powers; Australia later (but faster). If decolonization had become a global theme, it was played in many variations in the Pacific.

Part of the explanation lay in the muted and fragmented anti-colonial sentiments; another was physical closeness; but much had to do with the perceived damage inflicted by Japan to the legitimacy of prewar colonial authority. Japan's rapid conquest of coastal Melanesia shamed British, French and especially Australian administrators and some missions, whose helter-skelter retreat undercut the mystique of unruffled, invincible, paternal white authority. Partly to repair this wound to their self-esteem, Australian forces were deployed for the last two years of the war in re-occupying territory and then punishing 'collaborators' and rebuilding Australian prestige. When peace returned, the United Nations succeeded the League of Nations as supervisor of Australian rule in New Guinea, and endorsed a joint Administration over Papua and New Guinea in 1947.[12]

There was a brief contest for the ear of the minister. The Army's Directorate of Research and Civil Affairs, a clutch of scholars in uniform, reported to Minister Eddie Ward,[13] in opposition to the Department of External Territories, emerging from war-time hibernation. The department won, but Ward listened to neither, and the Territory Administration muddled along for several years with little policy advice or support.[14] With Menzies as prime minister, the West Australian Paul Hasluck took the portfolio of Territories which now included the Northern Territory as well as Papua New Guinea (and Nauru). A scholar and a wilful minister, he ruled for an unusually long term (1951–63), relishing 'a range of administrative experience that exceeded by far that of any … ministerial colleague, for in a country of two million people I was virtually the Premier and the whole of a state Cabinet'.[15] The real cabinet had scant interest in his work, the Opposition supported him, and parliament was indifferent; so he achieved a rare degree of policy autonomy and financial independence.

For the Northern Territory, his policy was clear: not only was it an intrinsic part of Australia, but Aborigines must be fully assimilated into white society. Addressing the destiny of Papua New Guinea, however, he was deliberately vague, exploiting the imprecision of 'Territory':

> I do not think that we can foresee the day when Papua and New Guinea will become a member of the Australian Commonwealth on exactly the same terms and in exactly the same constitutional relation as the six States of the Federation. There is no reason whatsoever why they should not enter into relation with the Commonwealth on terms to be negotiated ... when Papua and New Guinea can speak as one people. By that time ... the Australian Federation will itself have changed considerably.[16]

Realistically, Papua New Guineans could not be transformed into brown Australians, but whenever they did exercise 'self-determination' this might lead to full independence or (like the Northern Territory) incorporation into Australia, or some midway status. Ambivalence ruled because cabinet believed that self-government was decades away; so Hasluck happily set targets for social services but flatly declined target dates for decolonization.[17]

Hasluck left indelible marks. He insisted that Papua New Guinea had one destiny, which required 'even' economic and political development, so 'advanced' communities must wait for the others. Unlike the League of Nations, the United Nations began to ask for target dates for political change. Hasluck resisted: 'You know my views about target dates. I recognize that we have to supply some appropriate eye-wash'.[18] The UN's bite was less severe than the bark of the Committee of twenty-four. In particular they endorsed the unity of the territory. In 1962 a Visiting Mission did attract publicity, but mainly 'anticipated rather than initiated' policy choices.[19] It advised a survey of the economy by the World Bank, proposed a start for tertiary education and suggested a representative parliament. This was reform, not revolution.

Hasluck insisted that the territory was unique and he was 'revolted at the imitation of British colonial modes and manners by some of the Australians'.[20] He incited heads of territory departments to propose and implement projects, so the director of public health doubled the number of government hospitals in a dozen years and funded the missions to do the same. The director of education did the same for primary schools but could not satisfy Hasluck. What did not change was a heavy paternalism which (for example) banned people from drinking alcohol, playing contact sport, or (for men) wearing clothes above the waist. Entry to Australia was illegal except for domestic servants or students, whereas Australians entered the territory easily unless they held socialist or other 'subversive' opinions.

Social and economic change were therefore glacial. The World Bank in 1963 reported a population of two million, 99 per cent indigenous. Imports exceeded exports by 50 per cent and Australian grants provided three-quarters of government receipts. Planters (mainly Australian) grew the bulk of exports. A formal economy dominated by plantations had little need for skill, so only half of each age-cohort went to school at all, and only 14 pupils completed high school. Most schooling was provided by missions.[21]

It followed that there was no territorial elite at least until the 1960s. The courts teetered between Australian and 'traditional' Melanesian principles.

The Department of District Administration and Native Affairs ruled a rural population speaking several hundred languages. Its field officers enjoyed the prestige of 'outside men' who brought government to the frontiers. Until the mid-1960s field officers – *kiaps* – united the powers of prosecutors, magistrates and police, and their autocracy was tempered only by their discretion. In the 1950s they were still introducing 'government' to some highlanders. On the coast, however, some (reported a leading anthropologist)

> may be liked personally and others are undoubtedly hated, but as representations of an all-powerful 'Force'…they are all more or less feared.
>   In some cases this fear is exacerbated by dislike, distrust or contempt, in others it is tempered by genuine respect and even liking. But even in cases of the latter, natives…know by experience that postings are brief and that the next *Kiap* will probably be a wholly different kind of individual.[22]

The postwar administration enjoyed increased funding for economic and social (and even some political) development – but managed from the top. Economic change must be supervised by agricultural extension officers or co-operatives officers.[23] Political life must be channelled through Local Government Councils, also with Australian advisers. In these institutions there was little room for initiative by *kiaps*, and almost none by indigenes. An (advisory) Legislative Council was created in 1951, most of whose members were Australian. In 1964 a largely elected House of Assembly was opened. Its resolutions had moral authority but little bite; ordinances were drafted by officials, who steered them through debate. Many members were men of great eminence but narrow experience. Highlanders especially stood in awe of government, and seldom disregarded advice.

Britain might have left the Pacific Islands faster than she did, but progress towards self-government in Fiji was hampered by the anxiety of ethnic Fijians, outnumbered by Indo-Fijians and fearing a further erosion of their position. The strengthened Fijian Affairs Board, with the conservative Ratu Sir Lala Sukuna at the helm (see chapter 15), functioned like a chiefly state within a colonial state, avoiding the need for Fijians to consider a non-racial, democratic government.[24] Decolonization had to negotiate deep-dyed loyalism. In Solomon Islands the opposite predicament arose: Maasina Rule's programme of brotherhood and equality certainly challenged colonial ideology, but seemed an unlikely basis for government. The colonial powers were in no hurry to depart; where there were obvious successors they seemed in no hurry to inherit. Powers which were keen to decolonize elsewhere expressed no such urgency in the Pacific, and the resolutions of the United Nations General Assembly were hardly compelling.

Anxieties about national and regional security were significant; prosperity might be threatened by Britain's entry into the European Community, and the Cold War's threats were compounded by nuclear fears. Yet the 1950s were more 'comfortable' to more people than any previous decade in the region's modern history, promising a stable space in which societies could recover from six years of war. Governments in Australia and New Zealand

and rulers of island colonies at last inhabited a world of strategic security, social stability and economic progress. The Pacific Ocean – Spanish in the eighteenth century and British in the nineteenth – was now an American lake. China was recovering from civil war and posed little immediate threat. Japan's military machine was dismantled and her economy was importing almost anything that could be harvested or quarried. Colonial institutions were restored and islanders' millennial ambitions curbed. Anti-colonial nationalism and communism were happily remote. These circumstances implied an immutable hierarchy based on race. Japanese and Chinese were welcome trading partners but unwelcome immigrants; Melanesian products, but not people, entered Australia; while Polynesians might enter New Zealand for specific purposes, mainly education or work. Aboriginal Australians were too few, Maori too 'integrated' and Melanesians in New Caledonia too depressed, to destabilize structures of power and privilege created by Europeans and their descendants. Those illusions survived into the 1960s.

MIGRATION FROM EUROPE, POLYNESIA, ASIA

The scale of postwar migration to Australia set it apart from New Zealand. This was not just a matter of filling up the continent for its inhabitants' security. The need for both labour and consumers demanded 'settlers' rather than guest workers. The result was an exceptionally high rate of migration.[25] For a generation immigrants provided half the labour-force growth, allowing the highest rate of economic increase in the OECD. The migrant model also expanded. Immediate postwar migration remained predominantly British; but improved conditions in Britain shifted the focus to continental Europe. After 1947 the United Kingdom Assisted Passage Scheme imported entire families, increasing the British in Australia by 460,000. At £10 an adult and children free, the 'ten pound tourists' found it cheaper to migrate than to holiday at home.[26]

Australia turned to Europe's Displaced Persons camps for assisted migrants who travelled by troopships. While this strategy preserved White Australia, it ultimately changed the ethnic mix of Australians,[27] to an extent not experienced in New Zealand. The 1947 Mass Migration Act admitted thousands of (mainly Northern) Europeans in a very few years: Germans, Dutch, Hungarians, Poles, Romanians, Estonians, Latvians and Lithuanians. Young men began work on building and hydro-electric schemes, and provided cheap labour for BHP and manufacturers. Their families settled in the sprawling outer suburbs of Sydney, Melbourne and Adelaide, establishing ethnic clubs, islands in an alien landscape. The minister of immigration, Alexander Downer, believed that these 'New' Australians would assimilate: 'Holland is one of the few countries in Europe with people to export of a type that can quickly merge with the Australian community'.[28] Economic recovery in Europe eventually stemmed this flood, which was replaced by Italy, Greece, Yugoslavia (Slovenia, Serbia, Croatia) and other

Mediterranean nations as the catchment broadened for racially acceptable Europeans. Yugoslavs who worked on the Snowy Mountains scheme then built suburban houses in Canberra, the fast-growing federal capital. The largest wave of migrants came from Italy in the 1950s and 1960s, to Sydney and Melbourne, while Melbourne became the largest Greek city outside Athens. In 1947 White Australia was censused as 96 per cent British, with 25,000 'Asians' and 87,000 Aborigines in a population of over seven million.[29] In broadening the profile of the good migrant, the Mass Migration Act prepared the way for the end of the White Australia policy. Attitudes gradually shifted; the postwar need for relationships around the Pacific Rim invited the first easing of policy towards 'Asia' in the 1950s, favouring 'mixed race' Eurasians (including Japanese wives of servicemen) and elite Asians, and from the 1960s the barriers were lowered for non-Europeans as 'integration' replaced 'assimilation'. The radical shift in policies climaxed in 1973, when the Whitlam government denounced White Australia in the name of 'multiculturalism', attracting Asian migrants and refugees, in particular Vietnamese boat people and, through family reunion, their families. From the 1970s immigrants found citizenship relatively attainable. Through the 1990s, Asia constituted the largest single source of immigrants. In a short period the country emerged as one of the world's leading havens. Relative to its population, Australia accepted more Indochinese refugees than any other country. Between the Holocaust, Cold War and other diasporas of trauma from Europe, Asia (and even Latin America), fifty years brought in half a million refugees and displaced persons. In all, 5.5 million migrants came between 1947 and 1996, many from non-English speaking Europe.

Still overwhelmingly Anglo-Celtic in 1945, half a century later the proportion had radically changed. Taking second and third generations into account, 1 of every 3 Australians at the close of the twentieth century had origins outside the British Isles. The 1996 census found that more than 4 million people, 23 per cent of the population, were born overseas and a further 18 per cent were the children of immigrants; and 1 in 12 stemmed from places which had been proscribed not long ago. One in four Australians was either born in a non-English speaking country or had a parent from such a country. At least 17 per cent spoke a language other than English at home.

New Zealand stayed more homogeneous. Like Australia, 96 per cent British until the Second World War in its Pakeha component (95 per cent of the people), this dominion of 1.7 million people opted for much less migration. In 1946 a Dominion Population Committee reported:

> If it is proposed to encourage immigration of other European types, they should be of such character as will, within a relatively short space of time, become completely assimilated. ... The emergence of racial islands in such a small country as New Zealand must inevitably lead to serious maladjustment. The southern European tends at times to be merely an itinerant settler in this country. ... There is some evidence that when such settlers have accumulated a certain amount of wealth they tend to return to the country of origin. ... If any positive steps are taken to encourage immigrants other than from Great Britain they should be found in northern European countries.[30]

So New Zealand favoured northern Europeans, especially Dutch who comprised almost half the intake of migrant labour from continental Europe between 1945 and 1975.[31] 'New Zealander', at least in official eyes, still implied a distinctive 'Britishness'. The urge persisted to be more British than Australia. New Zealand resumed assisted migration from the United Kingdom in 1947, admitting fewer ten pound migrants. Numbers remained low: from 1945 to 1971 fewer than 77,000 came from Britain and 6,200 from the Netherlands. A mere 4,500 displaced persons migrated from 1949, and 1,100 Hungarian refugees, in a total of 90,000 assisted migrants from Europe.[32] Unassisted British migrants enjoyed easy entry until 1974, providing two-thirds of immigrants. Migrants consisted largely of kin, first from the United Kingdom, second from Australia until the late 1980s. Australia remained the second largest source, providing 23 per cent of permanent arrivals from 1946 to 1987, behind Britain's 47 per cent.

Like Canada and Australia, New Zealand created national citizenship separate from the British one in 1948, but this was a change in form, not substance. In Malcolm McKinnon's words, 'Citizenship was not a marker of membership in the New Zealand community, at least not for a British subject or a woman marrying a New Zealander'.[33] Ethnicity did remain a marker. The war brought a change in attitude to New Zealand-born Chinese because China had fought against Japan, and in 1952 the government restored their right to be naturalized. As the global climate changed, the Immigration Amendment Act 1961 required non-New Zealand citizens (except Australians but including Britons) to have a permit to enter. In practice, it was still hard for Chinese and Indians to gain entry unless they had family links.[34] With decolonization, however, the 'good migrant' embraced Polynesian kin – and Maori migrating to New Zealand's cities, especially Auckland. Changes in migration policy were tied to changes in the structure of the economy; and the need for cheap labour was met by Pacific Island and Maori migration. There are parallels of place in state, nation and economy between southern Europeans in Australia and Pacific Islanders in New Zealand, both recruited for unskilled labour.

From 1950 into the 1980s, just 23 per cent of New Zealand's population growth came from migration. Australia's population grew faster; New Zealand depended more on natural increase (higher among Maori and Island groups) and experienced faster ageing of population (mainly Pakeha). Since the 1880s natural increase largely shaped identity. Combined with continued kin migration from Britain and Australia, New Zealanders saw no discrepancy between citizenship and ethnicity until the 1980s. The dominant ethnic issue was still relations between Pakeha and Maori. This presented obstacles to multiculturalism, as the shift to Asia coincided with a resurgence of the Treaty of Waitangi in discourse and jurisprudence. Migrants were not all put on the same footing until 1987 when the Labour government introduced a points system.

Migration flows shape and are shaped by the nation imagined. The great change for New Zealand and Australia was that the Asia-Pacific regions supplemented and then displaced Britain and the empire as the leading source.

Plate 16.2 Fijians living in New Zealand: Abraham Foumaa, Iisireli Tawake, Lusiana Tuioneata, Sereana Yasa, Tomasi Tagicakibau, Fane Tagicakibau, Josaia Tuioneata and Tevita Yasa at a Kava ceremony in Christchurch, New Zealand. From the Press, Christchurch, *Celebrating Cultural Diversity*, Christchurch, 1999. Courtesy of The Press.

Plate 16.3 Tongan women. Back row from left: Fanelola Hodder, Morunga Tahaafe, Mele Piukala Tahaafe, Ema Valu Vakata, Mele Tasola; front row: Susana Leota and Suilolo Tauveli. Tonga is where the heart lies. From The Press, Christchurch, *Celebrating Cultural Diversity*, Christchurch, 1999. Courtesy of The Press.

Within that picture, Australia's focus shifted to East and Southeast Asia, and New Zealand's to the Pacific Islands – until the 1990s, when for the first time New Zealand's biggest slice of migrants came from North Asia. Australia with its broader intake of 'Europeans' became much more diverse in its non-indigenous population. There is no Australian equivalent to the term 'Pakeha', and the 'other' is harder to define.

Europeans largely provided New Zealand's needs for professional and skilled labour; the demand for unskilled and semi-skilled labour pulled Maori and Islanders into New Zealand cities, as they tugged women into paid work.[35] Patterns of migration suggest imagined linkages and compatibilities. Much of the immigration between 1950 and 1980 came from New Zealand's dependencies, the Cook Islands, Niue and Tokelau (the latter practically relocated to New Zealand in 1966). Migration from Western Samoa was promoted and regulated under a quota system after independence in 1962. Smaller numbers came from Tonga, Fiji and Tahiti, Polynesian societies with weaker real (and imagined) links to New Zealand. Islander migrants of the 1950s and 1960s were distinctive as neither British nor foreign, nor ethnically alien. Most came from former dependencies and arrived as New Zealand citizens. Pakeha saw them as similar to Maori (they and Maori knew better). Their numbers were absolutely small but proportionally large: 26,000 in 1966 and 61,000 in 1976 (including New Zealand-born).[36] Their issues resembled those of urbanizing Maori rather than continental Europeans. Occupying a narrow range of low-paid jobs and living mainly in low-cost housing, they are often misrepresented as a single community.

MAORI AND ABORIGINAL URBANIZATION

The movement of greatest salience for New Zealand identities is Maori urbanization. The drift of Aboriginal Australians from pastoral stations to urban centres is another important matter. The Second World War speeded the first phase of Maori migration to towns, drawn by the hope of work and a better life, and pushed by rural poverty arising from a shortage of land. From the 1950s the drift quickened, fuelled by economic growth on one hand and on the other by the relocation policy of the Department of Maori Affairs, which refused to build houses in areas which lacked jobs. Maori, 20 per cent urban by 1951, became 58 per cent urban by 1971, when 133,000 lived in towns, compared to 23,000 in 1951.[37] Largely separate peoples since the 1860s, Maori and Pakeha again encountered each other and engaged in new interactions, which were instrumental in changing values and in reshaping identities as young, single people and couples migrated to city centres, and families to the suburbs.

For Maori, the suburban ideal was obtained through state housing. The ideal of integrating Maori migrants into the host community by 'pepper potting' Maori housing among Pakeha, was tried in Rotorua and faltered. In

Auckland authorities instead built satellite estates of state houses on cheap land in outer suburbs, to which Maori migrated in the 1960s. Amid general prosperity, Maori and Island migrants found themselves in poorly paid jobs with little security or career structure. By 1960 70 per cent of Pakeha left school without qualifications, and 95 per cent of Maori. In Donna Awatere Huata's view the move to the cities proved disastrous: 'When we moved into town we encountered prejudice and harassment, and Pakeha ideas about noble, grass-skirted indigenes were shattered'. This encounter prompted a Pakeha backlash and Maori kin networks were broken as housing policy and the emphasis on integration rearranged them into nuclear rather than extended families.[38] Despite such disadvantage and dislocation, Maori communities forged new identities around urban marae. These pan-tribal marae provided the ground work for initiatives and new tensions between urban Maori and *iwi*-based groups by the 1990s.

The urbanizing experience of Aboriginal Australians was more diverse. In 1951 Hasluck urged the Commonwealth to set an example in the Northern Territory in a policy of active assimilation under which even indigenous people of full descent would be integrated into white Australia.[39] Under the Welfare Ordinance 1953, which came into effect in 1957, all Aboriginal people of full descent were defined as wards of the state, in need of special care, while it was assumed that those of mixed descent were already assimilated. In practice, children were declared wards, rather than whole families, which reinforced the practice of child removal. When entry to reserves was restricted in the 1960s, this too forced people to relocate to towns, and by 1967–8 almost 18 per cent of indigenous children in the Northern Territory were in state care.[40]

Urban Aboriginal Australians lived mostly in New South Wales and Victoria where, by 1957, fewer than 200 lived on the sole remaining reserve at Lake Tyers. The rest, forced into white society without land or resources, were denied government aid except for rations distributed by police, and faced harsh discrimination. They moved into shanty towns on the sites of former missions, on the margins of country towns and wherever there might be work, such as seasonal fruitpicking along the Murray River, where others joined them from New South Wales. They also moved to Melbourne and Sydney. Migration from outback Australia, combined with population recovery, produced a new generation of Aboriginal organizations and leaders who used direct action to have their grievances heard (see chapter 17).[41] By the 1970s, 'Mumshirl', Shirley Smith, identified in her autobiography a 'whole new level' of organizations among educated, urban Aborigines. But she also regretted that city dwellers had lost respect for their elders. When Margaret Tucker's elderly aunt died alone in a rural hospital, she mourned: 'I didn't even know she was ill but I should have and I still feel guilty'. Aboriginal youth lost their culture, kinship links and identity through removal (which amounted to forced urbanization, as well as assimilation) and the drift to towns and cities. By urbanization, however, Tucker perceived Aborigines hopefully as now 'one big tribe together'.[42]

SUBURBIA

Most Aboriginal people were barred from the suburban dream, as were Islanders in the Melanesian dependencies where government centres were essentially enclaves of white families and individuals. For other Australians and New Zealanders who met the small-family stereotype, the old ideal of a property-owning democracy came close to realization. Outer suburbs were built in cities which grew fastest from migration and manufacturing: Sydney, Melbourne, Adelaide, Newcastle, Wollongong, Auckland and Wellington. The governments of South Australia, Victoria and New South Wales did deals with manufacturers who promised to house their workers, often migrants, as in Elizabeth, an Adelaide satellite. Suburban development brought shopping malls and supermarkets consistent with the American Fordist model of mass production and consumption. Their shared identities as suburban nations facilitated American influence in Australia and New Zealand.[43] Suburbia also spread with the postwar baby boom, the result of couples postponing marriage in the Depression and marrying during or after the war: they begat a bulge of children, with family sizes increasing to four on average by 1960 in New Zealand (whose baby boom was more pronounced than in Australia), who crowded maternity hospitals, then kindergartens and primary schools. Their parents, having survived war and a housing shortage, aspired even more avidly to a suburban house and car. As one young couple explained in 1955, 'Because a home is the happiest place in the world, and the only perfect setting for family living, we decided that we'd do without anything to have a better-than-average house'. But they were anxious about borrowing.[44] In the uncertain boom of the 1950s, the state fostered reassertions of identity based on family and domesticity. The house with a front lawn (in New Zealand) and backyard (in Australia) came to symbolize their ways of life, the New Zealand emphasis hinting at a greater weight for respectability and privacy, and the Australian backyard and barbecue spoke of privacy and leisure.

In 1950s Australia and New Zealand, the goal became 'to own the dream'.[45] If 50 per cent of white Australians and New Zealanders owned their own homes by 1911, in the next 50 years rates of home ownership rose to nearly 70 per cent. The 1950s saw the steepest increase in ownership since the 1920s, incited by Cold War politics which inspired a conservative Menzies government in Australia and a conservative New Zealand National government to finance mortgages as a means of domestic defence as well as delivering material prosperity.[46] Conservatives presented the nuclear family as the bedrock of society. The great Cold War metaphor, containment, applied to the home as a source of virtues and containment of communism, the nuclear threat, or social pathology. Intellectuals concerned to contain the dubious social forces unleashed by prosperity and the Cold War favoured a civic personality, attuned to social structures, where the family served as 'antidote to the mass society', ensuring social stability and a democratic environment in which to rear children.[47] National identity framed by suburban family life was not a retreat, but a renewed expression of citizenship. Robin Boyd, in 1952, declared that owning a 'small house ... in a fenced allotment is as inevitable and unquestionable a goal of the average Australian as marriage'.[48]

Elizabeth, on the northern fringe of Adelaide (like Sydney's west, or south Auckland), was named for the queen. It had multiple identities, depending on the vision: a Housing Trust town (the equivalent of a state housing area in New Zealand), home of General Motors-Holden, and a 'government suburb'; postwar 'model town', and a problem housing area or postwar 'slum'. Mark Peel's term for such postwar suburbs is derived not from planners' views but from people who lived there: he sees Elizabeth as a 'workers' city', built by 'ordinary Australians' and working-class migrants who 'used the temporary resources of the postwar economic boom to build a better life'.[49] Naenae, a postwar suburb in Wellington's Hutt Valley, built according to Keynesian visions of postwar reconstruction, similarly acquired multiple identities as a model town, as monotonous and soulless, and a home of delinquent youth. Most occupants believed in, and lived, the suburban ideal of the nuclear family; but only a minority actively supported the community planning ideal. They were too busy, and if they did participate in collective activities, it was on their own terms. Community could not be 'designed into a new settlement'. A sense of community owes more to kinship and friendship than to material landscape.[50] In Naenae as in Elizabeth, and on urban marae, people again forged identities through interaction.

DECENTRALIZATION

The demands of war lowered barriers of several kinds. Air transport made it possible to travel to London from Auckland or Sydney – or from Noumea to Paris – in days rather than weeks by sea; Rabaul and Port Moresby, Apia and Rarotonga were now hours away from their metropoles. For a generation until the 1970s the cost of air travel ruled it out except for official purposes or personal emergencies, but these were important in themselves, and so was the boon of airmail. The increasing use of telegrams, and the introduction of telex in the 1960s enabled governments to exercise much closer supervision over local affairs than ever before. For colonial officers this was devastating. As one put it, 'matters which would, in the past, have been decided [in Papua New Guinea at] ... sub-district level were increasingly decided by persons [in Canberra] not qualified to judge situations in an environment beyond their experience'. The loss of independence was keenly felt by field officers, and noted with interest by those under their rule.[51] Equally significant was the development of medical drugs. Quarantine and racial segregation had been the main ways of containing infections until the 1930s. The magic bullets of sulfa and penicillin eventually eliminated the rationale for isolation, reducing the risks of movement between tropical and temperate countries, and promoting international travel.[52]

Shrinking distances, closer government and crumbling barriers were not always welcome. Decentralization programmes were widespread through the

Western world of the 1950s, usually linked to visions of economic reconstruction based on a partnership between public policy and private initiatives. The physical devastation of war stimulated a comprehensive economic purpose, whereas decentralization was more a response against interventionism and central authority.

However open to different forms of mobilization, decentralization has been a persistent theme in Australian political culture. It fostered both social ideals and conflict, and debate on issues at the heart of the Australian experience: the merits of mass society as against individuality; economic inequities between rural and urban areas; inaccessibility to political power; relations between community and nation, local needs and national policy; cultural ghettos outside the cities; the city jungle against the empty bush. The debate sharpened community and government focus on key terms and concepts including 'community' itself, 'citizenship', avenues of social and political participation, the role of privacy and the domestic in the social sphere, and acceptable limits of government control. Decentralism as an ethical point of reference provided a compelling focus more because it allowed for the divorce of social values from economic and technical change as a means of preserving traditional social forms, than as a useful way to meet such changes.[53]

The mark of Big Government is everywhere in Australia, from the cleared slums in inner cities to failed dreams of 'towns ringed with tiny farms, intensely cultivated market gardens, poultry farms and orchards'.[54] From the patterns of rural settlement to the early development of suburbia, the management of relations between classes, city and country, private and public spheres, has been the domain of central powers. Partly in response, decentralization has been a recurrent rallying cry. Many issues have been hitched to it, from the new statism campaigns of the 1920s, seeking to forge autonomous states by consolidating those communities outside the economic, political and social orbits of the capital cities;[55] a peculiar brand of collectivism of the 1930s; regionalism in the 1940s; to the advocacy of voluntarism in the 1950s through a new social contract.

After the Second World War the question re-emerged. Some measure of decentralization was advocated by all major parties and all levels of government. It also figured in public debate over political reform, economic development and social welfare, education, architecture, housing, even cultural criticism. To each interest group, community group and bureaucratic sector, it meant something different. Some treated it as utopian; others as a political rallying point, a way to discredit centralized government and comprehensive policies of social welfare. Political scientists were prominent in both arguments, seeing decentralization as an irrational desire to return to a pastoral ideal of family life, and the intimate interdependence of community and local economy it evokes. Proclaimed by several commissions of inquiry in the 1920s (a time of particular agitation for decentralization) as romantic or manipulative, it was portrayed as an impractical and foolhardy cause.

Others have read into decentralization a deeper meaning, linking it with essential aspects of Australian political development and social attitudes. This was particularly so during its 1950s heyday when it became identified with elements of conservatism in politics and culture, and part of a broader agenda to reduce the power of governments and check the growth of the welfare state. Its advocates, like their detractors, held many positions on relations between the individual and society. Some were fearful, others offended by the pace of modern life. Henry Tasman Lowell, professor of Psychology at Sydney University and president of the New South Wales Council of Social Service, argued in a 1944 report to the Commonwealth Housing Commission that 'a man deprived of space is reduced in stature':

> But as soon as he owns space in which to move and to realize himself, he begins to sense his own value, and to feel a self-respect which renders him socially amenable and contented; he then accepts and conforms to the law of the land of his own free will.[56]

Less government promised a return to a golden age. Some saw the hand of the state eroding private space, threatening civil liberties, choking community initiative, encouraging dependence. Decentralization promised a new social contract, a new accountability for citizens in a community where economic and technical progress were not at the expense of traditional roles and values.[57]

The impulse and nostalgia for space and freedom are embedded in the collective psyche of Australians, but the impulse sets up tensions, not least the gap between the image of lush English fields and outback reality. Tied both to the mythology of Bush Australia, and to the tradition of British pastoral, decentralization as escape from the strictures of government and order is a recurrent preoccupation of artists and writers.

In contrast with the conservative forces driving decentralization in the 1950s, the revival of the theme in fiction was led by the Left. Its mythology dovetailed with the Bush Legend in which the land is a site of freedom and redemption from the city, symbol of Progress and other Old World evils. For writers of the 1930s and 1940s, the first to mark the new parameters of an urban-based literature, the shift to celebrating rural Australia was dramatic. Some deem it cynical and shallow, a move pressed on them by the failure of the New Order and the advent of Menzies. Other critics saw the new developments not as regressive but as further evidence of the inevitable pull of the land, the elemental Australian urge.

Disillusioned with their society, fleeing the Cold War witch-hunts, Vance and Nettie Palmer, Flora Eldershaw and Frank Dalby Davison went in search of their own patch of pastoral, and for a time appeared to find it. Southeast Queensland, with mild weather and lush fields, was a popular destination. In fiction and travel literature, writers posed it as Camelot: green, fertile and well-watered, its winters at worst 'chilly', its summer nights never 'oppressive'. In its soil grew 'almost anything ... stuck into – or even dropped upon – the ground'. Plentiful harvests bore pineapple, bananas, tomatoes, strawberries, avocados, beans, passion fruit, macadamia nuts and other exotica.

Its absences also beckoned. Eleanor Dark, author of *The Timeless Land* (1941), chose with her doctor-husband to leave their elegant home and gardens in the Blue Mountains for a ramshackle macadamia farmhouse in a village on Queensland's Blackall Range. There the family spent most of the

1950s 'round the corner from the world, with not even a signpost to betray our whereabouts'.[58] Once removed from Cold War politics, mass culture and Big Government, the author in her last novel evoked her years as a 'farmer's wife'. Some absences, like an intellectual culture, were unfortunate but tolerated. Cultural impoverishment seemed a small price to pay, even if the writers' letters hinted at exile.

> Our Brisbane Library sends us pretty lightweight novels, and a remarkable assortment of Memoirs by the Duchess of this and the Countess of that with illustrations showing groups of aristocratic Edwardians posed in front of the Stately Homes of England.[59]

The sense of community, based on patterns of farming, was another culture shock. Small-town tyranny – the other side of the cozy network of kindred spirits – was confronted obliquely, more as quirk than affront. Intrusions and transgressions into their personal space were read as evidence of communal trust and loyalty.

> There are no secrets. ... There are conventions, however, one of which is that you do not appear to know your neighbours' business, but civilly wait until they see fit to inform you of it.[60]

The move to the bush was not an experiment in alternative life-styles, so much as a rewarding holiday-cum-political protest. As such they were cast by their peers in the city, some of whom portrayed the bush writers in grandiose terms, their efforts cast in terms of the national good. From writers of the people's literature, they had become toilers of the people's land. A visit to fellow-intellectuals-turned-farmers in Queensland persuaded a Sydney writer that they were visionary entrepreneurs: they had taken over 'an almost derelict farm, regenerated its soil, and raised some crops that point the way to new rural industries'.[61]

The doctor's wife did not really turn into a farmer's wife, nor the intellectual into a rural worker, although as a keen hobby-farmer she did her share of farm work. The concept rather than the fact of 'self-help' (with its own definitions of community and citizenship) was a sustaining element. Life, she conceded to friends at 'home', had 'become more strenuous instead of more leisured', but despite its 'harassments' something beckoned her to stay. Eleanor remembered these years as a time of 'sanity and sunlight', snatched from the claws of the Cold War pursuing her and other writers. For this generation of soured visionaries searching escape (from their society, not their country), rural life provided the chance to shed the political from their roles and responsibilities as writers.

The embrace of rural Australia for writers of the Left also required a different kind of shedding. In celebrating the family and community values underpinning that world, they aligned themselves with a political philosophy that was conservative to the core. Rural Australia is the heartland of the Country Party, of small-settler capitalism, its land worked by generations of White Australians, subdivided along European notions of management and cultivation, the domestic and working lives of its men – and women – governed by strict gender-based roles and responsibilities. And what of indigenous Australians and their claim to this land? The writers' shift from urban to rural represented a radical shift in perspective, and in sympathies.

If the politics of commitment defined their writings of the 1930s and 1940s, in the 1950s it was the politics of apathy. Advancing years and relentless conservative forces stamping out political dissent had broken their spirit. Not even the *bete noire* of censorship excited much heat. Invited to protest against a fellow writer's conviction for libel, few bothered. 'In making protests', one wrote,

> I really don't think it matters whether there are Communists associated with them or not. The present situation seems to be that anyone who doesn't see eye to eye with Menzies & Co. is a 'Communist' anyhow.[62]

Disengagement was reflected in their fiction. Dark's *Lantana Lane* (1950), an autobiographical novel of her farming years, is a salute to what in the 1990s would be called political incorrectness, and in Australia of the 1950s embodied the quintessential Australian's cynicism for politics and disregard for world affairs. The scene is a typical farmhouse in Lantana Lane:

> Henry went to sleep in his chair with an open book on his knee, and Sue went to sleep in hers with some knitting on her lap, and the nine o'clock voice of the ABC composedly reporting the sensations and disasters of the past twelve hours, fell upon two pairs of happily deaf ears.[63]

This contentment did not conform with the realities of chronic instability and declining relative incomes in many rural areas. Indeed, non-urban Australia was becoming a focus of official concern as it faced cultural impoverishment and economic insecurity, at least equal to that of the cities. The picture of affluence suggested by the postwar boom from 1945 to 1973 was shattered when a UNESCO inquiry described the 'typical' Victorian country town as locked into patterns of resentment, conformity and a level of class conflict comparable to, if not greater than, urban areas.

New Zealand's 'golden years', too, produced simmering resentment among those denied the suburban dream. By the 1960s the government began to withdraw from suburban home ownership. The costs of state investment palled in an environment of uncertainty magnified by dependence on Britain, which was turning towards Europe, while worries surfaced about suburban sprawl as a source of 'social pathology' rather than a panacea. New Zealanders did not abandon the suburban dream: the government did. 'Unlimited investment in the dream, which now included apparent social problems in the large mass housing suburbs of the late 1950s, had become too problematic.'[64]

NOTES

1   Cameron Hazlehurst, *Menzies Observed*, Sydney, 1979, 289–93.
2   G. C. Bolton, '1939–51', in F. Crowley, *New History of Australia*, Melbourne, 1974, 458–503.

3   Ibid., 471.

4   Ken Buckley, Barbara Dale and Wayne Reynolds, *Doc Evatt*, Melbourne, 1994.

5   W. J. Hudson, '1951–1972', in Crowley, *New History of Australia*, 504–55. The authoritative source on ANZUS is W. D. McIntyre, *Background to the ANZUS Pact: Policy-making, Strategy, and Diplomacy, 1945–55*, Basingstoke and Christchurch, 1995.

6   D. Wolfstone, 'The Colombo Plan after Ten Years', *Far Eastern Economic Review*, 3 August 1961; cited by Daniel Oakman, 'The Seed of Freedom: Regional Security and the Colombo Plan', Australian National University seminar paper, 1999.

7   Oakman, 'The Seed of Freedom'.

8   Stewart Firth, *Nuclear Playground*, Sydney, 1987; and Stewart Firth and Karin von Strokirch, 'A Nuclear Pacific', in Donald Denoon, Stewart Firth, Jocelyn Linnekin, Malama Meleisea and Karen Nero (eds), *Cambridge History of the Pacific Islanders*, Melbourne, 1997, 324–57.

9   Heather Goodall, ' "The Whole Truth and Nothing But … ": Some Intersections in Western Law, Aboriginal History and Community Memory', in B. Attwood and J. Arnold (eds), *Power, Knowledge and Aborigines*, Melbourne, 1992, 116–17.

10 Firth and von Strokirch, 'A Nuclear Pacific'.

11 David Hanlon, *Remaking Micronesia: Discourses over Development in a Pacific Territory, 1944–1982*, Honolulu, 1998.

12 Ian Downs, *The Australian Trusteeship: Papua New Guinea 1945–1975*, Canberra, 1980.

13 Ibid., 11–13.

14 D. Denoon, 'Capitalism in Papua New Guinea', *Journal of Pacific History*, 20 (1985), 119–34; Downs, *The Australian Trusteeship*, 82–3.

15 Quote from Paul Hasluck, *A Time for Building: Australian Administration in Papua and New Guinea 1951–1963*, Melbourne, 1976, 6. See Downs, *The Australian Trusteeship*; B. Jinks, 'Papua New Guinea 1942–1952. Policy, Planning and J. K. Murray', Ph.D. thesis, University of Sydney, 1975. Couve de Murville described him as his own inspector-general: Hasluck, *A Time for Building*, 407.

16 Ibid., 86, 239.

17 These are tabulated in Denoon, 'Capitalism in Papua New Guinea'.

18 60/374, minister's minute of 28 January 1960, cited in D. Denoon, *Getting Under the Skin*, Melbourne, 2000.

19 Downs, *The Australian Trusteeship*, 240.

20 Hasluck, *A Time for Building*, 14.

21 International Bank for Reconstruction and Development, *The Economic Development of the Territory of Papua and New Guinea*, Baltimore, 1965.

22 Douglas Oliver, 'Some Social–relational Aspects of CRA Copper Mining on Bougainville: A Confidential Report to Management', 1968, cited in Denoon, *Getting Under the Skin*.

23 Catherine Snowden, 'Cooperatives', in D. Denoon and C. Snowden (eds), *A Time to Plant and a Time to Uproot*, n.d., University of Papua New Guinea.

24 Ken Gillion, *The Fiji Indians: Challenge to European Dominance, 1920–1946*, Canberra, 1977; S. Firth, 'The War in the Pacific', in Denoon, Firth, Linnekin, Meleisea and Nero, *Cambridge History of the Pacific Islanders*, 291–322.

25 Jonathan Kelley, 'Ethnic Sympathies and Politics in Australia, 1995', *Worldwide Attitudes*, 19960115 (15 Jan. 1996).

26 James Jupp, *Immigration. Australian Retrospectives*, ed. David Walker, Sydney, 1991, ch. 5.

27 Ibid., 72.

28 Ibid., 77.

29 Ibid., 95–6.

30 Malcolm McKinnon, *Immigrants and Citizens: New Zealanders and Asian Immigration in Historical Context*, Wellington, 1996, 37–8, citing *Appendices to the Journals of the House of Representatives*, 1946, I-17, 99.

31 P. Ongley, 'Immigration, Employment and Ethnic Relations', in P. Spoonley, D. Pearson and C. Macpherson (eds), *Nga Patai*, Palmerston North, 1996, 18.

32 McKinnon, *Immigrants and Citizens*, 39.

33 Ibid., 35–7.

34 Ibid., 40–1.

35 Ongley, 'Immigration, Employment and Ethnic Relations'.

36 McKinnon, *Immigrants and Citizens*, 39–40.

37 M. McKinnon (ed.) with B. Bradley and R. Kirkpatrick, *New Zealand Historical Atlas*, Wellington, 1997, plate 91.

38 D. Awatere Huata, *My Journey*, Auckland, 1996, 22.

39 Human Rights and Equal Opportunity Commission, *Bringing Them Home: Report of the National Inquiry into the Separation of Aboriginal and Torres Strait Islander Children from their Families*, Sydney, 1997, 143.

40 Ibid., 145–6.

41 R. Broome, *Aboriginal Australians*, Sydney, 1994, 173.

42 B. Sykes, *Mumshirl: An Autobiography with the Assistance of Bobbi Sykes*, Richmond, Victoria, 1987, 110–11, 121; M. Tucker, *If Everyone Cared: Autobiography of Margaret Tucker M.B.E.*, Melbourne, 1983, 146, 25.

43 M. Rolfe, 'Faraway Fordism: The Americanization of Australia and New Zealand During the 1950s and 1960s', *New Zealand Journal of History*, 33: 1 (April 1999), 82–5.

44 *Australian House and Garden*, Nov. 1955, 19; cited in J. Murphy, 'The Commonwealth–State Housing Agreement of 1956 and the Politics of Home Ownership in the Cold War', Research School of Social Sciences, Australian National University, Urban Research Program Working Paper 50, Dec. 1995, 5.

45 G. Ferguson, *Building the New Zealand Dream*, Palmerston North, 1994, ch. 4.

46 See A. Greig, *The Stuff Dreams are Made Of: Housing Provision in Australia 1945–1960*, Melbourne, 1995; D. Thorns, 'Owner Occupation, the State and Class Relations in New Zealand', in C. Wilkes and I. Shirley (eds), *In the Public Interest: Health, Work and Housing in New Zealand*, Auckland, 1984, 213–30.

47 Nicholas Brown, *Governing Prosperity: Social Change and Social Analysis in Australia in the 1950s*, Melbourne, 1995.

48 R. Boyd, *Australia's Home: Its Origins, Builders and Occupiers*, 2nd edn, Melbourne, 1991.

49 M. Peel, *Good Times, Hard Times: The Past and the Future in Elizabeth*, Melbourne, 1995, 2, 4.

50 B. Schrader, 'A Brave New World? Ideal versus Reality in Postwar Naenae', *New Zealand Journal of History*, 30: 1 (April 1996): 61–79.

51 Downs, *The Australian Trusteeship*, 287.

52 Donald Denoon with Kathleen Dugan and Leslie Marshall, *Public Health in Papua New Guinea, 1884–1984: Medical Possibility and Social Constraint*, Cambridge, 1989.

53 Brown, *Governing Prosperity*, ch. 4, 126–65.

54 I. Harris, 'The Implications of Decentralization', in H. L. Harris et al., *Decentralization*, Sydney, 1948, 19–20.

55 Neville Cain, 'Political Economy and the Tariff: Australia in the 1920s', *Australian Economic Papers*, 12: 1 (1973), 3–4.

56 Preface to Phillip Matthews, K. Ogilvie and F. J. Walker, *Housing: A Report to the Commonwealth Housing Commission*, Sydney, 1944, iv; quoted in Brown, *Governing Prosperity*, 127–8.
57 Brown, *Governing Prosperity*, 126–30.
58 Eleanor Dark, *Lantana Lane*, London, 1950, 254.
59 Eleanor Dark to Dorothy Fitzpatrick, 8 Jan. 1957, NLA MS 5954/2/412.
60 Dark, *Lantana Lane*, 43–4.
61 J. Manifold, 'Our Writers, VIII: Eleanor Dark', *Overland*, 15 (winter 1959), 39.
62 Eleanor Dark to Miles Franklin, 17 May 1952, ML MSS 364/26/481.
63 Dark, *Lantana Lane*, 203–4.
64 Ferguson, *Building the New Zealand Dream*, 232, 197–206.

PART V

Reflections on Contemporary Identities

[17] EXPANDING CITIZENSHIP

Addressing a Global Cultural Diversity Conference in Sydney in 1995, the Australian Prime Minister Paul Keating spoke of a 'period of profound transition' for the nation-state, and the need to 'redefine the state and the nation'. As a quintessentially migrant nation, as well as a settler society skating over unresolved disputes with indigenous peoples, Australia was already confronting peculiar challenges to define its culture and identity, and then to shape political institutions to reflect its diversity. For New Zealand – as for New Caledonia and Fiji – the main challenge was to accommodate biculturalism; yet each polity was based on an increasingly remote eighteenth-century European model.

Their peculiar modern histories gave New Zealand and Australia a head start on most countries in addressing cultural difference arising from migration. Unlike other polities in the region, they could work out their own destinies, and their debates were not clouded by threats of secession, nor by sustained violence. Despite long commitment to the notion of White Australia (and the more discreet White New Zealand), they had experience and even success, compared to France and Britain – only recently acknowledging cultural difference through immigration. The contrast is even starker with Japan, whose otherwise modern nation-state does not easily accommodate ethnic difference.[1] Relations between ethnicity and polity mark the boundaries of societies' tolerance of ethnic and cultural difference. To what extent should the virtues of sameness be traded for those of difference? And at what price to the cohesion of the nation-state?

In 'Multicultural Citizenship'[2] Stephen Castles identifies three models for managing diversity: differential exclusion, whereby immigrants enter civil society in the labour force but are denied citizenship; assimilation, which incorporates immigrants who relinquish their cultural difference; and pluralism, which provides equal rights to minorities while protecting the qualities which distinguish them from the mainstream. Australian policy on indentured Pacific Islanders was an early example of differential exclusion: drafted into the labour force, they had no access to social services and hardly any to the state. Castles' categories can also extend to the management of relations with indigenous communities. Assimilation was the dominant policy on both sides of the Tasman for most of the twentieth century, to incorporate both the hosts of non-British European migrants, and the much small numbers of

Aborigines, and even the whole Maori population. All could become full and equal citizens – if they ceased to be Italian or Aboriginal or Maori. Only from the 1960s did that model dissolve into pluralism, as official racism and discrimination waned.

The liberal-democratic principle that all members of civil society should also be members of the political community settled into the Australian and New Zealand collective psyches earlier than in France or Britain. Acknowledged precedents were assimilationist policies aimed at integrating migrants into a new society, as had evolved in the United States. Massive immigration and urbanization, which triggered these policies in America, had the same effect in the antipodes. In time, doubts were cast on the idea that immigrants must relinquish their group identity in order to become citizens. Whether as assimilation or integration, such goals bespoke intolerance to difference, and prompted the reassessment of policy options.

Ethnocultural pluralism on the other hand celebrates difference as a way to avoid old divisions and build new cohesions. Federal Canada embraced that strategy (and coined the term 'multicultural') with an eye to defusing explosive tensions between itself and Quebec, the Francophone province whose aspirations were at least bicultural equality, if not secession.[3] Massive European immigration into Australia in the 1950s and 1960s created many different ways of experiencing Australia; but official policy maintained that the outcome should be (and one day would be) assimilation into a single Australian way of life. Assimilation formally yielded to pluralism only with the access to power of the Whitlam Labor government in 1972, and Al Grassby's adoption (as minister for immigration) of 'multiculturalism' both to describe a reality and to endorse a pluralist goal.[4] Conservative critics and right-wing politicians have denounced this sense of multiculturalism and non-Labor parties federally have often worried about it, but it became solidly entrenched in policy circles – possibly more so than it is in the general public.

For a variety of reasons then, 'classical immigration countries' like the United States, Canada and Australia, came to accept immigrant populations as ethnic communities, distinct in language, culture and social organization from other sectors of society. Citizenship in these societies does not demand the surrender of otherness, though it does assume conformity to basic values. The American version of pluralism involves a *laissez-faire* approach in which difference is tolerated but the state takes no responsibility to support it. Australia, like Canada, pursues a more aggressive line that foregrounds multiculturalism and acceptance by the majority of cultural difference and its implications for national identity and institutional structures. The fact that they share a tradition of state intervention in social affairs is no coincidence. As Castles argues, the success of their pluralist policies hinges on the state's commitment to ensuring that tolerance and social justice go hand-in-hand.[5] In the United States, with minimalist social policy, pluralism coexists with ethnic ghettos.

For Australia, and to a lesser extent for New Zealand, pluralism and its embrace of cultural difference continue to pose problems. One hurdle is the question of their relatively declining Anglo-Celtic populations and the implications for institutional structures based on the Anglo-Celtic values of their founders. As 'male' was once held to embrace 'female', so Anglo-Celtic values were believed to be universal across all cultural, social and political discourse. As in all attempts to bring mythology into line with real national identity, the polities need to coax communities to confront the challenge.

The status of citizen – a prerequisite but not a guarantee of equality – had different meanings in the diverse polities of our region; it was attained by different routes; and it opened doors to radically different rights and responsibilities. The Melanesians who became citizens of France after the Pacific war could point to the removal of disabilities, but few positive benefits flowed from being an ethnic minority in a global empire. Melanesians who became Indonesian citizens (instead of Dutch subjects) in the 1960s lost both the limited reality and the broader possibilities of autonomous development. Other Melanesians would become citizens of independent polities in the 1970s, by severing their constitutional links with the colonizing powers; whereas Polynesians who won citizenship of sovereign states gained and retained elements of dual citizenship and continuing access to the former colonial powers. Popular acknowledgement of Aboriginal Australians' citizenship from the 1960s secured no automatic benefits, though it did make possible the successful struggles of the 1980s and 1990s; but full citizenship has sometimes been invoked as an argument against programmes which target them as a group with specific and urgent needs.

The evolution of citizenship in different contexts is therefore complex and elusive. Australian assimilationism, for all its flaws, opened up citizenship to immigrants and to some indigenes. The 1970s debates on ethnicity and multiculturalism led to crucial shifts in the discourse of identity. As the principle of cultural homogeneity – once the security blanket of non-indigenous Australia – yielded to multicultural realities, a new citizenship linked cultural difference and social justice. The greatest changes touched indigenous communities.

ABORIGINAL AUSTRALIANS

Aboriginal Australians are now a minority of perhaps 280,000 in a population of 19,000,000. Despite colonists' expectations, already by the 1920s they were clearly not doomed (at least numerically).[6] The policy implications were less clear. Some thinkers on the Left as well as the Right assumed that only territorial segregation could ensure Aborigines' survival. Every strand of white opinion assumed special measures of some kind, although some reformists gave priority to 'social elevation' and education, and others insisted that nutrition and health measures were more urgent.[7] David Unaipon was a strong advocate for Aboriginal interests throughout his life (which ended in 1967). On Christian grounds he denounced segregation, but his enthusiasm for missions also implied a special nexus between governments and Aborigines. Governments usually proposed different programmes for 'full-bloods' and 'half-castes', the latter seen as assimilable into the white population. Aboriginal activists repudiated this division, but it was both pervasive and seductive. When the New South Wales Aborigines Progressive Association sought citizenship, they explained that they had 'no desire to go back to primitive conditions of the Stone Age. We ask you to teach our people to live in the Modern Age as modern citizens'.[8] Implicitly, only 'civilized' Aborigines should become citizens.

The consequences of legal inferiority were broad. State governments neglected their obligations in education, health and welfare, for people who were poor and powerless and often socially invisible. Many states licensed welfare and police officers to remove children from their parents to institutions, or to adoptive or foster parents: the 'stolen generations'.[9] Since colour-blind programmes were in practice delivered unequally, for many years the limit of Aboriginal aspiration was formal equality and the removal of discriminatory laws and institutions. In 'freedom rides' into country towns and other devices, they and some white allies uncovered the extent and nastiness of racism and made it a political issue; and in 1967 the Commonwealth proposed a referendum to acquire wider powers in Aboriginal affairs. Despite the explicit extension of Commonwealth powers over the states, and a dismal record of failed referenda, this passed by a great majority. Symbolically (though not legally) the passage of the referendum is often thought to mark the end of discrimination and the general public's acceptance of Aboriginal Australians into a common citizenship.[10]

Armed with this mandate, the Commonwealth nevertheless proceeded cautiously. An Anti-Discrimination Act was passed only in 1975 and the Aboriginal Land Rights (Northern Territory) Act a year later. These Acts reflected shifts in government policies, but did not entrench Aborigines' interests as constitutional rights: without full autonomy, they still relied on the government's good will. The latter sought bureaucratic solutions and the Department of Aboriginal Affairs was its first attempt to co-ordinate community development. Aboriginal people had no role in policy-making, except in consultative committees, until 1989 when the department was replaced by a unique body, the Aboriginal and Torres Strait Islander Commission. ATSIC was given administrative duties but it was headed by a board of elected commissioners, and it was designed to channel resources quickly to communities in need. This blend of features required ATSIC to meet two sets of (conflicting) criteria. Aboriginal clients had little interest in formal accountability, and their methods opened ATSIC to procedural criticism. On the other hand, ATSIC had none of the institutional powers enjoyed by Maori in New Zealand, or provinces in Papua New Guinea, or regions in New Caledonia. By the late 1990s when ATSIC came under siege from the (Liberal) Commonwealth government on grounds of accountability, it was also being denounced by Aboriginal groups whose needs had not been met.

The fragility of Aboriginal rights was demonstrated in 1996 with a change of federal government. In 1992, in Mabo & Others v. State of Queensland, the High Court found in favour of Torres Strait Islanders from Mer (Murray) Island, led by Eddie Mabo. The court found that the Meriam people had indeed possessed common law title to land, and that this had never been extinguished. Since that judgement overturned the doctrine of *terra nullius*, the Commonwealth had to legislate to resolve an anomalous situation.[11] Keating's cabinet was overtly committed to reconciliation between indigenous and non-indigenous Australians. The discovery of Native Title therefore provided an occasion to draft land laws in consultation with Aborigines, and to steer the package through a fragmented but mainly friendly Senate. The judgement itself and the legislation implied that black and white Australia must – and could – negotiate shared use of the land and even an equitable future.

The Mer people's title had survived partly through the Queensland government's oversight. The High Court next found (in the Wik judgement)[12] that although Native Title was extinguished by explicit government action in many circumstances, it could survive on land under pastoral lease – the bulk of Australia. By this time there was a new federal government whose response was less conciliatory. Drawing attention to other unresolved issues, the Human Rights and Equal Opportunities Commission investigated the systematic removal of some 100,000 children from indigenous parents[13] and described the policy as genocidal. John Howard's coalition reversed course, taking measures to limit or undo political and legislative gains. Keating's Redfern Speech in 1992 had acknowledged atrocities against Aboriginal people. Taking the opposite tack, Howard's sympathies lay with

> Australians who are insulted when they are told that we have a racist bigoted past. And Australians are told that quite regularly. Our children are taught that. ... Now, of course, we treated Aborigines very, very badly in the past – very, very badly – but to tell children whose parents were no part of that maltreatment ... that we're all part of a ... racist bigoted history, is something that Australians reject.[14]

So did the prime minister, in distinguishing Australians from Aborigines.

These policy shifts and their impact on people, land and identities are evident in the unfinished narrative of Elsey cattle station in the Northern Territory. This spread of half a million hectares became a cattle station in 1881 when a man bought it from two white 'owners' and drove 2,750 cattle across country from Queensland to stock it. A generation later (1902) Elsey was owned by Aeneas Gunn, whose wife Jeannie spent a year there. As a widow, she published *We of the Never-Never*, the most influential celebration of outback pioneering and paternalism. A second account, *The Little Black Princess*, a set text in Australian schools, introduced generations of pupils to Bett-Bett, 'a wild little nigger'. Elsey's fate became problematic with the passage of the Aboriginal Land Rights (Northern Territory) Act by the Fraser government in 1976. The minister introducing the legislation said that it would give Aborigines

> inalienable freehold title to land on reserves ... and provide machinery for them to obtain title to traditional land outside reserves. [The policy] clearly acknowledges that affinity with the land is fundamental to Aborigines' sense of identity.

Aboriginal interests in land came to be represented and managed by two Aboriginal Land Councils in the Territory, Northern and Central. In 1991, as the Act required, the Northern Land Council lodged a claim to Elsey on behalf of 'traditional Aboriginal owners'. The Northern Territory government, always sceptical and often hostile to Aboriginal claims, argued that the Aboriginal land commissioner had no authority to deal with the claim. It took six years for the commissioner to recommend that the federal government allow the claim.[15] A year later, the government acted as advised. After a century of alienation, the owners may yet regain Elsey, but they cannot unwrite the Never-Never. Legal equality within a common citizenship does not necessarily address historic wrongs or contemporary disadvantage.

TORRES STRAIT ISLANDERS

ATSIC's other constituents are Torres Strait Islanders. Around 30,000 people identify themselves as such, though only a quarter still live in the Islands. On several islands, cultural identity is delineated by self-selected Councils of Elders. Whether in the Islands or in mainland Queensland, Islanders see themselves as one people. Their lives were shaped by such paternalism that they yearned for integration into Australia 'without the mediation of administrators or missionaries'.[16] The opposite goal – independence – swelled in 1978 when Papua New Guinea proposed to annex the Islands to resolve what they saw as a boundary anomaly. Independence was first proposed by the Torres United Party, created by Islanders on the mainland. In 1978 they mounted a High Court challenge to Queensland's annexation, and appealed to the United Nations. Both ventures failed, and the issue lapsed until 1987, when a representative appealed to heads of Pacific Island governments. That gambit also failed, revealing the difficulty of bringing the Islanders' case (or even their grievances) to wider attention. Instead there were bureaucratic institutions: a Torres Strait Regional Council under the ATSIC umbrella, comprising Chairs of the Island Councils; an Office of Torres Strait Islander Affairs; and a Torres Strait Islander Advisory Board to serve Islanders outside Torres Strait. By now, some Islanders were asserting an identity separate from both white and Aboriginal Australia, to preserve *Ailan Kastom* and to escape from welfare colonialism. In 1992 the Mabo judgement incidentally re-launched the independence drive: the maverick James Akee declared secession in September 1993 and again in 1995. A straw poll found 18 per cent supporting his first 'Declaration of Sovereignty', while 48 per cent favoured a more moderate agenda of autonomy by 2001. The moderate agenda, promoted by Gaetano Lui Jr, aspired to limited self-government.[17] Prime Minister Keating took advice from his Office of Indigenous Affairs rather than ATSIC, and scuppered both options. The Commonwealth chose to see Torres Strait as an issue of regionalism and administration rather than ethnicity and politics. Lacking leverage, the Islanders had to accept this outcome.

SOUTH SEA ISLANDERS

Some 12,000 descendants of 'Kanakas' who escaped deportation in 1906 call themselves South Sea Islanders. The original cane workers suffered discrimination at work and in school; they came from many different islands, and almost all were male; but they survived and grew into a community whose identity was celebrated in biographies, family histories and novels. In the 1970s journalists took an interest in their lurid blackbird past – a clue that victimhood was the route to compensation.[18]

Most South Sea Islanders have Aboriginal or Torres Strait forebears, but in the 1970s there was bad blood between them. They began to be ousted from indigenous bodies, and by 1974 they had become ineligible for aid as indigenes. Some had learned lobbying in the struggle for Aboriginal rights. Faith Bandler, Secretary of the Federal Council for the Advancement of Aborigines and Torres Strait Islanders, was indeed the public face of the 1967 referendum campaign. Then she became concerned that South Sea Islanders continued to suffer the same racial discrimination as Aborigines and Torres Strait Islanders, without any compensatory measure. In 1974 she formed the Australian South Sea Islanders United Council, to win recognition and redress for 'descendants of those South Sea Islanders brought by force as indentured labour or who came voluntarily to work in Australia before 1906'.

After years of campaigning, the federal attorney-general acknowledged the South Sea Islander Community as a 'high-need group in equal opportunity, access and equity programmes'. Part of his rationale was their victimhood. They had been 'treated no better than slaves. ... No other group came to Australia with less status. ... Their historical experience in Australia has generally been one of lack of control over their own affairs and exclusion.' In brief, they were conceptually severed from indigenous Australia and joined the immigrant and multicultural mosaic. The government would provide educational support, and enable Islanders to help to rewrite school histories. In this venture they confronted academic historians who (seeking to transform victims into agents) insisted that Islanders had exercised real leverage in the labour trade, and became victims only by staying in Australia. Independent Islanders in Vanuatu and Solomon Islands cheerfully agree that their ancestors made things happen, but Australian Islanders insist that most recruits were kidnapped, that indenture was slavery, and their ancestors victims.[19] There is even convergence between 'blackbirding' and convictism. In 1999 Tumbulgum town named a park after Faith Bandler. People expressed their pride in hugs and kisses, and a local historian pronounced her 'the most significant [Tumbulgum person] in terms of her contribution to Australian society'. The mayor elaborated:

> Mrs Bandler had fought the 10-year campaign leading to the 1967 referendum which included Aboriginal people in the census, she had worked for Aboriginal housing, education and the rights of South Sea Islanders, she was a founding member of the Women's Electoral Lobby and the Australian Republican Movement, had written six books and received an honorary doctorate.

As to the broader context, a journalist explained that:

> Faith Bandler's father, Wacvie Mussingkon, was kidnapped in 1883 from the island of Ambrym in what is now Vanuatu. His kidnapping was part of an activity called blackbirding, a means of finding cheap labour which arose with the end of convict transportation from Britain. Wacvie ... was sold as a slave in Mackay and worked on sugar plantations until escaping in 1897, finally settling in Tumbulgum. He and his wife, Ida, had eight children.[20]

The cult of victimhood may enhance the prospects of the living and the not-yet-born by diminishing the agency of the dead. This disconcerts professional historians, but Australian South Sea Islanders have few other high cards, and this is a trump.

MAORI REVIVAL AND THE WAITANGI TRIBUNAL

Maori had been British (and then New Zealand) citizens just as long as Pakeha. It was not citizenship that they demanded, but an end to assimilationist notions which expected that – precisely because they were citizens – they should conform culturally to British and Pakeha norms and conventions. Profound changes in the place of Maori in the nation-state, and in Maori–Pakeha relations, occurred in the 1960s. Maori population recovery reached record rates between 1956 and 1966 at almost 4 per cent a year, twice the rate of the Pakeha baby boom and equal to the fastest recent rates in Africa.[21] This population was dominated by young people who would insist that Maori gain a greater stake and a fair share of resources, and have their status as *tangata whenua* acknowledged. They belonged to the youth culture of the 1960s, a counter-culture which also unsettled conservative, isolated New Zealand.

Maori urbanization itself prompted shifts in values. Maori were no longer a dispersed, rural people. At the end of the Second World War when three-quarters of Maori were still rural, Maori and Pakeha occupied largely separate worlds. By the mid-1970s three-quarters of Maori lived in cities, over a fifth in Auckland. This new engagement often led to marriage; in 1960, half of Maori marriages were with Pakeha.[22] Renewed culture contact also made Maori disadvantage more obvious. A generation politicized by and about disadvantages, better educated but outstripped by Pakeha, alert to the American civil rights movement, to United Nations advocacy of indigenous rights and decolonization, began to make a noise in the 1960s.[23]

In the Hunn Report in 1960, the government commissioned a stocktake of Maori people. Failure was clear: Maori suffered unequal employment, income and housing, and the report continued a hundred years of official commitment to amalgamation.[24] The current term was 'integration', meaning to make 'modern' Maori culture and society. Maori and Pakeha elements would be combined 'to form one nation', retaining 'only the fittest elements' of Maori culture – language, arts and crafts, and marae protocol – although these were seen as 'relics' of the 'ancient life' rather than part of the present. Modes of thinking about a dying race persisted. The aim of the state was to 'eliminate' a minority who were 'complacently living a backward life in primitive conditions' by integrating them with Pakeha, and then to allow the majority (deemed integrated) to choose whether to remain at home in either culture or become totally 'assimilated'.[25] Tribal authority would be undermined in the social order envisaged for urban Maori. There had been no consultation with Maori, who read the report's advocacy of 'integration' as 'assimilation'. Some academics and clerics protested, and the state of Maori housing received adverse publicity, but no general outcry ensued.[26]

Ten years later Maori protest erupted on television.[27] There had been a change in the mood of Maori–Pakeha relations matching changes in society, the economy and politics. Maori had missed the gains made in the 1960s, notably in education, and with the end of economic buoyancy in the 1970s, increased inequalities in work and housing in the cities hurt them particularly. Many young people left for Australia, including young Maori.

For Maori to resume their rightful place, New Zealand had to be decolonized, re-imagining itself as post-colonial, economically and culturally. Chief Judge Edward Taihakurei Durie, the first Maori on the bench of the Maori Land Court in the 1970s, later reflected that 'all Maori people brought up in areas of Maori concentration [were] aware that Maori people lost out'.[28] The burning issues had always been the loss of land and resources, and the Treaty of Waitangi. In Alan Ward's words, 'The situation of Maori by the mid-twentieth century was a travesty of their situation at 1840'. Mere vestiges remained of land and *tino rangatiratanga*. Formal equality as individuals had provided no basis for Maori as a whole, or for tribes, to engage with the modern economy and the state as they had expected in 1840:

> This realization became the dominant one for the increasingly educated, increasingly urbanized, but also increasingly unemployed, younger, postwar generation. It was that perception, as well as an awareness of specific injuries, that underlay the explosion of protest from the late 1960s. Maori people were fed up, not only with the sense of being left on the margins of a Pakeha-dominated economy but with still being ignored or patronized while other people were making decisions affecting their property and their lives.[29]

In the 1970s the Maori call was finally heard: that the state must restore their autonomy by honouring the treaty, arrest the loss of culture and language and instil respect for Maoritanga, and address inequalities by returning or compensating for resources and land.

Many global and local forces made this possible. After a century of Pakeha amnesia over the treaty, a growing sense of identity, Pakeha as well as Maori, sought symbolic outlet. Britain's moves towards the EEC made Pakeha recognize that their future lay in the Pacific. This consciousness coincided with the Maori cultural revival which compelled a response and gave new meaning (and reinforced old meanings) to being Pakeha: Maori had to educate Pakeha, as always. The Maori agenda for social justice entailed recourse to the treaty, but non-Maori first had to be educated over the treaty, since Maori and Pakeha had been travelling different roads guided by competing narratives.

Tensions had simmered on interpreting the treaty since 1840. Most Pakeha assumed that the English version was the treaty, and differences from the Maori text did not enter their narrative. The Land Wars marked a sharp divergence in view, tilting the balance of power and numbers from Maori to Pakeha. In the Pakeha narrative the treaty changed from being valid and binding, to not binding, the wars themselves violating treaty promises, as did the bitter dispossession and the ignominious descent into poverty. Henceforth Maori and Pakeha travelled separate roads over the significance of the treaty. On the Pakeha road, for many the treaty remained a 'simple nullity' as declared wrongly in the 1877 judgement, Wi Parata v. the Bishop of Wellington. For those who did recall the treaty, it was an instrument of assimilation to make New Zealand one people and one nation. Non-Maori assumed that the treaty's provisions were upheld, as the English text was the one acknowledged.

History known to Maori but not taught in schools assumed that much more had been intended by the treaty than inscribed in the British version. The treaty had *mana* as the deed of their *tupuna* (ancestors); the Maori text was the one venerated; after all, it contained the majority of signatures. The treaty was a living thing, a binding contract; it was invoked as a source of rights and redress, symbolic of Maori survival, physically and in terms of identity, and refusal to despair. From the mid-twentieth century this narrative began to affect Pakeha awareness.[30] The narratives clashed at Waitangi on 6 February, the anniversary of the treaty, which the government in 1960 declared a national day of thanksgiving. Routinely the Waitangi Day 'celebration' became the hot spot where narratives collided in fireworks and theatrics of spit and buttocks.

Protests over sporting contacts with South Africa were interwoven with the Maori cultural revival and the yearly buildup to Waitangi Day. In 1960 the New Zealand Rugby Football Union excluded Maori from the All Blacks team which toured South Africa, generating 'No Maori, No Tour' protests. Young Pakeha activists, who established Halt All Racist Tours in 1969 to fight apartheid, learnt from Maori radicals about racism at home.[31] Young Maori had lost patience with the conservative leaders of the Maori Council (created by the government in 1962) and with the marginality of Maori MPs. Some joined progressive social movements, including the New Left, forming the Maori Organization on Human Rights in 1968. MOOHR, with its trade union links, perceived racism through a New Left lens, arguing that Maori rights went hand in hand with class struggle. It grew from an underground newspaper, *Te Hokioi*, named for the nineteenth-century Kingitanga newspaper. Others formed the Maori Graduates Association and Maori Students Association following in the footsteps of the Young Maori Party.

Maori youth and elders united to declare Waitangi Day a day of mourning. The lead was taken by Nga Tamatoa, 'the young warriors', who from 1970 formed the cutting edge of activism. This Auckland group comprised radicals who modelled themselves on the American Black Power movement, and university students seeking Maori self-determination. Some sought black unity and co-operated with Pacific Island gangs in the Polynesian Panthers, while others fought for a narrower Maori unity. Nga Tamatoa, dressed in black – uniform of youth and mourning – initiated annual Waitangi Day protests, drawing attention to the treaty, and to the loss of the Maori language which these young warriors could not speak.[32] In a paradox of remembrance and forgetting, in 1973 the Labour government made 6 February a public holiday and whitewashed it as New Zealand Day; but such was Maori opposition that it reverted to Waitangi Day in 1976.[33] Waitangi remained the 'touchstone of protest', its vehemence varying with state responses on treaty grievances. From 1975, Maori protest made good television, and Pakeha New Zealand watched and listened.

The slow death of 'white New Zealand' began in 1975 with the land rights movement, triggered by three statutes: the 1967 Maori Affairs Amendment Act, whereby the state could alienate uneconomic Maori land compulsorily; the Rating Act 1967, which could compel the sale of land to recover unpaid rates (notably rural land vacated by urbanization); and power under the Town and Country Planning Act to restrict Maori land use through zoning without acknowledging ancestral dwelling places. The Public Works Act was another of many laws which contravened the treaty. Failing to stem the loss of land through official channels, Maori looked to more direct strategies. Lobbying would achieve more in the 1980s, but first the groundwork had to be laid, and Pakeha alerted to the issues.

The Maori Land March in 1975 launched protests to preserve Maori culture and identity. At its heart was land. Its slogan echoed the Kingitanga call: 'Not one more acre of Maori land'.[34] In contrast to Australia, 95 per cent of land had been alienated and was in private ownership, irrecoverable by Maori. The march wove its way from the north of the North Island to the steps of parliament, following the 80-year-old Whina Cooper, foundation president in 1951 of the Maori Women's Welfare League. She became a national figure, with the media title 'Mother of the Nation'. This march sent a powerful message of renewed Maori commitment, not just to persist with grievances over land but to reclaim their treaty rights as *tangata whenua*.[35] The occupation at Bastion Point in 1977–8 was even more compelling. Orakei, Bastion Point's original name, was the homeland of Ngati Whatua who sold Auckland to Hobson in 1840. The sit-in was the latest in a series of protests, including ten court actions; it was the first outside the law, and the first to etch itself into Pakeha consciousness through media coverage. The tribe's history was a typical tale of dispossession. In 1869 the Native Land Court vested the Orakei block of 700 acres in 13 members of Ngati Whatua, disinheriting the rest of the tribe, the inevitable result of individualized title under the 1865 Native Lands Act. In 1886, the state took land for defence on the pretext of a Russian naval scare and named it Bastion Point. Between 1914 and 1928 the state bought all but 2.5 acres of what remained of the Ngati Whatua marae, ignoring its own decisions that the *papakainga* be declared 'inalienable' to prevent Ngati Whatua being left entirely landless. In 1951 it compulsorily acquired the last sliver, except one acre (the cemetery); removed the remaining tribal members to state housing, and even burned their marae and houses. Bastion Point had become 'crown land', but in Maori eyes it

Plate 17.1 Watching for the first signs of a police convoy: Ngati Whatua occupation of Bastion Point, Auckland, during land protest. From *NZ Listener,* 24 June 1978. Photographer: Robin Morrison. The Robin Morrison Collection, Auckland, Auckland Museum, 1997.

rightfully belonged to Ngati Whatua. What compelled the protest was the last insult: the plan to sell the best of this real estate with harbour views to developers for expensive housing. Joe Hawke, later a member of parliament, led the protest. As a child he had watched the burning and dispossession of 1951 and sought *utu* 'by defying the state over the ownership of the land'.[36]

The 506-day occupation was televised. What shocked the general public in 1978 was the Muldoon government's deployment of police and army. Television viewers saw elderly people dragged away, the Riot Act read, and 222 people arrested (half of them Pakeha, as the protesters appealed to all New Zealanders). Bastion Point might have become crown land, but the state was not the 'real' owner because of the way the land had been acquired. Something was seriously wrong when *tangata whenua* had no land and no marae. The inequity issue struck home: first Ngati Whatua had been forced into state housing, and then the state proposed to sell its ill-gotten gains to privileged Aucklanders.

The water in the fishbowl was changing, globally and locally, and Pakeha cared enough to address the problem.[37] In the short term, the protesters were removed. Later they won redress through the Waitangi Tribunal in 1984, reaching a settlement acknowledging substantial losses through the state's breaches of the treaty. The settlement, a modest $3 million, was a step towards an economic base for the tribe, while Bastion Point became a public park, vested in Ngati Whatua.[38]

Another way in which 1975 marked the end of 'white New Zealand' was the creation of the Waitangi Tribunal. Matiu Rata, the minister of Maori affairs who embodied growing Maori influence, persuaded the third Labour government to pass the Treaty of Waitangi Act 'to provide for the observance, and confirmation, of the principles of the Treaty of Waitangi' by establishing a tribunal to deal with claims under the treaty and to determine where there were inconsistencies with the treaty.[39] The tribunal could consider claims dating from the passing of the Act, in October 1975. No longer was the treaty a nullity, though the tribunal was not very effective until 1981, with the appointment of E. T. Durie as chair, in his capacity as chief judge of the Maori Land Court. The first Maori to hold this post, Judge Durie was a product of Te Aute College and a graduate of Victoria University of Wellington. His wisdom, grace and *mana* won respect from Maori and Pakeha for the tribunal. In the early 1980s it comprised Judge Durie, (Sir) Graham Latimer of the Maori Council and Paul Temm QC. In the late 1980s an expanded tribunal comprised equal numbers of Maori and non-Maori. Judge Durie played a pivotal role in educating Pakeha in the need to redress injustices by honouring the treaty. The tribunal followed the protocol of each marae; it sat on marae and held hearings in Maori, then translated into English.[40] The culture of the tribunal with its Maori and English protocols exemplified respect for Maori, and biculturalism in practice.

In 1983 the tribunal faced down Prime Minister Muldoon in the first of four 'cornerstone decisions': the Motunui case about a synthetic fuel plant outfall in Taranaki. The state stood impugned as the polluter and offender against the treaty, because the plant was a 'think big' project devised in response to the second oil shock of 1979. Te Atiawa feared that the outfall would pollute their fishing reefs, and the tribunal agreed. As this was the first time the general public heard of the tribunal, Muldoon intended to ignore it, but an outcry incited by the media ensured that the outfall proposal was dropped. Indigenous rights in alliance with environmentalist politics had prevailed. For the moment, environmentalist politics seemed more important, but treaty politics soon soared to prominence. For the first time since 1877, it was 'brought to life' as a constitutional instrument, and Maoridom was abuzz.[41]

The Maori renaissance also affected the political arena. Matiu Rata, disenchanted with the two-party system, resigned from the Labour Party in 1979, ending the 40-year Ratana–Labour alliance. Rata formed the Mana Motuhake Party, reviving the cause of the nineteenth-century Kotahitanga for *Mana Motuhake*, or autonomy. The movements which contested the erosion of Maori power in the nineteenth century re-emerged with the treaty as their focus.[42] From the 1970s then, the treaty was pivotal in national discourse. Maoridom, the tribunal and the courts pursued the legal potential of the treaty while historians revised the national narrative, incorporating Maori narratives.[43] Unlike the case of Australian South Sea Islanders, documentary and oral sources were in substantial agreement – and so were the historians. Many Pakeha, moreover, had been politicized during the Springbok rugby tour in 1981. Facing batons and barbed wire in their own territory, they became more receptive to the Maori message. This was not the tolerant, diverse, open society they wanted. Gangs, alongside Maori feminists and nationalists, were highly visible in anti-tour protests, and Maori activists spoke out against the Muldoon government.

The year 1984 began a revolution in economic and social policy, another experiment which again fuelled debate on national identity (see chapter 19). Academics and publicists hyphenated the nation-state as Aotearoa/New Zealand. Nuclear-free New Zealand exuded pride of independence. At the helm of a small nation repositioning itself in a global economy, the zealously reformist fourth Labour government back-dated the tribunal's jurisdiction to 1840, in the Treaty of Waitangi Amendment Act 1985. Rata's heir as a Maori minister of Maori affairs, Koro Wetere, introduced the 1985 bill to address 'the mounting tension in the community' from outstanding griev-ances.[44] Maori shifted from protest to litigation and a flood of claims poured in. Cynics asserted that this achieved a conscious goal of defusing Maori mil-itancy by transferring their energies to the tribunal and the courts.[45] A more positive view maintained that retrospective jurisdiction altered Maori mind-sets from grudge to hope. The change called for a national review of indige-nous rights through due process of law, as tribes launched proceedings in the tribunal (whose powers resembled those of a commission of inquiry) and the courts.

As the state listened to treaty grievances for the first time, New Zealanders began to hear about them through political discourse rather than protest. Since the state neglected to specify any statutory goals for the tribunal in hearing claims, Judge Durie envisaged that an acceptable outcome would be to re-establish tribal groups with a 'reasonable economic base'.[46] (The tri-bunal itself lacked such a base whereas crown law was well funded to oppose claimants and the tribunal's judgements.) Treasury officials and others were confronted in the tribunal and the courts by a notion alien to the market economy: the 'honour of the crown'. The state stood guilty of impropriety in passing laws in breach of the treaty, and had to provide redress. But by what right? Who said so? Indigenous people began to question the fundamentals of citizenship.

New Zealand's massive deregulation also triggered an indigenous response which attracted wide support because of general alarm about the lack of consultation and the speed of the blitzkrieg. Maori moves to check state power revealed the lack of checks and balances in the political system and the absence of brakes on executive power. New Zealand had no federal sys-tem, and since 1950 had had no upper house to slow change. In this context the State Owned Enterprises (SOE) Act 1986 proved most provocative, prompting a long battle in the courts to prevent the privatization of public assets. The effect of the Act was to transfer state assets to the private sector where they would have been out of reach of treaty claims. The Maori Council therefore challenged the Bill in New Zealand Maori Council v. Attorney-General 1987, as far as the Court of Appeal. When the court found the Act contrary to the principles of the treaty, Maoridom had successfully challenged the supremacy of parliament.

The significance of the decision lay in the concept of treaty partners. 'Partnership' was not a word used in 1840; rather some chiefs used the strategic term 'alliance'. This modern interpretation of the essence of the treaty posed the question: 'who are the treaty partners today?'[47] The answer shifted rapidly from the 1980s to the 1990s (see chapters 19, 21). In the 1980s, the partners were defined as the 'crown' and *iwi*, as the identifiable, corporate representatives of the descendants of the signatories. The judges pronounced that the partners had a duty to act reasonably and in good faith, and that the supremacy of parliament rested on the treaty because the legitimacy of British sovereignty depended on it. Justice Casey ruled that Maori 'ceded rights of government in exchange for guarantees of possession and control of their lands and precious possessions for so long as they wanted to retain them'.[48] The courts accordingly backed tribunal decisions in the 1980s that the treaty was a living document. More than that, the tribunal was becoming the 'conscience of the nation'.[49]

A common thread in the roughly 650 'historical' claims before the tribunal was land. The expectation of chiefs that 'the tribes would not be left landless' had been fundamental to the treaty, yet landlessness in the 1980s was evidence that the treaty had been breached.[50] The tribunal's work ushered in a major rewriting of colonial history and an overlapping of narratives. The revisionist Pakeha narrative now recognized that the British government assumed sovereignty in the first place to wrest control of land. Land and sovereignty jostled for supremacy in this revisionist history (see chapter 6) but in the tribunal, land prevailed. Colonization had been a contest for resources. When Maori resisted the scale and pace of settlement, the crown broke the treaty. Grievances festered over the scale and pace and the manner of land loss. Since Maori had been denied the chance to develop their own land, they lost their *mana*, their autonomy and their place in the nation.[51]

Two cases before the tribunal elaborated the theme. The South Island Ngai Tahu claim turned on the state's failure to meet obligations under land purchase agreements made after the treaty, particularly those relating to the settlements of Dunedin and Christchurch, as well as breaches of the treaty itself. Part of the age-old grievance rested on failure to make adequate reserves and in neglecting to reserve for Ngai Tahu the land they expressly wished to keep. In the words of Tipene O'Regan,

> Instead the tribe was subjected to the demeaning process of having to beg the return of land, which it had not sold, from Pakeha who went amongst them handing out 'grants' of their own property. A fundamental breach of the treaty [lay] in the Crown agents' insistence on taking the title to the whole of an area (with unfulfilled promises to 'return' certain reserves later as determined by the Crown), whereas the treaty (and explicit instructions to the Governors) authorized only the purchase of such lands as the Maori freely wished to sell.[52]

As a result Ngai Tahu were reduced to poverty and landlessness. Tainui, on the other hand, had their land stolen through *raupatu*: confiscations in the wake of the wars of the 1860s. Robert Mahuta, who led the Tainui claim, was a grandson of Tawhiao, the second Maori king. The treaty, Kingitanga and *raupatu* issues endured in his upbringing, the confiscations limiting the tribe's participation in national life because of their bitterness and distrust.[53] Whole communities had been punished for the actions of a few, the land of 'loyal' Maori seized as well as that of 'rebels', and the best land taken.[54] The result was the same: landless poverty. The Kingitanga sought through the Tainui claim in the 1980s to restore land to the people of the Waikato. Both claims resulted in settlements in the 1990s of $170 million.

While native title in land had largely been extinguished, a distinctive contest emerged over fisheries. In 1986 the fourth Labour government moved to privatize rights in fish by creating tradeable property rights through a Quota Management System (QMS). The state advanced this in environmental terms, in response to overfishing (see chapter 18), but Maori saw that resources were again being privatized. They warned that this breached their rights to their fisheries under Article II of the treaty, but the state refused to budge. In 1987 the Ministry of Agriculture and Fisheries began to issue fishing quotas, and Maori claimants before the tribunal moved to halt this process.[55] A pan-Maori injunction succeeded in the High Court, and for the first time in a century the courts responded positively to native title. Justice Greig judged that native title in land might have been extinguished, but not in fish; so Maori had common law rights. In the courts as well as the tribunal, the QMS was held to be in conflict with the treaty, and the government had to negotiate with Maori.[56] From 1989, through the Maori Fisheries Commission, Maori once more became major players in fishing. An imperial instrument, the concept of native title, had facilitated the reclaiming of Maori *mana* and control over resources, as it did for Aboriginal Australians.

In 1986 the tribunal issued the landmark *Te Reo Report*, finding that the state had breached the treaty by failing to protect the language – a treasure under Article II. The treaty guarantee of the language entailed steps to ensure an education for Maori children in which they could learn their own language if their parents wished, and acknowledgement of Maori as an official language.[57] Loss of language as well as land and resources had led to a loss of *tino rangatiratanga*. The Maori nationalist and feminist activist, Donna Awatere Huata, had thrust into the spotlight the issue of *tino rangatiratanga* as guaranteed in the Maori text of the treaty, with an outburst on Maori sovereignty in 1982, asserting that New Zealand was Maori land. Published first in the feminist magazine *Broadsheet* as the 'issue for the eighties', *Maori Sovereignty* was reprinted in book form in 1984. It startled readers with its language.[58] While feminists sought parallels between struggles against patriarchy and for Maori sovereignty, tensions emerged in the feminist movement as well, because Maori women worked with Maori men (as did Aboriginal women with men), giving priority to indigenous issues.[59] To some the debate over *tino rangatiratanga* was academic, but to others it became a mantra. Awatere's view was influential in Fiji, for example, and wherever indigenous societies felt themselves under threat.

Maori continue to dispute what this concept means and whether it equates with sovereignty, while some 'corporate warriors' favour the free market as the source of Maori autonomy, claiming that welfare held Maori back.[60]

There is general agreement, however, that the treaty guarantee of *tino rangatiratanga* entailed Maori control of Maori affairs, and thus autonomy from the crown. According to Paul Temm QC, *te tino rangatiratanga* referred to 'the fullest authority of chieftainship'.[61] Justice Durie has cautioned that it has many meanings, and most generally refers to 'the authority of the people, of the *iwi*' to control and manage their own affairs, but it may also refer to personal *mana*, status and dignity.[62] People dispute whether this right to control and manage referred to the national or local level, and whether the latter is more appropriate in the context of globalization.[63] But there is a general argument that the state had no business telling *iwi* how to manage their assets. No longer would they tolerate a state paternalism which required tribes to gain approval before writing cheques of more than $200. *Te tino rangatiratanga* demanded that the state relinquish power it did not properly have. And if the state were to acknowledge *rangatiratanga*, consult its treaty partner and honour the treaty, the Maori–non-Maori relationship had to be transformed.[64]

Much of the vehemence of Maori protest flowed from exasperation at the refusal by non-Maori to acknowledge the 'extent and nature of avoidable injury' since 1840. In Maori eyes the spirit of the treaty required this acknowledgement. While there had been little discussion with Maori in the 1980s over how to handle the extensive review of history and provide redress,[65] the Waitangi tribunal did defuse tensions, providing a channel for grievances and public education. Aboriginal Australians were at least equally exasperated by denials of their dispossession and the destruction of families. A key difference has been the treaty, from which New Zealand's tribunal explicitly derived its powers.[66] In both countries the calls to account were first denied, and only reluctantly addressed. In these circumstances the campaigns had to challenge the supremacy of parliament, and make it subject to the law.

WOMEN'S LIBERATION AND FEMINIST POLITICS

Women also sought an expansion of citizenship through the women's liberation movement, which burst onto the scene in Australia and New Zealand in 1970–1. Its ideas came from America and the United Kingdom, and in New Zealand, from Australia, by way of personalities such as Germaine Greer who stunned New Zealand by using the word 'bullshit' at a public meeting in Auckland in March 1972. When asked if she understood that she had used the word, she repeated it. True to the counter-culture of the 1960s, she challenged notions of public decency in order to compel changes in values.

This 'second wave' of feminism which strove to liberate women from sexist, 'patriarchal' society was no mere import (we have seen that there was no hiatus between the 'first wave' feminist movement in the 1880s and the 1970s 'second wave'). It grew from the kaleidoscope of new interactions and interdependencies in our region, especially since the Second World War. As late as the 1960s, married women were denied permanent government employment, pregnant women could be fired, and women refused a job or study opportunities because they were female, or unwed mothers.[67] What society expected of women was rapidly transformed. The economy in Australia and New Zealand needed women in paid work as well as the home as the tertiary sector expanded. Families responded, and married women joined single women in paid work. This became essential if they wanted the benefits of mass consumption and homes no longer affordable for one breadwinner's wage. Reliable fertility control helped (the pill arrived in Australia and New Zealand in 1961 and 1962), as did white-goods with the belated mass arrival of washing machines and refrigerators. Daughters who carried their mothers' hopes attended university as higher education expanded, joined protests, and grew disillusioned by making the tea, serving unkempt young men and typing leaflets. If they graduated, equal pay and access to careers outside traditional women's spheres eluded them.

Politicized and angered by such constraints, these feminist activists sought autonomy outside the home through 'women's liberation' from the home and family. No longer was motherhood an empowering concept and the domestic hearth a source of strength, refuge and moral purity, but a prison. To overthrow the patriarchy which oppressed them as a class, women had to be liberated from the role of housewife, from 'sex roles', domesticity and marriage, and to transform daily life. Theirs was a radical agenda: to challenge the dominant society and culture, refashion feminine identities and demand places in the public world: 'the personal was political'. Women sought to control their bodies and lives. In order to claim the self, they had to ask 'who are you?' in body and mind. 'Equality' became a key word. Social justice and liberation demanded equal pay, won legislatively in Australia and New Zealand in 1972. Equity demanded child-care, sexual autonomy, including access to contraception and abortion, and an end to 'sexploitation'. These liberal demands were mostly won by the 1990s, at least for the white, middle-class women who fought the campaigns. Australia and New Zealand fared better in terms of gender equity than other countries, though equal pay (and wealth) remained elusive; on average, women's earnings reached 80 per cent of men's in New Zealand, and 85 per cent of men's in Australia.[68]

Once politicized, feminists felt oppressed by national histories and myths which portrayed men as shapers of identity. Those on the Left dismissed narratives of national identity as bourgeois, and supposedly neutral definitions and types (the 'convict' and the 'coming man') as patriarchal. War was rape, and Anzac mythology excluded women. Patriarchy defined national identity in a unified male image, controlled by men. Women's liberation, which aimed to free women from such oppression, itself saw 'patriarchy' as a constant; hence the initial efforts to assert a shared political identity for 'women', and the concept of 'sisterhood'. Such thinking characterized four seminal works in Australian feminist history, consciously part of the 'second wave', to mark International Women's Year in 1975. Anne Summers's *Damned Whores and God's Police*, Edna Ryan's and Anne Conlon's *Gentle Invaders*, Beverley Kingston's *My Wife, My Daughter and Poor Mary Ann* and Miriam Dixson's *The Real Matilda* exemplified the new genre in their focus on the oppression of women in Australian history. For Dixson, Australian women were the 'doormats of the Western world', while Summers termed Australia 'Manzone Country'. All destabilized certainties and helped to unsettle identities, like the movement whose message they carried. These books shared the 1970s feminist preoccupation with women's work and the sexual division of labour. They were 'gothic', relaying a dark history of gender relations. By contrast, New Zealand's women's history was presented as 'standing in the sunshine'. That genre was less apocalyptic, it recovered history for women and it restored women to that history, suggesting a rather different pattern of gender relations and of women's relations with New Zealand life and culture.[69]

All four Australian books, like second wave feminism itself, paid fleeting attention to race. The intellectual climate changed from the 1980s, with new politics and identities which saw the end of the essentialist category 'woman'. (Western) discourse shifted from 'sex' to 'gender', from 'sex roles' to 'gender relations' and 'the politics of difference'. Maori women organized their first national black women's *hui* (meeting) in 1980. The Treaty of Waitangi, revived, became the basis of Maori feminist politics. For Aboriginal women, Anglo-Australian culture (including the women's movement) often felt like 'the expression of power and not difference'. They were more preoccupied with survival and racism. Not only indigenous women, but migrant women were discovered as having race and ethnic as well as feminine identities which remained unexamined. Attention turned from elements uniting women to differences dividing them, and to multiple selves.[70]

The women's movement exerted more influence on government in Australia than in New Zealand through 'femocrats': feminist activists and academics-turned policy advisers such as Lyndall Ryan, who advised the Whitlam government, and Anne Summers who advised the Keating government. While Labor Party women could become state premiers if the political crisis were desperate (Carmel Lawrence in Western Australia and Joan Kirner in Victoria), they made much less impression federally. The different forms of politics again impinged, shaping relations between women and the state. Australian femocrats were part of a professional–managerial 'new class'. Women were differently positioned in New Zealand, with its more conservative tradition of politics, exerting a stronger presence in local government, as mayors, and in parliament. By 1993, Kate Sheppard was rediscovered as an icon for political women and a national mother figure representing women's citizenship, in time for the centennial of women's suffrage. Aotearoa/New Zealand had a woman governor-general (Dame Kath Tizard) and Kate Sheppard became the first woman (apart from the queen) depicted on a banknote. These were more than symbolic changes. New Zealand had six Maori women MPs in the late 1990s. In the 1999 election, the National Party's Jenny Shipley, New Zealand's first woman prime minister, was defeated by Labour's Helen Clark and their leadership was not deemed odd. Gender relations had shifted, and so had women's modes of writing history and doing politics.

In many ways in Australia and New Zealand national life and narratives, colonialism continued. To succeed as a public woman in New Zealand still required a strong, maternal image, the 'great New Zealand mum' – or aunt.

In Australia, mateship endured, suggesting to Dixson 'not "patriarchy" but a "fratriarchal" form of male domination, duly glossed for Australian circumstance.'[71] In her view – and ours – convictism was a foundational experience which darkened race and gender relations, and must be faced in order to be overcome.

NOTES

1 Donald Denoon, Mark Hudson, Tessa Morris-Suzuki and Gavan McCormack (eds), *Multicultural Japan: Palaeolithic to Postmodern*, Melbourne, 1997.
2 Stephen Castles, 'Multicultural Citizenship: A Response to the Dilemma of Globalization and National Identity?', *Journal of Intercultural Studies*, 18: 1 (April 1997), 5–22.
3 John Lack, 'Multiculturalism', in G. Davison, J. Hirst and S. Macintyre, *Oxford Companion to Australian History*, Melbourne, 1998, 442–3; and Freda Hawkins, *Critical Years in Immigration: Canada and Australia Compared*, Kingston, Ontario, 1989.
4 Lack, 'Multiculturalism'.
5 Castles, 'Multicultural Citizenship'.
6 Russell McGregor, *Imagined Destinies: Aboriginal Australians and the Doomed Race Theory, 1880–1939*, Melbourne, 1997.
7 For example, W. E. H. Stanner, 'The Aborigines', in J. C. G. Kevin (ed.), *Some Australians Take Stock*, London, 1939; Tom Wright, *New Deal for the Aborigines*, Sydney, 1939; both cited in McGregor, *Imagined Destinies*.
8 *Aborigines Claim Citizen Rights*, Sydney, 1937.
9 Human Rights and Equal Opportunity Commission, *Bringing Them Home: Report of the National Inquiry into the Separation of Aboriginal and Torres Strait Islander Children from their Families*, Sydney, 1997.
10 Adult Aborigines were enfranchised in 1962, by repealing a discriminatory provision in the Commonwealth Electoral Act. The gradual moves to inclusion by federal, state and territory governments are outlined in John Chesterman and Brian Galligan, *Citizens without Rights: Aborigines and Australian Citizenship*, Melbourne, 1997, ch. 6.
11 Tim Rowse and Murray Goot (eds), *Make a Better Offer: The Politics of Mabo*, Leichhardt, NSW, 1994.
12 Wik Peoples v. Queensland, 1996.
13 Human Rights and Equal Opportunities Commission, *Bringing Them Home*.
14 John Laws and Prime Minister Howard, 24 October 1996; transcript from the *Sydney Morning Herald*.
15 Alan Ramsay, 'Fighting for the Never Never', *Sydney Morning Herald*, 14 April 1999.
16 Steve Mullins, 'Decolonizing Torres Strait: A Moderate Proposal for 2001', in D. Denoon (ed.), *Emerging from Empire? Decolonization in the Pacific*, Canberra, 1997, 142–50.
17 Gaetano Lui, Jnr, 'A Torres Strait Perspective', in M. Yunupingu, et al., *Voices from the Land: 1993 Boyer Lectures*, Sydney, 1994, 68–71.
18 'Insider' accounts include Faith Bandler, *Wacvie*, Adelaide, 1977; *Welou My Brother*, Glebe (NSW), 1984, and *Turning the Tide: a Personal History of the Federal Council for the Advancement of Aborigines and Torres Strait Islanders*,

Canberra, 1989; Thomas Lowah, *Eded Mer* (My Life), Kuranda, 1988; Noel Fatnowna, *Fragments of a Lost Heritage*, Sydney, 1989; Mabel Edmund, *No Regrets*, St Lucia, 1992; Jacqui Wright with Francis Wimbis, *The Secret: The Story of Slavery in Australia*, Bundaberg, 1996. Academic accounts include Clive Moore and Trish Mercer, 'The Forgotten People: Australia's South Sea Islanders, 1906–1993', in Henry Reynolds (ed.), *Race Relations in North Queensland*, Townsville, 1993; Patricia Mercer, *White Australia Defied: Pacific Islander Settlement in North Queensland*, Townsville, 1995; Clive Moore, 'Decolonizing the History of Australia's South Sea Islanders: Politics and Curriculum Materials', in D. Denoon, *Emerging From Empire?*, 194–203.

19 Moore, 'Decolonizing the History of Australia's South Sea Islanders'.

20 Tony Stephens, 'A Proud Town Honours Fierce Daughter Faith', *Sydney Morning Herald*, 30 April 1999. For academic views, see Doug Munro, 'Revisionism and its Enemies: Debating the Queensland Labour Trade', *Journal of Pacific History*, 30: 2 (1995), 240–9.

21 Ian Pool, *Te Iwi Maori: A New Zealand Population Past, Present and Projected*, Auckland, 1991, 141.

22 G. Dunstall, 'The Social Pattern', in G. W. Rice (ed.), *Oxford History of New Zealand*, Auckland, 1992, 457; R. J. Walker, 'Maori People since 1950', in ibid., 503.

23 W. H. Oliver, *Claims to the Waitangi Tribunal*, Wellington, 1991, 9; Dunstall, 'The Social Pattern'.

24 Alan Ward, *A Show of Justice: Racial 'Amalgamation' in Nineteenth-century New Zealand*, Canberra, 1974.

25 J. K. Hunn, *Report on Department of Maori Affairs*, 1960, 14–16.

26 Barbara Brookes, 'Nostalgia for "Innocent Homely Pleasures": The 1964 New Zealand Controversy over *Washday at the Pa*', *Gender and History*, 9: 2 (1997), 242–61.

27 Dunstall, 'The Social Pattern'.

28 E. Durie, 'Not Standing Apart', in W. Ihimaera (ed.), *Vision Aotearoa: Kaupapa New Zealand*, Wellington, 1994, 23.

29 A. Ward, *National Overview*, Waitangi Tribunal Rangahaua Whanui Series, Wellington, 1997, vol. 1, 137.

30 R. J. Walker, 'The Treaty of Waitangi as the Focus of Maori Protest', in I. H. Kawharu (ed.), *Waitangi: Maori and Pakeha Perspectives of the Treaty of Waitangi*, Auckland, 1995, 275; Oliver, *Claims to the Waitangi Tribunal*, 3–4, 8; P. Temm, *The Waitangi Tribunal: The Conscience of the Nation*, Auckland, 1990, 17, 24.

31 Evan S. Te Ahu Poata-Smith, 'He Pokeke Uenuku I Tu Ai: The Evolution of Contemporary Maori Protest', in P. Spoonley, D. Pearson, and C. Macpherson (eds), *Nga Patai: Racism and Ethnic Relations in Aotearoa/New Zealand*, Palmerston North, 1996, 99–103; M. P. K. Sorrenson, 'Modern Maori: The Young Maori Party to Mana Motuhake', in Keith Sinclair (ed.), *Oxford Illustrated History of New Zealand*, Auckland, 1990, 348.

32 Poata-Smith, 'He Pokeke Uenuku I Tu Ai'; R. J. Walker, *Ka Whawhai Tonu Matou: Struggle Without End*, Auckland, 1990, 209–12.

33 Walker, 'The Treaty of Waitangi', 276; Oliver, *Claims to the Waitangi Tribunal*, 9.

34 Walker, 'Maori People since 1950', 513.

35 See Michael King, *Whina: A Biography of Whina Cooper*, Auckland, 1983, ch. 11; Walker, *Ka Whawhai Tonu Matou*, 212–15.

36 Walker, *Ka Whawhai Tonu Matou*, 217.

37 The 'water in the fishbowl' metaphor is courtesy of Tipene O'Regan.

38 Waitangi Tribunal Division Department of Justice, *Orakei (Bastion Point): Case Study of a Claim to the Waitangi Tribunal*, 1–11; see also Temm, *Waitangi Tribunal*, 61–6; R. J. Walker, *Nga Tau Tohetohe: Years of Anger*, Auckland, 1987, 51–3.

39 The Treaty of Waitangi Act, 1975.

40 Temm, *Waitangi Tribunal*, 3–8; Durie, 'A Peaceful Solution', in Witi Ihimaera, H. Williams, I. Ramsden and D. S. Long (eds), *Te Ao Marama: Contemporary Maori Writing*, Auckland, 1993, 2, 177–82.

41 *Motunui Report* (Te Ati Awa Claim), 1983; for a summary and assessment, see Temm, *Waitangi Tribunal*, 37–41.

42 L. Cox, *Kotahitanga: The Search for Maori Political Unity*, Auckland, 1993, 134–6.

43 For example, Claudia Orange, *The Treaty of Waitangi*, Wellington, 1987.

44 Wetere cited by Ward, *National Overview*, vol. 1, 137.

45 See, for example, J. Kelsey, 'From Flagpoles to Pine Trees', in P. Spoonley, D. Pearson, and C. Macpherson (eds), *Nga Patai: Racism and Ethnic Relations in Aotearoa/New Zealand*, Palmerston North, 1996, 183.

46 E. T. Durie, chairperson's foreword, in A. Ward, *National Overview*, vol. 1, xiii.

47 Durie, 'A Peaceful Solution', 2, 182.

48 Temm, *Waitangi Tribunal*, 96. See also 'Appendix: The Principles of the Treaty of Waitangi', in Ward, *National Overview*, vol. 2, 478.

49 Temm, *Waitangi Tribunal*, 97–8.

50 'Appendix: The Principles of the Treaty of Waitangi', in Ward, *National Overview*, vol. 2, 493.

51 Ward, *National Overview*, vol. 1.

52 T. O'Regan, 'The Ngai Tahu Claim', in I. H. Kawharu (ed.), *Waitangi: Maori and Pakeha Perspectives of the Treaty of Waitangi*, Auckland, 1989, 234, 242–3. On the Ngai Tahu claim see also Temm, *Waitangi Tribunal*, 118–22; H. C. Evision (ed.), *The Treaty of Waitangi and the Ngai Tahu Claim*, Christchurch, 1988; and the Waitangi Tribunal Report on the Ngai Tahu Claim.

53 R. Mahuta, 'From Raupatu', in Ihimaera, *Te Ao Marama*, 2, 144–9.

54 Waitangi Tribunal Report on the Tainui Claim.

55 Waitangi Tribunal, *Muriwhenua Report*.

56 T. O'Regan, lecture, University of Canterbury, 1997; Temm, *Waitangi Tribunal*, 70–82.

57 Waitangi Tribunal, *Te Reo Report*.

58 Donna Awatere, *Maori Sovereignty*, Auckland, 1984.

59 Donna Awatere, *Maori Sovereignty*, Auckland, 1984; Donna Awatere Huata, *My Journey*, Auckland, 1996; W. Larner, 'Gender and Ethnicity', in P. Spoonley, D. Pearson, and C. Macpherson (eds), *Nga Patai: Racism and Ethnic Relations in Aotearoa/New Zealand*, Palmerston North, 1996, 164–7.

60 Poata-Smith, 'He Pokeke Uenuku I Tu Ai', 98.

61 Temm, *Waitangi Tribunal*, 100.

62 Durie, 'A Peaceful Solution', 182.

63 Hugh Fletcher, then CEO Fletcher Challenge, argued that Maori should focus on increased tribal authority at the local level given global capital's effects on the nation-state; see C. Archie (ed.), *Maori Sovereignty: The Pakeha Perspective*, Auckland, 1995, 13.

64 Alan Ward, *National Overview*, vol. 1, 146, sees the articulation of non-Maori–Maori relations around the treaty concepts of *kawanatanga* and *tino rangatiratanga* as the central issue for all New Zealanders.

65 Ibid., 37.

66 Durie, 'Not Standing Apart', 25.

67 See, for example, Anne Summers, *Damned Whores and God's Police*, Melbourne, 1994; Sandra Coney, *Standing in the Sunshine*, Auckland, 1993.

68 Charlotte Macdonald (ed.), *The Vote, the Pill and the Demon Drink*, Wellington, 1993, ch. 7; Ann Curthoys, 'Doing it for Themselves: The Women's Movement since 1970', in Kay Saunders and Raymond Evans (eds), *Gender Relations in Australia: Domination and Negotiation*, Sydney, 1992, ch. 20; M. Cook, *Just Wages: History of the Campaign for Pay Equity 1984–1993*, Wellington, 1994.

69 Summers, *Damned Whores and God's Police*; Miriam Dixson, *The Real Matilda: Woman and Identity in Australia 1788 to the Present*, Melbourne, 1976; Edna Ryan and Anne Conlon, *Gentle Invaders: Australian Women at Work, 1788–1974*, Melbourne, 1975; Beverley Kingston, *My Wife, My Daughter, and Poor Mary Ann*, Melbourne, 1975. See the special issue of *Australian Historical Studies*, 27: 106 (April 1996) to mark the twentieth anniversary of these books. Cf. Coney, *Standing in the Sunshine*.

70 Chilla Bulbeck, *Living Feminism: The Impact of the Women's Movement on Three Generations of Australian Women*, Melbourne, 1997 (quotation from 164). For developments in New Zealand feminism, see Rosemary du Plessis and Lynne Alice (eds), *Feminist Thought in Aotearoa/New Zealand*, Auckland, 1998.

71 Miriam Dixson, 'The "Born-Modern" Self: Revisiting The Real Matilda: An Exploration of Women and Identity in Australia', *Australian Historical Studies*, 27: 106 (April 1996), 25.

[18] *Decolonization?*

Colonial Contexts

At least until the 1940s, most people of European descent accepted colonial relations as quite normal, even perhaps divinely ordained. Indigenous people (or anyone else) who found this unnatural, unbiblical or indefensible had few avenues for recourse. New Zealand and Australia enjoyed dominion status, so their governors and governors-general were largely ornamental, but reminders of an imperial nexus which they had not (yet) transcended. Settlers in New Caledonia had no such latitude and could aspire to no such devolution. They grumbled about high-handed metropolitan people and agencies, but relied massively on Paris for financial, logistical and military support. As colonists themselves, few white Australians or Pakeha or Caledonian settlers could challenge the ideological basis of their polities, economies and identities; nor could colonial officials who governed the islands.

Accepting colonial relations as normal, they also treated race (or pigmentation) as a reliable index of human capacity. With the perplexing exception of Japan, a racial hierarchy of power and wealth seemed natural. Japanese insistence that they too were distinct from Asia compounded (or for some people resolved) that paradox.[1] At any rate, the Pacific offered a barrier and perhaps a cultural buffer between the colonists and Asia. Yet in two generations some colonial relations were formally abandoned, and all were modified. Values also changed, though they are impossible to measure. Since these changes resemble the simultaneous global transformation of state institutions and inter-ethnic values, we might imagine that we are dealing merely with local variations of global trends. That would be a grievous error: we have seen (chapter 16) that the imperial powers were slow to decolonize in the Pacific, and in some cases reversed the process. And just as every colonial nexus is unique, so is every episode of decolonization.

European colonialism was attracting increasing opprobrium. The Soviet Union had long advanced a systemic critique of imperialism which targeted the capitalist mode of production generally, and Western powers in particular. During the Second World War the United States became another stern critic.[2] She did nevertheless demand a unique United Nations strategic trust over the Micronesian islands which her soldiers had wrested from Japan, insisting that a trust was definitely not a colony. European parties of the Left (and some of the Centre) queried the morality or the affordability (or both) of colonies. Their governments placed new emphasis on colonial welfare, development and participation. Partly this was to blunt criticism; but it cost something to provide development capital and to fund an expanding range of services. These moods encouraged scepticism about colonies, but did not provoke instant decolonization. It was not metropolitan sentiment which freed much of Asia, but mobilized populations. Independent Indonesia, India, Pakistan, Ceylon and Burma then added their weight to anti-colonial causes.

Failing to restore her rule, or to win American support, in 1949 the Netherlands grudgingly conceded sovereignty to the Indonesian Republic.[3] Nonetheless Dutch officials began a belated return to West Papua, partly to preserve the status of a colonial power, partly to re-settle Eurasians who rejected Indonesia, and perhaps to meet the claims of Papuans whose encounters with Javanese and other Malays had been unsettling. By detaching this province from the rest of the archipelago, the Dutch moved the border between Asia and the Pacific Islands brusquely west. To atone for long neglect, they accelerated the development of public works, education and health services, and began to localize the public service. Material progress was matched by constitutional advance: in 1961 a 28-member legislative Raad was created. Most were Papuans and a majority were elected: they resolved that they were Papuans, and their country West Papua, which adopted a flag and an anthem.

But West Papua's fate was decided elsewhere, as the Netherlands fought a losing diplomatic battle against Indonesia's claim to the whole of the former East Indies. During the Cold War, the United States and the Soviet Union were indifferent to Dutch colonizing proposals, and Australia gave much more weight to relations with the volatile Indonesian Republic. In 1963 the United Nations finally transferred sovereignty to Indonesia, on condition that a plebiscite be held in 1969. As soon as Indonesian officials took charge, they pre-empted the plebiscite and treated the province as part of the unitary Republic, disbanding local assemblies. The Act of Free Choice in 1969 was a tasteless charade conducted with overt coercion, but the United Nations General Assembly endorsed the verdict, with 30 countries abstaining. The western limits of the Pacific lurched east once more, translating Papuans into Irianese Indonesians and West Papua into Irian Jaya. Indonesian policy demanded that the people abandon what was bad (i.e. most) in their cultures, to be raised from ignorance to become as intelligent as their compatriots. Hunting and swidden cultivation must yield to market gardening, and 'eating root crops and wearing penis sheaths is uncivilized'. Indonesian officials shared with the Dutch the idea that Papuans must be elevated; they differed only in defining the goal-posts. Since then there has been sporadic resistance in the name of the Oposisi Papua Merdeka (Free Papua Movement) who insist that they were not decolonized but merely transferred to another colonizing power. Indonesia's economic crisis from 1998 onwards, the disgrace of President Suharto, the disarray of the Golkar regime, the separation and independence of East Timor and the election of Abdurrahman Wahid as president inspired separatists throughout the archipelago, but the OPM continued to be poorly armed, internally divided, and devoid of external support. Irianese have no immediate prospect of gaining autonomy – or rejoining 'the Pacific'.

Through the 1930s, British strategists assumed that the goal of political evolution in the empire was self-government and perhaps dominion status, rather than separation. Pakistan's and India's complete independence in 1947 subverted that scenario, but the Commonwealth Office still supposed that African, Caribbean and Pacific independence would depend upon their meeting some preconditions: economic viability, an effective public service, parliamentary government, an independent judiciary, non-governmental institutions including trade unions, and a population large enough to sustain viability.[4] Westminster did not expect island groups to meet all these criteria in the near future, or perhaps ever.

BRITISH WITHDRAWAL

The failed intervention in Suez in 1956 and the United States' refusal to endorse that adventure provoked Britain to begin to withdraw from east of Suez. Her nuclear tests had ended with the Partial Test Ban Treaty of 1963, so decolonization was now the goal of Britain's policy. Fiji was the obvious place to start, with a viable sugar economy and high levels of education and bureaucratic expertise. Throughout the 1960s there were industrial strikes (reflecting a strong trade union movement) and debates about constitutions to suit multi-ethnic Fiji (worrying, but evidence of political vitality).[5] From 1966, Legislative Council elections were contested by two major parties: the Federation Party was a platform for Indo-Fijians, pursuing independence for 'one country, one nation, one people'; and the Alliance Party, led by chiefly dynasties, who sought gradual change, political stability and the retention of communal rolls. British officials generally sided with the chiefs, an empathy which shaped the Independence constitution of 1970, which secured the Great Council of Chiefs' power and authority to protect Fijian interests. That concession, together with a complex electoral mechanism, persuaded the chiefs to accept independence, although descendants of *girmitiyas* were a majority of the population as well as the dominant force in commerce. For a generation, Alliance was the perennial government, and Prime Minister Ratu Sir Kamisese Mara the doyen of Pacific statesmen. That order enshrined 'the unity of *turaga* (chiefs) and *vanua* (people), bound indivisibly by the chiefly system'.[6] Public ritual as well as the constitution expressed Fiji's identity as a Pacific and chiefly polity with Christian values and British connections. Indo-Fijians were visibly and culturally subordinate, just as they were throughout the colonial era.

Dismantling the rest of Britain's Pacific dependencies was less demanding. In 1970 the kingdom of Tonga shed her British protectorate. The tranquil surface of Anglo-Tongan relations belied serious turbulences. One threatened the alliance in 1918 when the 18-year-old Queen Sālote Tupou III was the appropriate person to succeed her father. The British agent judged her incapable of ruling, and suggested annexation.[7] Another option was to treat her consort, Tungī Mailefihi, as king. The Colonial Office agreed but the despatch was lost in the muddle of war, and she was crowned Queen Sālote Tupou III before the despatch turned up. Given her chance, Sālote gained increasing favour with British officials. Her most urgent problem was to control an unruly parliament of fractious chiefs. In this dilemma the British made common cause with her, hinting that Tonga might be annexed if parliament was not reconciled with her. Sālote told the consul of her

> deep appreciation of the assistance and advice rendered to her by His Majesty's Government. I was deeply impressed with her personality, she is only twenty-five ... but she displays great dignity in her position, has acquired an intimate knowledge of native customs and traditions, and she undoubtedly commands the respect of the people.[8]

If Tāufa'āhau – as King George Tupou – created the kingdom and cemented it, Sālote remade and entrenched it in her 47-year reign. For both, the British alliance was critical. In the Second World War, therefore, Tongans contributed generously. Thereafter the Treaty of Friendship was renegotiated to allow greater autonomy. As a model 'native prince' Queen Sālote received four British imperial honours. At her funeral in 1965

> these four British honours were carried by two princes of the royal house ... alongside the mats and tapa that confirmed the wealth and pre-eminence of the royal house so personally secured by Queen Sālote of Tonga.[9]

Again, formal independence ratified rather than transformed the structure of the polity and its external relations. Like Christianity and constitutional monarchy, the British Commonwealth had been assimilated into Tonga's traditions and identity.

Several Pacific constitutions – Western Samoa, Nauru and Papua New Guinea – were devised mainly by their own people. British practice was more interventionist, taking the colony's representatives to London for the last round of debates. Yet in Pacific decolonizing, as in colonial rule, Britain waived some precedents. Solomon Islands gained independence in 1978 in textbook fashion as a unitary state with a constitution in the Westminster tradition, grafted onto the colonial advisory council. The division of powers between the central and local governments was not resolved, however. Landownership was likely to be contested, since Islanders assumed (but had no need to spell it out) that citizens (like foreigners) would be barred from buying land in each other's home islands.[10] Although Westminster practices were written into the constitution, there would be some awkwardness due to the frailty of political parties, which became ad hoc lobbying groups without ideology, discipline or binding loyalty.[11]

A more remarkable departure from British practice split the Gilbert and Ellice Colony into two states – Kiribati (1979) and Tuvalu (1978) – acknowledging ethnicity but defying the African imperative of unity, and overlooking the islands' lack of visible means of support. By then there was no population quorum: Nauru had become free with only 9,000 citizens (see below). Strict criteria for viability had all been abandoned: these states would be clients through their reliance on aid, or migration, or logistical and technical support. The only local delay was provoked by European complications rather than Pacific obstacles. It proved impossible to cut loose the New Hebrides Condominium until 1980 in the face of French determination to remain.

FRENCH DEPENDENCIES

France might have been expected to quit the Pacific faster than Britain. Since 1945 she had leaned towards colonial self-determination. The 1946 constitution recognized 'peoples and nations' in overseas France. As citizens they could (and did) form political parties, while discriminatory legal codes were abandoned. Devolution was slow but steady and (for example) in 1957 the Defferre Law gave partial autonomy to French Polynesia. But that proved the high-water mark; from then onwards Pacific dependencies increased in their material and perhaps symbolic value for Paris. In 1958 de Gaulle returned to power, began to reanimate Paris control, and transformed French Polynesia into a 'nuclear dependency' (see chapter 16).

France was determined to retain New Caledonia as well, although its strategic significance was slight.[12] One (diminishing) problem was the settlers' enthusiasm for autonomy. A self-conscious *caldoche* identity crystallized – according to Saussol and to Bobin[13] – between the world wars, in opposition to metropolitan French authority and personnel. Like white Australian readers of the *Bulletin* in the 1890s, *caldoches* cherished a self-image as 'the livestock breeder, the bushman, the pioneer of rural colonization, at home in wide open spaces and strongly individualistic', and some pastoralist language also reflected early Australian influence. The reality of many lives was more mundane: modest prosperity, less education than metropolitans, and careers as artisans in nickel mining. In the 1950s they supported the pursuit of autonomy by Maurice Lenormand's Caledonian Union party. Their populist agenda berated Paris's control together with dominant local enterprises – Ballande the trading firm and Le Société Nickel. By 1957 Lenormand was head of the territorial council, leading a regime which included canaque ministers and white trade unionists.

That was the limit of *caldoche* ambition: according to a dismissive Bobin they were 'hesitant, confused, incoherent and incapable of developing beyond an anti-metropolitan xenophobia or a folkloric belief in an up-dated pro-American cargo cult'. They could not become more than poor imitations of Australians or New Zealanders: outnumbered by indigenes, their living standards rested on subsidies. Bobin observes that metropolitan immigrants, and displaced settlers from Algeria and Indochina in the 1960s and 1970s (sustained by a nickel boom and public works investment) diluted the *Caldoche* identity. But he also pin-points their refusal to acknowledge their convict (as well as free settler) ancestry, and Kanak (as well as white) forebears.

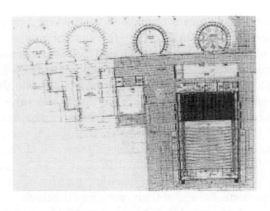

Plate 18.1 Colonialism and nationalism reconciled? One of the villages in the Tjibaou Cultural Centre, New Caledonia (see ch. 21). Courtesy Cultural Tjibaou www.adck.nc/presentation_generale/village_1.htm; copyright ADCK/Renzo Piano Building Workshop.

When Kanak proposed a different kind of independence, therefore, *caldoches* turned around and revived their loyalties to Paris.[14]

A Kanak nationalist position was developed by university students, inspired by the events of 1968 in Paris but also by folk memories of a rebellion in New Caledonia in 1878. They reclaimed the pejorative 'canaque' as Kanak, and chose Kanaky as the name for an independent country. Several parties agitated for independence, but Paris was intransigent, and multiple municipalities created many patronage networks and undercut the territorial assembly. They were also harassed by *caldoches*. The fractious parties persisted, but they came together at critical moments in the Front de Liberation Nationale Kanak et Socialiste, FLNKS, behind the charismatic Jean-Marie Tjibaou.

By 1988, Kanak were not only divided but outnumbered by immigrant communities. Tensions reached a catharsis when Kanak militants on Ouvea island captured gendarmes. Troops stormed the cave where hostages were held, and three soldiers and 19 Kanak died – three of them after their surrender. That tragedy made negotiations essential, and these gave rise to the Matignon Accord between French and FLNKS representatives. New Caledonia's destiny would be decided in 1998 by referendum; meanwhile the territory was split into three provinces, two of which elected Kanak governments. Some felt that the Accord conceded too much to France, and next year Tjibaou and his deputy were assassinated. However, the Accord survived and by the time of the referendum, Kanak and *caldoches* leaders had formulated a middle way. The Noumea Accords, signed in May 1998 and ratified by the November referendum, drafted the question for the voters, seeking (and receiving) endorsement for a new framework and timetable. For twenty years the territory would remain French, but enjoy increased powers of self-government. Once again Pacific conditions prompted a novel arrangement: New Caledonia did not become Kanaky, but nor was it quite colonial.

The preamble to the constitutional document declares that

> Kanak were pushed back to the geographic, economic and political margins of their own land. For a proud people not lacking in warrior traditions this could only provoke revolts which incited violent repression, aggravating the resentment and incomprehension.

Adrian Muckle notes that this formula still attributes original agency to France, but it does seek reconciliation, and tries to transcend the divisive rhetoric of the 1970s. He also observes the settlers' continuing preoccupation with their identity; and in that quest a key document is *Etre Caldoche Aujourd'hui*[15] (Being *Caldoche* Today), partly inspired by Michael King's study of New Zealand, *Being Pakeha*.[16] In that book, King illumined how Maori and Pakeha were mutually defining and interdependent, and strove 'to make it clear … that Maori had every right to be Maori in their own country and to expect Pakeha to respect them'. *Caldoches* identified more with his reworked *Being Pakeha Now* (1999), in which he asserted a Pakeha right to be themselves, and even to be 'another kind of indigenous New Zealander'.[17]

ANGLO-FRENCH CONDOMINIUM

British and French policies collided in the New Hebrides.[18] The condominium rested on two law codes, two police forces, two school systems and two administrations. These proved 'more of an obstacle to the economic and political "development" of the New Hebrides than an agent for the preparation of New Hebrideans to become rulers of their own country.'[19] Self-rule was not Paris's preference, since it might disrupt de Gaulle's Pacific strategy and France's nuclear programme. The French commissioner in 1969 explained that 'My instructions received from General de Gaulle were "we are staying"'. Two years later, his successor did expect political parties 'as soon as a small thinking elite will have been formed. All we hope for is that this elite will be francophone, trained in our way of thinking.'[20]

During the 1970s new political forms did emerge and seemed to mirror the dichotomy in government. Local protests against land alienation (the outcome of Higginson's misdeeds) failed, and revealed the need to capture government. In 1971 the New Hebrides Cultural Association formed, and was renamed the New Hebrides National Party. Its leaders were anglophone and non-Catholic: Donald Kalpokas, Father Walter Lini and Father John Bani, returning from studies abroad; and their journal, *New Hebrides View Points*, publicized land alienation and other grievances. Three years later NHNP recruited Barak Sope and Kalkot Matas, who helped to transform the party into a national body, emphasizing land to mobilize support among urban and rural, educated and unschooled.[21] In 1974 the party elected Father Lini as president, Barak Sope as secretary and Kalkot as publicist. The Presbyterian Assembly had already endorsed independence, and the Anglican Lini petitioned the United Nations, calling for independence by 1977.

In reaction, the Union des Communautes des Nouvelles Hebrides (UCNH) formed in 1974, explicitly representing francophones. One leader explained that

> the National Party was born on the English side and it therefore influenced the anglophones. The francophone Melanesians were not interested in this, and didn't understand too well why [it] had been born.[22]

A second francophone party, the Mouvement Autonomiste des Nouvelles Hebrides, also represented settler interests, but nursed separatist ideas and argued for 'autonomous status' for the country's regions. On Santo island it found an ally and zealous grassroots support in Nagriamel, a traditionalist (custom) movement led by Jimmy Stevens, protesting against new land alienation.

Britain and France now agreed to begin a transition to independence, with the election of an Assembly in 1975. NHNP won most of the Melanesian votes and 17 of 29 universal suffrage seats contested, but (renaming the party Vanua'aku) it boycotted the Assembly.[23] After sustained political pressure a government of national unity oversaw a Constitutional Planning Committee, and a new constitution was accepted by France and Britain in September 1979. Two months later the election under that constitution gave Vanua'aku a sufficient majority (26 out of 39) to amend the constitution at will. Faced with this disagreeable possibility, France sought to undermine the movement towards independence, and agreed to a date of 30 June 1980 – but only a month before the event. On the eve of independence there was a secession (led by Stevens and Nagriamel) on Santo. It was put down swiftly and almost bloodlessly by the Vanua'aku government and the Defence Force of the newly independent Papua New Guinea with logistical help from Australia. Those coalitions seemingly echoed and strengthened colonial cleavages, with 'anglophones' aided by the Anglican and Presbyterian churches, and by Australia, ranged against 'francophones' supported by France and the

Catholic church. Lini himself reported that

> Inspector-General Robert told the meeting that he did not care if civil war broke out. ... M. Dijoud appeared on TV and radio ... and encouraged French nationals and 'colons' to continue their activities against the legally elected government.[24]

Paradoxically, these discouraging circumstances helped to bring about something rare in Melanesia: a party with grassroots organization, a national vision and an explicit (and mildly socialist) agenda. Vanua'aku had made for themselves an independent identity. Several years passed before the fissiparous politics of land and ethnicity eroded this simple clarity.

NEW ZEALAND AND AUSTRALIAN DEPENDENCIES

These European manoeuvres offered little inspiration and less guidance for other colonists or for the colonized. Nor were Australians or New Zealanders exposed to ideas from newly independent polities: their selective isolation was maintained by migration controls which barred most non-Europeans, so there were few personal experiences to subvert old stereotypes of 'non-Europeans'. Decolonization was not a simple replication of events in other parts of the world.

New Zealand moved first. The Western Samoa administration had not regained the moral ascendancy from the *mau* movement. Constitutional change had to await the end of the Second World War, but began in 1948 when a new parliament designed a new form of government. The constitution was remarkable, since it set out to build post-colonial government on the bases of pre-colonial values. Many constitutions claimed to do so, but Western Samoa's took the aspiration seriously. At independence in 1962, only *matai* title-holders could vote or sit in parliament, and 'traditional' rules governed landownership.[25] No European power could conceivably have accepted this model.

An issue which faced all New Zealand's dependent peoples was how to reconcile economic frailty with political autonomy. Samoa's radically conservative constitution ignored the country's reliance on New Zealand's economic aid and the people's reliance on free movement into New Zealand and (via American Samoa) the United States. Partial decolonization was as difficult to imagine as partial pregnancy until Cook Islands leaders negotiated with New Zealand a new status, 'free association', which came into effect in 1965. Cook Islanders could hold dual citizenship, and their state would not exercise the full range of sovereign powers. The government relied on New Zealand in finance and foreign affairs, while Islanders entered freely and worked in New Zealand. This device then provided a template for Niue, which followed suit in 1974. As a direct consequence of these arrangements, Islanders soon amounted to almost 5 per cent of New Zealand's population – 167,073 people in 1991, half of them Samoan. This nexus stripped the islands of many young, ambitious, educated and energetic people – and many others.

By the 1990s 85 per cent of all Niueans, 70 per cent of Tokelauans, and 69 per cent of Cook Islanders lived in New Zealand. Without formal access, Tongans had become the third largest Island community in New Zealand.[26] Helpful for individuals and families, these movements were ominous for 'national' economies and cultures.

Free association was a model for constitutional development in the United States Trust Territory of Micronesia, but it was firmly rejected when mooted for Nauru.[27] A German protectorate from the 1880s, Nauru became a League of Nations mandate after the Great War. Britain delegated its powers to Australia. The British phosphate commissioners, appointed by Britain, Australia and New Zealand, held title to the phosphates and could sell them only to these countries: Nauru's main asset was excised from its political system.

Nauruans naturally sought control of their own affairs as well as a real share of phosphate profits. In response, the Australians constituted a Council of Chiefs which did negotiate slightly greater shares of profits. Nauru's war experience was appalling. Japanese forces occupied the island in 1942, but then the tide turned and Nauru was blockaded. The Japanese began moving Islanders randomly – 1,200 from Nauru to Chuuk, and 400 from Banaba to Nauru. In Chuuk, Nauruans survived on whatever they could grow or catch during intervals in American bombing. By the end of the war 1 in 3 Nauruans there had died.[28] They might therefore have expected more consideration than they received when a United Nations Trust replaced the League of Nations mandate; but the only change was the creation of a Local Government Council. From 1956 the council campaigned both for royalties and for independence. At this delicate moment the most serious threat to Nauruans' integrity was Australia's proposal to evacuate them all (as happened to the Banabans of Ocean Island, the other phosphate island, who were resettled in Fiji). Nauruans would share land with Aborigines; they would be Australian citizens; and they would lose their island, half of it yet to be mined. This plan meant assimilation, not free association. Full independence was preferred by the 9,000 Nauruans, who reached that goal in 1968. They could never provide the specialist skills implied by sovereignty, but they could buy these in a global market.[29]

The largest questions were posed in Papua New Guinea, whose destiny had been kept deliberately vague. Papua New Guinea stirred only indifference in Australia until the Labor Party opposition began to criticize government policies in the 1960s. Until then, ministers explained that it was not a colony but a territory, so that it might (like the Northern Territory) accede to the Commonwealth or (like the Antarctic) remain in limbo. As Leader of the Opposition in 1968, however, Gough Whitlam savaged the minister's argument that economic growth must precede political change, and that most people opposed independence: 'the minister's exploitation of a reluctance which he himself and his immediate predecessors have fostered sedulously is a tactic which reflects little credit upon him'.[30] In 1970 he insisted that independence was a decision for Australia: Papua New Guineans should decide its form, but the fact was already decided.[31]

The shape of the future came into focus in 1966 when a delegation of Papua New Guinean legislators asked the Australian government if they had a real option to become the Seventh Australian State. That may have been a debating point, but it was not illogical: free association had just been negotiated for the Cook Islands. What made it unthinkable was its timing: white and black Australians were not yet equal citizens at home and 'white Australia' still informed migration policy. Predictably, the Australian cabinet took fright at three million Melanesians crossing Torres Strait to demand jobs, schools, pensions and other rights of citizens. Instead, they resolved that Papua New Guinea's destiny was independence – eventually, after much economic development.[32] To make this scenario credible, Australians began to preach territorial (then national) unity and created its symbols and preconditions: a flag, anthem, national day, airline, university and a bureaucracy. When the Labor Party won office in late 1972, Prime Minister Whitlam simply accelerated the timetable, allowing only three years for the transition to independence. Some deplored Whitlam's approach:

> Australians, deeply and bitterly, and for years to come, will go on paying the cost of a frivolous prime minister's unwisdom. So will the oppressed and exploited people of Papua New Guinea.[33]

But the non-Labor parties had swung behind independence and even claimed credit for it.[34] By 1975 there was bipartisan support for decolonization.

Australia created a single state for a nation. Creating a nation was harder. In the territory there was some enthusiasm for freedom, but less for unity. In the 1960s the House of Assembly divided between members from Papua (an Australian territory since 1906) who believed that they had better claims to Australian citizenship than New Guineans who were 'Australian Protected Persons'. The country's 700 languages were a cliché but also a reality (Osmar White's popular *Parliament of a Thousand Tribes* publicized this difficulty).[35] It was local protests against development projects which undercut colonial power. In East New Britain, disputes over alienated land prompted the occupation of plantations and the formation of a dissident political movement in 1969, the Mataungan Association. On Bougainville, Conzinc Rio Tinto needed native-owned land for a mine (which Australia hoped would sustain the territory's economy). That provoked passive resistance in which women confronted police, and women and men lay down before bulldozers. Every metropolitan daily paper in Australia denounced the police as bloody thugs, and most wondered 'What will the world think of us?' These were minor incidents in global terms, but they brought colonial relationships into embarrassing focus.[36] A few Australians asked sceptically if Papua New Guinea was 'ready for independence', but the fact was that Australia was ready to delegate. The debates between Australian conservatives who wanted to maintain control, and liberals and radicals who were determined to decolonize, elided two questions: as the most vehement anti-colonial movements were less nationalist than secessionist, could Papua New Guinea's destiny be unitary? And must independence be complete?

When Whitlam's government set the goal of sovereignty in three years, that would be less than a decade since the Australian government first envisaged such an outcome, faster than most people in the territory absorbed the notion of unity, and sooner than anyone in either country expected. After the election of 1972, Michael Somare's Pangu Pati and Julius Chan's People's Progress Party formed the core of a coalition, with Somare as chief minister and Chan finance minister. Natives were becoming citizens; but citizenship was an awkward paradigm. The *de facto* chair of the Constitutional Planning Committee (CPC), Father John Momis, shared Bougainvilleans' suspicion of all central government; his colleague John Kaputin of East New Britain represented the separatist Mataungans. Separatist demands of varying strength were mounted in Papua as well, and many highlanders feared lest the future government be dominated by coastal people with longer access to schooling. The CPC proposed to devolve many powers to provinces (formerly districts) and curb executive power. Those proposals involved substantial changes to the manner of government and protracted debates which introduced tensions between the cabinet and the CPC.[37]

The difficulties of citizenship were broader than those of the constitution. While it was important to induct citizens into the public service, that programme might intensify highlanders' fears of coastal hegemony. It was also hard to build cabinet solidarity. As a backbencher, Momis introduced a motion to renegotiate the Bougainville Mining Agreement, and he and Kaputin issued a statement favouring wholesale nationalization, but Kaputin was a cabinet minister, and nationalization was certainly not government policy.[38] To handle this situation, Bougainville's leading politician, Paul Lapun, became minister for mines. He organized a successful renegotiation of the Agreement, and secured much increased benefits from mining – for the national government.[39]

The government did reach an aid agreement with Australia, and drew the teeth from most separatisms, but relations with Bougainville soured. Politicians could compromise, but public servants inherited the Australian enthusiasm for centralism and balked at providing resources to Bougainville. Sorely provoked, the Provincial Assembly lost patience and declared separate independence a fortnight before Papua New Guinea's. Lapun remained in cabinet, but Momis led a secessionist delegation to the United Nations. The UN predictably rebuffed them, the dispute was patched up, and Bougainville remained in the fold; but secessionism had not been dismantled, and landowners' discontents were the long, slow fuse. At the next opportunity they voted Lapun out of office, and a decade later the fuse ignited a savage civil war.

ISLAND INDEPENDENCE

As New Zealand's and Australia's colonial problems came to an end – or at least an interval – Island leaders inherited old and unresolved problems as well as new dilemmas. Especially in multi-ethnic Melanesia and bicultural

Fiji, independence aggravated problems of identity, loyalty and cultural coherence (see chapter 21). They also faced economic problems so severe as to threaten their autonomy.[40] That perplexity was sharpened by the popularity (in the 1970s especially) of a pessimistic dependency theory which asserted that dependent polities and economies in the periphery (i.e. far from Europe) necessarily suffered from unequal relations with metropolitan powers.[41] Part of the theory's popularity lay in its excuse for politicians who failed to transform their constituents' lives or even to maintain colonial services. Before long that theory came under attack – together with the politicians' alibi. One new paradigm wore the acronym MIRAB, a shorthand depiction and tentative analysis of polities and economies shaped by *MI*gration, *R*emittances, and *A*id sustaining a *B*ureaucracy. Two economists coined this term and applied it to micro-states: Kiribati, Tuvalu and New Zealand's associates Cook Islands, Niue and Tokelau. Although denounced by other scholars, and by political leaders, MIRAB and its variants remain influential in portrayals of island government. John Connell observes wryly that these economies enjoy 'considerable largesse ... [while] political incorporation has led to the construction of a welfare state ... [and] migration to the metropolitan country is a right that is jealously guarded'.[42] Against this perspective, Epeli Hau'ofa calculates that Australia and New Zealand are net winners: 'what they give you in aid they receive in return a great deal more in the forms of export earnings and repatriation of profits on investments'.[43] Be that as it may, international agencies, donors and recipients alike are easily persuaded by MIRAB's clarity and simplicity.

With low incomes and high expectations of government services, all newly independent countries except Nauru required financial aid, either bilateral (such as the Australian agreement with Papua New Guinea) or multilateral (from the World Bank or the Manila-based Asian Development Bank). That made governments timid, especially as they had no urgent agenda of social and economic reconstruction. Vanuatu's young turks had a rhetorical commitment to a Melanesian Socialism which had little specific content and less kinship with Marx; other leaders subscribed to an even looser 'Pacific Way' or 'Melanesian Way', which in practice meant the search for a populist consensus.[44] Neither formulation encouraged, or perhaps permitted, bold policy moves. In fact the new governments had more leverage than they knew, at least for some years. Colonial officials had seldom borrowed large sums; their successors could, and did. Colonial regimes had not proposed offshore banking or tax havens; the independent Cook Islands did. Australians in Papua New Guinea were disposed to accept any serious proposition from a mining company; a self-governing Papua New Guinea had the self-assurance to reject an ultimatum from the American giant Kennecott (for the Ok Tedi ore) and insist on better terms from Conzinc Riotinto of Australia (for the Bougainville mine).[45] At least until the new governments reached their credit limit, they were more expansive than their predecessors – a necessary quality when citizens expected improved services.

The honeymoon was brief. Soon after the last island group became free, the World Bank began to question its own policies, acknowledging the political and social dimensions of underdevelopment. Since its charter bars it from addressing domestic politics, the Bank described its new interest as 'good governance' – a term loose enough to cover new interests, but sounding sufficiently scientific to impress casual audiences.[46] That formulation allowed the World Bank to set conditions (and not only financial conditions) for financial aid. Bilateral donors followed suit, from concern for effective aid delivery and a desire to involve 'civil society' (churches and other non-governmental organizations) in project management.

The sometimes perverse impact of these policies are well illustrated in Papua New Guinea's financial and political crisis of 1999. While Australian aid still flowed, the untied portion had almost disappeared while the project segments expanded. In the mid-1990s, the World Bank and Australia had suspended funding for an adjustment package pending reform measures. As usual, the government yielded tactically but defaulted so long as its exports guaranteed a cash flow. Then in 1997 an opportunist government tried to escape the constraints by poaching the gamekeeper. The World Bank officer who had handled the latest negotiations was engaged to advise the prime minister on how to evade the bank's restrictions. That provoked even more tension with the bank, alleviated only when that government fell in mid-1999.

Reviewing the chaotic economy when he came to office, the economist and technocratic Sir Mekere Morauta introduced a supplementary budget to restore integrity to government institutions; to stabilize the budget and make it credible; to stabilize the plunging currency; and to remove obstacles to development. His account of 'what went wrong' began with the current budget:

> It did not respect our Parliament, or our Central Bank, or [the bureaucracy]. ... It was the work of [the Prime Minister's adviser], not the Treasury, not even the full Cabinet. ... It based big hopes for expenditure reductions and revenue increases, and access to external finance on wishful thinking. ...
> The 1999 Budget was based on the assumption that 7,000 public servants – more than 10 per cent ... be removed almost overnight. ... The retrenchment and retirement entitlements of these 7,000 public servants were estimated at 65 million Kina. But no funds were made available.

The true cost of retrenchment was three times the estimate: only a sixth of the target figure were retrenched; no retrenched officer was actually taken off the payroll; and despite the boast of shedding 7,000 employees, the number increased by 3,262.

The budget had cut funds to research and teaching institutions, and delegated functions to the provinces while cutting their funds. Many decisions had to be reversed at once, and provision had to be added to cover long-standing and concealed debts. In consequence of such mismanagement, the deficit for six months was three times the estimate for the whole year. Thwarted in international borrowing, the government had squeezed funds from a reluctant but dependent Bank of Papua New Guinea, and tried to sell recognition of Taiwan. As foreign exchange reserves fell, the exchange rate to the US dollar fell from 70 cents in 1997 to 29 cents, before stabilizing at 37 cents. Inflation exceeded 20 per cent, and interest rates touched 25 per cent. The new prime minister recognized that salvation required the favour of the International Monetary Fund, which had cleared the budget before it was presented, so that 'we look forward to timely resumption of lending from Fund facilities'. Australia and other 'Friends of Papua New Guinea' would also be asked for budgetary and technical assistance.[47]

As in this case, the imposition of 'good governance' needed a substantial crisis as a trigger. Cook Islands was near-bankrupt before bilateral donors and the Asian Development Bank prepared a rescue package. Cook Island small farmers had sold their produce in New Zealand until a free market undercut them. Many then left home – for New Zealand. The government's offshore banking also ran into trouble when the 'Winebox' affair of 1996 alleged systemic corruption. Because of free association, the scandal threatened New Zealand's reputation as much as that of the Cook Islands government, and stern measures followed. The donors' rescue package insisted on halving the public service and slashing salaries and allowances.

As in Papua New Guinea, in Solomon Islands donors all complained of her unsustainable logging, but export income from the logging sheltered the government from conditionality. Australia and New Zealand used meetings of the South Pacific Forum to hector Island governments and to preach the virtues of balanced budgets, free markets and financial accountability. Inevitably, Island governments came to see 'good governance' and conditionality as attacks on their sovereignty, and the donors' influence as more appropriate to colonialism than to relations between sovereigns. Whatever the donors' intentions, 'the outcome of good governance initiatives may ... be to make "them" appear to be more like "us" '.[48]

Some institutions already encouraged that convergence. Independent states inherited curricula shot through with colonial values which assumed that

> Formal education is more important and valuable than informal education.
>   Academic subjects such as Maths and English are accorded higher status than practical (vocational) subjects ...
>   The lifestyle led by formal education graduates is better than those who are educated and live in the villages.

Education did not prepare youngsters for the life that most people lead, but created 'frustrated school leavers, disillusioned parents who feel they have wasted their money and teachers and schools which are seen to have failed the community'.[49]

In any event full separation was difficult emotionally. In Papua New Guinea,

> We did not ... burn the Australian flag to pursue independence from Australia. That first day of independence was greeted with mixed thoughts and feelings of joy by the politicians with followers, sadness by those who had nurtured a relationship and confusion by the rural, uneducated majority who didn't understand what independence was all about.[50]

For many years it was a strangely deferential country in which every prime minister and leader of the opposition would

> congratulate the winner in Australian general elections...; where all normal official work comes to a stand-still on Melbourne Cup day; where fanatical partisanship during the state of origin rugby clashes in Australia seems to polarize the population; where telecasts from at least four Australian TV stations are available to the elite.[51]

If souring relations loosened those bonds, some inherited problems proved stubborn.

Nauruans came into possession of half an island, the other half having been stripped to a lunar landscape. The working of the remaining half raised the possibility that there would be no land with which people could identify. The purchase of real estate and less tangible assets elsewhere might address long-term financial needs, but Nauruans might share with Banabans the fate of absolute dispossession and the need to create a new identity. The government wondered if the colonial power had exercised its duty of care responsibly, and in 1986 created a 'Commission of Enquiry into the Worked out Phosphate lands of Nauru', with an Australian lawyer as its chief adviser.[52] Its task was to evaluate the colonial impact, allocating blame for damage from strip mining. The commission must determine who 'should accept responsibility for rehabilitating the environmental damage under international areas of phosphate land ... and the cost and feasibility of any proposed rehabilitation'.[53]

This enquiry found that Nauru had not in fact been colonized, that imperialism had served the interests of the British Phosphate Commissioners rather than the people, and that Australia had not observed the protocols for a Trust Territory. The international lawyer Weeramantry found that

> the natural resources of Nauru were the inviolable heritage of the Nauruan people, [and that] the principle of permanent sovereignty meant that neither title to the phosphate nor the right to exploit it could have been given away by the German government or acquired by the British Phosphate Commissioners in the manner claimed by the BPC and the partner governments on their behalf.[54]

Environmental damage was proven. The commission found mitigation – Australian attempts to redress some concerns, and the absence of malice – but the trustees were obligated to hand back the territory in at least as good a state as when they took it. On these bases a claim for compensation against the British Phosphate Commissioners was established in the Australian courts. When the case was dismissed by the Australian government, Nauru went to the International Court of Justice in the Hague, which found a case to be answered. Just when historians were relishing a definitive legal and economic decision about colonialism, however, in 1993 Australia settled out of court, and created a fund of $121 million to rehabilitate lands mined before 1970.

Decolonization might look simple, but it quickly proved indeterminate. In the Pacific it took novel forms which tried to embody the unique links created in strange colonial contexts. None could erase the colonial past. Not only was it impossible to recreate pre-colonial conditions (although Samoans tried), but every 'solution' generated a new problem. Since the former dependencies were bound to the former administering powers by sentiment, education, trade, investment, media and culture, decolonization abroad was no easier than decolonization at home.

NOTES

1 Donald Denoon, Mark Hudson, Tessa Morris-Suzuki and Gavan McCormack (eds), *Multicultural Japan: Palaeolithic to Postmodern*, Melbourne, 1997.

2 William Roger Louis, *Imperialism at Bay: The United States and the Decolonization of the British Empire*, Oxford, 1977.

3 Jan Pouwer, 'The Colonization, Decolonization and Recolonization of West New Guinea', *Journal of Pacific History*, 34 (1999), 157–80.

4 Barrie Macdonald, 'Decolonization and "Good" Governance: Precedents and Continuities', in D. Denoon (ed.), *Emerging from Empire? Decolonization in the Pacific*, Canberra, 1997, 1–9; W. David McIntyre, 'The Admission of Small States to the Commonwealth', *Journal of Imperial and Commonwealth History*, 24: 2 (1996), 262.

5 Brij V. Lal, *Broken Waves: A History of the Fiji Islands in the Twentieth Century*, Honolulu, 1992, and *Another Way: The Politics of Constitutional Reform in Post-coup Fiji*, Canberra, 1998.

6 Lal, *Broken Waves*; and *Power and Prejudice: The Making of the Fiji Crisis*, Wellington, 1988.

7 Elizabeth Wood-Ellem, 'Queen Sālote and the British Dual Mandate Policy', in D. Denoon (ed.), *Emerging from Empire?*, 22–5, citing Islay McOwan to high commissioner for the Western Pacific, 12 April 1918.

8 Ibid., high commissioner to secretary of state, 13 August 1925.

9 Ibid.

10 Yash Ghai, 'The Making of the Independence Constitution', in Peter Larmour with Sue Tarua (eds), *Solomon Islands Politics*, Suva, 1983.

11 See chs 6, 7 and 8 in Larmour, *Solomon Islands Politics*.

12 John Connell, *New Caledonia or Kanaky? The Political History of a French Colony*, Canberra, 1987.

13 Frederic Bobin, 'Caldoches, Metropolitans and the Mother Country', *Journal of Pacific History*, 26 (1991), 303–12.

14 Bobin, 'Caldoches, Metropolitans and the Mother Country'.

15 *Etre Caldoche Aujourd'hui*, Noumea, 1994.

16 Michael King, *Being Pakeha: An Encounter with New Zealand and the Maori Renaissance*, Auckland, 1985.

17 Michael King, *Being Pakeha Now: Reflections and Recollections of a White Native*, Auckland, 1999, 9, 239.

18 David Ambrose, 'From the New Hebrides to Vanuatu', in Denoon, *Emerging from Empire?*; Walter H. Lini, *Beyond Pandemonium*, Suva, 1980.

19 Barak Sope, 'The Colonial History of the New Hebrides', quoted in Ambrose, 'From the New Hebrides to Vanuatu'.

20 Howard van Trease, *Melanesian Politics Stael blong Vanuatu*, Suva, 1995; Barak Sope, 'The Colonial History of the New Hebrides', Suva, n.d.

21 Barak Sope, *Land and Politics in the New Hebrides*, Suva, 1974.
22 Chris Plant (ed.), *New Hebrides: The Road to Independence*, Suva, 1977, 47.
23 Van Trease, *The Politics of Land in Vanuatu*, Suva, 1987, 29; Lini, *Beyond Pandemonium*, 29.
24 Ibid., 51–4.
25 Malama Meleisea, Penelope Schoeffel Meleisea and Gatoloai Peseta Sio, 'Preparation for Independence 1945–1961', in Malama Meleisea (ed.), *Lagaga: A Short History of Western Samoa*, Suva, 1983.
26 Karen Nero, 'The End of Insularity', in Donald Denoon, Stewart Firth, Jocelyn Linnekin, Malama Meleisea and Karen Nero (eds), *Cambridge History of the Pacific Islanders*, Melbourne, 1997, ch. 13.
27 Nancy Viviani, *Nauru: Phosphate and Political Progress*, Canberra, 1970; Nancy Pollock, 'Nauru: Decolonized, Recolonizing, but never a Colony', in Denoon, *Emerging from Empire?*, 102–6.
28 Viviani, *Nauru*; Barrie Macdonald, *Cinderellas of the Empire*, Canberra, 1982.
29 Viviani, *Nauru*.
30 House of Representatives, 9 May 1968, quoted in Hank Nelson, 'The Talk and the Timing: Reputations and Reality, and the Grant of Self-government to Papua New Guinea', in Denoon, *Emerging from Empire?*, 107–17.
31 Nelson, 'The Talk and the Timing'.
32 Ian Downs, *The Australian Trusteeship: Papua New Guinea 1945–1975*, Canberra, 1980.
33 Peter Ryan, 'Some Unfinished Business from the Second World War', *Quadrant*, September 1995, 14–15.
34 Nelson, 'The Talk and the Timing'.
35 Osmar White, *Parliament of a Thousand Tribes*, London, 1965.
36 Downs, *The Australian Trusteeship*; Denoon, *Getting Under the Skin*, Melbourne, 2000.
37 James Griffin, *The PNG–Australia Relationship: Problems and Prospects*, Canberra, 1990; James Griffin, Hank Nelson and Stewart Firth, *Papua New Guinea: A Political History*, Melbourne, 1979; Paul Hasluck, *A Time for Building: Australian Administration in Papua and New Guinea 1951–1963*, Melbourne, 1976; Peter Hastings, *New Guinea: Problems and Prospects*, Melbourne, 1969.
38 Denoon, *Getting Under the Skin*.
39 Richard Jackson, *Ok Tedi: The Pot of Gold?*, Port Moresby, 1982.
40 Macdonald, 'Decolonization and "Good" Governance'.
41 For example, A. Amarshi, K. Good and R. Mortimer (eds), *Development and Dependency: The Political Economy of Papua New Guinea*, Melbourne, 1979.
42 John Connell, 'Island Microstate: The Mirage of Development', *The Contemporary Pacific*, 3: 2 (1991), 272.
43 Epeli Hau'ofa, 'The New South Pacific Society', in A. Hooper (ed.), *Class and Culture in the South Pacific*, Auckland, 1987, 9.
44 Jocelyn Linnekin, 'The Ideological World Re-made', in Donald Denoon, Stewart Firth, Jocelyn Linnekin, Malama Meleisea and Karen Nero (eds), *Cambridge History of the Pacific Islanders*, Melbourne, 1997, ch. 12.
45 Denoon, *Getting Under the Skin*.
46 Barrie Macdonald, '"Good" Governance and Pacific Islands States', in Peter Larmour (ed.), *Governance in the Pacific Islands*, Canberra, 1997; World Bank, *Governance and Development*, Washington, 1992, 58.
47 Address to parliament by the prime minister and treasurer, Tuesday 10 August 1999.

48 Macdonald, 'Decolonization and "Good" Governance'; David Hanlon, *Remaking Micronesia: Discourses over Development in a Pacific Territory, 1944–1982*, Honolulu, 1998.

49 Stanley Houma, 'Decolonizing the Mind: Towards an Alternative Vision for Education in the Solomon Islands', in Denoon, *Emerging from Empire?*, 172–4.

50 Rona Nadile, 'Decolonizing the Intellectual Mind-set: The Case of Papua New Guinea', in Denoon, *Emerging from Empire?*, 175–9.

51 Yao Saffu, cited by Rona Nadile, 'Decolonizing the Intellectual Mind-set'.

52 Pollock, 'Nauru: Decolonized, Recolonizing, But Never a Colony', in Denoon, *Emerging from Empire?*, 102–6; the report of the commission is Weeramantry, *Nauru: Environmental Damage under International Trusteeship*, Melbourne, 1992.

53 Weeramantry, *Nauru*.

54 Ibid., 336.

[19] GLOBALIZATION AND NATIONAL IDENTITIES

Local and national identities are challenged by pressures which we group together under the rubric of globalization. Definitions vary, and the broadest denounces globalization as a tendency towards eliminating all but one way of thinking about economics, society and politics. More modest is Le Heron's delineation of a 'process of deepening and changing links throughout the global economy'.[1] This entails the movement offshore of what we used to consider 'national' capital; growing emphasis on and salience of foreign companies supplying domestic markets, while domestic firms supply overseas markets; exposure of the domestic economy to global floods of capital; and the increasing power of external pressures in shaping domestic policy. These elements promote linkages between domestic and overseas individuals, companies and governments, at the expense of domestic networks.

In this limited sense, globalization has been the experience of this region at least since Captain Cook, even perhaps Magellan, and conceivably Lapita. On that view, local and national identities and distinctiveness do not merely survive but thrive on it. To anticipate: some global pressures reinforced regional links. One difficulty in discussing globalization, however, is its ambit. As a notion it is helpful, but as an organizing principle it is required to marshal every dimension of every society's life. Here we focus on economic integration, neglecting globalization's powerful ideological and cultural dimensions, which we address in chapter 20. But even this brief is dizzily ambitious. Self-sufficiency was an aspiration of many indigenous economic networks, and settler societies proudly insulated their working conditions from global norms. Even a narrow focus on economic integration therefore leads to the heart of each society's sense of itself.

THE CLOSER ECONOMIC RELATIONSHIP

The two polities best equipped to respond to new circumstances were New Zealand and Australia, and for each the early 1970s were ominous. For some years both had endured declining terms of trade, as demand ebbed for primary products. For the first time since the Second World War national incomes were falling, and living standards with them. Their economies were disfigured by unemployment, and also by inflation, a rare combination which baffled economists and policy-makers. They now had to restructure their economies and cap their ballooning overseas debts. An economic era was drawing to a close, forcing each country to reassess its place in the world. Three especially disturbing events marked this transition. One was the first 'oil shock' as oil-producing countries formed a cartel and increased prices dramatically. Another was the general abandonment of fixed exchange rates for national currencies. Britain's entry into the European Common Market was the third, felt almost as betrayal by New Zealanders, who had expected perpetual access to Britain's dinner table.

On either side of the Tasman, policy-makers concluded that salvation lay in freer trade, and in closer relations (even perhaps integration) with East and Southeast Asia, and with each other. They must develop manufactures and process primary products (adding value to them). The economy's service sector, long neglected, assumed greater importance, and education (reconceptualized as part of the 'knowledge economy') was an obvious element in strengthening trade with the Pacific Rim. That strategy meant lower tariff barriers to imports, making life harder for manufacturers; it also meant lower barriers to immigration (and especially Asian immigration) which occurred in Australia in the 1970s and in New Zealand in the 1980s.

The obvious place to begin was with each other, revisiting issues left unresolved when New Zealand withdrew from federation negotiations.[2] Since 1966, economic relations had been shaped by a Free Trade Agreement which (despite its name) did not espouse all free trade. Both governments believed that growth would come in manufacturing, which needed tariff protection. That loose device was replaced in 1983 by a more ambitious agreement, providing for Closer Economic Relations (CER). By then both economies had endured a decade of poor performance, and New Zealand's severe balance-of-payments problems were depressing living standards and provoking another exodus to Australia. New Zealand expected major benefits from links to a larger and wealthier economy. Trans-Tasman trade did increase significantly, and so did the flow of investment, people and capital, although it brought neither country closer to the grail of complete free trade in the South Pacific and Southeast Asia. Five years later the agreement was extended to include services, though they did exempt some areas of particular sensitivity, such as airlines and coastal shipping, and especially radio and television broadcasting with their special cultural sensitivity (an exemption later deleted by litigation). CER was very successful, perhaps because there was already an integrated labour market: no visa was needed for trans-Tasman travel, and until 1981 no passport; citizens of one country had for decades enjoyed free access to the other labour market. The same was true of capital markets. Six of New Zealand's ten biggest banks, including the two largest, are Australian-owned since the National Australia Bank acquired the Bank of New Zealand. Those affected were consumers as much as producers (especially in New Zealand), and the regions most affected (Auckland, the Bay of Plenty, and Canterbury; and Queensland) were already deeply committed to trans-Tasman trade.[3] A New Zealand company acquired the largest Australian chain of bookshops, supermarket chains buy goods on a trans-Tasman basis, New Zealand television programmes are treated as 'domestic' in Australian regulations, and a case has been put for a common currency.[4] Economically the countries are integrated in ways that would astound the political leaders of the 1890s.

MULDOON AND DOUGLAS

The two economic strategies and ideologies were converging in other ways. In each country exchange rates were floated. The New Zealand float was 'clean', according to the monetarism fashionable in the 1980s, in that the level that the New Zealand dollar ended up floating at relative to other currencies in the international money market (notably the US dollar and the Australian dollar) was left to the free market. According to the dominant market ideology (evident in these descriptions of 'clean' and 'dirty') the New Zealand float was 'clean' because it was not influenced by state intervention. The floating of the Australian dollar, however (i.e. the shift from a fixed to a floating exchange rate regime) was subject to more direct intervention from the Australian Treasury. This intervention from the state – the public sector – is what made it 'dirty'.

Tariff protection was lowered from the 1970s in Australia and the 1980s in New Zealand, and a new vocabulary shaped the agenda of policy-making: privatization, corporatization, restructuring, down-sizing (and right-sizing), labour market reform (dismantling arbitration and even trade unions) and welfare reform (reducing the scope and scale of benefits). Their strategic problems were similar and in each case it fell to a Labo(u)r government to organize responses, yet the two governments behaved in revealingly different ways. To a great extent this was due to the circumstances they inherited, notably the legacy left to New Zealand by the National Party government of Robert Muldoon when it lost office in 1984. His philosophy was encapsulated in his observation: 'For my part I look back to Britain',[5] and his earnest desire to preserve the 'New Zealand way of life'. New Zealand's first effective television politician, he took his messages into the nation's living rooms. Since his war veteran father was an invalid, Robert was raised by his mother and grandmother, and articulated the anxiety of generations which had endured Depression and war, convinced that the individual did not exist for the state – rather the state for the individual. Social security was the inalienable right of every New Zealander.[6]

How to pay for it was the trick. His 1975 election campaign slogan, 'New Zealand the way you want it', hardly answered the question, but it conveyed different meanings for different people. His unambitious vision was to leave New Zealand no worse than he found it. The captivating image of and nostalgia for a vanished New Zealand wilfully denied Britain's entry into Europe: it was the end of the golden weather portended in the 1960s, from which it followed that regional relations would become even more important. The national superannuation scheme initiated in 1976, a very expensive bribe, was a foundation for 'New Zealand the way you want it', providing a generous pension to everyone over 60. It manifested 'political age-ing', and breached an implicit contract between generations.[7] The Depression generation were obvious winners, but the fund was affordable only with high inflation. By 1980, national superannuation comprised two-thirds of the social welfare budget.

The Muldoon government also swam vigorously against the global tide in other matters. New Zealand had a mixed economy, which became increasingly a 'command economy'.[8] Under the rubric 'Think Big', ambitious economic development projects were launched, expressing a belief that the government should manage the economy and exercise its executive power fully. Since interest rates were high, they were regulated downwards; and to arrest infla-tion the government imposed a price and wage freeze in 1982. To smooth currency markets, exchange controls were retained. For six months, each car owner had to choose one day a week when they would not drive. If that exer-cise in executive power alerted the public to an energy crisis, the opposite was achieved by fast-tracking approval for the Clyde Dam, built in earth-quake country to provide power for the aluminium smelter at the southern port of Bluff. Environmental negligence and authoritarian decisions like this speeded up the emergence of new, green political activism. In a massive example of his confrontational style, Muldoon also endorsed a tour by the South African rugby union team in 1981, ignoring anti-apartheid sentiment and relying on batons and barbed wire to protect games from demonstrators. Here – as elsewhere – was a contest between competing ideas of Aotearoa/ New Zealand, acted out on sports grounds across the country.[9]

The National Party – and the 1950s – won the next election, but at the cost of widespread disillusion and a surge of emigration to Australia. In a snap election in 1984 on nuclear issues, electors revealed their exasperation with the Nationals – and opened the door to deregulation. The extent of the Nationals' liability for the mess of New Zealand's economy in the 1980s is still a matter of debate, especially since the revolutionary changes since then have not produced the outcomes promised. New Zealand continued to do worse than Australia, across all economic indicators. The formation of the (anti-Muldoon) New Zealand Party in 1983, and his electoral defeat in 1984, really do mark a turning point in terms of the role of the state, but in terms of historical narratives there are some remarkable continuities between 'Muldoonism' (1975–84) and 'Rogernomics' (1984–90) and even beyond.

Australia's federal structure, and a Senate which governments rarely con-trol, restrain sharp swings in policy. Governments in New Zealand enjoy a free rein between elections, allowing extreme measures which are almost inconceivable in Australia. Until 1996 New Zealand's first-past-the-post vot-ing system, unlike Australia's preferential voting, also gave excessive weight to electoral swings. Arguably Muldoon's conservatism did therefore precipitate a revolution by the Labour government of David Lange and his finance minister Roger Douglas. This was a radical commitment (nicknamed Rogernomics) with deregulation, privatization, corporatization, dismantling labour market regulation including arbitration, welfare cutbacks, reducing the role of the state, and sado-monetarism in all its forms. As the climax of many assaults on unionism, New Zealand recreated nineteenth-century norms of bargaining between the employer and individual employees, through the Employment Contracts Act 1991.

For Douglas's defenders such as his cabinet colleague Michael Bassett,[10] Big Government began to 'overreach itself' in the 1970s (under Labour as well as National). In this framework Muldoon's final years become 'Big Government's Last Hurrah', replete with statistics revealing how appalling were conditions. In sweeping terms Bassett argues that the 'jerry-built economic structure' needed 'drastic restructuring' as a 'matter of urgency', and there was really no alternative to Douglas's strategy. It is unthinkable that 'big government can produce the best outcomes for ordinary New Zealanders'. He points out that Big Business did well out of Think Big schemes which were introduced on the assumption that world oil prices would keep on rising. Fletcher Challenge, the oil companies, and Equiticorp (a 1980s corporate raider which became bankrupt) did very well.[11] However, Bassett does not mention that it was the Labour government which sold these assets at fire sale prices: there was as much of an alliance between business and government in the 1980s as there was in the 1970s.

There are other continuities. New Zealand governments may be animated by a persistent need to do things faster, better, more thoroughly, than their neighbour, as if this were intrinsic to national identity. At any rate the move from more to less government was as abrupt as a lurch. Many features were nevertheless common to Muldoon's and Lange's governments. One was the desperation of a small player, ill-equipped to meet dramatic changes in the world economy. Another was a yearning to be a first-world economy despite having third-world resources, with income dependent on primary commodities. As governments lurched one way, then the other, they all clung to myths of natural abundance. A third was their shared self-assurance in using executive power to push through policies and practices which the electorate did not necessarily endorse or even understand. Colonial myths had become a problem, if not *the* problem.

AUSTRALIA AND APEC

If New Zealand Labour's agenda was partly shaped as a reaction against Muldoon's National Party, it was an earlier Australian Labor Party government which served as the negative example for Bob Hawke's Labor government which took office in 1983. Rightly or wrongly the Whitlam government (1972–5) left an odour of extravagance and economic irresponsibility, which the Hawke government (and the treasurer, Paul Keating) was determined to eschew. There were problems to be sure, but not on New Zealand's scale. The contraction of the global agricultural market affected both, but in Australia it was offset by a mineral boom created by new discoveries and a strong market in industrializing Asia. Manufacturing was in trouble (in New South Wales and Victoria) but new forms of global integration in finance, trade and tourism generated new activities, especially along the eastern seaboard.[12] If 'the bush' was suffering, 'the beach' of coastal resorts and developments was not. The change of strategy would be neither as urgent as in New Zealand nor (thanks to the constitution) as easy to push through, nor perhaps was the Labor government quite so evangelical about it.

While each government was fully aware of the other's programmes, they sometimes made reference to them when a political point could be scored (Australian non-Labor reformers would point to New Zealand's Labor government as a model). For a variety of reasons that rhetoric ebbed in the 1990s; there was no mindless emulation. Where Douglas drew a bead on trade unions and arbitration, Hawke used his background in the union movement to negotiate agreements (the Accords) with the peak union body (the Australian Council of Trade Unions) throughout the 1980s. In each case unions were declining in numbers and proportions of the workforce and in industrial and political strength. In Australia the fall was cushioned during the Hawke and Keating years, whereas New Zealand Labour dismantled its arbitration system directly, in the belief that a more flexible labour market would respond more rationally, creatively and swiftly to change in the global economy and in technologies. It fell to the Howard Coalition government of the 1990s to launch an all-out assault on unions, collective bargaining and arbitration. Again, Douglas introduced a Goods and Services Tax as early as 1985. Although Treasurer Keating mooted the same reform at a similar date, he backed down in the face of political resistance, and it was the Howard government which eventually introduced it in 2000, after a long and difficult battle at the polls and in the Senate. These episodes demonstrate perhaps the most decisive difference between the political systems: New Zealand governments can – and do – introduce new measures without prior warning, and at great speed. The Senate makes that impossible in Australia, where governments are often required to argue and to show that they enjoy a 'mandate' from the electors over and above a lower-house majority.

These governments differed in style and pace, but they were dealing with a common set of problems which they analysed in similar ways, so that the substance of what they attained is very similar. In each case finance capital outstripped and out-muscled industrial capital. The fate of Broken Hill Proprietary Ltd is emblematic. BHP began as a mining company which expanded into iron and steel in time for the Great War. Especially during the 1980s, BHP was 'the big Australian', the largest enterprise whose shares were essential in any portfolio. As it diversified into energy and oil, and became increasingly international, it rose to number 120 in *Fortune*'s list of the world's largest corporations. In New South Wales, Newcastle was almost a BHP steel company town, and BHP exerted influence on every government's policies on wages, tariff protection and industrial relations. An over-ambitious programme of overseas acquisitions, and increasing global competition in steel-making, brought BHP low. During the 1990s, as banks and then communications companies overtook it, the board hired American top management; 'non-performing' assets were ditched; the steel operations were closed down; and BHP reverted to being a minerals company.[13]

BHP's board sat in Melbourne, and as financial surpassed industrial capital, so did Melbourne yield to Sydney as the main centre of Australian economic decision-making. However, as in this case, it became difficult to distinguish global from national corporations, and pointless to try. That was especially true of financial institutions. Largely deregulated in the 1980s, banks rapidly blurred their national identities by acquiring and being acquired by other financial institutions in the region and America and Europe. The dominance of finance capital then reinforced the constituency for neo-classical analyses which saw trade unions as obstacles to enterprise rather than partners in production. Unemployment, and the decline of labour-intensive sectors of the economy, also helped to unbalance old accommodations between capital and labour.[14] Deregulated banks stumbled in the stock market crisis of 1987, and paid a heavy price for their aggressive lending; but from then on they not only prospered, but adopted new technologies and 'down-sized' their workforces and their physical branches. More broadly, down-sizing shed employees through automation and multi-skilling; but the growth of the tertiary sector, and of electronics, also casualized and feminized – and de-unionized – the workforce. Although trade unions survived (more powerfully in Australia than in New Zealand) they lost much political strength, and came to be portrayed by governments as enemies of progress. 'Thus abandoned was the defensive Australian historic compromise of social protection against the market', tariff protection and job creation.[15] The workingman's paradise was pensioned off: if there was a new icon, it was the consumer rather than a producer. To orthodox analysts this was anathema. Bruce Jesson, for a typical example, summed up his reaction in *Only Their Purpose Is Mad*, denying that the market-place is rational: 'Modern capitalism is highly rational in the methods it uses but is ultimately deranged in the purposes to which it puts them'.[16]

Partly through their own efforts, but largely because of global changes in Australia's and New Zealand's economic environment, Europe receded and East and Southeast Asia advanced as their trading partners. Until the 1950s three-fifths of Australia's overseas trade flowed to and from Western Europe, and especially Britain (New Zealand was even more dependent). By the 1990s Europe accounted for only one fifth, and APEC (see below) three-quarters.[17] This was only partly a consequence of the Japanese economic miracle and the rapid development of the rest of East and Southeast Asia: those economies grew much faster in their importance to Australia, than to the rest of the world. Japan had been Australia's leading trading partner for some years, but that relationship was set in concrete in the 1980s. One striking consequence of that relationship, and Japanese infatuation with the eastern seaboard, was to inflate the value of property in the cities and coastal resorts; in short, the Australian beach.[18]

If New Zealand governments were first reluctant to accept the demise of Britain and the salience of East Asia, the Hawke government embraced these realities with energy and ardour. The economic forum APEC – Asia-Pacific Economic Cooperation, four adjectives in search of a noun, as Gareth Evans called it – aspired to flatten tariffs and integrate regional markets totally. Much of the academic planning and diplomatic pioneering was mounted by the Hawke government. The forum grew to include virtually all Pacific Rim countries, and its heads of government meet regularly to incite each other to more tariff cutting. So committed was Prime Minister Keating that he provoked a minor crisis by accusing Malaysia's prickly prime minister of 'recalcitrance' in resisting tariff reductions. Similarly, Australian governments committed themselves early and eagerly to free trade in farm products (through the Cairns Group of agricultural exporting countries) and to the World Trade Organization, and to the admission of China to that body.[19]

Unlike Australia, New Zealand found rhetorical continuity. The workers' paradise was defunct (at least as an ideal) but what about empiricism and experiment? Rogernomics could be marketed as another 'New Zealand experiment' or even 'the great experiment' precisely because the revolution was more extreme and abrupt in New Zealand than in most other sites.[20] The smallness of New Zealand's economy and a centralized political system could be glossed as laboratory conditions. The allusion to Reeves's *State Experiments* (see chapter 11) was explicit and the continuities were not merely rhetorical. The state experiments of the 1890s and 1900s were defensive reactions to globalization in economics and population movements; defensive reactions persistently characterized public policy on both sides of the Tasman through the first half of the twentieth century. This new phase was also a response to globalization, but this time embracing rather than resisting it. There were other continuities. The zeal of the deregulators was remarkable, almost religious in its nature – Jane Kelsey calls it 'evangelical fervour'.[21] Since it amounted to a crusade (like the prophets of civilized capital in the 1890s and Truby King's child-care nurses between the wars) it had no time for democratic norms and procedures. Many of the missionaries (or in their term 'change agents') had been graduate students in America, embarrassed by New Zealand's parochialism, and yearning to drag their country into the global village. Once established in policy-making positions they formed a managerial 'new class', enjoying first-world salary and severance packages while insisting that other New Zealanders (and especially Pacific Islanders) be paid less, to compete with the third world.

If it was another experiment, was it as successful as the first? A hit by the successful New Zealand pop group of the 1970s, Split Enz, was 'Rust in my car', an allusion to the many jokes about the country's backwardness – unkind Australians thought it quaint to see so many very old model cars on New Zealand's narrow roads. Twenty years later New Zealand's drivers enjoy late-model cars, but there is no local car manufacturing industry, and Split Enz have re-formed as an Australian band. Venerable institutions have been dismantled, such as the Post Office which split into Telecom, NZ Post, PostBank, which were then privatized. There is a new entrepreneurial spirit but – as in Australia also – a great and widening gap between haves and have nots. For good or ill, it is now quite implausible for Australians and New Zealanders to believe that their societies are egalitarian.

If the Australian economy could boast remarkable growth despite Southeast Asian and Japanese recession, New Zealand's economy had modest claims, including sluggish growth and increased unemployment to the point where

1 in 3 were receiving benefits of some sort. A floating exchange rate was expected to solve balance-of-payments problems. It did not, and it enabled the New Zealand dollar to become a speculative currency. Between 1989 and 1994 foreign shareholding in New Zealand's top forty listed companies leapt from 19 per cent to 51 per cent, and the foreign shareholders also diversified. Conversely local companies expanded overseas. Perhaps most important was the displacement of the producer by the consumer as the object of policy concern. Low tariffs certainly made consumer goods cheaper, but introduced insecurity to those workers whose jobs survived the wave of international competition.

More interesting than the performance of these economies is their adoption of the criteria of business. The state not only tried to shrink and to withdraw from many services, it adopted the mores of business, so that those functions which could not (or not yet) be delegated to the private sector were often corporatized so as to resemble private businesses. The cluster of values summed up in 'public service' was systematically dismantled. Under such legislation as New Zealand's State Sector Act 1988, department heads became chief executives charged with a mission of efficiency and effectiveness. Deficits must be reduced, costs cut, and the workforce trimmed. Despite such 'anomalies' as the 1987 share market crash, which revealed instances of private sector incompetence and venality, governments insisted that the private sector was more efficient than the public, and that regulation (of banks, for example) was adequate. By adopting the ethics of business, furthermore, the state changed the balance of power and influence.

Curiously, as governments on either side of the Tasman dismantled structures which had been their national defining characteristics, the relationship between them gained rather than lost its salience. Globalization made Australia even more important to New Zealand at the end of the twentieth century than a generation earlier; and the converse may also be true. Again, a return to embracing globalization encourages the re-emergence of narratives of progress, innovation and the pioneering of new frontiers, not unlike the rhetoric of the nineteenth century.

MINING

A feature of the region's economies and their interaction has been mining, first in rushes by small operators, but increasingly by corporations deploying immense capital and cutting-edge technology. The industry is in no sense 'typical', but its evolution reveals ways in which local, regional and global values have impinged on each other. Until the 1960s most companies (except Le Société Nickel in New Caledonia) were managed by Australians, who imposed their methods and values.[22] In the 1930s, New Guinea gold was worked by Australian managers, artisans, traditions and capital (though one company, Placer, incorporated in Vancouver).[23] Indentured New Guineans did the heavy work, but this was otherwise an extension of the Australian industry. Although Australian mining laws were amended to recognize landowners, prospectors and officials treated them as enemies rather than partners. Australian conditions applied to white men while plantation rates were benchmarks for New Guineans, and the colour bar was as rigid as South Africa's.[24] As in Australia, the hottest debates pitted highly capitalized companies against small operators. To balance these interests, the mining laws were amended following a Royal Commission and heroic editing of the 195 sections of the Mining Ordinance, 214 regulations and 49 forms.[25] Miners might still strut their militancy, but strife was contained within arbitration and political processes.

Australians expected that their values were consistent with their prosperity, and would continue to be acceptable to their trading partners. Most investors were British until the 1940s, when the US took the lead.[26] As this capital was notionally 'white', it did not threaten 'white Australia' policies on migration and employment. Through the 1950s Australians were sheltered from global competition, but enjoyed prosperity and full employment. Only in the 1960s did the government wonder if a prosperous white Australia was really assured by nature or by the global economy.

Between the wars Japan was Australia's fastest growing market, although the flows shrank in the 1930s, for fear that Japan was building her offensive capacity.[27] After the Second World War the notion of 'strategic minerals' gradually lost its force, to the dismay of some veterans. To many Australians, Japanese were not only recent enemies but also generic Asians, whose investment should be discouraged. Only in 1968 did the government resolve to treat Asian investment like any other. Even then there could be 'special restrictions'.[28] Nor should foreign capital expect much freedom. An official told a Japanese delegation in 1967 that Australia

> would expect foreign companies to follow the practices of established Australian producers ... to be good employers; follow good mining practices; undertake the maximum processing possible ... and to receive the going price in the market place.

Japanese investors must accept the protection of white wages and work practices, and refrain from integrating their operations.[29]

One source of change was the transformation of the industry's structure, as national mining companies yielded to transnationals and new technologies processed very low-grade ores on a large scale. A leader in this reinvention of mining was Rio Tinto Zinc (RTZ) of London, which acquired 85 per cent of Conzinc Rio Tinto of Australia (CRA), which then expanded into iron, aluminium and base metals.[30] In 1964 CRA tested the Panguna deposit in Bougainville island in Papua New Guinea, where large-scale and low-grade copper ores were now 'prospective'. This new style of mining required a new legal framework, which emerged in 1966. That framework retained the Australian principle that the crown owned all sub-surface minerals:

> If the law were to be changed so that the minerals were owned by the people who owned the surface of the land, a very few people could become rich and

the whole of the rest of the Territory would be deprived of its proper share of the benefits of the mining.[31]

The new mining also required that each large mine be the subject of its own legislation. The Bougainville Agreement was negotiated by Australians, and one of the first acts of a self-governing Papua New Guinea was to renegotiate it – in favour of the government, not the landowners. In a mood of great confidence, the new government also rejected terms offered by the American mining giant Kennecott, to mine the Ok Tedi ore on the border with Irian Jaya. The ore was later mined by a consortium led by BHP, still at that time the Big Australian. In these negotiations the government deployed consultants recruited in a global market. These consultants, their global reach, and their commitment to Papua New Guinea's national interest, placed the government in a much stronger position than the former administration, whose knowledge and expertise were limited by Australian Public Service traditions.[32]

So much for the government's hopes: it soon became clear that landowners presented a much more formidable impediment to government revenue, than mining companies. Since the 1970s every successive mining agreement strengthened the hand of landowners and reduced the benefits for the central government. The decline of the central government's powers in rural areas is immediately obvious, such that landowners require companies to provide the roads, schools, hospitals and other services which they would otherwise miss entirely. In Bougainville, landowner rebellion closed the Panguna mine and provoked a full-scale, island-wide secession in 1989, and a civil war which endured for eight years. Conversely landowners on the Fly River, whose environment was transformed by Ok Tedi mine tailings, insisted on the mine continuing to operate as the only possible source of compensation and remedies for their plight.[33] They first sought remedies through the Papua New Guinea courts, but were blocked when the government legislated to make that impossible. Undaunted, they engaged lawyers in Melbourne and sued BHP for environmental damage. After two years of legal manoeuvre, in June 1996 BHP settled out of court and committed itself to:

- implementing a tailings containment system,
- pay K40 million (then about $A80 million) in compensation to the worst-affected areas,
- pay K110 million to all affected people.[34]

The public image of this encounter was naturally simpler than the realities, but for that reason powerful. Journalists, stock-brokers, environmental activists and the general public on either side of Torres Strait could represent 'Ok Tedi' as a litigious alternative to the civil war option taken up in Bougainville.

'Ok Tedi' now stands for the image of an environmentally destructive, greedy multinational miner who … was prepared to collaborate with the state to refuse democratic and legal right to those rural Papua New Guineans who opposed them. In this David and Goliath rematch, popular opinion weighed heavily against Goliath. The subsequent settlement of the lawsuit was claimed as a victory for the landowners by activists and the media (though this perspective was played down by the actual participants in the dispute), and hence Ok Tedi has come to be seen as an example of international justice and of the benefits of foreign lawsuits over violence (that is, Bougainville) in resolving disputes of this kind.[35]

Whatever the realities of Panguna and the Fly River, the values of Melanesian landowners have decisively changed the ways in which mining companies behave.

GLOBAL OR REGIONAL?

The effects of globalization on Pacific Islanders are paradoxical. Rather than growing physically closer, some communities have become even more remote from the rest of the world, relatively and even absolutely. And when integration has occurred, it is more often regional than global. Gerard Ward spells out some of the unexpected and unintended effects of improved technology.[36] New telecommunications technology and serious competition in the 1990s enabled Australia and New Zealand in effect to bring North America and Western Europe closer (see figure 19.1), while the Pacific Islands remain where they were a decade ago. Conversely New Zealand and Australian cities remain the nearest metropolitan centres for most Pacific Islanders, as nobody has grasped the opportunity to bring these small markets closer to (say) Southeast Asia or America. Long-haul airliners carry passengers non-stop from Sydney or Auckland to Los Angeles, so that fewer flights land in Fiji than they did in the 1980s. Similar technicalities and economics affect other island destinations, so that some outer islands are now more remote from New Zealand or Australian emergency services than they were at any time in living memory. Again, containerized shipping benefits most producers and consumers unless they produce and consume too few goods to fill containers, in which case they may have to rely on expensive or unreliable coastal vessels.

Many of the Islander intelligentsia, and Epeli Hau'ofa in particular, rejoice in their creation of – and access to – a transnational Oceanian community.[37] That expanding universe certainly includes Hawaii and California (see map 3c), but has large concentrations in New Zealand and Eastern Australia. Although migrants usually enjoy higher standards of living than those who stay at home, they perform worse and have fewer jobs and receive less pay than their new neighbours. In 1991 in New Zealand, Islanders were twice as likely to be unemployed, with predictable effects on education and health. The Tokelau Islands Migrant Study, conducted among Tokelauans at home and in New Zealand in the 1970s and 1980s,[38] found disturbing rates of coronary troubles and obesity among migrants, higher than among stay-at-homes; but the migrants were confident that their lives had improved, in terms of 'improved living standards, more independence, and better educational and

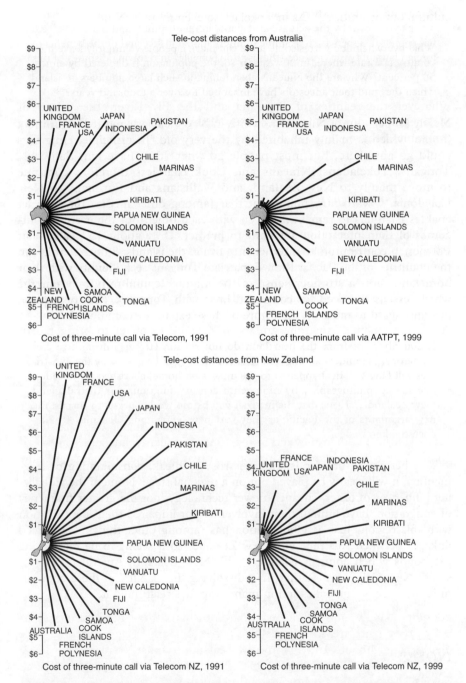

Figure 19.1 The world shrinking unevenly. The cost of a phone call expressed as distance from Australia and New Zealand. From 1991 to 1999 most of the world has come closer to Australia and New Zealand, but the Pacific Islands are no closer absolutely, and relatively more remote. Courtesy of R. Gerard Ward and the Cartography Unit, Research School of Pacific and Asian Studies, Australian National University.

421

cultural opportunities'.[39] As in Tokelau, so even more in Niue:

> What overwhelmingly irresistible force can make a people voluntarily leave their country at a rate where, in 20 years or so, the population is depleted by almost 50 per cent? Why are the Niueans abandoning in such large numbers an island which they and their ancestors have inhabited for over a thousand years?[40]

Nearly 90 per cent of Niueans now live in New Zealand, and few return to a 'home' which is mainly inhabited by the very old. In principle, emigrants could go anywhere, but most people go where they have kin. Samoans, Tongans, Tokelauans, Niueans and Cook Islanders therefore continue to move mainly to New Zealand, and Wallisians and Futunans to New Caledonia.[41] Ward now points out that (among other media) the internet enables Islanders to remain in touch with each other, but the eventual outcomes of that interaction are hard to predict. Only about 15 per cent of Polynesian contributors to internet sites live in the islands: 85 per cent live in the countries of the Pacific Rim. Expatriate Tongans seek identity with their homeland, but 'a stronger sense of the migrant community may emerge which lessens the need for continued links with Tonga'.[42] That perception prompts Ward to muse on the future of these expatriate communities:

> If contributions from the heartland do not remain strong, informative and numerous, the understanding and sense of identity to be gained by the expatriates will fade. ... This happened to the images of 'home' cherished for decades, like fading photographs, by nineteenth-century migrants to Australia and New Zealand. ... I fear that the internet will be too weak a vessel to sustain the new argonauts of the Pacific as they surf new, expanding Oceanias seeking ancestral knowledge.[43]

Whether the future for Islanders is rosy or bleak, consolidating or fragmenting, it will clearly be played out on a regional stage. None of the globalizing influences of faster, cheaper, newer technology, nor the greater frequency of emigration, have limited their involvement or impaired their identification with this region. Just as globalization has (among other things) reinforced linkages between Australia and New Zealand, so it seems to be reinforcing the bonds which connect Islanders with New Zealand, Australia and (for some) New Caledonia. Rather than dissolving the viability of these communities as a region, globalization in many ways has reaffirmed it.

NOTES

1   Richard Le Heron, 'Globalization and the Economy', in Richard Le Heron and Eric Pawson (eds), *Changing Places: New Zealand in the Nineties*, Auckland, 1996, 22.
2   Ian McLean, 'Trans-Tasman Trade Relations: Decline and Rise', in Richard Pomfret (ed.), *Australia's Trade Policies*, Melbourne, 1995.

3   Alan Bollard, Darcy McCormack and Mark Scanlan, *Closer Economic Relations: A View from Both Sides of the Tasman*, Wellington and Melbourne, 1986.
4   P. J. Lloyd, *The Future of CER: A Single Market for Australia and New Zealand*, Melbourne and Wellington, 1991.
5   R. D. Muldoon, *My Way*, Wellington, 1981.
6   R. D. Muldoon, *The Rise and Fall of a Young Turk*, Wellington, 1974.
7   David Thomson, *Selfish Generations?*, Wellington, 1991.
8   Michael Bassett, *The State in New Zealand 1840–1984: Socialism without Doctrines?*, Auckland, 1998, 17.
9   See Trevor Richards, *Dancing on Our Bones*, Wellington, 1999.
10 Bassett, *The State in New Zealand 1840–1984*.
11 Ibid., 367.
12 Robert H. Fagan and Michael Webber, *Global Restructuring: The Australian Experience*, Melbourne, 1994.
13 BHP Annual Reports; Fagan and Webber, *Global Restructuring*.
14 See, for example, R. Maddock and I. McLean (eds), *The Australian Economy in the Long Run*, Melbourne, 1987; B. Dyster and D. Meredith (eds), *Australia in the International Economy in the Twentieth Century*, Melbourne, 1990.
15 J. J. Pincus, in Pomfret (ed.), *Australia's Trade Policies*, Melbourne, 1995, 73.
16 B. Jesson, *Only Their Purpose is Mad*, Palmerston North, 1999, 10.
17 Pomfret, *Australia's Trade Policies*, 36.
18 Fagan and Webber, *Global Restructuring*, 68.
19 Pomfret, *Australia's Trade Policies*.
20 B. Easton, *The Commercialisation of New Zealand*, Auckland, 1997; J. Kelsey, *The New Zealand Experiment: A World Model for Structural Adjustment?*, Auckland, 1995; Francis G. Castles, Rolf Gerritsen and Jack Vowles (eds), *The Great Experiment: Labour Parties and Public Policy Transformation in Australia and New Zealand*, Auckland, 1996.
21 Kelsey, *The New Zealand Experiment*, 27.
22 For example, Hank Nelson, *Black, White and Gold: Gold Mining in Papua New Guinea, 1878–1930*, Canberra, 1976.
23 Ibid. Healey deals with Guinea Gold, Placer and Bulolo Gold Dredging companies.
24 Alan Healey, 'Bulolo: A History of the Development of the Bulolo Region, New Guinea', *New Guinea Research Bulletin*, 15, 1967; Donald Denoon, *Getting Under the Skin*, Melbourne, 2000.
25 Healey, 'Bulolo'; and A518/1, Z834/2, precis of Mr B. Dunstan's report of his investigations, 17 July 1931; T834/2, note of 19 July 1928.
26 Donald Denoon, *Settler Capitalism: The Dynamics of Dependent Development in the Southern Hemisphere*, Oxford, 1983.
27 Wray Vamplew (ed.), *Australian Historical Statistics*, Sydney, 1987.
28 Ibid.
29 A452/1, 67/3290, discussions, 6 April 1967. *Australian Financial Review*, 20 March and 6 April 1967; Denoon, *Getting Under the Skin*.
30 *Mining Journal*, 14 February 1969. Douglas Oliver, *Black Islanders: A Personal Perspective on Bougainville, 1937–1991*, Melbourne, 1991, ch. 8, is a clear introduction to this topic.
31 66/5311, unsigned departmental analysis, cited in Denoon, *Getting Under the Skin*.
32 Richard Jackson, *Ok Tedi: The Pot of Gold?*, Port Moresby, 1982, 82–3.
33 Glenn Banks and Chris Ballard (eds), *The Ok Tedi Settlement: Issues, Outcomes and Implications*, Canberra, 1997.

34 John Gordon, 'The Ok Tedi Lawsuit in Retrospect', in Banks and Ballard, *The Ok Tedi Settlement*.

35 Glenn Banks and Chris Ballard, 'Introduction: Settling Ok Tedi', in Banks and Ballard, *The Ok Tedi Settlement*, 1.

36 R. Gerard Ward, 'Widening World, Shrinking Worlds? The Reshaping of Oceania', the 1999 Pacific Lecture, Australian National University, Canberra.

37 Epeli Hau'ofa, 'Our Sea of Islands' and other contributors to E. Waddell, V. Naidu and E. Hau'ofa (eds), *A New Oceania: Rediscovering Our Sea of Islands*, Suva, 1993; Konai Thaman, 'The Defining Distance: People, Places and Worldview', *Pacific Viewpoint*, 26: 1 (1985), 106–15; Albert Wendt, 'Towards a New Oceania', in G. Amirthanayagam (ed.), *Writers in East–West Encounter: New Cultural Bearings*, London, 1982, 202–15.

38 C. Macpherson, 'Public and Private Views of Home: Will Western Samoan Migrants Return?' *Pacific Viewpoint*, 26 (1985), 242–64.

39 Albert Wessen et al., *Migration and Health in a Small Society: The Case of Tokelau*, Oxford, 1992, 383, 287.

40 H. Douglas, 'Niue: The Silent Village Green', in A. Hooper, *Class and Culture in the South Pacific*, Auckland, 1987, 186.

41 Karen Nero, 'The End of Insularity?' in D. Denoon, S. Firth, J. Linnekin, M. Meleisea and K. Nero (eds), *Cambridge History of the Pacific Islanders*, Cambridge, 1997, 439–67.

42 Helen Morton, 'Islanders in Space: Tongans Online', in John Connell and R. King (eds), *Small Worlds, Global Lives: Islands and Migration*, London, 1999.

43 Ward, 'Widening Worlds, Shrinking Worlds?'

[20] *POPULAR CULTURE*

Regional and national cultural traditions were secure while long-distance communication was slow, erratic and unevenly available. The advent of cable, telephone, radio, film and television, bringing remote communities into closer contact with centres of power and cultural production, enabled some colonists to emulate the speech and manners of the metropole. The New Zealand Department of Education, for an eloquent example, encouraged children to model their speech on recordings of the king's Christmas messages. Not for them would the future be tarnished by the 'colonial twang'.[1]

CULTURAL GLOBALIZATION

Every corner of the world is touched by cultural globalization and every debate asks whether this is more than the diffuse influence of American culture. Language gave English-speaking colonists – especially the well-connected – very easy access to the Atlantic centres of high culture. Richard Casey's diplomatic career took him from Melbourne to London and Versailles, then Washington and the Middle East, and he was British governor of Bengal before returning to Australia and the Menzies cabinet. After a term as minister for external affairs, he ended his career as Lord Casey, Australia's governor-general. Maie Casey's parallel career as artist, hostess and patron of the arts allowed her to relish the company of Australian painters (Sidney Nolan, Russell Drysdale) and writers (Patrick White, Rosemary Dobson) but also Katharine Hepburn, Noel Coward and Cecil Beaton.[2] Such exposure allowed some privileged individuals to present their wares on a broad stage, but wealth and connections were not essential. The scholar Peter Conrad's experience was not untypical, except in his description of it:

> I can remember the exact moment of my birth. It happened on Waterloo Bridge, on a morning in August 1968; I was twenty years old at the time.
> Those previous twenty years were, however, cancelled at that moment, relegated to a phase of pre-existence. I had spent them in Tasmania, reading about what my life would be like when I was reborn in the northern hemisphere. I was inclined to see this term of years as one of those penitential, ignominious lives you have to toil through in order to atone for crimes in some other incarnation.[3]

The penitential Tasmanian had no need to locate Waterloo bridge for his readers – near the spot where Macaulay had foreseen that 'some traveller from New Zealand shall, in the midst of a vast solitude, take his stand on a broken arch of London Bridge to sketch the ruins of St Pauls'.[4] Another Tasmanian, Helen Fraser, points out that the substitution of 'Australian' for 'English' school books in the 1960s exposed her to the arid outback, more alien to her than verdant England – and Tasmania.[5]

Easy access could also induce a 'cultural cringe', sowing doubt about one's own cultural production. Until the 1960s, the national broadcasters of both New Zealand and Australia insisted on BBC accents in their announcers (Papua New Guineans heard only Australian accents on the ABC local station). In reaction against the veneration of metropolitan culture, philistinism thrived. The conductor and composer Eugene Goossens ended his Australian career when customs officers found in his bags items to offend the puritan standards of the 1950s. He had, however, proposed an opera house for Sydney, and that led to a worldwide architectural competition in 1957. Joern Utzon's winning design was difficult and expensive: by the time Queen Elizabeth opened the Opera House in 1973 Utzon had been sacked, and the superb shells housed a modified concert hall and theatre which bore little resemblance to his vision, and the acoustics were miserable.

AN AUSTRALIAN HOAX

War between 'aesthetes' and 'Philistines' was not confined to architecture and opera. The conveniently deceased soldier-poet 'Ern Malley' was the 1944 brainchild of two young Australians, Harold Stewart and James McAuley, keen to expose what they saw as pretentious modernism and its arrogant advocates.[6] The poems of Ern Malley were hailed as work of genius by Max Harris, editor of the avant-garde journal *Angry Penguins*, which published the collection (*The Darkening Ecliptic*) in the autumn 1944 edition. In June the Sydney tabloid *Fact* published a statement by the authors explaining that their 'serious literary experiment' was designed to rescue literature and criticism from 'a literary fashion ... so hypnotically powerful that it can suspend the operation of critical intelligence':

> We have observed with distaste the gradual decay of meaning and craftsmanship in poetry. Mr Max Harris and other *Angry Penguins* writers represent an Australian outcrop of a literary fashion which has become prominent in England and America. [That fashion] rendered its devotees insensible of absurdity and incapable of ordinary discrimination.

Ern Malley's life-work had been produced in one afternoon, with the aid of the *Concise Oxford Dictionary*, the works of Shakespeare and a dictionary of quotations. The authors' principles were: no coherent theme, minimal attention to verse technique, and a style imitating 'the whole literary fashion as we knew it from the works of Dylan Thomas, Henry Treece and others'.

A bitter Harris later argued that, whatever the merits of the 'experiment', its timing and manner of handling ensured its success. In Australia and elsewhere, the press gleefully seized the chance to sensationalize and ridicule modernism.

Ern Malley was a *cause célèbre* throughout the English-language literary network, from the London *Times* to the American *Time* magazine. One publisher who was also 'taken in' published some Ern Malley poems in an anthology of Australian verse. The affair touched a sensitive chord among literati, and support for *Angry Penguins* came from leading British figures, including Sir Herbert Read, who confessed by telegram that

> I too would have been deceived by Ern Malley. But hoaxers hoisted by own petard as touched off unconscious sources of inspiration. Work too sophisticated but has elements of genuine poetry.[7]

Just as the discussion promised a considered debate, the tables turned again, and a youthful prank lurched into the ugly world of censorship. Charges were laid by the South Australian police against Harris and his journal, declaring seven of the poems 'indecent advertisements' and seven other items 'indecent, immoral or obscene'. It was no accident, Harris reflected, that charges were laid in Adelaide, 'a very small and small-minded regional city'. Modernism created more alarm there than in 'big cities or more advanced communities'. Whether Adelaide was exceptional or reflected the bowdlerism of federal and state censorship, 'a marathon police trial' eclipsed both the poems and the debate. A guilty verdict brought Harris a fine of £5 or twelve weeks' jail.

In 1952 Harris and others launched a new venture entitled *Ern Malley's Journal*, and the poems began to move from the modernist debate into broader fields of inquiry. Even their most consistent critics as poetry argue their merits as 'stimulus for paintings and sketches', poems and other writings. Most of all, the hoax became 'a focal point for modern Australian culture'. A critic concluded that the hoax

> touches on fundamental artistic issues of conscience, honesty, responsibility and artistic integrity. It is the kind of case that will always provoke interest as showing up conflicts between the conservatives and the radicals, the ancients and the moderns, the traditionalists and the experimentalists.[8]

In brief, the episode played differently in Adelaide than in overseas literary journals.

YOUTH REVOLUTION

Easy access also facilitated subversive relations. Richard Neville edited the student journal *Tharunka* at the new University of New South Wales. When the youthful President Kennedy was killed in 1963, Neville reflected that

> Our own Prime Minister, Sir Robert Menzies [monarchist, conservative and racist], was seventy. The NSW Premier, Mr Heffron, was seventy-three. The Chairman of the Literary Censorship Board was eighty-four. The Chancellor of Sydney University was in his nineties. ... In *Nation*, the writer Geoffrey Dutton contrasted this grim gerontocracy with the vibrant image of our country overseas, 'bounding from triumph on the tennis courts to bulldozing another million acres or two of virgin bush'. In reality 'youth in Australia controls nothing but the teenage gramophone business.' And not even that.[9]

The chief censor's age was germane, as *Tharunka*'s 'bad taste' brought down the wrath of the police as well as the university. Neville and others then created an independent magazine and named it *Oz* – alluding to the Yellow Brick Road rather than Australia. An outraged magistrate, fulminating against blasphemy and obscenity, launched the three editors' careers when he sentenced them to six months' hard labour, mercifully overturned on appeal. Soon afterwards Neville and others travelled overland to London and launched an English *Oz*. The 1970 obscenity trial of the London *Oz* – whose editors were defended by John Mortimer and Geoffrey Robertson – was a defining moment in liberalizing British censorship.

The trajectory of *Oz* is significant. Sydney was already a focus for libertarians (in the 'Push'), so the journal could attract the brilliant cartoonist Martin Sharp, Germaine Greer (on her way from Melbourne via Sydney to London, New York and Tuscany), Colin McInnes (established in London), Clive James (fleeing from Kogarah), Robert Hughes (en route to *Time* magazine from *The Fatal Shore*), Geoffrey Robertson (via Oxford to Amnesty, the English bench and television) and many others.[10] A pilgrimage to London was the birth-right of middle-class New Zealanders and Australians, though Neville was unusual in taking a side trip to New Caledonia and making his main journey overland. Robertson observes that British immigration laws formally affected the whole Commonwealth, though they were designed to limit the inflow of Africans, West Indians and Asians, but practice differed from principle, and Australians and New Zealanders found it easier than others to invoke officials' discretion and wriggle through loopholes.[11]

The ease with which protagonists of a youth revolution merged with their peers in Auckland, Sydney, London and New York gave them the illusion of global significance. It was as urgent in Auckland and Sydney as in London, to shrug off puritan supervision. Their commitments to peace (especially in Southeast Asia), non-racism (especially in South Africa and the USA), and rejection of puritan standards (especially on paper), reinforced their sense of globalism. To be Australian was no barrier to participation and leadership; and New Zealand and Australia were not mere consumers of journals and events in the cultural epicentres. Their sense of internationalism did perhaps blinker them to the boundaries of membership – educated youth – and the limited scope of their audience. New Caledonia was for Neville a mere holiday. Language kept France (let alone the rest of Europe and Asia) a closed book for most anglophone rebels, at least until 1968. The blend of a vague socialism infused by sexual liberation, anarchist ideas, marijuana and orientalism, sustained a youth counter-culture which was intolerable to older generations of New Zealanders, Australians and British outside the metropolitan centres.

It is significant that many rebels returned to Australia and New Zealand in the 1970s, to visit or to stay. Some returned from graduate school, determined to haul their countries into the global market-place. Partly this was a matter of transport economics. By 1970 the cost of air travel fell to the level of sea travel, so a traveller was no longer committed to at least three months away from home. Those with more time than cash trod the new Hippy Trail through Nepal and the Mediterranean. At the same time governments in the former dominions were eroding censorship, racism and Philistine smugness. An Australian critic described these, afterwards, as 'days of hope'.[12] One aspiration, especially among the young, was to end the generation-long reign of conservative parties and withdraw from the war in Vietnam. When both goals were realized by the end of 1972, with the election of the Australian Labor Party (proclaiming 'It's Time') and the New Zealand Labour Party ('It's Time for a Change'), the new governments explicitly attacked the 'cultural cringe', in Australia through the arts and New Zealand through a visionary foreign policy. No party had made so explicit an appeal to a creative intelligentsia and youth culture, and artists, filmmakers and writers – and anti-nuclear protesters – responded whole-heartedly, in the process dismissing the more timid reforms of earlier governments.

The assault may not have been totally successful, but in 1981 the commentator Vivian Smith declared that

> The era of cultural cringe and cringers is long over. The struggle for us now centres firmly on what sort of culture we have. How to represent adequately the rich yet controversial sites of our culture. ... How to articulate this new Australia of such abundance and diversity?[13]

POPULAR CULTURE

The new problem was no easier, but it has been approached with a new optimism, partly because the study of popular cultures everywhere has been transformed. Its rising status among academics has been dramatic since the 1970s, when it played a critical role in creating the 'New Humanities' in academia. As the author of *High Theory/Low Culture* argued, 'If anything needs defending now, it is that very high culture whose position in the university had once seemed so impregnable'.[14] Popular culture now enjoys the status of the foundation culture, the site of everyday life and everyday people. In New Zealand and Australia, the cult of the ordinary had been synonymous with authenticity, so the new respect for popular culture seems to formalize relations between popular and national cultures. It no longer situates itself specifically in the working classes, or among those without 'taste and education', but in the ordinary across age, gender, ethnicity and class.

At the same time 'class' was yielding to more sensitive tools (such as eth-nicity, or identity) for understanding social structures and values. The terms ruling class, middle class and working class no longer signify levels of culture. Raymond Williams's influential *Keywords* listed three categories of 'culture': processes, artefacts and way of life.[15] These are no longer helpful as organiz-ing concepts. Isolating categories of 'culture' denies their fluid and complex nature. It is 'the interconnectedness, contrasts and overlap of meanings' within this 'common life' that defines the new discourse.[16]

AMERICAN INFLUENCE AND LOCAL INVENTION

During the Second World War, GIs in Australia, New Zealand and the Islands presaged a more comprehensive American presence. The grip of American culture lies in the 1940s and 1950s when Hollywood's apparatus of fantasy-making captivated the war-weary, including New Zealanders and Australians, most vulnerable through their shared language. Indifferent to questions that troubled intellectuals, people embraced escapism in every medium. The glamour of American popular culture became synonymous with mass culture. British culture retained sentimental and cultural magnet-ism for many, but the drabness of postwar Britain could not compete with technicolor California.

For the priests of high culture in the West – the main critics of mass cul-ture – the process was slower and predicated on different values and needs. The Stalinism that tainted the Left prompted many to seek new political alignments. American culture might be vulgar but its values were grounded in concepts of freedom and choice with which New Zealanders and Australians could identify. The struggle for equality as enshrined in socialist Russia gave way to the celebration of freedom as symbolized by America. The 'pop' aesthetic of the early Cold War provided a new logic for the mass culture. 'Pop' problematized 'the nature of taste itself: what is valuable is not what is original but what is replicated, not what is timeless but what is by nature ephemeral and obsolescent.' If high culture with its emphasis on excellence was prohibitive, 'middle culture', gravitating towards the vulgar, was equally undesirable.[17]

In reality, most people in the region were sheltered from Americanism by remote location, language and colonial paternalism. The intrusive influences in Islanders' lives were Australian and New Zealand: they more often criti-cized their exclusion from cultural novelty than complained about cultural impositions. While censorship was unwinding in the dominions, a parallel movement dismantled many racial constraints in the Islands. The most dramatic was the abolition after the Pacific war of the *indigenat* which sub-jected Kanak to paternal laws and regulations. More slowly, ordinances were rescinded to allow Papuans and New Guineans to wear clothes above the waist, drink alcohol, play contact sports, commit adultery without break-ing the criminal code, and engage in inter-racial sex without incurring a death penalty.[18] More comprehensive was the liberalization of relations between Samoans, Cook Islanders and Niueans as they won self-government. For Melanesians, liberation movement was slower, but the normalization of race relations opened towns to internal migration: colonial towns began to evolve into Melanesian cities.[19] A few Melanesians (under escort or in domestic employment) had visited Australia for political education or with employers; more during the 1960s boarded at Australian high schools; and in 1969 the first two travelled freely.[20] While Australian radicals explored the London underground, Melanesians blazed trails to Brisbane and Sydney to allow a flow of kin, or commodities.[21]

As more encounters took place in the urban centres, questions of national language became urgent. Whereas Australians and New Zealanders (Pakeha) focused on accent, language itself was the issue in Melanesia. A World Bank survey of Papua New Guinea in 1963 was surprised that only half of each age cohort went to school at all, and only 14 pupils (in a population of 2 million) completed high school in the country (though some also studied in Australia). As in Solomon Islands and the New Hebrides, most schooling was provided by missions, and there was little technical education,[22] so that many political leaders were priests or ex-seminarians, infusing nationalist discourse with Christian values. English was the medium of government, but no language was widely enough spoken to serve a national purpose. Tok Pisin was a lingua franca for many men, especially in New Guinea; Hiri Motu served the same purpose along the Papuan coast; another pijin was spoken in Solomon Islands, and Bislama in New Hebrides; but they needed development if they were to become national languages like Bahasa or Hebrew. Constitutions conferred national status on these languages, but provided no resources for them to fulfil their task. Many members of the first parliaments had to speak in pidgin, but each election returned more Western-educated members, making English (or French in Vanuatu) the language of parliament as well as government, commerce and education. Maori became an official language in New Zealand in the Maori Language Act of 1987, following the *Te Reo* (language) report of the Waitangi Tribunal (see chapter 17); and some Maori MPs chose to speak in Maori to make a political point. But *Te Reo* needed more than this gesture to keep it alive: this demanded resources and commitment.

Language was one dimension of a general fascination with culture. Intellectuals often sought to revive tradition (or *kastom*) as a basis for national unity, but tradition was difficult to delineate and often divisive. Cultural engineering was not revolutionary: Melanesians had 'a tradition of remaking tradition' and cultural innovation was the hallmark of 'cargo cults' which dismayed colonial administrators.[23] By the 1960s *kastom* had embraced Christianity, as well as other elements of the colonial inheritance which were reassessed and – whenever possible – harnessed to the task of nation-building.

Among the new rhetorics were Melanesian socialism (for the Vanua'aku Pati in Vanuatu), *vakavanua* in Fiji (the 'way of the land'), and in Papua New Guinea the 'Melanesian Way'. The leading ideologist of the Melanesian Way, Bernard Narakobi (a Catholic lawyer) denied that Melanesian cultures were 'so varied and contradictory as many have claimed. ... We are a united people because of our common vision'.[24] Constitutions and politicians wove *kastom* into national institutions. Thus Vanuatu's constitution defined the state as based on 'traditional Melanesian values', and the government promoted Bislama – and even installed *kava* as the national drug. Like Fiji, Vanuatu acknowledged a leading role for chiefs in elucidating tradition. Reference to Melanesian values marked off the successor-states from their predecessors, but *kastom* and tradition were frail foundations for nationhood:

> This rhetoric smiles with promises of cultural identity and social regulation, but Vanuatu and Papua New Guinea have felt *kastom*'s teeth. ... *Kastom* can serve as an idiom of national identity and as a mechanism of state regularization and control; but it may enunciate opposition and resistance with equal facility.[25]

FROM BUSH TO BEACH AUSTRALIA

Debates about national culture touch raw nerves: multicultural tensions exist in many Islands, while in New Zealand, New Caledonia and Fiji bicultural issues are explosive. Australian debates address reconciliation between Aboriginal and non-Aboriginal Australia, multicultural citizenship, the republic and the feminist agenda. Australian and New Zealand 'new histories' question the identification of high culture with empire, and of low culture with the 'real' community. They also challenge the privileging of Anglo-Celtic societies as the mainstream, and the dominance of the male in representing popular culture.

In 1968 Craig McGregor drew up a constellation of symbols to represent Australian experience: 'bush picnics, Anzac Day, the Melbourne Cup, surf lifesavers, poker machines, transistors, on the beach, backyard barbecues and Sunday in the car'.[26] A quarter of a century later he reflected on 'meaning and significance in everyday Australia' in a piece called 'The beach, the coast, the signifier, the feral transcendence and pumpin' at Byron Bay'. His argument was not novel: 'Today it is the beach, rather than the bush, and the beach-goer, rather than the bushman, which [identifies] what is typical about Australia'. More significant was the brash language and style. The form more than the content signalled the arrival of popular culture in academia.

A new generation of white, Anglo-Celtic, urban male intellectuals entered debates on national identity, bearing a new icon: still in the bronzed image of the male, holding the torch of mateship between drinking bouts, still seeing women as sexual objects (though 'Damned Whores' had become 'Randy Tarts'). For all their critique of the Bush Legend – 'male chauvinist, racist, historically flawed' – advocates of the Beach argued a similar case. Beach Australia, they conceded, may be as unrealistic as the bush, as neither took account of the powerful urban pull, but the beach – like the bush – has 'enormous mythic power' for Australians. A new icon was crowned, arguably more irrelevant, ahistorical and marginal than its predecessor.[27]

Members of the First Fleet saw Aborigines swimming in the ocean, and took to the water themselves with delight; but recreational use of the beach declined through the next century, in response to official discouragement. By the end of the century it was a crime to swim at the beach except in very limited circumstances. The breakthrough occurred only in the early 1900s. Young white men once again envied Aborigines swimming at Manly in sub-urban Sydney, and noticed that they were not taken by sharks. Sea-bathing became common (but still illicit) until middle-class activists made it a politi-cal issue. So successful was this campaign that sea-bathing was not only decriminalized, but in a decade almost mandatory. The beach became the prime site for building strong, tanned colonial bodies.[28]

In a later but equally decisive shift in images in advertisements and tourist icons, the Bush yielded to the Beach as the quintessential site also of Australian culture. This shift and its implications eventually reached acade-mia, which embraced 'popular culture' fervently. This about-face has implica-tions for the way common people are understood, their choices legitimated, their agency confirmed. The consumer of mass culture, once seen as both vic-tim and perpetrator of mass culture, a thoughtless consumer of vulgar com-modities, is now credited with more complex discernment. 'Consumption is not a sign of passive acceptance of the dominant ideology but a form of "utterance".'[29]

Australian popular culture had been defined both as the people's lowly culture, and the product of the true Australian. This knot is hard to untie. Class associations located the culture among the working masses as well as at the heart of Bush Australia. Self-styled 'radicals' of the Left saw no tension between espousing the cause of the masses and contempt for those who com-prised them: in the words of a radical of the 1900s, 'the swearing, sweating, tobacco-juicing proletariat – the "breeders"'.[30] The irony that began with the wedding of popular culture and Australian identity, consecrated by white male intellectuals, came full circle when lowly popular culture entered academia.

The writers and artists to whom this challenge fell between the 1930s and the 1950s had perhaps the best conditions in which to exploit links between art and country, high and popular culture and audiences. Yet they drew the sharpest lines between themselves and their compatriots, between 'good' and 'popular' art and entertainment. A few grasped the implications of the estrangement: at the height of the Depression, William Baylebridge won-dered whether 'the best bread for a literary worker in Australia might easily, under present conditions, be the bread earnt at something beyond literature'.[31]

Patterns of settlement made 'the coast' and 'the beach' a feature of the 'Australian way of life' throughout the twentieth century, but acknowledge-ment of this fact was tardy because of the Bush's grip on popular imagina-tion. The Bush did recede in the national imagination as mechanization displaced rural workers, transforming many farms into family operations – and replacing Labor Party with Country Party members. The Bush also suf-fered from the decline of the Old Left. The Bush was shaped by 'second wave' radical nationalists – strong and articulate voices in cultural, literary and political circles in postwar Australia, all white urban male intellectuals of the Left like the novelist Vance Palmer and the historians Russel Ward and Brian Fitzpatrick. In their hands the Bush became a heartland of anti-imperial ideology. Shaped and flavoured by their writings, the Bush became identified with the 'true' Australia, free of the Mother Country: it seemed almost un-Australian to challenge it. The Labor Party therefore sought to retain its links to it and the Left best understood and exploited its possibilities.

The rise of the New Left in the 1970s was the beginning of the end. From its leading voices – Humphrey McQueen in particular – came a critique of the Bush as outdated. The Bush drew its force from receding realities: convicts and the empire. At its core lay an assumption about Australians committed to a radical path of change which failed time and again, in two depressions, two world wars, and Chifley's use of federal troops to break the miners' strike of 1948. The Bush focused attention inward, ignoring the Vietnam War, the 'woman problem' or indigenous politics. Nor could it translate fluently into global debate. The Bush, then, was unsettled by globalization. It was not buried overnight, nor was its demise altogether the product of New Left inter-nationalism, but it needed movement and vision from within to begin and to legitimize its overthrow.

The vacated space allowed new icons to appear: the city as the central site of modern Australia, suburbia as home to most Australians, the coast linking capital cities, and the beach as playground and sacred site. The move from the centre to the margins required finesse. To make a metropolitan European Australia of the city, the Austerica of the suburbs, the coast-dweller's discovery of Asia-Pacific neighbours and affinities, the cult of the beach with its emphasis on youth, sun and fun – how could these be brought into focus without seeming to betray the egalitarian and collectivist values of the Bush?

If the 1970s and 1980s saw an explosion of interest in urban Australia, the 1990s focus was on coast and beach cultures. The implications were diffuse. The Great Australian Emptiness – as the novelist Patrick White called it on his return 'home' from Europe in the 1960s – had little resonance in the lives of ordinary people. The tyranny of distance – explored by the historian Geoffrey Blainey – no longer dismayed people at home in the region. Images of Australian emptiness and distance were more imagined than real, the province of intellectuals who imported the preoccupations of high culture. Ordinary Australian leisure activities, their icons – often sports icons – and their sense of 'home' were securely anchored, and mostly to the coast. Many sports heroes were already showing the friendly, sunburnt, outdoors Australian face to the wider world.

Beach Australia borrows from earlier images. The bronzed surfer is kin to the bushman and the digger, more physical than intellectual, fearless and defiant; his, too, is a body on display. He has little attachment to a particular place, but lifesaving clubs manifest his commitment to fellow surfers. Mateship wears fewer clothes, but is no less a religion. The Beach presents a friendlier, cosmopolitan Australia. The designer Ken Done's images of a sunny people on perpetual holiday draw strength from the elements of Beach Australia: primary colours, endless coastline, a people worshipping their birthright of sand, sun and surf. From the weary stalwart bushman to the young surfer lies a transformation of visions and values. Anti-imperialism yielded to internationalism, and to the demands of a global economy.

CLEAN, GREEN NEW ZEALAND

The shift from bush to beach rendered Australia an island, and part of the Pacific. Beach Australians became beach-crossers in a globalized world. But New Zealanders had no great distance to travel from bush to beach; in their archipelago, as tourism brochures emphasized, mountain and beach are side by side. 'Our Aotearoa. A young island nation at the end of the earth, like nowhere else', enthused an advertising leaflet for APEC meetings in Auckland and Christchurch in 1999. 'We came as adventurers and pioneers and our questing spirit remains ... we are the world's greatest travellers', its writers gushed. The pioneer myth and myth of natural abundance persisted: 'Lush, rich and productive, grass, bush, forests, farmlands, fiords, waterfalls, glaciers, lakes, rivers, beaches and fresh air.' All ingredients of an invented settler culture and identity lived on in clean, green New Zealand, including the cliché 'Godzone', from the nineteenth-century 'God's Own Country', the slogan of Premier Richard Seddon in the 1890s and early 1900s.[32]

This suggests a resettlement by colonial icons, but it is more a transmutation of colonial into global icons that New Zealanders, collectively, have undertaken. That shift is illustrated by the continued esteem for Sir Edmund Hillary. The conqueror of Everest enjoyed a state birthday party (on turning 80) in 1999, held in his honour at Government House. Sir Edmund is the only living New Zealander with his head on a banknote – the $5 note, which has the highest rate of circulation. This mountaineer and adventurer encapsulates what is valued in Kiwi culture: a pioneer and an imperial icon, knighted for climbing Everest for the (young) queen's coronation, for being the first and the best; a gentleman with a larrikin streak, adventurous and courageous, practical, and a family man. He strides through bush, snow, ice and rapids.[33] He moved easily from imperial to global icon. Already a symbol of overseas success, climbing Everest was by definition a global achievement, as were his later exploits, driving a tractor to the South Pole.

FILM

Creators of identity in the 1890s worked mainly in print: poets, novelists and propagandists in Australia and New Zealand, travel writers and anthropologists in the Islands. First film, then television, became increasingly important thereafter. For the Islands this transition replaced one set of foreign imagemakers with another. New Guinea generated ethnographic documentaries of high quality, beginning with *Dead Birds* set in Irian Jaya, and including *Trobriand Cricket* and *Ongka's Last Moka*.[34] These have been matched by accounts of the Pacific war in *Angels of War* and *Senso Daughters*.[35] Indigenous servicemen and civilian women are the focus of these Australian and

Japanese accounts, but they do not control their own images. The same is true of the Leahy family trilogy: *First Contact* reconstructs the first meetings of prospectors and Highlanders; *Joe Leahy's Neighbours* follows an unacknowledged son in creating a plantation in partnership with customary landowners; and *Black Harvest* describes the tragic outcome of this collaboration.[36] Dennis O'Rourke made political films on television (*Yap: How Did You Know We'd Like TV?*) and nuclear testing (*Half Life*),[37] powerfully presenting Islander perspectives, but nonetheless an outsider's vision. The closest that Islanders have so far come to control is as advisers, as in *Auckland Fa'aSamoa* where Albert Wendt was consultant.[38] Only in New Zealand and Australia has filmmaking become an instrument for creating and disseminating people's views of themselves, their ancestors, and their countries' place in the world.

Australian film was for many years constrained by a small local market, a cultural cringe, and a chronic lack of funding and expertise. Unlike literature and painting, it was not British or European imports that threatened local producers, but Hollywood's grip on the genre as well as the market. Through the 1940s, 1950s and 1960s film remained a Cinderella. *The Adventures of Barry McKenzie* (1972) and *Alvin Purple* (1973) with their penchant for 'cleavage and crudity' did little to help,[39] but the pendulum then swung to aesthetic period films. The 1975 *Report of the Interim Board of the Australian Film Commission* (AFC) recommended retention of the essential and distinctive, shedding the provincial and crass. A new aesthetics was emerging to define 'Australian art', and the second birth of Australian film reflects this. Heading the commission's priorities was 'ocker...out', and '"quality" films in'. The first crop – full of 'quality' – therefore became known as 'the AFC genre'. *Picnic at Hanging Rock* (1975), *Caddie* (1976), *The Getting of Wisdom* (1977), *The Last Picture Show Man* (1977), *My Brilliant Career* (1979), *Breaker Morant* (1980) and *Gallipoli* (1981) all raised the stature of Australian film at home and abroad. Ranging across the bush, battlers, the spirit of place, war and the empire, working-class *vs* genteel culture, they shared attention to period detail, a keen aesthetic eye, and superior photography. Several of their creators (Peter Weir, Bruce Beresford) and actors (Judy Davis, Mel Gibson, Sam Neill, Wendy Hughes, Angela Punch-McGregor and Jack Thompson) became international stars.

For all its virtues, 'the AFC genre' became a strait-jacket. Conceived as cultural flagships, the films projected stereotypes of colonial society, waving the banner of radical nationalism, still burdened with the imperial connection. Just as Whitlam's Labor government was setting an agenda of tolerance, shattering the illusion of homogeneity, the period films reaffirmed colonial Australia.[40] A few challenges to the stereotypes – *Promised Woman* (1975), *The Chant of Jimmie Blacksmith* (1978), *Kostas* (1978) – proved the point. By contrast *Crocodile Dundee* (1986) made a fortune by endorsing stereotypes: for Meaghan Morris it reveals some of the obstacles to national self-definition in international cultural markets.[41] By the late 1980s the industry was facing crises in both funding and imagination. Government rebates had ceased, and the period formula was exhausted.

Opting to develop an 'idiosyncratic vernacular' distinct from the broad canvas of contemporary Western film, Australian cinema in the 1990s shed the formula and the cultural cringe. In one record-breaking week in 1992 *Strictly Ballroom* and *Romper Stomper* topped earnings around the country. The next year, 3 of 23 films chosen to compete at the Cannes Film Festival were Australian. They were contemporary, urban and multicultural.[42] Ben Gannon, producer of *The Heartbreak Kid* (1993), noted that

> we found that in the majority of inner-city schools, the percentage of Asians, Greek, Lebanese and Muslim students far outweighed the Anglos. I don't believe that any recent Australian film has really reflected just what a total melting pot contemporary Australian society is.[43]

New Zealand film flourished and was all but destroyed, through greed, in the early 1980s because the New Zealand Film Commission identified and exploited a tax shelter for investors. Once the loophole closed, investment collapsed; globalization required overseas investment and an international product, or small-budget, boutique films as a way of telling, and seeing, New Zealanders' own stories. Until *Once Were Warriors* (1994), *Goodbye Pork Pie* (1980) was the most-seen New Zealand film. A road movie, it was the first New Zealand feature, with Albert Wendt's Samoan–New Zealand tragedy *Sons for the Return Home*, to screen at Cannes. A sexist movie of 'blokes' on the run, it nonetheless ended the cultural cringe in New Zealand film, by earning acclaim at home and a profit abroad. If its themes were shared with Australian narratives, the film's star was not: an ageing yellow Mini, a comment on New Zealand cars at the time (and a British icon). The New Zealand landscape starred in Vincent Ward's gothic *Vigil* (1984), a success at Cannes. With the Maori cultural revival Maori voices and faces emerged, in the Maori-directed *Patu!* (by Merata Mita, 1983), a documentary account of the Springbok tour from the protesters' point of view, and the Pakeha-framed *Utu*, a fictitious account of the land wars (1983). Jane Campion's *The Piano* (1993) lifted New Zealand film not only to celebration at Cannes, where it won the Palme d'Or, but in Hollywood, at the Academy Awards. Anna Paquin, aged nine, became the second-youngest winner, for supporting actress, as the daughter of the 'mute mail-order bride' in *The Piano*, while Campion won the Oscar for best original screenplay.[44] This was not an insider's film, but an expatriate view of New Zealand. Jane Campion had left New Zealand because she could not be herself. The male lead, the New Zealander Sam Neill, had also become Australian. The film's evocative images, of the *waka* (canoe), the piano on the wild beach, and mud, resonated with New Zealand dreamings from Sydney. Technically *The Piano* was not a New Zealand film but an Australian production, funded by French money. Campion insisted it was a New Zealand film: most of the cast and crew were local, and the theme of womanly sensibility and pioneering belonged to Pakeha narratives. Aesthetically, it belonged to New Zealand but the representation of Pakeha–Maori relations no longer convinced Pakeha audiences in Aotearoa. A product of economic integration, this film reflected the end of the cultural cringe.

The imprimatur of overseas success, however, still resonated in the New Zealand psyche. The blockbuster *Once Were Warriors* (1994) marked another phase in the formation of collective identity. Based on the dark novel by the Pakeha–Maori author Alan Duff, it exposed simmering anger among urban Maori and domestic violence. This movie was a product of the deregulation of broadcasting. Its Maori director, Lee Tamahori, was a commercial television producer whose independent production company became the most prolific after deregulation. Tamahori had earned a reputation for slick television advertisements (notably for Anchor butter and milk). For two months, *Once Were Warriors* was the most successful film at the box office in New Zealand history (until again overtaken by Hollywood). Hollywood itself claimed Tamahori, although Peter Jackson stayed home. The director of *Heavenly Creatures* (1994), which recreated the infamous Parker-Hulme murder case of 1954 in Christchurch, where two teenage girls murdered the mother of one, he went on to produce *The Frighteners*, starring Michael J. Fox, and *Lord of the Rings*, also filmed locally, using New Zealand laser technology and landscapes.[45]

A new confidence and creativity marks these films, their artistic successes widely attributed to the industry's embrace of cultural pluralism. Globalization has also embraced the industry, providing a world audience and funding for local products, and bringing a local audience their own stories.

SPORT

The labour movement's victories in colonial Australia and New Zealand reduced working hours, liberated Saturday afternoons and created the weekend. For young men especially, organized sport filled the gap. That gender preference persisted: men may not outnumber women players, but their games have attracted larger audiences (in the flesh, in print, on radio and television) than women's. Cricket, hockey, rugby union and league, soccer and netball were adopted from England, but Australian Rules Football was a Melbourne invention of the 1850s, to occupy cricket ovals and cricketers through the winter. Suburbs identified with clubs, which found their way to the heart of community life, in Melbourne but also in country towns. Competitive team sport became an immediate means of separating colonial from imperial loyalties, yet there was always ambiguity. Australians and New Zealanders had facilities (level fields and lawns, balls, bats, pads) but they also possessed the inclination to play by British rules: the body presiding over the laws and traditions of cricket, for example, was the Imperial Cricket Conference (becoming 'International' much later). The first Australian cricket tour of England involved exclusively Aboriginal players, who also displayed the boomerang, but colonists soon replaced them as the proper representatives of their country.[46] Neither the whole-village cricket of Samoans, nor the feathered splendour of Trobriand Islanders, nor the more conventional women's cricket matches of Papua acknowledged these rules and conventions. It was rare for Papuan mission station men's teams to play

Australian residents,[47] and unthinkable until the 1950s that they would travel abroad or even form a 'national' team.

Sport reflected race relations in other ways. Maori eagerly adopted rugby union, and from an early date the New Zealand All Blacks included Maori. Other Polynesians also adopted rugby union, and in New Zealand they played for established clubs. By contrast (but consistent with colonial paternal values) New Guineans and Papuans were banned from all contact sports until the 1950s, lest they rupture spleens, swollen by malaria. The pre-eminent rugby union nations were Wales, England, New Zealand and segregated South Africa. To indulge white South African sensibilities, Maori were not selected to tour South Africa. Similarly, racial integration did not transform Australian sports until the 1950s, thereby barring one of the broadest avenues for social advance by working-class boys. Boxing offered a career for some Aboriginal men, team sports did not. On a larger scale, international cricket became distinctively white in Victorian times. There was an Australian cricket team for years before Australian federation, but the ultimate prize was 'the ashes' – the remains of English cricket, following defeat by Australians in 1882 – contested only by Australia and England. There was also a West Indian cricket team before West Indian federation, but captained by white men; and Indian princes played for England, but Indian (and Pakistani and Sri Lankan) teams were slow to win imperial acceptance. Cricket remained largely a white man's preserve until the Second World War.

Sport allowed Australians and New Zealanders to display their prowess at Olympic and Empire (later Commonwealth) Games, as well as the tennis circuit and test series in cricket, rugby union and rugby league. Only Australian Rules flourished in the fervent parochialisms of Victoria, South Australia, Western Australia and Tasmania; yet Australian Rules clubs always had more members, and drew bigger gates, than the other codes. (In the 1990s international games were played between Irish and Australian teams, under hybrid rules.) To accommodate a sports-hungry public, councils and state governments built massive stadia, and national governments chipped in to help win the right to host Olympic games (Melbourne in 1956, Sydney in 2000), Empire (Auckland in 1950) then Commonwealth games (Christchurch in 1974, Brisbane in 1982) as well as every code of football competition, cricket and hockey.

Befitting their English cultural traditions, team players were not paid, which implied that they took part for pleasure and patriotism. On this issue English rugby split in the 1890s between (amateur) union and (paid) league, the latter drawing mainly working-class and northern support. In 1907 that split reached Sydney, where league appealed more to Catholic and to Labor supporters than to Protestants and non-Labor.[48] Cricket would unite Australians, but each winter revealed divisions. Rugby union and league were dominant winter sports in Queensland and New South Wales; Australian Rules everywhere else; while soccer attracted mainly first-generation migrants. That division was blurred at the edges. Australian Rules was always played along the New South Wales border with Victoria; Maori were quicker than Pakeha to enlist in rugby league; and rugby union players in New Zealand

and Australia developed a tradition of 'boot money' which was really covert wages. Without such funds, many amateurs could not represent their country, especially when a trip to England took players away for most of a year.

It was cricket in which a global revolution first erupted. From the 1920s to the 1940s cricket reached the peak of its appeal as an amateur code. Don Bradman was acknowledged as the greatest living cricketer, perhaps greater even than the nineteenth-century English icon W. G. Grace. In 1932–3 England's methods of curbing his talents by 'bodyline' bowling (legal, but in Australian eyes 'not cricket') rallied the Australian nation like no other issue.[49] By the 1960s, however, the pace of five-day test cricket was repelling audiences, whether live or on television. Australians were winning tennis championships at Wimbledon, Paris, New York and Melbourne, and the Davis Cup in most years, offering a patriotic public a compelling and more tightly packaged spectacle. The problem was alleviated by improved televised coverage from the 1970s, but that accentuated the contrast between amateur players and their commercial value. Tennis shed its amateur fig-leaf in 1968, but cricket's tensions festered until Kerry Packer, proprietor of an Australian television company, recruited leading players, offered them real incomes, and organized the first 'one-day' matches. As against traditional cream flannel, lengthy (and often drawn) matches, and mainly live audiences, World Series Cricket offered coloured uniforms, quick results, and a game whose rhythms were tailor-made for television advertising. The transition from feudalism to capitalism was no more dramatic nor more complete. The World Series 'circus' survived only for two seasons before cricket was reunited, on Packer's terms. One-day matches became part of the normal season (attracting colossal crowds and subsidizing conventional matches), a more-than-living wage was paid to players, Packer won access for his television station, cricket was restored as a focus of chauvinism, and a chastened board resumed control.[50]

World Series Cricket demonstrated a global change. Until sports were formalized in the nineteenth century, more people played than watched. That remains true of club-level games, and of most women's sports, but even the Melbourne Cricket Ground's 100,000 capacity (now matched by Sydney's Olympic Stadium) pales beside the almost-infinite audiences for television. Television had dramatic effects. Rugby League and Australian Rules expanded beyond their catchments when their peak bodies sponsored League teams based improbably in Adelaide, Perth, Melbourne and even Auckland, while Australian Rules teams migrated to Brisbane and Sydney. Small live audiences ('scenery' in television's dismissive jargon) were of little consequence so long as games drew television ratings. It became necessary, too, to abandon the tradition of playing all ARL and rugby union games on Saturday afternoons and league games on Sundays. A spread of times over a weekend made commercial sense.

The leading winter codes were then acquired (or enchanted) by television stations. As the New South Wales Rugby League competition became a national contest, it came to depend upon Packer's Channel Nine for revenue to allow the clubs to pay over-priced players. In 1994 the other Australian media mogul Rupert Murdoch (now an American citizen) and his interests (News Corporation) engineered a breakaway competition. Like World Series Cricket, Rugby SuperLeague bought players' contracts wholesale, in England and France as well as Australia and New Zealand, and tried to create a global competition. Meanwhile News Ltd initiated a global programme to professionalize and control rugby union. For a century, amateurism lay at the heart of union's identity, but 'the game they play in heaven' capitulated at once. Murdoch's real opposition came from Packer, until the corporations compromised, leaving proletarian league largely in Packer's control and patrician union mainly in Murdoch's. And in each case the competing clubs (or provinces and states) were 'rationalized' and the contests streamlined to suit television coverage.

The commercialization of sport reshaped identities at every level. Players sell their services on the market, weakening links between fans, clubs and national teams. Again, the Islands' small urban middle classes sustain only nominal television coverage which relies on content from Australia, New Zealand or France. The market therefore discourages full international status for their national teams. Samoan, Fijian and Tongan teams have excelled internationally, but rugby union's premier competition – Super Twelve – involves none of them among the provincial teams from New Zealand, Australia and South Africa. Ambitious players of either rugby code move to Australian and New Zealand clubs.

One effect is the browning of the All Blacks and rugby, and other team sports, including netball. New Zealand immigration policy has promoted this trend, as have fast-growing populations of Pacific Islanders and Maori, proportionately more youthful than the ageing Pakeha population; the free market; and the economic reality that team sports are less expensive (we may contrast tennis, an individual sport, more expensive, and whiter). Gaining selection for the All Blacks or the national netball team, the Silver Ferns, offers possibly the best chance to 'get on'. The Pacific presence also reflects the cultural renaissances among Maori and Pacific Islanders and their growing autonomy. Sports heroes and heroines wear multiple identities: New Zealand-born, they are Kiwi first and Samoan, or Tongan, second. To excel in sport leads to doing well in school, so that some schools in poorer urban areas (with Polynesian populations) are establishing sports academies. There is a 'brawn drain' in sport from the Pacific to New Zealand as well as to Australia.[51]

By contrast, ambitious Australian and New Zealand soccer players gravitate to Munich, Manchester and Milan and are often lost to their national team. If soccer is the only genuinely global sport, its centre is Western Europe and our region is marginal. Perhaps the best-known Kanak of the 1990s was not a politician but Christian Karembeu who played soccer for France and was targeted by leading European clubs.[52] The centres of gravity of rugby codes include New Zealand and Australia, so the best-known Papua New Guineans of the 1990s were Adrian Lam and Marcus Bai, playing league in Australia. As in cricket, commercialization and internationalization need not centralize power in Europe or America. For individual sports however, the picture is

Plate 20.1   Anna Rowberry, Wing Attack, Silver Ferns v. Australia, 1999. Australia won by a single goal scored in the closing seconds of the game. Reproduced courtesy of The Press, Christchurch.

Plate 20.2   The browning of the All Blacks (All Blacks against South Africa, 1999). T. Umaga, shown in the centre of the picture, is a Pacific Island New Zealander. Courtesy of The Press, Christchurch.

different. Leading golfers (women as well as men) and tennis players usually take up residence in the United States, near the most lucrative competitions.

The local consequences are clear in Greg Ryan's account of Christchurch.[53] As in other provincial centres after the war, shorter working hours, higher incomes, increased education, the proliferation of cars and globalization all affected the sporting culture. The emphasis on team games of English origin was gradually eroded by (American) basketball and softball and by the increasing affordability of tennis and golf. Skiing, climbing, tramping and yachting also became popular as people found time and money for them. As fixtures grew in number, and television removed the need to attend in person, provincial games lost some significance as community events, and a wide range of other sports came onto the menu. The infrastructure which enabled Christchurch to digest these changes was in place by the 1930s. Even the hosting of the 1974 Commonwealth Games was neither a radical innovation nor a defining epoch.

The street parades for successful Canterbury rugby teams in the 1990s indicate the survival of sporting passion. Equally, the city continued to enjoy its horse-racing carnival (while watching the Melbourne Cup on television) and to toast winning athletes in an increasing range of sports; but the sporting culture is shaped by sponsorship, global conglomerates and contrived spontaneity. A few at the top enjoy the benefits of professionalism, but little sponsorship money trickles down to the clubs; and as talent scouts secure children on professional contracts or draft them into sports academies, the role of the local club becomes marginal. Weekend work restricts many players. The senior rugby competition shrank from sixteen to nine teams in the decade after 1987 and the standard of competition declined. There are signs of two cultures, one of dedicated volunteers, the other inhabited by high performers, image-makers and lawyers.

The transformation of Lancaster Park to Jade Stadium in 1998 may be seen in the context of earlier efforts to clear debt and generate finance to redevelop a premier venue. But there is no longer room for the Lancaster Park Cricket Club or other 'local' users. Corporate viewing areas reduced ground capacity; and these facilities were put in place while those for traditional spectators remained on the drawing board and ticket prices increased. The reservation of grounds for televised games, and amalgamations as clubs struggle to survive, suggest that opportunities for club players are far from certain.

EXPATRIATES

These players may not be the most significant expatriates: the departure of Australian and New Zealand cultural performers was more serious than any American invasion. Expatriatism is a long tradition in New Zealand and Australia. For classical musicians it was almost inevitable. From Nellie Melba and Peter Dawson to sopranos Joan Sutherland and Kiri Te Kanawa, overseas performance was more an obligation than an option. Victoria-born Percy Grainger went further, training in Germany and settling in England before 1914, and in America thereafter. Whatever their preferences and their accents, they were exponents of European classical music, and neither Melbourne nor Auckland could provide the audiences they deserved.

For writers the situation was different. Katherine Mansfield might have lived in New Zealand and mailed manuscripts to London; it was a milieu, not readers, that drew her to London and Middleton Murry. As a New Woman, she was a metropolitan creature. Besides, rejection of the colonies and a return 'home' were implicit in the original exile. In the 1890s William Lane added an ideological twist. A utopian socialist, after some years in America he settled in Queensland to edit the *Boomerang* and then the *Worker*. He was appalled by the failure of the shearers' strike and wrote *The Workingman's Paradise* in 1892 partly to raise funds to defend unionists. The next year he led his disciples to found a new colony in Paraguay. When 'New Australia' crumbled, he sailed to Auckland and edited the conservative *New Zealand Herald*.[54]

Expatriation was seldom so circuitous or so political. In the twentieth century it acquired a more culture-specific meaning, almost an expression of cultural cringe in the embrace of the Old World. It signifies a return 'home' to the centre of British/European culture by intellectuals, artists, writers, musicians. The departure of leading high- and popular-culture artists appeared to signify that the colonies could not sustain their gifted sons and daughters. Mansfield and Henry Handel Richardson, the first Australian writer to be nominated for a Nobel Prize (for *Ultima Thule* (1929), the last volume of her trilogy *The Fortunes of Richard Mahony*), were early examples. Among later writers were Janet Frame, Christina Stead and Patrick White, and Ruth Park, who migrated from New Zealand to Australia.

Expatriate artists and writers were usually cast as victim, setting 'serious' high-culture writers against a grim background of community neglect, Philistine society, repressive government, paranoid censors, and American and British cultural empires. Henry Lawson was among the first to foster this image. *A Song of Southern Writers* (1892) encapsulates its main elements:

O the critics of your country will be very proud of you
When you're recognized in London by an editor or two
In the land where sport is sacred, where the labourer is a god
You must pander to the people, make a hero of a clod![55]

The tradition had its apotheosis in cultural and political histories of the inter-war years. The official historian of the Fellowship of Australian Writers referred to the Australian writer of that early period as 'almost an endangered species': 'nothing... could be done to secure for Australian writers the dignity and respect – and the bread and butter – that were needed for the carrying out of their all-important work'.[56] The writer-as-victim tradition revived with revisionist histories of the Cold War which posed the author as victim of security organizations.[57] This emphasis overlooks basic sympathies and values shared with fellow Australians. It also underestimates the agency exercised by writers in community life. Being a New Zealander or Australian usually enriched as well as complicated their work. The film industries suggest the advantages of distance in releasing the native imagination. A distinctive flavour legitimizes the work, yet risks its failure with global audiences.

In Australia and New Zealand, 'expatriate' assumed culture-centric associations and remains ambivalent. Often expatriates are understood to have returned 'home' – to Europe and specifically Britain – to the culture and values of the Old World. It is not surprising that 'expatriate' is reserved mainly for Anglo-Celts and Pakeha living abroad, mainly in England and America. In such terms and assumptions about a lost 'British' Australia and residual British New Zealand we may see a hierarchy of 'Australianness' and 'Kiwiness' that mocks 'multiculturalism' and 'biculturalism'. Australian or New Zealand citizenship is one thing at home, but many things abroad. So ingrained is this hierarchy in some older Australian and New Zealand intellectuals, that the issue itself – who may constitute an expatriate? – has yet to be raised. In New Zealand this category technically includes New Zealanders who have become Australians, in search of a larger world than their islands, but who wish still to live 'here' as opposed to 'over there'. Among these are the comic archetype Fred Dagg (John Clarke), the quintessential 'Kiwi bloke' of the 1970s, in black singlet and gumboots; Footrot Flats, the cartoon strip, and its main character, an Australasian sheepdog; the rock band Split Enz, later Crowded House; Sam Neill; Jane Campion; and Fred Hollows the opthalmic surgeon who worked with Aborigines. 'New Zealand' artists and professionals on one side of the Tasman are 'Australians' on the other, and even Australian of the Year. From New Zealand, going to Australia is merely an extension of staying home.

The most perceptive treatment of recent Australian expatriates is Ian Britain's *Once an Australian*.[58] His expatriates – Barry Humphries, Clive James, Germaine Greer and Robert Hughes – are celebrities with an 'aptitude for self-publicity' and a talent for 'privacy and self-effacement, if not self-concealment'. In their stories he found in varying degrees an 'integral relationship between the life and the work'. They are all 'Word Children', writers as well as 'verbal performers' in various media. Curiously, in listing their shared features, Britain neglects ethnicity. The commonalities he identifies – in their personal and professional backgrounds, in the issues and impulses prompting their decisions to work abroad – lie elsewhere, in time, region, class, religion. All were born in the same decade into middle-class, Christian homes in the suburbs of Melbourne or Sydney. All left between 1959 and 1964 as young adults to settle in England where – except Hughes, who went to America – they remained. Typically, much time elapsed before they revisited Australia, which most had hoped to leave forever. Expatriatism in this context involves misplaced Britons who endured Australia's backwardness and then found their way 'home'. It is not too far-fetched to see these as orphans of empire, pulled back into the fold by their cultural roots. They could equally be termed exiles from the Old World. Tension between what constitutes Australian and

British cultures, 'home' and 'exile', resonates with a major stream of the debate of Australian national identity.

Expatriatism in Australia and New Zealand has usually been cultural rather than political or economic, growing from the same values that bred the cultural cringe: the need to reach back to the Old World for high culture. William Lane is so far the only celebrity to leave on ideological grounds. For all the radical rhetoric and industrial unrest that punctuated the twentieth century, Australia seemed a good place to its non-indigenous population in which to live, work and raise a family. Lane's disillusion was not that of the workingman but of the visionary, much like Ian Britain's expatriates.

This expatriatism does not easily embrace escapees who do not 'go home' to the Old World, but to the United States. Some, like Jill Ker Conway, author of *The Road from Coorain: An Australian Memoir* and *True North*,[59] also left Australia in the 1950s, dismayed by the parochial and aggressively masculine culture of the public service. Ker Conway climbed the heights of American academia, and belongs to a different breed than Ian Britain's celebrities. Her attack on her backward compatriots earned few supporters at home. It is one thing to prefer the Mother Country, but quite another to opt for an ex-colony. It is all right, however, to emulate the New Zealand historian of political thought, J. G. A. Pocock, and write about a British heritage from the United States.

Britain remained the 'mother country' culturally, for many people. In 1999 the Australian High Court again took the lead in an identity issue when it upheld an objection to the election to the Senate of One Nation's leading Queensland candidate. The grounds for protest were her dual citizenship of Australia and 'a foreign power'. Although she insisted that she was 'an Aussie' and had felt like one 'ever since I came here', she had not renounced her British citizenship. That judgement caused general surprise (and anxious moments for some parliamentarians). In view of the widespread sense that Britain is not foreign (or is less foreign than other places) it has been easy to ignore another kind of expatriate, growing in numbers: non-British, born overseas or born to parents born overseas. The decade that saw the departure of Ian Britain's expatriates greeted hosts of Europeans. The children of these diasporas ventured 'home' in the 1980s and 1990s, to revisit their childhoods, reconnect with families and cultural roots. Some opted to stay, but most returned. Either way, these journeys are a critical link in the story of migration, exile and expatriatism that began in 1788. We need to look beyond the imperial connection to trace this journey and its implications. If the history of Anglo-Celtic expatriates suggests a bland cultural landscape where milk and honey and little else flow, the histories of other expatriates emphasize the promise of the land. To many, human rights and political freedom are paramount criteria in the search for a new 'home'. Globalization has not only reconfigured individuals' and groups' notions of home and exile; it also demands new approaches to issues of identification with place and community. 'Expatriatism' in academic discourse remains fixed to notions of society increasingly out of touch with the dynamics of migration and settlement, 'home' and exile since the 1950s.

GLOBALISM AND PAROCHIALISM

In sporting domains there are 'global' and 'parochial' alternatives (World Cup soccer or Trobriand Island cricket), but there are also traditions which are touched by globalizing pressures and develop into distinctive regional or national formations. Some (like World Cup cricket) disguise their English origins and imperial provenance, and pretend to universality. Others (like Australian Rules Football) adapt the financial and sponsorship techniques of global sport in order to entrench a local following. Much the same lush diversity can be teased out in the domains of popular pastimes and amusements. Homogeneous globalism may not be our future, idiosyncratic parochialism may not be restricted to the past, and many options lie between these poles.

NOTES

1 Elizabeth Gordon, 'That Colonial Twang: New Zealand Speech and New Zealand Identity', in David Novitz and Bill Willmott (eds), *Culture and Identity in New Zealand*, Wellington, 1989.
2 Diane Langmore, *Glittering Surfaces: A Life of Maie Casey*, Sydney, 1997.
3 Peter Conrad, *Where I Fell to Earth: A Life in Four Places*, London, 1990, 25.
4 In 1840, when New Zealand seemed immensely remote from him, T. B. Macaulay ruminated on an equally remote time 'when some traveller from New Zealand shall, in the midst of a vast solitude, take his stand on a broken arch of London Bridge, to sketch the ruins of St Paul's' (Macaulay's essay on Leopold von Ranke).
5 Helen Fraser, *Your Flag is Obscuring our Sun*, Sydney, 1990.
6 Vivian Smith, 'Poetry', in Leonie Kramer (ed.), *Oxford History of Australian Literature*, Melbourne, 1981, 370; Cassandra Pybus, *The Devil and James McAuley*, Brisbane, 1999.
7 *Ern Malley's Poems*, with an introduction by Max Harris, Melbourne, 1961, introduction, 8–10.
8 Smith, 'Poetry', 371.
9 Richard Neville, *Hippie Hippie Shake: The Dreams, the Trips, the Trials, the Love-ins, the Screw-ups ... the Sixties*, Melbourne, 1995, 32–3.
10 Neville, *Hippie Hippie Shake*; Ian Britain, *Once an Australian: Journeys with Barry Humphries, Clive James, Germaine Greer and Robert Hughes*, Melbourne, 1997.
11 Geoffrey Robertson, *The Justice Game*, London, 1998.
12 Donald Horne, *Time of Hope: Australia, 1966–72*, Sydney, 1980.
13 David Headon, Joy Hooton and Donald Horne (eds), *The Abundant Culture: Meaning and Significance in Everyday Australia*, Sydney, 1995, xiii–xvi.
14 Peter Goodall, *High Culture, Popular Culture: The Long Debate*, Sydney, 1995, 69.
15 Raymond Williams, *Keywords*, London, 1983.
16 Headon, Hooton and Horne, *Abundant Culture*.
17 Goodall, *High Culture, Popular Culture*, 68–9.
18 E. P. Wolfers, *Race Relations and Colonial Rule in Papua New Guinea*, Sydney, 1975.
19 Nigel Oram, *Colonial Town to Melanesian City: Port Moresby 1884–1974*, Canberra, 1976.

20 Donald Denoon, *Getting Under the Skin*, Melbourne, 2000.
21 Joel Bonnemaison, *The Tree and the Canoe: History and Ethnogeography of Tanna*, Honolulu, 1994.
22 International Bank for Reconstruction and Development [World Bank], *The Economic Development of the Territory of Papua and New Guinea*, Baltimore, 1965.
23 Lamont Lindstrom, 'Culture Remade', in D. Denoon, S. Firth, J. Linnekin, M. Meleisea and K. Nero (eds), *Cambridge History of the Pacific Islanders*, Melbourne, 1997, 407–15.
24 Bernard Narakobi, 'The Melanesian Way', in Lindstrom, 'Culture Remade'.
25 Lindstrom, 'Culture Remade'.
26 Craig McGregor in *People, Politics and Pop: Australians in the 1960s*, Sydney, 1968.
27 Craig McGregor, 'The Beach, the Coast, the Signifier, the Feral Transcendence and Pumpin' at Byron Bay', in Headon, Hooton and Horne, *The Abundant Culture*, 51–60.
28 Leonie Huntsman, *Sand in our Souls: The Beach in Australian History and Culture*, Melbourne, forthcoming.
29 Michel de Certeau, *The Practice of Everyday Life*, trans. Steve Rendall, Berkeley, Calif.; first published in French, 1974; cited in Goodall, *High Culture, Popular Culture*.
30 Dowell O'Reilly to 'Molly' Miles, 18 September 1916, quoted in M. O'Reilly (ed.), *Dowell O'Reilly from His Letters*, London, 1927.
31 William Baylebridge to Nettie Palmer, 8 March 1933, NLA MS 1174/1/4214-15.
32 APEC Task Force, *The Real Colours of New Zealand*, Wellington, 1999.
33 See, for example, Edmund Hillary, *Nothing Venture, Nothing Win: His Autobiography*, London, 1975. A new autobiography is just published. New Zealanders also watched his life serialized on television in 1998 and can buy the series on video.
34 McGraw-Hill, *Dead Birds*, 16mm and video, 1963, CRM; PNG Office of Information, *Trobriand Cricket: An Indigenous Response to Colonialism*, 16mm and video, 1976, Ronin Films; Charlie Nairn, *Ongka's Big Moka*, 16mm and video, 1974, Granada TV.
35 Andrew Pike, Hank Nelson and Gavan Daws, *Angels of War*, 16mm and video, 1983, Ronin Films; Noriko Sekiguchi, *Senso Daughters: Senjo no Onnatachi*, 16mm and video, 1990, Ronin Films.
36 Bob Connolly and Robin Anderson, *First Contact*, 16mm and video, 1983, Ronin Films; *Joe Leahy's Neighbours*, 1988, Ronin Films; *Black Harvest*, 1992, Film Australia.
37 Dennis O'Rourke, *Yap: How Did You Know We'd Like TV?*, 16mm and video, 1982, Film Australia; *Half Life: A Parable for the Nuclear Age*, 16mm and video, 1986, Film Australia.
38 George Andrews, *Auckland Fa'aSamoa*, 1982, Television New Zealand.
39 Tom O'Regan, 'Cinema Oz: The Ocker Films', in Albert Moran and Tom O'Regan (eds), *The Australian Screen*, Ringwood, Victoria, 1989, 80.
40 Jock Collins, 'Migrant Hands in a Distant Land', in Gillian Whitlock and David Carter (eds), *Images of Australia: An Introductory Reader in Australian Studies*, St Lucia, 1992, 115.
41 Meaghan Morris, *The Pirate's Fiancee: Feminism, Reading, Postmodernism*, London, 1988. In 1999 the character on whom Crocodile Dundee was based, disgruntled with his small share of the proceeds of the film, launched an attack on a Northern Territory road block and was shot dead by police.

42 David Headon, 'Strictly Stomper: The New Australian Films', in Headon, Hooton and Horne, *Abundant Culture*, 71–9.
43 *Daily Telegraph–Mirror*, 28 June 1993, 29; cited in Headon, 'Strictly Stomper', 75.
44 Peter Calder, 'Would-be Warriors: New Zealand Film since *The Piano*', in J. Dennis and J. Bieringa (eds), *Film in Aotearoa New Zealand*, 2nd edn, Wellington, 1996, 183.
45 For an overview, see Helen Martin and Sam Edwards, *New Zealand Film 1912–1996*, Auckland, 1997.
46 D. J. Mulvaney, *Cricket Walkabout: The Australian Aboriginal Cricketers on Tour, 1867–8*, Melbourne, 1967.
47 David Wetherell, *Charles Abel and the Kwato Mission of Papua New Guinea, 1891–1975*, Melbourne, 1996.
48 Chris Cunneen, 'The Rugby War: The Early History of Rugby League in New South Wales 1907–1915', in Richard Cashman and Michael McKernan (eds), *Sport in History*, Sydney, 1979.
49 Ric Sisson and Brian Stoddart, *Cricket and Empire*, London, 1984.
50 Richard Cashman et al., *Oxford Companion to Australian Cricket*, Melbourne, 1996.
51 On the growing Polynesian influence in New Zealand sport, see T. Hyde, 'White Men Can't Jump', *Metro*, 157 (Sept. 1993), 62–9. On the 'brawn drain', see Atama Raganivatu, 'Rugby Becomes Big Business', *Pacific Islands Monthly* (May 1998), 32–5. With thanks to Greg Ryan.
52 David Small, 'Prospects for New Caledonia: The Challenge of Ouvea', in D. Denoon (ed.), *Emerging from Empire? Decolonization in the Pacific*, Canberra, 1997, 60–8.
53 Greg Ryan, 'Sport', in J. Cookson and G. Dunstall (eds), *Southern Capital*, Christchurch, forthcoming.
54 Gavin Souter, *A Peculiar People*, Sydney, 1968.
55 *Bulletin*, 28 May 1892.
56 Len Fox (ed.), *Dream at a Graveside: The History of the Fellowship of Australian Writers 1928–1988*, Sydney, 1988, 3.
57 Fiona Capp, *Writers Defiled: Security Surveillance of Australian Authors and Intellectuals 1920–1960*, Melbourne, 1993.
58 Britain, *Once an Australian*.
59 Jill Ker Conway, *The Road from Coorain: An Australian Memoir*, New York, 1992 (first published in Great Britain, 1989); *True North*, London, 1994.

[21] CONTEMPORARY IDENTITIES

It is a commonplace that the end of the Cold War loosened many bonds which had strait-jacketed the world into two camps. Exposing sheltered communities to global competition (it is argued) also prompted the reassertion of ethnic identities. Anxious people seeking solidarity in the face of cut-throat competition were likely to imagine new communities or reimagine old ones, especially when the collapse of communism dashed hopes of class unity. Europe offers more cases than our region to support this thesis. Although the Cold War had diffuse influence here (see chapter 16), assertions of ethnic identity had little relation to global trends, other than some emulation of the United States civil rights movement. We cannot link separatism in Melanesia or Polynesian transnational ethnicities to such global forces. No settler society generated strong separatist sentiment – Western Australia's threatened secession in the 1930s was unique and perhaps rhetorical. On the contrary it was possible (see chapter 17) to expand the political community towards multiculturalism (especially in Australia) or biculturalism (in New Zealand and New Caledonia) and to make women generally more welcome in formal politics.

Western Europe did influence local opinions. Australia's Prime Minister Robert Menzies mistrusted the political capacity of non-Europeans but was given pause when the Tories decided to quit tropical Africa.[1] Maori and Kanak students in Europe and North America met other dependent people, or made connections in the literature of 'emerging' countries. Aboriginal Australians encountered the notion that they might strive for something beyond mere legal equality and the end of specific discrimination. Despite such connections, governments' own agendas shaped events. New Zealand's Free Association concept (see chapter 18) had no precedent; nor did the 1998 compromise in New Caledonia. Papua New Guinea remained a Territory in the 1960s partly because that suited Australia then. The hopes of Torres Strait Islanders and South Sea Islanders were provoked and curbed by Canberra's changing priorities. That government unilaterally reclassified South Sea Islanders as immigrants after a century as 'natives' (see chapter 17). The Howard government had the power to represent and treat Aborigines not as a community but as individuals and families whose problems could be addressed by mainstream services. Australia's rulers could accommodate multicultural tensions more easily than sovereignty claims.

By 2000 the region had shed many outward features of its varied colonialisms. Every native had become a citizen, most had been born into that condition and they were subjects of a government with some legitimacy. To be sure, many Irianese would prefer not to be Indonesian citizens, and Kanaky did not yet exist, but neither did the odious *indigenat*, and Kanak enjoyed a fair prospect of gaining control of government. But the region had not reached the fabled end of History.[2] For decades these peoples had seen each other – and themselves – through colonial spectacles. Our neighbours are most visible when back-lit by our sense of their past – and our own. The identities we consider rest largely upon other histories, mainly within the region. To put it over-simply, the categories of Maori and Pakeha exist because of, and in relation to, each other; Kanak and *caldoches* are aware of, and moved by, analogies with Aotearoa/New Zealand. Ethnic Fijians and Indo-Fijians are even more alert to bicultural parallels: each yin knows its yang, and other yins and yangs. Australia has been both an exception and a regional yardstick. Its history was used (or misconstrued) by French penal reformers and by French settlers. Many New Zealanders still distinguish themselves from their trans-Tasman neighbours by superior sporting prowess, gentility, closer ties with Britain, or sensitivity to indigenous issues and the possession of a treaty. Papua New Guineans are also not-Australians because their proposal was rejected, whereas New Zealanders made their own fate. Similar awarenesses connect and divide Solomon Islanders from Papua New Guineans, and so on *ad infinitum*.

The management of crises suggests the scope and limits of inter-state and inter-communal co-operation and opposition within a network of real and imagined links. The most durable of these is the pursuit of a nuclear-free Pacific. British, American and French nuclear tests provoked regional hostility of uneven quality but cumulative strength. While the Islands were colonies, Islanders' objections could be ignored, but when they gained their own voice, opposition became articulate. A nuclear-free zone – a New Zealand proposal – gave focus to this hostility. Island leaders were quick to follow. The first South Pacific Forum meetings in 1971 and 1972 objected to French tests, and the 1975 meeting approved a nuclear-free zone. Agitation developed more slowly in Australia, partly because Australia exported uranium.

The struggle of Palauans to combine nuclear-freedom with United States aid suggested some obstacles and considerations. In 1979 they wrote a constitution which declared that 'harmful substances' such as nuclear weapons should not be 'used, tested, stored or disposed of… without the express approval of not less than three-fourths of the votes cast in a referendum'.[3] This clause inhibited the United States from agreeing to the Free Association and massive aid which was conceded elsewhere in Micronesia, and Palauans held seven referenda to try to reconcile the constitution with aid and Free Association. A 1992 referendum finally achieved that outcome. Firth observes that more issues impinged than the nuclear one; but the world chose to see Palau as 'a nuclear-free David menaced by a nuclear-armed Goliath'.[4]

Many Australian towns made the popular if rhetorical gesture of declaring themselves nuclear-free. That sentiment embarrassed the Australian Labor

Party, elected in 1983 and keen to prove itself a reliable American ally. When New Zealand barred United States nuclear-armed ships from her ports, the ANZUS treaty ceased to mean much. Prime Minister Hawke also feared that French nuclear testing would provoke Islanders to reject all nuclear phenomena, including United States ships. Australia therefore placed itself at the head of the campaign for a Nuclear Free Treaty and campaigned to moderate its terms, targeting French tests rather than American ships. Melanesian states wanted tighter controls but Australia prevailed and twelve of the sixteen Forum countries signed the treaty. There was a brief reprise in 1995 when a new French president, Jacques Chirac, authorized another series of tests. The region was again united against France: public figures from Australia, New Zealand, Japan and Europe marched alongside Polynesians; there was rioting in Pape'ete, and the series was brought to a close. In brief, Australia purposefully and successfully held the spotlight on France, and channelled protests away from American interests.[5]

REGIONAL CRISES AND SECURITY

Their management of the nuclear issue reinforced the view that Australia and New Zealand were responsible for regional security. Their electorates also expected their governments to exercise control over the Islanders' domestic political affairs, although Islanders were adept in resisting paternal advice. That dilemma is evident in Fiji affairs. From Independence Fiji was ruled by Prime Minister Ratu Sir Kamisese Mara and the Alliance Party, blending chiefly style with Western business acumen. The quasi-traditional order seemed divinely ordained until 1987, when an election produced an unthinkable victory for a coalition dominated by Indo-Fijians. The upstart Fiji Labour Party campaigned on an anti-nuclear and social-democratic platform. Labour's leader, Dr Timoci Bavadra – a doctor and a commoner, though married to the high-ranking Adi Kuini Bavadra – became prime minister with decisive support from the National Federation Party (NFP). Although he described the chiefly system as 'a time-honoured and sacred institution of the *taukei* [Fijian people]',[6] his government was sacked within a month in the first of two coups by Colonel Sitiveni Rabuka. The populist Taukei Movement portrayed Bavadra as the bullet, but NFP as the gun aimed at Fijians: Rabuka agreed that Fijian interests were menaced by an illegitimate regime. A new constitution laid even more stress on Fijian control. The Great Council of Chiefs – *Bose levu Vakaturaga* – was made guardian of Fijian affairs, nominating the president and two-thirds of the Upper House. All 70 Lower House seats had segregated electorates, 37 of them for ethnic Fijians, reaffirming that Indo-Fijians were neither real Fijians nor equal citizens.[7]

Around 70,000 Indo-Fijian entrepreneurs and professionals emigrated in the decade after the coup, mainly to Australia and New Zealand. Governments in Australia and New Zealand were shocked and dismayed, but unable to change the course of events. They did organize the suspension of Fiji's Commonwealth membership, but no heavier sanction could be imposed on a regime which enjoyed some acceptance at home and more abroad. Island governments accepted Rabuka's rationale and even his methods, while some Maori applauded both the coups and the consequent constitution.[8]

Under the stress of these events Labour lost most of its ethnic Fijian support. When elections were held in 1992, Labour won only Indian seats, sharing them with the NFP. Seemingly secure, the Fijian vote splintered. Partly this reflected a division between Ratu Mara (who was sidelined until he became President of the Republic), and Rabuka, the leader of government. Although *Soqosoqo ni Vakavulewa ni Taukei* was formed to reunite Fijian voters, in 1992 SVT won 30 Fijian seats but only two-thirds of Fijian votes. SVT itself split on the choice of a prime minister and, amazingly, Rabuka enlisted Labour to help him defeat Ratu Mara's candidate. When this government fell a year later, Mara's man formed a new party – which Fijian voters buried. The constitution had been too successful in reassuring Fijians. The decline in Indo-Fijian numbers (and birth-rate) removed a perceived threat, while urbanization and economic complexity undermined chiefly authority. As Rabuka claimed in almost Napoleonic terms, Fiji was about to experience 'the replacement of traditional aristocracy with meritocracy.'[9]

Fijian factionalism, vanishing Indians and fiscal mismanagement persuaded Rabuka that the constitution must be revised, and a review commission was created, comprising one nominee each by the prime minister and the leader of the opposition, and an independent chair. For this role the Maori Paul Reeves, former Anglican archbishop and governor-general of New Zealand, was designed by God to embody Christian values, ethnic conciliation, Commonwealth traditions and constitutionalism. The commission heard opinions at home and abroad, and steered debate towards inter-ethnic collaboration and accountability. They proposed a move towards inclusive, non-racial representation, while protecting each community and shielding many functions from ministerial control.[10] These proposals were slightly amended and written into a constitution which was approved unanimously by parliament and even blessed by the Great Council of Chiefs.[11]

The 1999 election was contested, as intended, by inter-ethnic coalitions. Rabuka signified the shift in values by apologizing for the coups. Signifying new realities, not only did his party lose, but his NFP allies lost every seat. The revived Labour Party swept to power with enough seats to govern alone (though Prime Minister Mahendra Chaudhury honoured his electoral pact with smaller Fijian parties). The inter-ethnic coalitions promised success for liberal democracy, yet victory went to the parties least committed to inter-ethnic co-operation. Labour voters dumped the coup-maker; but one Labour ally was led by Aposai Tora, former leader of the Taukei Movement. The other was led by Adi Kuini Bavadra Speed (widow of Dr Timoci), who demanded to be prime minister until President Ratu Mara persuaded her to accept the deputy's post. In her maiden speech she then prayed for Chaudhury's conversion to Christianity.[12] What held this league – and the president – together was little more than shared dislike of Rabuka. The bewildering dynamics of Fijian politics are wholly domestic. New Zealand and Australian influence rests not on superior force, but overlapping values.

Much the same is true of relations between Australia and Papua New Guinea, although the links are closer and often fraught. Australian rule had not separated clans from their land, nor did it create many territory-wide institutions. As landowners negotiated directly with mining and logging companies for royalties, compensation and services, the outcome was constant renegotiation and often corruption. Members went to parliament to win local projects. They joined parties as ad hoc lobbying groups, and parliament embodied parochialism and pork-barrelling. Back-benchers readily crossed the floor to create new majorities, and no cabinet held office for a five-year parliament. As members voted themselves high salaries and K500,000 (US$250,000) per annum to spend locally, cabinet lost control over back-benchers, and thereby lost control of the budget (see chapter 18). In 1994 in Rabaul, premiers of the Island provinces threatened to secede unless the government stopped trying to take control over them. Fortuitously the crisis was eclipsed by a volcanic eruption which destroyed Rabaul.[13]

Secession was a chronic threat to the central government. Although the country averted Bougainville's secession in 1975, landowner anger persisted. John Momis, Bougainville's longest-serving member of parliament and often a member of cabinet, began to analyse politics in apocalyptic terms: 'Each time a few of our leaders surrender to the politics of greed, the nation as a whole moves closer to the rule of money, of a rich few holding onto power, backed by an army which protects them from the wrath of the dispossessed.'[14] The mining company, CRA, addressed landowner anger by paying more compensation through the Panguna Landowners' Association. The PLA however failed to contain volcanic tensions generated by 'distortion of customary land rights; arguments over the distribution of cash benefits; the economic stratification of the landowning community; and the difficulty of sustaining or adapting rules for the inheritance of property and for the orderly succession to … leadership.'[15] In the late 1980s younger landowners created the New PLA and ousted their elders in a putsch which also launched a huge compensation claim (14 billion US dollars) against CRA. The national government dismissed the claim, and in 1988 dissidents began to sabotage the mine. Secession ensued and the island descended into war.

The rhetoric of secession stresses the distinctiveness of Bougainvilleans, either innate or flowing from colonial history. A contrary view represents Bougainvilleans as typically Melanesian, and their revolt only one of many signs of the government's palsy: Papua New Guinea had a 'weak state' with little leverage over a 'strong society'.[16] As state power wanes, resource companies provide roads, schools, hospitals, and other services normally managed by government. Citizens lost faith in their political leaders, who in turn were frustrated by a constitution which rewards parochialism. Successive cabinets were also irritated by Australian paternalism, as budgetary support was replaced by funding for specific projects. Defence aid also came with conditions:

> [Apart from infantry training, Australia] consistently refused PNG's requests for additional support, special forces training or anything else that might have given [the army] a fighting chance [to defeat the Bougainville Revolutionary Army]. Canberra had clearly decided that such expenditure would be wasted, that the PNGDF simply couldn't win a guerilla war.

When Canberra did supply helicopters, they insisted that these must never be deployed offensively.[17] That rider guaranteed perpetual and mutual mistrust.

Some cabinet ministers sought a negotiated outcome, while others insisted that the PNGDF could strike a decisive blow; but the decay of state capacity, the loss of Panguna's income and the cost of the war meant that soldiers were paid and supplied irregularly, and morale declined. When Julius Chan became prime minister in 1995, he promised a resolution. Negotiations and a fresh assault both failed, but some ministers glimpsed a cunning solution. Out-sourcing was the fashion in government, why not in war? Agreement was reached with Sandline, a London company which contracted Executive Outcomes, expert in capturing mining centres in African wars.[18]

Lobbying ministers for the Sandline agreement, Colonel Tim Spicer argued that Australia and New Zealand were prolonging the war to prevent Papua New Guinea from becoming the region's industrial giant.[19] Ministers were easily persuaded and the contract was signed; but at the last minute Defence Force Commander General Jerry Singirok aborted the mission and arrested Sandline's officers. Explaining his action – on talk-back radio – he demanded the resignations of the prime minister, the minister of finance, Chris Haiveta, who had organized the finance of the project, and the minister of defence.[20]

Much as the Australian government deplored mercenaries, it was even more opposed to military interventions in politics, no matter that Singirok insisted that this was not a coup. By whatever name, his action drew support. The army's denunciation of corrupt politicians and a dysfunctional political system made immediate sense; so students and other citizens besieged parliament to support the demand that ministers resign. The crisis was defused when ministers stepped aside and a commission of enquiry examined the Sandline contract. An election – scheduled independently – gave equivocal judgement. Chan lost his seat but Haiveta increased his majority: several professedly moralist candidates were elected (albeit on local issues), but joined in the usual factionalism and office-seeking. As the reformists splintered, normal horse-trading made Bill Skate (the most vigorous critic of Sandline) prime minister, supported as deputy by Haiveta, the organizer of that adventure.

Serendipitously, these events opened the door to peace after nine years of devastating civil war. Singirok's action gave Bougainville Revolutionary Army (BRA) leaders confidence to open discussions. Since the BRA saw Australia as partisan, the New Zealand government played the role of honest broker,

Plate 21.1   Don McKinnon (New Zealand minister of foreign affairs) presides over the signing of the Burnham Declaration by Gerard Sinato (left), leader of the PNG-backed Bougainville Transitional Government, and Joseph Kabui (right), leader of the Bougainville separatists. Reproduced courtesy of The Press, Christchurch. Published 19 July 1997.

bringing all sides to two rounds of talks at Burnham in the South Island. There, BRA and PNGDF officers chipped away some of their distrust and recommended a truce. Bougainville's destiny would not be addressed at once, fighting would cease, and truce monitors would give people confidence to resume normal living.

Truce monitors were organized by the New Zealand army, which hardly pleased Australian officers, yet their friendly rivalry proved constructive. Monitors also came from Fiji and Vanuatu. Fijians' tradition of peace-keeping in Lebanon gave them an edge, while the cultural closeness of niVanuatu gave them exceptional insights. Maori were prominent in New Zealand's teams, whereas Aboriginal Australians were scarce, so that Australians found themselves the element least attuned to their milieu. When truce monitors yielded to peace monitors, the Australian Defence Force succeeded New Zealanders in command, but at all times most monitors were civilians. Many found that the chasm between soldiers and civilians was as wide as that which divided both from villagers. Military command sharpened the masculinism of the teams, such that women monitors struggled to bring their insights to their commanders' notice. More important for all monitors was their absolute dependence on villagers for survival. A decade of disputes and betrayals made politics more complex than monitors could grasp, especially as they were isolated by language. Had Bougainvilleans not desired peace, it would not have been kept; had they mistrusted the monitors, the operation would have collapsed. The multinational force therefore experienced 'post-colonial' relations radically different from the paternalism of the 1960s.

Negotiations offered Papua New Guinea's and Bougainville's negotiators some perspective by reflecting on New Zealand society and polity. At one crisis in 1999, the Papua New Guinea *National* gave the orthodox line, when it reported that all factions learned the reasons

> why New Zealand is the most racially tolerant society on earth. They learnt that differences over land do not always have to be resolved by violent conflicts. They learnt that a people do not need political independence to enjoy the full realization of their rights and inheritance. ... This was the purpose the New Zealand head of the Pacific division... had in mind when he organized the [study] tour.

How well he delivered his lecture![21] Alas, the hard core of secessionists reported in contrary terms. The Secretary to BRA leader Sam Kauona concluded that

> The Maori experience... is no precedent for Bougainville to follow. They are just merely fighting to get their land and fishing rights back, which were stolen from them by white New Zealanders in the 1800s. We are fighting for... self-determination of our people. The Maori Nations as far as we can understand are being advised not to fight for self-determination and independence outside of the New Zealand political framework, but merely to be economically and socially independent within the existing structure.[22]

For Papua New Guineans, however, the more important comparator was still Australia. Despite the country's divisive parliamentary politics, a fragile national sentiment did take root, which redefined relations with Australians. Independence hardly changed that link, since Australia remained the chief source of aid, logistical support and private capital. Many Papua New Guineans chafe at Australian oversight, yet for most Australians there is no issue to address; independence wiped the slate clean, making Papua New Guinea just another undeveloped country. A Port Moresby newspaper reflected on this development, while musing on Anzac Day:[23]

> The old and familiar father figure, Australia, has long been expected to fill the role of major donor and supporter. ... Our own politicians... acknowledge how that relationship has changed. ... But still the relationship is seen in a false light, because the emphasis is always on the pace of change in PNG.
>
> Australia has changed even more fundamentally than PNG; the old familiar image of the tough, sunbrowned Aussie, underpinned by two generations of kiaps and the soldiers of the Second World War, is as unreal as the perception of Papua New Guineans as fuzzy wuzzy angels. ...
>
> The 'old' Australia had a special affinity with PNG because many of those kiaps and soldiers returned to government or private sector employment in Australia and carried their knowledge of this country with them. ...
>
> Today's Australia bears little resemblance to the isolated Anglo-Saxon outpost of even 40 years ago. ... Cities reflect the multicultural nature of what is both economically and socially a highly diversified people.

In such refracted forms do political actors plot their destinies on the regional grid.

Papua New Guinea, and especially Bougainville, might be deemed unique, until violence erupted next door in Solomon Islands. The independence constitution had not tackled land. In that vacuum, passions mounted and then exploded on Guadalcanal island. Until the Pacific War the administrative centre was Tulagi, an islet too small for postwar needs; so a new town, Honiara, was built on Guadalcanal. The town and nearby plantations attracted people from other islands, especially from densely settled Malaita. As migrants settled down, landowners became restive and violent incidents were noted (see chapter 10). When some called themselves the Guadalcanal Revolutionary Army (GRA) and in 1999 began to harass Malaitans, the government was cornered. Prime Minister Bartholemew Ulufa'alu, as a Malaitan, was seen by the militants as partisan. The police (relying on British principles) saw all citizens as equal, so the militants were simply law-breakers to be arrested and charged. Guadalcanal people recalled colonial narratives in which 'savage' Malaitans struck fear into the hearts of police. Every action therefore confirmed stereotypes and escalated tensions.

The GRA was clearly influenced by the Bougainville Revolutionary Army, although there was probably no direct contact. Happily, other regional links helped to settle this impasse. When the Commonwealth Secretariat was asked to mediate, Sitiveni Rabuka (recently voted out of office) was called in.[24] His prestige and skills resolved the immediate problem, although the structural difficulty clearly persists. Governments cannot treat land as a commodity in the 'modern' fashion, so long as landowners enforce 'traditional' values. This is a pan-Melanesian dilemma. Vanuatu's government tried to accommodate 'kastom' principles in land management, but the logic of a commercialized economy is near-impossible to reconcile with the customs on which personal, communal and national identities are based.

NEW CALEDONIA

Vanuatu's and Papua New Guinea's efforts to engineer national identity seem perfunctory compared with the French creation of the Tjibaou Cultural Centre in New Caledonia. This innovative structure (see plate 18.1) was designed by the great architect Renzo Piano, co-creator of the Pompidou Centre in Paris, following a request by Jean-Marie Tjibaou, Kanak political leader of the 1980s, architect of the Matignon Accord. When he became a political martyr (see chapter 18) the project adopted his name and perhaps reputation. The Centre aspires to reconcile European and Oceanian civilizations:[25] in this context 'Oceanian' includes Tahitian, Wallisian and Indonesian as well as Kanak, reflecting the ethnic mix of New Caledonia. The term therefore sets Kanak in a context somewhat broader than 'the South Pacific'. Equally singular is a biculturalism which does not match Maori/Pakeha, much less Fijian/Indo-Fijian, but does echo the rhetoric of the new political order. The architects were possibly not aware of Fijian or New Zealand resonances, but each attempt to move beyond colonialism and reconcile settlers with indigenes inevitably comments on other such attempts.

The metropolitan financial and creative resources showered on the Tjibaou Cultural Centre eclipse other structures in the Islands, and invite comparison with the investment in Te Papa, Our Place, the immensely popular new Museum of New Zealand, and the long-delayed Australian National Museum. Yet in other respects the ambition to emulate these settler colonies has evaporated. Most obviously the economy rests uncomfortably on French government subsidies and the proceeds of the nickel-mining industry. As Kanak find places in the new political structure, and opportunities in the commercial economy, the fissiparous tendencies of independent Melanesia become increasingly evident here as well.

Over the same period – the 1980s and 1990s – the distinctiveness of Vanuatu also fell away. The seemingly clear ideological division crumbled between francophone and Catholic (with some 'traditionalist' allies) on one side and anglophone and Protestant niVanuatu on the other. First Vanua'aku Party split; then other parties began to behave as ad hoc lobbying and jockeying associations, abandoning any attempt at popular mobilization, in every way approximating the parliamentary factions which made governments unstable in both Papua New Guinea and Solomon Islands.

WALLACE'S OTHER LINE

Australia and New Zealand clearly exercise such hegemony as is possible in this region, but see their roles in rather different ways. Since the 1890s Pakeha as well as Maori New Zealanders saw themselves as island people, even perhaps the hub of a mainly Polynesian island empire (see chapter 9). Official Australia (represented by New Zealanders as continental in outlook) never saw itself in such intimate relations with Melanesia, a region to be subdued, converted, elevated or developed, but surely not incorporated. In the 1990s the government was embarrassed that the minister for foreign affairs found so little time to meet Island leaders. One remedy was a junior minister for Pacific Island affairs, responsible also for aid. An able politician was appointed, and Island issues did find a focus in the Australian bureaucracy, but Island governments naturally felt down-graded. The Howard government abolished the junior ministry and a new minister for foreign affairs did devote time and attention to Papua New Guinea and other Islands. Briefly, Islanders could believe that they occupied a leading place in Australian hearts and minds. That illusion exploded in East Timor.

Australian relations with Indonesia began propitiously. As minister for external affairs, H. V. Evatt promptly recognized the fledgling Indonesian Republic (see chapter 18). Despite Australia's continuing support (for example, recognizing Irian Jaya as a province of Indonesia), relations were embittered by *konfrontasi*. Not until John Gorton in the late 1960s did an Australian prime minister visit Jakarta. From then on, however, each government treated Indonesia as its most important neighbour. That nexus gained more importance as the Association of South East Asian Nations took shape, with Indonesia at its core. The greatest care went into diplomatic links; aid programs were initiated; and special attention was paid to co-operation with the armed forces. Successive ministers talked of a 'special relationship'.

Special, but not popular among Australians. Prime Minister Lee Kwan Yew of Singapore inspired dislike for his severe industrial and social discipline, balanced by awe for the commercial growth of the island state. Businessmen would invite him to lecture Australians on the need for hard work and compliant trade unions. No such respect offset the image of President Suharto's New Order in Indonesia as incompetent as well as repressive and corrupt. Indonesian forces moved into East Timor in 1975, dousing the unruly democracy unleashed in that Portuguese colony by a military coup in Lisbon. Both Gough Whitlam's Labor government and Malcolm Fraser's coalition recognized the integration of East Timor, although no other government followed suit. As governments espoused the economic integration of Australia into Southeast and East Asia, the Indonesian connection seemed ever more important. Prime Minister Paul Keating negotiated a security treaty with Indonesia, in a secrecy which acknowledged that public opinion would not approve so intimate an alliance. After the economic crisis of 1998 the financially austere Howard government offered a billion dollars towards Indonesia's economic recovery. Self-interest was the public rationale, as much as the desire to be a good neighbour.

The East Timor crisis of 1999 followed several events suggesting that Australia's relations with Southeast Asia had been misperceived. Australia (like the Netherlands and Scandinavian countries) offered asylum for Suharto's opponents, and Australian newspapers published occasional critiques. Sporadically in the 1980s and 1990s academics and journalists debated 'Asian values'. Set out most lucidly by Lee Kwan Yew, Asian values were said to buttress family life and subordinate individual to national interests. On one view this was merely a rationale for repressive government; from another it was enlightened neo-Confucianism. Since there were grounds for both perceptions, the argument was never resolved, but it did highlight the fact that the 'universal' human values to which most Australians and New Zealanders subscribed were variants of explicitly Western traditions. These background issues ensured that diplomacy between the governments needed constant nurturing.

Equally tricky was Australian governments' enthusiasm for Asia Pacific Economic Cooperation, and lower tariffs. Not everyone else was keen, and in 1995 this difference prompted an exchange of well-polished insults between Prime Minister Keating and Malaysian Prime Minister Mahathir Mohamed. Again, when Thailand sank into financial crisis in 1997 and the rest of Southeast Asia followed, the Australian economy continued to enjoy a long and strong boom. Perhaps Southeast Asia was less vital to Australian prosperity than Japan, America, China and even Europe. The collapse of the Suharto regime in 1998, widely welcomed by Australians and New Zealanders, caused some anxiety to government officials who understood how much the 'special relationship' depended upon personal diplomacy.

Australians and New Zealanders – almost as much as Indonesians – were stunned when President B. J. Habibie (Suharto's vice-president and successor) offered a referendum on East Timor's future.[26] The territory and its people were cherished by Australian veterans who had sheltered there during the Pacific War, and Catholics and ex-servicemen alike argued that Australia had a special obligation. This was anathema to the realists who developed foreign policy: for thirty years Australia, New Zealand and other governments had ritually expressed concern for East Timorese human rights and autonomy, confident that Suharto would never budge. In August 1999, when the great majority of East Timorese took their chance and voted for full independence, anarchy was the immediate result: savage reprisals by pro-Indonesian militia groups, assaults on United Nations personnel, and evidence of detailed military planning, made outside intervention inevitable. The United Nations itself was unable to mobilize and deploy a force to intervene, and the Association of Southeast Asian Nations clearly could not endorse intervention in a crisis which could be represented as the internal affairs of a member country. In consequence the Australian Defence Force led a multinational military force to East Timor (INTERFET) to enforce peace. That force was boosted by New Zealand but deployed few Southeast Asians, despite Indonesia's clear preferences. INTERFET won praise (especially from the United States) for its swift and effective restoration of peace, but the regional diplomatic consequences were problematic. If Indonesian military and even civilian authorities were annoyed by the rest of the world, they felt deeply betrayed by Australia. The security treaty had had no effect (and Indonesia suspended it), and Australia's public protests stood in clear contrast to the 'quiet diplomacy' exercised by ASEAN members in dealing with each other. A generation of diplomatic effort had not averted the burning of flags on each side of the Timor Sea.

Conflicting notions of 'Asia' had modified Australian identity. But, alas, Southeast Asian governments could manage rather well without Australia: 'In 1978 a senior Indonesian official likened Australia to the appendix of South-East Asia – its function was not properly understood, it was only taken notice of when it hurt, and nobody would miss it if it was removed.'[27] A generation of diplomacy, deepening commercial relations, and joint venture projects modified that view, but a Wallace's Line of sensibility had re-emerged, once more separating 'Asia' decisively from the settler societies to the south.

DEFINING AOTEAROA/NEW ZEALAND

Before 'Asia' entered national consciousness, New Zealand focused on Maori–Pakeha relations, driven by financial and military crises which troubled governments. Multiculturalism then challenged the dichotomy of biculturalism. Moving beyond Maori–Pakeha relations required first settling them. In the sequelae to Waitangi, the treaty and treaty principles re-established themselves, at least at the level of political identity, and treaty claims began to produce results. With three big settlements of $170 million each: commercial fisheries, Tainui (in the Waikato) and Ngai Tahu (the South Island), nearly $600 million was allocated from 1992 to 1998. At $100 million a year, treaty settlements approached one per cent of GDP.[28]

Maori and government motives continue to diverge, as they have for decades. Maori motives are described by the lawyer Joe Williams as 'Maori survival on Maori terms'.[29] The objective of Justice (then Judge) Eddie Durie, as Chair of the Waitangi Tribunal, was to restore a Maori economic base. The government, by contrast, aims to acknowledge past injustices, reach a settlement within political and economic constraints, and settle grievances. The claims settlement process had been criticized on the grounds that it locks both sides into combat in the 'old politics of domination', 'their identities rigidly confined to "the Crown" versus "the tribe".' According to Paul McHugh and Ken Coates, 'not only do claim-centred relations lock out any Maori expression of identity which is not based on tribe, but there is an assumption that once the claim is settled the relationship is over'.[30] Layered, multiple and permeable identities, as we argue, offer less dichotomy and more co-operation. Mason Durie, head of Maori Studies at Massey University, avers: 'the Treaty of Waitangi was always about the future; righting a wrong was a by-product of colonial domination but it was not the whole story'.[31] What matters is planning a future together for Maori and Pakeha.

Across a range of opinion, there is 'increasingly hesitant, conditional, and fragile' Pakeha support for the settlement process.[32] From those who target the Treaty of Waitangi's restoration as 'divisive' comes an occasional diatribe against 'Treaty Mania'. But is the treaty the problem, or the erosion of settler identity and living standards which some regard as their birthright? David Round asserts that:

> If most people who wanted jobs had them; if more and more of our assets were not sold to foreigners; if we all had a modest share in what remains of our prosperity; if ... government respected the environment and genuinely consulted with people, both Maori and European ... [he chose not to write 'Pakeha']

then New Zealand would be 'decently governed'.[33] Here are echoes of Wakefield and the New Zealand imagined in chapter 11. Yet there is general public acknowledgement that no choice exists about an enduring relationship between the 'crown' and Maori, and Maori and other New Zealanders: what matters is the quality of those relations.

Since the 1980s Pakeha have gained more confidence in their collective identity; institutions such as Te Papa, the new people's museum, dispel doubts about Pakeha culture. More contentious are questions of Maori identity. There is a contest between advocates of tribal – *iwi* – identity, and urban Maori who want to share the treaty settlements cake.[34] The latter invoke ethnicity, a sharing of culture rather than blood, yet ancestry is central to being Maori, and *whakapapa* the heart of Maori identity. There are debates, too, over '*Iwi* Inc.': the relevance of tribal structures, and unease at the tribal embrace of globalization; for example, Ngai Tahu has adopted the corporate model in order to be taken seriously by governments and in business ventures.

Treaty narratives have multiple threads. As we conclude this book a group of northern Maori who claim descent from the Confederation of United

Tribes of Nu Tireni, who adopted a flag and a declaration of independence in the 1830s, and whose members were among the first to sign the Treaty of Waitangi, were caught selling 'citizenship' of an independent Aotearoa to Pacific Islanders for $1,000 to $2,000, a practice familiar to Islanders accustomed to governments' sale of passports. The *whakapapa* of those who now call themselves the Confederation of the United Tribes of Aotearoa is contested. There is ample evidence that sovereignty is layered: not least in New Zealand, as the signatories of the Treaty of Waitangi probably knew, despite their misunderstandings. Roger Maaka, head of Maori at the University of Canterbury, seeks to reconceptualize a relationship 'built on interlocking sovereignties'. In his view, 'self-determination is about relationships of autonomy within a unified nation'. He sees a trilogy of critical relationships, with Maori as a whole, tribes, and individuals. Treaty matters are 'a discourse on a multi-tiered relationship, not one on a socio-political problem. It is not a problem to be solved but a relationship founded on mutual respect, to be continually managed and even celebrated, it is an ongoing relationship where both parties have to contribute to their shared destinies.'[35] One argument is that national myths inhibit the capacity to find common ground, but myths can also help to find that common ground.

It is symptomatic of New Zealand nationalism (relative to Australian) that the Ministry of Justice commissioned essays on the way ahead for Maori–Pakeha relations (published as *Living Relationships*) from two authorities, one in constitutional law, the other in history, both enjoying the imprimatur of overseas success. In this salute to the emergence of post-colonial identities we hear echoes of colonial narratives.

In the 1990s, New Zealanders voted to change the electoral system from First Past the Post to Mixed Member Proportional Representation (MMP), disillusioned by the relentless use of executive power to implement changes which the majority did not want. The first parliament elected under this system, in 1996, produced an unwieldy coalition between the National Party and New Zealand First. Winston Peters and New Zealand First represented a reaction against globalization, and an unlikely alliance between ageing Pakeha – the 'grey' vote – and Maori. He enlisted elderly Pakeha, concerned at the unsettling of settler identity and anxious to protect their privileges in a shrinking welfare state, and Maori, who ended their 60-year allegiance to Labour and sought a platform for Maori autonomy. Peters is of Maori and Scottish descent (a wily lawyer in the Muldoon mould, he is the 'comeback king' of New Zealand politics). New Zealand First campaigned against economic rationalism; support for tariffs; opposition to the sale of state assets, and opposition to Asian immigration. It is over immigration that older, Pakeha New Zealand shared concerns with Maori who insisted that treaty issues be resolved before New Zealand could move towards multiculturalism. New Zealand First capitalized on the bogey of Asia. However, five MPs soon defected to form a new party, Mauri Pacific, whose name suggests Pacific kinship and identity.

Although New Zealand First had fragmented by the time of the 1999 election, MMP again demanded coalitions of interest groups. On the surface, the battle was represented as a contest between two 'Xena Warrior Princesses',[36] National's Jenny Shipley and Labour's Helen Clark. There were other themes, reflected in Labour's return to power as a minority government and the entry to parliament of the Greens, representing the environmentalist movement, with 5.2 per cent of the vote. Laments had been growing for a lost 'decent society'. In 1997 National's Prime Minister Jim Bolger had borrowed the concept of 'social capital' from the author of the *End of History*; but his call for decency was a summons to New Zealand's own past rather than an imported concept. Calls increased for economic policies to 'fit in with New Zealanders'.[37] Globalization should be made to fit New Zealand's myths, identities and beliefs. Astronomy and global convention made New Zealand one of the first countries to welcome the millennium. More broadly, her collective identity had come to depend less on being first. Instead, the tradition of social experiment has been modified to signify New Zealand being once again the best; but growing numbers of people suspect that the Chicago-based theories imposed since the 1980s were, and remain, second-best.

DEFINING AUSTRALIA

Much the same global forces, and many similar domestic tensions, had to be addressed in Australia as well. The global pressures were brought to bear mainly in economic domains, favouring lower tariffs, the freer flow of capital, technology and commodities, and reducing the government's presence in the market-place; domestic tensions expressed themselves in reaction against these tendencies, but also centred upon unresolved issues of relations with Aboriginal Australia and multiculturalism. Not surprisingly these diverse forces were accommodated and resisted in different proportions and in very different ways.

With the Hawke Labor Party's victory in the 1983 election, the new treasurer, Paul Keating, embarked on two arresting projects. One was to reconcile the Labor party to a steady dismantling of the remains of the workers' welfare state. The other was to popularize economic policy debate, and especially the rhetoric of the economic rationalism which steadily took over all policy discussions. Whereas New Zealand's government could simply implement a new orthodoxy, Australia's independent Senate and federal constitution made it essential to generate popular understanding at least, and if possible public acceptance. That meant a slower swing of the pendulum and the full support of the formal trade union movement. Hawke himself had been president of the Australian Council of Trade Unions, as well as president of the ALP, before his entry into parliament. Those links were critical in gaining ACTU support for the steady reduction of its political and even its industrial roles: never again would the ALP and ACTU see each other as indispensable partners.

Labor's policy was defended as an essential element of a strategy to build links with the tiger economies of the East and Southeast Asia region. When the Liberal–National coalition came to power in 1996, their rhetoric was more global than regional, consistent with the coalition's general coolness towards 'Asia'. Labor had presided over a relative decline in the size and authority of the public service; the coalition determined to reduce absolutely its size and responsibilities. Where Labor enlisted ACTU support for policy initiatives, the coalition launched an explicit and sustained assault on trade unions generally, and the ACTU in particular. A leading target was the Maritime Union of Australia, which enjoyed a vice-like control over stevedoring; and in this campaign the government identified its interests completely with the employer. In the event the MUA survived, the non-union labour force was disbanded, and the workforce was 'down-sized' to a substantial degree. Similar alliances marked mining disputes. Since every major piece of legislation requires negotiation with independent or Australian Democrat senators, the government has not been able to achieve quite as draconian effect as it would like or as New Zealand's government achieved. In this rerun of the 'social laboratory', New Zealand stands alone.

Parliament's response to the High Court's Mabo judgement (see chapter 17) seems, in retrospect, the acme of co-operation between the government and Aboriginal people. In an altered political climate (see below) the coalition government's response to the Wik judgement was much less positive, and its refusal to apologize to the 'stolen generations' strikingly ungenerous. The frustration of Aboriginal leaders paralysed moves towards reconciliation, and denied the government credible negotiating partners. An impasse which would be catastrophic for New Zealand's politicians was endurable by their Australian counterparts. It was multicultural rather than indigenous affairs that drew the more creative attention.

One way in which Australian governments represent themselves is in terms of national economic performance. Economic statistics always place Australia and New Zealand in the frame of the Organization for Economic Cooperation and Development. As most OECD members are European or North American, the substance and the form of presentation emphasize the incongruity of little Europes in the South. Eurocentrism was almost inevitable after a century of efforts to eliminate every non-European trait. Andrew Markus makes this point statistically (see table 21.1).

Policy-makers were blind to the racism of the exclusionist policy which gave rise to these outcomes (see chapter 12). Prime Minister Menzies explained in 1959: 'It is our national desire to develop in Australia a homogeneous population in order that we may avert social difficulties which have arisen in many other countries. [Nevertheless] we are...a friendly

Table 21.1 Non-Europeans in Australia, 1901–1947[38]

	Country of origin			
Year	China	Melanesia	India	Japan
1901	32,997	9,654	7,637	3,593
1933	14,249	3,098	3,098	2,466
1947	12,094	1,638	2,898	335

people not given to making distinctions among people on grounds of race or religion.'[39]

Thereafter Australia changed significantly through a more varied pool of immigrants and greater tolerance of visible, and audible, difference among its citizens (see chapter 16). Rhapsodists of Australia's multicultural diversity are prone to exaggerate the extent of the transformation. A variety of ethnic minority cultures supplement the Anglo-Celtic culture without challenging its dominance. Each interacts with that culture and its institutions and agencies, but only rarely with each other. Furthermore, from the 1960s onwards, policy was modified almost surreptitiously and with minimal debate. The consequences were more visible in the cities than in provincial centres and the countryside. Many people – thinking of themselves as simple battlers – were therefore disconcerted to find their society committed to cultural diversity, non-discriminatory immigration, and the dismantling of tariff protection.

These anxieties shaped the election campaign of 1996, which more explicitly than usual canvassed questions of national identity, from multicultural and Aboriginal affairs to the significances of 'Asia'. Prime Minister Keating and Labor advanced self-consciously 'progressive' views on social policy fronts, and the Liberal–National coalition chose to draw attention to these policies without articulating alternatives. The Liberal leader John Howard, professedly the most socially conservative leader in a generation, was widely understood to want to wind back these policies and practices. Together with his commitment to the monarchy and test-match cricket, and his scepticism on feminist issues, he was caricatured as yearning for the Australia of the 1950s.

But the candidates who most hotly stated conservative positions were two independents: Graham Campbell, the member for Kalgoorlie in Western Australia, recently expelled from the Labor Party; and Pauline Hanson, running for the Labor seat of Ipswich in Queensland but disendorsed by the Liberal Party following remarks deemed racist. Both castigated programmes to address Aboriginal disadvantage; both demanded less immigration, especially from 'Asia'; both questioned tariff reductions and integration with Asian economies; and both denounced multiculturalism. Each won a seat, but it was the novice Hanson who captured attention at home and abroad. While Campbell looked and spoke like most middle-aged male politicians, the red-haired, tongue-tied and often scowling Hanson was a caricaturists' delight, and her lack of finesse strengthened her credibility among 'battlers'. Creating her own party (Pauline Hanson's One Nation) with populist rhetoric which attacked programmes for specific communities, she drew in opponents of gun control, enemies of Aboriginal land rights and remedial programmes, defenders of tariff protection, foes of immigration generally and Asian migrants in particular, and occasional white supremacists.

The issues which agitated One Nation supporters were legion, but common to most were the grievous difficulties of provincial towns. Government offices (social security, taxation, post office and employment) closed as agencies were corporatized, and in some instances privatized. Bank branches were also shutting, whether or not each was viable. Some rural products (pork in particular) were hurt by the imports permitted by lower tariffs, even if more farmers benefited. On this view One Nation's racism was merely idiomatic, not the core of its appeal; but the urban intelligentsia responded with rage to One Nation's social programme rather than its critique of economic rationalism. One Nation explicitly threatened the heartland of the National (formerly Country) Party. Queensland, Hanson's own state and that with the most dispersed population, was especially propitious. Although she lost her federal seat at the next election, her party astonished everyone in 1998 when they captured eleven seats in a Queensland state election. Within months the parliamentary party again astonished themselves. Like New Zealand First across the Tasman, One Nation's reliance upon a charismatic but erratic leader, its explicit critique of mainstream political parties and their organization, and its appeal to temperamental malcontents, courted dissension and schism. Over the next two years they disintegrated in defections and resignations.

The government's response to this inchoate threat was cagey. Ministers criticized ATSIC and reduced its mandate and funding, implying endorsement of some of One Nation's critique of 'the Aboriginal Industry'. On several occasions offered to him, the prime minister flatly refused to apologize for past injustices to the stolen generations or to Aborigines generally. Immigration quotas were cut, economic links with Asia were defended exclusively on economic grounds, and pig-farmers were bought off. Responding to overseas crises, Australia offered temporary asylum to (white) Kosovars but not to (black) Congolese or Rwandese. Government policy in these areas moved perceptibly to deflate One Nation's threat to the National Party.

These encounters reflected the vitality of national images which had departed from realities. The prime minister's distinction between Australians and Aborigines (see chapter 17), and the implicit dichotomy between Australians and Asians, endorsed 'the authentic Australians' as Europeans, whose lineage stretched back via the diggers of two world wars to the bushman and perhaps to the convict. This backdrop informed debate on two identity issues in referenda in 1999. One was whether or not to move from a constitutional monarchy to a republic. Despite the prime minister's passionate monarchism and divisions within the Liberal Party, a constitutional convention recommended such a plebiscite, the Labor Party was near-unanimous in its favour, and the issue could not be dodged. In the event the status quo prevailed, not because it commands majority support, but because republicans were divided: a 'minimalist' republic was on offer, with the president appointed by parliament and accountable to the prime minister; but those who favoured a directly elected president voted against the proposition, denouncing it as merely 'a politicians' republic'. Once again political change was inhibited by scepticism about politicians, and disunity among reformists.

The second question sought endorsement for a preamble to the constitution. The great and conservative poet Les Murray was consulted, but the resulting text was John Howard's (as Murray insisted with some asperity). It merely acknowledged that Aborigines were present before 1788, and insisted on mateship as a core value. Opposed in the Senate, Howard negotiated with the cross-bench Australian Democrats and their Aboriginal senator, Aiden Ridgeway. The final text (see Appendix) was nationalistic but free of mateship; it conceded Aboriginal and Torres Strait Islanders' 'deep kinship with their lands... [and] ancient and continuing cultures'; and it genuflected towards ethnic pluralism and environmental responsibility; but its anodyne terms failed to command attention. If Australians wanted their identity delineated, they were not about to accept a politicians' text any more than a politicians' republic.

A COHERENT REGION

Australia and New Zealand have become increasingly vital to most of the Island countries of the Pacific. At the same time, Australia has grown more important to New Zealand since the 1970s: as a home away from home, as a point of comparison, and because of closer economic and defence relations. The converse was not true: the hub of this region was relatively unaware and uninterested in their neighbours. As imperial connections faded, Australian policy aspired to learn about and benefit from the 'near North' rather than the Pacific. The main centre of the putative region in material terms, Australia was (and alone could afford to be) an exception in terms of consciousness.

Here are paradoxes and perversities. In 1999 and 2000 Australia and New Zealand had soldiers in Southeast Asia, empowered to use weaponry to create and enforce peace. Conversely, representatives of East Timor were contemplating a geopolitical shift of some moment – fudging the boundary between Asia and the Pacific by declaring themselves to be Melanesians and taking their country diplomatically out of Asia and into the South Pacific through joining the Pacific Commission and the South Pacific Forum.[40] At the same time Australia and New Zealand sustained unarmed civilian and military peace monitors in the Pacific island of Bougainville. Their power could be projected into 'Asia' only by force: only in the Pacific Islands could they project their influence without weapons. One perversity was the determination of Australian political leaders to create photo-opportunities with heavily armed soldiers, and never to mention the civilian and military volunteers risking their lives in Bougainville.

In 2000, Australia and New Zealand and the Islands do not conform to the model of post-Cold War fragmentation. Nor do they vindicate another model which perturbs critics of globalization. Political and ideological forces do pull us towards lower tariffs, freer flows of capital, technology, goods and people, and the creation and consumption of homogenized culture. But this is not unprecedented. Austronesian, Polynesian, British and French migrations also had homogenizing tendencies; and the universalist claims of Christian missions even more so. British sterling, then the American dollar, and for several decades the gold standard, aimed to be accepted as global measures of value. Diverse and divergent value systems survived these pressures, by part-accommodation more often than rejection. Today, when globalizing pressures may be more diffuse and powerful, rejection is not the only possible (nor perhaps the most effective) response, nor are states the only (nor the most creative) sites of resistance.

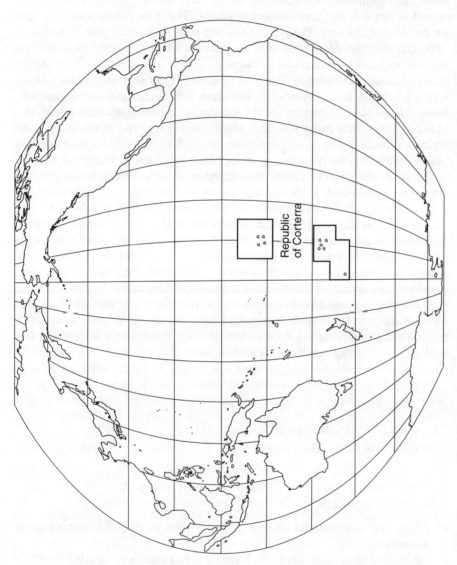

Figure 21.1 Republic of Corterra visualized by a Hong Kong entrepreneur, 1989; paradise with Chinese characteristics? Corterra's multi-racial population of 80,000 love democracy and freedom, speak English and have a British-derived legal system, and levy neither customs duties nor income tax. Quoted from the *Australian* of 28 March 1990. Courtesy of R. Gerard Ward and the Cartography Unit, Research School of Pacific and Asian Studies, Australian National University.

Many groups in our region exercise some control over their destinies. Samoans and other Polynesians, Tannese and other Melanesians, multiply their life-chances in extended families with far-flung links.[41] Urbanization from rural Melanesia should be seen in the same way, since Vila is as foreign to Aneityumese as Auckland to Tongans or Noumea to Wallisians.[42] Long-range opportunism is less obvious, and perhaps less common in other communities, but it is an option widely available. These movements and linkages are not bounded by the Pacific, but the region is their predominant focus.

We pay more heed to imagined communities which formed in dialectical opposition to each other and perhaps in dialectical sympathy with neighbours: Maori and Pakeha, Kanak and *caldoche*, Fijians and Indo-Fijians, South Sea Islanders, Torres Strait Islanders, Aborigines and non-indigenous Australians. Their concerns dominate the agendas of the region's states. Many governments insist that the 'main game' concerns relations between their own country and 'Asia', or its surrogates ASEAN, APEC, or individual 'Asian' countries. So they should: the prosperity of every country is affected by the economies to our north. On the other hand individuals, families and ethnicities focus much more strongly within the region.

Australians and New Zealanders of all descriptions feel comfortable with their Pacific neighbours. The extent and the warmth with which Islanders reciprocate is another question. In a critical sense, however, those sentiments hardly matter. It would be rash to suggest that the people of this region understand one other. Quite the reverse: what gives the region some of its coherence is that communities identify themselves by misunderstanding their neighbours in a mesh of dubious analogies. It is the accumulation of perceptions, misperceptions and concerns which makes ours such a dynamic region; and by reifying the region we make it a significant player in the layered impacts of, and reactions to, globalization.

APPENDIX

PREAMBLE PROPOSED IN 1999 FOR THE AUSTRALIAN CONSTITUTION

With hope in God, the Commonwealth of Australia is constituted as a democracy with a federal system of government to serve the common good.
We the Australian people commit ourselves to this constitution

- proud that our national unity has been forged by Australians from many ancestries;
- never forgetting the sacrifice of all who defended our country and our liberty in time of war;
- upholding freedom, tolerance, individual dignity and the rule of law;
- honouring Aborigines and Torres Strait Islanders, the nation's first people, for their deep kinship with their lands and for their ancient and continuing cultures which enrich the life of our country;
- recognizing the nation-building contribution of generations of immigrants;

- mindful of our responsibility to protect our unique natural environment;
- supportive of achievement as well as equality of opportunity for all;
- and valuing independence as dearly as the national spirit which binds us together in both adversity and success.

NOTES

1   R. G. Menzies, *Afternoon Light: Some Memories of Men and Events*, Melbourne, 1969; and David Goldsworthy, 'Menzies, Britain and the Commonwealth', in Frank Cain (ed.), *Menzies in War and Peace*, Sydney, 1997.

2   cf. Francis Fukuyama, *The End of History and the Last Man*, New York, 1992.

3   Stewart Firth, *Nuclear Playground*, Sydney, 1987; Bengt and Marie-Therese Danielsson, *Poisoned Reign: French Nuclear Colonialism in the Pacific*, Harmondsworth, 1986; Guy Smith, *Micronesia: Decolonization and US Military Interests in the Trust Territory of the Pacific Islands*, Australian National University Peace Research Centre, 1991.

4   Stewart Firth and Karin von Strokirch, 'A Nuclear Pacific', chapter 10 in Donald Denoon, Stewart Firth, Jocelyn Linnekin, Malama Meleisea and Karen Nero (eds), *Cambridge History of the Pacific Islanders*, Melbourne, 1997.

5   Ibid.

6   Brij Lal, 'Coups in Fiji', in Denoon, Firth, Linnekin, Meleisea and Nero, *Cambridge History of the Pacific Islanders*, 415–18; quotation from p. 416.

7   Brij Lal, *Broken Waves: A History of the Fiji Islands in the Twentieth Century*, Honolulu, 1992; and *Power and Prejudice: The Making of the Fiji Crisis*, Wellington, 1988.

8   Lal, *Power and Prejudice*.

9   *Fiji Times*, 29 August 1991. Lal, 'A Time to Change: The Fiji General Elections of 1999', seminar paper, Australian National University, Canberra, 1999; and his *Another Way: The Politics of Constitutional Reform in Post-coup Fiji*, Canberra, 1998.

10 Fiji Constitution Review Commission, *The Republic of the Fiji Islands: Towards a United Future*, Suva, 1996. See Brij Lal, 'Towards a United Future: Report of the Fiji Constitution Review Commission', *Journal of Pacific History*, 32: 2 (1997), 71–84.

11 Lal, *Broken Waves* and *Another Way*.

12 *Fiji Times*, 4 June 1999.

13 See annual Political Chronicles of Papua New Guinea in the *Journal of Pacific History*.

14 Momis's 'Bougainville Initiative' of 1987, reproduced as an appendix in Paul Quodling, *Bougainville: The Mine and the People*, Sydney, 1991.

15 Colin Filer, 'The Bougainville Rebellion, the Mining Industry and the Process of Social Disintegration in Papua New Guinea', in R. May and M. Spriggs, *The Bougainville Crisis*, Bathurst, 1990, 73–112; and 'The Escalation of Disintegration and the Reinvention of Authority', in M. Spriggs and D. Denoon, *The Bougainville Crisis: 1991 Update*, Bathurst, 1991, 112–40.

16 For example, chapters by Colin Filer, Rolf Gerritsen and Richard Jackson in Donald Denoon, Chris Ballard, Glenn Banks and Peter Hancock (eds), *Mining and Mineral Resource Policy Issues in Asia-Pacific*, Canberra, 1995.

17 Mary-Louise O'Callaghan, *Enemies Within: Papua New Guinea, Australia, and the Sandline Crisis: The Inside Story*, Sydney, 1999, 62.

18 Sean Dorney, *The Sandline Affair: Politics and Mercenaries and the Bougainville Crisis*, Sydney, 1998.
19 O'Callaghan and Dorney both cite the Sandline sales pitch.
20 Dorney, *The Sandline Affair*, 11–12, 347.
21 Papua New Guinea *National*, 23 April 1999.
22 BRA media release, 29 April 1999. A summary is published as 'BRA: NZ Deal "A Sell-out"', in *PNG Post Courier*, 30 April 1999.
23 Papua New Guinea *National*, 30 April 1999.
24 Tarcissius Kabataulaka and John Naitoro, seminar paper, Australian National University, Canberra, May 1999. See also the *Journal of Pacific History*'s annual Political Chronicles.
25 Alban Bensa, 'Culture Kanak et art contemporain: le Centre Tjibaou', in Darrell Tryon and Paul de Deckker (eds), *Identites en mutation dans le pacifique a l'aube du troisieme millenaire*, Bordeaux, 1998.
26 For the unfolding saga of East Timor, we rely on reports over CNN, the Australian Broadcasting Commission, the *Sydney Morning Herald*, and the *Australian*.
27 John Ingleson, 'Indonesian–Australian Relations', in Graeme Davison, John Hirst and Stuart Macintyre (eds), *Oxford Companion to Australian History*, Oxford, 1998, 341–3.
28 Alan Ward, *An Unsettled History: Treaty Claims in New Zealand Today*, Wellington, 1999, 173.
29 Joe Williams, 'Quality Relations: The Key to Maori Survival', in Ken S. Coates and P. G. McHugh, *Living Relationships: Kokiri Ngatahi*, Wellington, 1998, 263.
30 Coates and McHugh, *Living Relationships*, introduction.
31 Justice Durie's brother; quotation in Coates and McHugh, *Living Relationships*, 11, 193.
32 Bill Oliver, quoted in ibid., 11.
33 David Round, *Truth or Treaty? Commonsense Questions about the Treaty of Waitangi*, Christchurch, 1998, 11, 25, 201, 203.
34 See, for example, Waitangi Tribunal, *Te Whanau O Waipareira Report*, Wai 414, Wellington, 1998.
35 Roger Maaka, in Coates and McHugh, *Living Relationships*, 15, 204–5.
36 A common media reference to *Xena, Warrior Princess*, a Hollywood television production starring New Zealand actor Lucy Lawless and produced in New Zealand.
37 Tim Hazeldine, *Taking New Zealand Seriously: The Economics of Decency*, Auckland, 1998, 11.
38 Andrew Markus, *Australian Race Relations 1788–1993*, Sydney, 1994.
39 Ibid., 172.
40 Jose Ramos-Horta, in the *East West Observer*, Honolulu, spring 1999, 3.
41 Grant McCall and John Connell (eds), *A World Perspective on Pacific Islander Migration: Australia, New Zealand and the USA*, Sydney, 1993; Joel Bonnemaison, *The Tree and the Canoe: History and Ethnogeography of Tanna*, Honolulu, 1994.
42 John Connell (ed.), *Migration and Development in the South Pacific*, Canberra, 1990.

BIBLIOGRAPHY

Adams, Ron, *In the Land of Strangers: A Century of European Contact with Tanna*, Canberra, 1984.

Aldrich, Robert, *The French Presence in the South Pacific, 1842–1939*, London, 1990.

Aldrich, Robert and John Connell (eds), *France's Overseas Frontiers: Departments et Territoires D'Outre-Mer*, Cambridge, 1992.

Alford, Katrina, 'Colonial Women's Employment as Seen by Nineteenth-century Statisticians and Twentieth-century Economic Historians', *Labour History*, 51 (1986): 1–10.

Alford, Katrina, *Production or Reproduction? An Economic History of Women in Australia, 1788–1850*, Melbourne, 1984.

Allen, Colin H., 'The Post-war Scene in the Western Solomons and Marching Rule: A Memoir', *Journal of Pacific History*, 24: 1 (1989): 89–99.

Allen, Jim and Chris Gosden, *Report of the Lapita Homeland Project*, Australian National University Prehistory Occasional Paper 20, Canberra, 1991.

Allen, Jim, Jack Golson and Rhys Jones (eds), *Sunda and Sahul: Prehistoric Studies in Southeast Asia, Melanesia and Australia*, London, 1977.

Allen, Michael, 'The Establishment of Christianity and Cash-cropping in a New Hebridean Community', *Journal of Pacific History*, 3 (1968): 25–46.

Amherst, Lord and Basil Thomson (eds), *The Discovery of the Solomon Islands by Alvaro de Mendaña in 1568*, London, 1901.

Amirah Inglis, *Not a White Woman Safe: Sexual Anxiety and Politics in Port Moresby, 1920–34*, Canberra, 1974.

Anderson, Athol (ed.), *Traditional Fishing in the Pacific: Ethnographic and Archaeological Papers from the 1st Pacific Science Congress*, Honolulu, 1986.

Anderson, Athol, *Prodigious Birds: Moas and Moa-hunting in Prehistoric New Zealand*, Cambridge, 1989.

Anderson, Benedict R. O., *Imagined Communities: Reflections on the Origin and Spread of Nationalism*, 1st edn, London, 1983.

Andrews, C. Lesley, 'Aspects of Development: The Maori Situation, 1870–1890.' MA thesis, University of Auckland, 1968.

Archie, Carol (ed.), *Maori Sovereignty: The Pakeha Perspective*, Auckland, 1995.

Arnold, Lorna, *A Very Special Relationship: British Atomic Weapon Trials in Australia*, London, 1987.

l'Association des français contre la bombe, *Le Bataillon de la paix*, Paris, n.d.

Asterisk [Robert James Fletcher], *Isles of Illusion: Letters From the South Seas*, London, 1986.

Atkinson, Alan, *The Europeans in Australia: A History*, 2 vols, Melbourne, 1997.

Attwood, Bain (ed.), *In the Age of Mabo: History, Aborigines and Australia*, Sydney, 1996.

'Atu Emberson-Bain, *Labour and Gold in Fiji*, Cambridge, 1994.

Auchmuty, J. J., '1810–30'. In Frank Crowley (ed.), *A New History of Australia*, Melbourne, 1974, 45–81.

Aveling [Quartly], Marian, 'Bending the Bars: Convict Women and the State.' In Kay Saunders and Ray Evans (eds), *Gender Relations in Australia: Domination and Negotiation*, Sydney, 1992, 144–57.

Awatere, Donna, *Maori Sovereignty*, Auckland, 1984.

Bain, Wilhelmina Sherriff, 'Peace and Arbitration.' In Margaret Lovell-Smith (ed.), *The Woman Question: Writings by the Women Who Won the Vote*, Auckland, 1900, 224–8.

Baines, Dudley, *Emigration from Europe 1815–1930*. Studies in Economic and Social History. Houndmills and London, 1991.

Ballara, Angela, *Proud to be White? A Survey of Pakeha Prejudice in New Zealand*, Auckland, 1986.

Ballara, Angela, *Iwi: The Dynamics of Maori Tribal Organization from c.1769 to c.1945*, Wellington, 1998.

Ballard, Chris, 'The Centre Cannot Hold: Trade Networks and Sacred Geography in the Papua New Guinea Highlands', *Archaeology in Oceania*, 29: 3 (1994).

Ballard, Chris, 'The Death of a Great Land: Ritual, History and Subsistence Revolution in the Southern Highlands of Papua New Guinea.' Ph.D. thesis, Australian National University, Canberra, 1995.

Banks, Glenn and Chris Ballard (eds), *The Ok Tedi Settlement: Issues, Outcomes and Implications*, Canberra, 1997.

Bann, Stephen, 'From Captain Cook to Neil Armstrong.' In Simon Pugh (ed.), *Reading Landscape: Country – City – Capital*, Manchester, 1990.

Barnett, Stephen and Richard Wolfe, *New Zealand! New Zealand! In Praise of Kiwiana*, Auckland, 1989.

Barrett, J. W. 'Presidential Address', *Intercolonial Medical Journal of Australasia*, 6 (1901): 1–28.

Barwick, G. F., *New Light on the Discovery of Australia as Revealed by the Journal of Captain Don Diego de Prado y Tovar*. In H. N. Stevens (ed.), Hakluyt Society Works, London, 1930, series 2, vol. 64.

Bassett, Michael, *The State in New Zealand 1840–1984: Socialism Without Doctrines?* Auckland, 1998.

Bate, Weston, *Victorian Gold Rushes*, Melbourne, 1988.

Bates, Arthur P., *The Bridge to Nowhere: The Ill-fated Mangapurua Settlement*, Wanganui, 1982.

Bates, Daisy, *The Passing of the Aborigines: A Lifetime Spent Among the Natives of Australia*, 1st edn, London, 1938.

Beaglehole, J. C. (ed.), *The Journals of Captain James Cook on his Voyages of Discovery*, 3 vols, Cambridge, 1955–74.

Beaglehole, J. C. (ed.), *The 'Endeavour' Journal of Joseph Banks 1768–1771*, vol. 1, Sydney, 1963.

Beaglehole, J. C., *The Life of Captain James Cook*, London, 1974.

Beaglehole, J. C. (ed.), *The Voyage of the 'Endeavour' 1768–1771*, London, 1988.

Beaumont, Joan (ed.), *Australia's War, 1914–18*, Sydney, 1995.

Becke, Louis, *By Reef and Palm*, Sydney, 1955.

Bedford, R. D. and A. F. Mamak, *Compensating for Development: The Bougainville Case*, Christchurch, 1977.

Belich, James, *The New Zealand Wars and the Victorian Interpretation of Racial Conflict*, Auckland, 1986.

Belich, James, *Making Peoples: A History of the New Zealanders from Polynesian Settlement to the End of the Nineteenth Century*, Auckland, 1996.

Bell, Claudia, *Inventing New Zealand: Everyday Myths of Pakeha Identity*, Auckland, 1996.

Bell, Clive (ed.), *The Diseases and Health Services of Papua New Guinea*, Port Moresby, 1973.

Bellwood, Peter, *The Polynesians: Prehistory of an Island People*, London, 1987.

Bellwood, Peter, James Fox and Darrell Tryon (eds), *The Austronesians: Historical and Comparative Perspectives*, Canberra, 1995.

Bennett, James Ewan, 'Redeeming the Imagination: A Trans-national History of Australia and Aotearoa/New Zealand, 1890–1944.' Ph.D. thesis, University of Melbourne, 1997.

Bennett, Judith, *Wealth of the Solomons: A History of a Pacific Archipelago, 1800–1978*, Honolulu, 1987.

Bennett, Neville, 'Bitter Fruit: Japanese Migration and Anglo-Saxon Obstacles, 1890–1924', *Transactions of the Asiatic Society of Japan*, 8 (1993): 67–83.

Bennett, Samuel, *The History of Australian Discovery and Colonization*, Sydney, 1867.

Best, Elsdon, *Fishing Methods and Devices of the Maori*, 1929 edn, Dominion Museum Bulletin No. 12, Wellington, 1977.

Binney, Judith, *Illustrated History of New Zealand*, Auckland, 1990.

Binney, Judith, Gillian Chaplin and Craig Wallace, *Mihaia: The Prophet Rua Kenana and His Community at Maungapohatu*, 2nd edn, Auckland, 1990.

Blainey, Geoffrey, *The Rush that Never Ended: A History of Australian Mining*, 2nd edn, Melbourne, 1969.

Blainey, Geoffrey, *The Triumph of the Nomads: A History of Ancient Australia*, Melbourne, 1975.

Bobin, Frederic, 'Caldoches, Metropolitans and the Mother Country', *Journal of Pacific History*, 26: 2 (1991): 303–12.

Bollard, Alan, Darcy McCormack and Mark Scanlan, *Closer Economic Relations: A View from Both Sides of the Tasman*, Wellington and Melbourne, 1986.

Bolton, Geoffrey (ed.), *Oxford History of Australia, Vol. 5: The Middle Way 1942–1995*, 5 vols, 2nd edn, Melbourne, 1996.

Bonnemaison, Joel, *The Tree and the Canoe: History and Ethnogeography of Tanna*, Honolulu, 1994.

Boot, H. M. 'Government and the Colonial Economies', *Australian Economic History Review*, 38 (1998): 74–98.

Borrie, W. D., *The European Peopling of Australasia: A Demographic History, 1788–1988*, Canberra, 1994.

Bougainville, Louis-Antoine de, *A Voyage Round the World … in the Frigate 'La Boudeuse' and the Store Ship 'L'Etoile' …* , trans. J. R. Forster, London, 1772.

Boutilier, James, Daniel Hughes and Sharon Tiffany (eds), *Mission, Church and Sect in Oceania*, Lanham, MD, 1978.

Boyd, Mary, 'The Military Administration of Western Samoa, 1914–1919', *New Zealand Journal of History*, 2: 2 (1968): 148–64.

Boyd, Robin, *Australia's Home: Its Origins, Builders and Occupiers*, 2nd edn, Melbourne, 1991.

Bradley, David, *No Place to Hide, 1946/1984*, Hanover, 1983.

Brooking, Tom, ' "Busting Up" the Greatest Estate of All: Liberal Maori Land Policy, 1891–1911', *New Zealand Journal of History*, 26 (April 1992): 78–98.

Brooking, Tom, 'Use It or Lose It: Unravelling the Land Debate in Late Nineteenth-century New Zealand', *New Zealand Journal of History*, 30 (October 1996): 141–62.

Brooking, Tom, *Lands for the People?* Dunedin, 1996.

Brooking, Tom and Roberto Rabel, 'Neither British nor Polynesian: A Brief History of New Zealand's Other Immigrants.' In Stuart W. Greif (ed.), *Immigration and National Identity in New Zealand*, Palmerston North, 1995, 23–49.

Broome, Richard, *Aboriginal Australians: Black Responses to White Dominance, 1788–1994*, 2nd edn, St Leonards, NSW, 1994.

de Brosses, Charles, *Histoire des navigations aux terres australes*, Paris, 1756.

Brunner, Edmund de S., *Rural Australia and New Zealand: Some Observations of Current Trends*, Studies of the Pacific no. 2, San Francisco, 1938.

Bryant, Jenny, *Urban Poverty and the Environment in the South Pacific*, Armidale, 1993.

Bryder, Linda and Derek Dow (eds), *New Countries and Old Medicines*, Auckland, 1995.

Buckley, Ken and Ted Wheelwright, *No Paradise for Workers: Capitalism and the Common People in Australia 1788–1914*, Melbourne, 1992.

Bulbeck, Chilla, *Australian Women in Papua New Guinea: Colonial Passages 1920–1960*, Cambridge, 1992.

Bulbeck, Chilla, *Living Feminism: The Impact of the Women's Movement on Three Generations of Australian Women*, Melbourne, 1997.

Burns, Patricia, *Fatal Success: A History of the New Zealand Company*, Wellington, 1989.

Burridge, K. O. L., *New Heaven, New Earth: A Study of Millenarian Activities*, Oxford, 1969.

Burton, John, 'Axe Makers of the Wahgi.' Ph.D. thesis, Australian National University, Canberra, 1984.

Butlin, N. G., *Investment in Australian Economic Development 1861–1900*, Canberra, 1976.

Butlin, N. G., *Our Original Aggression: Aboriginal Populations of Southeastern Australia, 1788–1850*, Sydney, 1983.

Butlin, N. G., 'Australian Wealth and Progress since 1788: A Statistical Picture.' In *The Bicentennial Diary*, Brisbane, 1987, 221–32.

Butlin, N. G., *Economics and the Dreamtime: A Hypothetical History*, Cambridge, 1993.

Butlin, N. G., *Forming a Colonial Economy: Australia 1810–1850*, Cambridge, 1994.

Butlin, N. G., A. Barnard and J. J. Pincus, *Government and Capitalism: Public and Private Choice in Twentieth Century Australia*, Sydney, 1982.

Butterworth, Graham, *Sir Apirana Ngata*, Wellington, 1968.

Byrnes, Giselle M., 'Inventing New Zealand: Surveying, Science, and the Construction of Cultural Space, 1840s–1890s.' Ph.D. thesis, University of Auckland, 1995.

Byrnes, Giselle M., 'Surveying – the Maori and the Land: An Essay in Historical Representation', *New Zealand Journal of History*, 31 (1997): 85–98.

Camm, J. C. R. and John McQuilton (eds), *Australians: A Historical Atlas*, Sydney, 1987.

Camm, J. C. R. and John McQuilton (eds), *Australians: A Historical Library*, Sydney, 1987.

Campbell, I. C., 'European–Polynesian Encounters: A Critique of the Pearson Thesis', *Journal of Pacific History*, 29 (1994): 222–31.

Campbell, I. C.,'Culture Contact and Polynesian Identity in the European Age', *Journal of World History*, 8 (1997): 29–55.

Campbell, Ian, *A History of the Pacific Islands*, Christchurch, 1989.

Campbell, Ian, *Island Kingdom: Tonga, Ancient and Modern*, Christchurch, 1992.

Carter, Paul, *The Road to Botany Bay: An Essay in Spatial History*, London, 1987.

Castles, Francis G., *The Working Class and Welfare: Reflections on the Political Development of the Welfare State in Australia and New Zealand, 1890–1980*, Wellington, 1985.

Castles, Frank, Rolf Gerritsen and Jack Vowles (eds), *The Great Experiment: Labour Parties and Public Policy Transformation in Australia and New Zealand*, Auckland, 1996.

Chapman, R. M., 'No Land is an Island.' In Keith Sinclair (ed.), *Distance Looks Our Way: The Effects of Remoteness on New Zealand*, Auckland, 1961, 42–62.

Chapman, Valerie and Peter Read (eds), *Terrible Hard Biscuits: A Reader in Aboriginal History*, Sydney, 1996.

Chappell, David, 'Shipboard Relations between Pacific Island Women and Euroamerican Men, 1767–1887', *Journal of Pacific History*, 27: 2 (1992): 131–49.

Chappell, David, 'Secret Sharers: Indigenous Beachcombers in the Pacific Islands', *Pacific Studies*, 17 (2), 1994: 131–48.

Chappell, David, 'Active Agents versus Passive Victims. Decolonized Historiography or Problematic Paradigm?', *The Contemporary Pacific*, 7: 2 (1995): 303–26.

Chesterman, John and Brian Galligan, *Citizens without Rights: Aborigines and Australian Citizenship*, Melbourne, 1997.

Choi, C. Y., *Chinese Migration and Settlement in Australia*, Sydney, 1975.

Chowning, Ann, 'The Development of Ethnic Identity and Ethnic Stereotypes on Papua New Guinea Plantations', *Journal de la societé des oceanistes*, 42 (1986).

Clancy, Patricia and Jeanne Allen (eds), *The French Consul's Wife: Memoirs of Celeste de Chabrillan in Gold-rush Australia*, Melbourne, 1998.

Clark, C. M., *A History of Australia*, 6 vols, Melbourne, 1962–87.

Cleave, Peter, *The Sovereignty Game: Power, Knowledge and Reading the Treaty*, Wellington, 1989.

Clifford, James, *Person and Myth: Maurice Leenhardt in the Melanesian World*, Berkeley, CA, 1982.

Coates, Ken S. and P. G. McHugh, *Living Relationships: Kokiri Ngatahi: The Treaty of Waitangi in the New Millennium*, Wellington, 1998.

Condliffe, J. B., *New Zealand in the Making: A Study of Economic and Social Development*, London, 1930.

Coney, Sandra, *Standing in the Sunshine: A History of New Zealand Women Since They Won the Vote*, Auckland, 1993.

Connell, John, *New Caledonia or Kanaky? The Political History of a French Colony*, Canberra, 1987.

Connell, John (ed.), *Migration and Development in the South Pacific*, Canberra, 1990.

Connell, John, 'Island Microstate: The Mirage of Development', *The Contemporary Pacific*, 3: 2 (1991), 251–87.

Connolly, Bob and Robin Anderson, *First Contact: New Guinea's Highlanders Encounter the Outside World*, New York, 1988.

Cooper, Matthew, 'Economic Context of Shell Money Production in Malaita', *Oceania*, 41: 4 (1971).

Corney, B. G., J. Stewart and B. H. Thomson, *Report of the Commission Appointed to Inquire into the Decrease of the Native Population*.

Corris, Peter, *Passage, Port and Plantation: A History of Solomon Islands Labour Migration*, Melbourne, 1973.

Cox, Lindsay, *Kotahitanga: The Search for Maori Political Unity*, Auckland, 1993.

Craven, Edward, 'Mineral Resources: A Discussion about an Irian Jaya Experience.' In B. Farrell (ed.), *Views of Economic Development in the Pacific*, Santa Cruz, CA, 1975.

Crosby, Alfred W., *Ecological Imperialism: The Biological Expansion of Europe, 900–1900*. Studies in Environment and History, ed. Donald Worster and Alfred Crosby, Cambridge, 1986.

Cross, Gary, 'Labour in Settler-state Democracies: Comparative Perspectives on Australia and the US, 1860–1920', *Labour History*, 70 (1996): 1–24.

Crowley, Frank, *A New History of Australia*, Melbourne, 1974.

Curthoys, Ann and Andrew Markus (eds), *Who are our Enemies? Racism and the Working Class in Australia*, Sydney, 1978.

Dacker, Bill, *Evidence for the Ngai Tahu Claim before the Waitangi Tribunal*, Waitangi Tribunal vol. 24, Otakou Marae, 1988.

Dacker, Bill, *The People of the Place: Mahika Kai*, Wellington, 1990.

Dacker, Bill, *Te Mamae me te Aroha: The Pain and the Love*, Dunedin, 1994.

Dagmar, Hans, 'Banabans in Fiji: Ethnicity, Change and Development.' In M. C. Howard (ed.), *Ethnicity and Nation-building in the Pacific*, Tokyo, 1989.

Dairy Board, New Zealand, 'Interview with William Pember Reeves', *New Zealand Dairy Produce Exporter*, 30 April 1926, 24–5.

Dalton, B. J., *War and Politics in New Zealand, 1855–1870*, Sydney, 1967.

Dalziel, Raewyn, *Julius Vogel: Business Politician*, Auckland, 1986.

Dalziel, Raewyn, 'Men, Women and Wakefield.' In *Edward Gibbon Wakefield and the Colonial Dream: A Reconsideration*, Wellington, 1997, 77–86.

Damousi, Joy, 'Socialist Women and Gendered Space: The Anti-conscription and Anti-war Campaigns of 1914–1918', *Labour History*, 60 (May 1991): 1–15.

Damousi, Joy, *Depraved and Disorderly: Female Convicts, Sexuality and Gender in Colonial Australia*, Melbourne, 1997.

Davidson, James, 'Problems of Pacific History', *Journal of Pacific History*, 1 (1966): 5–21.

Davidson, James, *Samoa mo Samoa: The Emergence of the Independent State of Western Samoa*, Melbourne, 1967.

Davidson, Janet M., *The Prehistory of New Zealand*, 2nd edn, Auckland, 1992a.

Davidson, Janet M., 'The Polynesian Foundation.' In G. W. Rice (ed.), *Oxford History of New Zealand*, Auckland, 1992b, 3–27.

Davis, Lance E. and Robert A. Huttenback, *Mammon and the Pursuit of Empire*. Interdisciplinary Perspectives on Modern History, eds Robert Fogel and Stephan Thernstrom. Cambridge, 1986.

Davison, Graeme, 'The Australian Energy System in 1888', *Australia 1888 Bulletin*, 10 (1982): 3–37.

Daws, Gavan, *A Dream of Islands: Voyages of Self-discovery in the South Seas*, Brisbane, 1980.

Day, David, *Claiming a Continent: A History of Australia*, Sydney, 1996.

Deacon, Desley, 'Seeing the State.' In Terry Irving (ed.), *Challenges to Labour History*, Sydney, 1994, 136–49.

Dening, Greg, *Islands and Beaches: Discourse on a Silent Land, Marquesas 1774–1880*, Honolulu, 1980.

Dening, Greg, *Mr Bligh's Bad Language: Passion, Power and Theatre on the Bounty*, Cambridge, 1992.

Denoon, Donald, *Settler Capitalism: The Dynamics of Dependent Development in the Southern Hemisphere*, Oxford, 1983.

Denoon, Donald, 'Pacific Island Depopulation: Natural or Unnatural Causes?' In Linda Bryder and Derek Dow (eds), *New Countries and Old Medicines*, Auckland, 1995, 324–39.

Denoon, Donald, *Getting Under the Skin*, Melbourne, 2000.

Denoon, Donald and Catherine Snowden (eds), *A History of Agriculture in Papua New Guinea*, Boroko, n.d. [1981].

Denoon, Donald with Kathleen Dugan and Leslie Marshall, *Public Health in Papua New Guinea, 1884–1984: Medical Possibility and Social Constraint*, Cambridge, 1989.

Denoon, Donald, Chris Ballard, Glenn Banks and Peter Hancock (eds), *Mining and Mineral Resource Policy Issues in Asia-Pacific*, Canberra, 1995.

Denoon, Donald, with Stewart Firth, Jocelyn Linnekin, Malama Meleisea and Karen Nero (eds), *Cambridge History of the Pacific Islanders*, Melbourne, 1997.

Dexter, David, *The New Guinea Offensives: Australia in the War of 1939–1945*, Australian War Memorial Series 1, VI, Canberra, 1961.

Diamond, Jared, *Guns, Germs and Steel: The Fates of Human Societies*, New York, 1997.

Dirlik, Arif, 'The Asia-Pacific Idea: Reality and Representation in the Invention of a Regional Structure', *Journal of World History*, 3 (1992): 55–79.

Dixson, Miriam, *The Real Matilda: Woman and Identity in Australia 1788 to the Present*, 3rd edn, Melbourne, 1994.

Dodson, J. (ed.), *The Naive Lands: Prehistory and Environmental Change in Australia and the South-west Pacific*, Melbourne, 1992.

Douglas, Bronwen, 'Discourses of Death in a Melanesian World.' In Donna Merwick (ed.), *Dangerous Liaisons: Essays in Honour of Greg Dening*, Melbourne, 1994, 353–78.

Douglas, Ngaire, *They Came for Savages: 100 Years of Tourism in Melanesia*, Lismore, 1996.

Dow, Derek, ' "Smoothing Their Dying Pillow" Lingering Longer', *New Zealand Doctor*, (1998): 45.

Downs, Ian, *The Australian Trusteeship Papua New Guinea 1945–75*, Canberra, 1980.

Drake-Brockman, Henrietta, *Voyage to Disaster*, Sydney, 1963.

Drummond, J., 'The Guardians of Papawai', *New Zealand Historic Places*, 63 (1997): 22–3.

Dumont d'Urville, J. S. C., *Voyage de la corvette l'Astrolabe … pendant les années 1826, 1827, 1828, 1829*, Paris, 1830.

Dunmore, John (trans. and ed.), *The Journal of Jean-François de Galaup de la Pérouse*, London, 1994–5.

Durie, Mason H., *Te Mana Te Kawanatanga: The Politics of Maori Self-determination*, Auckland, 1998.

Durie, Mason H., *Whaiora: Maori Health Development*, Auckland, 1994.

Dyster, Barrie and David Meredith, *Australia in the International Economy in the Twentieth Century*, Melbourne, 1990.

Easton, Brian, *The Commercialisation of New Zealand*, Auckland, 1997.

Easton, Brian, *In Stormy Seas: The Post-war New Zealand Economy*, Dunedin, 1997.

Elsmore, Bronwyn, *Like Them That Dream: The Maori and the Old Testament*, Tauranga, 1985.

Elsmore, Bronwyn, *Mana from Heaven: A Century of Maori Prophets in New Zealand*, Tauranga, 1989.

Engels, Dagmar and Shula Marks (eds), *Contesting Colonial Hegemony: State and Society in Africa and India*, London, 1994.

Epeli Hau'ofa, 'A Pacific Islander's View.' In R. G. Ward and A. Proctor (eds), *South Pacific Agriculture: Choices and Constraints*, Canberra, 1980.

Epeli Hau'ofa, 'Our Sea of Islands.' In Eric Waddell, Vijay Naidu and Epeli Hau'ofa (eds), *A New Oceania: Rediscovering Our Sea of Islands*, Suva, 1993.

Epstein, T. S., *Capitalism, Primitive and Modern: Some Aspects of Tolai Economic Growth*, Canberra, 1968.

Evatt, Elizabeth, 'The Acquisition of Territory in Australia and New Zealand.' In C. H. Alexandrowicz (ed.), *Grotian Society Papers 1968: Studies in the History of the Law of Nations*, The Hague, 1970.

Evison, Harry C. (ed.), *The Treaty of Waitangi and the Ngai Tahu Claim*, Ka Roimata Whenua Series, No. 2, Christchurch, 1988.

Evison, Harry C., *Te Wai Pounamu: The Greenstone Island*, Christchurch, 1993.

Fagan, Robert H. and Michael Webber, *Global Restructuring: The Australian Experience*, Meridian: Australian Geographical Perspectives, ed. Deirdre Dragovich and Alaric Maude, Melbourne, 1994.

Fairburn, Miles, 'The Rural Myth and the New Urban Frontier: An Approach to New Zealand Social History, 1870–1940', *New Zealand Journal of History*, 9: 1 (April 1975): 3–21.

Fairburn, Miles, *The Ideal Society and Its Enemies: The Foundations of Modern New Zealand Society, 1850–1900*, Auckland, 1989.

Feil, D. K., 'Women and Men in the Enga tee', *American Ethnologist*, 5 (1978): 263–79.

Ferguson, Gael, *Building the New Zealand Dream*, Palmerston North, 1994.

Field, Barron (ed.), *Geographical Memoirs on New South Wales*, London, 1825.

Filer, Colin, 'The Bougainville Rebellion, the Mining Industry and the Process of Social Disintegration in Papua New Guinea.' In R. May and M. Spriggs (eds), *Bougainville Update*, Bathurst, 1990.

Fingleton, Jim, 'Pacific Values and Economic Development? How Melanesian Constitutions Deal with Land.' In P. Sack (ed.), *Pacific Constitutions*, Canberra, 1982.

Firth, Raymond W., *Economics of the New Zealand Maori*, 2nd edn, Wellington, 1959.

Firth, Stewart, *New Guinea Under the Germans*, Melbourne, 1983.

Firth, Stewart, *Nuclear Playground*, Sydney, 1987.

Fitzpatrick, Brian, *The British Empire in Australia: An Economic History, 1834–1939*, Melbourne, 1941.

Flannery, Timothy Fridtjof, *The Future Eaters: An Ecological History of the Australasian Lands and People*, Melbourne, 1994.

Flinders, Matthew, *A Voyage to Terra Australis...*, London, 1814.

Formisano, Luciano (ed.), *Letters From a New World: Amerigo Vespucci's Discovery of America*, New York, 1992.

Forster, Colin, *France and Botany Bay: The Lure of a Penal Colony*, Melbourne, 1996.

Forster, Johann Reinhold, *Observations Made During a Voyage Round the World* [1778], ed. Nicholas Thomas, Harriet Guest and Michael Dettelbach, Honolulu, 1996.

Frances, Raelene, 'Marginal Matters: Gender, Skill, Unions and the Commonwealth Arbitration Court – A Case Study of the Australian Printing Industry, 1925–1937', *Labour History*, 61 (1991): 17–29.

Frances, Raelene, Linda Kealey and Joan Sangster. 'Women and Wage Labour in Australia and Canada, 1880–1980', *Labour History*, 71 (1996): 54–89.

Francis, Mark, *Governors and Settlers: Images of Authority in the British Colonies, 1820–60*, London, 1992.

Frankel, Stephen, *The Huli Response to Illness*, Cambridge, 1986.

Frankel, Stephen, and Gilbert Lewis (eds), *A Continuing Trial of Treatment: Medical Pluralism in Papua New Guinea*, Boston, 1989.

Frazer, Ian, 'Walkabout and Urban Movement: A Melanesian Case Study', *Pacific Viewpoint*, 26 (1985): 185–205.

Freeman, Derek, *Margaret Mead and Samoa: The Making and Unmaking of an Anthropological Myth*, Canberra, 1983.

Frost, Alan, 'Towards Australia: The Coming of the Europeans 1400 to 1788.' In D. J. Mulvaney and J. Peter White (eds), *Australians to 1788*, Sydney, 1987: 368–411.

Frost, Lionel, *Australian Cities in Comparative View*, Melbourne, 1990.

Frost, Lionel, *The New Urban Frontier*, Sydney, 1991.

Fry, Eric (ed.), *Common Cause: Essays in Australian and New Zealand Labour History*, Wellington, 1986.

Fry, Greg, 'South Pacific Regionalism.' MA thesis, Australian National University, Canberra, 1979.

Furnas, J. C., *Anatomy of Paradise: Hawaii and the Islands of the South Seas*, London, 1948.

Galbreath, Ross. 'Colonization, Science and Conservation.' D. Phil. thesis, University of Waikato, 1989.

Gallagher, John and Ronald Robinson, 'The Imperialism of Free Trade', *Economic History Review*, 6 (1953): 1–15.

Gallagher, Timothy Martin, 'New England Whalers and the Maori Economic Frontier 1815–1840.' MA thesis, Victoria University of Wellington, 1994.

Gammage, Bill, 'The Rabaul Strike, 1929', *Journal of Pacific History*, 10: 2 (1975): 3–29.

Gammage, Bill, *The Sky Travellers: Journeys in New Guinea 1938–1939*, Melbourne, 1998.

Ganter, Regina, *The Pearl-shellers of Torres Strait: Resource Use, Development and Decline, 1860s–1960s*, Melbourne, 1994.

Gardner, Robert and Karl Heider, *Gardens of War: Life and Death in the New Guinea Stone Age*, New York, 1968.

Gardner, W. J. 'The Founding of Nelson and Canterbury: A Comparative Study', *Historical News*, 48 (1984): 1–9.

Garrett, John, *Footsteps in the Sea: Christianity in Oceania to World War II*, Geneva and Suva, 1992.

Garton, Stephen, *Out of Luck: Poor Australians and Social Welfare 1788–1988*, Sydney, 1990.

Garton, Stephen and Margaret E. McCallum, 'Workers' Welfare: Labour and the Welfare State in 20th-century Australia and Canada', *Labour History*, 71 (1996): 116–41.

Gegeo, David, 'Tribes in Agony: Land, Development and Politics in Solomon Islands', *Cultural Survival Quarterly*, 15: 2 (1991).

Gibbons, P. J., 'Non Fiction.' In Terry Sturm (ed.), *Oxford History of New Zealand Literature in English*, Auckland, 1998.

Gilbert, Alan D., and K. S. Inglis (gen. eds), *Australians: A Historical Library*, 10 vols, Sydney, 1988.

Gillion, Ken, *The Fiji Indians: Challenge to European Dominance 1920–1946*, Canberra, 1977.

Gilson, Richard, *The Cook Islands 1820–1950*, ed. Ron Crocombe, Wellington, 1980.

Gilson, Richard, *Samoa 1830–1900: The Politics of a Multi-cultural Community*, Melbourne, 1970.

Goddard, Michael, 'The Rascal Road: Crime, Prestige, and Development in Papua New Guinea', *The Contemporary Pacific*, 7: 1 (1995): 55–80.

Goldsmith, Paul, 'Medicine, Death and the Gospel in Wairarapa and Hawke's Bay, 1845–1852', *New Zealand Journal of History*, 30 (1996): 163–81.

Gollan, Robin, *The Coalminers of New South Wales: A History of the Union, 1860–1960*, Melbourne, 1963.

Goodman, David, *Gold Seeking: Victoria and California in the 1850s*, Sydney, 1994.

Gotschalk, J., 'Sela Valley: An Ethnography of a Mek Society in the Eastern Highlands, Irian Jaya, Indonesia.' Ph.D. thesis, University of Amsterdam, 1993.

Gourevitch, Peter A., 'The Pacific Rim: Current Debates', *Annals of the American Academy of Political and Social Science*, 505 (1989): 8–23.

Grattan, C. Hartley, *The United States and the Southwest Pacific*, Cambridge, MA, 1961.

Grattan, C. Hartley, *The Southwest Pacific Since 1900: A Modern History*, 2 vols, Ann Arbor, MI, 1963.

Graves, Adrian, *Cane and Labour: The Political Economy of the Queensland Sugar Industry*, Edinburgh, 1993.

Green, R. C., 'Near and Remote Oceania: Disestablishing "Melanesia" in Culture History.' In A. Pawley (ed.), *Man and a Half: Essays in Pacific Anthropology and Ethnobiology in Honour of Ralph Bulmer*, Auckland, 1991.

Greenfeld, Liah, *Nationalism: Five Roads to Modernity*, Cambridge, MA, 1992.

Greif, Stuart W. (ed.), *Immigration and National Identity in New Zealand: One People, Two Peoples, Many Peoples?* Palmerston North, 1995.

Grey, Alan H., *Aotearoa and New Zealand: A Historical Geography*, Christchurch, 1994.

Griffin, James, Hank Nelson and Stewart Firth, *Papua New Guinea: A Political History*, Melbourne, 1979.

Grimshaw, Anna and Keith Hart, *Anthropology and the Crisis of the Intellectuals*, Cambridge, 1993.

Grimshaw, Patricia, Marilyn Lake, Ann McGrath and Marian Quartly, *Creating a Nation*, Melbourne, 1994.

Grove, Richard H., *Green Imperialism: Colonial Expansion, Tropical Island Edens and the Origins of Environmentalism 1600–1860*, Cambridge, 1995.

Grove, Richard H., *Ecology, Climate and Empire*, Cambridge, 1997.

Guiart, Jean, *Un Siècle et demi de contacts culturels tanna, Nouvelles-Hebrides*, Paris, 1956.

Guiart, Jean, *La Terre est la sang des morts*, Paris, 1984.

Gunson, W. N., *Messengers of Grace: Evangelical Missionaries in the South Seas, 1797–1860*, Melbourne, 1978.

Hackshaw, Frederika, 'Nineteenth-century Notions of Aboriginal Title and their Influence on the Interpretation of the Treaty of Waitangi.' In I. H. Kawharu (ed.), *Waitangi: Maori and Pakeha Perspectives of the Treaty of Waitangi*, Auckland, 1989.

Hagan, Jim and Andrew Wells (eds), *The Maritime Strike: A Centennial Retrospective*, Five Islands Press Associates with University of Wollongong Labour History Research Group and the Australian Society for the Study of Labour History, 1992.

Haines, Robin, 'Indigent Misfits or Shrewd Operators? Government-assisted Emigrants from the United Kingdom to Australia, 1831–1860', *Population Studies*, 48 (1994): 223–47.

Haines, Robin and Ralph Shlomowitz, 'Immigration from the United Kingdom to Colonial Australia: A Statistical Analysis', *Journal of Australian Studies*, 34 (1992): 43–52.

Hamer, David, *New Towns in the New World: Images and Perceptions of the Nineteenth-century Urban Frontier*, New York, 1990.

Hamer, David, *The New Zealand Liberals: The Years of Power, 1891–1912*, Auckland, 1988.

Hammerton, A. James, *Emigrant Gentlewomen: Genteel Poverty and Female Emigration, 1830–1914*, London, 1979.

Hancock, W. Keith, *Australia*, London, 1930.

Hanlon, David, *Upon a Stone Altar: A History of the Island of Pohnpei to 1890*, Honolulu, 1988.

Hanlon, David, *Remaking Micronesia: Discourses over Development in a Pacific Territory, 1944–1982*, Honolulu, 1998.

Hanson, Elizabeth, *The Politics of Social Security*, Auckland, 1980.

Hargreaves, R. P., 'The Maori Agriculture of the Auckland Province in the Mid-nineteenth Century', *Journal of the Polynesian Society*, 68 (1959): 61–79.

Hargreaves, R. P., 'The Golden Age: New Zealand About 1867', *New Zealand Geographer*, 16 (1960a): 1–32.

Hargreaves, R. P., 'Maori Agriculture After the Wars (1871–1886)', *Journal of the Polynesian Society*, 69 (1960b): 354–67.

Hargreaves, R. P., 'Maori Flour Mills of the Auckland Province 1846–1860', *Journal of the Polynesian Society*, 70 (1961): 227–32.

Hargreaves, R. P., 'Waimate–Pioneer New Zealand Farm', *Agricultural History*, 36 (1962): 38–45.

Hargreaves, R. P., 'Changing Maori Agriculture in Pre-Waitangi New Zealand', *Journal of the Polynesian Society*, 72 (1963): 101–17.

Hargreaves, R. P., 'Farm Fences in Pioneer New Zealand', *New Zealand Geographer*, 21 (1965): 144–55.

Hasluck, P., *A Time for Building: Australian Administration in Papua and New Guinea 1951–1963*, Melbourne, 1976.

Hastings, Peter, *New Guinea: Problems and Prospects*, Melbourne, 1969.

Hastings, Peter, *Papua New Guinea: Prospero's Other Island*, Sydney, 1971.

Havemann, Paul (ed.), *Indigenous People's Rights in Australia, Canada, and New Zealand*, Auckland, 1999.

Hawke, Gary R., *The Making of New Zealand: An Economic History*, Cambridge, 1985.

Hazledine, Tim, *Taking New Zealand Seriously: The Economics of Decency*, Auckland, 1998.

Head, Lyndsay, 'The Gospel of Te Ua Haumene', *Journal of the Polynesian Society*, 101 (1992): 7–44.

Healey, A. M., *Bulolo: A History of the Development of the Bulolo Region, Papua New Guinea*, New Guinea Research Bulletin 15, 1967 (reprinted 1968).

Healy, Chris, *From the Ruins of Colonialism: History as Social Memory*. Studies in Australian History, ed. Alan Gilbert, Patricia Grimshaw and Peter Spearritt. Melbourne, 1997.

Hearn, Terry. 'The Wealth of Miners A Study of the Gold Miners of Central Otago, 1861–1921'. In *Proceedings of the 1998 Conference of the New Zealand Society of Geographers*, University of Otago, Dunedin, April 1998.

Hempenstall, Peter, *Pacific Islanders under German Rule: A Study in the Meaning of Colonial Resistance*, Canberra, 1978.

Hempenstall, Peter, *The Meddlesome Priest: A Life of Ernest Burgmann*, Sydney, 1993.

Hempenstall, Peter and Noel Rutherford, *Protest and Dissent in the Colonial Pacific*, Suva, 1984.

Henderson, J. M., *Ratana: The Man, the Church, the Political Movement*, 2nd edn, Wellington, 1972.

Henningham, Stephen, *France and the South Pacific: A Contemporary History*, Sydney, 1992.

Le Heron, Richard and Eric Pawson (eds), *Changing Places: New Zealand in the Nineties*, Auckland, 1996.

Hezel, Francis, *The First Taint of Civilization: A History of the Caroline and Marshall Islands in Pre-colonial Days, 1521–1885*, Honolulu, 1983.

Hicks, Neville, *'This Sin and Scandal': Australia's Population Debate 1891–1911*, Canberra, 1978.

Hill, A. V. S. and S. W. Serjeantson (eds), *The Colonization of the Pacific: A Genetic Trail*, Oxford, 1989.

Hilliard, David, *God's Gentlemen: A History of the Melanesian Mission 1849–1942*, St Lucia, 1978.

Hirst, J. B., 'The Pioneer Legend', *Historical Studies*, 18 (1978): 316–37.

Hirst, J. B., *Convict Society and its Enemies: A History of Early New South Wales*, Sydney, 1983.

Hirst, J. B., 'Australian Defence and Conscription: A Reassessment, Part I', *Australian Historical Studies*, 25 (1993): 608–27.

Hirst, John, 'Constitutions.' In Graeme Davison, John Hirst and Stuart Macintyre (eds), *Oxford Companion to Australian History*, Melbourne, 1998, 153–4.

Hobsbawm, Eric, *Bandits*, London, 1969.

Hobsbawm, Eric, *Age of Extremes: The Short Twentieth Century 1914–1991*, London, 1995.

Hogbin, H. I., *Experiments in Civilization: The Effects of European Culture on a Native Community of the Solomon Islands*, London, 1939.

Holt, James, *Compulsory Arbitration in New Zealand: The First Forty Years*, Auckland, 1986.

Holt, Stephen, *Manning Clark and Australian History, 1915–1963*, Brisbane, 1982.

Howard, Alan and Eric Kjellgren, 'Martyrs, Progress and Political Ambition: Re-examining Rotuma's "Religious Wars"', *Journal of Pacific History*, 29: 2 (1994): 131–52.

Howard, Michael, *Mining, Politics, and Development in the South Pacific*, Boulder, CO., 1994.

Howe, Kerry, 'The Fate of the "Savage" in Pacific Historiography', *New Zealand Journal of History*, 11: 2 (1977): 137–54.

Howe, Kerry, *The Loyalty Islands: A History of Culture Contact 1840–1900*, Honolulu, 1977.

Howe, Kerry, *Where the Waves Fall: A New South Sea Islands History from First Settlement to Colonial Rule*, Sydney, 1984.

Howe, Kerry, *Nature, Culture and History*, Honolulu, in press.

Howe, Kerry, Robert Kiste and Brij Lal, *Tides of History: The Pacific Islands in the Twentieth Century*, Honolulu, 1994.

Hudson, Wayne and Geoffrey Bolton (eds), *Creating Australia: Changing Australian History*, Sydney, 1997.

Hughes, Robert, *The Fatal Shore: The Epic of Australia's Founding*, New York, 1987.

Human Rights and Equal Opportunity Commission, *Bringing Them Home: Report of the National Inquiry into the Separation of Aboriginal and Torres Strait Islander Children from their Families*, Sydney, 1997.

Hutching, Megan, '"Mothers of the World": Women, Peace and Arbitration in Early Twentieth-century New Zealand', *New Zealand Journal of History*, 27 (1993): 173–85.

Hviding, Edvard, *Guardians of Marovo Lagoon: Practice, Place and Politics in Maritime Melanesia*, Honolulu, 1996.

Hyde, Tom, 'White Men Can't Jump', *Metro*, September 1993, 62–9.

Ihimaera, Witi (ed.), *Te Ao Marama: Regaining Aotearoa: Maori Writers Speak Out*, vol. 2, Auckland, 1993.

Ihimaera, Witi (ed.), *Vision Aotearoa: Kaupapa New Zealand*, Wellington, 1994.

Ihimaera, Witi, H. Williams, I. Ramsden and D. S. Long (eds), *Te Ao Marama: Contemporary Maori Writing*, Auckland, 1993.

Inglis, K. S., 'War, Race and Loyalty in New Guinea, 1939–1945'. In K. S. Inglis (ed.), *The History of Melanesia*, Port Moresby, 1969.

Inglis, K. S., *The Australian Colonists: An Exploration of Social History, 1788–1970*, Melbourne, 1974.

Inglis, K. S., *The Rehearsal: Australians at War in the Sudan, 1885*, Sydney, 1985.

Inglis, K. S., *Anzac Remembered: Selected Writings of K. S. Inglis*, ed. John Lack, Melbourne, 1998.

Inglis, K. S., assisted by Jan Brazier, *Sacred Places: War Memorials in the Australian Landscape*, Melbourne, 1999.

International Bank for Reconstruction and Development, *The Economic Development of the Territory of Papua and New Guinea*, Baltimore, 1965.

Ip, Manying, 'Chinese New Zealanders.' In Stuart W. Greif (ed.), *Immigration and National Identity in New Zealand*, Palmerston North, 1995, 161–99.

Ip, Manying, *Dragons on the Long White Cloud: The Making of Chinese New Zealanders*, Auckland, 1996.

Irving, Helen, *To Constitute a Nation: A Cultural History of Australia's Constitution*. Studies in Australian History, ed. Alan Gilbert, Patricia Grimshaw and Peter Spearritt, Melbourne, 1997.

Irving, Helen (ed.), *The Centenary Companion to Australian Federation*, Melbourne, 1999.

Irwin, Geoffrey, *The Emergence of Mailu, Terra Australis*, Canberra, 1985.

Irwin, Geoffrey, *The Prehistoric Exploration and Colonisation of the Pacific*, Cambridge, 1992.

Jaarsma, S. R., ' "Your Work is of No Use to Us ... ": Administrative Interests in Ethnographic Research (West New Guinea, 1950–1962)', *Journal of Pacific History*, 29: 2 (1994): 153–71.

Jack-Hinton, Colin, *The Search for the Islands of Solomon, 1567–1838*, Oxford, 1969.

Jackson, Richard, *Ok Tedi: The Pot of Gold?*, Port Moresby, 1982.

Jebb, R., *Studies in Colonial Nationalism*, London, 1905.

Jesson, Bruce, *Only Their Purpose is Mad*, Palmerston North, 1999.

Jolly, Margaret, ' "Ill-natured Comparisons"? Racism and Relativism in European Representations of ni-Vanuatu from Cook's Second Voyage', *History and Anthropology*, 5: 3 (1992): 31–64.

Jolly, Margaret, *Women of the Place: Kastom, Colonialism and Gender in Vanuatu*, New York, 1994.

Jolly, Margaret and Martha Macintyre (eds), *Family and Gender in the Pacific: Domestic Contradictions and the Colonial Impact*, Cambridge, 1989.

Jolly, Margaret and Kalpina Ram (eds), *Maternities and Modernities: Colonial and Post-colonial Experiences in Asia and the Pacific*, Cambridge, 1997.

Jolly, Margaret and Nicholas Thomas (eds), *The Politics of Tradition in the Pacific*. Special issue 62 of *Oceania*, 1993.

Jones, Eric, Lionel Frost and Colin White, *Coming Full Circle: An Economic History of the Pacific Rim*, Melbourne, 1993.

Jones, Pei Te Hurinui, *King Potatau: An Account of the Life of Potatau Te Wherowhero, the First Maori King*, Auckland, 1959.

Jupp, James, *Immigration*. Australian Retrospectives, ed. David Walker, Sydney, 1991.

Kawharu, I. H. (ed.), *Waitangi: Maori and Pakeha Perspectives of the Treaty of Waitangi*, Auckland, 1989.

Keenan, Danny, 'Nga Pakanga Whenua O Mua: Wars without End.' Paper presented at the NZHA Conference, Palmerston North, 1997.

Keesing, Roger, 'Creating the Past: Custom and Identity in the Contemporary Pacific', *The Contemporary Pacific*, 1: 2 (1989): 279–301.

Keesing, Roger, 'Colonial History as Contested Ground: The Bell Massacre in the Solomons', *History and Anthropology*, 4 (1990).

Keesing, Roger and Peter Corris, *Lightning Meets the West Wind: The Malaita Massacre*, Melbourne, 1980.

Keesing, Roger and Robert Tonkinson (eds), *Reinventing Traditional Culture: The Politics of Kastom in Island Melanesia*. Specil issue 13 of *Mankind* (1982).

Kelsey, Jane, *The New Zealand Experiment: A World Model of Structural Adjustment?* Auckland, 1995.

Kennedy, Brian, *Silver, Sin, and Sixpenny Ale: A Social History of Broken Hill, 1883–1921*, Melbourne, 1978.

Kidd, Rosalind, *The Way We Civilise: Aboriginal Affairs – The Untold Story*, Brisbane, 1997.

King, Michael, *Te Puea: A Biography*, Auckland, 1977.

King, Michael, *Moriori: A People Rediscovered*, Auckland, 1989.

King, Michael, *Maori: A Photographic and Social History*, Auckland, 1996.

King, Michael, *Being Pakeha Now: Reflections and Recollections of a White Native*, Auckland, 1999.

Kingston, Beverley, *My Wife, My Daughter, and Poor Mary Ann: Women and Work in Australia*, West Melbourne, 1977.

Kirch, Patrick, *The Evolution of the Polynesian Chiefdoms*, Cambridge, 1984.

Kirch, Patrick and T. Hunt (eds), *Archaeology of the Lapita Cultural Complex: A Critical Review*, Seattle, 1988.

Kituai, Augustin, *My Gun, My Brother: The World of the Papua New Guinea Colonial Police, 1920–1960*, Honolulu, 1998.

Knapman, Bruce, *Fiji's Economic History, 1874–1939: Studies of Capitalist Colonial Development*, Canberra, 1987.

Knapman, Claudia, *White Women in Fiji 1835–1930: The Ruin of Empire*, Sydney, 1986.

Knapman, Claudia, 'Reproducing Empire: Exploring Ideologies of Gender and Race on Australia's Pacific Frontier.' In Susan Magarey, Sue Rowley and Susan Sheridan (eds), *Debutante Nation: Feminism Contests the 1890s*, Sydney, 1993, 125–35.

Kociumbas, Jan, *Australian Childhood: A History*. The Australian Experience, ed. Heather Radi, Sydney, 1997.

Kundera, Milan, *The Book of Laughter and Forgetting*, trans. M. H. Him, Harmondsworth, 1983.

Kunitz, Stephen J., *Disease and Social Diversity: The European Impact on the Health of Non-Europeans*, New York and Oxford, 1994.

Kuper, Adam, *Anthropologists and Anthropology, the British School, 1922–1972*, London, 1973.

Kuper, Adam, *The Chosen Primate: Human Nature and Cultural Diversity*, Cambridge, MA, 1994.

Lake, Marilyn, 'Helpmeet, Slave, Housewife: Women in Rural Families 1870–1930.' In Patricia Grimshaw, Chris McConville and Ellen McEwen (eds), *Families in Colonial Australia*, Sydney, 1985, 173–85.

Lake, Marilyn, 'The Politics of Respectability: Identifying the Masculinist Context', *Historical Studies*, 22 (1986): 116–31.

Lake, Marilyn, *The Limits of Hope: Soldier Settlement in Victoria 1915–38*, Melbourne, 1987.

Lake, Marilyn, 'A Revolution in the Family: The Challenge and Contradictions of Maternal Citizenship in Australia.' In Seth Koven and Sonya Michel (eds), *Mothers of a New World: Maternalist Politics and the Origins of Welfare States*, New York and London, 1993, 378–95.

Lake, Marilyn, 'Women and Nation in Australia: The Politics of Representation', *Australian Journal of Politics and History*, 43 (1997): 41–52.

Lal, Brij V., *Girmitiyas: The Origins of the Fiji Indians*, Canberra, 1983.

Lal, Brij V., *Power and Prejudice: The Making of the Fiji Crisis*, Wellington, 1988.

Lal, Brij V., *Broken Waves: A History of the Fiji Islands in the Twentieth Century*, Honolulu, 1992.

Lal, Brij, Doug Munro and Ed Beechert (eds), *Plantation Workers: Resistance and Accommodation*, Honolulu, 1994.

Lambert, Sam, *A Yankee Doctor in Paradise*, Boston, MA, 1941.

Landor, E. W., *The Bushman, Or Life in a New Country*, London, 1847.

Langdon, Robert, *The Lost Caravel*, Sydney, 1975.

Langdon, Robert, *The Lost Caravel Re-explored*, Canberra, 1988.

Lange, Raeburn, *May the People Live: A History of Maoii Health Development 1900–1920*, Auckland, 1999.

Langmore, Diane, *Missionary Lives: Papua, 1874–1914*, Honolulu, 1989.

Laracy, Eugenie and Hugh Laracy, 'Beatrice Grimshaw: Pride and Prejudice in Papua', *Journal of Pacific History*, 12: 3–4 (1977): 154–75.

Laracy, Hugh, *Marists and Melanesians: A History of Catholic Missions in the Solomon Islands*, Canberra, 1976.

Laracy, Hugh (ed.), *Pacific Protest: The Maasina Rule Movement, Solomon Islands, 1944–1957*, Suva, 1983.

Latukefu, Sione, *Church and State in Tonga*, Canberra, 1974.

Latukefu, Sione, 'Oral History and Pacific Island Missionaries', in D. Denoon and R. J. Lacey (eds), *Oral Tradition in Melanesia*, Port Moresby, 1981.

Lawrence, Peter, *Road Belong Cargo: A Study of the Cargo Movement in the Southern Madang District*, Manchester, 1964.

Lawrey, John, *The Cross of Lorraine in the South Pacific: Australia and the Free French Movement 1940–1942*, Canberra, 1982.

Lawson, John A., RN, *Wanderings in the Interior of New Guinea*, London, 1875.

Leach, Helen, 'In the Beginning.' In Jock Phillips (ed.), *Te Whenua, Te Iwi: The Land and the People*, Wellington, 1987, 18–26.

Leenhardt, Maurice, *Notes d'ethnologie Neo-Caledonienne*, Paris, 1930.

Leenhardt, Maurice, *Do Kamo: Person and Myth in the Melanesian World*, Chicago, 1979.

Levine, Stephen and Paul Harris (eds), *The New Zealand Politics Source Book*, Palmerston North, 1999.

Lewis, David, *The Plantation Dream: Developing British New Guinea and Papua, 1884–1942*, Canberra, 1996.

Lindstrom, Lamont, *Cargo Cult: Strange Stories of Desire from Melanesia and Beyond*, Honolulu, 1993.

Lini, Walter H., *Beyond Pandemonium*, Suva, 1980.

Linnekin, Jocelyn, 'Ignoble Savages and Other European Visions: The La Perouse Affair in Samoan History', *Journal of Pacific History*, 26: 1 (1991): 3–26.

Linnekin, Jocelyn and Lyn Poyer (eds), *Cultural Identity and Ethnicity in the Pacific*, Honolulu, 1990.

Lissington, M. P., *New Zealand and Japan 1900–1941*, Wellington, 1971.

Livingston, K. T., *The Wired Nation Continent: The Communication Revolution and Federating Australia*, Melbourne, 1996.

Livingston, William S. and W. Roger Louis (eds), *Australia, New Zealand, and the Pacific Islands Since the First World War*, Canberra, 1979.

Lloyd, P. J., *The Future of CER: A Single Market for Australia and New Zealand*, Melbourne and Wellington, 1991.

Loeliger, Carl and Gary Trompf (eds), *New Religious Movements in Melanesia*, Suva, 1985.

Long, Gavin, *The Final Campaigns: Australia in the War of 1939–1945*, Australian War Memorial Series 1, vol. 7, Canberra, 1963.

Long, Jane, Jan Gothard and Helen Brash (eds), *Forging Identities: Bodies, Gender and Feminist History*, Perth, 1997.

Love, Ngatata, 'Edward Gibbon Wakefield: A Maori Perspective.' In *Edward Gibbon Wakefield and the Colonial Dream: A Reconsideration*, Wellington, 1997, 3–10.

Lukere, Vicki, 'Mothers of the Taukei: Fijian Women and the Decrease of the Race.' Ph.D. dissertation, Australian National University, Canberra, 1997.

Lynn, Martin, 'British Policy, Trade, and Informal Empire in the Mid-nineteenth Century.' In Andrew Porter (ed.), *Oxford History of the British Empire*, vol. 3, *The Nineteenth Century*, Oxford, 1999, 101–21.

Maaka, Roger, 'The New Tribe: Conflicts and Continuities in the Social Organization of Urban Maori', *The Contemporary Pacific*, 6 (1994): 311–36.

McAllister, Ian and Jack Vowles, 'The Rise of New Politics and Market Liberalism in Australia and New Zealand', *British Journal of Political Science*, 24 (1994): 381–402.

McArthur, Norma, *Island Populations of the Pacific*, Canberra, 1967.

McCall, Grant and John Connell (eds), *A World Perspective on Pacific Islander Migration: Australia, New Zealand and the USA*, Sydney, 1993.

McCalman, Janet, *Struggletown: Public and Private Life in Richmond, 1900–1965*, Melbourne, 1984.

McCalman, Janet, *Journeyings: The Biography of a Middle-class Generation, 1920–1990*, Melbourne, 1993.

McCarthy, Dudley, *South-west Pacific Area – First Year. Kokoda to Wau, Australia in the War of 1939–1945*, Australian War Memorial, Series 1, V, Canberra, 1959.

McCarty, J. W., 'Australian Capital Cities in the Nineteenth Century.' In J. W. McCarty and C. B. Schedvin (eds), *Australian Capital Cities*, Sydney, 1978, 9–25.

McCarty, J. W. and C. B. Schedvin (eds), *Australian Capital Cities*, Sydney, 1978.

McClure, Margaret, *A Civilised Community: A History of Social Security in New Zealand 1898–1998*, Auckland, 1998.

Macdonald, Charlotte, *A Woman of Good Character: Single Women as Immigrant Settlers in Nineteenth-century New Zealand*, Wellington, 1990.

McEvedy, Colin, *Penguin Historical Atlas of the Pacific*, New York and London, 1998.

McGee, W. A. and G. R. Henning, 'Investment in Lode Mining, Papua 1878–1920', *Journal of Pacific History*, 25: 2 (1990), 244–59.

McGibbon, Ian, 'Australia–New Zealand Defence Relations to 1939.' In Keith Sinclair (ed.), *Tasman Relations*, Auckland, 1987, 164–82.

McGibbon, Ian, *The Path to Gallipoli: Defending New Zealand 1840–1915*, Wellington, 1991.

McGrath, Ann (ed.), *Contested Ground: Australian Aborigines under the British Crown*, Sydney, 1995.

McGregor, Russell, *Imagined Destinies: Aboriginal Australians and the Doomed Race Theory, 1880–1939*, Melbourne, 1997.

McHugh, Paul, *The Maori Magna Carta: New Zealand Law and the Treaty of Waitangi*, Auckland, 1991.

Macintyre, Stuart, *Oxford History of Australia, Vol. 4: 1901–1942: The Succeeding Age*, 5 vols, Melbourne, 1986.

Macintyre, Stuart, *The Labour Experiment*. Themes in Australian Economic and Social History, ed. Boris Schedvin, Melbourne, 1989.

Macintyre, Stuart and Richard Mitchell (eds), *Foundations of Arbitration: The Origins and Effects of State Compulsory Arbitration 1890–1914*. Australian Studies in Labour Relations, Melbourne, 1989.

McIntyre, W. D., 'From Dual Dependency to Nuclear Free.' In Geoffrey W. Rice (ed.), *Oxford History of New Zealand*, 2nd edn, Auckland, 1992, 520–38.

McIntyre, W. D. (ed.), *Journal of Henry Sewell, 1853–7*, 2 vols, Christchurch, 1980.

McIntyre, W. D. and W. J. Gardner (eds), *Speeches and Documents on New Zealand History*, Oxford, 1971.

Mackay, Ross, 'The War Years: Methodists in Papua 1942–1945', *Journal of Pacific History*, 27: 1 (1992): 29–43.

Mackinnon, Alison, *Love and Freedom: Professional Women and the Reshaping of Personal Life*, Melbourne, 1997.

McKinnon, Malcolm, *Immigrants and Citizens: New Zealanders and Asian Immigration in Historical Context*, Wellington, 1996.

McKinnon, Malcolm, Barry Bradley and Russell Kirkpatrick (eds), *New Zealand Historical Atlas*, Wellington, 1997.

MacLeod, Roy and Philip Rehbock (eds), *Darwin's Laboratory: Evolutionary Theory and Natural History in the Pacific*, Honolulu, 1994.

McNab, R. (ed.), *Historical Records of New Zealand*, vol. 1, Wellington, 1908.

MacNaught, Timothy, *The Fijian Colonial Experience: A Study of the Neotraditional Order under British Colonial Rule Prior to World War II*, Canberra, 1982.

McNeill, J. R., 'Of Rats and Men: A Synoptic Environmental History of the Island Pacific', *Journal of World History*, 5 (1994): 299–349.

Macpherson, C., 'Public and Private Views of Home: Will Western Samoan Migrants Return?' *Pacific Viewpoint*, 26 (1985): 242–62.

Macrae, John Tait, 'A Study in the Application of Economic Analysis to Social Issues: The Maori and the New Zealand Economy.' Ph.D. thesis, University of London, 1975.

Maddock, Rodney, and Ian W. McLean (eds), *The Australian Economy in the Long Run*, Melbourne, 1987.

Maddocks, Ian, 'Medicine and Colonialism', *Australian and New Zealand Journal of Sociology*, 11: 3 (1975): 27–33.

Magarey, Susan, Sue Rowley and Sue Sheridan (eds), *Debutante Nation: Feminism Contests the 1890s*, Sydney, 1993.

Maher, Robert F., *New Men of Papua: A Study in Culture Change*, Madison, WI, 1961.

Malinowski, Bronislaw, *Argonauts of the Western Pacific: An Account of Native Enterprise and Adventure in the Archipelagos of Melanesian New Guinea*, London, 1922.

Mamak, F. and A. Ali (eds), *Race; Class and Rebellion in the South Pacific*, Sydney, 1979.

Maori Kiki, Albert, *Ten Thousand Years in a Lifetime*, Melbourne, 1968.

Marais, J. S., *The Colonisation of New Zealand*, London, 1968.

Markham, Clements (ed.), *The Voyages of Pedro Fernandez de Quiros 1595 to 1604*, London, 1904.

Markus, Andrew, *Governing Savages*, Sydney, 1990.

Markus, Andrew, *Australian Race Relations 1788–1993*, Sydney, 1994.

Martin, Helen, and Sam Edwards, *New Zealand Film 1912–1996*, Auckland, 1997.

Martin, John E., *The Forgotten Worker: The Rural Wage Earner in Nineteenth-century New Zealand*, Wellington, 1990.

Maude, Harry, *Of Islands and Men: Studies in Pacific History*, Melbourne, 1968.

Maude, Harry, *Slavers in Paradise: The Peruvian Slave Trade in Polynesia, 1862–1864*, Canberra, 1981.

May, P. R., 'Gold on the Coast (1) and (2)', *New Zealand's Heritage*, 3 (1972): 841–6, 879–81, 884–5.

May, P. R., *The West Coast Gold Rushes*, Christchurch, 1962.

May, R. J. (ed.), *Change and Movement: Readings on Internal Migration in Papua New Guinea*, Canberra, 1977.

May, R. J . (ed.), *Micronationalist Movements in Papua New Guinea*, Canberra, 1982.

Mead, Margaret, *New Lives for Old: Cultural Transformation – Manus 1938–1953*, New York, 1956.

Meaney, Neville, *The Search for Security in the Pacific, 1901–14*, Sydney, 1976.

Meek, Ronald L., *Social Science and the Ignoble Savage*, Cambridge, 1976.

Mein Smith, Philippa, *Maternity in Dispute: New Zealand 1920–1939*, Wellington, 1986.

Mein Smith, Philippa, *Mothers and King Baby: Infant Survival and Welfare in an Imperial World: Australia 1880–1950*, Basingstoke, 1997.

Meleisea, Malama, *The Making of Modern Samoa: Traditional Authority and Colonial Administration in the Modern History of Western Samoa*, Suva, 1987.

Meleisea, Malama, 'Pacific Identity.' Lecture to HIST 243, Kiwi Culture, University of Canterbury, 1995.

Meleisea, Malama et al., *Lagaga: A Short History of Western Samoa*, Suva, 1987.

Mercer, Patricia, *White Australia Defied: Pacific Islander Settlements in North Queensland*, Townsville, 1995.

Merle, Isabelle, 'The Foundation of Voh 1892–1895: French Migrants on the West Coast of New Caledonia', *Journal of Pacific History*, 26: 2 (1991): 234–44.

Merle, Isabelle, *Expériences coloniales: la Nouvelle-Calédonie 1853–1920*, Paris, 1995.

Merle, Isabelle, 'Le Mabo case: l'Australie face a son passe colonial', *Annales HSS*, March–April (1998): 209–29.

Merwick, Donna (ed.), *Dangerous Liaisons: Essays in Honour of Greg Dening*, Melbourne, 1994.

Métin, Albert, *Socialism Without Doctrines* [first published in French in 1901], trans. R. Ward, Sydney, 1977.

Molony, John, *Eureka*, Melbourne, 1984.

Moloughney, B. and J. Stenhouse, ' "Drug-besotten, Sin-begotten Fiends of Filth": New Zealanders and the Oriental Other, 1850–1920', *New Zealand Journal of History*, 33: 1 (1999): 43–64.

Monin, Paul, 'The Maori Economy of Hauraki 1840–1880', *New Zealand Journal of History*, 29 (1995): 197–210.

Moore, Clive, *Kanaka: A History of Melanesian Mackay*, Port Moresby, 1985.

Moore, Clive, Jacqueline Leckie and Doug Munro (eds), *Labour in the South Pacific*, Townsville, 1990.

Moorehead, Alan, *The Fatal Impact: An Account of the Invasion of the South Pacific 1767–1840*, London, 1966.

Morison, S. E., *The Struggle for Guadalcanal August 1942–February 1943: History of United States Naval Operations in World War II*, Boston, MA, 1966.

Morison, S. E., *Coral Sea, Midway and Submarine Actions May 1942–August 1942: History of United States Naval Operations in World War II*, Boston, MA, 1967.

Morrell, W. P., *The Provincial System in New Zealand 1852–76*, 2nd revd edn, Christchurch, 1964.

Mouat, Jeremy, 'Mining in the Settler Dominions: A Comparative Study of the Industry in Three Communities from the 1880s to the First World War.' Ph.D. thesis, University of British Columbia, 1988.

Muldoon, R. D., *The Rise and Fall of a Young Turk*, Wellington, 1974.

Muldoon, R. D., *My Way*, Wellington, 1981.

Mulvaney, D. J., *Cricket Walkabout: The Australian Aboriginal Cricketers on Tour, 1867–8*, Melbourne, 1967.

Mulvaney, D. J. and J. H. Calaby, *So Much that is New: Baldwin Spencer, 1860–1929*, Melbourne, 1985.

Mulvaney, D. J. and J. Peter White (eds), *Australians to 1788*, Sydney, 1987.

Narokobi, Bernard, *The Melanesian Way*, Boroko and Suva, 1980.

Nash, Jill and Eugene Ogan, 'The Red and the Black: Bougainville Perceptions of other Papua New Guineans', *Pacific Studies*, 13: 2 (1990).

Nelson, Hank, *Black, White and Gold: Gold Mining in Papua New Guinea, 1878–1930*, Canberra, 1976.

Nelson, Hank, 'Taim Bilong Pait: The Impact of the Second World War on Papua New Guinea.' In W. McCoy (ed.), *Southeast Asia under Japanese Occupation*, New Haven, CT, 1980.

Nelson, Hank, *Taim Bilong Masta: The Australian Involvement with Papua New Guinea*, Sydney 1982.

Neumann, Klaus, *Not the Way It Really Was: Constructing the Tolai Past*, Honolulu, 1992.

Neumann, Klaus, Nicholas Thomas and Hilary Ericksen (eds), *Quicksands: Foundational Histories in Australia and Aotearoa New Zealand*, Sydney, 1999.

New South Wales Royal Commission on the Decline of the Birth-rate and on the Mortality of Infants in New South Wales, *Report and Minutes of Evidence*, vols 1 and 2, Sydney, 1904.

New Zealand Institute of International Affairs, *Western Samoa: Mandate or German Colony?* Wellington, 1937.

Nicholas, Stephen (ed.), *Convict Workers: Reinterpreting Australia's Past*, Melbourne, 1988.

Nolan, Melanie, 'Sex or Class? The Politics of the Earliest Equal Pay Campaign in Victoria', *Labour History*, 61 (1991): 101–22.

Nolan, Melanie, 'Employment Organisations.' In Anne Else (ed.), *Women Together: A History of Women's Organisations in New Zealand*, Wellington, 1993, 195–206.

Novitz, David and Bill Willmott (eds), *Culture and Identity in New Zealand*, Wellington, 1989.

'NSW Family Endowment Act.' *George V, No. 39, 1927*, Sydney, 1927.

Obeyesekere, Gananath, *The Apotheosis of Captain Cook: European Mythmaking in the Pacific*, Princeton, NJ, 1992.

O'Connor, P. S. 'Keeping New Zealand White, 1908–1920', *New Zealand Journal of History*, 2 (1968): 41–65.

O'Faircheallaigh, Ciaran, *Mining in the Papua New Guinea Economy, 1880–1980*, Port Moresby, 1982.

Offer, Avner, *The First World War: An Agrarian Interpretation*, Oxford, 1989.

Ogden, Michael, 'MIRAB and the Marshall Islands', *ISLA*, 2 (1994): 237–72.

Oliver, Douglas, *Bougainville: A Personal History*, Melbourne, 1973.

Oliver, Douglas, *The Pacific Islands*, 3rd edn, Honolulu, 1989.

Oliver, W. H., *Claims to the Waitangi Tribunal*, Wellington, 1991.

Oliver, W. H. and B. R. Williams (eds), *Oxford History of New Zealand*, Oxford, 1981.

Olssen, Erik, *A History of Otago*, Dunedin, 1984.

Olssen, Erik, *Building the New World: Work, Politics and Society in Caversham 1880s–1920s*, Auckland, 1995.

Olssen, Erik, 'Wakefield and the Scottish Enlightenment, with particular reference to Adam Smith and his *Wealth of Nations.*' In *Edward Gibbon Wakefield and the Colonial Dream: A Reconsideration*, Wellington, 1997, 47–66.

Olssen, Erik, 'Families and the Gendering of European New Zealand in the Colonial Period, 1840–80.' In Caroline Daley and Deborah Montgomerie (eds), *The Gendered Kiwi*, Auckland, 1999, 37–62.

Olssen, Erik and Marcia Stenson, *A Century of Change: New Zealand 1800–1900*, Auckland, 1997.

Ongka: A Self-account by a New Guinea Big-man, trans. Andrew Strathern, London, 1979.

Oram, Nigel, *Colonial Town to Melanesian City: Port Moresby 1884–1974*, Canberra, 1976.

Orange, Claudia, *The Treaty of Waitangi*, Wellington, 1987.

Orange, Claudia, 'Introduction.' In Claudia Orange (ed.), *The Maori Biographies from the Dictionary of New Zealand Biography, Vol. 2: The Turbulent Years, 1870–1900*, Wellington, 1994.

O'Regan, Tipene, 'Maori Battalion and Maori Peace.' Lecture to HIST 124, New Zealand History, University of Canterbury, 1998.

O'Sullivan, M., 'Presidential Address', *Australasian Medical Gazette*, 26 (1907): 55–64.

Owens, J. M. R., 'New Zealand Before Annexation.' In W. H. Oliver with B. R. Williams (eds), *Oxford History of New Zealand*, Wellington, 1981, 28–53.

Oxley, Deborah, *Convict Maids: The Forced Migration of Women to Australia*. Studies in Australian History, ed. Alan Gilbert, Patricia Grimshaw and Peter Spearritt. Melbourne, 1996.

Panoff, Michel, 'The French Way in Plantation Systems', *Journal of Pacific History*, 26: 2 (1991): 206–12.

Park, Geoff, 'Edward Gibbon Wakefield's Dream, Thomas Shepherd's Eye and New Zealand's Spatial Constitution.' In *Edward Gibbon Wakefield and the Colonial Dream: A Reconsideration*, Wellington, 1997, 135–42.

Parsonson, Ann R., 'The Expansion of a Competitive Society: A Study in Nineteenth-century Maori History', *New Zealand Journal of History*, 14: 1 (1980): 45–60.

Parsonson, Ann R., 'The Pursuit of Mana.' In W. H. Oliver with B. R. Williams (eds), *Oxford History of New Zealand*, Wellington, 1981, 140–67.

Parsonson, Ann R., 'The Challenge to Mana Maori.' In G. W. Rice (ed.), *Oxford History of New Zealand*, Auckland, 1992, 167–98.

Parsonson, G. S., 'The Literate Revolution in Polynesia', *Journal of Pacific History*, 2 (1967): 39–57.

Pawley, Andrew and Malcolm Ross, 'Austronesian Historical Linguistics and Culture History', *Annual Review of Anthropology*, 1993: 425–59.

Payton, Philip, *The Cornish Overseas*, Fowey, 1999.

Pearson, W. H., 'The Reception of European Voyagers on Polynesian Islands, 1568–1797', *Journal de la societé des oceanistes*, 26 (1970).

Peattie, Mark, *Nan'yo: The Rise and Fall of the Japanese in Micronesia, 1885–1945*, Honolulu, 1988.

Peel, Mark, *Good Times, Hard Times: The Past and the Future in Elizabeth*, Melbourne, 1995.

Phillips, Jock, *A Man's Country? The Image of the Pakeha Male – A History*, Auckland, 1987; revd edn 1996.

Phillips, Jock, 'Our History, Our Selves: The Historian and National Identity', *New Zealand Journal of History*, 30 (1996): 107–23.

Pickles, Katie, 'Feminist Movements.' Lecture to HIST 124, New Zealand History, University of Canterbury, 1998a.

Pickles, Katie, 'Urbanization and Migration.' Lecture to HIST 124, New Zealand History, University of Canterbury, 1998b.

Pike, Douglas, *Paradise of Dissent: South Australia 1829–1857*, London, 1957.

Plant, Chris (ed.), *New Hebrides: The Road to Independence*, Suva, 1977.

Du Plessis, Rosemary and Lynne Alice (eds), *Feminist Thought in Aotearoa/New Zealand: Differences and Connections*, Auckland, 1998.

Ploeg, Anton, 'First Contact, in the Highlands of Irian Jaya', *Journal of Pacific History*, 30: 2 (1995): 227–39.

Pomfret, Richard (ed.), *Australia's Trade Policies*, Melbourne, 1995.

Pool, Ian, *Te Iwi Maori: A New Zealand Population Past, Present and Projected*, Auckland, 1991.

Porter, Frances and Charlotte Macdonald (eds), *My Hand Will Write What My Heart Dictates: The Unsettled Lives of Women in Nineteenth-century New Zealand as Revealed to Sisters, Family and Friends*, Auckland, 1996.

Press, The, *Celebrating Cultural Diversity: Canterbury's Rainbow Community*, Christchurch, 1999.

Price, A. Grenfell, *White Settlers in the Tropics*, New York, 1939.

Price, Charles, 'The Asian and Pacific Island Peoples of Australia.' In J. T. Fawcett and B. V. Cario (eds), *Pacific Bridges: The New Immigration from Asia and the Pacific Islands*, New York, 1987.

Price, Charles A., *The Great White Walls are Built: Restrictive Immigration to North America and Australasia 1836–1888*, Canberra, 1974.

Pugsley, Christopher, *Te Hokowhitu a Tu: The Maori Pioneer Battalion in the First World War*, Auckland, 1995.

Raganivatu, Atama, 'Rugby Becomes Big Business: Professionalism Creates New Challenges for Pacific Rugby', *Pacific Islands Monthly*, May 1998: 32–5.

Rallu, J. L., 'Population of the French Overseas Territories in the Pacific, Past, Present and Projected', *Journal of Pacific History*, 26: 2 (1991): 169–86.

Ranger, T. O., 'Connexions between "Primary Resistance" Movements and Modern Mass Nationalism in East and Central Africa, Part I', *Journal of African History*, 9 (1968): 437–53.

Ravuvu, Asesela, *Fijians at War 1939–1945*, Suva, 1974.

Ravuvu, Asesela, *The Facade of Democracy: Fijian Struggles for Political Control, 1930–1987*, Suva, 1991.

Read, K. E., 'Effects of the Pacific War in the Markham Valley, New Guinea', *Oceania*, 18: 2 (1947): 95–116.

Read, Peter, *A Hundred Years War: The Wiradjuri People and the State*, Sydney, 1988.

Renwick, William, *The Treaty Now*, Wellington, 1990.

Reynolds, Henry, *Aborigines and Settlers: The Australian Experience, 1788–1939*, Melbourne, 1975.

Reynolds, Henry, *Frontier: Aborigines, Settlers and Land*, Sydney, 1987.

Reynolds, Henry, *Dispossession: Black Australians and White Invaders*, Sydney, 1989.

Reynolds, Henry, *With the White People*, Ringwood, 1990.

Reynolds, Henry, *The Law of the Land*, 2nd edn, Melbourne, 1992.

Reynolds, Henry, *Aboriginal Sovereignty: Reflections on Race, State and Nation*, Sydney, 1996.

Reynolds, Henry, *This Whispering in Our Hearts*, Sydney, 1998.

Reynolds, Henry, *Why Weren't We Told? A Personal Search for the Truth about Our History*, Ringwood, 1999.

Rice, G. W. (ed.), *Oxford History of New Zealand*, Auckland, 1992.

Rice, Geoffrey, *Black November: The 1918 Influenza Epidemic in New Zealand*, Wellington, 1988.

Richards, Eric, 'Wakefield and Australia.' In *Edward Gibbon Wakefield and the Colonial Dream: A Reconsideration*, Wellington, 1997, 89–105.

Richards, Trevor, *Dancing on our Bones: New Zealand, South Africa, Rugby and Racism*, Wellington, 1999.

Richardson, Len E., *Coal, Class and Community: The United Mineworkers of New Zealand 1880–1960*, Auckland, 1995.

Rickard, John, *Class and Politics: New South Wales, Victoria and the Early Commonwealth, 1890–1910*, Canberra, 1976.

Rickard, John, *Australia: A Cultural History*, 2nd edn. The Present and the Past, ed. Michael Crowder and Juliet Gardiner, London and New York, 1988.

Riseborough, Hazel, *Days of Darkness: Taranaki 1878–1884*, Wellington, 1989.

Rivers, W. H. R., *The History of Melanesian Societies*, Cambridge, 1914.

Rivers, W. H. R. (ed.), *Essays on the Depopulation of Melanesia*, Cambridge, 1922.

Riviere, Henri, *Souvenirs de la Nouvelle-Caledonie*, Paris, 1881.

Robertson, Stephen, 'Women Workers and the New Zealand Arbitration Court, 1894–1920', *Labour History*, 61 (1991): 30–41.

Robinson, Neville, *Villagers at War: Some Papua New Guinean Experiences of World War II*, Canberra, 1981.

Robinson, Portia, *The Women of Botany Bay: A Reinterpretation of the Role of Women in the Origins of Australian Society*, Sydney, 1988.

Roe, Michael, *Australia, Britain, and Migration, 1915–1940: A Study of Desperate Hopes*. Studies in Australian History, ed. Alan Gilbert, Patricia Grimshaw and Peter Spearritt, Melbourne, 1995.

Roper, Brian and Chris Rudd (eds), *State and Economy in New Zealand*, Auckland, 1993.

Rosi, P., 'Papua New Guinea's New Parliament House: A Contested National Symbol', *The Contemporary Pacific*, 3: 2 (1991): 289–324.

Ross, Angus, *New Zealand Aspirations in the Pacific in the Nineteenth Century*, Oxford, 1964.

Ross, Angus (ed.), *New Zealand's Record in the Pacific Islands in the Twentieth Century*, Auckland, 1969.

Round, David, *Truth or Treaty? Commonsense Questions about the Treaty of Waitangi*, Christchurch, 1998.

Routledge, David, 'Pacific History as Seen from the Pacific Islands', *Pacific Studies*, 8: 2 (1985), 81–99.

Roux, J. C. 'Traditional Melanesian Agriculture in New Caledonia and Pre-contact Population Distribution.' In D. E. Yen and J. M. J. Mummery (eds), *Pacific Production Systems: Approaches to Economic Prehistory*, Canberra, 1990.

Rowley, C. D., *The New Guinea Villager: A Retrospect from 1964*, Melbourne, 1965.

Rowse, Tim, *After Mabo: Interpreting Indigenous Traditions*. Interpretations, ed. Ken Ruthven, Melbourne, 1994.

Roy, T. M., 'Immigration Policy and Legislation.' In K. W. Thomson and A. D. Trlin (eds), *Immigrants in New Zealand*, Palmerston North, 1970, 15–24.

Ryan, Edna and Anne Conlon, *Gentle Invaders: Australian Women at Work 1788–1974*, Melbourne, 1975.

Ryan, Greg, ' "Handsome Physiognomy and Blameless Physique": Indigenous Colonial Sporting Tours and British Racial Consciousness, 1868 and 1888', *International Journal of the History of Sport*, 14 (August 1997): 67–81.

Sack, P. G. (ed.), *Problem of Choice: Land in Papua New Guinea's Future*, Canberra, 1974.

Sahlins, Marshall, *Moala: Culture and Nature on a Fijian Island*, Ann Arbor, MI, 1962.

Sahlins, Marshall, 'The Stranger-King or Dumezil among the Fijians', *Journal of Pacific History*, 16 (1981): 107–32.

Sahlins, Marshall, *Islands of History*, Chicago, 1985.

Sahlins, Marshall, *How 'Natives' Think – About Captain Cook for example*, Chicago, 1995.

Said, Edward, *Orientalism*, London, 1978.

Said, Edward, *Culture and Imperialism*, London, 1994.

Salisbury, Richard, *From Stone to Steel: Economic Consequences of a Technological Change in New Guinea*, Melbourne, 1962.

Salmond, Anne, *Two Worlds: First Meetings between Maori and Europeans 1642–1772*, Auckland, 1993.

Salmond, Anne, *Between Worlds: Early Exchanges Between Maori and Europeans 1773–1815*, Auckland, 1997a.

Salmond, Anne, 'The Trial of the Cannibal Dog/The Death of Captain Cook.' Paper presented at the Histories in New Zealand, NZHA Conference, Massey University, December, 1997b.

Satchell, William, *The Toll of the Bush*, London, 1905.

Saunders, Kay and Raymond Evans (eds), *Gender Relations in Australia: Domination and Negotiation*, Sydney, 1992.

Scarr, Deryck, *Fiji: A Short History*, Sydney, 1984.

Scarr, Deryck, *Fiji: Politics of Illusion*, Sydney, 1988.

Scarr, Deryck, *The History of the Pacific Islands: Kingdoms of the Reefs*, Melbourne, 1990.

Schapper, Henry P., *A Survey of Dairy Farming in the Far South-west of Western Australia*, Perth, 1953.

Schieffelin, E. and R. Crittenden (eds), *Like People You See in a Dream: First Contact in Six Papuan Societies*, Stanford, CA, 1991.

Schieffelin, E. and D. Gewertz, *History and Ethnohistory in Papua New Guinea*. Oceania Monographs 28, Sydney, 1985.

Serle, Geoffrey, *The Golden Age: A History of the Colony of Victoria 1851–1861*, Melbourne, 1963.

Serpenti, L. M., *Cultivators in the Swamps: Social Structure and Horticulture in a New Guinea Society*, Assen, 1965.

Sharp, Andrew, *The Voyages of Abel Janszoon Tasman*, Oxford, 1968.

Shaw, A. G. L., *Convicts and the Colonies*, London, 1966.

Sheridan, Susan, 'The *Woman's Voice* on Sexuality.' In Susan Magarey, Sue Rowley and Susan Sheridan (eds), *Debutante Nation: Feminism Contests the 1890s*, Sydney, 1993, 114–24.

Shineberg, Dorothy, *They Came for Sandalwood: A Study of the Sandalwood Trade in the Southwest Pacific, 1830–1865*, Melbourne, 1967.

Shineberg, Dorothy, *The People Trade: Pacific Island Laborers and New Caledonia, 1865–1930*, Honolulu, 1999.

Shute, Carmel, 'Heroines and Heroes: Sexual Mythology in Australia 1914–18.' In Joy Damousi and Marilyn Lake (eds), *Gender and War: Australians at War in the Twentieth Century*, Melbourne, 1995, 23–42.

Simkin, C. G. F., *The Instability of a Dependent Economy: Economic Fluctuations in New Zealand, 1840–1914*, London, 1951.

Sinclair, Keith, *The Origins of the Maori Wars*, Auckland, 1976.

Sinclair, Keith, 'Australasian Inter-government Negotiations 1865–80: Ocean Mails and Tariffs', *Australian Journal of Politics in History*, 16 (1970): 151–76.

Sinclair, Keith, *A History of New Zealand*, revd edn, Auckland, 1980.

Sinclair, Keith, 'Why are Race Relations in New Zealand Better than in South Africa, South Australia, or South Dakota?' *New Zealand Journal of History*, 5: 2 (Oct. 1971): 121–7.

Sinclair, Keith, *Kinds of Peace: Maori People After the Wars, 1870–85*, Auckland, 1991.

Sinclair, W. A., *The Process of Economic Development in Australia*, Melbourne, 1976.

Slobodin, Richard, *W. H. R. Rivers*, New York, 1978.

Smith, Bernard, *European Vision and the South Pacific 1768–1850*, 2nd edn, Sydney, 1985 [1st edn, 1960].

Smith, Bernard, *Imagining the Pacific: In the Wake of the Cook Voyages*, Melbourne, 1992.

Smith, F. B., *The Conscription Plebiscites in Australia 1916–17*, Melbourne, 1971.

Smith, F. B. (ed.), *Historical Studies: Eureka Supplement*, Melbourne, 1965.

Smith, M. A., M. J. T. Spriggs and B. Fankhauser (eds), *Sahul in Review*, Australian National University Prehistory Occasional Paper 24, Canberra, 1993.

Smith, T. R., *South Pacific Commission: An Analysis after Twenty-five Years*, Wellington, 1972.

Smyth, B., *Limitation of Offspring*, Melbourne, 1893.

Somare, Michael, *Sana*, Port Moresby, 1975.

Sorrenson, M. P. K. 'The Maori King Movement, 1858–1885.' In Robert Chapman and Keith Sinclair (eds), *Studies of a Small Democracy: Essays in Honour of Willis Airey*, Auckland, 1963, 33–55.

Sorrenson, M. P. K., 'Maori Land Development', *New Zealand's Heritage*, 6 (1973): 2309–15.

Sorrenson, M. P. K., *Maori Origins and Migrations: The Genesis of some Pakeha Myths and Legends*, Auckland, 1979.

Sorrenson, M. P. K., 'Maori and Pakeha.' In W. H. Oliver with B. R. Williams (eds), *Oxford History of New Zealand*, Wellington, 1981, 168–93.

Sorrenson, M. P. K., 'Modern Maori: The Young Maori Party to Mana Motuhake.' In Keith Sinclair (ed.), *Oxford Illustrated History of New Zealand*, Auckland, 1990, 323–51.

Sorrenson, M. P. K., 'Maori and Pakeha.' In G. W. Rice (ed.), *Oxford History of New Zealand*, Auckland, 1992, 141–66.

Sorrenson, M. P. K., 'Ngata, Apirana Turupa.' In Claudia Orange (ed.), *Dictionary of New Zealand Biography*, vol. 3, Auckland, 1996, 359–63.

Souter, G., *New Guinea: The Last Unknown*, Sydney, 1965.

Spate, O. H. K., *The Pacific since Magellan, Vol. 1: The Spanish Lake*, Canberra, 1979.

Spate, O. H. K., *The Pacific since Magellan, Vol. 2: Monopolists and Freebooters*, Canberra, 1983.

Spate, O. H. K., *The Pacific since Magellan, Vol. 3: Paradise Found and Lost*, Canberra, 1988.

Spate, Oskar, ' "South Sea" to "Pacific Ocean": A Note on Nomenclature', *Journal of Pacific History*, 12: 4 (1977): 205–11.

Spate, Oskar, 'The Pacific as an Artefact', in Niel Gunson (ed.), *The Changing Pacific: Essays in Honour of H. E. Maude*, Melbourne, 1978, 32–45.

Spenceley, Geoffrey, *A Bad Smash: Australia in the Depression of the 1930s*, Melbourne, 1990.

Spoonley, Paul, *Racism and Ethnicity*, 2nd edn. Critical Issues in New Zealand Society, ed. Steve Maharey and Paul Spoonley, Auckland, 1995.

Spoonley, Paul, David Pearson and Cluny Macpherson (eds), *Nga Patai: Racism and Ethnic Relations in Aotearoa/New Zealand*, Palmerston North, 1996.

Spriggs, M. J. T., 'Vegetable Kingdoms, Taro Irrigation and Pacific Prehistory.' Ph.D. thesis, Australian National University, Canberra, 1981.

Spriggs, M. J. T. et al., *A Community of Culture: The People and Prehistory of the Pacific*, Canberra, 1993.

Stannard, David E., *Before the Horror: The Population of Hawai'i on the Eve of Western Contact*, Honolulu, 1989.

Stanner, W. E. H., 'The Aborigines.' In J. C. G. Kevin (ed.), *Some Australians Take Stock*, London, 1939.

Stanner, W. E. H., *The South Seas in Transition: A Study of Post-war Rehabilitation and Reconstruction in Three British Pacific Dependencies*, Sydney, 1953.

Stenhouse, John, ' "A Disappearing Race Before We Came Here": Doctor Alfred Kingcombe Newman, the Dying Maori, and Victorian Scientific Racism', *New Zealand Journal of History*, 30 (1996): 124–40.

Stevenson, Robert Louis, *In the South Seas*, London, 1987.

Stokes, Geoffrey (ed.), *The Politics of Identity in Australia*, Melbourne, 1997.

Stout, Robert, 'New Zealand and an Island Federation', *Review of Reviews*, 20 October 1900.

Strathern, Marylin, *The Gender of the Gift: Problems with Women and Problems with Society in Melanesia*, Berkeley, CA, 1988.

Summers, Anne, *Damned Whores and God's Police*, 2nd edn, Melbourne, 1994.

Sutherland, William, *Beyond the Politics of Race: An Alternative History of Fiji to 1992*, Canberra, 1992.

Sutton, D. G., 'The Whence of the Moriori', *New Zealand Journal of History*, 19 (1985): 3–13.

Sutton, D. G., 'Maori Demographic Change, 1769–1840: The Inner Workings of "A Picturesque but Illogical Simile"', *Journal of the Polynesian Society*, 95 (1986): 291–339.

Szabo, Michael, *Making Waves: The Greenpeace New Zealand Story*, Auckland, 1991.

Temm, Paul, *The Waitangi Tribunal: The Conscience of the Nation*, Auckland, 1990.

Thakur, Ramesh (ed.), *The South Pacific: Problems, Issues and Prospects*, London, 1991.

Thomas, Nicholas, 'The Force of Ethnology: Origins and Significance of the Melanesia/Polynesia Division', *Current Anthropology*, 30 (1989): 27–41.

Thompson, V. and R. Adloff, *The French Pacific Islands: French Polynesia and New Caledonia*, Berkeley, CA, 1971.

Thomson, Arthur S., *The Story of New Zealand: Past and Present – Savage and Civilized*, 2 vols, London, 1859.

Thomson, David, *A World Without Welfare: New Zealand's Colonial Experiment*, Auckland, 1998.

Thomson, J. Mansfield (ed.), *Farewell Colonialism*, Palmerston North, 1998.

Tippett, A. R., *Solomon Islands Christianity*, London, 1967.

Tolerton, Jane, *Ettie: A Life of Ettie Rout*, Auckland, 1992.

Tomkins, Sandra M., 'The Influenza Epidemic of 1918–19 in Western Samoa', *Journal of Pacific History*, 27 (1992): 181–97.

Treadgold, M. L., *The Regional Economy of Bougainville*, Occasional Paper 10, NCDS, Australian National University, Canberra, 1978.

Van Trease, Howard, *Melanesian Politics Stael blong Vanuatu*, Suva, 1995.

Tremewan, Peter, *French Akaroa: An Attempt to Colonise Southern New Zealand*, Christchurch, 1990.

Tremewan, Peter, 'The French Alternative to the Treaty of Waitangi', *New Zealand Journal of History*, 26 (April 1992): 99–104.

Trompf, Gary (ed.), *Cargo Cults and Millenarian Movements: Transoceanic Comparisons of New Religious Movements*, Berlin, 1990.

Tuimaleali'ifano, Morgan, *Samoans in Fiji: Migration, Identity and Communication*, Suva, 1990.

Tulloch, Tracy, 'State Regulation of Sexuality in New Zealand 1880–1925', Ph.D. thesis, University of Canterbury, 1997.

Tyler, Linda (ed.), *Shane Cotton*, Dunedin, 1998.

Uriam, Kambati, *In Their Own Words: History and Society in Gilbertese Oral Tradition*, Canberra, 1995.

Vail, John, 'The Impact of the Mt Kare Goldrush on the People of the Tari District.' In T. Taufa and C. Bass (eds), *Population, Family Health and Development*, Port Moresby, 1993.

Vasil, Raj, *What Do the Maori Want? New Maori Political Perspectives*, Auckland, 1990.

Ville, Simon, 'Networks and Venture Capital in the Australasian Pastoral Sector before World War II', *Business History*, 38: 3 (1996): 48–63.

Viviani, Nancy, *Nauru: Phosphate and Political Progress*, Canberra, 1970.

Waiko, John, 'Be jijimo: A History According to the Traditions of the Binandere People of Papua New Guinea.' Ph.D. thesis, Australian National University, Canberra, 1982.

Waiko, John, *A Short History of Papua New Guinea*, Melbourne, 1993.

Waitangi Tribunal, *Te Whanau O Waipareira Report*, Wellington, 1998, Wai 414.

Wakefield, Edward Jerningham, *Adventure in New Zealand*, abridged, ed. Joan Stevens, Auckland, 1975.

Wallace, Alfred Russel, *The Malay Archipelago: The Land of the Orang utan and Bird of Paradise*, London, 1874.

Wallace, Alfred Russel, *The Geographical Distribution of Animals*, London, 1876.

Wallace, Alfred Russel, *Australasia*, London, 1883.

Ward, Alan, *A Show of Justice: Racial 'Amalgamation' in Nineteenth-century New Zealand*, Canberra, 1974.

Ward, Alan, *Land and Politics in New Caledonia*, Canberra, 1982.

Ward, Alan, *National Overview*, 3 vols. Waitangi Tribunal Rangahaua Whanui Series. Wellington, 1997.

Ward, Alan, *An Unsettled History*, Wellington, 1999.

Ward, R. G., 'Contract Labor Recruitment from the Highlands of Papua New Guinea, 1950–1974', *International Migration Review*, 24: 2 (1990): 273–96.

Ward, R. G. and E. Kingdon (eds), *Land, Custom and Practice in the South Pacific*, Cambridge, 1995.

Ward, R. G. and A. Proctor (eds), *South Pacific Agriculture: Choices and Constraints*, Canberra, 1980.

Ward, Russell, *The Australian Legend*, Melbourne, 1966.

Weiner, Annette, *Women of Value, Men of Renown: New Perspectives in Trobriand Exchange*, Austin, TX, 1976.

Weiner, Annette, *The Trobrianders of Papua New Guinea*, New York, 1987.

Wendt, Albert, 'Guardians and Wards: A Study of the Origins, Causes and First Two Years of the Mau Movement in Western Samoa.' MA thesis, Victoria University of Wellington, 1965.

White, Geoffrey, *Identity Through History: Living Stories in a Solomon Islands Society*, Cambridge, 1991.

White, Geoffrey and Lamont Lindstrom (eds), *The Pacific Theater: Island Representations of World War II*, Honolulu, 1989.

White, Geoffrey and Lamont Lindstrom (eds), *Custom Today*. Special issue 6, *Anthropological Forum*, 1993.

White, Geoffrey, David Gegeo, David Akin and Karen Watson-Gegeo (eds), *The Big Death: Solomon Islanders Remember World War II*, Honiara and Suva, 1988.

White, J. Peter and D. John Mulvaney, 'How Many People?' In D. J. Mulvaney and J. Peter White (eds), *Australians to 1788*, Sydney, 1987, 114–17.

White, Richard, *Inventing Australia*. The Australian Experience, ed. Heather Radi, Sydney, 1981.

White, Richard, *Inventing Australia: Images and Identity 1688–1980*, Sydney, 1981.

White, Richard, '*Inventing Australia* Revisited.' In Wayne Hudson and Geoffrey Bolton (eds), *Creating Australia: Changing Australian History*, Sydney, 1997, 12–22.

Whittaker, J. L., N. G. Gash, J. F. Hookey and R. J. Lacey (eds), *Documents and Readings in New Guinea History: Prehistory to 1889*, Brisbane, 1975.

Williams, David V., 'The Queen v. Symonds Reconsidered', *Victoria University of Wellington Law Review*, 19 (1989): 385–402.

Williams, Maslyn and Barrie MacDonald, *The Phosphateers: A History of the British Phosphate Commissioners and the Christmas Island Phosphate Commission*, Melbourne, 1985.

Wolf, Eric R., *Europe and the Peoples Without History*, Berkeley, 1982.

Woods, Megan C., 'Re/producing the Nation: Women Making Identity in New Zealand, 1906–1925.' MA thesis, University of Canterbury, 1997.

Worsley, Peter, *The Trumpet Shall Sound*, New York, 1968.

Wright, Harrison M., *New Zealand, 1769–1840: Early Years of Western Contact*, Cambridge, MA, 1959.

Wurm, S. A., *Papuan Languages of Oceania*, Tübingen, 1982.

Yarwood, A. T. and M. J. Knowling, *Race Relations in Australia: A History*, Sydney, 1982.

Yen, D. E. and J. M. J. Mummery (eds), *Pacific Production Systems: Approaches to Economic Prehistory*, Canberra, 1990.

Young, John, 'Lau: A Windward Perspective', *Journal of Pacific History*, 28: 2 (1993): 159–80.

Young, Michael, *Fighting with Food: Leadership, Values and Social Control in a Massim Society*, Cambridge, 1971.

Young, Michael, ' "Our Name is Women: We Are Bought with Limesticks and Limepots": An Analysis of the Autobiographical Narrative of a Kalauna Woman,' *Man* (n.s.), 18 (1983): 478–501.

INDEX

Aboriginal Australians: careers in sport, 439; and Cook, 44, 56; creation of Northern Territory, 203; discrimination in welfare, 297; diseases, violence and depopulation, 75–6, 80–1; dispossession of, 81–2; early colonial view of, 18, 37, 44, 79–81; in European exploration, 85; exchange of goods, 46; and the First Fleet, 19; gender relations, 45; half-caste policy, 369–70; land rights, 4, 122–5, 370–1; legal status of, 82, 354; Maori views on, 67–8; postwar assimilation policy, 33, 346; pre-invasion society, 40, 44–5; Second World War service, 324; suffrage rights, 208, 369, 370 in 1990s, 369

Aboriginal labour: in coastal industries, 173; pastoral 171

Aboriginal Land Councils, Northern and Central, 372

Aboriginal Land Rights (Northern Territory) Act 1976, 370; and Elsey cattle station, 371–2

Aboriginal and Torres Strait Islander Commission (ATSIC), 370, 372

Aboriginal women: in domestic service, 242; double oppression, 171; and feminism, 385

Advances to Settlers, 232, 234

Age of Discovery, 13, 18, 37

agriculture: 1930s policies, 228; Maori, 4, 105

All Blacks, 441

Alliance Party (Fiji), 392

Amalgamated Miners' Association of Australasia (AMA), 152

amalgamation *see* assimilation policy

America: alliance with, 341–2; Australian and New Zealand ambivalence to, 340, 343; Curtin and, 320; French ambivalence to, 343; GIs in Australia and New Zealand, 326; Islander enthusiasm for, 343

American Board of Missions, 103

Andesite Line, 15, 18

Anglo-Celtic values: continued dominance in Australia, 466; in multicultural society, 369

Anglo-French Condominium, New Hebrides, 189, 396

Anglo-Japanese Treaty of Commerce and Navigation 1894: negative reaction to, 252–4

Angry Penguins, 426

Anker, Lorna: *Ellen's Vigil,* 281–2

anthropology, 20–1

Anti-discrimination Act 1975 (Australia), 370

Anzac Cove: as birthplace of two nations, 273

Anzac Day, 267; as ritual, 273

Anzac histories: language of, 276; recent, 275

Anzac legends, 267; Bean's role in, 274–5; bushman and digger, 274; and conscription, 279; in film, 276; and the gender divide, 286; New Zealand gentlemen, 271; New Zealand, official, 277–9; New Zealand, private, 277, 282, 286; non-white roles, 268; significance of, 274. *See also* Gallipoli

Anzac memorials, 273

ANZUS pact, 342–3

APEC *see* Asia-Pacific Economic Co-operation

arbitration: in Australia and New Zealand, 232; centrality of, 233; and equal pay, 238; eugenist elements of, 237; as expression of identity, 233; and gender division of labour, 240, 241; and pacifism, 284; realizing the workingman's paradise, 233; reinforces ethnic solidarity, 235; and small farmers, 234; and women's unionism, 241

Arcadianism, 135; in New Zealand, 32, 230, 435

Archibald, J. F., 204, 214

505

Rivers, W. H. R., 20–1; on depopulation
problems, 76–7
Riviere, Henri, 102
Road from Coorain, The, 446
Roberts, Tom, 219
Rogernomics (New Zealand), as state
experiment, 416
Rotuma Island, Christianity on, 106
Rout, Ettie, campaign for safe sex, 286
Royal Commission on the Decline of the
Birth-Rate and on the Mortality of Infants in
New South Wales 1903–4, 256
Ruatara and missionaries, 104
rugby: codes on television, 440; league, 440;
Polynesian players, 439; union,
professionalization of, 441–2
rural decline, 360; and One Nation support,
466
rural life and writers of the Left, 360
Ruse, James, 99
Rye, Maria, 69

Sahul, 17
Sâlote, Queen Tupou, 392–3
Samoa: anti-New Zealand movement, 311;
Black Saturday 1929, 311; Christianity in,
104; influenza epidemic, 1918, 311;
Mau, 311; plantations, 177
Samoan Offenders Ordinance 1922, 311
Sandakan death march, 322
scholarships, Colombo Plan, 342
sealers and Aboriginal labour, 173
Second Australian Imperial Force (2AIF),
318
Second World War: Australia and New
Zealand commitment, 318; civilian
detainees, 319; feminine identities, 326; GIs
in Australia and New Zealand, 326; soldier
images, 325. *See also* Pacific War
selectors, 126–7
self-government, Australian colonies, 122
self-help, decentralization, 359
Seligman, C. G., 20
settlement, indigenous narratives of, 38–40
settler capitalism, dependence on Britain, 230
settler societies: civic baggage, 31;
constitutions, 122; gender imbalance in,
204; governors of, 30; and states, 30;
systematic colonization, 166
sexual freedoms in Second World War, 326
Shadbolt, Maurice, 277

Shapiro, Karl: *News to Australia*, 334
Sheppard, Kate, 208, 385; suffrage campaign,
207
Shipley, Jenny, 464
shipping companies in the Pacific, 129
Silent Division (New Zealand, First World
War), 272
silver mining: at Broken Hill, 149; flotation
technique, 149
Simpson and his donkey, 275
Singapore, fall of, 320
Singirok, General Jerry, and abortion of
Sandline mission, 455
Skate, Bill, 455
skill: as masculine, 241; and wage hierarchy,
237
small settlers, Australia, 86. *See also* selectors
smallpox, 67, 75
Smith, 'Mumshirl' Shirley, 354
Smith, Vivian, 429
Smith, William Mein, 86
Snowy Mountains hydro-electric scheme, 327
soccer players, Australia and New Zealand
overseas, 441
social justice (Australian), 235; and family
wage, 237
social realism, 308–9
social security: New Zealand, 411;
non-contributory, 297
socialism: postwar, 328, 334; 1930s, 306
soil erosion, 41
soldier settlement schemes: failure of, 294;
home loans, 292
Solomon Islands: as British protectorate, 188;
decolonization, 349, 393; depopulation, 77;
Maasina Rule, 330; Malaita, 209
Solomon Islands Defence Force, 322
Somare, Michael: Pangu Pati, 401; on Second
World War, 323
South Pacific Commission, 342
South Pacific Forum, 451
South Sea Islanders: Australian South Sea
Islanders United Council, 373; in Australian
labour market, 202; discrimination against,
373–4; and victimhood, 373–4
Southeast Asia: financial crisis in 1997, 460;
views on Australia, 461
sovereign (British-born), 31
Spain in the Pacific, 51–2
Spanish Civil War and Australians, 306
Spate, Oskar: *The Pacific Since Magellan*, 17